A History of Korea

A History of Korea

From Antiquity to the Present

Michael J. Seth

ROWMAN & LITTLEFIELD PUBLISHERS, INC.
Lanham • Boulder • New York • Toronto • Plymouth, UK

Published by Rowman & Littlefield Publishers, Inc.
A wholly owned subsidiary of The Rowman & Littlefield Publishing Group, Inc.
4501 Forbes Boulevard, Suite 200, Lanham, Maryland 20706
http://www.rowmanlittlefield.com

Estover Road, Plymouth PL6 7PY, United Kingdom

British Library Cataloguing in Publication Information Available

Library of Congress Cataloging-in-Publication Data

Seth, Michael J., 1948–
  A history of Korea : from antiquity to the present / Michael J. Seth.
    p. cm.
  Includes bibliographical references and index.
  ISBN 978-0-7425-6715-3 (cloth : alk. paper) — ISBN 978-0-7425-6716-0 (pbk. :
alk. paper) — ISBN 978-0-7425-6717-7 (electronic)
  1. Korea—History. 2. Korea—Civilization. I. Title.
  DS907.18.S426 2011
  951.9—dc22

                                                                    2010032330

Printed in the United States of America

Contents

Primary Source Readings

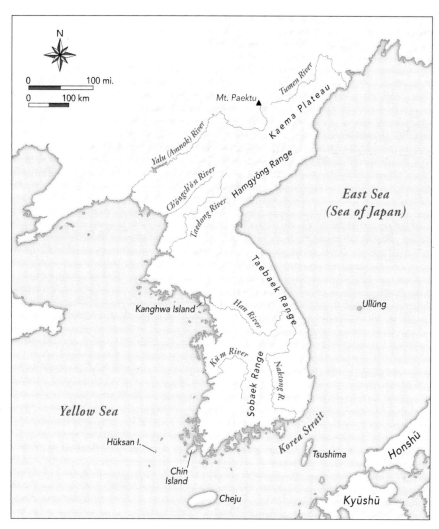

Physical Map of Korea

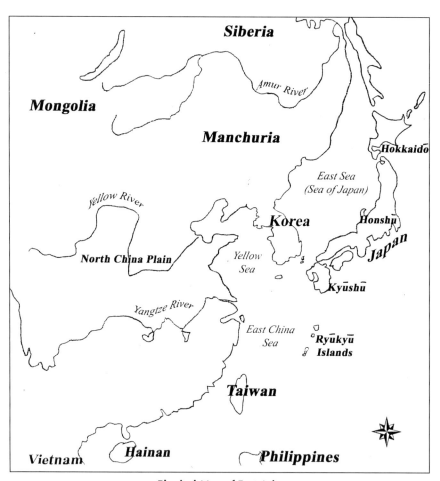

Physical Map of East Asia

Korea in the Fifth Century

Silla and Parhae Kingdoms

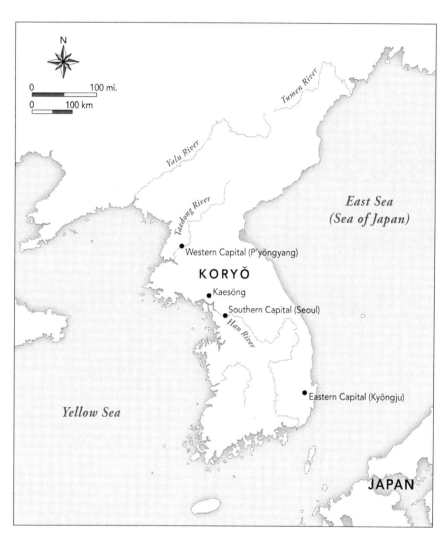

Koryŏ in the Eleventh Century

HAMGIL
(Hamgyŏng)

P'YŎNGAN

Hamhŭng
•

P'yŏngyang
•

HWANGHAE

KANGWŎN

Haeju

KYŎNGGI

Hanyang
(Seoul)
•

Wŏnju
•

CH'UNGCH'ŎNG

Kongju
•

KYŎNGSANG

Taegu
•

Chŏnju
•

CHŎLLA

Tongnae
•

Chosŏn Korea

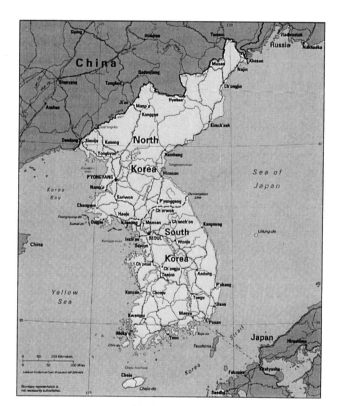

Modern Korea

Introduction

Korea is an ancient land with 2,000 years of recorded history and a rich and distinctive cultural tradition. The various peoples that lived in the peninsula gradually forged a society characterized by cultural homogeneity and political unity. Korea today is divided into two rival states, but this is a fairly recent development. Before being effectively partitioned by the United States and the Soviet Union in 1945, Korea had been one of the oldest continuously unified states in the world. The peninsular heartland of what is today Korea was united in 676, and except for one brief period, remained so until the end of World War II. It had also become one of the most homogeneous societies in the world. A number of peoples entered the peninsula in antiquity, but gradually all merged into a single ethnicity, sharing one language and participating in one political system. In modern times there have been no significant ethnic minorities.

Binding Koreans together and distinguishing them from their neighbors has been their language. Korean, while showing some similarities to Japanese and to the Altaic languages of Inner Asia, is also quite distinct from them. In modern times all Koreans spoke the Korean language, which since the fifteenth century has been written in a unique alphabet. Before the twentieth century, there were no significant Korean-speaking groups outside of Korea. Thus, Korea became one of the few lands where ethnicity, membership in a language community, and a state were coterminous. This unity and homogeneity that emerged over the centuries has become an important part of Korean identity.

In the late nineteenth century few if any states could match Korea's territorial and institutional stability, its historical continuity, its ethnic unity

1

and its isolation. The last earned it the sobriquet "the hermit kingdom." As with so much of the non-Western world Korea became a victim of the age of imperialism. Its colonial experience was atypical, however, in that it was ruled by Japan, another non-Western society, a familiar neighbor with which it shared many cultural affinities. But what makes Korea's modern history unique was its division in 1945 by the United States and the Soviet Union at the thirty-eighth parallel. Korea was divided along a totally arbitrary line that had no historical, geographical, cultural, or economic logic; just a line that conveniently separated the country into roughly two halves—dividing provinces, valleys, and families. A nation that was arguably the most ethnically homogeneous in the world, with thirteen centuries of political unity, with national and provincial boundaries older than almost any other state, was cut into halves by the two superpowers.

While in theory this was only a temporary measure, almost immediately two separate regimes emerged. In 1948, the United States and the Soviet Union set up their client states: the Republic of Korea, better known as South Korea, and the Democratic People's Republic of Korea, or North Korea. The two "Koreas" had different leaders, different political and economic systems, and different external orientations. Both saw the division as an unacceptable and temporary condition, but the attempts to unify the country led to one of the bloodiest conflicts since the end of World War II. Despite horrific destruction and loss of life, both regimes survived and continued on their markedly different trajectories of development. North Korea evolved into one of the world's most totalitarian and militant states, ruled by a family with a cult of personality unequaled in its extreme intensity. It was the world's most closed and enigmatic state, with a leadership busy developing missiles and nuclear weapons while millions of the nation's children were stunted from malnutrition. South Korea, by contrast, after a rocky and uncertain start evolved into an open, democratic society, whose spectacular economic growth and internationally competitive industries made it an outstanding success story among the postcolonial states.

Nowhere else was a nation so arbitrarily divided and the peoples of the two halves so effectively isolated from each other; nowhere else did such radically different political and social systems emerge. The boundary between the two Koreas is not only the world's most heavily armed and until recently most hermetically sealed, it marks two different living standards and lifestyles. Nowhere else is there such a sharp contrast between two contiguous states—one rich, democratic, and cosmopolitan; the other impoverished, totalitarian, and isolated. And arguably the history of no other society in the past century offers such contrasting examples of how societies can undergo modern development. Korea's modern history is both a remarkable story and an incomparable example of how the interplay of historical contingency, policy choices, and cultural heritage can shape societies in contrasting ways.

Korea is also a fascinating land with a rich and distinctive culture that continues to evolve in interesting and even surprising ways. Yet Korea and its history have often been overlooked in the past. Except for the Korean War it has not, at least until recently, drawn much attention from the rest of the world. Partly this is due to the fact that it has been overshadowed by it larger neighbors, China and Japan.

Today Korea is emerging from its past obscurity. On the negative side there is the notoriety of Kim Jong Il and the North Korean nuclear threat. But South Korea has become a major world economy whose corporate names LG, Samsung, and Hyundai are globally recognized and whose popular culture has a huge audience among its Asian neighbors and is beginning to be known beyond Asia. Yet its remarkable history, with its important implications, is still not widely known or appreciated.

Geographically, Korea is a mountainous peninsula about 600 miles long and an average of 120 miles wide with a mixture of maritime and continental climates. The mountains are not high, reaching only 9,000 feet with Mount Paektu on the border between North Korea and Manchuria. Yet no place in Korea is not within sight of them.

Arable land is limited but well watered and fertile. Winters vary from short and mild in the south to long and bitter cold in the north; summers are wet and humid almost everywhere. The wet, humid summer and dry autumn are ideal for growing rice, and except in the far north where it is too cold to cultivate, rice has been the staple crop for several millennia. Wet rice agriculture is labor intensive but produces high yields per acre. Therefore, despite the limited amount of land suitable for farming, Korea has been for centuries a densely populated country and until quite recently an overwhelmingly rural, agricultural one.

No part of Korea is far from the seas. The seas, however, while filled with abundant fish and seafood, important components in the Korean diet, are not friendly to navigation. The east coast on the Sea of Japan (or "East Sea" as the Koreans call it) has few good harbors and is cut off from the major population centers by rugged mountains. Navigation on the western Yellow Sea coast is made difficult by shifting sandbars and some of the world's highest tides. Confined to a geographically well-defined peninsula with ample resources to support a fairly populous agricultural society Korea developed its own distinctive society and identity while borrowing heavily from China.

Korea is a modest-sized country surrounded by much larger neighbors: China, Japan, and Russia. The fact that it has been lodged between the important and culturally rich Chinese and Japanese societies helps account for the lack of attention its history has attracted. It has been difficult for Koreans to emerge from the shadow of their East Asian neighbors and to make their presence and their culture known to the rest of the world. Yet Korea, small as it seems next to its neighbors, is not all that small. The area of North and South Korea combined is 84,000 square miles, about the same as Utah. This sounds unimpressive, but it is also the same size as the United Kingdom and a little smaller than another peninsular society, Italy, which it roughly resembles in shape. In population today North Korea has about 23 million inhabitants and South Korea 47 million for a total of 70 million, a little larger than that of Britain, France, or Italy, and a little smaller than that of Germany.

Korea has been a part of an East Asian civilization centered in China. China was one of the earliest homes of agriculture, urbanization, state structures, and literacy. As long as three and a half millennia ago a culture emerged in northern China that was recognizably Chinese. This culture profoundly influenced its neighbors, Korea, Vietnam, and Japan, to the extent that the cultures of these societies can be viewed as offshoots of Chinese civilization. Literate states emerged first in Korea and then Japan in the early centuries of the first millennium CE. From China the Koreans received their writing system. Although in the fifteenth century the Koreans invented their own unique alphabet, Chinese characters were the main means of writing until the twentieth century. The Korean language borrowed much of its higher vocabulary from Chinese, much as English borrowed most of its educated vocabulary from Latin and Greek. Koreans then brought literacy farther eastward to their Japanese neighbors. Written classical Chinese was studied by all educated Koreans before the twentieth century, and it served as the means for communicating with their Chinese, Japanese, and Vietnamese neighbors.

China provided the model for literature, art, music, architecture, dress, and etiquette. From China Koreans imported most of their ideas about government and politics. They accepted the Chinese worldview in which China was the center of the universe and the home of all civilization, and its emperor the mediator between heaven and earth. Koreans took pride in their adherence to Chinese cultural norms. For most of the period from the seventh to the nineteenth century they accepted their country's role as a subordinate member of the international hierarchy in which China stood at the apex, loyal adherents of Chinese culture such as Korea ranked next, and the barbarians outside Chinese civilization stood at the bottom. Close adherence to civilized standards was a source of pride. But this did not result in a loss of separate identity. On the contrary, in adapting Chinese culture to their own society Koreans defined their own cultural distinctiveness. Nor did Korea's membership in the "tributary system" in which the Korean king became a vassal of the Chinese emperor mean that

Korea was less than fully independent, as was sometimes misunderstood by Westerners. In fact, Koreans were fiercely independent. Much of their history has been the story of resistance to outside intruders. Korea's position as a tributary state was usually ceremonial, and for Koreans it did not imply a loss of autonomy. Chinese attempts to interfere in domestic affairs were met with opposition. Indeed, some today view the Korean past as a saga of the struggles of a smaller society to resist control or assimilation by larger, more aggressive neighbors: the Chinese, the Japanese, and the Inner Asian peoples that border them on the north, the Russians being the successors of the last.

Missionaries from China and Central Asia introduced Buddhism to Korea. For much of its history Korea was a Buddhist land. Millions of Koreans are still adherents to Buddhism, which until recently has been the most influential religious tradition. Buddhism originated in India from where it spread throughout most of Asia, coming to Korea via China. When it reached Korea it had absorbed a number of Chinese and other Asian traditions. Buddhism had a profound impact on Korean art, music, and literature. Buddhism inspired the earliest sculptures and the first monumental architecture other than tombs, and importantly, its missionaries brought literacy. It included the idea of reincarnation, that the suffering in life is inevitable, but escape from the cycle of births and rebirths is possible. For many Koreans it meant a hope for a future life of bliss through faith in the Buddha. It also taught a respect for all forms of life. Buddhist practices of meditation and the escape from daily concerns that temples provided were an important outlet for those who found the obligations and pressures of everyday life too strong.

Confucianism had an especially profound impact on Korean society, forming the basis for ethical standards and for ideas about government, society, and family relationships. Confucianism was a tradition of thought in China, a dynamic tradition that evolved over the centuries. It taught that the world was a moral universe, that all humans were connected to the universe and to each other. For Koreans it was important in that it made the family, and the roles and responsibilities of each member of the family, the foundation for morality. Each individual had the duty to adhere to his or her role as mother, father, son, daughter, elder brother, and so on. These relations were given cosmic significance. At a political level Confucianism emphasized the importance of loyalty, hierarchy, and authority. It made obedience to a ruler a moral duty and correctly carrying out rulership a moral obligation. It also influenced the Korean concern for social rank. Koreans viewed the world as a hierarchical order in which everyone has a place. The young were subordinate to their elders, women to men, commoners to members of the upper class, and subjects to the ruler. Yet in each of these relations both were bound by moral obligations.

While Buddhism and Confucianism came to Korea from China, the Korean love and respect for nature has indigenous origins. Koreans have looked to the natural world—the mountains, rivers, trees, rocks, flowers, animals, and seashores—as sources of artistic and spiritual inspiration. The changing of the seasons and the beauties of nature have always been among the most popular topics of painting, poetry, and song. Prominent features of nature, especially mountains, but also rocks, trees, and rivers, have been seen as sources of spiritual power. This took the form of directly worshiping the spirits of nature, spirits that were not personified as gods and goddesses but accepted as part of nature. Nature worship blended with geomancy, the belief imported from China that certain topographical settings are auspicious. The location of buildings, the layout of cities and towns, and the placement of graves, as well as architecture and everyday activities, took note of their natural settings.

While in general the Koreans adhered to Chinese models more closely than did the more distant Japanese, Chinese culture imports did not erase indigenous cultural traditions and beliefs. Shamanism and nature worship remained a strong component of religious life, particularly for the non-elite. Folk dances, folk art, and craft traditions drew upon domestic sources. Koreans often selectively borrowed and adapted from China. Korean homes, for example, with their heated paper floors, were unlike those of their neighbors. Their cuisine took on its own style, evolving into a highly spiced culinary tradition in sharp contrast to the blander fare of the northern Chinese and Japanese. The social system evolved differently from that of China. Korea retained a fairly rigid hierarchical tradition, with an aristocracy made up of families who often could trace their ancestries back many generations, in contrast to the Chinese ruling class with its greater social mobility and lesser stability. Yet the Korean aristocracy gradually moved from a warrior aristocracy to a civilian one that held military skills in contempt in contrast to the Japanese warrior elite. In many ways, such as ritual practices, marital customs, the role of women, the structure of the family, and the patterns of governance, Korean society provided a distinctive variant within East Asian civilization.

Another way Korean history was distinctive was its remarkable continuity. From the seventh to the twentieth century only three dynasties ruled Korea. The second ruled for almost five centuries and the third for more than five centuries; both were among the longest-ruling dynasties in history. The two dynastic changes that did take place did not bring about a vast upheaval. Elite families as well as institutions were carried over from one dynasty to another. This, along with a Confucian concern for examining the past, contributed to a strong sense of historical consciousness among Koreans.

This history traces the origins and development of the Korean people and their culture from the varied tribal peoples who settled in the peninsula to the two Koreas today. The first chapter deals with the origins of the Korean people, from the earliest human inhabitants to the emergence of indigenous literate states in the third century CE. The second chapter deals with the "Three Kingdoms" period, in which three states—Silla, Paekche, and Koguryŏ—competed for supremacy in the peninsula, and ends with the unification of most of the peninsula under Silla in the seventh century. The next six chapters deal with the evolution of Korean society and culture under a unified state structure. The third chapter examines developments during Late Silla (676–935); the fourth and fifth during Koryŏ (935–1392), the second dynastic state; and chapters 6, 7, and 8 survey the social, political, and cultural evolution of Korea during the third and longest dynastic state, Chosŏn (1392–1910). Chapter 9 looks at the entry of Korea into the modern world and the age of imperialism in the late nineteenth century and traces its loss of independence to Japan. The tenth chapter surveys the thirty-five-year period of colonial rule, from 1910 to 1945, and its impact on later Korean history. Chapter 11 narrates the division of Korea, the development of two separate regimes and the horrendous Korean War. Chapter 12 examines the evolution of North Korean society from the end of the Korean War in 1953 to the early 1990s. Chapters 13 and 14 cover South Korea's development during this time. More attention is given to South Korea than to the North since not only does it contain a majority of the Korean people, its history is far better documented. Chapters 15 and 16 deal respectively with North and South Korea since the late 1980s.

To place Korean history into global perspective one or two short essays entitled "Korea in Global Perspective" appear at the end of each chapter. This is followed by one or more short primary sources. Korean names and terms are transliterated according the modified McCune-Reishauer system used by the Library of Congress and most English-speaking scholars (see appendix). Most dates for premodern Korea are based on the lunar (Chinese) calendar. Since the lunar calendar usually begins between mid-January and mid-February they may vary slightly with our solar calendar.

The remarkable continuity of Korea's social and political history, its turbulent modern history, the creation of two Koreas, and the radically divergent paths they followed offer many insights for understanding economic, social, and political development. Korea is also an important part of the global community, with a rich and dynamic culture. That alone makes its history worthy of study.

1

✦

The Origins

THE KOREANS

The Koreans today are one of the world's most ethnically homogeneous peoples. In recent times there have been no significant ethnic or linguistic minorities. Ethnicity is a very difficult term to define, but language is simpler. All Koreans speak Korean as their native tongue, and all people who speak Korean as their first language identify themselves as ethnically Korean. No other language is known to have been spoken by any large group on the peninsula in recent centuries.

Korean is not closely related to any other language. Most linguists classify it as related to Japanese and remotely related to the Altaic languages of Inner Asia, which include Mongolian, the Turkic languages, and the Tungusic languages such as Manchu. Korean shares a grammatical structure with Japanese and the Altaic languages. All are agglutinative, that is, one adds components to a root to form words that are often long. This linguistic relationship, if accurate, is often interpreted as meaning that the ancient ancestors of modern Koreans came from Central Asia and entered the peninsula through Manchuria, with some of them going on to occupy the Japanese archipelago. According to one current theory, the ancestral Koreans spoke Proto-Altaic, one branch of which evolved into the Tungusic languages and another into Proto-Korean-Japanese, which eventually became the modern Korean and Japanese languages.[1] Korean shares many similarities in sentence structure with Japanese, and it is probable that the two languages are genetically related, but linguists differ on whether both languages are related to the Altaic languages. A

9

recent linguistic theory places Korean and Japanese along with Ainu in its own language group and does not see a direct connection between this proposed Japanese-Korean-Ainu language family and those of any other. Genetic evidence lends some support for both theories. Analysis of Y-chromosome DNA suggests that at least some of the ancestors of Koreans entered from Manchuria and Northeast Asia, and that after a long period in the peninsula some of their descendents moved into Japan. The migration into Japan may have taken place 4,000 years ago. Koreans and Japanese share a cluster of genetic markers that is uncommon among other Asians. Whatever the origins of Koreans and their relations with their neighbors, in the 2,000 years of Korean history that can be supported with written records, no documented large-scale migrations of people into the peninsula took place.

Although most probably related to Japanese, the unusual sound system of Korean and most of its native vocabulary are very different. Korean consonants make a distinction between aspiration and nonaspiration, and between tense and lax sounds, but do not make phonemic distinctions between voiced and unvoiced consonants. This means that Korean has no initial *b*, *d*, hard *g*, or *j* sounds but has three *p*, three *t*, three *ch*, and three *k* sounds. This plus the complex system of sound changes makes it a difficult language for most nonnative speakers to pronounce. It is highly inflected and has no tones. Although modern Korean is filled with many Chinese loanwords it does not resemble Chinese at all. The distinctiveness of Korean native vocabulary and phonology is a source of pride to some modern Korean nationalists who like to emphasize Korean uniqueness. For the historian it presents a linguistic puzzle, making it hard to trace Korean origins. It should be added that historians do not know much about how the language sounded before the invention of the Korean alphabet in the fifteenth century and can only guess at its structure in ancient times.

EARLY INHABITANTS

Humans have lived on the Korean peninsula since very early times. Remains of Paleolithic hominids have been found at Kulp'ori in Unggi-gun in the extreme northeast of Korea that have been tentatively dated back 400,000 years. North Koreans have claimed to have found evidence of human habitation as early as 600,000 years ago. Stone implements and evidence of the occupation of caves by Paleolithic people have been reported at a number of sites in South Korea. The dating of these early inhabitants is uncertain. It is also unclear if the peninsula was continuously inhabited since these early times. At the minimum, we can say that human activity in Korea goes back hundreds of thousands of years.

The search for the origins of Korean culture begins during the post-Pleistocene climatic optimum, 6000 to 2000 BCE. This period of warming climate roughly coincided with the early Neolithic period in Korea. Our chief source of information on Neolithic peoples in Korea comes from pottery. The earliest pottery is found on top of layers of pre-pottery sites. This, along with a continuity in the stone tools, suggests that the pottery cultures may have emerged from the preexisting cultures rather than being the product of new peoples entering the peninsula.[2] The earliest pottery dates back to perhaps 6000 BCE and is found in connection with shell middens along the Korean coasts. This early pottery is known as *chŭlmun*, or comb-patterned pottery (also known in Korean as *pitsal munŭi*), after the characteristic decorative pattern that consisted of incised parallel lines. The early forms show considerable regional variation. After 3500 BCE the classic *chŭlmun* emerged in the Han and Taedong River basins on the west coast. Regional variations in pottery remained. Along the east coast a flat-based pottery has been found, while on the south coast, pottery vessels are typically round-based vessels with wide mouths. The early cultures associated with these pottery remains appear to have had a subsistence base that was heavily dependent on fishing. In addition to shell middens, the importance of fishing is apparent from the abundant stone net sinkers and fishhooks that have been found at these early Neolithic sites.[3]

Villages associated with *chŭlmun* pottery resemble earlier ones, being small clusters of semisubterranean dwellings made by digging a pit into the ground and covering it with wood, mud, and thatch. A central hearth lined with stones provided heat. This was a practical adaptation to the climate, since the homes would likely be cool in summer and relatively warm in winter. The complex relationship between the peoples of the peninsula and their relationship with their regional neighbors China, Manchuria/Siberia, and the Japanese archipelago are apparent in this early period. Pottery in Korea shows some similarity to that of Japan and the Yellow Sea region of China. Some scholars have also noted some resemblances in regional Korean styles to Siberian pottery. Similarity in pottery styles suggests these early inhabitants of Korea were part of a larger complex of Northeast Asian peoples and cultures. Some scholars see a distinctiveness in the pottery of Korea from what has been found in either the Asian mainland or in Japan. Others, however, find the evidence for a distinctive Korean culture at such an early date unconvincing.

The *chŭlmun* period, which lasted until about 2000 BCE, is a period of transition from hunting, fishing, and gathering to agriculture as the basis

of subsistence. To understand this transition, we can best see developments in Korea as part of a worldwide change in human patterns of
existence. About 10,000 years ago, people in various parts of the world
shifted from economies based on specialized hunting with minor subsidiary gathering of plants and some fishing to a broad-spectrum strategy
for existence. This involved hunting a wider variety of game, including
many smaller animals, and relying more on fishing and on plant collection for food. In many parts of the world this was followed by the gradual
domestication of plants and animals until societies became sedentary and
once again specialized, relying on one to several species of cultivated
plants or livestock. The reasons for this development remain somewhat
mysterious, although the transition to agriculture is possibly related in
some complex way to the end of the most recent glacial period about
10,000 years ago and the subsequent global warming.

Archaeological evidence shows Korea fitting very much into this
pattern. During the Neolithic, the peoples of the peninsula lived by
fishing; shellfish collecting; hunting deer, wild pigs, and oxen; and
collecting wild plants. The forests of Korea, especially during the post-
Pleistocene climatic optimum from 6000 to 2000 BCE, contained great
bounties of edible plants: acorns, chestnuts, arrowroots, turnips, green
onions, garlic, and Japanese camellia. The stone implements left behind
show that these foods became increasingly important in the diet.[4] In
the fourth millennium, the beginnings of agriculture appear. Millet,
native to Korea, was probably the first major domesticated plant, and
by the end of the *chŭlmun* its cultivation was widespread, as was the
domestication of the pig. Evidence for plant domestication is found in
the existence of grinding stones, hoes, and stone sickles at archaeological sites. Agriculture is extremely important for historical development,
for it makes possible dense populations of sedentary communities,
transforms the landscape, and creates the possibilities for more complex forms of social organization to emerge. But agriculture developed
slowly as the basis of subsistence, and settlements remained small.
Hunting, fishing, and wild plant collecting were still important. The
changes brought about by the *chŭlmun* peoples were laying the foundation for the future developments in Korea, but who these peoples were
and what their relationship was to the peoples and cultures outside the
peninsula or to the later Korean peoples are unclear. Early agriculture
was probably introduced into the peninsula from what is now central
and southern China, perhaps brought by migrations of people into
Korea. A cluster of genetic markers has been linked with the spread
of Neolithic agriculture from southern China to the rest of East Asia
including Korea and Japan.

THE AGE OF RICE FARMING BEGINS

Rice has been a staple crop in Korea for the past several millennia.[5] Korea is well suited for rice cultivation. There are two main varieties of rice: *Oryza sativa indica* and *Oryza sativa japonica/sinica*, both of which were cultivated in the Yangzi basin in central China by the third millennium BCE. *Oryza sativa japonica/sinica* is best suited for Korea, since it germinates and ripens at lower temperatures and is more resistant to cold weather. Rice can be grown on dry fields, but the best yields are in wet paddies. During earlier times, most rice was grown in dry fields, but after the sixteenth century wet rice farming emerged as the dominant form of agriculture in Korea. In wet rice farming, water is kept in small reservoirs or diverted from small streams to flow into fields. Rice seedlings are first planted in seedbeds and then transplanted into the main field. In Korea the transplanting is usually done in June just before the start of the summer monsoon season. Weather patterns in Korea are ideal for this type of rice cultivation. The summer monsoon brings most of the year's rainfall, which amounts to about sixty inches a year in the southern areas and about fifty inches in the central Han River basin and declines further as the monsoon proceeds northward. Rice grows fast in Korea's warm, humid, tropical-like summers and ripens in the bright, cloudless, dry autumns. Although there are no broad plains in Korea, the many river valleys provide rich alluvial soils, and the numerous streams that trickle down the mountainsides into the valleys make for a ready supply of water for the paddies.

A number of other crops, such as soybeans, barley, and millet, have been important components of the Korean diet, but rice occupies a place in the culture unrivaled by any other food source. The word for meal, *pap*, means "cooked rice." Most Koreans from the beginnings of recorded history 2,000 years ago until the mid-twentieth century were rice farmers. The rhythms of rice production have been dictated by the planting and harvesting of rice. Rice production has been the prime determinant of the population distribution. The majority of Koreans in historical times have lived in the warmer and moister regions of southern and central Korea; the northern regions, less suitable for rice, have been less populated and more marginal. The elite derived their wealth primarily from their ownership of good rice lands and their control over those that farmed them.

It is not yet clear when rice farming began in Korea. Between 2000 and 1500 BCE the *chŭlmun* pottery culture gave way to the *mumun*, or plain, pottery style, so named after the characteristic undecorated double-rimmed vessels. It was during this period that agriculture clearly emerged as the dominant way of life. During the early *mumun* culture, hunting, fishing, and foraging were still important, and archaeological evidence suggests that cultivation of rice was not extensive until the first millennium BCE, indicating not an abrupt change but a slow transition as the peoples of the peninsula adapted to rice farming.[6] But by the late first millennium, a great transformation had taken place, as rice cultivation was beginning to be the basis for the Korean way of life, which it would continue to be until the twentieth century. The impact of rice cultivation on the peoples and cultures of Korea was profound. Rice cultivation made it possible to support dense populations. It bound this expanded population to the soil and to the seasonal rhythms associated with the cultivation of rice. Collecting wild plants, the planting of a variety of vegetables, the raising of pigs and oxen, fishing, shellfish collecting, and the cultivation of barley and millet as secondary crops were also important, but only as supplements to rice farming.

Some archaeological evidence suggests that the early peoples of Korea were influenced by developments of China. Around 700 BCE, or perhaps a little earlier, the use of bronze began in Korea. Western scholars, impressed by the impact of technology on social and cultural change, have tended to regard the arrival of bronze tools and weapons as of epochal significance. In the case of Korea, however, the appearance of bronze knives and tools was in itself probably of only minor significance. During the Bronze Age, some graves are accompanied by bronze mirrors, daggers, and bells, which are sometimes found in stone cists. These would appear to be precious goods, setting off their possessors from those whose graves had simpler, more common stone burial possessions. Characteristic among Korean bronze artifacts are a dagger shaped like a *pip'a* (Chinese lute) and a multiknobbed mirror; both are found in adjacent areas of Manchuria, and the dagger is also found in Shandong and parts of northern China. Neither appears to be of Chinese origin, and these may be indicators of a broad Northeast Asia cultural zone.[7] Interestingly enough, not a single bronze ritual vessel, which is characteristic of China's Bronze Age, has been found in Korea. This suggests that although bronze metalworking most probably spread to Korea from China, where it developed around 1800 BCE, Korea remained culturally different from the Chinese mainland. Also interesting is the fact that bronze was not associated with state formation in Korea as it has been elsewhere. Despite efforts by some nationalist Korean historians to claim bronze artifacts as evidence of early states, it is unlikely that any organization above the tribal level existed at this time. Iron also probably came to the peninsula from China sometime before 300 BCE. Iron is important not only because it is superior to stone for cutting trees, clearing fields, and eliminating enemies, but also because it contributed to economic specialization and the development of trade. Both are key elements in the creation of complex societies.

Another artifact that suggests Korea was part of a Northeast Asian cultural zone distinct from most of China is the megalith. About 10,000 dolmens have been found in Korea, most probably built in the first millennium BCE. These are not unique to Korea but are found in Manchuria, northern Shandong Province of China, and northern Kyushu. They usually mark grave sites and consist of two basic types. The northern type, called *t'akcha* (table) style, has typically three or four stones covered by a large stone; the southern *paduk* (Korean name for the game of *go*) type consists of a large capstone resting on a number of much smaller stones or directly on the ground. Less is known about them and the people who constructed them than is known about the more famous megaliths in Western Europe. The construction of elaborate stone megaliths suggests formation of social stratification and of social units larger than simple villages. Presumably it took large numbers of people, more than would inhabit a small village, to construct the megaliths, and burials there would be for persons of high or important status.[8] Many mysteries remain about the megaliths. For example, why do the artifacts found in stone cists and dolmens vary considerably? Do they represent different ethnic groups or social strata? If the latter, then why are bronze artifacts more likely to be found in the stone cists than in the more impressive dolmens?

Early peoples in Korea lived in small self-sufficient communities, originally hunting bands and later farming or fishing settlements. It was most probably only in the late first millennium BCE that larger political units were formed. By the middle of the second millennium BCE states appeared in northern China. The formation of states and later empires in the north of China had a profound impact on Korea. The emergence of early kingdoms in Crete and mainland Greece was influenced by the more ancient societies of Egypt and the Near East. Likewise, state formation in Northeast Asia—Manchuria, Korea, and Japan—occurred under the influence of the earlier and more complex societies of China. This, however, does not mean that Northeast Asian state formation was always and only the product of the direct impact of Chinese developments. For throughout the history of Korea cultural processes took place that were often very different from those in China, indicating a high degree of autonomous development based in part on cultural roots and ecological factors that were quite distinct. From the beginning of Korean history, proximity to the great Chinese civilization was one of the main determining factors in the evolution of Korean culture. Consequently, the absorption of Chinese cultural patterns and their adaptation to indigenous and non-Sinitic patterns have been a major part of the process that created a clearly definable Korean culture and society.

SOURCES FOR EARLY KOREA

Our knowledge of the early Korean states comes from several sources: written records, archaeological evidence, and myths and legends. The earliest Korean written sources are inscriptions; the earliest of these dates from 414 CE. The most important written sources are two histories, the *Samguk sagi* (*History of the Three Kingdoms*) (see chapter 4) and the *Samguk yusa* (*Memorabilia of the Three Kingdoms*) (see chapter 5). But these were compiled in 1145 and 1279 respectively, centuries after the events they describe. Although they are based on earlier sources that are no longer extant and remain extremely important for our understanding of ancient Korean history, their usefulness is greatly enhanced when they can be confirmed and supplemented by other sources. Chinese sources also bring considerable light to early Korean history. During the Han dynasty, the first great dynasty that unified all of China on a long-term basis (202 BCE–220 CE), the first detailed accounts of events on the Korean peninsula appear. The most important of these are the Chinese history *Shiji* (*Historical Record*), written by Sima Qian around 100 BCE, and the *Dongyizhuan* (*Account of the Eastern Barbarians*) section of *Sanguozhi* (*Record of the Three Kingdoms*), compiled in 297 CE. The latter is probably the single most important contemporary document on ancient Korean history. Archaeologists have also provided valuable information that is no less important in understanding this period. And although it seems unlikely that major new written sources will be found, new archaeological evidence is providing a continuously better picture of early Korea.

Still another source is the myths and legends associated with this period. The study of myths for historical information is a difficult and controversial field, but it too can yield clues about the past. The most famous myth is that of Tan'gun. In this myth a celestial deity mates with a compliant bear that gives birth to Tan'gun (Sandalwood Prince), who in turn establishes the first Korean state of Chosŏn in 2333 BCE. While this story was not recorded until the thirteenth century, it is probably of much more ancient origin. It hints of animal totems; mountain worship, since most of the action takes place on a sacred mountain; and perhaps at the semidivine claims for early ruling families. In the twentieth century, the Tan'gun myth would be interpreted by nationalist writers as supporting claims for the antiquity and uniqueness of the Korean people.

CHOSŎN

An early recorded name associated with Korea is Chaoxian (Korean: Chosŏn). The name is derived from the Chinese characters *chao*, meaning "dawn" or "morning," and *xian*, meaning "fresh" or "calm." Often translated in English as "Land of the Morning Calm," it is one of the names Koreans call their country. The name comes from the geographic position of Korea in relation to China. Korea was to the east of China; hence it was an early morning country in the same way that Japan, still farther east, was later designated Riben (anglicized as Japan) or "sun origin" land.[9] By the second century BCE, Chinese works such as the *Zhanguoce* (*Strategies of the Warring States*) and the *Shangshu dazhuan* (*Commentary on the Esteemed Documents*) refer to an area called Chaoxian. Although some later Korean histories would assert that the state was founded by Tan'gun in 2333 BCE, the earliest uncontested date for a political entity called Chosŏn is 109 BCE[10] At that time, the Chinese, under Emperor Han Wudi, attacked and conquered Chaoxian, or Chosŏn. Almost everything about the origin and nature of this Chosŏn is obscure. It was likely to have been more a tribal federation than a state. Perhaps originally located in southern Manchuria, it fell after the Chinese besieged a fortress located in northern Korea, probably near P'yŏngyang.[11] The people of the Chosŏn were most likely illiterate. Modern Koreans see ancient Chosŏn as an ancestor to their nation, but there is no clear evidence linking it with any particular ethnic group or culture. Its chief historical importance is that it brought the Chinese into direct involvement in Korea.

In 221 BCE the Qin unified all China for the first time, although only briefly. After 210 BCE the Qin Empire began to fall apart, and in the struggle for power that ensued Liu Bang emerged and reunified China, establishing the Han dynasty that lasted from 202 BCE to 220 CE, an empire comparable to its contemporary, the Roman Empire, in area and population. Liu created a number of *wang* (kings) to function as vassals; the king of Yan was one of these. In 195 BCE, the Yan king revolted and went over to the Xiongnu, a steppe nomad people. One of his lieutenants, Wiman (Chinese: Weiman), is recorded in the *Shiji* as having fled with 1,000 followers to Chosŏn, where the ruler Chun appointed him a frontier commander. Wiman, however, seized power with the aid of Chinese who had already settled in Chosŏn and set himself up as king. This occurred sometime between 194 and 180 BCE. His descendants ruled until 108 BCE.

Wiman and his successors probably served as foreign vassals of China, perhaps acting as middlemen between the tribal peoples in the area and the Chinese. But if this was so, Chosŏn's relationships with China were often uneasy. It had become a place of exile for dissidents in the northeastern part of the empire. The rulers of Chosŏn also blocked attempts by tribal groupings in the area to directly contact and trade with tribal peoples to the south. When the Han emperor Wu (141–87 BCE) sought to bring the frontier regions of his empire under direct control, he conquered this troublesome neighbor. During 109–108 BCE Emperor Wu launched a land and sea invasion. Following initial setbacks, the Chinese occupied the Chosŏn capital of Wanggŏm, and the last king, Ugŏ, a grandson of Wiman, was killed by his own ministers. For the next four centuries a northwestern part of the Korean peninsula was directly incorporated into the Chinese Empire, the first and only time the Chinese exerted direct rule in Korea.

THE CHINESE COMMANDERIES

The Chinese, having conquered Chosŏn, set up four administrative units called commanderies (Chinese: *jun*; Korean: *kun*). The Taedong River basin, the area where the modern city of P'yŏngyang is located, became the center of the Lelang (Korean: Nangnang) commandery. Three other commanderies were organized: Xuantu (Korean: Hyŏndo), Lintun (Korean: Imdun), and Chenfan (Korean: Chinbŏn). The locations of these commanderies are not altogether certain, but most likely Xuantu originally was farther inland from Lelang, and Lintun was just south of it in the area inhabited by a people known as the Okchŏ. The site of Chenfan is less easy to determine but was probably south of Lelang. After Emperor Wu's death in 87 BCE a retrenchment began under his successor, Emperor Chao (87–74 BCE). The remote Chenfan commandery was abandoned in 82 BCE, the Lintun commandery was merged with Xuantu in 75 BCE, and Xuantu in the same year was relocated farther east, most probably in the Yalu River basin. Thus, the history of the Chinese presence in Korea was mainly the story of Lelang and Xuantu, with the former being the more populous and prosperous of the two outposts of Chinese civilization.

The creation of the Chinese commanderies is important in the development of Korean history. It brought the peoples of the peninsula into direct contact with the advanced civilization of the Chinese, launching the process of the sinicization of the Korean peoples. With the establishment of the commanderies, the various peoples of the peninsula became involved in a web of trade and cultural ties that connected them with the vast empire of the Han. The Han Empire radiated out from its base in the North China Plain to the Yangzi and southward to Vietnam, and from the Pacific coast to the oases of Central Asia. Thus Korean history became a part of a larger history of East Asia.

These Chinese commanderies have been likened to colonies. However, the commanderies were not foreign territories, but were an integral part of the Han Empire, with the same administrative structure that characterized the rest of China. The inhabitants included many Chinese settlers. Just how many is not known, nor is it possible to estimate the percentage of the population that was ethnically Chinese. In any case, a good deal of intermarriage and cultural assimilation is probable. The Chinese presence was not a sudden break in the history of the region, for Chosŏn had already absorbed Chinese refugees, and the ruling house of Chosŏn was, at least according to the recorded accounts, of Chinese descent. The Lelang commandery produced textiles and fine Chinese ceramics locally. It imported silk, lacquerware, jade, and gold and silver jewelry, and the elite rode in carriages made from imported equipment. The way of life maintained by the elite at the capital in the P'yŏngyang area, which is known from the tombs and scattered archaeological remains, evinces a prosperous, refined, and very Chinese culture.[12] The existence of imported goods in large numbers from all over the Han Empire testifies to the prosperity of Lelang.

The prosperity of the commanderies was derived from trade. Lelang, and to a lesser extent Xuantu, sat in the center of a network of trade that incorporated the peoples of Manchuria and of northeastern Korea and the tribes in the southern peninsula, and even extended to the peoples and polities of the Japanese archipelago. Bronze mirrors, silk brocade, jade, vermillion, and gold seals from China were exchanged for the hardwood timber, fish, salt, iron, and agricultural produce of the region. Many of the imports into Lelang from the surrounding peoples were locally consumed, but the wealth of goods that were imported from the Chinese mainland suggests that any local products may have been re-exported to the rest of China. Many of these goods were of symbolic nature: caps, robes, seals, and precious items that were status goods enhancing the prestige and authority of native elites. This policy was termed *heqin*, "peace and kinship," buying peace with nomadic and settled peoples along the frontiers with entertainments and sumptuous gifts.[13] In the time-honored practice of successful imperialists, the Chinese extended their authority beyond the territory they physically occupied by incorporating surrounding indigenous peoples into the imperial system. Tribal and clan leaders received prestige goods, along with Chinese titles and symbols of authority, and were able to engage in a profitable trade in return for their loyalty and cooperation. In this way, most of the peoples of Korea became tied to the Han Chinese imperial system.

Economic considerations may have entered into the original conquest; however, it seems clear that the primary concern was strategic, to protect the eastern flank of China's northern frontier with often warlike and aggressive tribal peoples. Tribal leaders were required to come to the Xuantu or Lelang capitals to "pay tribute," that is, to trade and receive the caps, gowns, seals, and titles that were bestowed upon them by Chinese officials as vassals of the emperor. Throughout Korean history this use of the Chinese emperor as a source of authority would prove mutually advantageous to the Chinese and to Koreans. In return, tribal leaders were

called upon to aid in fighting other tribal groups beyond the control of
the Chinese. In the southern part of the Korean peninsula, tribal groups
appear to have generally been militarily less formidable and perhaps
less organized. Their relationship with the Chinese may have been more
ruthlessly exploitative, and tribute goods, food, timber, iron, and other
resources may have been forcibly extracted from local peoples. But even
if this was the case, the tribute relationship still held many of the same
advantages for the elite groups among the southern peoples.

CHINESE COMMANDERIES AND THEIR NEIGHBORS: THE NORTHERN PEOPLES

Chinese sources from the time of the commanderies provide us with the
earliest written descriptions of Korean societies and cultures. What is
now Korea was inhabited by a confusing array of tribal groups that had
not merged into a single culture. The Chinese sources refer to the Dongyi
(the "Eastern Barbarians"), a general term for the non-Chinese people
of the northeast region. According to the third-century *Sanguozhi* there
were nine Dongyi: Puyŏ (Chinese: Fuyu), Okchŏ, Ŭmnu (Chinese: Yilou),
Eastern Ye (Chinese: Hui), Koguryŏ (Chinese: Gaogouli), the three Han
tribes of southern Korea, and the Wa of Japan. The actual classification of
peoples is a complex matter, as different tribes were called by different
names, peoples moved about, and groups split off from other groups.
Trying to sort out these groups and their relationships to each other has
been a problem for historians of early Korea.

Along the northern borders of the Chinese commanderies were several
major groups, among which the Puyŏ were the first to be recorded by the
Chinese. The Puyŏ, who attracted the notice of the Chinese in the third
century BCE, lived in the plains and valleys of the upper Sungari River
basin in central Manchuria. Although very much on the fringe of the Chinese world, they were influenced by Chinese culture and often served as
allies against the warlike Koguryŏ, who lived south of them. They were
not organized as a state but were ruled by tribal chiefs who apparently
met to elect a supreme chieftain for all the Puyŏ. This Puyŏ tribal confederacy emerged by the second century BCE as the most powerful force in
the region.

South of the Puyŏ lived the Koguryŏ, a people who according to the
Chinese spoke a similar language and had similar customs but who differed from the Puyŏ in their emotional and volatile temper. The Koguryŏ
may have originally been a branch of the Puyŏ who settled farther into
southern Manchuria in the region of the Yalu headwaters. Not only were

they linguistically and culturally related to the Puyŏ, but their legends as well suggest Puyŏ origins. Unlike the Puyŏ, the Koguryŏ appear in Chinese records only in 12 CE, by which time a long-standing client relationship had been established between them and the commandery of Xuantu. Living in marginal lands less suitable for agriculture than the fertile plains the Puyŏ occupied, the Koguryŏ were more dependent on hunting for their livelihood and maintained a more aggressive and warlike way of life that caused considerable concern for the Chinese. In fact, the principal function of the Xuantu may have been to attempt to control the Koguryŏ. The Koguryŏ were in frequent conflict with the Chinese after 12 CE, which no doubt accounts for the more negative assessment of them as an emotional and volatile people.

From 75 BCE to 12 CE the Koguryŏ paid tribute to the Chinese. Then they established a tribal federation, in the Hun River, a tributary of the Yalu; and the ruler began to call himself *wang*, or king, a sign that he no longer accepted subordinate status as a mere marquis but wished to be treated as the ruler of a sovereign state.[14] The Koguryŏ began a territorial expansion that included establishing a suzerain relationship with the Okchŏ on the eastern coast of Korea. From there they launched frequent raids against their neighbors, including many clashes with the Chinese. Our information on the culture of the Koguryŏ in this period is limited. The religion of the Koguryŏ appears to have had an astral element similar to that of more nomadic steppe peoples from which they themselves were most probably descended. It also included a "Spirit of the Underground Passage," and worship of rivers and other natural features. We also know that they were divided into five main tribes or clans: the Yŏnno, Chŏllo, Sunno, Kwanno, and Kyeru. The next several centuries saw the gradual evolution from a loose confederacy of these five tribes into a centralized state (see chapter 2).

In terms of the future history of Korea the Koguryŏ were by far the most important of the northern peoples; however, several other groups played an active role during this period. The Ŭmno were a people subordinate to the Puyŏ who never organized themselves into a state. From their home in Manchuria, they conducted raids during the summer into northeastern Korea; the peoples along the coast appear to have been their chief victims. Famed as archers and as pig breeders, the Ŭmno were probably less closely related to modern Koreans. They may have been related to the Suksin (Chinese: Suzhen), another people based in Manchuria who earned a reputation for their use of poison arrows. Two other groups that lived in what is now Korea were the Eastern Ye (Tongye) and the Okchŏ. The Puyŏ, Koguryŏ, the Okchŏ, and the Eastern Ye are collectively known as the Yemaek; most were associated with Manchuria as much as they were with the modern boundaries of Korea.

CHINESE COMMANDERIES AND
THEIR NEIGHBORS: THE SOUTHERN PEOPLES

To the south of Lelang were the Han tribes.[15] Present-day South Koreans generally trace their ancestry to the Han tribes. In South Korea the official term for the Korean nation is Han'guk, "country of the Han." Since they were farther away from the center of Chinese civilization, less was recorded about these peoples. Much of the knowledge we do have about them comes from the *Sanguozhi,* written at the end of the third century. It describes the Samhan (the three Han): the Mahan, the Chinhan, and the Pyŏnhan. These terms refer not to states or organized groups but to three related peoples that lived in different regions of Korea south of the Han River. Collectively their homeland roughly covered the area of modern South Korea. They were organized into petty statelets of varying size, ruled by chiefs. By the middle of the third century the Mahan inhabited the rich farmlands of the southwestern part of Korea, which have been the rice basket of Korea. Not surprisingly they were listed as the most numerous of the Han, constituting fifty-four of the statelets, what the Chinese called *guo* (countries). The *guo* varied in size. Some were reported as having up to 10,000 households, and the total number of households was said to be 100,000.[16] The Chinhan, who lived in the middle and upper Naktong basin in southeast Korea, constituted twelve *guo.* Along the lower Naktong River basin and along the southeast coast were the Pyŏnhan, who also lived in twelve *guo.*

It would be inaccurate to regard the *guo* as states. Their small size and the lack of any clear archaeological evidence of organized states confirm the observations made by the ancient Chinese that the rulers of the *guo* were not *wang.* Most probably these were chiefdoms, that is, small polities ruled by hereditary chiefs who controlled at least a few villages but lacking any state administrative structure. Although most were farmers, an elite stratum existed who, the Chinese recorded, wore silk garments and leather shoes, in contrast to the common people, who wore hemp clothes and straw shoes. The elite were also fond of earrings and necklaces. The Mahan, who lived in earthen huts, were an agricultural people. As with most agricultural peoples they held festivals in the spring and at harvest time in which sacrifices were made. The Chinese sources describe the Mahan as backward people who did not value horses or money. The Mahan traded with an island people called Hoju who lived on a large island in the western sea, perhaps referring to Cheju Island.

The Chinhan lived in settlements, the Chinese reported, enclosed by wooden stockades; they practiced sericulture and used oxen and horse carts. Of particular note is that they traded in iron, which appears to have been an important export from the southeastern region. The Chinhan were reported to have been fond of dancing and drinking, an observation that has been made by many subsequent foreign observers to the Korean countryside. The Mahan and the Chinhan spoke the same (or similar) languages, but the Pyŏnhan, who shared the same dwellings and customs as the Chinhan, were said to have spoken a different language.[17] The general assumption has been that the languages spoken by the Samhan were directly ancestral to the modern Korean language. And while there is no proof of that assertion, it seems a reasonable one. Thus in terms of ethnicity and language the Samhan can be said to be early Korean peoples. Most lived in semisubterranean homes in little villages near river terraces where they were able to grow rice, barley, and other crops. These villages were likely to have been largely self-sufficient. Sustained contact with the Chinese commanderies was probably a key factor in stimulating organizational development among the people of the peninsula, especially the southern folk.

Further to the south of the Han were the T'amna of Cheju Island, cattle and pig breeders who spoke a language different from the Samhan. Farther still were the Wa peoples, long considered to be the earliest reference to the Japanese. The first contact with the Wa was in 57 CE, when an embassy arrived in Lelang. Another was recorded in 107, and four were recorded from 238 to 248. Evidence indicates that the Wa had close connections with the Pyŏnhan and probably imported iron from the Kimhae area. A regular trade between the Korean peninsula and the Japanese archipelago must have existed, since Korean and Chinese artifacts from this period are frequently found there. The *Sanguozhi*, the first detailed description of both the Samhan and the Wa, makes a clear distinction between the two peoples, whose customs are described as very different. Who were the Wa? In traditional accounts they are simply equated with the Japanese. It is highly unlikely, however, that a definable Japanese ethnic group existed at such an early date. Rather, the peoples of both the peninsula and the archipelago consisted of various tribal cultures. The Wa probably lived in western Japan and perhaps on both sides of the Korean Strait. Just as tribal peoples in southern Manchuria and Korea overlapped, so the peoples along the southern coast of Korea were probably linked with those of western Japan. Only later did separate and distinct Korean and Japanese peoples emerge.

POLITICS OF THE THIRD CENTURY

The fortunes of the Chinese commanderies fluctuated with those of the Chinese heartland. Toward the late second century the Han dynasty went into decline. In 220 CE, the Han Empire broke up into three states. Wei, the northernmost, controlled the North China Plain, the heartland region of ancient China and the region closest to Korea. As part of the efforts by the Wei to consolidate their power, they launched a series of campaigns against the belligerent peoples of the northeast from 238 to 245, which became one of the most impressive displays of Chinese power in the history of Korea. A main target of the campaign was Koguryŏ, which the Chinese defeated, destroying its capital in 244. The revival of Chinese authority, however, did not last long, and the Jin dynasty that temporarily reunited the Chinese Empire rapidly declined in the early fourth century. A civil war broke out in northern China in 301. In 311, the Xianbei, a steppe nomad people, sacked the imperial Chinese capital, Luoyang. Six years later, the Jin relocated their capital to the lower Yangzi region and all effective administration in northern China collapsed. This inaugurated a period of Chinese history whose troubled nature is exemplified in the convention of referring to it as the Period of the Five Dynasties and the Sixteen Kingdoms (317–589).

The Lelang and Taifang commanderies, the latter created south of Lelang, cut off from the rest of China by a series of nomadic intruders who had overrun northern China, continued a shadowy existence. By tradition, Lelang was conquered by a resurgent Koguryŏ in 313 and its southern outpost Taifang by the emerging kingdom of Paekche in 316. It appears, however, that some sort of rule by local Chinese elites continued well into the fourth century.[18] After four centuries the Chinese presence in Korea disappeared. One reason for the lack of a continued Chinese presence was the geographic remoteness of Korea. The commanderies in Korea were distant outposts of the empire that could not be maintained in troubled times. With the withdrawal of China, the people of the Korean peninsula had several centuries to develop their societies without direct Chinese intervention. It was during these centuries that the first literate indigenous states emerged.

KOREA IN GLOBAL PERSPECTIVE: 5,000 YEARS OF HISTORY

Modern Koreans have been proud of their "5,000 years" of history. A rather arbitrary figure based on the idea that their history began with Tan'gun in the third millennium BCE. In proclaiming an ancient national lineage, they resemble other twentieth-century nationalists, from the Chinese, with their "4,000 years of history," to the Turkish historians of the 1920s and 1930s, who established a new national history tracing the Turkish nation to earliest antiquity.

How old is Korea? The question cannot be answered because it supposes that the modern concept of Korea, of a nation of people with a common heritage and a common destiny living as an autonomous unit within a global community of nations can be connected back in time in linear fashion. But this is misunderstanding history. Korea, although politically divided today is still thought of as one nation by the people of North and South Korea. As a state that has occupied most of the Korean Peninsula, it has existed since 676, making it one of the oldest continuous political units in the world. No modern state in Europe, and few if any in Africa or in Southwest and Southeast Asia, can be so clearly traced in recognizable form from such an early period as this. Only China and Japan are comparable. China, far older, was a vast multiethnic empire rather than a geographically compact state. Yet all the historical evidence suggests that no distinctive "Korean" ethnic group or culture existed before this, and even after political unity in 676 there is no clear evidence that all within the state shared the same language and identity. Moreover, the cultural and ethnic boundary between peninsular Korea and Manchuria was still a blurred one at best.

It is a common tendency for modern peoples to project their strong sense of national identity further back into the past than can be reasonably supported by historical evidence. While Koreans can justifiably point to a long history as distinctive peoples existing within a single political framework, when they interpret the varied peoples and polities that existed in ancient times as "Koreans" in the modern sense, they too are projecting their own identity on the past in an unrealistic manner.

The Tan'gun Myth

The Wei shu tells us that two thousand years ago, at the time of Emperor Yao, Tan'gun Wanggŏm chose Asadal as his capital and founded the state of Chosŏn. The Old Record notes that in olden times Hwanin's son, Hwanung, wished to descend from Heaven and live in the world of human beings. Knowing his son's desire, Hwanin surveyed the three highest mountains and found Mount T'aebaek the most suitable place for his son to settle and help human beings. Therefore he gave Hwanung three heavenly seals and dispatched him to rule over the people. Hwanung descended with three thousand followers to a spot under a tree by the Holy Altar atop Mount T'aebaek, and he called this place the City of God. He was the Heavenly King Hwanung. Leading the Earl of Wind, the Master of Rain, and the Master of Clouds, he took charge of some three hundred and sixty areas of responsibility, including agriculture, allotted life spans, illness, punishment, and good and evil, and brought culture to his people.

At that time a bear and a tiger living in the same cave prayed to Holy Hwanung to transform them into human beings. He gave them a bundle of sacred mugworts and twenty cloves of garlic and said, "If you eat these and shun the sunlight for one hundred days, you will assume human form." Both animals ate the species and avoided the sun. After twenty-one days the bear became a woman but the tiger, unable to observe the taboo, remained a tiger. Unable to find a husband, the bear-woman prayed under the altar tree for a child. Hwanung metamorphosed himself, lay with her, and begot a son called Tan'gun Wanggŏm.

[Tan'gun later was often considered the first Korean and/or founder of the first Korean state. This account goes on to say that in the "fiftieth year of the reign of Emperor Yao," on a date calculated as October 3, 2333 BCE, Tan'gun was said to have established the state of Chosŏn. This date has become a national holiday in South Korea. Koreans today often refer to the "5,000 years of Korean history," a phrase based on this legendary date.]

—from the *Samguk yusa* 1:33–34[19]

2

✦

The Period
of the Three Kingdoms,
4th Century to 676

The fourth century is an important period for Korean history. It was a time when the welter of peoples, polities, and imperial outposts that had characterized Korea was replaced by three large, well-developed states: Koguryŏ, Paekche, and Silla. The next three centuries saw the development of Korean society and culture within the frameworks of these three states and their struggle for the mastery of the peninsula.

The term *Three Kingdoms* is somewhat misleading, for in addition to Silla, Koguryŏ, and Paekche, there were a number of small states in the southeast that are collectively known as Kaya, and Puyŏ. However, the states of Kaya failed to consolidate themselves into a centralized political unit and as a result were swallowed up one by one by their northern neighbor Silla, a process that was completed in 562 CE, while Puyŏ disappeared earlier, in 494. For about a century there were only three states on the peninsula. In 660, Silla and its Chinese ally conquered Paekche, and in 668 Silla and the Chinese destroyed Koguryŏ. Silla then drove the Chinese out of southern Koguryŏ and by 676 emerged as the sole peninsular power.[1] The origins of the three kingdoms are somewhat obscure. The traditional dates for the founding of the Three Kingdoms as recorded in the *Samguk sagi*, the oldest extant Korean history, are 57 BCE for Silla, 37 BCE for Koguryŏ, and 18 BCE for Paekche. And these dates are dutifully given in many textbooks and published materials in Korea today, but their basis is in myth; only Koguryŏ can be traced back to a time period that is anywhere near its legendary founding.

THE EMERGENCE OF THE THREE KINGDOMS

The Koguryŏ peoples, most probably a branch of the Puyŏ, were living in the Hun River basin just north of the Yalu from 75 BCE to 12 CE. The early Koguryŏ kingdom was more of a tribal federation than a centralized state. From 12 to 207 CE it was independent of China, and it was a formidable military power that conducted frequent raids on its neighbors. In 207, after suffering a series of retaliatory attacks by the Liaodong commandery, Koguryŏ relocated to the Yalu valley. Its leaders set up a stone-walled capital at Hwando (Chinese: Wandu) in the Tonggou region of what is now Jilin Province in Manchuria. From there the kingdom expanded to the mouth of the Yalu, gaining an access to the Yellow Sea. When China in the third century became divided into three rival dynasties, Koguryŏ carried out diplomatic relations with the southern dynastic rivals of the northern Chinese state of Wei. In retaliation the Wei state of north China destroyed the capital in 245. After disappearing from the historical record, Koguryŏ reemerged as a strong state during the reign of King Mich'ŏn (reigned 300–330).[2] The rise of Koguryŏ at this time coincides with the decline of Chinese power in the region, and the two are no doubt related. Koguryŏ's rise was probably aided by the fact that it was able to move into a power vacuum that existed at the time.

Paekche emerged from the area of the Mahan in southwestern Korea. According to tradition, it was founded in 18 BCE by the two sons of Chumong, Onjo and Piryu, who were given some land by the Lord of Mahan. Onjo then became the first king of this new state, and his descendants ruled until 660 when the last king, Ŭija, was defeated by his Silla rivals and their Chinese allies. The foundation legend places the founding of Paekche much too early; nonetheless, many historians assume that Paekche grew out of one of the fifty-four *guo* mentioned in the *Sanguozhi*, although the ruling family may have been of Manchurian Puyŏ origin. Evidence suggests that there may have been a migration into the Mahan region by some Puyŏ or related Manchurian peoples; however, the links between the Paekche and Puyŏ are not well understood. Whatever its origins, unlike Koguryŏ, Paekche appears rather suddenly in the historical records with the reign of Kŭnch'ogo (r. 346–375), who ruled a state that inaugurated diplomatic relations with the Chinese state of Jin in 372. The first capital of Paekche was Hansŏng, believed to have been in the Han River area.[3] This served as the capital until 474. The inhabitants of Paekche were probably ethnically and linguistically Han and thus more closely related to the people of Silla and Kaya than to Koguryŏ or Puyŏ. But it is hard to untangle the ethnic and tribal links between the peoples within the peninsula and the peoples in Manchuria and the Japanese archipelago at this time.

The emergence of the Paekche kingdom coincides with the crumbling of Chinese power in Northeast Asia. The Chinese appear to have conducted a divide-and-rule policy in the peninsula, bestowing honors and status on local chieftains but intimidating them from extending their power. The collapse of Chinese authority led to a power vacuum, in which indigenous polities were left to contend for mastery of the region. In the decades after 290, when the Chinese position in Korea began to decline, consolidation of Korean states proceeded rapidly, with Koguryŏ in the north making a strong revival after 300. Quite possibly the rise of Paekche begins at this time as well.

Located in the southeastern part of the peninsula farthest from direct contact with China, Silla was last to receive influences from the continent, and its institutional development showed a time lag compared with Koguryŏ and Paekche. But Silla was the state that unified most of the Korean peninsula and whose language, customs, and institutions dominated the subsequent historical development of Korean society and culture. The Silla state began in the Kyŏngju basin, a small fertile area sheltered by surrounding hills. The nucleus of the state was Saro, one of the twelve Chinhan *guo*. According to tradition, Silla was founded in 57 BCE by Pak Hyŏkkŏse, who was miraculously born from an egg. His name Pak was perhaps derived from *palk*, meaning "bright," since sunlight shone from his body. In the recorded legend, Saro prior to Pak had been made up of six villages. It was their headmen who unanimously chose this strange youth as their leader.[4] Subsequently, the villages were under his united rule. The date 57 BCE is far too early for the likely founding of the Silla state. It is of symbolic importance for later Silla historians who established this traditional chronology because it makes their state older than its two neighbors. The date itself is derived by counting back twelve sixty-year cycles (these cycles were the principal unit of measuring years in East Asia) from 663 CE, the year that Paekche was finally destroyed.

The legend does suggest that Saro was formed by a voluntary union of the six villages/descent groups: Kŭmyang, Saryang, Ponp'i, Maryang, Hanji, and the Sŭpp'i. The Pak kings came from the Kŭmyang, and the queens, starting with Pak Hyŏkkŏse's bride, Aryŏng, came from the Saryang. This legend would appear to hint that the founder of Saro or at least its first major ruler was an outsider, since he arrived mysteriously when an egg was discovered. His supernatural birth could also be a means of justifying the elevated status of the later rulers of Silla, since they could lay claim to being descendents of no ordinary men. The Paks, however, were not the sole ruling family, for the Sŏk and the Kim families supplied rulers as well. The Sŏk founder was also born from an egg and is reported to have come from the east coast. When in the fourth century Silla emerges as a fully historical state, the ruling family was from the Kim descent group and would remain so until the tenth century. Several million Koreans today claim membership in this royal Kim descent group (the Kyŏngju Kim). The Kim rulers chose their consorts from the Pak family.

The first fully documented ruler of Silla was Naemul (r. 356–402), who held the title of *maripkan*, a word that denotes an elevated ridge.[5] In 377, Silla is recorded as having sent envoys who accompanied a Koguryŏ embassy to the former Qin rulers of northern China. It is not clear, however, how far state development had proceeded in Silla at this time, or to what extent it ruled or dominated the former Chinhan territories. The adoption of a new title (previous Silla rulers are said to have called themselves *isagŭm*, "successor princes"), and its active role in international politics, would suggest that Silla was undergoing a new phase in its history. Most probably Silla was still in the process of completing its consolidation of the former Chinhan *guo* in the late fourth century. As it did so, it began associating itself with Koguryŏ and competing with Paekche and the Kaya states for mastery of the entire Samhan region, roughly the region that makes up what is now South Korea.

The fourth century also saw the emergence of a loose federation of small states collectively known as Kaya. The Kaya states may have evolved out of the Pyŏnhan peoples who inhabited the fertile middle and lower Naktong basin and the southeast coast. They actively engaged in commerce and iron production. Despite their prosperity and apparent commercial sophistication, the Kaya states were never consolidated into a large kingdom. The price they paid for this was their gradual annexation and absorption by Silla. Yet, Kaya had a distinctive culture that exerted considerable influence on its neighbors, as illustrated by its pottery, which became the basis for both Silla pottery and Japanese *sue* ware, as well as the *kayagŭm*, a kind of zither that is still one of the most popular of traditional Korean musical instruments. There were six main loosely confederated Kaya polities. The two most important were Pon Kaya (Original Kaya) and Tae Kaya (Greater Kaya). Pon Kaya, also known as Kŭmgwan Kaya, was located near Kimhae. Iron slags dating to at least the first century BCE testify to the long importance of this area as a center of commerce and industry. Tae Kaya was located in the rich farmlands of the middle Naktong River valley.

The origins of the Kaya states are best known from the eleventh-century work *Karak kukki*. In the legend it records, the kings of the Kaya states emerged from golden eggs that descended from heaven to Mount Kuji (Turtle Mountain) during a festival. This occurred as local chieftains sang a song about a turtle at the command of a strange voice from the mountain. As with Silla, we have dynastic founders emerging from supernatural origins (eggs again).[6] The Kaya had close connections with the Wa of Japan, probably involving trade based on the Kaya area's rich iron deposits. Recent archaeological excavations of the royal tombs of Tae Kaya reveal a wealthy state. The size of the mounded tombs and the considerable wealth of the royal family indicate a highly developed society where the kings were not merely local chieftains but rulers of exalted status with considerable power to command labor and resources.[7] The fertile rice land, the existence of iron deposits, and its location on an ancient trade route that reached from central Japan to northern China were the sources of this wealth. Despite their prosperity, the Kaya states were too small to remain viable political entities. Consequently, they fell victim to an expanding Silla that absorbed Pon Kaya in 532 and Tae Kaya in 562.

THE WA AND THE MIMANA

Another political presence in fourth-century Korea was the Wa. If little is known for certain about the formation of states in Korea before the late fourth century, even less is known about what transpired in Japan. The peoples of Japan were an important factor in northeast Asian politics even in this early period, yet information about them is sparse and almost anything that is said is bound to be caught up in controversy. Both the Japanese and Korean peoples are proud of their uniqueness and concerned about their origins. Furthermore, the bitter legacy of Japan's twentieth-century conquest of Korea has made the study of the relationship between the two peoples an emotionally laden topic. In the late nineteenth and early twentieth centuries Japanese expansionists cited the evidence that Wa peoples were in Korea to support their claims that in ancient times Korea was ruled by Japan. Much of this was based on the existence of the territory of Mimana, also identified with Kaya. According to the eighth-century Japanese history *Nihon shoki* (*The Chronicles of Japan*), Empress Jingu in the fourth century conquered a region in southern Korea and set up the Mimana territory, which was administered by a Japanese official. Later the territory was turned over to Yamato's ally Paekche and then lost to Silla. Japanese imperialists used this historical claim to justify imperialist expansion into the peninsula. When the Japanese annexed Korea in 1910 they could claim to be "restoring" the ancient unity of the two countries.

Most historians today regard the story of Empress Jingu's conquests with skepticism, and many question whether Mimana ever existed at all. Some scholars have suggested that rather than Japanese peoples conquering Korea, horse riders from the peninsula invaded and subdued the peoples of Japan.[8] The "horse rider theory" has been used to account for the appearance of weapons, armor, and tomb decorations found in Japan from the fourth and fifth century that are similar to those found in Korea. More likely, the peoples on both sides of the Korea Straits were related and interacted with each other.

Evidence suggests that between 300 BCE. and 300 CE large numbers of peoples migrated from the Korean Peninsula to the Japanese archipelago, where they introduced rice agriculture, bronze and iron working, and other technologies. Thus rather than the existence of Korean and Japanese peoples there was a continuum of peoples and cultures. The Wa of western Japan, for example, may have lived on both sides of the Korean Straits, and they appeared to have close links with Kaya. It is even possible that the Wa and Kaya were the same ethnic group. The fact that Japanese and Korean political evolution followed similar patterns is too striking to be coincidental. On both sides of the straits the collapse of Chinese authority at the end of the third century and in the early fourth century was followed by the formation of large and durable states. In Japan the rise of Yamato apparently began during or shortly after the formation of the three kingdoms. Its rise was probably related to influences, and possibly migrations, from the peninsula. Northeast Asia formed an interacting and intermingling complex of peoples and cultures. The task of historians to sort out the links and patterns within this complex has been made more difficult by the strong nationalist sentiments that prevail in the region today, and by the tendency to project modern notions of national and ethnic identity anachronistically onto these early times.

Thus, by the second half of the fourth century a number of clearly defined states emerged. These are no longer tribal units or chiefdoms but strong centralized states that were ruled by kings who governed through administrative officials and who were cut off from ordinary subjects by their supernatural origins and their exalted status. They possessed considerable territory and something else as well: literacy. For in the confusion that entailed the fourth-century collapse of Chinese authority north of the Yangzi River valley, Chinese scribes and officials found their way into the courts of these "barbarian" states. They supplied a veneer of sinicization (Chinese cultural influence) as they tutored their masters in the use of Chinese characters, a development that would ensure that these newly rising states and their successors would have the means of sophisticated recordkeeping that is needed by advanced civilizations. The use of Chinese characters as the basic form of writing also meant that the Korean people would be linked by a shared written medium with the civilization of China.

KOREA AND NORTHEAST ASIA
IN THE FOURTH AND FIFTH CENTURIES

The fourth-century events of the Korean peninsula developed in the larger context of Northeast Asia and beyond. For reasons that historians are still trying to determine, the fourth century was a period of profound upheavals in much of Eurasia. In Europe, the Roman Empire, weakened by demographic and economic decline, split into two halves, abandoned its traditional panoply of gods, and adopted a new religion of other-worldly salvation: Christianity. In the next century it saw its western half crumble and lapse into semibarbarism. The other great Eurasian empire, the Chinese, similarly went into economic and military decline and saw half its empire, the northern half, collapse under the strain of nomadic invaders who, like their European equivalents, set up a number of ephemeral semibarbarian successor states. And the Chinese too accepted a foreign religion of otherworldly salvation: Buddhism.

The collapse of the Chinese imperial authority in the north gave the peninsular peoples breathing space for purely indigenous forces to come into play; this led to the rise of large-scale centralized native states. The process was assisted by the diaspora of Chinese who, fleeing turmoil in north China or its Northeast Asian commanderies, took refuge in the newly emerging Korean kingdoms. Korean rulers, in turn, sought the skills of the Chinese as a means of strengthening their own states. Although there was no direct Chinese intervention into Korea for several centuries, all three states sought trade and diplomatic support from the various states of divided China during this period. They were also greatly influenced by Chinese culture. The chief avenue for Chinese influences was Buddhism. Buddhist missionaries from China converted all three kingdoms. In 372, the former Qin sent a monk, Sŏndo, to introduce Buddhism to the Koguryŏ court, and Buddhism became a state religion. Buddhism was adopted by Paekche in 384 when the Jin state of China sent the Indian monk Marananda to the Paekche court. In more remote Silla, another century and a half would pass before the rulers converted to Buddhism.

Koguryŏ was a Manchurian-based power that moved into the peninsula in the fifth century. Under Kwanggaet'o (r. 391–413), Koguryŏ won an impressive series of victories known chiefly through the Kwanggaet'o Inscription, a stele put up by his son and successor Changsu (r. 413–491) in 414 to commemorate his father's achievements.[9] This is the earliest dated Korean inscription. Kwanggaet'o defeated the Murong tribal people that had emerged as a power in Manchuria; expanded his domain to the Liao River; conquered the Yilou, a tribal people in the northeast; and captured 64 walled towns and 1,400 villages. He also boasted of inflicting a defeat on the Wa. Kwanggaet'o, whose name means "broad expander of the realm," took on a reign name, Yŏngnak ("Eternal Rejoicing"), an act that symbolically placed him on terms of equality with the rulers of China, since in Chinese practice only the Chinese emperor could hold a reign title. His successor, Changsu ("Longed Lived"), moved the Koguryŏ capital from the Yalu to P'yŏngyang on the Taedong River in 427, and thus planted the center of the kingdom firmly in the Korean peninsula. This provided Koguryŏ with a large area of fertile rice lands as a reliable economic base. Changsu continued to press southward, and in 474 Paekche was forced to move its capital from Hansŏng on the Han River south to Ungjin (modern Kongju) in the Ch'ungch'ŏng region. Koguryŏ then gained control of the Han River basin.

The expansion of Koguryŏ threatened the survival of the southern states and led to the alliance between Paekche and Silla in 433. The next 120 years was largely the drama of Paekche and Silla fighting the attempts at further southern encroachments by Koguryŏ. Despite this alliance, Paekche, which experienced the main brunt of the Koguryŏ advance, suffered a series of setbacks, including the death of King Kaero (r. 455–474) in battle as Changsu took Hansŏng. But by the sixth century it was Silla that began to go on the offensive. The period from the middle sixth century until 676 saw Silla's emergence as master of the Korean peninsula.

CULTURE AND SOCIETY OF THE THREE KINGDOMS

During the period from the late fourth to the mid-fifth century, a process of political and cultural change occurred in each of the Three Kingdoms. Selectively borrowing from the states that ruled China, the Korean states carried out administrative reforms, adopted Buddhism as a state-protective cult, and acquired bits of Chinese cultural forms and learning. Chinese models were adopted because these were the only models of state organization available to the peoples of the region. These proved useful to the growth of state power and appealed to the elites as forms of cultural enrichment. Yet Chinese culture was introduced to Korea at a time when China itself was politically weak and divided and much of the northern heartland was ruled by alien dynasties of Inner Asian origin. Chinese states were useful sources of cultural ideas and practices, but during this period of political disunity in China they were not in a position to threaten the existence of the Korean states. Nor was there any great empire with universalistic pretensions and the ability to dazzle its neighbors with cultural brilliance or intimidate them with military might. As a result, the process of state building during the Three Kingdoms period was largely an indigenous development, and Chinese cultural borrowing was done on a purely voluntarily basis. A process of sinicization occurred, but the native institutions and cultural forms were still dominant in this period.

Another feature of this time was the armored mounted warrior. In East Asia, the appearance of these horse-riding warriors with coats of bone or iron, similar to the medieval knights of the West, began around the fourth and fifth centuries. Impressive bone armor has been discovered in Paekche and elaborate iron armor has been uncovered in Kaya dating from at least the fifth century.[10] Surviving depictions of Korean warriors show them formidably outfitted in armor and deer antler helmets. Armored warriors fought for all three kingdoms, and this style of warfare spread to Japan, where it formed the basis for the elaborately attired horse warrior of medieval Japanese samurai lore.

The earliest of these three kingdoms, Koguryŏ, was a society dominated by a warrior aristocracy. Rulers and high-ranking nobility built elaborate tombs during this time, which are one of the main sources of information about this period. Most of Koguryŏ's tombs have been looted, but tomb paintings provide some information about this society. One of the best-known of these is the Ssangyŏng-ch'ong (Tomb of the Twin Pillars) that depicts broad streets, and rouge-faced ladies dressed in skirts and three-quarter-length coats engaged in conversation with upper-class men. Other tombs show hunters, mounted archers, dancers, and wrestlers engaged in what appears to be an early form of *ssirŭm*, Korean-style wrestling. Paintings show people in the kinds of activity expected to be found in a warrior aristocracy: horse-riding, hunting, vigorous sports, and warfare. This artistic style, so different from later Korean art, shows less Chinese influence; instead it shares more traits with the art of the peoples of Central Asia, Manchuria, and Siberia. The murals, such as those in the Tomb of the Four Spirits in South P'yŏngyang Province, which contains pictures of a dragon, tiger, phoenix, tortoise, and snake, were probably of religious and cosmological significance. Interestingly, tomb paintings show little Buddhist influence. The name of one Koguryŏ artist, Tamjing, who went to Japan, has been recorded, but generally the producers of some of the most splendid works of art in Korean history are anonymous. The Koguryŏ are recorded to have been fond of music and dance. The most renowned of Koguryŏ musicians was Wang San-ak, master of the *hyŏnhakkŭm* (black crane zither), a modified Chinese seven-string instrument.

Buddhism was the official state religion, but its influence on Koguryŏ society was initially limited as indicated by the tomb murals. By the sixth century, however, the dominant Vinaya (Rules) school of Buddhism had become a major institution that provided learned advisors to Koguryŏ rulers. In the sixth century, Koguryŏ was able to act as a point of dispersal for the spread of Buddhism. In 551, a Koguryŏ monk was appointed by the king of Silla to head that kingdom's monastic organization, and in 594, the monk Hyeja went to Japan, where he became an advisor to Prince Shōtoku (573–621). A generation later, in 628, the monk Hyegwan introduced the important Samnon (Three Treatises; Japanese: Sanron) school of Buddhist philosophy to Japan. No Koguryŏ Buddhist temples have survived, but a gilt bronze statue of Tathagata Buddha and a gilt bronze half-seated Maitreya testify to the high level of Buddhist art that flourished by the sixth century.

Koguryŏ gradually adopted elements of Chinese culture in a pattern that Paekche and Silla repeated. To promote learning and train government clerks, an official academy, the T'aehak, was established in 372, where the curriculum included the study of Confucian learning. This is the first known center where Confucianism was studied in Korea. The Han histories *Shiji* and *Hanshu* (*Book of Former Han*) were studied as well as the Chinese literary anthology the *Wenxuan* (*Literary Selections*). Knowledge of the Chinese literary tradition may not have been very deep or profound, but the aristocratic class had some exposure to it. Little is known of the popular religion or customs except that the tenth lunar month was a time of harvest festivals, as it was in all three kingdoms. Although the aristocracy practiced Buddhism, it probably remained only a marginal part of the spiritual life of the people, who sought shamans rather than monks when dealing with the supernatural. One Koguryŏ institution worthy of notice was the *kyŏngdang*, communal bodies of unmarried men, presumably of aristocratic background, who were organized in each locality, trained in archery, and given instruction in Chinese texts.

Paekche, too, was a state dominated by a warrior aristocracy and a monarch who had by the end of the fourth century developed a centralized administration. As with the case of Koguryŏ, much of what we know of Paekche culture comes from the tombs of Paekche rulers and high-born aristocrats. Paekche tombs show a strong affinity with those of Koguryŏ that may be due to the fact that both were derived from the Puyŏ or perhaps from the geographic proximity of Paekche to Koguryŏ. By the fifth century, large mounded tombs with horizontal passageways leading to stone-walled high-ceilinged burial chambers were constructed. Since these proved rather easy to pillage, the contents have long since been looted. The discovery of the undisturbed Tomb of Muryŏng (r. 501–523) in the 1970s near Kongju, however, provides a glimpse of the splendid and refined culture of the Paekche kingdom. The tomb murals are more refined and less animated than those of Koguryŏ. They were a product of a gentle culture more removed from the rough nomadic influences of Manchuria and Central Asia and in closer contact with the maritime courts of southern China. Paekche bronzes, with their thin, elongated bodies, are perhaps the most famous product of the kingdom's artistic tradition. The best example is the Kudara (Paekche) Kannon in the Hŏryūji Temple in Nara, Japan. The cultural high point of Paekche is considered the reign of King Sŏng (r. 523–553). It was at this time that the famous Paekche mission to Japan took place (either in 538 or 552) that has traditionally been credited with introducing Buddhism to that country.

Buddhism played the same role in Paekche as it did in Koguryŏ, as a state-protective cult patronized by the court. The most influential form of Buddhism before the seventh century was Vinaya, which emphasized monastic discipline and, as its meaning ("rules") implies, systematic organization. The Vinaya-trained monks offered an array of practical information about administration, law, and systematic procedure as well as knowledge of literacy and the traditions of other lands. This was a valuable aid to early Korean rulers as they attempted to consolidate their rule and strengthen their states.

Our knowledge of Buddhist architecture in the Three Kingdoms period is limited, but we do know that Paekche pagodas were highly regarded in medieval times. Of the many Buddhist temples that must have dotted the landscape only a few stone pagodas remain; the most famous was the Nine Story Wooden Pagoda of the master craftsman Abiji that was destroyed by the Mongol invasion in the thirteenth century. As with Koguryŏ, it is questionable how deeply the influence of Buddhism penetrated among the peasant majority, but at least among the court it was profound. Paekche king Pŏp (r. 599–600) went so far as to ban killing animals and hunting. He ordered the release of all domestic animals and the destruction of hunting weapons. Not surprisingly, he was soon deposed. It is clear, however, that by the end of the fifth century Buddhism as a way of life was being taken seriously by some.

Although the last to emerge in recorded annals, Silla is today the best known of the Three Kingdoms, for it was Silla that unified the peninsula and implanted its language and culture as the dominant element in the evolution of Korea. Most of our knowledge of this period comes from histories written by later historians who saw themselves as heirs to the Sillan tradition. As a result, there is an inherent pro-Silla bias in most Korean history. Also, because Silla became the dominant power, its traditions have been best preserved and have served as the models for later Koreans. Thus more is known about Silla and its culture than of Paekche and Koguryŏ. It would be wrong, however, to regard Silla as the most advanced of the states; rather the opposite is closer to the truth. Archaeological evidence suggests that Silla, tucked in the southeast corner of the Korean peninsula out of direct contact with the East Asian heartland, developed somewhat later than Koguryŏ and Paekche in terms of social stratification, the creation of institutions of a centralized state, and the adoption of literacy. And it maintained its indigenous cultural traditions longer. Compared to Koguryŏ, Silla was very much a latecomer as an organized state, and compared to Paekche, Sillan culture was less refined and sophisticated. Yet this does not mean that Silla remained a primitive backwater, for it developed into one of the medieval world's more sophisticated societies. Its cultural legacy, which can be seen today in the museums of South Korea, is impressive by any standard. The Sillan mounded tombs, a prominent feature of modern Kyŏngju, differed some-what in their design from Koguryŏ and Paekche mounded tombs.[11] This indicates the cultural autonomy of Silla, which appears in general to show less pronounced Manchurian influences. These tombs were less easy to loot, and as a result, vast cultural treasures have survived to the present. Not all tombs have been opened by modern archaeologists, but those that have reveal a splendid artistic heritage.

As with Paekche and Koguryŏ, a major theme in the early history of Silla was the emergence of a centralized monarchical state. The concept of kingship had to contend with strong local, tribal, and aristocratic tradi-tions. Buddhism was important in strengthening the power of the early kings. Under Pŏphŭng (r. 514–540) Silla adopted Buddhism. Silla resisted the alien religion long after Buddhism had been accepted in Koguryŏ and Paekche, a testimony to the comparative remoteness of the state and the strength of its indigenous culture. In 527, a noble, Ich'adon, was martyred for his beliefs. According to later tradition, a set of miracles followed this event and the Silla king converted to Buddhism, adopted the name Pŏphŭng ("rising of the dharma"), and officially sponsored the new faith. Buddhism was initiated by the Silla monarchs, as it provided a source of religious sanction to the monarchy and an impressive ritual tradition that when closely aligned with its royal patrons served to greatly enhance the majesty and prestige of the royal house and of the state. In Silla, Bud-dhism would retain a close association with the state.

Silla kings borrowed Chinese institutional practices to add to their power and prestige. Pŏphŭng's reign also saw the first code of adminis-trative law, issued in 520. The content of this code is unknown, but it is believed to have included a seventeen-grade official rank system with dif-ferent ranks distinguished by distinctive attire. The *kolp'um*, or bone-rank system, the basis of Silla's social structure, may have been formalized around this time. To further add to monarchical prestige Pŏphŭng in 536 took on an independent era name, "Kŏnwŏn" (Initiated Beginning). In the Chinese tradition, an era name was given only to the emperor and it sig-nified his role as a mediator between heaven and earth. An era name by a ruler other than the Chinese emperor was a declaration of equality. In times when China was united and strong this would be a direct challenge to the authority of the Chinese emperor. At this time, of course, China was politically divided; nevertheless, the adoption of an era name was at the very least a sign of the growing influence of Chinese culture and the pretensions of the Silla monarchs.

Pŏphŭng expanded his domain by conquering Pon Kaya, the largest of the Kaya states, in 532. His successor, Chinhŭng (r. 540–576), expanded the state further, making Silla a serious contender for control of the entire peninsula. With Silla's ally Paekche, Chinhŭng launched an invasion of the Han River basin during the years from 551 to 554. Under his general Kŏch'ilbu, the Silla forces and their Paekche allies were successful in driving Koguryŏ out of the Han valley. Then turning against his erstwhile partner and severing a 120-year alliance, Chinhŭng attacked Paekche, whose King Sŏng perished at the battle of Kwansan in 554. The Han River basin was now part of the Silla state. This gave Silla access to the Yellow Sea and brought Silla into direct contact with China. It also separated Paekche from Koguryŏ, making cooperation between the two states more difficult. Perhaps most importantly, the Han River basin with its rich farmlands and its iron deposits enriched the kingdom. Chinhŭng then conquered Tae Kaya in 562, ending the independent existence of the Kaya states and bringing the entire Naktong valley under Sillan control. This step excluded direct Japanese influence in Korea for over 1,000 years. Silla forces then invaded the former territory of the Okchŏ along the Hamgyŏng coast, inflicting another defeat on Koguryŏ. Chinhŭng celebrated his military triumphs by erecting what are known as the Four Chinhŭng Stelae. These were placed at strategic points in his domain at Chungnyŏng Pass, at Pukhansan in north Seoul, and in the Hwangch'o and Maullyŏng passes in Hamgyŏng Province and have survived to the present, providing us with among the earliest Sillan written documents.

THE BONE-RANKS, THE HWABAEK, AND THE HWARANG

Silla's strength was drawn in part from its three prominent social and political institutions: the bone-rank system, the *Hwabaek* (Council of Notables), and the *hwarang* (flower boys). The *kolp'um* (bone-rank) was a system of hierarchical ranks in Silla corresponding to hereditary bloodlines. Each rank conferred a variety of special privileges such as qualification for office or the right to possess certain kinds of material goods.[12] The two top bone-ranks were the *sŏnggol* (sacred bone), which was confined to the main branch of the royal Kim descent group, and the *chin'gol* (true bone), whose members were the cadet branches of the royal family, perhaps members of the Pak and Sŏk royal consort families, and the royal house of Pon Kaya. These made up the highest level of the aristocracy. Originally the *chin'gol* may have been formed by those lineages that were related to the royal family through marriage and were probably expanded to include the Kaya royal descent group that was absorbed into the bone-rank system. The *chin'gol* held the highest offices and served on the *Hwabaek* council. The *sŏnggol* line, however, died out when King Chinp'yŏng left no male heir and was succeeded by his daughter Sŏndŏk (r. 632–647) and her female cousin Chindŏk (r. 647–654). Thereafter the royal family was drawn from the *chin'gol* line. The name *sŏnggol*, which can be translated as "hallowed" or "sacred," implies a sacred or priestly authority for the Silla kings, a role that is also hinted at by the term *ch'ach'aung*, used by an early ruler and believed to refer to a shaman or priest. It is possible that the Silla royal line may have been evolving in a pattern similar to the imperial line of the Yamato in Japan, where the ruling family took on a sacerdotal (priestly) function. With the extinction of the royal line, the Silla kings became merely first among *chin'gol* equals. Silla kings after 654 were frequently challenged by powerful aristocrats, their throne never entirely secure. The extinction of the sacred bone line then may have been a factor contributing to the less exalted status of the Silla and later Korean kings. Throughout Korean history, the position of the monarch was more humble than in many premodern Asian societies.

Beneath the two bone-ranks was a system of *tup'um* (head-ranks), of which there were theoretically six; but only the head-ranks six, five, and four, the three highest, appear to have functioned as meaningful groupings. The most important was the *yuktu-p'um* (head-rank six), which was the highest aristocratic ranking after the *chin'gol*. Head-rank-six members held many of the middle-level offices and provided a sizeable portion of the country's scholars. The bone-rank system was an early manifestation of the propensity toward hierarchical social structure with sharply defined status distinctions and a stress on hereditary bloodlines that were to characterize Korean society throughout its history. While little is known about women in this period, in later Silla at least, social status was determined by the maternal as well as the paternal lines, and women of the upper classes appeared to have considerable freedom of movement. Burials also suggest the Silla queens had high social status and perhaps wielded considerable power.[13]

A Silla institution of particular importance was the *Hwabaek* or Council of Notables. The *Hwabaek* was a council headed by the single aristocrat who held "extraordinary rank one" and was composed of those of "extraordinary rank two," all of whom are thought to have been of true-bone lineage. Its function was to deliberate on the most important matters of state, such as succession to the throne and the declaration of war. The decision to formally adopt Buddhism also was made by the *Hwabaek*. The principle of unanimity governed the *Hwabaek*, which convened at four sites of special religious significance around Kyŏngju. Significantly, the *Hwabaek* typified another feature of the political process of Silla that was to characterize most Korean governments: political decision making by councils of high aristocrats. Throughout most of Korea's history, rulers shared power with aristocratic families who governed through various councils or committees.

Another key Silla institution was the *hwarang*, a state-supported organization of aristocratic adolescents. It served as a way of educating youths to prepare for adulthood and to perform their duties to the society. The *hwarang* were originally connected with native cults and rituals, and pre-Buddhist religious practices remained a part of their ceremonies. Later their education gradually became more linked with Buddhism and eventually Confucianism as these belief systems penetrated Silla. Boys just beyond puberty would meet at sacred sites outside the Silla capital, swear oaths of loyalty to each other, and participate in initiation ceremonies. According to a later recorded tradition, they were selected for their beauty, and they painted their faces.[14] Whatever the sexual connotations these ceremonies may have had, it is clear that the institution was useful for the state. It taught an attitude of defiance toward death that prepared the members for service in warfare and taught moral values that the state was promoting. Only sons of the elite could be *hwarang*. These young men traveled around the country getting to know the land and each other before later serving as the elite warrior-aristocrats who would govern the state. Some *hwarang* went on to distinguish themselves in battle. Silla's aristocrats were first of all warriors, and the greatest honor for a parent was to have a son die a hero in battle. An example of this is the story of General P'umil, whose sixteen-year-old son, Kwanch'ang, later venerated as an exemplary youth, died in battle against Paekche. Upon hearing of his son's death the general is reported to have remarked that he regretted having only one son to give his kingdom. Most of the prominent military and political figures of Silla, such as the famed general Kim Yu-sin, served in their youth as *hwarang* warriors. Although as much an institution to teach moral values as to train warriors, twentieth-century Korean nationalists would later glorify the military bravery of these *hwarang* and extol the *hwarangdo* (the way of the *hwarang*) as an example of dedication to the nation.[15]

The bone-ranks, the *Hwabaek*, and the *hwarang* do not appear to have been unique to Silla; similar institutions are known to have existed in Koguryŏ and Paekche. Each was dominated by warrior-aristocracies ranked in sharply defined status hierarchies. The *Hwabaek* had its parallel in the Paekche *chŏngsa-am*, and councils of high aristocrats are known to have made decisions in Koguryŏ. The *hwarang* had a parallel in the *kyŏngdang* of Koguryŏ. But less is known about these social institutions. It is principally in Silla that we see clearly the patterns of rigid status hierarchy and councilor governance that characterized later Korean social and political history.

Silla kings and queens were buried in luxurious style. There is no sign of human sacrifice as in ancient Chinese royal burials, although royal members were interred with the emblems of their authority. These included the Silla crown, whose shape is derived from deer antlers, and the *kogok*, or curved jewel, stylized bear claws that also served in Japan as symbols of royal authority. Both the crowns and the *kogok* suggest totemism and Manchurian and Siberian religious influences. In addition to the tombs, a gilt bronze statue of a meditating half-seated Maitreya Bodhisattva shows a more linear style of sculpture than the more famous Paekche statue. Painting was apparently prized, and the names of a few masters have survived but not their works. In Kyŏngju, the stone-brick pagoda of the Punhwang-sa temple and the Ch'ŏmsŏngdae observatory hint at the architecture of this period, but not enough has survived for us to make sound evaluations of the nature of Silla architecture.

One of the main purposes of the Silla state was to make war, so it is not surprising that the military organization of the state was well developed. Each of the six *pu* contained a *chŏng* (garrison) headed by a general of the *chin'gol* bone-rank. In 583 a more centralized *sŏdang* (oath banner) system was organized. Somewhat resembling the banner system of later Qing China, the *sŏdang* were named after the different-colored fringed banners that each of the six military groups had. Each banner had specialized units of armored troops, catapult teams, ladder teams, teams for breaching walls, composite bow units, and crossbow units. After Silla's conquest of Paekche and Koguryŏ, three additional banners were formed containing troops of those former kingdoms. Commoners were allowed to serve in the banners, and they swore an oath to its commanders.

THE CHANGING ENVIRONMENT
OF THE LATE SIXTH AND SEVENTH CENTURIES

The late sixth and seventh centuries saw important changes throughout East Asia. In 589, after more than three centuries of division, China was reunified under the Sui dynasty (581–618). The new Chinese rulers sought to strengthen the tributary system. Under the imperial order of the Han, the tributary system was fully developed and functioned in East Asia as the main method of handling foreign affairs. According to the usual practice, foreign peoples would be granted permission to establish trade and diplomatic and cultural contact with China on the condition that their ruler or the ruler's representatives demonstrate their subservience to the Chinese emperor by personally bearing him tribute. This was usually in the form of local products or of rare precious goods. The presentation of tribute was accompanied by ceremonies in which the ruler or his representatives offered to accept Chinese suzerainty in an exchange of seals and patents of authority, and he was presented with a Chinese calendar that symbolically incorporated his state into the Chinese cosmological scheme. The seals of ranks, robes, caps, and paraphernalia of authority were important symbols of the tributary's legitimacy and status. New rulers, when they came to power, were expected to present themselves or their representatives to the imperial court to be formally enfeoffed. Besides the symbolic value this offered them, the tributaries received permission to trade. Much of this trade was under the guise of an official exchange of gifts, but in practice this often amounted to a lucrative trade for the tributary state. It also provided an opportunity to travel and study in China and participate in China's rich cultural life. During the fourth through sixth centuries the Korean states regularly sent tribute missions to states in China. While this in theory implied a submission to Chinese rulers, in practice it was little more than a diplomatic formality. In exchange, Korean rulers received symbols that strengthened their own legitimacy and a variety of cultural commodities: ritual goods, books, Buddhist scriptures, and rare luxury products. Different Korean states, however, had paid tribute to different Chinese states. Now the Sui wanted to bring the whole peninsula into its diplomatic orbit.

The second Sui emperor, Emperor Yang, was determined to bring the northeast frontier under control and to match the achievements of the Han by controlling all the lands that were once part of the Han Empire, including Liaodong and northern Korea. But Koguryŏ was an obstacle to resurgent Chinese expansionary plans, and Yang directed his attention at subjugating the northern Korean state. In 612, after an unsuccessful naval attack, he embarked upon a major campaign against Koguryŏ. This was a large-scale undertaking that involved forces and resources from across the Chinese Empire. A confident Emperor Yang, fresh from successful campaigns against the Turks, sent a reported 1,130,000 men 1,000 *li* into Koguryŏ.[16] About 300,000 troops were detached from the main force and unsuccessfully besieged P'yŏngyang. On their return, they were ambushed by Koguryŏ general Ŭlchi Mundŏk at the Salsu (Ch'ŏngch'ŏn) River, a defeat that only 2,700 Chinese forces are reported to have survived. The size of the forces and the magnitude of the defeat were recorded by Tang China historians, who no doubt inflated these figures to discredit their Sui predecessors. Nonetheless, Koguryŏ won an impressive victory that became part of Korean legend. Ŭlchi Mundŏk later became a symbol of national resistance for modern Koreans. Emperor Yang made two more unsuccessful attempts on Koguryŏ in 613 and 614, and those costly defeats were a major factor in the collapse of the Sui and the rise of the Tang.

The newly established Tang dynasty (618–907), one of the most brilliant in Chinese history, inherited the same foreign policy objectives of its predecessors—to secure the northern frontier and bring all the former Han lands under its control. When in 628 the Tang defeated the Turks, it began to reconsider Silla's appeals for assistance. Silla, seeing an opportunity to deal a fatal blow to its northern rival, justified its need for Chinese intervention in much the same way that Han chieftains may have called for Han help in overcoming Wiman's Chosŏn blockade of the overland route to China. Tang emperor Taizong (r. 626–649) attacked Koguryŏ and was defeated at Ansi Fortress by Koguryŏ general Yang Man-ch'un. Taizong was again defeated in 648, and his successor, Tang Gaozong (r. 649–683), launched unsuccessful attacks in 655 and in 658–659. Koguryŏ's consistent success against the world's mightiest military force was an impressive achievement in Korean annals. It also shielded the states of Paekche and Silla from the brunt of Chinese expansionism, allowing them time for autonomous development.

While Koguryŏ was engaged in its wars of resistance, Paekche fought Silla. In 642, it seized forty border forts. Silla, seeking assistance, sent the official Kim Ch'un-ch'u on diplomatic missions to Japan, to Koguryŏ, and twice to China. In 650 he presented the Tang emperor with a poem written by Queen Chindŏk requesting Tang military aid against Paekche. At the same time, Silla sought to move culturally closer to Tang. In 649, the state adopted Tang court dress, and in 651, it reorganized its administration closer to the Chinese model. This cooperative policy toward China continued when in 654 Kim Ch'un-ch'u, known by his posthumous title Muyŏl (r. 654–661), was elected by the *Hwabaek* as king.

THE UNIFICATION OF KOREA UNDER SILLA

In 660, the Tang, frustrated by their inability to overcome Koguryŏ resistance, decided on a plan to invade Paekche by sea, and after subduing Paekche, to invade Koguryŏ from the south. This plan was implemented, with Admiral Su Dingfang, who had recently defeated the Turks, leading the Chinese forces. His ships sailed up the Kŭm River while Silla forces under General Kim Yu-sin crossed the Sobaek range that separates the Kyŏngsang heartland of Silla from the Chŏlla and Ch'ungch'ŏng regions of Paekche. On the Hwangsan Plain, the Paekche forces under General Kyebaek were defeated. Paekche king Ŭija surrendered at Ungjin, and in the seventh lunar month of 660 the Tang forces were in control of most of Paekche.

Tang now concentrated on its major goal of destroying Koguryŏ. In 668, Tang land and naval forces, and Silla forces under Kim In-mun, captured P'yŏngyang. As a result, Koguryŏ fell. It was clear that Tang efforts were now aimed at directly controlling the entire Korean peninsula, with the former Koguryŏ and Paekche territories to be directly incorporated into the empire and Silla to survive only as a satellite state. The Chinese emperor proposed that Silla become the Great Commandery of Kyerim—in essence a Chinese territory—and offered to appoint the Silla king as its head. The Silla monarch Munmu (r. 661–681) rejected the offer and instead invaded the Chinese-controlled territory in Paekche. Sillan forces drove out the Chinese by 671, and then moved north into Koguryŏ. In a series of battles in the Han River basin in 676 Silla forced the Tang into retreat, gaining control of all the territory south of the Taedong River, that is, almost all of peninsular Korea. Although Chinese and Korean accounts of this period vary, it is clear that Silla emerged as the victor.[17] Most of the peninsula was now under Silla's control. The Korean peninsula, and Silla especially, proved too much of a logistical problem for permanent occupation by China. China had a hard time supplying its troops in the peninsula. Silla had provided its Chinese forces with food. Once Silla turned against them the logistical problems proved too much for the Chinese, contributing to their defeat and withdrawal. Tang settled for the destruction of a strong Koguryŏ contiguous to its northeast frontier and ceased further efforts to intervene militarily in the peninsula. To further secure their frontier, the Chinese set up a small puppet state of Lesser Koguryŏ in the Liaodong region of Manchuria.

Silla's victory in unifying most of the peninsula can be attributed to several factors. The political and military institutions of the kingdom proved capable of providing a stable and effective government that could successfully carry the country's expansion. The kingdom itself enjoyed considerable prosperity and had an economic base and a system of extracting the surplus from that base sufficient to support large military undertakings. Nonetheless, it is not certain that this was any less the case with its rivals. Most probably it was geography that provided the greatest opportunities for the kingdom. Koguryŏ had to wage wars on its northwestern and southern boundaries, and Paekche was vulnerable to Koguryŏ to the north, Silla to the south, and China from the sea. Silla in the southeast corner of Korea, however, had easier boundaries to defend and was out of reach of direct assault by China. China assisted in the unification, but unintentionally, since its motive was to establish control over Korea, not to create a strong united state there.

The unification of most of the peninsula by Silla in 676 was a pivotal event in Korean history. From the late seventh century to the twentieth, a single state dominated the peninsula, including most of the agricultural heartland of what was to become Korea. Gradually, within the framework of the peninsular state, a culturally well-defined and ethnically homogeneous Korean society emerged. This process, however, was only beginning in the seventh century.

KOREA IN GLOBAL PERSPECTIVE:
STATE FORMATION

The emergence of indigenous states in the Korean peninsula from the fourth century followed a pattern common in world history. The early kingdoms in Korea were part of a process called secondary state formation. Pristine states, those that evolve autonomously, are relatively uncommon, emerging in the original centers of complex societies in the Middle East, the Indus Valley, China, Mesoamerica, and Peru. Secondary societies emerged as a result of interaction with these early societies. Just as literate, urban-centered societies emerged in the Mediterranean basin and in southern and central India as a result of trade and other cultural interactions with earlier centers, states emerged among agricultural peoples along the periphery of the Chinese cultural heartland. These included the peoples of the Red River basin in northern Vietnam and the peoples of Manchuria and the Korean peninsula. It is not yet clear just how far the process of state formation in Northeast Asia had progressed when Chosŏn, one of the earliest states or proto-states in the region, became absorbed into the Chinese Empire.

It was the weakening and collapse of the Chinese Empire in the third and fourth centuries that gave the indigenous people free reign to develop autonomous states that were culturally distinct from China. The process was analogous to contemporary developments at the other end of Eurasia when the declining Roman Empire disintegrated in Western Europe, allowing tribal peoples to develop their own heavily Roman-influenced states. A further parallel was the role of Buddhism in Northeast Asia as a vehicle for the spread of Chinese culture among indigenous rulers and elites, similar to the role of Christianity in Western Europe. And just as Christian missionaries extended the zone of Western civilization into areas beyond the boundaries of the former Roman Empire—northern Germany, Ireland, Scandinavia, and Poland, so Buddhist monks spread elements of Chinese civilization to southern Korea and Japan. To the south of China, Buddhist and Hindu missionaries along with Indian traders similarly extended Indian cultural influences to emerging states in Southeast Asia in the first millennium CE.

Unlike the Roman Empire, China's period of disunity lasted only until the late sixth century. But this relatively short period of political fragmentation from the fourth through sixth centuries may have been crucial in allowing the peoples of Korea to develop strong, independent states based in part on indigenous cultural patterns.

Origins of the Hwarang

The *wŏnhwa* ["original flowers," female leaders of the *hwarang*] were first presented at the court in the thirty-seventh year [576] of King Chinhŭng. At first the king and his officials were perplexed by the problem of finding a way to discover talented people. They wished to have people disport themselves in groups so that they could observe their behavior and thus elevate the talented among them to positions of service. Therefore two beautiful girls, Nammo and Chunjŏng, were selected, and a group of some three hundred people gathered around them. But the two girls competed with one another. In the end, Chunjŏng enticed Nammo to her home and, plying her with wine till she was drunk, threw her into a river. Chunjŏng was put to death. The group became discordant and dispersed.

Afterward, handsome youths were chosen instead. Faces made up and beautifully dressed, they were respected as *hwarang*, and men of various sorts gathered around them like clouds. The youths instructed one another in the Way and in rightness, entertained one another with song and music, or went sightseeing to even the most distant mountains and rivers. Much can be learned of a man's character by watching him in these activities. Those who fared well were recommended to court.

Kim Taemun, in his *Annals of the Hwarang* [*Hwarang segi*], remarks: "Henceforth able ministers and loyal subjects shall be chosen from them, and good generals and brave soldiers born therefrom."

—from the *Samguk sagi* 4:40[18]

King Hŭngdŏk's Edict on Clothing, Carts, and Housing

There are superior and inferior people, and humble persons, in regard to social status. Names are not alike, for example, and garments too are different. The customs of this society have degenerated day by day owing to the competition among the people for luxuries and alien commodities, because they detest local products. Furthermore, rites have now fallen to a critical stage and customs have retrogressed to those of barbarians. The traditional codes will be revived in order to rectify the situation, and should anyone transgress the prohibition, he will be punished to the law of the land.

—from the *Samguk sagi* 33:320–26[19]

3

⬤

Late Silla, 676 to 935

THE PENINSULAR KINGDOM

Silla's victories created a kingdom that controlled most of the Korean Peninsula. Historians often refer to the period from 676 to 935 CE as Late Silla, or sometimes United Silla. This unification of Korea needs some qualification. Although Silla ruled most of the agricultural heartland of Korea, it did not control the northern third of the modern boundaries of Korea. It is also somewhat controversial to speak of a single Korean state after 676 since the demarcation between Korea and Manchuria was not well defined, and a northern kingdom, Parhae, emerged in the early eighth century that occupied much of the former Koguryŏ. Nor was there a single "Korean" ethnic group. Over the centuries, however, under the peninsular kingdom of Silla and its successor states, an increasingly well-defined Korean culture and society emerged. For the next twelve centuries, from 676 to 1876, Korea underwent two major political reformations, suffered several assaults from the outside, and experienced continual sociocultural evolution. In the process, it developed a society that possessed a strong sense of its own identity and historical continuity. Then after 1876, Korea entered the emerging Western-dominated global civilization, and the Korean people faced the challenge of adapting their culture and applying their historical experience to the modern world.

During the twelve centuries of the premodern peninsular kingdom, historical events can be put into context by placing them within several broad patterns of change. First, the kingdom became increasingly homogeneous. In terms of language, cultural identity, and shared values and traditions, the Koreans became one people. Second, the peoples of Korea continued absorbing Chinese notions of government, religion, ethics, art, music, family structure, and fashions. Chinese-derived cultural values and habits penetrated further down the social hierarchy. As this happened, Koreans combined these with indigenous traditions and developments. Thus Korea was able to become a full participant in, and at the same time a distinctive component of, the cosmopolitan East Asian civilization centered in China. Third, the kingdom gradually expanded in population and wealth. It expanded internally by absorbing more marginal lands and internal frontiers into its sociopolitical system, while externally there was a slow, fitful extension of its northern frontiers until by the middle of the fifteenth century they were stabilized at their present Yalu and Tumen river boundaries.

The periodization of Korean history generally follows dynastic demarcations. From 676 to 935 there was the Silla state that was ruled by the Kim and Pak kings from the southeastern capital of Kyŏngju. From 918 to 1392 the kingdom, renamed Koryŏ, was governed from Kaesŏng under the Wang family, and from 1392 to 1910 the Chŏnju Yi family from Yŏnghŭng governed the state, renamed Chosŏn, from Seoul. Within this chronological outline, it is helpful to see Korea as undergoing several stages and transitions. From 676 to the late eighth century the state under Silla experienced a period of growth and consolidation accompanied by an artistic and literary efflorescence. The period after 780 to the end of the ninth century was one of political if not socioeconomic and cultural decline. The tenth century was truly a transitional period that saw the disintegration of Silla, a brief period of political disunity, and the reformulation of the kingdom under the early Wang kings. Their Koryŏ state lasted nearly five centuries until another transitional period in the fourteenth century saw the establishment of the remarkably durable and stable Chosŏn state of the Yi dynasty, which survived to the annexation of Korea by Japan in 1910.

CONSOLIDATION OF CENTRAL
MONARCHICAL RULE UNDER SILLA, 676–780

Silla's rulers sought to consolidate their power and create a centralized state. This proved difficult because the society was dominated by powerful aristocratic families, especially those of the highest true-bone rank. The true-bone aristocrats monopolized higher political offices, possessed private armies, and through the *Hwabaek* chose the king and participated in policy making. In 654, King Muyŏl (r. 654–661) the first *chin'gol* monarch began a line of kings that remained on the throne to 780. These

Silla rulers struggled to establish a centralized state under monarchical control. The task was made more difficult by the fact that the *sŏnggol* (sacred-bone) line died out with Queen Chindŏk (r. 647–654). Although Muyŏl's mother was of the royal Kim clan and his primary queen was the younger sister of Kim Yu-sin and a member of the Kaya royal family, Muyŏl and his descendants were of *chin'gol* (true-bone) rank, that is, of the same rank as the great aristocratic families. This meant that in terms of caste they were merely first among equals. The term *sacred-bone* implies a magico-religious function that may have contributed royal authority. It is not clear if, in fact, the early rulers actually possessed priestly functions; it is apparent, however, that the status of the Silla kings after Muyŏl was far from secure and they had to struggle to maintain their supremacy. Because of this they were eager to seek alternative sources of legitimacy.

The chief rivals of the Silla kings were other higher aristocrats of true-bone rank who were represented in the *Hwabaek* and who held the top administrative posts. Muyŏl was challenged by the *sangdaedŭng*, as the chief of the *Hwabaek* was called, a man named Pidam, and later by another *sangdaedng*, Alch'ŏn. Another king, Sinmun (r. 681–692), was challenged by Kim Hŭm-dol, the father of his first queen, and purged another *sangdaedŭng*, Kun'gwan, forcing him and his son to commit suicide. To secure his authority Sinmum reorganized the army to bring it under closer royal control. The *yuk chŏng* (six garrisons) were replaced by the *sŭdang* (oath banner) system as the main military force. Recruits were selected from Koguryŏ, Paekche, and from the Mohe (Korean: Malgal) tribes along the northern border. He placed these under direct royal authority and supplemented them with the *sip chŏng* (ten garrisons). These forces, primarily concerned with internal security, were stationed outside the capital, Kyŏngju. One garrison was placed in each province, with two in the capital area, and two in Hanju, the strategic province between the Han and Taedong rivers. Since earlier Silla armies are believed to have been headed by powerful aristocrats, and perhaps organized along clan lines, the new royal forces marked the beginning of a truly centralized military. Meanwhile, the *hwarang* continued to exist as an organization of aristocratic youth. Sinmun also attempted to strengthen the fiscal basis of the state by reforming the tax system.

Under Sinmun the regional administration was reorganized, and in 685, nine *chu* (provinces) were created: three out of the Silla homeland, three out of the former Paekche, and three out of former Koguryŏ territories; at the same, time five secondary capitals were created, a measure important in controlling the country, since the capital Kyŏngju was awkwardly situated in the extreme southeastern corner of the country. Following Chinese practice, each province was subdivided into *kun* (prefectures), which totaled over 100, and into *hyŏn* (smaller counties), of which

there were more than 300. At the lowest level of administration were *ch'on*
(villages) headed by village chiefs. An elaborate administrative hierarchy
of governors, prefects, and county magistrates administered the country.
There were also subcounty units called *hyang* and *pugok* that were places
of settlement for outcaste groups.

On the surface, Silla appeared to be an impressively centralized state
with royal administration penetrating down to smaller units of administration, much like, on a bigger scale, Tang China. In reality, however,
Silla functioned more as an alliance of powerful families in the capital
and prominent provincial families. Royal authority was limited by the
fact that the top officialdom was recruited from a small segment of the aristocracy, the true-bone aristocrats of the Kyŏngju area. Local elites were
appointed to serve as functionaries in the local administrations, perhaps
a recognition of the need to rule with the support of these prominent
families. To insure the loyalty of non-Sillan and other local elites a hostage
system was believed to exist in which family members served at court on
a rotation basis (this was later dubbed the *sangsuri* system). In the capital,
a complex central bureaucracy existed headed by the *Chipsabu* (Chancellery Office), which had been created in 651 and was headed by a *chungsi*,
or chief minister.[1] Eleven ministries, a board of censors, and hundreds of
departments administered the court and the state. It is generally believed
that after unification the *Hwabaek* declined in importance and the royal
bureaucracy under the *Chipsabu* administered the kingdom.

SILLA AND THE CHINESE MODEL

Silla, a close ally of Tang and an exemplary tributary in many ways,
modeled itself on Tang China. Yet for all the adoption of court robes and
rituals; Chinese legal concepts and administrative nomenclature; and the
careful study of Chinese literature, art, and philosophy, Silla maintained
some distinctive features. This is evident in its administration. Tang China
was administered by three chancelleries and six ministries: revenue, rituals, military, personnel, justice, and public works, a system later adopted
by the Koryŏ state. In contrast, Silla's bureaucratic structure included
many different ministries, including a Ministry of Horses and a Ministry
of Marine. There were also, on paper at least, hundreds of departments,
including offices that dealt with monasteries, astronomy, medicine, and
translation. There was even an office of water clocks. It is not clear how
many of these offices functioned or whether they existed only on paper.
Many or most may have been sinecures for the well connected. Provincial
administration was based on the nine *chu* (Chinese: *zhou*) of the ancient
Zhou dynasty, not the circuits (Korean: *to*; Chinese: *dao*) of Tang. Silla's

society was also evolving differently from China's. While the Tang state was gradually reducing the hereditary aristocracy's control over government posts, despite efforts by monarchs to assert their personal authority, the aristocracy's monopoly of government was strengthened under Silla. In fact, it can be argued that Silla was not so much a centralized state as a coalition of local and central elites. Furthermore, while anti-Buddhist sentiment asserted itself in late Tang, the links between Buddhism and the state remained strong in Silla. Thus, while the Silla state faithfully adopted much of Chinese culture and nomenclature, it was not a miniature Tang China.

SUPPORTING THE SILLA STATE

As with other premodern states, Silla consisted of a small elite of officials and courtiers on top of a mass of farmers. To support itself, the state exacted tribute from its peasants and fishers to feed and clothe its officials and their retainers. How this taxation was organized during the Three Kingdoms period is not clear, but by the seventh century we have enough information to give a general description. *Sigŭp* (tax villages) were granted to prominent members of the elite as a reward for their services to the state. Apparently the owners of these estates were free to extract what produce and labor they could. It is not known how often this was done or how much of the countryside was controlled in this manner. The famous general Kim Yu-sin was granted 500 households and six horse farms, but as he was a national hero this might not have been typical. Most officials were supported by *nogŭp* (stipend villages), which are believed to have included the right to collect a stipulated grain tax and perhaps corvée labor (use of labor service as a form of taxation) on the part of the recipients. In 687, a new system, the *chikchŏn* (office-field), was introduced, which assigned land to specific offices and entitled the officeholder only the right to collect the grain tax. Two years later the stipend village system was abolished. Both moves were an apparent attempt to gain greater control over the nation's resources by the state. The office-field system was abandoned in 757, and the *nogŭp* restored. More ambitious was the *chŏngjŏnje* ("able-bodied land system") that was initiated in 722. Based on the Chinese term "equal field" (Chinese: *juntian*; Korean: *kyunjŏn*), this was an attempt to establish state control over all land and periodically redistribute it to individual households, the amount depending upon the number of able-bodied adult males each contained. Upon the death of an adult male, his portion of land reverted to state control and was redistributed. This would insure that the state had access to the surplus produce and labor of its peasantry, and would prevent great landowners from controlling these resources and denying the state access to them. This too was abandoned; just when is not known. Along with the failure of the *chikchŏn,* the failure of the "able-bodied land system" indicates the limits of the state's control over its aristocracy and peasantry.

However, a chance discovery of four village registers found in the form of a wrapper over another document in the Shōsōin Imperial Repository in Nara, Japan, in 1933 belies this impression of limited government control. This fascinating peak into Silla administration, while highlighting the fragmentary knowledge of this period of Korean history, also testifies to the ingenuity of historians who have managed to derive a wide range of insights and interpretations of Korean history from a single scrap of documentation. The document contains portions of a census register of four villages near modern Ch'ŏngju. The dating of this document is given in a sexagesimal cycle year used in East Asia to count by giving each year in a sixty-year cycle a name. The year name given is generally believed to refer to 755, although 815 is a possibility. With surprising detail, the villages were classified into nine grades of households based on the number of able-bodied adults and others available for corvée duty. Fields were divided into paddies, dry fields, and hemp fields. Horses, oxen, and mulberry, pine nut, and walnut trees were all listed. Certain fields appear to have been set aside for the support of village heads. There are other categories of fields of uncertain purpose.[2] These were perhaps office lands in accordance with the *chikchŏn* system, that is, for the support of the state officials.

All this would indicate that the Silla state made a considerable effort to consolidate its control over the peasantry and its resources, and possessed an impressive level of administrative organization and recordkeeping. An important form of taxation was corvée. Peasants were required to work on major public construction projects. Skilled workers owned or controlled by the state provided it with services and needed goods that were produced in state workshops. Metalsmiths, leather workers, butchers, guards, spinners and weavers of cotton and hemp, makers of medicinal goods, temple officials, street cleaners, and bookkeepers worked for the state in varying degrees of servitude. The state's ability to extract taxes and labor was the key to its effectiveness as a political institution. Potential revenues were lost to grants of tax-free land given as rewards, such as the impressive grant to Kim Yu-sin. Buddhist temples owned farmland that was also exempt from taxes. How much land was owned by temples is not clear, but it may have been considerable. Revenue gathering reached its peak efficiency in the late seventh and eighth centuries as monarchs consolidated their power. In the ninth century, especially in the latter half, there appeared to have been a sharp drop-off in state revenues, and a concomitant decline in the power of the Silla monarchy.

At the apex of the state was the monarch. The king, however, had to compete for authority and revenue with the great landowners, who were generally the high-born aristocrats. To shore up their legitimacy Sillan kings made use of the Chinese tributary system. The Chinese emperor was recognized as the Son of Heaven, and the Silla king as his enfeoffed representative on the peninsula. The Chinese imperial calendar was official, and in the eighth and early ninth centuries each king sought to confirm his position by sending an envoy to the Tang capital upon coming to the throne.

Kings also used Confucianism to strengthen state authority. Confucianism was a line of teachings derived from the Chinese philosopher Kongfuzi, known in the West as Confucius (551–479 BCE). In Silla times, its most important teachings were its emphases on filial piety, loyalty to the ruler, and respect for authority, all useful for the state. Confucian ideas would gradually penetrate Korean culture until by the fourteenth or fifteenth century they became the principal basis for moral, social, and political philosophy. In Silla times, however, Confucianism was primarily useful for training literate and loyal officials. The full implications of this school of thought were not felt until much later. As early as 636, Queen Sŏndŏk appointed scholars to teach the Confucian classics. Her successor, Queen Chindŏk, followed Koguryŏ and Paekche practice by designating certain scholars as *paksa* (erudites). In 682, a *Kukhak* (National Academy) along Tang lines was established to promote the study of the Chinese classics. This institution was open to sons of aristocratic families between eighteen and thirty years of age. In 717, portraits of Confucius and the "ten philosophers" and seventy-two worthies were brought back from Tang China, and in 750, the National Academy was reorganized as the *T'aehakkam* with a curriculum based on Confucian works. Examinations on Chinese classics were held to select worthy officials. Confucianism, however, was strictly secondary to Buddhism as a source of moral and political authority. It is also unlikely that the examinations were more than a short-lived modest experiment. Only later, with the reintroduction of the civil examinations in the Koryŏ state, did the Chinese practice of selecting officials by examination begin to play a significant role in Korean political culture.

A number of scholars trained in the Chinese classics served that state. Some were historians. Historical compilation played an important role in Silla society as it did throughout Korean history. Two erudites of history served the Sillan kings. The most distinguished historian was Kim Taemun, active in the early eighth century, who authored a history of the *hwarang*, the *Hwarang segi* (Chronicles of the Hwarang), *Kosŭng chŏn* (Biographies of Eminent Monks), the *Kyerim chapchŏn* (Tales of Silla), and the *Hansan ki* (Record of Hansan). Unfortunately none of these has survived.

The men like Kim Tae-mun who served as officials became the forerun-
ners of the Confucian scholar-bureaucrat who would characterize later
Korean history. Another early scholar official was Kangsu (d. 692), who,
as with most of the men of Chinese learning, came from the lower head-
rank aristocracy (see below). Most famous of the early masters of classical Chinese learning was Sŏl Ch'ong (c. 660–730), a contemporary of the
historian Kim Tae-mun. Son of the Silla monk Wŏnhyo by a Silla princess,
Sŏl Ch'ong was one of the outstanding learned men of Silla. He served as
a royal advisor, and his letter to the throne *P'ungwang so* (*Parables for the
King*) urged monarchs to renounce pleasure seeking and strictly observe
moral standards. This is one of the earliest examples of the Confucian
moralistic admonitions to the monarch that would remain a major feature
of premodern Korean politics. Sŏl Ch'ong was also incorrectly credited
with inventing the *idu* (or *kugyŏl*) transcription system used to facilitate
the reading of the Chinese classics, but he may have standardized it.

A distinction existed between these men of the head-rank-six class, who
were generally better educated so they could carry out the clerical functions of the state, and the higher aristocracy of the true-bone that monopolized the top posts. Many of the early Confucian scholars such as Kangsu
and Sŏl Ch'ong were locally educated men, and their knowledge of the
Chinese classics was still a rare and valuable skill. By the ninth century a
large number of men who had studied in Tang and were fluent in Chinese
emerged to take an increasingly active part in government serving the
kings. They were mostly from the lower aristocratic head-rank-six class.
These educated head-rank-six officials insisted, as men of learning and
merit, on the right to serve government at the higher levels despite their
lower rank. Ch'oe Ch'i-wŏn (857–?) was the most famous of these. Ch'oe
went to Tang China where he studied Chinese classics and literature. He
distinguished himself in the Tang examinations in 874 and served in the
Tang bureaucracy. After returning to Korea in 885, Ch'oe served as an
advisor to Queen Chinsŏng (r. 887–897), to whom he submitted a number
of memorials proposing reforms. The content of those proposals has not
survived, but he is believed to have been an early champion of the employment of the Chinese civil examination system. When his proposals
were not adopted, he retired to self-imposed exile, setting a pattern for
many subsequent scholars and reformers. Ch'oe Ch'i-wŏn was regarded
in his day as an outstanding poet and essayist both in China and in Korea.
A collection of his writings, the *Kyewŏn p'ilgyŏng chip* (*Plowing the Laurel
Grove with a Writing Brush*), has survived. They represent the earliest extant collection of literary works of an individual Korean author. He was
also highly thought of as a calligrapher and samples of his calligraphy
have survived in the "four mountain inscriptions."[3]

Daoism (Taoism) was another school of thought that shaped Korean culture at this time, albeit to a much lesser extent than Buddhism or Confucianism. The Daoist classic, the *Laozi*, was known in Koguryŏ. Religious Daoism was actively promoted as an alternative to Buddhism by the state in the seventh century. Even earlier references to the *Laozi* and the *Zhuangzi*, the other great Daoist classic, appear in Paekche. In Silla, the official transmission of Daoism came in 738 when the Tang envoy presented King Hyosŏng with a copy of the *Laozi*. It was, however, only during the period of decline during the eighth and ninth centuries that Daoism had a significant influence in Korea.

SILLA SOCIETY

Silla's elaborate formal government apparatus was imposed over a society structured along hereditary class lines. Bureaucratic positions were limited to corresponding hereditary ranks. At the top was the *chin'gol* (true-bone) aristocracy. The true-bone aristocrats, for the most part, resided in the capital and monopolized the first five of the seventeen bureaucratic ranks, including the highest position, the *sangdaedŭng*; the *yŏng* (heads) of the ministries; the provincial governors; and the generals. Many of these high-ranking aristocrats possessed private armies of armed retainers. According to one Chinese source, these private armies numbered as many as 3,000 men.

Below the true-bones were the *tup'um* (head-ranks). The *yuktup'um*, the topmost head-rank six, formed the second tier of the aristocracy. Also primarily residents of the capital, Kyŏngju, they played an increasingly significant political and cultural role. The head-rank-six members held positions of lesser bureaucratic rank and provided the state with many of its scholars and court scribes. Beneath the aristocratic class were commoners. We hear little of these people, who probably made up the majority of the population. One historical question has been whether the peasantry was free or in some state of servitude. Evidence is too fragmentary to make conclusions as to whether they were free to move or to buy and sell land. In view of the powerful grip the aristocracy had on society, it is not likely that peasants possessed much freedom of movement. That peasants enjoyed at least some rights and privileges is implied by the fact that they were distinguished from people of more servile status. Free or not, in Silla's hereditary class-based society, the opportunity to rise in status, serve in government, or change occupation was at best extremely limited.

Koreans adopted the Chinese classification of non-elites into *p'yŏngin* ("good people") and "mean" or "base" people. The *p'yŏngin* lived in villages (*ch'on*) and were subject to the supervision of village elders, farming their own fields as well as those designated for government and elite support. "Mean" people ranged from skilled craftsmen and specialists to chattel slaves. While slavery certainly existed, it does not appear to have been the primary economic basis of society. It appears that there were no large landed estates, only scattered parcels of land that could have been worked by slaves; public construction, however, was carried out by peasant corvées, not slaves. But that slaves were probably fairly numerous and could be held by commoners is suggested by the few records that have survived.[4] The four village census registers list 25 slaves among the 442 members of the agricultural communities.

Available evidence indicates that Silla was a rigidly hierarchical society where rank, status, and privilege ran along hereditary class lines. Incidences of social mobility, if it existed, must have been rare. Strict sumptuary laws reinforced class differences. Clothing, footwear, utensils, the size of houses, the designs on tiles, size of carts, and room sizes were all regulated. Commoners were forbidden from having big entry gates to their homes and could have no more than three horses in their stables. Nevertheless, commoners could become wealthy, and the flourishing maritime trade of late Silla must have afforded many opportunities for lower-ranked merchants to amass wealth and influence. The records state, for instance, that in 834, King Hŭngdŏk issued an edict prohibiting the possession of luxurious foreign goods by commoners because this was leading to confusion in social ranks. Family descent was extremely important, as it was in later periods in Korea. The main kinship organization was the *chok*, a large descent group. Later Koreans would have family shrines and elaborate rituals honoring their ancestors, but this was probably not the case in Silla.[5]

The status of women in Silla was higher than in subsequent periods and perhaps higher than it was in Paekche and Koguryŏ. Much of our knowledge of Silla's family structure and the role of women, however, remains a matter of speculation. It is believed that the status of women was high compared to most contemporary Asian societies, that men and women mingled freely and participated together in social functions, and that families traced their ancestry along both their father's and mother's line. Women were able to succeed as the family head, and failure to produce a son was not grounds for divorce. Three women ascended to the throne—the last was Chinsŏng (r. 887–897)—although only when there was no male heir. Among royalty, about whom much more information is available, girls married between sixteen and twenty, and there was often a considerable difference in ages between partners. No strict rule seems to have existed concerning the use of paternal surnames. Succession was not limited to sons, but also included daughters, sons-in-law, and grandsons by sons and daughters. Equal importance was given to the rank of the father and the mother in determining the status of the child.[6] Kings selected their queens from powerful families. A careful reading of the historical records that were edited in later times suggests that Silla queens may have exercised considerable authority.[7]

In all these ways, Korean society at this time differed from later periods, in which the position of women weakened considerably. If the above represents an accurate picture of Silla society, then the pattern of the next 1,000 years of Korean history is one of a steady decline in the status of women, of the greater segregation of sexes, and of a shift to a more patrilineal society.

Agriculture was the basis of the economy and the vast majority of the population lived in small villages and hamlets where they farmed rice, barley, and vegetables. Little is known about farming methods in this period, but enough surplus was produced to support a sizeable urban population. Kyŏngju was the largest city. The thirteenth-century history *Samguk yusa* states that at one point it had 178,936 households. The city is said to have had 1,360 residential quarters in its fifty-five wards, thirty-five great private estates, and four royal palaces, one for each season. While these figures no doubt are greatly exaggerated, archaeological evidence suggests that it was indeed a sizeable city, among the major urban centers in Asia. It was apparently a prosperous city of parks, bridges, and large official markets. The *Samguk yusa* records that when King Hŏn'gang (r. 875–886) looked out from his palace he could see "homes with tiled roofs in rows from the capital to the seas, with not a single thatched roof in sight."[8] Historical demography for Korea is still largely undeveloped, but Korea under Silla probably had a population of at least 2 million, possibly twice that, making it one of the larger states in Eurasia.

Religion and Aristocratic Culture

Silla was a Buddhist kingdom. The religion had taken deep roots, at least among the ruling class, by the time of unification. Both kings Chinhŭng and Pŏphŭng, for example, abdicated late in their reigns to be ordained as monks.[9] Originally from India, Buddhism eventually spread across most of Asia. Through Buddhism Korea was linked to the wider world that included not only China and Japan but the Buddhist lands in Central Asia, Southeast Asia, and India. A few Korean monks even journeyed to India in search of Buddhist teachings. Best known was Hyech'o (b. 704), who described his pilgrimage to India in *Wang och'ŏnch'ukkuk chŏn* (*Record of a Journey to the Five Indian Kingdoms*).

The basic teachings of Buddhism included the ideas that the world was full of suffering and that this suffering was the result of karma or deeds done in this or past lives. The goal of Buddhism was to break the cycle of births and rebirth and achieve Nirvana, a state of nonexistence that was free from suffering. The forms of Buddhism that reached Korea had undergone considerable change from the original teachings that had emphasized moderation and avoidance of excessive attachment to worldly affairs. These modifications were, in part, due to the Chinese practice of *ge-yi*, that is, finding suitable Chinese equivalents to Indian Buddhist terms, a process that did much to reinterpret and perhaps dilute the original meanings. Chinese Buddhism during the Tang also reflected the influence of Daoism and other indigenous beliefs.

In Silla Buddhism was a source for legitimizing authority, adding to the prestige of the monarchy, and providing the state with scribes and advisors. It was especially, perhaps principally, valued for the supernatural aid it provided. This role gradually declined with the absorption of Chinese secular learning, especially Confucianism, and with the consequent growth of a literate segment of the aristocracy trained in the Chinese classics and in Chinese principles of law and government. Yet, Buddhism still provided the chief source of artistic inspiration, continued to attract many of the best minds in Korea, and pervaded all aspects of secular culture. It was the fundamental belief system of the dominant groups of society. The Buddhist scholarship produced during this period was one of the finest outpourings of intellectual creativity in Korean history.

Tang Buddhism was characterized by its division into many doctrinal sects. Most were named after a particular sutra that was regarded by the sect as the embodiment of the true essence of Buddha's teachings. Korean Buddhism inherited this multiplicity of doctrines and the focus on certain sutras from Tang. It also shared, if not inherited, the Chinese practice of doctrinal tolerance and the absence of sectarian strife as well as a tendency toward syncretism. Sects tended to borrow from one another so that distinctions between them gradually became blurred.

One of the most important sects was Hwaŏm (Flower Garland). Named for the Avatamsaka (Flower Garland) Sutra, this sect tried to incorporate various doctrines by classifying them into varying degrees of truth. The tenets of Hwaŏm were complex and intellectually demanding, making little concession for the follower who was unable to devote his life to them. It appealed to the small number of monks of aristocratic background who spent their lives mastering esoteric knowledge and thereby gaining awe and respect. It also appealed to other members of the elite who were attracted to its rich rituals and ceremonies, and who could afford to finance the construction of temples, perform elaborate ceremonies and prayers, and support monks who could study on their behalf. Ŭisang (625–702), founder of the Hwaŏm school in Korea, was one of the major intellectual figures of Korean history. Ŭisang went to China at sixteen, where he studied under the Hwaŏm master Zhiyan, along with Fazang, who became one of China's seminal Buddhist thinkers. Among Ŭisang's many disciples were Simsang, who later propagated the doctrine in Japan. Ŭisang's later reputation was such that he was credited with saving Silla from an invasion by Chinese emperor Tang Gaozong. He emphasized strict learning, the performance of rituals, and monastic life. In this, he typified the Korean Buddhism of his age.

While Silla kings did not abandon the patronage of Buddhism or its use as a source of legitimacy, Silla Buddhism became less court centered and at the same time less confined to the aristocratic elite. Newer, less esoteric forms of Buddhism with simpler doctrines appeared that did not require constant sponsorship of costly ceremonies. A precursor of this popular Buddhism came with Wŏnhyo. Wŏnhyo (617–686) was one of the major Buddhist thinkers of Korea.[10] He preached to the common people at a time when Buddhism was confined mainly to the court and the aristocracy. Most of the eminent monks of Silla derived their fame from introducing some new teaching from China. Wŏnhyo, however, did not journey to China. Instead he traveled throughout the countryside as an act of penance after having broken his vows and sired a son, Sŏl Ch'ong, by a Silla princess. He was also the founder of the Pŏpsang (Dharma-nature) school of Buddhism, sometimes called the Haedong (Korea) school, since it was the only indigenous sect. Wŏnhyo's aim was to create a school of Buddhism that would harmonize the doctrines of the various other schools. He would be the first major figure in a distinctively Korean tendency to seek a unifying school of doctrine and practice.

Two forms of Buddhism that appeared in Silla times had their major impact on Korean religious beliefs later on: Pure Land Buddhism and Meditative Buddhism. The Pure Land sect centered around devotion to Amitabha (Amit'a-bul), who helped the troubled reach Happy Land (Sukhavati). This belief spread among those of humble status as early as the mid-eighth century, becoming of greater importance in subsequent centuries. Meditative Buddhism, or Sŏn (called Chan in Chinese but better known in the West by its Japanese pronunciation, Zen), was first introduced by Pŏmnang (c. 632–646) after returning from Tang. Another monk, Sinhaeng (d. 779), founded one of the world's oldest extant Sŏn temples. Sŏn became important in the ninth century with the teachings of Toŭi (d. 825), the first major figure in that tradition, and it had a profound impact on Korea during the Koryŏ period.

Buddhism was the inspiration for much of the art of this period. The most outstanding examples are the Pulguk-sa temple and the Sŏkkuram grotto. Pulguk-sa, built near Kyŏngju in the mid-eighth century, is still one of the great architectural monuments of East Asia. Of special interest is the Muyŏng-t'ap (pagoda that casts no shadow), built in 751. During its reconstruction in 1966 a dharani, a magical formula, was found that was apparently placed in the pagoda at the time of its construction. This is the world's oldest known printed document. The justly famed Sŏkkuram Grotto, located in a mountain near Kyŏngju facing the East Sea, contains among its many excellent carvings an exquisite eleven-foot stone Buddha that is situated so that it catches the first rays of dawn as the sun rises above the East Sea. The bronze Buddhas and bodhisattvas are of a high standard and were never equaled in Korea. Also impressive are the bronze bells. The Samwŏn-sa Bell, cast in 725, the oldest extant, weighs 1,500 kilograms. The Pongdŏk-sa Bell, cast in 770, is the second largest in the world. Silla bells were decorated with delicate bas-reliefs of flowers, clouds, and flames. Most famous of all is the Emille Bell in Kyŏngju.

Beneath the Buddhism of the Silla was a rich and complex tradition of indigenous religion and practices. We know little of these, however, because they did not leave behind written records. The peoples of Korea worshiped the spirits of mountains and rivers and of various natural features. Dragon spirits were worshiped. The popularity of the cult of Maitreya (Korean: Mirŭk), the Buddha of the future, may have been linked to dragon worship, since the word for dragon is the same in Korean. A chilling hint of indigenous beliefs is the story of the Emille Bell. According to legend, the craftsman who cast the magnificent bronze bell was successful only after sacrificing his daughter by throwing her into the molten metal. The cry of her name could be heard, it was said, calling out when the bell was rung.

Silla rulers continued to construct tombs in the Chinese manner. A distinct feature of these tombs, not found on the mainland, is the zodiacal animal deities bearing weapons. One of the interesting surviving monuments from Silla is the Ch'ŏmsŏng-dae, a bottle-shaped granite tower in the ancient Silla capital of Kyŏngju, often cited as the world's oldest astronomical observatory. According to the *Samguk yusa*, the Ch'ŏmsŏng-dae was built during the reign of Queen Sŏndŏk (632–647). Its original purpose is not clear but it is widely believed that it served as an observatory, and it has been suggested that its shape was designed to hold a large armillary sphere. If so, it is the world's oldest extant observatory.[11] Due to the central role that Buddhism played as a state-protective cult it has been suggested that the tower was built as a replica of the holy Mount Sumeru, and that it was a place where praying and incantations took place. It is known that astronomy was an important science for compiling the calendar and for prognostication. One eighth-century astronomer, Kim Am, the great-great-grandson of Kim Yu-sin, enjoyed a high reputation. Kim studied in China and was also remembered as a master of military science and of yin-yang theory.

Educated members of the elite wrote poetry in Chinese, and some of their works have survived in Chinese anthologies. The great anthology of Chinese literature, the *Wenxuan*, was taught in Korea, and the Tang poets Bo Juyi and Du Fu were highly esteemed by the educated elite, while some Korean writers in Chinese, such as Ch'oe Ch'i-wŏn, were highly admired in Tang. Ch'oe was considered a master of poetry and parallel prose. A collection of his writings was compiled in 886 and published in both China and Korea. In general, Koreans used Chinese ideographs (called *hanmun* or *hanja* in Korean) for writing, although, of course, they spoke one of the several dialects of Korean used in the peninsula during that time. All three kingdoms apparently employed systems for writing in their native languages using Chinese characters. One method of writing in the vernacular was called *idu*. Idu used *hanmun* sentences and placed them in Korean syntax by using certain characters to indicate grammatical markers. Another system, *Kugyŏl* or *t'o*, also employed a system of markers and was used as an aid in reading Chinese. Writing Korean in Chinese characters presented problems, as can be seen in the Oath Inscription of 612 where Chinese characters are put in Korean word order. The complicated sound system of Korean made development of a phonetic script difficult, and it was not until the fifteenth century that the Korean alphabet *han'gŭl* was developed (see chapter 7).[12]

Koreans in Silla times also wrote poetry in Korean. In the late ninth century an anthology of hundreds of vernacular Korean poems, the *Samdaemok* (*Collection from the Three Kingdoms*), was compiled, but it has been lost. Much Korean poetry was written in a system called *hyangch'al*, which was devised to transcribe entire Korean sentences with Chinese characters. Using this system, Korean-language poems known as *hyangga* were composed. Unfortunately, few *hyangga* have survived (see below). Although we have the titles of many *hyangga*, only twenty-five *hyangga* now exist: fourteen dating to Silla times are in the *Samguk yusa*; the other eleven, attributed to the tenth-century monk Kyunyŏ, are in the *Kyunyŏ chŏn* (*Tale of Kyunyŏ*). These poems provide us with the earliest forms of purely Korean literature. They are invaluable in providing a window into the language and indigenous poetry of the period. Seventeen are Buddhist in inspiration and content; others show a shamanistic influence. Among the latter the "Song of Ch'ŏyong" is probably the best known. This eight-line poem refers to the legend of Ch'ŏyong, one of the seven sons of the Dragon King of the Eastern Sea, who married a beautiful woman. Seeing that the wife was extremely attractive, an evil spirit transformed himself into a man and attacked her in her room while Ch'ŏyong was away. But Ch'ŏyong returned and, witnessing the scene, calmly sang the words of the poem, which so moved the evil spirit that it went away. The Ch'ŏyong mask was later used to exorcize evil spirits, usually on New Year's Eve. It is apparent that many of the *hyangga* were to be accompanied by music and dance. Indigenous religious undertones are strong in surviving Silla literature. Even many of the Buddhist poems appear to have been Buddhified shamanistic invocations to mountain spirits and other nature deities and are perhaps of remote origin.

Saenae-mu, mask dances, were performed on festival days such as the three-day *T'aep'o* (Festival of Wine), which was imported from China. The first was recorded in 615. In 746, at a *T'aep'o* given by King Kyŏngdŏk, a general amnesty was declared, and 150 novices were ordained monks. This was celebrated in Kyŏngju, which was the great center for aristocratic life. In fact, there appear to have been no significant regional cultural centers, and to a much greater degree than in later Korea, the higher culture was confined to the aristocratic elite living in the capital. An inkling of what this life may have been like is revealed in the Imhae-jŏn (Pavilion on the Sea) banquet hall, which was built over the man-made Anapchi Lake and in the P'osŏkchŏng. The latter was a slightly winding water channel carved out of stone in which wine cups were floated. Revelers took turns composing verse before the wine cups floated down to them. Little is known, however, of the art, music, and festivities of the non-elites.

SILLA AND ITS NEIGHBORS

Silla relations with Tang began to improve in the eighth century. There were several reasons for this. After the reign of Gaozong, the expansionary phase of Tang was largely over, and fear of a direct invasion lessened. Furthermore, the creation of Parhae, a new state in Manchuria, acted both as a buffer between Silla and Tang and as a mutual enemy. It controlled part of what is now Korea, posing a threat to its southern neighbor. An alliance between Tang and Silla against Parhae in 733 brought a long period of amiable relations between the two. Tang's interests in the Korean peninsula were largely strategic, and as it became obvious that Silla posed no threat to its security, relations warmed. China found instead that its policy of using trade and cultural exchanges and offering legitimacy and prestige to the Silla monarchy was effective in keeping Silla safely in the tributary system. Indeed, the relationship that was worked out in the late seventh and early eighth centuries can be considered the beginning of the mature tributary relationship that would characterize Sino-Korean interchange most of the time until the late nineteenth century.

Cultural relations with China were significant. Forty-five of the fifty Silla monks known to have traveled to China did so after unification. Many Korean students studied in Tang. There is no way of knowing how many, but it must have been a considerable number, for in 844, 105

Koreans who were studying at the national academy were sent back to Silla. Eighty-eight Sillans passed the highly competitive and prestigious civil examination during the Tang. A few Koreans even rose to high office in China. Koreans who succeeded academically or who achieved fame in China returned to the homeland as celebrated heroes. In addition to students, frequent embassies were exchanged. One Chinese embassy is said to have had 800 members. The resultant process of sinicization among the elite was profound. Silla courtiers wore Chinese dress; aristocrats wrote verse in the best Chinese; and Chinese fashions in eating, drinking, music, and imported luxuries of all sorts were necessary accoutrements to high-born status. It is not certain how far Chinese cultural influences penetrated down the social scale. Most probably, the interest in Chinese culture was largely confined to the elite.

In contrast to those with China, relations between Silla and Japan were often hostile. In 733, the Yamato government participated in an alliance with Parhae and sent ships to attack Korea. Japanese leaders hoped to gain a foothold on the Korean peninsula. Attacks by the Japanese from the sea were a threat in early Silla. In 746, 300 Japanese ships are reported to have attacked Silla. This was followed by a treaty of amity that initiated a period of peaceful exchange. Good relations with Silla served the Japanese well because during the next century the chief maritime route to China passed along the south coast of Korea. A bureau for Silla was established in Dazaifu in Kyushu in western Japan, and embassies were exchanged. One Japanese embassy had a reported 204 members. During 761–764, during the An Lushan rebellion in China, a Japanese court official, Fujiwara no Nakamura, planned another invasion; but this was called off by rivals at court and no further organized invasions of Korea took place for the next eight centuries. Instead, it was Sillan pirates who plagued the Japanese coast in the ninth century.

Silla was also tied to its neighbors by trade networks. This included the official tribute given to Tang and the "gifts" received in return. A great deal of private trade flourished as well. Silla silver and gold wares were prized in China. Especially famous were silver and gold basins that became known in China through Song times as "Silla" and copper basins that were called "copper Silla." Silla silver and gold gained a reputation as far as the Middle East where early Arab references to al-Sila describe it as rich in precious metals.[13] Silla exported silver and gold bullion, textiles, and ginseng, for which Korea has always been famous in East Asia. Sometimes Silla took advantage of its location to re-export Chinese goods and furs and horses from the tribal peoples on its northern border to Japan. From China books, tea, textiles, swords, a variety of ceremonial goods such as court robes, and various luxurious goods were imported. Chinese coins were also imported; they served as a medium of exchange,

since Silla did not mint coins. Some of these goods were re-exported to
Japan, where they were traded along with Silla crafts for pearls, fans, and
screens.

Silla was the greatest period of maritime activity in Korea's history. Koreans dominated the commerce of Northeast Asia in the eighth and ninth
centuries; most of the commerce between Korea, north China, and Japan
was carried out in Korean ships. Koreans established communities in the
port of Dengzhou, the historic gateway into north China from Korea, and
in Lianshui and Chuzhou on the Huai River. Korean ships sailed to Yang-
zhou at the junction of the Yangzi River and the Grand Canal, but did not
generally venture into southern China where international commerce was
dominated by Arabs. In the ninth century Japanese going to China sailed
on Korean vessels, and the account of one these travelers, the monk Ennin
(794–864), provides a valuable description of Korean maritime activities
and of the Korean naval commander Chang Po-go.

Chang Po-go's (788?–846) career illustrates this interesting chapter of
Korean history. Born on Ch'ŏnghae (Wando) Island off Korea's south-
western coast of humble family background, Chang Po-go immigrated to
Tang, where he became a military officer in the lower Huai River basin.
Chang returned to Korea and gained royal permission to establish the
Ch'ŏnghae Garrison on his home island in 828 by arguing for the need to
control Chinese piracy and to protect Korean trade and travelers. From
his stronghold he operated a private navy that was a major power in the
Yellow Sea. According to the Japanese monk Ennin in his *Account of a Pilgrimage to Tang in Search of the Law*, which tells of his 840 voyage to Tang
China in one of Chang Po-go's ships, the Korean commander operated a
large Buddhist temple in Shandong Province with twenty-eight Korean
monks and nuns.[14] Chang Po-go's maritime trade and connections were
so extensive that he was called "King of the Yellow Sea." According to
Korean accounts he was given command of the Ch'ŏnghae Garrison because he wanted to end the marauding of pirates who were kidnapping
Koreans and selling them as slaves. However, this official position was
probably just an official acknowledgment of his already accumulated
power. Chang supported Kim U-jing in his successful bid for the throne
in 839, when he became King Sinmu. When the newly installed king died
the same year, Chang attempted to marry his daughter to King Sinmu's
son and successor, King Munsŏng. For an islander and a man outside the
aristocratic elite of Silla, this bid for influence was a bold move, which
failed when a member of the capital aristocracy assassinated him in 846.
The Ch'ŏnghae Garrison was abolished in 851. Chang Po-go's rise from
a maritime trader to a major power broker in late Silla was unusual but
probably indicative of the growth of maritime lords during this period.
Two other maritime lords were Wang Pong-gyu in Chinju and Wang

Kŏn (877–943), the Koryŏ founder, who came from a maritime family in the Kaesŏng area. Korea's dominance of Northeast Asian sea lanes ended after the ninth century.

PARHAE

Silla was not the only state to occupy the Korean peninsula. To the north was the state of Parhae. After the collapse of Koguryŏ, remnants from that state and a number of Manchurian tribal peoples set up a state in southern Manchuria at the end of the seventh century that dominated most of Manchuria and the northern third of Korea for two centuries. From 713 to its destruction by the Khitans in 926, Parhae was a formidable power. Its relations with its neighbors were often tense. Parhae, an extensive state, was strong enough to launch a naval raid on the Chinese port of Dengzhou in 732. Despite the tense relations with Tang, Parhae was quickly brought into the Chinese cultural orbit, modeling its administrative structure, its laws, and its literature after its giant neighbor. In general the Parhae administrative structure conformed more closely to the Tang model than to Silla. The state impressed the Chinese enough to earn from them the sobriquet the "flourishing land in the East." A high-water mark of its wealth and power was reached under the tenth king, Sŏn (r. 818–831).[15] Sŏn expanded the kingdom to the Amur River.

For Silla, Parhae was a menacing neighbor. This was heightened when the second king, Tae Mu-ye, known also as King Mu (r. 719–737), completed the tasks of subjugating the western Manchurian tribes and then turned south and established control over the Hamhŭng plain and the Hamggyŏng coast. In 721, Silla was forced to construct what is recorded as a wall but was more likely a chain of fortifications along its northern border that extended from the mouth of the Taedong to Wŏnsan Bay on the east coast. In terms of geopolitics, Parhae occupied the former position of Koguryŏ. With the consolidation of the Parhae state under Mu, Silla found itself in the same position that it was in the 660s when, after the fall of Paekche, it allied itself with Tang to remove the threat in the northern part of the peninsula. But the Tang-Silla military campaign of 733 was no repeat of 668. Half the Sillan army, including two grandsons of Kim Yu-sin, perished in the snows of the northern mountains. Parhae remained a powerful state that outlived by a couple of decades Silla's effective control over most of the peninsula. The war did bring one benefit for Silla. Tang, in return for its support against Parhae, recognized Silla's sovereignty over all the territory south of the Taedong. Again in 762, during the An Lushan rebellion in China, Silla felt compelled to fortify its northern border in anticipation of a joint Parhae-Japanese invasion. Relations between the two states, however, were not always hostile, and diplomatic missions to Parhae are recorded for 792 and 812. Trade also was carried out between them, and there is a reference to thirty-nine stations along a trade route stretching from the Parhae city of Tonggyŏng to Silla.

Parhae's relations with Japan were of a much more consistently friendly nature. For two centuries, the two nations exchanged diplomatic embassies. Parhae dispatched thirty-five embassies to Japan and the Japanese court sent thirteen embassies to Parhae.[16] A lively trade existed between the two, Parhae selling furs for Japanese textiles. Parhae also acted as an important avenue for the transmission of Chinese culture into Japan, assuming the role formerly played by Koguryŏ. The Japanese were impressed by the cultural attainments of Parhae's envoys; surviving poems composed by Parhae diplomats for the Japanese hosts remain the only extant examples of Parhae literature. Twice in 733 and again in 762 joint attacks on Silla were planned, the second one abortive. And when the Parhae state fell to the seminomad Khitans, a last embassy came in 929 unsuccessfully seeking assistance in restoring the kingdom. In the early eighth century Parhae also sought alliance with the Tujue (Turkish) confederation that arose in Mongolia, briefly making Korea the focal point of a vast East Asian military alliance system that pitted Tang and Silla against Parhae, the Tujue, and Japan.

Only fragmentary knowledge has survived about Parhae society and culture. The economy was based on agriculture with the rich central Manchuria plains supporting a population that according to one Chinese source consisted of 100,000 households or about half a million people. Ethnically, the population was a mix of various Manchurian peoples of Tungusic linguistic stock along with possible admixtures of Koguryŏ-speaking people. Recently, archeological work in Manchuria has begun to give us a glimpse of an amalgamated cultural style of Chinese, Korean, and indigenous elements. Interestingly, an *ondol* system for heating homes characteristic of Korean houses was used. Many Parhae students studied and sat for the examinations in Tang, where the Chinese diplomatically admitted the same number of Sillan and Parhae applicants to the exams. But the Chinese were not always so even-handed and gave Sillan envoys a higher place in imperial audiences. Since only a few fragments of literature have survived, little can be said except that the elite at least had absorbed a great deal of Chinese culture and wrote eloquent Chinese verse. Buddhism was patronized and a purple porcelain was produced that gained a high reputation in Tang.

Since the eighteenth century many Korean historians have considered Parhae part of Korean history, which has led some historians to regard the Late Silla period as the "two Kingdoms period."[17] The implications of this for Korea are significant. Considering Parhae part of Korean history strengthens the argument of those modern Korean nationalists who seek to incorporate much of Manchuria within the historical homeland of Koreans, and it provides support for modern ultranationalists who hold irredentist claims for all or portions of Manchuria. For contemporary Koreans it also provides a historical echo for their current north-south division. Still the questions remain: Was Parhae a Korean state? And what role does it play in Korean history? It did occupy the northernmost parts of what is now Korea, including the modern Hamgyŏng Province, and its ruling dynasty of non-Korean ethnic origins proudly laid claim to Koguryŏ's heritage. The rulers of Parhae often referred to their state as the successor to Koguryŏ, and many of the leading families traced their ancestry to that state. But Parhae's population was predominately of groups different from those that evolved into modern ethnic Koreans. In this respect it resembled Koguryŏ, a state that lay mostly outside of the peninsula and that most likely had many ethnic groups that were not ancestral to modern Koreans. If fact, even the Koguryŏ language appears to have been quite different from that spoken in Silla and Paekche and perhaps less closely related to modern Korean. Some historians, therefore, regard it as illogical to include Koguryŏ and exclude Parhae as part of Korean history. But to a greater extent than Koguryŏ, Parhae's population base and its primary capital (as well as three of four of its secondary capitals) lay outside the Korean peninsula.

Whether or not it is included as a part of Korea, Parhae's role in Korean history is important because for all its tensions with its southern neighbor, it acted as a protective barrier both from Tang and from potential seminomadic invaders. That is, Parhae stabilized the always-troublesome northern frontiers of Manchuria and Siberia and enabled Silla to enjoy two centuries of relative peace and prosperity. This, perhaps, was Parhae's most important contribution to Korea's historical development.

THE DECLINE OF SILLA

After the mid-eighth century Silla began a political decline. The central government became weaker, powerful local warlords emerged, and the countryside was plagued by banditry. In part, this was related to the changes in its international environment. Throughout East Asia the eighth century was a period of cultural brilliance and prosperity while the ninth century was a time of decline. All three cultural/geographical areas that surround Korea—China, the northern frontiers of Manchuria and Siberia, and Japan—experienced troubles. The Tang Empire, after reaching a political and cultural apogee under Xuanzong (r. 712–756), began to weaken. By the late ninth century China saw internal rebellions and intrusions by tribal invaders, and at the beginning of the tenth century the Chinese Empire broke up into smaller rival states. The Manchurian state of Parhae was weakened by external pressures from seminomadic neighbors. In Japan, Nara was abandoned in 784 and the capital moved to Heian a decade later. While the early Heian period was one of cultural creativity, the central Japanese state declined and effective power gravitated toward regional warlords. Contacts between Japan and China diminished, hurting Korea, since it had benefited as an intermediary in Chinese-Japanese trade. In the south, Annam (Vietnam) became restless, and in the tenth century it broke free from Chinese rule. Tribal peoples along the northern borders of the East Asian cultural realm became increasingly powerful, with the Khitans (or Qidans) emerging in the ninth century as the most formidable in the northeast. In the early tenth century they contributed to the fall of the Tang, destroyed Parhae, and threatened the Korean peninsula with invasion. It is important to see the weakening of central authority in Silla, the rise of local warlords, and the resultant civil disorder within the context of the great fragmentation of authority and breakdown in order that characterized all of East Asia at this time. But the Silla state's decline was also part of the internal pattern. After 780, local landed aristocrats consolidated their landholdings, built *sŏngju* (walled towns), and commanded private armies. These local aristocrats in effect became warlords, even styling themselves as *changgun* (generals). Eventually these warlords formed alliances and competed with each other for power.

THE LATER THREE KINGDOMS

Toward the end of the ninth century the central government's control over most of the peninsula disintegrated. During Chinsŏng's reign (887–897) the bandit Kihwŏn overran much of south-central Korea. Yanggil, another bandit, controlled much of the north-central region; a third, Ch'onggil, lorded over parts of the south and central areas, while a group known as the Red Pantaloons terrorized the southeast and raided the outskirts of Kyŏngju in 896. Eventually three separate states emerged, so that the period from 901 until 936 is known as the Period of the Later Three Kingdoms. It became another three-way struggle for the mastery of the Korean peninsula. Later histories portrayed the struggle for the mastery of Korea among three personalities, Wang Kŏn, Kyŏnhwŏn, and Kungye, whom historian C. Cameron Hurst has called respectively the good, the bad, and the ugly.[18] Kyŏnhwŏn (867–936), the bad one, a son of a farmer, served in the coast guard in southwest Korea, was commissioned as an army officer, and with his private army occupied the provincial capital of

Muju, installing himself as military governor in 892. Initially he was still an officer in the Silla army, but then he aligned himself with the rebel-bandit Yanggil before setting himself up in 900 as the king of Paekche. This state is often referred to as Later Paekche to distinguish it from the earlier Paekche.

Kungye (d. 918), the ugly one, according to traditional sources was either born from a liaison between King Kyŏngmun and a woman outside his court or was the son of a low-ranking concubine of King Hon'an (r. 857–861); the accounts vary. A Silla prince, as a victim of a power struggle he was exiled from the court and eventually became a supporter of the bandit-rebel Kihwŏn and later of another rebel leader, Yanggil. As one of Yanggil's commanders in northern Silla, he is said to have brought large areas of Kyŏnggi, Kangwŏn, and Hwanghae provinces under the former's control. In 901, after having killed Yanggil, Kungye established what he called the state of Koguryŏ (often referred to as Later Koguryŏ) at Songak (Kaesŏng). He renamed his state twice; it is best known as Later Koguryŏ. As leader of one of the Later Three Kingdoms he engaged in a three-way power struggle with Later Paekche and Silla. Kungye is depicted in Korean histories as cruel and tyrannical with a deep hatred of Silla. Announcing "revenge on Silla for the fall of Koguryŏ" and declaring Kyŏngju the "City of Destruction," he is said to have killed anyone who ventured into his kingdom from the old Silla heartland, although his staff included Silla aristocrats. In an effort to sanctify his rule he claimed to be the Maitreya Buddha, proclaimed his sons bodhisattvas, dressed himself and his sons in colorful garb, and composed sutras. He rode on a white horse preceded by youths and maidens burning incense, followed by 200 monks chanting mantras. Kungye, claiming to have the power of mind reading, carried out frequent purges of his officials whose disloyal intentions he could anticipate.[19] In 918, he was murdered by one of his commanders, Wang Kŏn, the good one, and the founder of Koryŏ.

Silla was the weakest of the three states. The monarchy's control was limited to the extreme southeast corner of the country. Internal instability is suggested by the fact that between 912 and 927 three monarchs came from the ancient Pak line. In 921, the weakened Silla state allied itself with Wang Kŏn and his renamed Koryŏ state, a move possible only with the death of Kungye. Silla paid for this alliance with a devastating attack by Kyŏnhwŏn in 927 in which Kyŏngae (r. 924–927) committed suicide and Kyŏngju was sacked. A member of the royal Kim clan was then placed on the throne as Kyŏngsun (r. 927–935). Wang Kŏn, whose base of support appeared to be maritime, captured the islands off the west coast of Korea. But these early victories were followed by two decades of stalemate during which Silla just managed to survive and gradually came under the protection of Koryŏ. In 930, Wang Kŏn defeated Later Paekche at Mount

P'yŏng north of Andong; a year later he visited Kyŏngju and probably effectively controlled that state from then on. In 932, he was recognized as Korean ruler by the Later Tang dynasty that ruled northern China. His position was also strengthened by the arrival of refugees from Parhae including the crown prince, Tae Kwang-hyŏn, in 934.

Later Paekche, increasingly isolated, was defeated at Ungju in 934 and lost all land north of the Kŭm River. Kyŏnhwŏn sought unsuccessfully to obtain military support from Japan in 935. In the end his older son, Sin'gŏm, murdered his younger son, Kŭmgang, whom Kyŏnhwŏn had set up as his successor, and imprisoned his father. Escaping, the aging Kyŏnhwŏn marched with Wang Kŏn's army to Ilsŏn-gun. There Wang Kŏn, now able to act as an avenger for unfilial conduct, defeated the Later Paekche forces at Ilsŏn-gun in September 936. Sin'gŏm surrendered and died a few days later. The previous year, 935, the last Silla king, Kyŏngsun, abdicated and recognized Wang Kŏn as his successor. Thus Korea was reunified by Wang Kŏn and the Koryŏ period began.

Our information on this period comes from official sources written in the twelfth century under the sponsorship of the dynasty that Wang Kŏn founded. Much about the events remains unclear. For example, how did Silla manage to survive so many years? Why did Kyŏnhwŏn not annex it in 927? What were the bases of support for Kyŏnhwŏn, Kungye, and Wang Kŏn? Was the conjuring up of the names Paekche and Koguryŏ indicative of a resurgence of regional/ethnic sentiment in those regions? And, if so, does this mean that the unification of Korea under Silla was far from complete at the end of the ninth century? Or was the use of these names simply part of the search for sources of legitimacy by the rebel leaders? None of the answers to these questions are clear.

Silla rulers had only limited success in establishing a centralized polity. Powerful true-bone aristocrats resisted attempts to create a more Chinese-style centralized bureaucracy. After 780 real power seems to have slipped from the king and his officials in the capital to aristocrats in the country-side. By the end of the ninth century the king could no longer maintain control much beyond the capital, and a power struggle emerged among regional warlords. The use of the old names of Paekche and Koguryŏ suggests that the Korean peninsula was not as homogeneous as it later became; regional loyalties were still considerable. Evidence indicates that people in different areas probably still spoke distinctive languages. They also probably possessed local and ethnic identities apart from and/ or stronger than any shared Korean/Sillan identity. Much of this is not yet understood. Whatever the reasons for the creation of the later three kingdoms, they were short-lived. Most of the Korean peninsula was soon reunited, and would remain united until the division of the peninsula by the United States and the Soviet Union in 1945.

KOREA IN GLOBAL PERSPECTIVE:
SILLA'S RISE AND FALL

Silla went through a period of cultural brilliance in the eighth century, then declined in the ninth, and disintegrated in the early tenth century. This was a pattern shared by many other societies at the time. For China as well, the seventh and eighth centuries under the Tang were one of the most brilliant in its history, with a great outpouring of poetry and art, an expanding population, growing cities, and administrative efficiency peaking in the mid-eighth century. From the second half of the eight century, following the An Lushan Rebellion, 755–763, Tang went into a political decline, although it continued to flourish well into the ninth century, when the decline began to accelerate. After 906, a number of short-lived dynasties and weak governments existed until the establishment of the Song in 960 brought about an economic and cultural revival. That this matched events in Korea in terms of chronology is certainly too much to be a coincidence. Silla's peak and decline roughly coincides with events in Japan, where the eighth century saw a great outpouring of creative energy in poetry and architecture and the Japanese state at Nara flourished. In 794 the capital was transferred to Heian (Kyoto), which also flourished culturally, but by the late tenth century the central Japanese state was in decline.

The eighth and early ninth century was a time of political consolidation, economic prosperity, and cultural creativity in the Middle East as well. The Umayyad Caliphate was replaced by the Abbasid Caliphate centered in Baghdad in 750, which marked a sort of high point of the great Arab Empire as Arab and Persian cultural traditions creatively blended. Then from the mid-ninth century the Abbasid Caliphate began a long decline, and smaller polities emerged in the Middle East. The eighth century saw a political and cultural revival in Western Europe with the rise of the Carolingian Empire, which then split up into weaker units in the mid-ninth century. Invasions by Norsemen, Bulgars, and Magyars in the ninth and early tenth centuries threatened the political and economic institutions of Europe until they were contained in the mid-tenth century. The eighth century was a period of political centralization and outward trade and prosperity in most of Eurasia, while the late ninth was a period of political fragmentation and decline.

Historians do not understand all the links among the societies of the Old World, but they are increasingly appreciating just how interconnected they were. Korea, geographically on the periphery of Eurasia was not only embedded in the larger historical developments of East Asia, but a part of the larger Afro-Eurasian world.

Sŏl Kye-du

Sŏl Kye-du was a descendant of a Silla official. Once he went drinking with his four friends, each of whom revealed his wishes. Sŏl said, "In Silla the bone rank is the key to employment. If one is not of the nobility, no matter what his talents, he cannot achieve a high rank. I wish to travel west to China, display rare resources and perform meritorious deeds, and thereby open a path to glory and splendor so that I might wear the robes and sword of an official and serve close to the Son of Heaven."

In the fourth year, *sinsa*, of Wu-te [621], Sŏl stealthily boarded an oceangoing ship and went to T'ang China.

—from the *Samguk sagi*, 47:436[20]

Great Master Kyunyŏ: Eleven Poems on the Ten Vows of the Universally Worthy Bodhisattva
Worshiping and Honoring the Buddhas

I bow today before the Buddha,
Whom I draw with my mind's brush
O this body and mind of mine,
Strive to reach the end of the dharma realm
He who is in every mote of dust;
He who pervades every Buddha field;
He who fills the realm of dharma—
Would that I could serve him in the nine time periods.
Ah, idle body, mouth, and mind—
Approach him and be with him, unimpeded.

Rejoicing in the Merit of Others

The truth of dependent origination tells me
That illusion and enlightenment are one.
From the buddhas down to mortal men,
The other and myself are one.
Were I able to practice his virtues,
Were I able to master his ways,
I would rejoice in the merit of others;
I would rejoice in the good of others.
Ah, were I to follow in his footsteps,
How could the jealous mind be aroused

Transfer of Merit

Would that all my merit
Might be passed on to others,
I would like to awaken them—

Those wandering in the sea of suffering.
When we attain the vast realm of dharma,
Removed karmas are jewels in dharmahood;
Since aeons ago
Bodhisattvas, too, have devoted their merit to others.
Ah, he whom I worship and I are one,
Of one body and one mind.

   —from the *Kyunyŏ chŏn* 7, in *Korean Tripitaka* 47:260c–261b [21]

4

꧁

Koryŏ, 935 to 1170

THE NEW KORYŎ STATE

The disunity of Korea in the tenth century was short-lived and soon the peninsula was reunited under the Wang Kŏn. He named the state Koryŏ after Koguryŏ, the ancient state that ruled the northern part of the peninsula as well as parts of Manchuria. The English name Korea is derived from Koryŏ. The Wang dynasty he founded in 918 ruled all of the peninsula for the better part of five centuries from 935 to 1392, making it among the longer-reigning dynasties in world history and inaugurating a sense of stability and continuity in Korean history. Under Koryŏ the peoples of Korea became integrated into a single, distinctive culture and society to a far greater extent than under Silla. In fact, it may not be too much to say that a truly Korean society and ethnicity that was coterminous to the state emerged during this time.

Toward the end of the ninth century and into the early tenth century as centralized rule broke down, Korea became in effect a land where local military warlords ruled. Considering the rugged mountainous terrain of Korea, the strength of local traditions, and the great difficulty that even the ablest of Silla's rulers had in trying to create a centralized state in the face of powerful aristocratic clans, the disintegration of the Silla is not surprising. What is more surprising is how quickly Korea was reunified in the tenth century under Wang Kŏn. Several factors help explain this. Silla left a two-century legacy of unified, bureaucratic government that may have become accepted as the norm. Furthermore, under the Silla a strong cultural unity among the peoples of the peninsula emerged, although

77

it is difficult to gauge its extent or depth. Korea was also influenced by outside events. The nomad threat posed by the Khitans (or Qidan), a proto-Mongol group that emerged as dominant in Manchuria in the tenth century, made the need for a centralized authority more obvious. Korea may have also been influenced by the model of a strong unified state that Tang presented, a model reinforced by the reunification of China by the Song in 979.

Wang Kŏn's new state was far from a strong centralized bureaucratic state, however, but was rather an alliance of warlords. Much of the work in creating a strong, centralized kingdom was left to his successors during the next two centuries. It was a slow process of building effective state institutions and creating an elite class that owed its prime allegiance to the dynasty. The result was largely successful in that Wang and his successors created a kingdom that lasted for nearly half a millennium and that was inherited largely intact by the Yi dynasty that ruled for another five centuries. Together the two dynasties ruled a state that forged its inhabitants into one of the most homogeneous peoples in the world, a people with a strong sense of cultural identity and historical consciousness.

Wang Kŏn's base was in the Kaesŏng area, meaning the Imjin and Yesŏng basin area and the adjacent coastal area. There is some doubt about his real name, since Wang Kŏn simply means "kingly founder," but it is believed that he was from a prominent local family with military and merchant connections. His grandfather reportedly was a merchant and his father a military naval commander. The name Koryŏ suggests that the new dynasty saw itself as a successor to the old Koguryŏ. Certainly the name still symbolized power and greatness in Northeast Asia at that time. Wang Kŏn established his capital at Kaesŏng, a more centrally located city to the north of the Han River. Soon after establishing his capital at Kaesŏng he made P'yŏngyang his secondary capital, naming it Sŏgyŏng (Western Capital), further suggesting the link between the once formidable state and the new kingdom. Perhaps he also sought to draw upon the geomantic power of the ancient city as well. But Koryŏ was strictly a peninsular state, possessing none of the Manchurian lands of its earlier namesake.

Major changes in government and society took place that marked Koryŏ as more than simply a change of ruling houses, yet there was also a great deal of continuity. As the dynastic founder, Wang Kŏn sought to underline this continuity and establish himself as the legitimate successor to Silla. He did this by marrying into the Kyŏngju Kim family of Silla and by incorporating many elite families of Silla into the power structure of Koryŏ. Indeed it would be more accurate to consider Koryŏ as a reformulation of the Silla state rather than a radical break in Korean history. Wang Kŏn took great care to establish his state as the legitimate successor to Silla, pensioning off the last king, appointing members of the Silla aristocracy to positions in the new state, and taking two members of the Silla royal family as consorts. Later Korean historians would largely accept this claim that Koryŏ was the successor to Silla, and that the "Mandate of Heaven" had simply been passed on to a new dynasty.

One of the dynastic founder's primary tasks was to consolidate power over a land where local families had their own powerful armies. In fact, as historian John Duncan has pointed out, the early Koryŏ was as much a confederation of powerful warlords and aristocratic families as a centralized state.[1] To establish his authority Wang claimed the Mandate of Heaven, the Chinese practice in which authority was legitimized by asserting that the ruler governed with Heaven's blessing. His invocation of Heaven's authority is reflected in the reign name he chose, Ch'ŏnsu (Heaven-Given). To further establish his authority he formed alliances with powerful warlords and prominent members of the old Silla aristocracy, including the Silla royal family, acquiring twenty-nine wives in total. His death in 943 consequently created succession problems due to the vast number of in-laws jockeying for power. Wang Kŏn's philosophy of government is summed up in his Ten Injunctions, which sought to promote Buddhism as a protective cult and warned against appointment of people from Paekche (see below). He sought the protection of the spirits of the land and was concerned that Buddhism be supported. His injunctions made it clear that while China was to be looked to as a model, Korea had its own customs and should not imitate the Chinese unnecessarily. In contrast to China, according to the injunctions, the seminomadic tribal peoples of the north were barbarians and their customs should never be copied at all.

The Wang court initially held little direct power over the countryside, where control was in the hands of local lords with their private armies and their walled towns. In realistic recognition of the entrenched power of these lords, the central government appointed them as officials in their home areas. Gradually the Koryŏ developed a *kun-hyŏn* (prefecture-county) system of local administration. Under this system, the more powerful aristocrats headed *yŏng* (control prefectures) and control counties, occupied the local offices in administrative units, and also collected taxes from the less powerful families that held offices in the *sok* (subordinate prefectures) and counties. It was an odd arrangement that had no Chinese precedent. Most likely the system reflected the hierarchical order of local aristocrats who actually governed the countryside. The bone-rank system was replaced by the *pon'gwan* (ancestral-seat) system. Under this system, aristocratic clans were identified by their place of origin. This clan-seat system closely linked aristocrats with a particular area where they generally held the key local offices.

The fragility of the new state was evident by the succession struggle after Wang's death. He named his eldest son, Mu, as his heir in 921. By the time of Wang Kŏn's death, Mu, who is better known as King Hyejong (r. 943–945), had long prepared for the assumption of his father's position. Yet he had to defend his throne against Wang Kyu, one of the powerful warlords whom Wang Kŏn had sought alliances with through marriage. Wang Kyu (?–945) had married two daughters to Wang Kŏn and supported a grandson by one of these marriages for the throne. Hyejong died after only two years on the throne and his brother Chŏngjong (r. 945–949) defeated Wang Kyu and ended the rebellion.[2] But the private armies threatened the stability of the state. To counter the private armies of great aristocrats Chŏngjong created the Kwanggun (Resplendent Army), an important step in consolidating royal power.

The fourth Koryŏ king, Kwangjong (r. 949–975), took further measures to consolidate monarchical power. He created a large military force from the provinces loyal to him, declared himself *hwangje* (emperor), and renamed Kaesŏng the Imperial Capital (Hwangdo). This was an unusual step, since Koreans generally accepted the idea that there was only one emperor, the Chinese emperor. Not until 1897 would a Korean king again claim the imperial title. The pretension was abandoned when the Song dynasty was able to reassert Chinese authority in the region. In 956, Kwangjong issued a Slave Investigation Act aimed at determining those who had been illegally or unfairly enslaved during the Later Three Kingdoms period. During that time many peasants had been captured as prisoners of war, while others had fallen into debt, and in both cases they had become slaves. The king sought to reduce the power of the great lords by limiting the number of their slaves and returning the freed peasants to the tax rolls. Kwangjong also carried out bloody purges among the high aristocracy. In 960, he launched a purge of powerful aristocrats who held posts as Meritorious Subjects. Under Wang Kŏn and his immediate successors many individuals who had aided or allied with the monarchs as they established the new state or who helped them secure their throne had been granted the post of Meritorious Subject as a reward. The purge was designed to reduce their number and influence.

The next king, Kyŏngjong (r. 975–981), abandoned the imperial pretension but strengthened the central government by issuing the *chŏnsi-kwa* (Field and Woodland) system. This was a system by which officials were given fixed incomes from designated lands according to rank. By providing support for officials, the Field and Woodland system helped to transform the government from an aristocratic confederation into a central bureaucracy of officials recruited by and loyal to the throne.[3] Another early step in consolidating state power was carried out by Sŏngjong (r. 981–997), who created among other institutions a Finance Commission

(*Samsa*) to handle financial affairs, the Hallim Academy to draft royal edicts, and an inspectorate, the *Ŏsadae*, to check on the conduct of officials.

After early experiments with different types of institutions Koryŏ adopted the Tang Three Chancelleries system. The *Samsŏng* (Three Chancelleries) were the chief administrative organs of the Koryŏ state. The *Chungsŏsŏng* (Secretariat) was responsible for drafting policy, the *Munhasŏng* (Chancellery) reviewed policy, and the *sangsŏsŏng* (Secretariat for State Affairs) was responsible for executing policies through the *Yukpu* (Six Ministries). Following the Chinese practice the six ministries were war, rituals (that included foreign affairs), finance, personnel, punishments, and public works. Heads of the Secretariat of State Affairs were often concurrently heads of the six ministries, but their positions were less prestigious than those of the directors of the first two chancelleries. The first two formed a *Chungsŏ-Munhasŏng* (combined Secretariat-Chancellery) under a *Munha-sijung* (supreme chancellor), the highest of all officials. Officials were divided Chinese-style into nine grades. At the top of this hierarchy were the eight first- and second-grade officials of the *Chungsŏ-Munhasŏng*, who become known as the *chaesin* or *chaesang*. Another important organ was the *Ch'ungch'uwŏn* (Royal Secretariat, later called the *Ch'umirwŏn*), which was responsible for military affairs and for transmitting royal orders. The top-ranking officials of the *Ch'unch'uwŏn* formed a lesser elite group known as the *ch'usin*.

This complex system of administration was closely modeled on the administration of Tang China. Indeed, Koryŏ adhered much closer to the Tang model of administration than Silla did. But in reality Koryŏ functioned quite differently. In practice, the distinctions between the various organs of government were less sharply defined than in China. Furthermore, unlike China where members of nonaristocratic families and eunuchs held key positions, the government of Koryŏ was dominated by the members of the great pedigreed families. In what was a common Korean pattern, effective decision making was carried out by these men in the form of councils of high-ranking officials. These were represented in the *chaesin* and *ch'usin* elite officialdom, who collectively became known as the *Chaech'u* or Privy Council that met at joint sessions. Later in the dynasty, the top council was called the *Todang*. The Three Chancelleries were typical of the councilor organs that characterized policy making and administration in premodern Korea. The desire to achieve positions on the Three Chancelleries and to be able to participate in the key *Todang* policy-making sessions led to intense competition among the major aristocratic families.

Another characteristic of this system was civilian dominance. Military officers were drawn from military lineages that had less prestige than civilian lineages. The top military post was the *sang changgun* (grand general), whose rank was only senior third-grade, lower than the second-grade rank of the *chaesin* and *ch'usin*. In times of crisis civilians were given military commands. The division of officialdom into civil and military lines resulted in tensions that emerged in the political upheavals of the twelfth century.

A significant innovation of the early Koryŏ was the introduction of the *kwagŏ* or civil service examinations in 958. Until its abolition in 1894 this was a key institution in Korea for recruiting and appointing officials. Although Silla experimented with civil service exams, they only became significant when they were reintroduced in the tenth century. The civil examination system was developed in China in the first centuries CE and became an important avenue for recruiting officials under the Tang dynasty. Its purpose was in part to free the Chinese emperors from reliance on powerful aristocrats for their officials by selecting talented men from the provinces. In theory the exams were open to all commoners, and in practice, too, members of non-elite families often rose to high positions. It was also based on the Confucian ideal that the state should be ruled by men of merit. Although not all officials in China were recruited through this method, it gradually came to undermine the power and status of the old aristocracy, replacing it with a merit-based service elite of scholar-officials. In Korea, the civil examinations were less a tool for the recruitment of officials than a means of training members of the aristocratic elite for government office. Thus they did not undermine the old landowning aristocratic class but helped to transform it into a service nobility that needed to validate its status by producing sons who scored well in the state examinations.

King Kwangjong established the civil examination system as part of his effort to consolidate monarchical control over the state. He was assisted by a Chinese advisor, Shuang Ji (Korean: Ssang Ki). Shuang Ji was an official of the Later Zhou dynasty that controlled northern China just prior to the reunification under the Song dynasty. He came to Korea in 956 as part of a Later Zhou (951–960) embassy, fell ill, and stayed behind. Apparently impressed by his erudition and administrative knowledge, Kwangjong persuaded him to stay on in Korea as an advisor. With Shuang Ji's help the king organized the first civil service exams in 958.[4] Three men were chosen on the basis of their mastery of the Chinese classics and two on their demonstration of literary skills, and two others passed an examination on geomancy. It was a modest beginning for an institution that would eventually transform the character of the aristocracy.

Koryŏ's civil service system was primarily modeled after that of Tang. There were three types of *kwagŏ*: the *chesul ŏp* (Composition Examination), the *myŏnggyŏngŏp* (Classics Examination), and the *chap ŏp* (Miscellaneous Examinations). In the Composition Examination the examinees were tested on their skill in various Chinese literary forms such as poetry, rhyme prose, and sacrificial odes, and in writing problem-solving essays. The Classics Examination tested the candidates' knowledge of Chinese classics. Less prestigious than the first two were the Miscellaneous Examinations that were used to find officials with knowledge in such areas as law, medicine, divination, and geomancy. Of the two prestige degrees the Composition Examination was by far the most popular. From its implementation in 958 to the end of the dynasty four centuries later, 252 exams were given; over 6,000 received the composition degree and about 450 the classics degree.[5]

The *kwagŏ* never served as the sole or even primary method of recruiting officials during the Koryŏ; most still owed their position to family connections rather than success in examinations. Higher-ranking officials, for example, held the *ŭm* privilege, by which their sons received automatic appointment to office. The exams did, however, establish the principle of rule by merit and provided an avenue for the rise in power and status for some aristocrats, including some from minor families. Furthermore, the exams were important in enhancing one's prestige; even men from powerful families often took the exam. One study shows that during the period from 1070 to 1146, twenty-four of fifty-seven men who held the supreme and associate chancellor posts were examination graduates; five were ŭm privilege beneficiaries; and five were from military, clerical, or palace backgrounds. The rest were of unknown background. Ten had served as examiners or *tong chigong-gŏ* (associate examiners).[6] Although some of humble background may have risen to high office through the exams, it is most likely that they functioned as a way of selecting offices among competing members of elite families. The civil exams were in theory a method of selecting the ablest officials to serve the state; they also had the effect of establishing the loyalty of officials to the ruler and to the bureaucracy that served him. They also promoted literacy among the elite. Many Koreans identified the civil examination system as a mark of their land's civilized attainment. They had successfully emulated China or even surpassed it in this respect. A famous writer and official of the thirteenth century and successful exam passer said, "The success achieved in recruiting men of merit [through the examination system] under our dynasty cannot be matched even by [that of the golden age of] Yao and Shun."[7]

Throughout the Koryŏ period a concern for education grew as a means of preparing men for the examinations and of promoting Confucian learning and moral training. To aid in this task a national academy, the *Kukchagam*, was established in 982. More important was the role played by private schools. In 1055 Ch'oe Ch'ung (984–1068), a distinguished official who held many top posts, retired at the age of seventy-four and established a school, the Nine Course Academy, that trained young men for the civil exams and government service. Ch'oe became known as the "Confucius of Korea," and his school produced many of the kingdom's leading officials and scholars. Following his example, other high-ranking officials established schools, until there were twelve, which became known as the *Sibi to* (Twelve Assemblies). The bureaucracy became dominated by their students. To further ensure a supply of educated officials and to provide an alternative to these schools, King Injong in 1127 ordered that each *chu* (large districts) and *hyŏn* (district) establish a school, but schooling remained largely a private affair for sons of the elite.

Local administration was in the effective hands of local aristocratic families. Koryŏ rulers made attempts to create a Chinese-style regional administration, but had great difficulty in penetrating their governance to the local level. An early attempt to adopt the Tang system of dividing the country into *dao* (administrative circuits) under appointed officials was abandoned. Another attempt at orderly local administration was made by creating eight regions headed by an appointed official called the *moksa*. By the early twelfth century the eight original circuits were re-created, each administered by an *anch'alsa* (appointed governor). These formed the basis of the eight provinces of Korea today. Real power was at the local level, following the Chinese practice of dividing the countryside into prefectures and counties. But in practice the local county and prefecture officials were simply the local aristocratic lords. Gradually, however, the state gained more control over the countryside. By 1170, the central government appointed perhaps half the prefectural and county heads.[8] The slow process of appointing royal officials to local posts, along with the system of control and subordinate counties, meant that the countryside was ruled in a hierarchical fashion, with weaker regional lords under the control of greater ones. The latter in turn had their power recognized by the king with the appointment of an official title such as prefectural head. *Sŏri* (central clerk) positions were often filled by sons of local officials, and this became a route to the ranks of the regular bureaucracy. Increasingly men were drawn from the countryside to the capital as the offices of the central government grew in prestige and in real power.

The state supported itself primarily by the Field and Woodland system. Under this system land was divided into *kongjŏn* (public land), whose tax receipts went to the central government, and *sajŏn*, which referred to land assigned to various classes of persons who provided services to the state. *Sajŏn* is sometimes referred to as "private land," but it was probably state-owned land for which people were allowed to collect rents. In theory, at least, these lands reverted to the state upon the death of an official. In practice, they were passed down in families over generations, becoming in effect private. Some smaller plots of land were made hereditary to families of deceased officials. Officials also received salaries paid in rice. Since there was a big difference between the theory of central and local bureaucratic power and the reality of aristocratic rule and authority, the Field and Woodland system was in practice different from its formal structure. It was probably little more than a legal confirmation of private land holdings of the elite or de facto tax exemptions on lands owned by the elite. Koryŏ also continued the Silla practice of assigning certain locales known as *so* to produce items of special economic importance such as gold, silver, paper, and porcelain. Other agricultural lands were assigned for the support of various government agencies, military camps, and schools.

The Koryŏ state modeled many of its formal institutions and nomenclature on Tang rather than on the contemporary Song state. China experienced a great cultural resurgence under the Song (960–1279), which modified many of the institutions of government, and it evolved into a very different society, less aristocratic, with greater social mobility. The Song state also made far less use of Buddhism to legitimize itself and saw a great revitalization of Confucianism. Koryŏ did not follow this pattern. Partly this was due to the fact that Korea's contact with Song was more sporadic than it had been with Tang. This in turn was a result of Song's military weakness, which left Korea's immediate frontier in the hands of powerful seminomadic Khitan and Jurchen (or Ruzhen) peoples. Furthermore, the Tang impacted the society of Korea when it was at an earlier, more formative stage of political and social development. Korea's own native worship, patterns of marriage and kinship, and cultural traditions may also have coincided more with those of China in Tang times. Of course Song culture and its diplomacy did exercise considerable influence on Korea. Yet the Koryŏ dynasty with its attachment to Buddhism, its rule by great aristocratic families, and its adherence to Tang political institutions remained quite distinct from Song China.

KORYŎ IN EAST ASIA

Koryŏ's great external challenge was dealing with its northern frontier. The tenth-century upheaval resulted in a great influx of peoples from Manchuria to the Yalu and Tumen Rivers. Some of them entered the peninsula. The most troublesome of the new peoples along the frontier were the Khitan. The Khitan helped bring about the collapse of Parhae in 926, then laid claim to its land. They also claimed to be the heirs of Koguryŏ. For Wang Kŏn and his successors these tribal peoples posed a threat to their efforts to consolidate Koryŏ's position on the frontier. Wang Kŏn made his hostility to the Khitans clear when in 942 they sent envoys with fifty camels as gifts. He banished the envoys to an island and let the camels starve. His successor, King Chŏngjong, planned to move the capital to P'yŏngyang and created the armed force called the Kwanggun (Resplendent Army) to prepare against Khitan invasions. As part of the effort to expand northward, the Koreans from 949 to 975 established garrison forts beyond Ch'ŏngch'ŏn River.

The Khitan meanwhile created the state of Liao on the northern borders of China and ruled much of Manchuria. The Liao emperor Shenzong (983–1031) led a series of campaigns against the Song that ended with the Treaty of Shanyuan in 1005. Under this treaty the Chinese emperor recognized the frontier state as an equal. At the same time they were fighting the Chinese, the Khitans began to tighten their pressure on Koryŏ. In 993, the Khitan ruler Xiao Sunning led an invasion force. This invasion resulted in negotiations with the Koreans and a brief period of nonhostile relations began. The Koreans built six garrisons on the Yalu River, establishing it as their northern boundary for the first time. But the Khitan demanded that Koryŏ turn over the six garrisons to them. When Koryŏ refused, the Khitan emperor, Shenzong, launched another invasion in 1010. Initially Koryŏ under Yang Hyu was victorious, but an overconfident general Kang Cho was defeated and the invaders burnt Kaesŏng. King Hyŏnjong fled south and then agreed to pay homage in person at the Khitan court. Koryŏ did not fulfill this promise, however, which led to the invasion of 1018 under the Khitan leader Xiao Paiya. The Koreans defeated this force at Kuju fortress under the military command of Kang Kam-ch'an. According to the Korean chroniclers, only a few thousand of the 100,000 Khitan invaders survived. Whatever the true scale of victory, it was not enough for Koryŏ to avoid submitting to the powerful invaders from the north. Korea kept its independence but was forced to pay tribute to the Khitan state of Liao.

After 1022, Koryŏ raised a corvée of 300,000 to reconstruct the destroyed capital and finished it seven years later. Between 1033 and 1044 the Koreans constructed a long wall and fortifications against the Khitans and another Northeastern Asian tribal group, the Jurchens (or Ruzhen). Meanwhile, despite its resistance, Korea was forced to not only pay tribute to the powerful Liao state but in 994 to adopt the Liao calendar. Thus in effect the kingdom became a tributary state of Liao as it had in the past been a tributary of Tang. These were simply concessions to reality; the Koreans continued to regard the Khitan as barbarians. After 1054 the Liao yoke over Korea lightened, and there appears to have been no tribute after that date.

The Khitan cut Korea off from the militarily weak but prosperous and culturally dynamic Song. Because of the existence of the powerful and hostile Liao state between them, there was little direct contact between Korea and China for a century. Taking advantage of a lessening of Liao militancy, China opened relations with Koryŏ in 1062. For a while, considerable trade flourished between China and Korea, enabling Koreans to participate in some of the intellectual and cultural activities in China. China sought to bring Korea into its tributary system, but relations between the two were not especially close. Partly this was because Korean-Chinese relations were complicated by the fact that Korea was a tributary of the Liao. Fearing close relations with China that might arouse Khitan hostility, the Koreans appear to have been cautious and selective in their relations with their great continental neighbor. There was a suspicion of Korea among the Chinese officials as well, some of whom saw the country as a potential ally of the Khitans and Jurchens. Some Song officials complained that vital information given to Korean embassies could find its way to the Khitan; consequently they restricted the Koreans' access to books.

Koryŏ was part of the network of trade that linked Northeast Asia. The government established regulated markets in the northwest with Liao and in the northeast with Jurchen tribes. On its northern border Koryŏ supplied grain, iron, agricultural implements, and weapons to the Khitans and Jurchen peoples in exchange for horses. Koreans also carried out an active trade with Japan, importing folding fans and swords. After the reopening of relations with Song, trade with China greatly overtook that with Japan and the Manchurian-Siberian frontier in volume. Korean merchants sailed to the Song ports of Gwangzhou, Quanzhou, Hongzhou, and Mingzhou. Quanzhou merchants took the initiative in reestablishing trade. In 1078, Song sent two "divine ships," which were given a tumultuous welcome in Korea.[9] Most merchants traveled on Chinese vessels, although some trade was conducted on Koryŏ ships, mostly to the north China port of Dengzhou. The voyage from Mingzhou to the Hŭksan Islands off the southwestern coast of Korea took three weeks; from there it took several days along the Korean coast to reach Yesŏng. The voyage was dangerous and frequently resulted in wrecks.[10] Yet it could be highly profitable. Koreans imported Chinese teas, lacquerware, books, medicines, ceremonial robes, and a variety of luxury goods. Korea's most important import was probably porcelain. Merchants from Fujian in southern China sailed to Korea in large ships loaded with the highly prized products from their kilns. Even Arab merchants arrived in Korea from China to trade in 1024 and 1025. Koryŏ exports were copper, gold, silver, utensils, ginseng, pine nuts, silks, ramie cloth, paper, furs, and even horses. The balance of trade seemed to favor China, but this is not certain.[11] This foreign trade was a stimulus to commercial development. Major towns had permanent marketplaces, and in the thirteenth century Kaesŏng is reported to have had over 1,000 shops and stalls. A government bureau regulated weights and measures.

The era of active foreign trade and contact came to an end with the rise of a new seminomadic power on the northern frontier, the Jurchens. The Jurchens created the state of Jin, conquered the Khitan in 1126, and then conquered northern China in 1127. Interestingly, the Jurchens claimed Koguryŏ ancestry. This testified to the reputation of Koguryŏ, but it also suggested that Jurchen ambitions included the peninsula. In response to this new threat, Korea in the early twelfth century created a special military force, the *Pyŏlmuban*, to deal with the Jurchen challenge. After an internal debate, the Koreans established a tributary relationship with the Jurchen state of Jin and broke off relations with China. The period that followed was a peaceful one on the northern frontier, allowing the Koreans to concentrate on their own domestic developments. Not surprisingly, during this period of relative isolation and external calm, Korean political and cultural institutions moved somewhat further away from the Chinese model. Another important result of this peaceful period was that it led to a further downgrading of the military and the ascendancy of civil officials. The decline of the military's prestige led to the 1170 coup that can be seen as a delayed reaction to these events (see chapter 5).

INTERNAL POLITICS, 935–1170

Politics in Koryŏ centered on competition between powerful clans for high offices in government. Studies indicate that a small number of clans held a large percentage of high offices in the period from 981 to 1146. Some of these clans were of Silla true-bone origin such as the Kyŏngju Kim, Kangnŭng Kim, and P'yŏngsan Pak. These were among the greatest producers of high officials. But leading clans came from all parts of the kingdom, indicating that the early Koryŏ state sought to win support from the aristocracy throughout the country. It also showed that the elite were being integrated into a common society, helping to establish a common social order and common culture.

One of the themes of Koryŏ history during the first two centuries was the attempts by the dynastic government in the capital to gain greater control over the countryside. Another was the intrigue among powerful clans. The problem of containing the power of great clans was compounded by the practice begun by Wang Kŏn of marrying members of the royal family into these clans to cement alliances with them. The result was powerful in-law families that could threaten the dynasty. In the early eleventh century, the Ansan Kim clan achieved a degree of dominance when an aristocrat, Kim Ŭn-bu, married three of his daughters to King Hyŏnjong (r. 1009–1031). After dominating the court for half a century the power of the Ansan Kim clan was eclipsed by that of the Kyŏngwŏn Yi.

In the middle of the eleventh century, a member of that clan, Yi Cha-yŏn, emerged as the dominant figure in the government. He bound the royal family to his by marrying three daughters to King Munjong (r. 1046–1083). The Kyŏngwŏn Yi thereafter produced by far the most officials and continued to marry into the royal family. The clan grew in power until it posed a threat to the throne. In 1095, the clan leader, Yi Cha-ŭi, attempted to dethrone the king and replace him with a son of King Sŏnjong by Yi's sister, but he failed and was removed from power. Again in 1127, another leader of the clan, Yi Cha-gyŏm, purged many opponents and tried to depose the teenage King Injong (r. 1123–1146), who was both his son-in-law and grandson. His plan was to place himself on the throne with the aid of less illustrious clans, including new arrivals from the countryside. Rivals defeated Yi Cha-gyŏm and his clan fell from power.[12]

As happened so often in Korean history, factional rivalry during the Koryŏ was aggravated by external threats and tensions. Yi Cha-gyŏm attempted to align the dynasty with the rising Jurchen state of Jin in Manchuria and northern China. Accordingly he sent an envoy to the Jin in 1126 following the Jin conquest of Liao. His opponents wanted to maintain good relations with Song rather than submit to yet another northern barbarian state. Yi was eventually overthrown, but his realistic policy of acknowledging the power of the Manchuria-based empire that was gaining control over the northern half of China prevailed. The fall of the Kyŏngwŏn Yi shifted power to a number of northwestern-based clans that aimed at moving the capital near the northern frontier at P'yŏngyang. This group remained hostile to Jin. They were led by the monk Myoch'ŏng (?–1135), who used *fengshui* (Korean: *p'ungsu*) theory to argue that the geomantic forces around the capital of Kaesŏng had waned but that those of P'yŏngyang were strong. Myoch'ŏng urged the king to move there, declare himself emperor, and launch an attack on the Jin. When his effort failed, he and his supporters attempted to establish a new state called Taewi in 1135, but this revolt was destroyed by forces loyal to the dynasty that included the Confucian scholar and historian Kim Pu-sik. Koryŏ then refrained from military adventurism.

To deal with the growing number of competing clans, the number of top officials was increased and the councils of aristocrats such as the privy council swelled in number, the latter eventually having seventy *Chaech'u* officials. Competition was aggravated by men from the *hyangni*, the local hereditary elite, seeking central government offices. Meanwhile there was growing domestic tension between the dominant lineages that supplied civil officials and the lineages that supplied the less prestigious and less influential military officials that resulted in a military uprising in 1170 (see chapter 5). While all this gives an impression of constant political tension, it is important to note that politics was a struggle among great aristocratic families for power and privilege; it had little to do with most ordinary non-aristocratic peoples. As for the common people, we hear little of them in the historical records except for an occasional peasant uprising.

KORYŎ CULTURE

The introduction of the civil exams in 958 did much to foster the spread of Confucianism in Korea. Exam questions included some from the *Analects* and the *Classic of Filial Piety*. Eventually scholars established twelve private academies known as the Twelve Assemblies to spread Confucian teaching as well as to educate the aristocratic youth. Some Confucian scholars became famous in the early Koryŏ. Among them was the eleventh-century teacher Ch'oe Ch'ung. Confucianism, with its stress on order, hierarchy, and the importance of good government led by an enlightened monarch, was appealing to the state and was promoted by it.

While Confucianism was important in shaping ideas of government and morality, Koryŏ was very much a Buddhist kingdom in the sense that Buddhist ceremonies and rituals were at the center of social and cultural life. The state sought to utilize the power of the Buddha and bodhisattvas (Buddhist saints) to protect it from invasions and natural calamities. Most monks protected the kingdom through prayers and rituals, but there were also warrior monks who fought for it. Some of the most effective fighters against the Mongols in the thirteenth century and against the Japanese in the sixteenth century were monks. Accordingly, the court generously patronized Buddhist temples. Buddhist holidays punctuated the year as times of national celebration. Well supported by the state, a vigorous Buddhist intellectual life flourished. Buddhist thought and practice was roughly divided into Kyo (Textual) and Sŏn (Meditative) schools. Each school had a hierarchy of Buddhist officials and its own set of examinations modeled on the state civil exams. The highest ranks among Buddhist officials were Royal Preceptor and National Preceptor. Both held enormous prestige.

Korean Buddhism was characterized by greater concern for unity than was found in Chinese or Japanese Buddhism. When Buddhism arrived in Korea from China, it was part of an established tradition divided into many different doctrinal traditions and practices. The diversity of Buddhism in China reflected both the richness and the diversity of Indian and Central Asian Buddhism, and the diversity and vitality of Chinese civilization. But Korea was a much smaller country, more homogeneous and conscious of its comparable smallness and its vulnerability to invasion. Partly for this reason, Koreans frequently sought unity in intellectual thought. A tendency toward syncretism appeared as early as Silla with Wŏnhyo. In the early half of the Koryŏ period the most important effort at bringing the schools of Buddhism together was undertaken by Ŭich'ŏn (1055–1101), fourth son of King Munjong, known posthumously as Master Taegak. Ŭich'ŏn sought to compile as complete a set of Buddhist sacred works as possible in order to create a vast library of all known Buddhist wisdom. Against the wishes of his father he surreptitiously traveled to Song China in 1085, where he collected more than 3,000 treatises and commentaries. He dispatched agents to China, Japan, and Khitan Liao to gather more Buddhist texts. He eventually had woodblocks carved for 1,010 Buddhist texts that were intended to supplement the *Tripitaka Koreana* (the complete Buddhist canon) that was also published. Unfortunately this vast collection of texts, along with the first edition of the *Tripitaka Koreana*, was destroyed in the 1231–1232 Mongol invasion. As he gathered his great collection he also attempted to merge the Sŏn schools of meditative Buddhism and the five Kyo textual or scholastic sects into Ch'ŏnt'ae (Chinese: Tiantai; Japanese: Tendai). Ch'ŏnt'ae was not a new Buddhist teaching. It was known in Silla times, and in 960 the monk Ch'egwan went to China, where he became one of its masters. But it had not been an independent sect before Ŭich'ŏn. Despite royal patronage and the enormous respect he had acquired as a pious and learned man, Ŭich'ŏn's efforts to unify Korean Buddhism failed. Instead his activities resulted in still another flourishing sect.[13]

Buddhist ecclesiastical organizations were wealthy. Temples owned extensive holdings in land and slaves. Exempted from taxation, these temples, which were also monasteries since monks and nuns lived year round in them, grew to become wealthy and play a major role in economic life. Temples engaged in trade, wine making, and grain and money lending. The problem of monasteries possessing a considerable amount of land and many slaves, all exempt from taxes, came to worry state officials. Later in the dynasty it would contribute to anti-Buddhist sentiment. Aristocratic families used temples as a means of extending their power by sending off sons to them. These were often younger sons not needed to supervise the family estates. As monks they advised the officials, served at court, and carried considerable influence. Kings and officials also complained that too many peasants were taking up orders, thereby depriving the state of military conscripts and productive farmers. To avoid some of these abuses, the state promulgated laws restricting the number of peasants who could become monks, barring children of monks who had married before they had taken vows from sitting for the monk exams, and prohibiting monks from staying overnight outside of the monasteries.[14]

In addition to Buddhism, Koreans believed in the hidden spiritual power of prominent features of nature such as rivers, rocks, and especially mountains. From at least the thirteenth century the most sacred mountain was Paektusan on the Korean-Manchurian border. Other mountains, such as Chirisan in the southern part of the country, were also venerated. This worship of nature was blended with geomantic ideas imported from China. In the twelfth century the Chinese visitor Xu Jing, in his *Illustrated Record of an Embassy to Korea in the Xuanhe Reign Period* (1124), stated of the Koreans that "it is their habit to make excessive sacrifices to spirits."[15] Shamanism was also widely practiced. However, Koryŏ elites were often critical of shamanism, accusing it of sponsoring vulgar and indecent rituals. Thus while Buddhism ceased to be an elite religion and instead was practiced by every sector of Korean society, a new religious boundary emerged during Koryŏ between the elite and commoners. The common people sought the solace of shamans as well as of Buddhist monks, while the educated aristocrats turned away from them, at least publically. To this day shamanism has been treated with disdain, and more recently as an embarrassing part of their cultural heritage, by middle- and upper-class Koreans, while it has continued to maintain a strong hold on many of the less educated and poor.

The aristocracy read and memorized Chinese poetry and wrote verse in Chinese, the literary language of the elite. Tang and Song poets were immensely popular, and Koreans wrote poems in their style. Koryŏ aristocrats sometimes left collections of their literary writings that often included both prose essays and large numbers of poems. Noted writer and scholar Yi Kyu-bo (1168–1241), for example, left 1,500 poems. Poems in the vernacular were popular but were mostly sung or recited orally. Derived from folk songs, they were often bawdy and satirical. Only a few were written down after the invention of the phonetic alphabet in the fifteenth century, and even some of these may have been edited to conform to the more prudish taste of later times. Among the best known are *Ch'ŏngsan pyŏlgok* (*Song of Green Mountain*) and *Ssanghwa chŏm* (*The Dumpling Shop*).

As in Silla, Buddhism remained a major inspiration for art. A rich tradition of Buddhist paintings in the form of wall paintings, hanging scrolls, and illustrated manuscripts developed. Although few wall paintings have survived, in recent years a number of Koryŏ-period Buddhist scrolls and illustrated manuscripts have been discovered in Korea, in Japan, and in Western collections. These paintings can be distinguished from Chinese Buddhist art by the less extensive use of gold paste and by a preference for duller shades of red and green than their Chinese counterparts. The use of less bright colors would remain characteristic of the aristocratic art tradition in Korea. These paintings are an important source of information on the costumes of the time.[16] Secular painting and calligraphy in Chinese styles flourished. Among the most famous were the twelfth-century painters Yi Yŏng and his son Yi Kwang'p'il. Famous also were three Koryŏ calligraphers, Yu Sin (d. 1104), the monk T'anyŏn (1070–1159), and Ch'oe U (d. 1249). They became known, along with the Silla calligrapher Kim Saeng, as the "Four Worthies of Divine Calligraphy." Unfortunately, virtually all the secular paintings and calligraphy of the Koryŏ have been lost. The Silla traditions in sculpture continued in early Koryŏ. Later Koryŏ sculpture showed the influence of Lamaistic Buddhism from the Mongol court. The high standards of metallurgical craftsmanship continued with fine bronze and silverware. Koryŏ did not, however, produce the great bronze bells of the Silla. Since buildings were made of wood, it is not surprising that none survive from the early Koryŏ. The oldest extant wooden temple buildings are the Pongjong in Andong and the Hall of Eternal Life (Muryangsu-jŏn) at Pusŏk temple in Yŏngju, both from the thirteenth century. The latter with its tapered columns, three-tiered roof supports, dual roof edge, and its interior without a ceiling provides a sense of both refinement and grandeur.[17]

Perhaps the greatest of the art forms of the period was ceramics. The most famous of the ceramics of this period is a porcelaneous stoneware with a fine bluish-green glaze known by the French term *celadon*. Koryŏ celadon was developed early in the dynasty by potters who had imported the technique from Song China. It was produced throughout the Koryŏ period, although the quality declined from the thirteenth century. The center of celadon production was in Chŏlla in the southwest part of the peninsula. Korean potters derived a distinctive style by turning the straight lines of Song pottery into curves and the cold blue of Song into a soft greenish tone. In the twelfth century the style reached a peak of perfection when potters developed a variety of innovative techniques such as painting in brown and red under the glaze and in gold over the celadon glaze. Today Koryŏ celadon is regarded as among the greatest ceramic masterpieces ever created. It is highly prized by connoisseurs in Asia and throughout the world. Korean potters also created innovative vessels in the shapes of animals and vegetables, as well as white wares, black wares, and unglazed stonewares.

THE *SAMGUK SAGI*

A rich tradition of historical writing existed during the Koryŏ period. The most important historical work was the *Samguk sagi* (*History of the Three Kingdoms*). The oldest extant Korean history, it was written in 1145 by Kim Pu-sik (1075–1151), a high court official. The *Samguk sagi* set out to give the history of the three kingdoms—Koguryŏ, Paekche, and Silla—from their founding to the end of Silla and the establishment of the Koryŏ state. An orthodox, Confucian history, the *Samguk sagi* is the most important single source for early Korean history. Much of the material is based on earlier, now lost sources, although the author seldom directly cites them. The work is an official history written in the Chinese *kijŏn* (Chinese, *jizhuan*) format, meaning it contains annals, that is, a chronological year-by-year history, treatises on various topics, and then a section of biographies. Kim with ten assistants compiled this history after collecting many sources. One hundred twenty-three Chinese and sixty-nine Korean titles are given as sources; the most important is the *Ku samguk sa* (*Old Three Kingdoms History*), a work now lost. Adhering to the "praise and blame" concept of history, Kim Pu-sik added his personal comments on historical issues.

Following a tradition of history writing that began in China with Sima Qian's *Shiji* written over twelve centuries earlier, Kim Pu-sik viewed history as a guide to correct government and personal behavior. This East Asian tradition of history held that one can learn from the past, not just practical lessons of statecraft, but more importantly lessons on moral and ethical conduct. Modern scholars have sometimes criticized Kim's work for repressing the nativist traditions in favor of a Sinocentric Confucian view of history. It has also been criticized for excluding Parhae from Korean history and therefore placing Manchuria outside the definition of Korean history. The *Samguk sagi*, however, was not a slavishly pro-Chinese work. The author states that the work was intended to create a more accurate record of early Korean history that had not received the attention or accuracy it deserved in Chinese histories. The history also reflects the author's desire to affirm the Koryŏ dynasty as the legitimate and logical successor to the Silla state. The work also reflects the southern orientation of Kim Pu-sik, a man of Sillan descent, who led armies against Myoch'ŏng. Kim set Korean history firmly in the peninsula, with the northern Korean/southern Manchurian region of Koguryŏ and its successor Parhae marginalized. This is an important development in the evolution of a Korean ethnic identity, since the *Samguk sagi* was influential in shaping Korean views of themselves and their history.

The *Samguk sagi* represents the high historical standards of the time. If translated into English (which it has not been) it would be several thick volumes long. It is an invaluable historical source for Korean history during the Three Kingdoms and Silla period. Our modern knowledge of that period, especially from the fourth to tenth centuries when the history becomes more reliable, is heavily dependent on this single source. It also reminds us how much of Korean history has been lost to us. Sadly, none of the sixty-nine Korean historical sources cited by the author exists today.

The *Samguk sagi* is also a rich source of stories, given as historical accounts, not as literature, but serving as both. Especially useful is the *yŏlchŏn* (biographical) section, although there are also many good stories in the annals section. Some of these stories, especially those set in earlier times, appear to be imaginative legends, some with magical elements. For example, in one well-known story, Prince Hodong, a handsome son of the king of Koguryŏ, was offered the virgin daughter of the Chinese governor of Nangnang, but the prince refused to accept her unless she destroyed a mysterious drum-and-horn that sounded by itself at the approach of the enemy. The daughter surreptitiously destroyed the drum-and-horn and had word of her deed sent to Prince Hodong. He then had his father, the Koguryŏ king, attack the Nangnang (Lelang) capital. The governor put his daughter to death and then surrendered. In another episode, Hodong, who was the son of a secondary consort, aroused the jealousy of the queen, who feared the king would make him, not her son, the heir. She falsely accused him of making sexual advances on her. Rather than clearing his name by disgracing his father's wife and causing the king further grief, he committed suicide. The commentary praises his filial piety.[18] The story represents the mixture of ancient tales, whose meanings are somewhat obscure, and the later Confucian gloss given them. The stories also suggest the strong warrior code of early Korea, a code that still made sense in Kim Pu-sik's time. Another example of this warrior code is the story of Wŏnsul, who after a distinguished career lost a battle against the army of Tang China and returned home in disgrace. Kim Yu-sin recommended that he be beheaded for dishonoring the kingdom and his family. The king, however, pardoned him. Yet his parents refused to forgive him or even see him even after he restored his honor on the battlefield.

KORYŎ SOCIETY

The spread of literacy encouraged by the civil exams along with the study of a common curriculum, the establishment of private schools, the gradual penetration of the state into local government, and the attraction of the capital that drew members of the elite from around the country all contributed to the creation of a shared cultural identity among the upper class. Yet even as Korea during the Koryŏ period was being integrated into a single society it maintained a three-part division that remained characteristic to the end of the nineteenth century. At the top was a hereditary aristocracy that became known as the *yangban*. The name *yangban*, literally the "two sides," referred to the two divisions of officials: *muban* (military officials) and the *munban* (civil officials). The term eventually was used to refer to the aristocracy from which the bureaucracy was derived. This class dominated politics, the economy, and culture. Next were commoners: some were probably small free farmers, and others were tenants working the fields of the aristocracy. A much smaller number of commoners served as merchants and skilled craftsmen. At the bottom of society were the low born. The low born consisted mostly of slaves. These were divided into public slaves owned by government agencies and private slaves owned by the aristocracy. Slaves were, along with land, a measure of elite status. How many Koreans were slaves? This is not known and estimates vary widely. The number probably fluctuated; perhaps slaves accounted for up to one-third of the population. Most worked the land of the aristocracy, but not on large estates. Large landholdings consisted of scattered parcels of land, and most slaves lived away from any direct supervision. Their living conditions probably resembled that of poor tenant farmers.

Most of the information we have on Koryŏ society is about the elite families, and even here there is much that is not clearly understood. Social status was based primarily on family ancestry. This became determined not only by family surname but by the *pon'gwan* (ancestral-seat) system. Each family became identified with its place of origin. For example, the surname Kim was a very common one, but there were many different Kim clans with different places of origin such as the Kyŏngju Kim and the Kangnŭng Kim. The concept of an ancestral-seat remained a permanent feature of Korean society, and to this day Korean descent groups are identified in this way. Some of the Koryŏ's great descent groups descended from Silla true-bone ranks such as the Kyŏngju Kim, the Kangnŭng Kim, and the P'yŏngsan Pak. A few were originally from head-rank-six families. Most, however, were descended from local strongmen who were incorporated into the Koryŏ elite. Unlike China and Japan there were no official lists of great descent-groups, so their number is not certain. But it is clear from the records of officeholders that a small number of great families dominated society. One study found that from the mid-tenth to the mid-twelfth centuries twenty-nine elite descent groups held two-fifths of high government posts.[19] Descent groups, which could be very large, were divided into different lineages or segments. Some of these segments became more prominent than others. Most descent groups had their base in the countryside, deriving income from their estates worked by tenants and slaves. Gradually, however, some identified their status with office holding, lived entirely in the capital, and lost ties with their rural roots. They came to form a small upper stratum of capital-based aristocracy linked together by marriages. There is some controversy over whether one inherited social status from both parents or whether social status was primarily inherited from the male side of the family. It seems clear, however, that a good marriage was key to maintaining or enhancing the status of an aristocrat, especially a marriage to a member of the royal family. Under the influence of Tang and Song China greater importance was gradually placed on the direct male lineage. Koryŏ, however, especially in earlier times, gave much more weight to the female side of the family in determining status than did China. This in turn gave greater status to women.

As historian Martina Deuchler and others have pointed out, compared to later periods, the social position for women in Koryŏ times was high. Women could inherit property, and an inheritance was divided equally among siblings regardless of gender. A woman's property was hers and could be passed on to her children. Some women inherited homes and estates. Ownership of property often gave upper-class women considerable independence. Korean women remained to a considerable extent members of their natal families, not those of their husbands. For example, if a woman died without children, her property passed on to her siblings, not to her husband. Wives were not merely servants of their husbands. Their importance was reflected in the practice of conducting marriages in the house of the bride. There was no bride wealth or dowry, and men often resided in their wife's home after marriage. The two sexes mingled freely. The twelfth-century Chinese traveler Xu Jing was surprised by the ease with which men and women socialized.

We do not yet have a clear picture of marriage in Koryŏ.[20] Evidence suggests that marriage rules were loose. Divorce was possible, but seems to have been uncommon; separation may have been more common. Koreans may have also practiced short-term or temporary marriages; however, the evidence of this is unclear. Remarriage of widows was an accepted practice. Marriage between close kin and within the village was also probably common. Later Korean society was characterized by extreme endogamy in which marriage between people of even the remotest relationship was prohibited, but this was not yet the case in Koryŏ times. Plural marriages may have been frequent among the aristocracy. Xu Jing said that it was common for a man to have three or four wives. Concubinage existed, but it is not known how customary it was. Evidence suggests that upper-class men married at about twenty and women at about seventeen. Men lived with their wife's family until about the age of thirty. Widows as well as widowers appear to have kept their children. All this is a sharp contrast with later Korean practices (see chapter 7).

The Koryŏ elite was not strictly patrilineal. Instead, members of the elite traced their families along their matrilineal lines as well. This gave importance to the wife's family, since her status helped to determine that of her children. Although high status and rights of women in Koryŏ were in contrast to later Korean practice, in many ways it was similar to Japan in the Heian period (794–1192). Much less is known about either Sillan or early Koryŏ society than about Heian Japan, but it is likely that the two societies shared a number of common practices relating to family, gender, and marriage. It is possible that these practices may, in fact, be related to the common origins of the two peoples. This is still a matter of speculation; further study needs to be made before the relationship between Korea and Japan is clearly understood.

Some changes took place over the nearly five centuries of the Koryŏ period. The adoption of the civil examination system in the tenth century led to careful records of family relations. At the same time, the strengthening of Chinese influences resulted in the gradual adoption of the Chinese practice of forbidding marriage among members of patrilineal kin. As Koreans began to place more importance on direct male descent and the Confucian ideas of the subordination of women to men became more accepted, the position of women declined. The state, for example, enacted laws prohibiting a wife from leaving her husband without his consent. Most major changes in family and gender relations, however, took place only after the Koryŏ period.

KOREA IN GLOBAL PERSPECTIVE: KORYŎ'S EXAMINATION SYSTEM

The introduction of the civil exam system in tenth-century Koryŏ proved to be a major development in Korean history, helping to transform the aristocracy into a highly educated, service nobility, strengthening the central state, culturally homogenizing the country's elite, and acting as a conduit for the dissemination of Chinese culture, especially Confucianism. It also marked Korea off from most other premodern societies, since only China and later Vietnam among major states had such a system. Rulers nearly everywhere faced the problems of how to select officials and how to impose their authority over their nobilities. Most commonly, officials served by inheritance like the hereditary class of *kshatriaya*, which provided the officials of Indian states, or the inherited aristocracies of Europe or Japan. States often required strong, charismatic leaders to impose stability; when such leaders failed to emerge, power struggles, administrative decline, and political fragmentation took place. The civil examination system provided an institutional framework that contributed to the remarkable political stability and continuity of the Korean state and ruling elite after the tenth century.

The examination system that developed in Korea differed from China. From the eighth century the Chinese examination system, because it was opened to commoners, served to break the dominance of the inherited aristocracy over office holding and led to a society with greater social mobility. In Korea, the examinations remained confined to members of the elite and reinforced hereditary status and privileged rather than undermined it.

Wang Kŏn: Ten Injunctions

I have heard that when great Shun was cultivating at Li-stan he inherited the throne from Yao. Emperor Kao-tsu of China rose from humble origins and founded the Han. I too have risen from humble origins and received undeserved support for the throne. In summer I did not shun the heat and in winter did not avoid the cold. After toiling, body and mind, for nineteen years I united the Three Han [Later Three Kingdoms] and have held the throne for twenty-five years. Now I am old. I only fear that my successors will give way to their passions and greed and destroy the principle of government. That would be truly worrisome. I therefore wrote these injunctions to be passed on to later ages. They should be read morning and night and forever used as a mirror of reflection.

His injunctions were as follows:

1. The success of every great undertaking of our state depends upon the favor and protection of Buddha. Therefore, the temples of both the Meditation and Doctrinal schools should be built and monks should be sent out to those temples to minister to Buddha. Later on, if villainous courtiers attain power and come to be influenced by the entreaties of bonzes, the temples of various schools will quarrel and struggle among themselves for gain. This ought to be prevented.

2. Temples and monasteries were newly opened and built upon the sites chosen by the monk Tosŏn according to the principles of geomancy. He said: "If temples and monasteries are indiscriminately built at locations not chosen by me, the terrestrial force and energy will be sapped and damaged, hastening the decline of the dynasty." I am greatly concerned that the royal family, the aristocracy, and the courtiers all may build many temples and monasteries in the future in order to seek Buddha's blessings. In the last days of Silla many temples were capriciously built. As a result, the terrestrial force and energy were wasted and diminished, causing its demise. Vigilantly guard against this.

3. In matters of royal succession, succession by the eldest legitimate royal issue should be the rule. But Yao of ancient China let Shun succeed him because his own was unworthy. That was indeed putting the interests of the state ahead of one's personal feelings.

Therefore, if the eldest is not worthy of the crown, let the second eldest succeed to the throne. If the second eldest, too, is unworthy, choose the brother the people consider the best qualified for the throne.

4. In the past we have always had a deep attachment for the ways of China and all of our institutions have been modeled upon those of T'ang. But our country occupies a different geographical location and our people's character is different from that of the Chinese. Hence, there is no reason to strain ourselves unreasonably to copy the Chinese way. Khitan is a nation of savage beasts, and its language and customs are also different. Its dress and institutions should never be copied.

5. I achieved the great task of founding the dynasty with the help of the elements of mountain and river of our country. The Western Capital, P'yŏngyang, has the elements of water in its favor and is the source of the terrestrial force of our country. It is thus the veritable center of dynastic enterprises for ten thousand generations. Therefore, make a royal visit to the Western Capital four times a year—in the second, fifth, eighth, and eleventh months—and reside there a total of more than one hundred days. By this means secure peace and prosperity.

6. I deem the two festivals of Yŏndŏng and P'algwan of great spiritual value and importance. The first is to worship Buddha. The second is to worship the spirit of Heaven, the spirits of the five sacred and other major mountains and rivers, and the dragon god. At some future time, villainous courtiers may propose the abandonment or modification of these festivals. No change should be allowed.

7. It is very difficult for the king to win over the people. For this reason, give heed to sincere criticism and banish those with slanderous tongues. If sincere criticisms are accepted, there will be virtuous and sagacious kings. Though sweet as honey, slanderous words should not be believed; then they will cease of their own accord. Make use of the people's labor with their convenience in mind; lighten the burden of corvée and taxation; learn the difficulties of agricultural production. Then it will be possible to win the hearts of the people and to bring peace and prosperity to the land. Men of yore said that under tempting bait a fish hangs; under a generous reward an able general wins a victory; under a drawn bow a bird dares not fly; and under a virtuous benevolent rule a loyal people serves faithfully. If you administer rewards and punishments moderately, the interplay of yin and yang will be harmonious.

8. The topographic features of the territory south of Kongju and be-yond the Kongju River are all treacherous and disharmonious; its inhabitants are treacherous and disharmonious as well. For this reason, if they are allowed to participate in the affairs of state, to intermarry with the royal family, aristocracy, and royal relatives, and to take the power of the state, they might imperil the state and injure the royal safety—grudging the loss of their own state [which used to be the kingdom of Paekche] and being resentful of the unification.

   Those who have been slaves or engaged in dishonorable trades will surrender to the powerful in order to evade prescribed ser-vices. And some of them will surely seek to offer their services to the noble families, to the palaces, or to the temples. They then will cause confusion and disorder in government and engage in treason through crafty words and treacherous machinations. They should never be allowed into government service, though they may no longer be slaves and outcasts.

9. The salaries and allowance for the aristocracy and the bureau-cracy have been set according to the needs of the state. They should not be increased or diminished. The classics say the sala-ries and allowance should be determined by the merits of those who receive them and should not be wasted for private gain. If the public treasure is wasted upon those without merit or upon one's relatives or friends, not only will the people come to resent and criticize such abuses, but those who enjoy salaries unde-servedly will also not be able to enjoy them for long. Since our country shares borders with savage nations, always beware of the danger of invasions. Treat the soldiers kindly and take good care of them; lighten their burden of forced labor; inspect them every autumn; give honors and promotions to the brave.

10. In preserving a household or a state, one should always be on guard to avert mistakes. Read widely in the classics and in his-tory; take the past as a warning for the present. The Duke of Chou was a great sage, yet he sought to admonish his nephew, King Cheng, with *Against Luxurious Ease* (*Wu-i*). Post the contents of *Against Luxurious Ease* on the wall and reflect upon them when entering and leaving the room.

—from *Koryo sa* 2:14a–17b[21]

5

Military Rulers and Mongol Invaders, 1170 to 1392

Three developments shaped the latter part of the history of Koryŏ. In the twelfth century, generals seized power and inaugurated a century of military rulers. In the thirteenth century, the Mongols launched a highly destructive series of invasions and eventually reduced Korea to a vassal state of the vast Mongol Empire centered in northern China. During the century of Mongol domination, a third major development occurred, less dramatic than the first two but more profound in its long-term impact on Korean society, the introduction of Neo-Confucianism. This school of thought, which had developed in China in the eleventh and twelfth centuries, provided the ideological basis of the establishment of a new Yi dynasty in the late fourteenth century.

MILITARY RULE

Koryŏ was a society dominated by a civil aristocracy (*munban*). Wealthy landed families held the key posts in the state, advised and intermarried with the Wang kings, controlled most of the land and economy, and supplied most of the leadership of Buddhist temples. It was from the ranks of the elite aristocratic civil officials that most of the kingdom's writers and scholars were drawn. There was, however, an inferior line of military officials (*muban*). Although they were aristocrats, they held less prestige and generally did not rise to the highest ranks in the bureaucracy. In general, their voices were seldom heard. Even Korea's military victories such as those against the Liao were usually attributed to the leadership of civil officials. It should be noted, however, that the civil officials wrote the official histories. Then in 1170, officers of the military aristocracy revolted and seized power.

Military-civil tension had existed long before the 1170 revolt.[1] For example, in 1014, the military revolted when civil officials tried to limit their salaries. Yet something changed in the twelfth century that gave the military leaders the desire and confidence to wrestle power from the civilian aristocracy. Perhaps when the military helped to defeat Yi Cha-gyŏm in 1126 and Myoch'ŏng in 1135 they realized their potential power. King Ŭijong (r. 1146–1170), a patron of the arts, was not an effective king, and disputes between civil and military officials appeared to have gotten worse under his rule. The military grew more restless; as early as 1164 some military officials plotted to overthrow the state.

The leader of the 1170 coup was Chŏng Chung-bu (1106–1179). Chŏng belonged to the influential Haeju Chŏng clan but represented the less powerful and prestigious *muban* military lineages. Before coming to power Chŏng Chung-bu served as commander of the royal guards. According to tradition, Chŏng had been humiliated when Kim Ton-jung, son of historian Kim Pu-sik, set fire to his beard. Whatever its accuracy, the story symbolizes the growing tensions between the dominant civil aristocracy and the military aristocrats that led to the military revolt. The coup was carried out as King Ŭijong and his entourage of court officials visited a temple near the capital. Chŏng, along with two other generals, Yi Ŭi-bang and Yi Ko, massacred the entire court, sparing only the king, whom they exiled to Kŏje Island off the south coast, and the crown prince, whom they banished to Chindo, another island off the south coast. Ŭijŏng was later executed by drowning. Once in power, Chŏng Chung-bu carried out an extensive purge of civil officials and managed state affairs through the *Chungbang* (Supreme Military Council). He replaced King Ŭijong with the king's brother Myŏngjong, who was more compliant. But the new monarch had little real power. Power was now in the hands of military officers. The Wang line of Koryŏ kings continued to reign, and a civil government continued to carry out the formal functions of government. Actual authority, however, was wielded by generals who developed a parallel government administration based on military clan organs. Military leaders derived their support from their own clans based on *mun'gaek* (retainers) and *kadong* (house slaves).

The first quarter century of military rule was characterized by competition for power among rival military clans. Having seized control, the military rulers do not seem to have had a clear plan of how to rule the state. As a result, the period from 1170 to 1196 was one of instability in which a number of generals plotted against each other. At first, Chŏng ruled along with Yi Ŭi-bang and Yi Ko, two other military officers, but Yi

Ŭi-bang killed Yi Ko, who in turn was assassinated by Chŏng's faction. Chŏng then ruled alone for several years until 1179 when the young military commander Kyŏng Tae-sŏng killed him. Eventually another general, Yi Ŭi-min (d. 1196), became paramount leader. Meanwhile, the countryside saw numerous rebellions. Peasants rose up against landowners and local officials, slaves revolted against masters, and even soldiers in the provinces revolted. The most famous of these revolts was that of the slave Manjŏk (?–1198), a sort of Korean Spartacus. Manjŏk gathered an army of government and private slaves that met at North Mountain outside of the capital Kaesŏng in 1198 (see below). The leaders of this group were betrayed. Their revolt and those of others were eventually suppressed, but they reflect a general breakdown of authority that took place in the land during the first three decades of governance by military officials.

Stability came when in 1196 Ch'oe Ch'ung-hŏn (1149–1219) seized power and established the rule of Korea by the Ch'oe family house that lasted fifty-eight years. Of the Ubong Ch'oe clan, Ch'oe Ch'ung-hŏn's father was an officer who had reached the top of the military hierarchy.[2] Ch'oe served as the *toryŏng* (military commander) and wrote a *Ten-Point Memorial* expressing dissatisfaction with the military rule under King Myŏngjong (r. 1170–1197), its corruption, its inferior officials, and the interference of Buddhism in politics. He killed Yi Ŭi-min and became the new paramount military leader, thus the de facto ruler of Korea. Ch'oe restored order to the areas that had been plagued by frequent peasant and slave revolts. He did this in part by offering some rebel leaders ranks and offices, and by freeing low-born inhabitants of special districts called *pugok* and *hyang* and merging them into the regular county system of local administration. He also broke the power of the Buddhist monasteries and temples that had ties to the courts and that had even threatened Ch'oe's authority with their armed monks. He crushed the armed monks and forced many of the clergy, especially the illegitimate princes who had become monks, to leave the capital. Ch'oe's twenty-two-year rule stands out in Korean history. Seldom did a single individual, who was not a king, manage to concentrate so much power in his hands.

Ch'oe created a stable rule by developing an innovative set of institutions. These institutions amounted to the establishment of two sets of government.[3] The monarchy, the court officials, and civil bureaucracy were maintained, while he created a new parallel government based on house institutions that were under his direct control. The latter, in fact, became the real locus of power. The house institutions were staffed by his own retainers and slaves and by officials personally loyal to him. The most important of these was the *Kyojŏng Togam* (Office of Decree Enactment), which served as the effective center of political authority. The *Kyojŏng Togam* functioned as the highest administrative organ of his

government. It had the power to collect taxes and investigate wrongdo-
ing by officials. Having gathered effective power in his hands, Ch'oe
preferred to create personal house organs that now had the actual civilian
and military functions of government while preserving the older court-
centered institutional structure that held only nominal power. Members
of these organs were nominally appointed by the king, but were generally chosen by Ch'oe Ch'ung-hŏn. Ch'oe in effect created a sort of parallel
dynasty to the Wang royal dynasty, passing his rulership to his son Ch'oe
U, and his grandsons Ch'oe Hang and Ch'oe Ŭi.

Ch'oe Ch'ung-hŏn's son Ch'oe U, who governed Korea from 1218 to
1249, further elaborated on the structure of house organs. He created the
Chŏngbang (Personnel Authority), an institution through which civil officials could enter government, the *Sŏbang* (Household Secretariat) that was
formed from the men of letters among his retainers, and the *Sambyŏlch'o*
(Three Elite Patrols) that served as a clan-controlled military force. The
Sambyŏlch'o were elite military units that carried out police and combat
duties. This military force originated in the two (left and right) *Yabyŏlch'o*
(Night Patrols) Ch'oe U created as military units that would be outside
the regular army command. A third unit, the *Sinŭigun* (Army of Transcendent Righteousness), was formed from fighters who escaped after
being captured by Mongols. The Ch'oe rulers financed their house organs
through *sigŭp*, extensive lands theoretically granted by the court, in which
the Ch'oe family was allowed to directly collect taxes and tribute. In effect these lands provided an independent base of economic support for it.

Essential to the new government was the use of *mun'gaek. Mun'gaek*
were private military retainers of great clans. The *mun'gaek* were important in the armies of the military clans that gained control of the Koryŏ
government in 1170. After 1196 the clan of Ch'oe Ch'ung-hŏn was especially effective in promoting its *mun'gaek*. Under the Ch'oe military rulers
many scholars became *mun'gaek* and served in the *Chŏngbang* (Personnel
Authority) and other offices. The *mun'gaek* played an important role in
the competition for power throughout the Koryŏ period. In addition to
mun'gaek who were freedmen, *kadong*, male house slaves, also served as
armed retainers.

Ch'oe Ch'ung-hŏn asserted more direct control over local institutions.
His task was an enormous one because under his military predecessors
authority of all sorts had broken down in the provinces. Ch'oe had to
deal with six peasant rebellions during his first twelve years. He uti-
lized a variety of methods to reassert control over the countryside. The
military ruler reinvigorated the power of the *hojang* (local headmen) and
expanded the *kamugwan*, a central government office that oversaw rural
jurisdictions. Ch'oe had officials called *anch'alsa* (appointed governors)

meet directly with peasants and elevated or demoted a district's status as a reward or punishment.

The Ch'oe rulers sponsored a vigorous intellectual life through their encouragement of Confucianism as a means of legitimizing their rule. They carried out civil examinations with considerable frequency, and despite the disdain of civil officials (*munban*) toward military officials (*muban*), the Ch'oe succeeded in attracting a large proportion of the former to serve in their government as civil officials or personal retainers. The military rulers were also patrons of Sŏn Buddhism, and through their support Buddhism entered a period of intellectual vigor. At the same time, the military rulers struggled to undermine the power of the capital-area monasteries that were often headed by members of cadet branches of the royal family and by court-connected aristocratic families. These efforts led to a rebellion by armed monks in 1217 that Ch'oe Ch'ung-hŏn suppressed. Overall, the Ch'oe rulers appeared to have stabilized the government and developed a set of effective institutions that secured their power. Hardly, however, had they accomplished this when they were faced with the Mongol invasions. The stubborn resistance of the Ch'oe rulers to the Mongols from 1231 to 1258, for the most part directed from the island fastness of Kanghwa, eventually contributed to their downfall when a faction suing for peace with the Mongols overthrew the last Ch'oe ruler, Ch'oe Ŭi.

SŎN BUDDHISM

Perhaps the most important cultural legacy of this period was the promotion of Sŏn Buddhism under the Ch'oe. At this time, Buddhism in Korea had become divided into Kyo, or textual, Buddhism, which emphasized the study of sutras and elaborate rituals, and Sŏn, or meditative, Buddhism. The civil aristocracy patronized Kyo and lavished great wealth on temples that supported a large number of monks. Kyo temples became major land and slave owners. The military rulers, while patronizing shamanist shrines, also sought to support Sŏn, which was more austere and centered in mountain temples far from the capital and its politics. By shifting patronage to Sŏn temples they also weakened the Kyo temples as a power base for the aristocrats that supported them. Partly as a result of this support, meditative Buddhism flourished during the late twelfth and thirteenth centuries.

A key development in Korean Buddhism at this time was its revitalization under the monk Chinul, also known as Pojo Kuksa (National Preceptor Pojo) (1158–1210). Born in an aristocratic family, he took and passed the monk exams. But he quickly became disenchanted with the atmosphere of official Buddhism with its wealthy temples and politically ambitious monks. He sought to reestablish the spirit of Buddhism by working outside the official court-sponsored religious hierarchy. Trained in the Sŏn tradition, he spent most of his active years in remote mountain areas and founded Sŏngwang-sa temple in Chŏlla Province, which became an important center for his teachings. Chinul was the first Korean Buddhist to practice koans (to use the Japanese term), the insoluble or nonsense problems that are designed to jolt one into sudden intuitive enlightenment. Derived from Chinese practice, the koan came to be practiced in Korea about the same time it was introduced to Japan. But for Chinul it was only a minor "supplementary" technique.[4] His aim was to bring together and reinvigorate the various Buddhist practices.

More successfully than the earlier effort by Ŭich'ŏn, Chinul established a Buddhist doctrine and practice that could embrace the many scholastic teachings with the antitextual Sŏn, a form of Sŏn that became known as Chogye. He did so by developing an original synthesis combining the emphasis on sudden enlightenment of the Sŏn and the stress on careful study emphasized by the Kyo lineages of Korean Buddhism. This synthesis was summed up in the terms *tano chŏmsu* (sudden enlightenment and gradual cultivation) and *chŏnghye ssangsu* (twofold training in quiescence [meditation] and activity). Chinul has been credited with unifying Korean Buddhism by creating a broad-based doctrine that was able to incorporate the major strands of Buddhism into a blended whole. Under his immediate successor, Hyesim (Chin'gak Kuksa), Chogye received the patronage of the military rulers of Korea, beginning with Ch'oe U.

Under Chinul and his successors Korean Buddhism deviated somewhat from the path of development of Buddhism in China, evolving its own distinctive body of tradition and practices. One of the major features of Korean Buddhism became the tradition of syncretism. Kyo and Sŏn practices began to blend, and sects were defined more by separate lines of transmission from a master than by sharp doctrinal differences. Within this syncretic tradition, Sŏn practices of meditation, austerity, and the disciplined seeking of enlightenment became central, and the influence of Chinul profound. To this day, the majority of Korean Buddhists belong to the Chogye sect of Buddhism.

KOREA, JAPAN, AND FEUDAL EUROPE

Korea under the military governments developed institutions that in some ways resembled feudalism. Feudalism is usually defined as a decentralized political system in which a landowning or land-controlling warrior aristocracy supported by peasantry bound to the land is linked in a hierarchical scheme of political loyalty. It became a fully developed and dominant political-social system only in medieval Western Europe and in medieval Japan. Historians have long noted the similarities between Japanese feudalism and Western European feudalism. Less well appreciated is that many of the important transformations in Japanese society that took place in the twelfth century to establish the classic Japanese feudal society took place simultaneously in Korea. As historian Edward Shultz has observed, "Civil aristocratic societies characterize both Korea and Japan at the start of the twelfth century."[5] In Japan as in Korea, the court and dynasty lost effective power to new military lineages, and in both after a period of struggle among military leaders a strong military leader emerged. In Japan this leader was Yoritomo, who in 1185 became paramount ruler of Japan, taking the title of Shogun in 1192; and in Korea Ch'oe Ch'ung-hŏn emerged as the effective ruler in 1196. In both countries the military hegemons established a parallel clan government with effective power while maintaining the dynastic organs of government. Both Ch'oe and Yoritomo made use of an elaborate system of personal retainers and military leaders who pledged to serve their military ruler through ties of loyalty, and who derived income from their extensive personal landholdings. Both recruited men of letters to serve in their private agencies and relied on these educated men to help them in administering the country. In both cases members of the old clans that had supplied the court with officials continued to serve as officials, although without the power and influence they previously had. Both patronized Zen (Sŏn) Buddhism, which became the religion of the warriors. In Japan, as well as in Korea, the late twelfth and thirteenth centuries became the great age of meditative Buddhism, which with the help of official support emerged as a major religious and cultural force. Military rulers in both Korea and Japan fiercely resisted the Mongol invasions.

But there were important differences. Yoritomo came out of a Heian order that witnessed the expansion of warrior and regional autonomy, while Ch'oe emerged from the Koryŏ system in which the military was closely tied to the dynasty. In Japan local autonomy and military culture grew stronger, while in Korea the Ch'oe, searching for appropriate forms of governance, restored many dynastic agencies, working closely with the king and his officials, thus reaffirming the importance of civil traditions in Korea. While in Japan the military traditions emerged as dominant, in Korea the civil traditions prevailed. Partly this was due to the use of the civil exams by the Ch'oe family to recruit men of learning for office, thus reinforcing the importance of scholarship. There was no civil exam system in Japan. In Japan, the emergence of military rule was a consolidation of trends that had been taking place for several centuries as power slipped away from the court and into the hands of local military elite. By contrast, in Korea, the emergence of military rule was a more dramatic break with tradition. Koryŏ monarchs were active in governing in the twelfth century, private armies had been effectively uprooted in the tenth century, the military was clearly subordinated to civil authority, and the central hierarchy was more clearly defined than in Japan.

Even under the Ch'oe the Korean government remained more centralized than was the case in either Europe or Japan. The military rulers of Koryŏ were based in the capital and maintained an orientation toward centralized rule. Yoritomo, by contrast, led a coalition of warriors rooted in the countryside. Furthermore, he had his own large provincial power base on the Kanto plain. Ch'oe had no such power base and was much more reliant on key court and military officials to support him.[6] Also the *mun'gaek* retainers were considerably smaller in number than those available to Yoritomo and the shoguns who succeeded him. More significantly, retainers in Korea could not own land, unlike the vassals who served their lords in Europe and in Japan. An entire system of feudal law emerged in Japan and in Europe, but in Korea the Chinese-patterned legal system continued to function. So for all the parallels with developments in Japan, Korea never developed a truly feudal system. It is possible, of course, that with time Korea might have developed a more feudal-like system, but the tendency to recruit ever more civil officials during the Ch'oe clan's rule does not suggest this was going to happen. Perhaps Korea, unlike Western Europe and Japan, which were relatively free from outside invasions, simply could not function without a centralized state. Geography made Korea less secure. Unlike Europe or Japan, Korea had to deal with powerful and often aggressive neighbors from the Manchurian plains and grasslands of Inner Asia.

The final question is why such institutions appeared in Japan and Korea around the same time, in fact, at almost exactly the same time. The answer to this is not well understood, but the fact they did suggests that Korean and Japanese historical developments are more closely linked than most scholars have previously appreciated. Both were in contrast to China, where no similar trends occurred in the twelfth and thirteenth centuries. The power of the Chinese military aristocratic clans had declined sharply in the eighth to tenth centuries and saw no revival.

THE MONGOL INVASIONS

Would the Ch'oe family or another family have developed a dynastic system similar to the Japanese shogunate? We simply do not know, since Korea's period of rule by military warlords came to an end with the Mongol invasions. Emerging as a unified group in the thirteenth century under their leader Chinggis (Genghis) Khan and his successors, the Mongols built a great empire based on the grasslands of Inner Asia and subjugated the greater part of Eurasia. Few countries suffered more from the ravages of the Mongols than Korea. From 1217 to 1258 Korea endured repeated invasions as a result of the rise of the Mongols. In 1217, Khitan tribes fleeing the Mongol invasions of northern China crossed the Yalu and plundered northern Korea.[7] In 1218 the Mongols, pursuing the Khitans, aided Koryŏ forces in defeating them. The Mongols then demanded tribute from the Koreans: clothes, furs, and horses. They also demanded virgins, which the Koreans refused. For the Koreans the tribute demands were burdensome, especially horses in a country with little grazing land. In 1224, the Koryŏ stopped tribute payments and murdered the Mongol envoys. In retaliation the Mongols invaded in 1231.

The Mongols withdrew the following year after the Koryŏ government agreed to accept tributary status and to accept the placing of Mongol representatives, called *darughachi*, in Korea to oversee tribute collections. Later, in 1232, the Ch'oe house military rulers ordered the Koryŏ court to retreat to Kanghwa Island and killed the *darughachi*. The military rulers then declared all-out resistance. From the protection of Kanghwa Island the Ch'oe rulers and their successors carried out a fierce and stubborn resistance that lasted four decades. The Ch'oe transferred the entire government to the small ten-by-seventeen-mile island, constructing palaces, temples, and administrative buildings where thousands of officials, soldiers, and monks carried out the functions of government. Some officials objected to abandoning the people; nonetheless, the small but easily defendable island proved to be an effective stronghold against the Mongols. The state was not, however, able to protect the countryside, where the Mongol destruction was devastating. Much of the country's heritage, including the 80,000 wood blocks for the *Tripitaka*, was destroyed.

The 1232 invasion ended when the Mongol commander Sartaq was killed from an arrow shot by the monk Kim Yun-hu. In 1233, the Mongols launched a new series of invasions, led by Tanqut-batu and Prince Yeku, that dragged on for several years and eventually resulted in a six-year truce from 1241 to 1247. During this time, distant members of the royal family were sent to the Mongol court as hostages under the pretense that they were crown princes. But the Koryŏ government continued to resist the Mongols, refusing to send tribute. As a result, further invasions occurred in 1247–1248. The most destructive invasions were a series that began with the Mongol attack of 1254 led by Jalairtai. Small bands of Mongol warriors were sent to lay waste to the countryside in an attempt to wear down Korean resistance and cut off the grain supply to the court on Kanghwa. According to later Korean accounts, the Mongols killed vast numbers of people and took away over 200,000 as prisoners. Historians recorded that "The fields were covered with the bones of the dead; the dead were so many that they could not be counted"; wherever the Mongol army passed, "the inhabitants were all burned out, so that not even dogs and chickens remained."[8] These tactics proved effective, and in 1258 the Ch'oe clan, still adamant in resisting the Mongols, was overthrown. A new leader, Kim Chun, attempted to seek an end to the invasions. Mongol military activity continued in Korea, however, when in 1269 the military leader Im Yŏn ousted the Mongol-supported king. The king was restored to power in 1270 with Mongol assistance, and resistance was limited to holdouts in the provinces. The *Sambyŏlch'o* forces, led by Pae Chung-son and by Kim T'ong-jŏng, continued to fight the Mongols until they were defeated respectively on Chindo Island in 1271 and Cheju Island in 1273.

From 1270 to 1356 Korea was under Mongol domination. While the court and bureaucracy continued to govern, Koryŏ was, in reality, an appendage of the Yuan or Mongol Empire that moved its center from Mongolia to what is now Beijing. Korea is sometimes called the *Pumaguk* (Son-in-law Nation) during this period, since King Wŏnjong (r. 1259–1274) married his son, later King Ch'ungnyŏl (r. 1274–1308), to a daughter of the Yuan emperor Shizu (Kubilai Khan). He thus began a line of Koryŏ kings who had princesses of the Yuan imperial house as their primary consorts. The sons of these queens usually succeeded to the throne so that Koryŏ kings were sons-in-law of the Yuan emperors. During this period Koryŏ crown princes resided in Beijing as hostages until ascending to the throne. Even while reigning, Koryŏ kings spent much of their time in Beijing rather than in Kaesŏng.

Kings under the Mongol hegemony saw their authority weaken. They were sometimes at the mercy of the Yuan emperors, who could depose them at will. Several were removed, sometimes with the support of members of the Koryŏ aristocracy. Yuan emperors appointed some monarchs as King of Shenyang, a region of southern Manchuria. Thus they created two courts among the members of the Wang royal family as a means of manipulating them by playing royal relatives against each other. To reinforce Koryŏ's subordinate status, the organs of government were renamed to give them titles that carried less prestige or hint of sovereignty. For example, the *Samsŏng* (Three Chancelleries) were merged to form a single Council of State, and the *Chungch'uwŏn* (Royal Secretariat) was renamed the *Milchiksa*, which had the same meaning but was less exalted sounding.

As a vassal of the Yuan (Mongol) state, Korea became a member of one of the world's most cosmopolitan societies. Korean court officials, scholars, and others seeking opportunities traveled and resided in Beijing, where they encountered Chinese, Mongols, Vietnamese, Central Asians, and a handful of other peoples. For some it was a time of opportunity for social advancement. A number of Koreans, following the tradition of marrying into influential and wealthy families, formed marriage alliances with Mongols and Central Asians and rose to prominence in Beijing or back in Korea. Many Koreans adopted Mongol clothing and hairstyles. A number of foreigners also made their way to Korea and served as members of government. Often they filled the need for personnel fluent in Chinese and Mongol, or familiar with the complexities of the Yuan court. As Peter Yun has found in his research, foreigners in Korea numbered in the thousands. Several foreigners became members of the *Chaech'u* and others became military officers. Even after Korea broke with the Yuan court, three Mongols, In Hu, Hwang Sang, and Na Se, served as military commanders during Red Turban invasions in the fourteenth century.[9]

Korea was also the base of two efforts to conquer Japan. Having subdued the last resistance to their rule in 1273, the Mongols drafted Korean shipbuilders and sailors to construct and pilot a large Mongol fleet that invaded Japan in 1274. The invasion, launched in typhoon season, was forced to retreat when a typhoon that the Japanese called the *kamikaze* (divine wind) came. A second invasion in 1281 also failed when another typhoon destroyed much of the fleet. For the Japanese this would remain until 1945 a sign that theirs was a special land of the gods protected from invasion, and it contributed to the myth of their uniqueness and invincibility. To the Koreans the two invasions and an aborted planned third invasion were a costly burden. Furthermore, along with the tribute of horses and women the Mongols extracted, the forced participation in the invasions of Japan was a humiliating reminder of their subordinate status. Yet, the Mongol rule was indirect, not direct. The court and bureaucracy in Kaesŏng continued to function. After the invasions of Japan there was little direct interference in Korean affairs. As a result Korea maintained itself as a separate kingdom with its own court and culture.

THE LEGACY OF THE MONGOL PERIOD

Historians differ in their evaluation of the importance of the Mongol invasions and their domination of Korea. Some emphasize the continuity in Korea. They argue that there was no change in dynasty, the bureaucracy underwent relatively minor changes in organization, and while some new powerful families emerged, the social structure remained essentially the same with most of the old elite lineages continuing to dominate society. Korea's vassalage to China was not a radical break with tradition. The Mongol rulers of China took on the role of Chinese emperors and assumed the big brother role that China often took toward Korea. When Korean kings paid homage to the Yuan rulers they were continuing a practice of seeking legitimacy by having their positions confirmed by the Celestial (Chinese) emperor.

Nevertheless, the destruction that resulted from the invasions was an enormous loss to Korea. To this day, few structures before this period still exist. The scorched-earth policy and the repeated and systematic invasions at least partially account for the fact that so few of Korea's pre-fourteenth-century literary and artistic works have survived. One has only to read the lists of compilations of poetry, the praise and descriptions of famous painters given in the fifteenth-century *Koryŏ sa* (*History of Koryŏ*), and the many works of history cited in the *Samguk sagi* to sense how much has been lost. The Mongol invasion may have contributed to a growing consciousness of Korean cultural identity. It was, for example, during the Mongol period that the legend of Tan'gun appeared in the written record in the *Samguk yusa* (see below) and in the long history in verse *Chewang un'gi* (*Song of Emperors and Kings*). During the Mongol period Korean monks also compiled the extant version of the *Tripitaka Koreana.*

The Mongol invasions may have made Koreans more cautious of outsiders. Ming China, which drove out the Mongols, maintained a policy of greater isolation and wariness of outsiders than earlier dynasties. This is generally explained as a reaction to the Mongol invasion and rule. Similarly, Korea maintained a policy of limiting foreign contact that would eventually earn it the sobriquet of "the hermit Kingdom." Most probably the experience and memory of the Mongols contributed to this idea that foreigners meant trouble. Korea's stubborn resistance and ability to maintain itself as a separate state even during this period may have also contributed to a sense of pride, and of being the inheritor of a distinctive cultural and historical tradition.

No less important was the fact that for a short time Korea was closely connected with the truly vast cosmopolitan Mongol Empire, the largest the world had ever seen. At its peak the Mongol Empire stretched from Russia and Persia to Korea. At this time Koreans at the Mongol court met peoples and ideas from all over Eurasia. Concepts about mathematics, astrology, and medicine reached some Koreans from as far away as the Middle East. But it was the relatively close contact the royal family members, courtiers, and others in Beijing had with their Chinese counterparts that made the greatest impact. This influenced painting, calligraphy, literature, and clothing fashions. Cotton and cotton cloth making became known to Koreans at this time. By tradition, cotton was brought back from Yuan China in 1363 by Mun Ik-chŏm (1329–1398), who had gone there as part of a diplomatic mission. He gave the seeds to his father-in-law, who successfully planted them. Gunpowder too spread to Korea during this period. Credit for this introduction is given to Ch'oe Mu-sŏn (1326?–1395), a minor official who learned the formula from the Chinese.

In 1377 Koryŏ established an office for the manufacture of gunpowder and cannons, which were first used to fight Japanese pirates. The Mongol period was one of close contact between Korean scholars and officials and their Chinese counterparts whom they met at the Yuan court in Beijing. This contact resulted in what is perhaps the most significant legacy of the Mongol period, the introduction of Neo-Confucianism to Korea. (See below.)

LATE KORYŎ SOCIETY

For all the turbulence of the latter two centuries of Koryŏ, the basic structure of the social and the political order remained largely intact. At the top of society was the dynastic family. The king reigned, if not always effectively. Under him, the upper strata of the aristocracy that was based in the capital dominated the organs of government. A lower stratum of rural-based aristocrats sometimes referred to as *hyangni* controlled much of the countryside and held local offices. Underneath them were commoners and the large number of slaves and certain outcaste groups. Military rule did little to change this, since most of the military rulers were quick to acquire *nongjang* (landed estates) and intermarried with the civil-official aristocracy in the capital. The Mongol period saw a number of new families emerge, but recent studies indicate that while some elite families fell in status and a few new ones appeared, the old aristocracy largely survived. The central aristocracy may have actually strengthened its dominance over society. Furthermore, new families adopted the style of the old.

There were some changes. The devastation brought about by the Mongol invasions destroyed much of the wealth of the *hyangni*. Because of this development and the gradual penetration of the central government into the countryside, the rural aristocracy probably declined in power. Significantly, while late Koryŏ was still an aristocratic society dominated by powerful families deriving much of their wealth from landed estates, increasingly, the dominant aristocracy, or *yangban* as it eventually became known, associated itself with service to the state. Korea evolved into a bureaucratic polity with a ruling class that identified with the state and shared a common set of values.

The struggle of Koryŏ kings to gain some independence from the aristocracy continued. The situation of late Koryŏ kings was worsened by the loss of taxable lands. During the Mongol period a great deal of taxable public land (*kongjŏn*) slipped into private hands, and powerful families had consolidated their power in the capital. Furthermore, raids by Japanese pirates known as *wakō* (*waegu* in Korean) devastated much of the

coastal areas, and countermeasures against them drained the public trea-
sury. Late Koryŏ kings tried to check the power of the powerful families
by appointing eunuchs, slaves, and other outsiders to office. Most notable
of these efforts was King Kongmin's (r. 1351–1374) selection of a slave
monk, Sin Ton (?–1371), as his chief officer to carry out a redistribution
of lands and slaves. This move was taken to undermine these powerful
families and restore land and peasants to the tax rolls. Kongmin, however, was reported to have gradually lost interest in politics following the
death of his Mongol wife in childbirth in 1365. According to the historical
records, he had a large shrine to his deceased wife constructed, hung a
portrait of her that he painted himself, and spent hours in front of it griev-
ing. Kongmin's efforts to rein in the power of the elite then failed. Sin Ton
was exiled and killed, and the king was assassinated in 1374.

THE END OF THE KORYŎ

The mid-fourteenth century was a time of upheaval in continental East
Asia. Uprisings occurred in China against the Yuan dynasty, and a
number of rebel bands emerged. One of these, led by former monk Zhu
Yuanzhang (or Hongwu) (r. 1368–1398), gained control over most of central and southern China. In 1356, Zhu set up a capital at Nanjing. Twelve
years later, in 1368, Zhu's forces drove the Mongols out of Beijing and
back to their Mongolian homeland. In that year Zhu proclaimed a new
Ming dynasty. The Mongols formed a northern Yuan rump state and carried on the struggle with Ming, but China was now unified and free from
the Mongols.

Taking advantage of Yuan weakness, Kongmin in 1356 destroyed the
pro-Mongol faction led by Ki Ch'ŏl (?–1356), brother of Empress Ki, the
second wife of Shun, the last Mongol emperor. Korea was now independent of Mongol control. Kongmin then pursued an anti-Mongol, pro-
Ming policy. He abolished the Eastern Expedition Field Headquarters, an
institution through which the Mongols kept an eye on events in Korea,
and his army annexed the Yuan commandery of Ssangsŏng based in what
is now the northeastern province of Hamgyŏng. He also abolished the
Chŏngbang (Personnel Authority), the organ of administration created under the military rule. In 1369, the Ming recognized Kongmin as king, and
the Korean court adopted the Ming calendar. The old tributary relationship between Korea and the Chinese court was reestablished.

Mongol domination had ended, but the last years of the Koryŏ were
troubled ones. The collapsing Mongol power and the rise of the Ming
dynasty in China created turmoil on the northern border, and Ming and
Mongol forces fought each other in Manchuria. A product of this turmoil,

a Chinese rebel/brigand army known as the Red Turbans plundered their way across Manchuria and twice invaded Korea, first, in 1359, with a force reported to have been 40,000 men, and two years later with a larger force of 100,000, forcing the Korean court to flee to Andong in the southeastern part of the kingdom. Another threat came from the son of Ki Ch'ŏl, who led a group of Yuan refugees in Manchuria that menaced Koryŏ. Meanwhile along the southern coast *wakō* raided, plundered, and spread terror, even attacking Kanghwa Island and threatening the capital, Kaesŏng.

When Kongmin was assassinated in 1274, his ten-year-old son came to the throne as King U (r. 1374–1388). The real power, however, was in the hands of Yi In-im (?–1388), head of an important clan. The Ming were suspicious of the new administration in Korea. Consequently, the Ming emperor refused to recognize King U. Yi In-im then abandoned the pro-Ming policies of Kongmin. But attempts to establish friendly relations with the Northern Yuan failed when the Mongols demanded the Koreans join them in attacking the Ming. Relations with the Ming were briefly restored but broke down when the new Chinese dynasty began to build a garrison at Ch'ŏllyŏng and create a commandery out of the former Mongol Ssangsŏng commandery in Hamgyŏng Province. Domestically politics was torn between pro-Yuan factions, which included many families that had risen to prominence under the Yuan, and pro-Ming officials and aristocrats.

In 1388, the Yi In-im faction was driven out, led by a general, Ch'oe Yŏng (1316–1388), who became military commander. He appointed two of his supporters, generals Yi Sŏng-gye (1335–1408) and Cho Min-su, as deputies. Ch'oe and King U then mobilized the country for an attack on the Ming and an expedition was launched under Ch'oe's leadership. Yi Sŏng-gye was given a command of some of the forces, but he opposed the launching of a military campaign against the Ming. At Wihwa Island in the mouth of the Yalu, Yi turned back, and with the support of general Cho Min-su ousted Ch'oe Yŏng. Yi and his supporters then deposed King U and replaced him with Ch'ang, his nine-year-old son. In the following year, 1389, he ousted the recently installed King Ch'ang on the grounds that he was really the son of Sin Ton and replaced him with Kongyang (r. 1389–1392), a distant relative. Yi then removed Cho Min-su and made him a commoner. Yi's rise to power was relatively bloodless; a few high officials such as Yi Saek (1328–1396) and Kwŏn Kŭn (1352–1409) were banished, but otherwise he ruled with cooperation of the existing bureaucracy. With the aid of reform-minded scholar-officials he began to carry out sweeping changes. Yi supervised a new land survey, and then in 1390, he burned all registers in a big bonfire in the market. The next year he carried out a major land reform. With his supporters secure in high positions, he removed Kongyang in 1392. The deposed king was sent into exile and later murdered. Yi Sŏng-gye then became King T'aejo (r. 1392–1398), the first of the new Yi dynasty, and renamed the state Chosŏn. The Wang dynasty and the Koryŏ state had come to an end.

LATE KORYŎ CULTURE

During the nearly five centuries of the Koryŏ, the process of borrowing and adapting from China continued. With these adaptations a distinctive Korean cultural style and identity emerged. Among the most important cultural achievements in late Koryŏ were those dealing with papermaking and printing. Papermaking had been introduced from China in the Silla period. Under Koryŏ high-quality paper made from the mulberry shrub was valued as an import by the Chinese. Woodblock printing, also borrowed from China, became highly developed, spurred by the demand for printed Buddhist sutras. Blocks were made from wood that was soaked and boiled in salt water then coated with lacquer. The greatest publishing project of the Koryŏ was the *Tripitaka Koreana*. This is the most complete extant edition of the *Tripitaka* (*The Three Baskets*), which contains the Buddhist canon, anywhere in the world today.[10] The first copy was printed during the Liao invasions in the eleventh century and destroyed in the Mongol invasion of 1232. During the years 1235 to 1251, 81,137 woodblocks, enough to print 160,000 pages, were carved at Kanghwa and are now stored at Haein-sa temple in Mount Kaya. This is one of the great cultural treasures of Korea and an invaluable resource for Buddhists.

In addition to the woodblock tradition, Koryŏ craftsmen, drawing upon their highly skilled metal-casting techniques, produced the world's first moveable metal type. Exactly when this happened is not known for certain. The first known use of moveable metal type was in 1234 to print twenty-eight copies of *Sangjŏng kogŭm yemun* (*Prescribed Ritual Texts of the Past and Present*). This was more than two centuries before Gutenberg. Indeed, some historians have speculated that knowledge of Korean moveable metal type may have reached Europe and inspired the development of printing there.[11] The Koreans, however, did not invent a printing press. In 1392, at the end of the dynasty, a National Office for Book Publication was established to cast type and print books. Moveable type was useful, since many different books could be published. Woodblocks were still used to print books, especially when a large number of copies of a single book were needed.

Late Koryŏ scholars produced a number of medical texts. The oldest existing Korean medical text, *Hyangyak kugŭp pang* (*Emergency Remedies of Folk Medicine*), was produced in the thirteenth century during the times of the Mongol invasions. Korea's medical tradition was derived from China but incorporated folk practices as well. A special problem for Koreans was that Chinese medical practice relied heavily on the use of medicinal herbs and had created a vast materia medica. But many of these plants were not available in Korea. Searches for indigenous medicines in the fourteenth century led to impressive compilations of native Korean *hyangyak ŭisul* (prescriptions) using local materials. These efforts led to the eighty-five-volume *Hyangyak chipsŏngbang* (*Compilation of Native Korean Prescriptions*) published in the early fifteenth century.

The East Asian tradition of short prose essays, still popular in Korea, flourished in Koryŏ times. Koryŏ essays were classified as follows: admonition, disquisition, dirge, appreciation, proclamations, announcement, memorials, letters, and descriptions (or records). There were didactic and humorous stories written in Chinese and often set in ancient China. Authors of these essays and little stories were members of the elite, often leading officials. Among the most noted was Yi Kyu-bo (1168–1241), who passed the civil service exam in 1190 and rose to first privy councilor. Yi took the pen name "White Cloud" and styled himself as master of the lute, poetry, and wine. Yi Che-hyŏn (1287–1367), another highly regarded writer, placed first in the state exam in 1301 and had a distinguished public career.[12] Other prose writers of note were Yi Il-lo (1152–1220) and Ch'oe Cha (1188–1260). History and biographies modeled on the Chinese works, especially Sima Qian's *Shiji*, were popular as well.

With the Mongol threat and the relative isolation of Korea from China during the period of military rule, there appeared to be an interest in ancient history and legends. In the early thirteenth century Yi Kyu-bo wrote *Tongmyŏng wang p'yŏn* (*The Saga of King Tongmyŏng*). This was a narrative poem that dealt with the legendary founder of Koguryŏ. The purpose in writing this, Yi Kyu-bo states, was "simply to let the world know that our country always has been a land of hero-sages." Yi Sŏng-hyu (1224–1300) composed the *Chewang un'gi* (*Song of Emperors and Kings*), a long poem recounting the rulers of Korea starting with Tan'gun. Scholars also wrote a number of other works on Korean history, now lost. All this suggests a growing sense, among the educated Koreans at least, that they were part of a society with its own history and traditions distinct from that of its neighbors.

The most important result of this interest was *Samguk yusa* (*Memorabilia of the Three Kingdoms*). The *Samguk yusa* is a history of Korea from its mythical origins to the end of the Silla kingdom in the tenth century written in 1279 by the monk Iryŏn (1206–1289). Along with the *Samguk sagi*, the *Samguk yusa* remains one of the two major sources for early Korean history. The work contains a chronological table that is often more accurate than the *Samguk sagi* and is an important source of historical information. This is followed by a long section, "Records of Marvels," that contains valuable material on ancient Korea, including the earliest recorded legend of Tan'gun, a story, incidentally, not recorded in the *Samguk sagi*. The *Samguk yusa* is based on many now lost sources, such as the *Karak kukki* (*Record of the Karak Kingdom*) written in 1076, of which a synopsis is given. It also preserves some of the *hyangga* poems, the earliest literature written phonetically in Korean. The *Samguk yusa*, although an invaluable historical source, is better thought of as a collection of tales and stories containing many folk traditions, in contrast to the *Samguk sagi*, which is an official history. It was written at the aftermath of the Mongol invasions by a Buddhist monk and has been viewed as part of a heightened awareness of a Korean cultural identity that many must have felt at this time. As such, it has been praised by twentieth-century nationalist historians who find the *Sam'guk sagi* to be too Chinese and who see the real spirit and sentiment of Korea in Iryŏn's work.[13]

The *Samguk yusa* contains an especially rich collection of Buddhist legends and tales. The themes of these stories reveal the importance of Buddhist morality in Korean thought and literature at this time. In some, beggars, outcastes, servants, poor peasants, and children turn out to be bodhisattvas. In one story, a poor girl servant keeps trying to attend a temple service but is constantly blocked by her mistress. She becomes airborne and flies directly to the Buddha land. In another tale the famed monk Silla Wŏnhyo meets another monk, Hyegong. They go fishing, eat their catch, and then defecate on a rock. Hyegong, pointing to the excrement, says "Your fish is my shit," the meaning being that all things are part of the eternal changing world.[14] In a famous story known as "Chosin's Dream" a monk falls in love with the daughter of a magistrate. He prays for assistance in his love, but the daughter marries another man. He has a dream where she appears and tells him that she secretly loves him and decides to spend her life with him. They live together for fifty years, have five children, and struggle with poverty. A son dies of starvation; a daughter becomes a beggar. Realizing their love has led only to their suffering they decide to part. Waking from the dream Chosin visits the spot in his dream where he buried his son and finds a Buddha statue buried instead. He establishes a monastery at the spot and dedicates his life to good deeds.[15]

THE RISE OF NEO-CONFUCIANISM

Late Koryŏ saw a period of military-dominated government, the Mongol invasions, and the Mongol domination of the state. As important as these developments may be, neither probably had as much impact on Korean society as did the rise of Neo-Confucianism. Neo-Confucianism is a modern term for the school of Confucian thought that emerged during the Song period in China, culminating in the interpretations of Zhu Xi (1130–1200). Confucianism has had an enormous influence on Korea since the time of the Three Kingdoms. It was an ethical philosophy that taught that each individual should strive to pursue a virtuous life. This involved carefully and sincerely carrying out one's social obligations and serving family and society. It was also a political philosophy that stressed the duty of rulers to act as moral exemplars and to attend to the needs of the people in order to create a harmonious society. Confucianism respected formal learning and accepted a hierarchical society, a patriarchal family structure, and an authoritarian state. It viewed human nature as basically good if properly led, and saw human affairs as connected with natural affairs. Sometimes Confucianism is called familism in that Confucian thinkers saw the family as the primary unit of society and the state as a kind of superfamily with the ruler playing the role of the patriarchal family head. The ruler should be stern and proper but possess a fatherly love and a concern for those he rules.

But Confucianism was vague about the big questions such as: What is the nature of reality? Who is the real me? How am I connected with reality? Buddhism and to some degree Daoism supplied answers to these questions along with impressive rituals, practices of meditation, and the Buddhist concept of enlightenment. In China during the eleventh and twelfth centuries, Confucian scholars began to borrow metaphysical concepts and meditative practices from the Buddhists, and to a lesser extent from the Daoists. They began to reinterpret the Confucian classics, and to derive meaning and inspiration from them. Under Song thinkers such as Cheng Yi (1033–1107) and Cheng Hao (1032–1085) in the eleventh century and Zhu Xi in the twelfth these new formulations of Confucianism, called by modern scholars Neo-Confucianism, were carefully elaborated in a set of works that became canonical to later generations.

The Yuan emperors sponsored this school of thought. Whatever its metaphysical teachings, the Yuan rulers saw Neo-Confucianism as a secular ideology that would assist them in the administration of their hybrid Chinese-Mongol state. When they revived the Chinese civil service exams in 1313 they made Zhu Xi's interpretations of Chinese classics authoritative for the exams. The close relations between Korea and Beijing in the late thirteenth and fourteenth century meant that there were many opportunities for Korean scholars and court officials to come in contact with Chinese scholars and Chinese intellectual activity. In addition, the Yuan was a cosmopolitan empire in which Koreans, Vietnamese, Central Asians, and others mingled. Foreigners were allowed to sit for the Chinese civil exams. Some Koreans studied and passed them, immersing themselves in Neo-Confucian learning. Many of these Koreans brought back to their country these new exciting formulations of Confucian thought. The introduction of Neo-Confucian learning brought more than just some new lines of interpretation. It caused many educated Koreans to reexamine their government, their society, and their personal behavior. This in turn led to a revolution that transformed Korean society and formed the basis of cultural norms, ethical standards, and conceptions about state and society that still influence Koreans in the twenty-first century.

During the period of Mongol domination some Koreans tried to promote Neo-Confucian learning in their own country. Starting with An Hyang (also known as An Yu) (1243–1306), they encouraged the rebuilding of the *Kukhak* (National Academy) and the *Munmyo* (National Shrine to Confucius). Both were carried out during the reign of King Ch'ungnyŏl (r. 1274–1308). These were important steps in the revival of Confucianism that marked the fourteenth century. By the late fourteenth century a group of eager scholars saw in Neo-Confucianism a blueprint for perfecting Korean society. Their basic ideas were: educate the ruler to act as a good moral exemplar for society; select only the virtuous to serve the monarch and govern society; eliminate the influence of Buddhism and any other rival and false schools of thought; and remodel both government institutions and family practices such as marriage on the ideals of Confucianism, especially the Zhu Xi interpretation of them. Foremost among these zealous scholars were Chŏng Mong-ju (1337–1392) and his rival Chŏng To-jŏn (1337?–1398). They were especially hostile to Buddhism, which was "foreign" (that is, not from China or Korea); selfish, since it stressed individual enlightenment instead of serving family and society; and too otherworldly.

The last years of the Koryŏ saw a continuation of the movement by some members of the aristocracy to promote Neo-Confucianism. In 1367 the state established the *Sŏnggyun'gwan* (National Confucian Academy) under the leadership of Yi Saek (1328–1396) and Chŏng Mong-ju. There Zhu Xi's commentaries on the Four Books formed a central part of its curriculum. The faculty included Chŏng To-jŏn, who later played a central role in establishing the Yi dynasty. Its curriculum was a departure from previous schools. Education at private schools that aristocratic sons attended before serving in government included Confucian texts among the Chinese classics, but the emphasis was on belles lettres and developing formal literary polish. The scholars at this new school trained their students to examine the Chinese classics in order to grasp the underlying moral principles that governed the individual, society, and the cosmos. Not surprisingly they were highly critical of the society around them. They saw in Confucian principles the learned rules for ordering society and government, and they eventually sought to use their knowledge of these principles to assist a willing king. By the late fourteenth century, Neo-Confucian scholars joined with elements among the elite and military disgruntled with the court to establish the new Yi dynasty. Under this new dynasty Korea would undergo a significant cultural transformation.

KOREA IN GLOBAL PERSPECTIVE:
THE MONGOLS AND KOREA

Korea was greatly impacted by the Mongols in two main ways. First the Mongol invasions devastated the country. The repeated attacks and especially the scorched-earth tactics they employed that systematically destroyed cities, towns, and temples resulted in a horrendous loss of the country's cultural heritage. Very little in the way of physical remains survives from pre-Mongol times. In this, Korea shared the fate of many other parts of the world. The Mongol invasion of Iraq in 1258, for example, led to the utter destruction of Baghdad, the greatest city of the Islamic world. The Tigris River, legend has it, turned black from the ink of the many books the Mongols dumped into it as they destroyed the city's great libraries and numerous bookstores. Even the elaborate irrigation system that made Mesopotamia a highly productive agricultural region was destroyed. As a result, little remains today of Iraq's legacy as the former center of Islamic civilization. Similar destruction was heaped upon many of the great cities of Kwarezm and other parts of Central Asia, and across much of China and Russia. This contrasts with Western Europe and Japan, which were largely spared this devastation.

The other legacy of the Mongols was Korea's unprecedented integration into the larger Eurasian world. Once the Mongols had created their great steppe-based empire, they settled in on the task of extracting revenue from it. This involved promoting trade. Nomadic peoples had always been dependent on trading as well as raiding the settled agricultural societies they bordered. They provided meat, skins, and horses, and they traded plunder for metal goods such as swords, knives, and pots; for grain; and for other items they could not produce themselves. In addition to encouraging trade, the Mongols, with their control over most of the steppe and adjacent lands, were able to ensure safety and stability for long-distance merchants and were concerned with maintaining good communications. They also searched for and hired or drafted talent—clerks, administrators, and skilled craftsmen—from the lands they conquered, having them serve in their capital or other administrative centers. As a result, the period from the late thirteenth century, when the Mongols' conquests were largely completed, to the collapse of the Mongol Empire in the mid-fourteenth century was a period of unprecedented cosmopolitanism in much of Eurasia. Some historians call this period the Pax Mongolica. Western Europe, for example, for the first time had direct contact with China.

Korea became a part of this cosmopolitan world. Perhaps as never before in its history, Koreans serving the Mongols in their capital at Beijing or elsewhere came into contact with people from all over Eurasia. This is when gunpowder, cotton, and other imports and innovations entered or were established in the peninsula. And it was during the Mongol period that Koreans began to adopt Neo-Confucianism. For Korea, being more integrated into the cosmopolitan world of the Pax Mongolica resulted in the greater flow of influences from China, while the cultural influences of Central Asia, the Middle East, and other parts of the world were less significant. Thus, like much of Eurasia, the Mongol period brought about enormous destruction and loss of heritage but also facilitated technological and cultural innovation through greater contact with distant cultures.

The Mongols were part of a long-term historical process in which mobile, horse-riding nomads from the steppe posed a constant threat to their neighbors. Koreans had endured the Murong, the Khitans, the Jurchens, and others. The Koreans themselves were partly of nomadic origin. The Mongols were the latest and most formidable of these invaders. But they also were among the last. The development of firearms and conquest of most of the steppe by the Russian and Qing empires in the seventeenth century brought this era of history to an end.

Many historians have argued that the Mongols brought about a more defensive, withdrawn attitude among some of their neighbors, especially the Chinese. They see China under the Ming dynasty, 1368–1644, as more xenophobic, less open to foreign culture, placing more restrictions on contacts with outsiders as a legacy of the Mongol period. It is difficult to see this trend in Korea. Korea, after the Mongol period was not marked by more restrictions on contact with outsiders. Historians have also attributed Mongol rule of China to the growth of a more autocratic style of rule by the Chinese emperors from the late fourteenth century, but this also had no parallel in Korea, where monarchs faced institutional restraints and had to contend with a powerful aristocracy.

Manjŏk's Slave Rebellion

In King Sinjong's first year [1198], the private slave Manjŏk and six others, while collecting firewood on a northern mountain, gathered public and private slaves and plotted, saying, "Since the coup in the year *kyŏngin* [1170] and the countercoup in the *kyesa* [1173], the country has witnessed many high officials rising from slave status. How could these generals and ministers be different from us in origins? If one has an opportunity, anybody can make it. Why should we still till and suffer under the whip?"

The slaves all agreed with this. They cut several thousand pieces of yellow paper and on each put the graph *chŏng* [adult man] as their symbol. They pledged: "We will start from the hallways of Hŭngguk Monastery and go to the polo grounds. Once all are assembled and start to beat drums and yell, the eunuchs in the palace will certainly respond. The public slaves will take control of the palace by force, and we will stage an uprising inside the capital, first killing Ch'oe Ch'unghŏn and others. If each slave will kill his master and burn the slave registers, there will be no people of humble status in the country, and we can all become nobles, generals, and ministers."

On the date set to meet, their numbers did not exceed several hundred, so they feared they would not succeed and changed their plans, promising to meet at Poje Temple this time. All were ordered: "If the affair is not kept secret, then we will not succeed. Be careful not to reveal it." Sunjŏng, the slave of Doctor of Legal Studies Han Ch'ungyu, reported this incident to his master. Ch'ungyu told Ch'oe Ch'unghŏn, who seized Manjŏk and more than one hundred others and threw them in the river. Ch'ungyu was promoted to the warder in the Royal Archives, and Sunjŏng was granted eighty *yang* of white gold and manumitted to commoner status. Since the remaining gang could not all be executed, the king decreed that the matter be dropped.

—from *Koryŏ sa*, 129:12–13a [16]

6

✠

The Neo-Confucian Revolution and the Chosŏn State, 1392 to the 18th Century

ESTABLISHING THE YI DYNASTY

Few events in Korea's premodern history are more important than the establishment of the Chosŏn state under the Yi dynasty. It was more than a change of dynasties; it was a long-term attempt to create a society in conformity to Confucian values and beliefs. The effort, while involving close study of Chinese models, contributed to the further evolution of a distinctive Korean cultural and political entity. Today when Koreans talk of "traditional society" they generally are referring to the culture and society that emerged during this period.

The dynastic founder, Yi Sŏng-gye, after deposing the last Koryŏ monarch, made himself king. He was posthumously designated King T'aejo, the first of the Yi dynasty that was to rule Korea to 1910. Yi Sŏng-gye placed his supporters, whom he named "Dynastic Foundation Merit Subjects," in key positions, and these men dominated Korea for the next few decades. They established the institutions of the new state and promoted the ideals of Neo-Confucianism. The new government officially named the state Chosŏn, so the period of Korean history from 1392 to 1910 is referred to as either the Chosŏn or the Yi dynasty period. To mark a new start for his new dynasty Yi Sŏng-gye and his supporters in 1394, believing the geomantic force of Kaesŏng was exhausted, established a new capital at Hanyang (today called Seoul). Careful consideration based on geomantic principles went into the selection. The city was protected on the north by mountains and on the south by the Han River. It was also a practical location, since it was in the agriculturally rich and centrally

127

located Kyŏnggi region. The location on the Han River, one of the major
rivers of Korea, assisted in communicating with the interior. The actual
construction of the city was largely left to King T'aejong (r. 1400–1418),
who in 1404 and again in 1412 summoned more than 100,000 corvée laborers to build the palaces, government buildings, city walls, and gates.
The city was modeled on Chinese imperial capitals, albeit on a smaller
scale, with the main streets laid on a north-south, east-west grid. Seoul
soon came to be the great city of Korea, the center of government, learning, the arts, and commerce—a place it has occupied ever since.

Yi Sŏng-gye justified the new dynasty with the concept of the Mandate
of Heaven (Chinese: *Tianming*; Korean: *chŏnmyŏng*). According to Yi and
his supporters, the last years of the Koryŏ saw rule by immoral men who
ruled through puppet kings. Confucian belief was that the ruler must
be a person of integrity and virtue who sets a moral example or else the
harmony between Heaven and Earth can not be maintained, there will
be calamities, and the people will become restless. This, according to Yi,
had happened in the years after Kongmin, when self-serving, evil officials ruled through weak monarchs. To further justify his assumption
of power, the dynastic founders argued that the legitimate line of Wang
kings had died out with Kongmin. In such a situation there was no re-
course but to assume the throne:

> The ancestral altar must surely be returned to the man of virtue and the great
> throne should not be left vacant too long. With merit and virtue, the public
> mind can be won. The ranks and offices [of government] should be correctly
> reestablished to pacify the people's discontent. I, lacking virtue, decline [the
> offer of the throne] repeatedly for fear that I may not be competent to carry
> the burden. Everyone is saying, however, that the Heavenly mandate has
> already been manifested in the popular will. No one should resist the public
> will. Nor should he go against Heaven. Holding this [principle] firmly, I have
> decided, with humility, to follow the public will and to accept the throne.[1]

The new dynasty carried out important reforms, most notably land
reform. Prior to his assumption of the throne Yi Sŏng-gye carried out
a comprehensive land survey, destroying old registrars of public and
private land. The court created a new set of land registrars with the intention of making sure that less land escaped taxation. The king confiscated the huge holdings of the Buddhist temples, a move that weakened
institutional Buddhism and that was enthusiastically embraced by the
anti-Buddhists among his followers. The former temple holdings were
redistributed to his supporters and added to the tax base.

The new dynasty was largely the creation of an alliance of military men
such as Yi and a group of scholar-officials eager to reform society by creating a new state based on Neo-Confucian principles. The most important

of these officials was Chŏng To-jŏn. Chŏng was from the Ch'ungch'ŏng region in southern Korea. His father was a government official from the lesser aristocracy. He was a descendant of a *hyangni* (local government official). A student of Neo-Confucian scholar Yi Saek, he was appointed to the National Confucian Academy faculty when Yi Saek became its head. Chŏng To-jŏn was driven into exile for pro-Ming sentiments by Yi In-im in 1375. After living in poverty in a small village he went to Yi Sŏng-gye's remote frontier camp and became his chief political advisor. When Yi came to power, Chŏng used his influence to secure key positions. As a civilian head of the armed forces command he worked toward abolishing private armies and creating a new central army under civilian control. His most important contribution was drawing up the *Statutes for the Governance of Chosŏn*, an outline for the new government.[2] Many of the institutions of the new dynasty were based on this outline.

A central part of Chŏng To-jŏn's program was land reform. In late Koryŏ most land was in the hands of large landholders. Most peasants worked as tenants paying a customary one-half their crops in rent. Based on the Confucian ideal that the ruler governed in the interests of the welfare of his people, as well as the practical need to bring more land under government taxation, he called for converting all land into public land. This would then be distributed equally among all the peasants, who would then pay a small portion in taxes. Chŏng To-jŏn cited the idealistic picture of Zhou China in the *Rites of Zhou*, which had become part of the Confucian canon, to justify this proposal. While too radical for adoption, it illustrates the idealistic zeal of Chŏng and many of his colleagues.

Chŏng and others wanted to end the relationship between Buddhism and the state. Late Koryŏ Neo-Confucianists such as Yi Saek had been critical of Buddhism. They chided monks for their moral laxity and their involvement in politics. The example of Sin Ton, who served as King Kongmin's chief advisor, was a case in point. Neo-Confucianist reformers were also critical of the expense of supporting temples and of elaborate rituals. Temples, they felt, owned too much land, reducing the tax base. Some officials of the new dynasty such as Chŏng To-jŏn regarded Buddhism as an undesirable alien faith. Buddhism, in their opinion, did not respect the social relations that held society together. Its tradition of celibacy was a threat to family and lineage, and its concept of abstract universal love was inimical to the graded love of Confucianism that gave primacy to family, then to friends, and then to neighbors. It encouraged withdrawal from society, not active participation in it. This harsh antipathy was not shared by Yi Sŏng-gye or by many of the members of court. It was a minority view at the start of the dynasty; however, it gradually prevailed. Consequently, Buddhism retreated from playing an active role in state affairs. There was some backsliding. King Sejo (r. 1455–1468), for example, was a vigorous patron of Buddhism, but the connection with Buddhism and the state was eventually broken.

Yi Sŏng-gye, nonetheless, emphasized continuity, not radical change. At the onset of his reign he ordered that all the rites of the Koryŏ be observed. Most Koryŏ officials were kept. Only a small number of them were purged, such as the distinguished scholar Chŏng Mong-ju, who, while supporting the movement for reform, remained loyal to the old dynasty. In general, the change of dynasty was relatively smooth and bloodless. One of the major issues in Korean history has been whether the establishment of the Yi dynasty marked a revolution or simply a change of dynasties. The answer may be that, while it was more than a simple change of dynasties, it was not quite a revolution. The new dynasty brought a number of new individuals and clans into the seats of power and restructured or newly created the institutions of government. Most of all, the promotion of Neo-Confucianism gave the new Chosŏn state a more rigid ideological orientation than had been the case in Koryŏ or Silla.

Many, if not most, of the great families that dominated late Koryŏ society survived into the new dynasty. Rather than a replacement of one dominant social group by another, a number of new people joined the ruling aristocracy of landed officials and scholars. Indeed, most of the Neo-Confucian reformers came from aristocratic families. Kwŏn Kŭn (1352–1409), one of the leading members of the new government, came from the Andong Kwŏn clan, one of the most illustrious families under the old dynasty.[3] Yi Sŏng-gye himself represented one of the small number of new men, mostly of a military background, who joined the old elite. The Yi family was originally from Chŏnju in southern Korea; later they moved to the northern frontier. Yi's father, Yi Cha-ch'un, rose to prominence during the Mongol period as a military commander and cooperated with Kongmin to retake the northeast region occupied by the Mongols. Yi Sŏng-gye, his second son, distinguished himself in campaigns against the Red Turbans, the Japanese pirates, and the Mongols. But while the dynastic family and some of its supporters were new members of the elite, most of officialdom came from the old aristocratic families.

Furthermore, the change of dynasty did not mean a sharp ideological change. Neo-Confucianism had already begun to gain adherents in late Koryŏ. Nor was Neo-Confucianism itself an entirely new way of thinking. To a large extent it was a revitalization of Confucian values and ideas of government and society that had long influenced Korean culture. One major change was the anti-Buddhism of the new dynasty. But as mentioned above, most Yi officials did not completely reject Buddhism, and it continued to have some hold on society; even many members of the royal family supported temples and consulted monks.

If the establishment of the Yi dynasty did not mark an immediate radical change, it nonetheless helped to set in motion a significant transformation in Korean society. Although Neo-Confucianism grew out of the long tradition of Confucian thought, it was revolutionary in its insistence that the state and society be structured according to the moral principles that governed the universe. While the initial changes were not revolutionary, eventually under the influence of Neo-Confucianism Korean society and culture went through profound changes. As a result of Neo-Confucianism, Korea under the new dynasty did see major changes in the family, the role of women, the conduct of the *yangban*, and art and literature. In the long run, then, what took place in Korea is sometimes called a Neo-Confucian Revolution. These changes, however, took place gradually over several centuries. Only by the eighteenth century did Korea become the model Confucian society that most modern Koreans see as "traditional." Therefore, the dynasty inaugurated profound change, but in a more evolutionary fashion. Indeed, one could argue that the continuity between early Chosŏn Korea and the Korea of Silla and Koryŏ is just as striking as the changes.

THE CHOSŎN STATE

At the apex of the Chosŏn state was the king. Under him was a complex set of bureaucratic institutions to carry out his rule. The highest organ of government was the *Ŭijŏngbu* (State Council).[4] It was similar to the Privy Council of Koryŏ except that it had fewer members, only seven. Members reviewed important matters then gave their opinion to the king. After receiving his decision the State Council then transmitted it down the bureaucracy. The State Council had general powers of surveillance over all government offices and affairs, which were known as *sŏsa*, general supervisory authority. The three highest-ranking members, the high state councilors, were especially important. The king frequently referred to them, and they often carried out public policy independently of the other members. No other position held as much prestige as being a high councilor, and they tended to hold their positions for long periods of time. The four junior members tended to have little influence and held positions for shorter periods. In the early days, merit subjects, people appointed to high office by the king in return for aiding him in some way, dominated high state councilor positions. Most State Council members, however, came up through the civil examination system. Gradually during the long Yi dynasty the State Council declined in importance.

The day-to-day administration was carried out by the *Yukcho* (Six Ministries): Personnel, Taxation, Rites, Military Affairs, Punishments, and Public Works. Personnel was in charge of nominations for office, certification of appointments, ranks, titles, evaluation of the performance of officeholders, and conducting special procedures for recruiting personnel. Taxation carried out censuses, maintained population registers, made land surveys and land registers, collected taxes, distributed funds, and maintained warehouses. Rites handled foreign relations, supervised the schools and examinations, licensed monks, and supervised state ceremonies. War included the supervision of post roads, beacon fire communication systems, fortifications, and weapons production. Punishments was the judicial branch of government, in charge of both civil and criminal cases. Works dealt with construction and repair of public buildings, bridges, roads, state mining and lumbering operations, and the production of articles for state use by the corps of state artisans. Each ministry was headed by a board consisting of three or four ministers. Their direct access to the king made the ministers important.

Another important institution was the *Sŭngjŏngwŏn* (Royal Secretariat), an organ that transmitted documents to and from the king. At times it acted on its own without regard to other government bodies. There were six members, each in charge of dealing with one of the Six Ministries. Two recorders in the Royal Secretariat kept diaries of daily activities; their careful recordings were one of the sources for the *Sillok*, the official record of the reign (see below). These institutions were modeled on those of China but fit the Korean pattern of rule by councils or committees of aristocrats.

There were eight provinces, which are still the provinces of Korea today: Kyŏnggi, Ch'ungch'ŏng, Kyŏngsang, Chŏlla, Hwanghae, Kangwŏn, Hamgil (today called Hamgyŏng), and P'yŏngan. Each had a centrally appointed governor and six government departments based on those of the central government. The provinces were divided into counties of which there were several types. The number of counties varied somewhat, but were around 300. Each was headed by a centrally appointed county magistrate. The county magistrate was an important figure who represented the state at the local level. Each county also had a *Hyangch'ŏng* (Local Agency) organized by *yangban* residents, which wielded considerable influence. The Local Agency was directed by a *chwasu* (overseer) and his assistants and undertook responsibilities for assisting the magistrate, rectifying public morals, and scrutinizing the conduct of the county's petty functionaries, called *hyangni*. The Local Agency served as a power base for the local *yangban*. To counter the power of the local elite, a *Kyŏngjaeso* (Capital Liaison Office) existed in Seoul for each county, headed by central government officials from that county, to see that the Local Agency served the central state's, not local, interests.

The Yi rulers maintained the basic classification of officials into the *yangban* (two sides) consisting of *munban* (civil officials) and the less prestigious *muban* (military officials). The tradition of discrimination against military officials resumed and became more pronounced in the later years of the dynasty. Officials as in Koryŏ were graded into nine ranks, a practice developed in China a millennium earlier. Each rank was subdivided into senior and junior ranks such as senior first rank and junior first rank to make a total of eighteen grades of officials. The most elite of the officials were those of senior third rank and above, known as the *tangsanggwan*. Strict protocol and sumptuary laws governed the behavior and respect given to each rank.

THE CENSORATE AND THE CLASSICS MAT

One of the important institutions of Korea was the censorate, an institution with no exact counterpart in Western institutional history. Although borrowed from China, the censorate in Korea had far more power. The censorate existed in the Koryŏ period, when it was known as the *Ŏsadae*. It played a greater role during the Yi dynasty. Under the Yi the censorate was known as the *Samsa*, or three institutions. The two chief institutions that made up the censorate were: the *Sahŏnbu* (Office of Inspector-General) with six members, which dealt with political issues, official conduct, and public morals, and the *Saganwŏn* (Censor-General), which scrutinized and criticized the conduct of the king. A third institution, the *Hongmun'gwan* (Office of Special Advisors), was created in 1478. Its members maintained books in the royal library, composed royal epitaphs and eulogies, and compiled state-sponsored texts. It also served as a panel of advisors to the king on policy and principle, and gave lessons on history and the orthodox Chinese writers. The *Hongmun'gwan* had seventeen members, mostly younger officials.

The censoring organs were the moral guardians or moral police of the state. They had the unique right to investigate the backgrounds of all those who were appointed to office to find out if they were morally fit to serve or if they had the proper aristocratic background. They also saw to it that no one with dishonorable or disloyal ancestors would serve the state. They reviewed the actions of officials and of the king himself and issued moral condemnations for improper conduct. Since good Confucians made no distinction between private and public conduct, the censors carefully scrutinized the private as well as public lives of officials. They also reviewed the behavior of the general public and issued ethical guidelines. Most officials served as censors for only short periods, yet

while in office, censors, often quite young, frequently carried out their responsibilities with persistence and zeal. At times the censorate was used
as a base for power by ambitious individuals and factions. Since most
censors were well schooled in the tenets of Neo-Confucianism and were
firm adherents of them, the organs acted as one of the institutional bases
for the great undertaking of making Korea a model Confucian society.

Another base for Neo-Confucian reformist zeal was the Classics Mat
(*Kyŏngyŏn*). Modeled on the Song China *jingyan* advocated by the Neo-
Confucianist thinkers Cheng Yi (1033–1108) and Zhu Xi, the Classics Mat
was instituted as a lecture program that in 1392 was organized with a
staff of twenty-one. Although the first three Yi kings seldom attended,
the fifteenth-century king Sejong attended daily. Later in the fifteenth
century it met three times a day. Censors, historians, and a royal secretary
attended. Since members of the censorate often supplied and conducted
the lessons, the Classics Mat contributed to an increase in the power of
censorial organs. At these sessions the reader would read and lead a
discussion of the Confucian classics and commentaries on the classics by
such luminaries as Zhu Xi. To further edify the monarch, historical works
were included in addition to the Neo-Confucian texts. Readers could
digress from texts to discuss implications for current affairs. The Classics
Mat was designed to guide the monarch, and it served as an agency for
promoting Neo-Confucian concepts at court.

HISTORIANS

Another feature of the Yi dynasty was the significant role of the state
historians. They too promoted Neo-Confucian ideals. The monarchs and
officials of the Yi dynasty took history seriously as a guide to statecraft.
Three high state councilors supervised the *Ch'unch'ugwan* (Bureau of
State Records), the official government archives. Daily records were kept
by officials from the *Yemun'gwan* (Office of Royal Decrees). Low-ranking
posts were usually held by young bureaucrats who held great prestige
despite their age. Due to their importance, a careful and elaborate procedure took place for selecting them. They were to be free of vested interests
and it was thought that their youthful idealism would keep "their brushes
straight."[5] Careful daily records of all proceedings at court were kept.
Historians followed the king and recorded both his conversations with
officials and his facial expressions as well. No official business could be
transacted without their presence. The records were not made available to
the king. In contrast to Ming China, where the first Ming emperor insisted
on seeing what had been recorded, similar requests from Yi monarchs
were denied. At the end of each reign the *Sillok* (*Veritable Records*) was
compiled. This was a multivolume, detailed account of each reign.

Chosŏn-era Koreans regarded history and the role of the historian as matters of great importance. As good Confucian scholars, they viewed history as an indispensable source of guidance for those that governed and as a source of moral tales providing examples of virtue and vice that would instruct all who read it. Since history was valuable for instruction for both governance and morality, historical works were included in the Classics Mat. Through their writing of history, Yi dynasty historians promoted the ideals and principles of Neo-Confucianism. Because of history's vital role in governance, great efforts were made to preserve the historical records. Four copies of the daily record of proceedings at court were kept, one in Seoul, and one each in the provincial cities of Sŏngju, Ch'ungju, and Chŏnju. This precaution served the dynasty well when the Japanese invasions destroyed all but the Chŏnju archives. The government then had all records copied and established new archives at remote islands and mountains.

To understand the past in order to guide them in their endeavor to create a moral society, scholars at the beginning of the dynasty began the work of compiling an official history of the Koryŏ. The *Koryŏ sa* (*History of Koryŏ*), after going through several versions, was completed in 1451. It reflected the Confucian commitments of its authors, who neglected to give any special attention to Buddhism. Furthermore it justified the establishment of the new dynasty by painting the later years of the Koryŏ as a time of decline when the dynasty had lost its mandate from heaven. Today it is the primary source for the Koryŏ period. In 1452, the *Koryŏ sa chŏryo* (*Abridged Essence of the Three Kingdoms*), a shorter official history in the *p'yŏnnyŏn* (annalistic format), was independently compiled. It contains information not found in the *Koryŏ sa*. Several other officially sponsored histories were compiled during the early Yi. One of the most significant is the *Tongguk t'onggam* (*Comprehensive Mirror of the Eastern Kingdom*), compiled by Sŏ Kŏ-jŏng (1420–1488) in 1485. This covered all of Korean history from Tan'gun to the fall of the Koryŏ, and was possibly the most widely read history in the Chosŏn dynasty period. Another important work was Han Paek-kyŏm's (1552–1615) *Tongguk chiri chi* (*Treatise on Historical Geography*). Han's history influenced later historiography with his theories on the origins of the Three Kingdoms and the location of the three Han tribes.

THE EXAMINATION SYSTEM

Most officials in Chosŏn Korea were selected through the examination system. Since serving in office was the most prestigious occupation as well as a vital way to protect a family's interest, it became the goal of most ambitious families to have a son who passed the exams. In a society where no other culturally sanctioned avenue to power and prestige existed, the exam system was of enormous importance. While education was recognized as an end in itself, in practice, it was also understood to be a means of social mobility and status selection. Potential office seekers had to go through a series of highly competitive examinations. These civil examinations were divided into the lower-level *sokwa* or *sama* exams, where a student could choose to take either the *saengwŏn* (classics licentiate) or the *chinsa* (literary licentiate) exam. The passage of these exams did not secure an official post, but it did bring certain privileges, such as eligibility for government office and exemption from military duties. Most importantly it qualified its successful passers for the higher civil exam called the *taekwa* or *munkwa*, which was the real vehicle to high government office.

The lower-level *sama* or *sokwa* exams began at the provincial level. First, hopefuls took the *ch'osi*, or preliminary, exam at their province's capital. Those who succeeded in these provincial exams could take the metropolitan exam in Seoul. To insure representation from all parts of the country a quota was established for the number of candidates from each province and from Seoul. Those selecting the classics exam wrote two essays. In the first they explicated the meaning of a short passage that was given from one of the Five Classics of ancient China: *The Classic of Changes, The Classic of History, The Classic of Songs, The Spring and Autumn Annals,* and the *Classic of Rituals.* For the second essay they wrote on the issues involved in several passages given from the Four Books, the most revered works of Confucianism: The *Analects* of Confucius, *The Book of Mencius, The Great Learning,* and *The Doctrine of the Mean.* Those who chose the literary exam were required to compose one *pu* (rhyme-prose) and one old-style poem, each based on a topic and rhyme given at the examination. A candidate could sit for both exams. Passing both brought great honor. Successful examinees received a white diploma presented by the king. This degree enabled the recipient to enroll in the National Academy in Seoul and to sit for the higher-level civil examinations. It generally did not result in an appointment for office. Since the Yi dynasty, holding a degree was important to confirm social status; for many this was enough, and they returned home to play prominent roles in their local communities.

The higher-level exam, the *taekwa* or *munkwa*, was the real gateway to public office holding. Passing the higher civil examination was not easy, and most lower-exam passers never succeeded. There was no limit to how often one could take the exam, and some persistent candidates took it many times, well into old age. There were three stages to this exam. The first was a preliminary provincial-level exam. In taking the classics exam one had to write an essay on the Five Classics and the Four Books and another essay on an assigned topic. For the literary exam candidates had to compose a formal memorial or report and a dissertation on an assigned topic. The second stage was the metropolitan exam in Seoul. The third stage was the *chŏnsi* (palace exam), taken under the supervision of the king. The top thirty-three examinees received the coveted *munkwa*. All exams were triennial and were held throughout the dynasty until they were abolished in 1894, with the exception of 1594 and 1597 during the Japanese invasions and 1636 during the Manchu invasions. In addition to the triennial exams special exams were held from time to time. This practice of holding special exams became more common during the late Yi period.

Although, as historian Ch'oe Yong-ho has pointed out, a few men of commoner status may have been allowed to take the exams in the early years of the dynasty, they served chiefly to allocate official positions among members of the *yangban* aristocratic elite. The examination system acted as the main selection device for the limited number of government posts. Formal education was largely organized around preparation for the exams. Another feature of education and the examination system during this period is the incongruity between the ideal of meritocracy implied by the system and the reality of a society that emphasized bloodlines and kinship. For while in many ways Korea became the Confucian society par excellence, it was dominated by a hereditary aristocratic elite. The Neo-Confucianism that developed in Song China and that became the reigning orthodoxy in Korea in the fourteenth century had a strong egalitarian streak that emphasized the perfectibility of all men. It assumed that each individual was capable of benefiting from education and of achieving moral enlightenment. Neo-Confucianism emphasized the need for society to be governed by men of talent and virtue, which could best be demonstrated by mastery of the classics, self-discipline, and personal conduct. In conformity with this ideology, the schools and the civil examinations were opened to all except outcaste groups (see chapter 7), but in reality a number of practices arose that limited access to both state schools and the exams. In addition, preparation for the examinations required many years of study. Those parents who could afford to finance lengthy studies and hire tutors had an enormous advantage. And as studies have shown, Korean society was one where family lines, along with rank and hierarchy, were of vital importance. In reality, therefore, the examination system and the schools associated with it primarily served as a means of allocating power, privilege, and status, all closely associated with office holding, among members of the *yangban* aristocracy.

Unlike in China there were no exam halls in Korea. All exams were conducted in the open. A fence would be put up around an area and candidates would have to take the exams with no protection from the elements. Many complained of enduring rain and snow. In the eighteenth century some examinees began to set up tents. Cheating was always a problem. Common forms of cheating were having someone take the exam for a candidate and collusion between the examinees. Bribery and nepotism were also a problem. Others cheated by smuggling notes written on thin paper and stuffing them up their nostrils, which led to the slang term "wisdom storage" for nostrils.[6]

The degree holders formed an important elite. Because of the law of avoidance, another Chinese practice, officials could not serve in their home localities. This meant that the local country magistrates and other local officials were usually not familiar with the area they administered. Degree holders living in the community were able to advise the official on local conditions. Degree holders also formed organizations such as *samaso* that acted as both social organizations and local pressure groups. Since taking the exams was such an intense experience, those who took and passed the same examinations often formed *tongnyŏnhoe* (classmate organizations) whose members met at regular reunions.[7]

Not all officials were recruited through civil examinations. Some came to office through the *ch'ŏn'gŏ* (recommendation system). Senior civil and military officials of the third rank and above submitted lists of three worthy men every third year to the Ministry of Personnel. If the ministry approved, the men could be appointed to office. Appointment was not automatic, and the candidate would be tested on one book of the candidate's choice from the Four Books and the Five Classics. Provincial governors, too, would sometimes recommend local men for submission to the Ministry of Personnel as candidates to be examined. The total number of officials appointed this way was not large, and it never rivaled the use of civil examinations as a way of recruiting the men who administered the state. Nonetheless, the recommendation system had its supporters among the elite. The recommendation system appointees were called *yuil* (people of merit and integrity). The practice went back as early as Han China and was used during the Koryŏ. It was based on the same Confucian principle of government by men of merit as the civil examinations. Many scholars and officials regarded the examinations as an inadequate or incomplete method of selecting worthy individuals. Recommendations were seen as a way to find such worthies who had been overlooked by the exams. Some scholars, such as Cho Kwang-jo (1482–1519) in the sixteenth century, wanted to abolish the examination system and rely exclusively on recommendations.[8] Despite its champions, the recommendation system was strictly of secondary importance as a method of recruiting officials. In general *yuil* possessed less prestige than the exam passers and held only low-ranking posts. Another method of securing an office was through purchase. This practice, called *napsok pogwan* (appointment through grain contributions), was usually done during emergencies. This was a method of the state to raise money; often it meant only that a prestigious rank or office was purchased, not an actual appointment to office. Many ranks and offices were sold this way during the Japanese invasions of the late sixteenth century, but at most times it was not common.

EDUCATION

Education in traditional Korea was valued as a means of personal self-cultivation and as a way of achieving status and power. An individual could become virtuous through the study of ethically oriented Confucian classics. He could go on to play an informal role as a moral exemplar and as a teacher and advisor to others, thus enhancing his status and influence in society. As in other East Asian societies, Koreans highly esteemed the written word and the prodigious efforts needed to master the accumulated body of literary and scholarly works. Furthermore, the examination system reinforced the importance of learning.

In order to have a supply of educated men from which to select officials, the early Yi dynasty leadership established a fairly comprehensive network of schools. These schools were seen as a means of establishing loyalty, maintaining orthodoxy, and recruiting officials. Basic education was provided for by village schools known as *sŏjae* or *sŏdang* and by private tutoring. The *sŏdang* remained the most common institution of formal education in Korea until well into the twentieth century. At a more advanced level, a system of *hyanggyo* (state-sponsored local schools) existed to prepare students for the civil examinations. These included the *sahak*, four schools organized in four of the five districts of Seoul, and schools established in each of the provinces. The *sahak* in Seoul accepted 160 and later just 100 students in each of its schools. There were over 300 *hyanggyo* (the figure varied somewhat over time) throughout the countryside. The state fixed the number of students assigned to each of these schools in the fifteenth century, ranging from thirty to ninety. Students entered at around the age of sixteen and at about the age of eighteen or nineteen were allowed to sit for the lower-level civil exams. Admittance to a *hyanggyo* brought with it the coveted status of *yuhak*, which included exemption from military duty and eligibility for taking the civil service exams. At the pinnacle of Chosŏn education were those who passed the *sama* (lower-level examinations) and entered the *Sŏnggyun'gwan* (National Confucian Academy). These students were generally eighteen or nineteen years old when admitted. Sometime between the ages of twenty and twenty-three they would compete for the *munkwa*, the higher civil service examination.

The basic structure of Chosŏn schooling was set up in the early fifteenth century; however, there were significant changes during subsequent centuries. The official schools experienced a gradual decline. Although they continued to function until the end of the nineteenth century, their role as agents of advanced schooling was challenged by the *sŏwŏn* or private academies that emerged in the middle of the sixteenth century. Unlike the *hyanggyo*, which were usually located in administrative centers, the *sŏwŏn* sprang up in the countryside. They functioned as rural retreats for the literati and as shrines to honor scholars and officials as well as centers of learning. About 680 *sŏwŏn* were founded by the end of the eighteenth century, and they served as important bases for political factions until most of them were closed in the decade after 1864.

Education trained the cultivated generalist. There was disdain for the specialist and for technical training that prevailed into recent times. Although *chapkwa*, specialized technical exams, existed for certifying doctors, astronomers, interpreters, and other needed professionals, they remained far less prestigious; education was basically of a nonspecialized, literary nature, which has remained the preference of most Koreans. The people who took the specialized exams were largely from the *chungin* class, not the *yangban* aristocracy (see chapter 7).

Literacy in Korea among males was probably high by premodern standards, and most likely increased in the eighteenth and nineteenth centuries. An indication of this is the growth in private academies that promoted education among the *yangban* class. But even commoner boys attended village schools where an ability to read basic moral texts was considered essential to being a good husband, father, and neighbor. In addition, literacy no doubt brought about advantages in legal disputes and enabled individuals to keep informed of government regulations. Literacy among commoners was facilitated by the use of the Korean alphabet, *han'gŭl* (see below). There was also a thriving popular literature of adventure stories and romances, an indicator of high rates of literacy. For commoners schooling was confined to *sŏdang* village schools. These consisted of a teacher and boys of different ages, often quite young. The *sŏdang* became a feature of Korean village life. Literacy among females was very low and largely confined to a small number of elite women; some of these, however, were highly educated by private tutors. Another exception was the *kisaeng*, the refined female entertainers (see chapter 7).

The scholar-teacher held an exalted position. Since organized religion was peripheral to Chosŏn society, it was the school and the teacher, rather than the temple and the priest, that served as the principal source of ethical counsel. Consequently, the scholar obtained an almost sacred status. The learned man was more than a scholar or teacher: he was the moral arbiter of society and source of guidance at the village as well as the state level. Thus, the value placed on learning and the position of the teacher in society were extremely high. Teachers, scholars, and earnest students were vested with considerable moral authority. This was the basis for the tradition of remonstrance, the right to issue formal protests based on ethical principles. It was the duty of the scholar to criticize the actions of the government, including the king; since Confucianism perceived the universe as a moral order, improper behavior on the part of officials and rulers threatened that order. Scholars and lower-ranked officials wrote memorials, and students at the *Sŏnggyun'gwan* held protest demonstrations when they felt that those in positions of authority were not adhering to ethical standards or were improperly performing rituals. Students in the Academy periodically withdrew from school in mass protests, with nineteen such incidents recorded in the reign of King Sukchong (r. 1674–1720) and twenty in the reign of King Sunjo (r. 1800–1834).[9] This tradition of equating education and scholarship with moral authority, hence giving students and scholars the right and duty to criticize officialdom, has been one of the most persistent features of Korean education. It is a tradition still felt in Korea today.

AGRICULTURAL IMPROVEMENTS AND THE STATE

The Chosŏn state was based on an agricultural society. The prosperity of the state was a result of the improvements in farming that eventually resulted in an increase in the population. Since the bulk of the population consisted of peasants and it was they who paid most of the taxes and provided most of the labor, the state was vitally concerned with agriculture. New farming methods developed during the Song period in the Yangzi River valley and in southern China known as the "Jiangnan Farming Techniques." These involved improved strains of rice, intercropping, and the use of wet field rice production in which rice was planted and then transplanted in shallow flooded paddies. Wet field farming allowed for repeated cultivation of the same field. Korea's climate, colder and drier than the southern Chinese regions, hindered the spread of these techniques, but in the middle of the fourteenth century the new methods of transplanting rice were beginning to be practiced in Korea. It was not until the seventeenth century that this more intensive style of agriculture became dominant in the southern part of the country. However, it was already increasing the ability of the southern provinces Chŏlla and Kyŏngsang to increase production and support denser populations in the early Chosŏn dynasty.

A number of other improvements in farming occurred. Farmers were beginning to make greater use of fertilizers; that meant less time letting the land remain fallow. Under local government supervision hundreds of small reservoirs were constructed to minimize the impact of drought, and better strains of seed came into use. Interest in agricultural improvements by the elite is reflected in the appearance of agricultural manuals. Koreans had long been familiar with Chinese agricultural manuals; now they produced their own, adapted to local conditions. The first known agricultural manual, *Nongsa chiksŏl* (*Straight Talk on Farming*), was compiled in 1430. It was followed by other published works on farming. New land was brought under cultivation. According to the national land-tax records the amount of arable land, which totaled about 930,000 *kyŏl* at the beginning of the fifteenth century, had reached 1,700,000 *kyŏl* by the middle of the sixteenth.[10] These records are notoriously unreliable and much of the land went unreported to evade taxation, but they do suggest that a considerable expansion of agriculture occurred during the early Chosŏn dynasty.

MILITARY AND FOREIGN AFFAIRS

With potentially dangerous tribal peoples to the north and Japanese raiders on the coast, the Yi rulers were aware of the need for a strong military. Indeed, the dynasty was founded by a general. One of the first challenges of the early monarchs was to create an effective central army. With this in mind, T'aejo, the first Yi king, established the *Ŭihŭng Samgunbu* (Three Armies Headquarters) to provide central control over the military. In the early years of the dynasty, members of the royal family maintained personal armed retainers. King T'aejong (1400–1418) abolished these private forces, bringing all soldiers under the authority of the Three Armies Headquarters. The era of private armies came to an end in Korea. Only the central state now had military forces. Sejo, in 1464, reorganized the army into the *Owi Toch'ongbu* (Five Military Commands Headquarters). The five commands were named after the regions of the country where they were stationed: Center, West, East, North, and South. The divisions were divided into five *pu* (brigades), which consisted of four *t'ong* (regiments), and these in turn were divided into *yŏ* (companies) and *tae* (platoons). Professional soldiers had to pass a series of tests, and these soldiers were supplemented by *chŏngbyŏng* (conscripts) in the capital garrisons. Beyond this were the provincial armies. Each province had an Army Command and Navy Command with control of provincial garrison forces called *chinsugun* stationed in *chin* (garrisons). Under this *chin'gwan* system district magistrates would assume defense of their own walled towns. Peasants were assigned as garrison forces serving on a rotation basis.

In the fifteenth century Korea maintained a policy of military vigor. But with the frontiers secured (see below), the army and navy went into a decline. The rise of Neo-Confucianism also contributed to this decline. Confucian officials tended to take less interest in military affairs and viewed military men with contempt. *Yangban* avoided the military, while soldiers were recruited primarily from the peasantry and treated poorly. Since few volunteered, the state supplied the armed forces with men through the *popŏp* (Paired Provisioner) system. A team of two or three able-bodied men was supported while on active service by the provisioners, who supplied the conscripted soldiers with fixed amounts of cotton cloth. They were similarly supported when their turn to serve came up. This system was unpopular and ineffective. Conscripts under the Paired Provisioner system were poorly trained and had low morale. Peasants evaded service whenever they could. The decline in the military forces led to the disastrous defeats when the Japanese invaded in the late sixteenth century and the Manchus invaded in the early seventeenth.

Early Chosŏn foreign policy centered around securing its legitimacy, establishing correct relations with China, and securing its borders from the threats of its tribal neighbors on the Manchurian border and from Japanese pirates along the southern coasts. Establishing friendly relations with Ming China was a central component of the new political and social order established by the founders of the Chosŏn dynasty. Yet relations remained tense between the Ming and the Chosŏn courts during the first years of the Chosŏn. The Chinese looked at Korean attempts to establish their borders at the Yalu and Tumen rivers with great suspicion. Memories of Koguryŏ and Parhae control over Manchuria mixed with fears of a Korean-Jurchen alliance. Several embassies were turned back on various excuses, such as that the horses sent as tribute were unfit. To mollify the Chinese, members of the royal family such as Prince Pangwŏn were sent to the Ming court at Nanjing as hostages. The Yi officials wanted good relations with China for ideological as well as practical reasons. China was the home of the sages, of Confucius, Zhu Xi, and of civilization. The Yi kings sought Chinese recognition as a way of legitimizing themselves as bearers of civilized values. Ming suspicions soon waned and relations improved in the early fifteenth century.

The Chosŏn court operated in a hierarchical world order. Its external relations were a matter of placing foreigners in that hierarchy and treating them accordingly. At the top of the hierarchy was Ming China, with which it maintained friendly relations in China's tributary system. The first Ming emperor limited Korean tribute missions to once every three years, but these later became annual and then three times a year. The court dispatched regular embassies to Beijing at New Year's, the emperor's birthday, the birthday of the crown prince, and the winter solstice. It also sent special embassies when an emperor died or when a new Korean king was enthroned. Technically these were tributary missions in which the Korean king offered tribute to the Chinese embassies, but in reality they were opportunities for both sides to engage in trade.

Koreans traded horses; furs; cloth; and above all, prized Korean ginseng and imported silk, medicines, books, and Chinese porcelains. These embassies also served as opportunities for Korean scholars to collect books, meet with their Chinese counterparts, and keep abreast of cultural trends in China by attaching themselves to the embassies. Korean kings claimed legitimacy by being enfeoffed by the Chinese emperors. The Chinese emperors, by confirming the right of Korean kings to rule, ensured peaceful relations with Korea and reinforced their own pretensions to being universal rulers. Koreans were generally well regarded in China for their scholarship and adherence to Confucian cultural norms, and Korean officials were usually seated closest to the Chinese officials at diplomatic functions, indicating the high rank of Korea in the Chinese world order.

This did not mean that relations were always free from problems. Ming officials were sometimes suspicious of Korea's attempts to establish friendly relations with the Jurchen tribes of Manchuria. Disputes arose over official Chinese histories. In one it was reported that Yi Sŏng-gye had murdered the last four Koryŏ monarchs, confusing him with Yi In-im. Korea sent an embassy to the Ming capital of Nanjing to ask that the correction be made. Yet the mistake continued to pop up in Chinese records. From time to time other incidents arose between Seoul and Beijing when the Koreans became offended at what they thought were erroneous and unflattering accounts of Yi kings in the Chinese records.

Early Chosŏn kings gave considerable attention to pacifying the nomads along their northern border. The principal threat came from the Manchurian Jurchen tribes. Yi Sŏng-gye, himself a skilled horseman and archer, had extensive experience fighting Manchuria-based warriors, including the Red Turbans, who invaded in 1361. He began a policy that was pursued with some success by T'aejong (1400–1418) and Sejong (1418–1450) in using a threefold approach of launching vigorous military campaigns against the Jurchens, encouraging them to trade peacefully, and seeking to "civilize" them. The Koreans did this by opening trading posts where the tribal people could peacefully exchange their horses and furs for agricultural products and manufactured goods. Borrowing from an old Chinese practice, the Chosŏn court rewarded tribal leaders with degrees and titles. One tribal leader, Yi Chi-ran, was awarded the highest honor of Merit Subject. Some Jurchen were enrolled in the Korean military, including the Royal Palace Guard. Tribal people living along the border were encouraged to marry Korean women and adopt Korean customs. Some of the tribal peoples did so and became assimilated into Korean society.

Nonetheless, tribal unrest still occurred. King Sejong launched more military campaigns, built six forts along the Tumen River, and carried out a resettlement policy. Sejong established the borders of Korea along the

Yalu and Tumen rivers, approximately where they have remained to the present day. To make sure these new borderlands became a permanent part of Korea, he colonized them between 1431 and 1447 with thousands of Koreans, mostly from the heavily populated southern provinces. This action largely fixed the northern borders of the kingdom, and these areas have been an integral part of Korea ever since. Despite these efforts the rugged, mountainous northeastern region that made up Hamgyŏng Province remained for generations a frontier at the periphery of central government control. In 1453, the area's military commander, Yi Ching-ok, revolted against the government in Seoul with the support of some Jurchen tribes, declaring himself king of a new dynasty. The royal forces put down the revolt, but another sprang up in 1467 led by a local official, Yi Si-ae, who attempted to gain Jurchen support. This too was suppressed by dynastic forces.

Japanese pirates posed another problem. The increased frequency of *wako* raids in the fourteenth century contributed to the troubles of the last Koryŏ kings. Japanese pirate raids started becoming common in the thirteenth century; after 1350 they increased in frequency and scale. Some consisted of more than 300 ships and penetrated deep inland where they looted and abducted thousands of Koreans to be sold as slaves. Koryŏ tried to negotiate with the government of the shogun in Kyoto, sending a mission as early as 1367. The weak central government of Japan, however, had little control over the western region of the country where local feudal lords found the raids highly lucrative. A successful military expedition against the pirate base of Tsushima in 1389 brought only temporary relief.[11] The early Chosŏn rulers applied a policy of military raids against pirate bases coupled with attempts to persuade pirates to trade peacefully.

Particularly troublesome was the island of Tsushima across the Korea Straits, whose feudal lords were among the principal sponsors of pirate raids. In 1419, the Koreans launched a massive attack with 250 ships to destroy that base. Shortly afterward the Japanese shogun Yoshimitsu offered to suppress pirates in exchange for a copy of the *Korean Tripitaka*. The Yi government then presented him the Buddhist collection in over 6,000 volumes. But the central government of Japan maintained little control over the lords in the western part of the country. In 1443, Seoul established an agreement that allowed Japanese merchants to trade at several authorized ports along the southern coasts. This proved profitable enough for the rulers of western Japan that they no longer encouraged pirate raids. The ports were temporarily closed in 1510 when Japanese residents in the ports rioted and again in 1544 following a pirate raid.[12] Thus the Koreans eventually adopted an effective carrot-and-stick policy toward the Japanese similar to that used to control the Jurchens. This kept the coasts mostly peaceful until the end of the sixteenth century.

Besides the relations with China, Japan, and the northern tribal peoples, Korea maintained trade and contact with other Asian lands. Active trade and diplomacy existed with Okinawa (Ryukyu Islands), which until 1609 was an independent state. An embassy was sent to Thailand in 1393, and envoys from Java arrived in Korea in 1397.[13] There were some Korean merchants in Okinawa and in Southeast Asia. However, trade with Southeast Asia was generally carried out indirectly through Ryukyuan and Japanese merchants in the fifteenth and sixteenth centuries. Thus Korea participated in a wider Asian world of trade and contact beyond East Asia, but only peripherally. Korea had no direct contact with Europe before the seventeenth century. The first European known to visit Korea was a Jesuit priest, Gregorio de Cespedes, who arrived in 1597 in the company of Japanese invaders.

THE JAPANESE AND MANCHU INVASIONS

After a century and a half of peaceful relations with its neighbors Korea suffered from a destructive series of invasions. The first, and most devastating, came from the Japanese. In Japan, a bloody struggle for power among feudal lords temporarily ended when a powerful warlord, Toyotomi Hideyoshi (1536–1598), unified the country. Hideyoshi then launched an invasion of Korea with the intention of using the peninsula as a base to conquer China. It is unclear if he was motivated by megalomania or a desire to direct the energies of warriors harmlessly abroad. Or perhaps the invasion of Korea was merely a continuation of his drive to extend his power, the next step after he had brought the autonomous domains of western Japan under his control. Hideyoshi assembled a quarter of a million men for what was probably the largest overseas invasion in history before the twentieth century. Korean officials received rumors of preparations for an invasion by 1591, but debated among themselves over the reality of the threat and only made some inadequate efforts to strengthen their defenses. When the initial contingent of 52,000 troops landed in Pusan on May 23, 1592 (by the solar calendar), they overran the coastal fortifications that were defended to the death by the local commander. The Japanese forces then advanced quickly up the peninsula. Their foot soldiers were armed and well trained in musketry, which they used to great effect. One unit of Japanese would fire volleys of muskets into the Korean forces, overwhelming them with musket power, while other units would attack with swords on the right and left flanks, decapitating as many as they could. Korean troops, who would defend themselves by massing together, were then slaughtered in great numbers. So effective were Japanese tactics that three weeks after the start of the invasion the Japanese captured Seoul and then pushed north.

The Chosŏn court fled ahead of the enemy advance, abandoning the defense of the capital to slaves and commoners. Disgusted onlookers jeered and even threw stones at the royal entourage as it made its way to Ŭiju on the Chinese frontier. Slaves in Seoul took advantage of the chaos to burn palaces and offices and to destroy the registers that documented their status. After a pause for regrouping and supplying their forces, the Japanese under General Konishi Yukinaga captured P'yŏngyang on July 23. A second wing under General Katō Kiyomasa and General Nabeshima Naoshige advanced northeast to the Yalu and Tumen rivers. The Korean army disintegrated under this massive and well-organized invasion. In desperation the Koreans appealed to China for help. The Chinese, fearful of this new threat from the east, responded with assistance. Led by General Li Rusong, himself of Korean descent, the Ming forces entered in January 1593 and defeated Konishi in battle at P'yŏngyang in February. The Chinese then advanced south, but did so too fast and were halted. Then the war began to stalemate in a way similar to the later Korean War.

Unlike the Korean War where Koreans fought on both sides, Koreans were united in their resistance to Japan, and after a poor initial showing they resisted more effectively. Peasants often fiercely fought to defend their villages from these strange, dangerous outsiders. Local *yangban*, monks, and others formed resistance bands called *ŭibyŏng* ("righteous armies"). Among the more effective groups were ones led by Cho Hŏn in Ch'ungch'ŏng province in south-central Korea, Kwak Chae-u in the southeastern province of Kyŏngsang, and Kwŏn Yul in the southwestern province of Chŏlla. While most were defeated, they made the Japanese position difficult, and along with the pressure from the Chinese forces they forced Hideyoshi's troops to withdraw to the southern coastal areas. Especially successful was Admiral Yi Sun-sin (1545–1598), who waged a naval campaign that destroyed hundreds of Japanese ships and made supplying and reinforcing Japanese troops costly. Yi came from a family of civil officials but chose to take the military rather than the civil examinations. He served as an officer along the northern frontier and later in Chŏlla. Alarmed by the reports of a possible invasion, he launched a last-minute shipbuilding effort. Yi experimented with new weapons and tactics. His most ingenious innovation was the *kŏbuksŏn* ("turtle ship"), an ironclad ship designed to withstand Japanese cannon fire and to ram and sink its opponents' vessels. These were the world's first ironclad ships. The turtle ships proved to be highly effective. The first ship was completed just days before the Japanese landed. Yi with the help of his turtle ships led an effective naval campaign that prevented the Japanese from using the western coastal route to transport supplies and reinforcements to their army in the north of Korea, making resupplying their army in Korea from Japan hazardous.

With the war stalemated by 1594, the Chinese withdrew their forces to Manchuria and the Japanese to the southern coastal ports. A period of diplomacy began. Chinese diplomats came to Japan, but the negotiations revealed how little the Chinese and Japanese knew each other. The Chinese were willing to recognize Hideyoshi as the "king" of Japan and allow the Japanese to enter the Chinese tributary system. Hideyoshi in turn offered to form a marriage alliance with the Chinese emperor. Interestingly Hideyoshi offered to divide Korea, with the southern provinces coming under Japanese control and the northern parts under Chinese authority, thus roughly anticipating the division of Korea that the United States and the Soviet Union carried out three and half centuries later. Eventually negotiations broke down and the Japanese launched a second massive invasion in 1597. This time the Koreans and the Chinese under General Yang Hao were better prepared and limited the advance of the Japanese. Meanwhile, Yi Sun-sin, who had been removed from his post due to court intrigue, was given back his naval command. He scored a major victory at Myŏngnyang near Mokp'o. While chasing the retreating Japanese ships he was killed by a chance shot. Today he is remembered as a national hero and one of the world's great naval geniuses. Suffering defeats at sea and stalemate on land, the Japanese generals withdrew their forces to Japan to participate in the jockeying for power that followed Hideyoshi's death in late 1598.

The invasions, while a failure, were highly destructive, since the Japanese, like the Mongols earlier, used a scorched-earth policy to overcome resistance. As a result, they left behind a ruined countryside and a legacy of bitterness and fearfulness of the Japanese among Koreans. The viciousness of the conflict was symbolized by the 38,000 ears of Chinese and Korean forces sent back to Japan by military commanders as proof of their military successes. These were pickled and buried in Kyoto in the Mimizuka (Mound of Ears). The conflict provided later generations of Koreans with heroes from the fighting monks and peasants to Admiral Yi. It also led to a temporary and partial breakdown in the social order as slaves took advantage of the war to seek freedom. A court in desperate need of money sold official titles to commoners and even outcastes. These titles, however, did not become hereditary. While the Ming only intervened when it became clear that the Japanese were a threat to Chinese security, the invaluable assistance of China reinforced Korea's tributary ties and its emotional connection with the Middle Kingdom. The conflict also brought Korean influence to Japan. Japanese forces brought back thousands of Korean captives. These included the scholar Kang Hang, who played a major role in introducing Neo-Confucian philosophy to that country, and potters whose rough-hewn Korean wares would influence Japanese ceramic traditions.

Hardly had Korea recovered from the Japanese invasions when it faced a new threat to the north with the rise of the Manchus. The Manchus were a Jurchen group who under their leader Nurhaci united the tribal peoples of what is now called Manchuria. In 1616, Nurhaci established the new state of Later Jin, a name derived from the Jurchen state of the twelfth century that conquered northern China. The Manchus then began attacking Chinese garrisons in the northeast. The Ming court called upon the Korean king for assistance. Realizing how vulnerable Korea was to a Manchu invasion, King Kwanghaegun (r. 1608–1623) sought to avoid becoming involved. When he sent forces to assist the Ming he secretly instructed his military commander to observe which way the battle was going, and when Manchu forces appeared to be emerging victorious the Koreans surrendered without fighting. Korea did not remain neutral for long. Kwanghaegun was overthrown in a power struggle led by some who were angered by his lack of support of the Ming, who had a generation earlier come to Chosŏn's rescue. The new group that placed Injo on the throne in 1619 pursued a pro-Ming, anti-Manchu policy.

Shortly afterward, Yi Kwal, a military officer who felt that his family had not been properly rewarded for his part in the coup, seized control of Seoul, forcing the court to flee. Yi Kwal was soon defeated. The new pro-Ming court then provoked a Manchu invasion of Korea in 1627. The court fled to its traditional refuge of Kanghwa Island while the Manchu forces looted P'yŏngyang. Bowing to reality the Koreans negotiated a tributary relationship with the Manchus, recognizing them as elder brothers and agreeing to make tribute payments of gold, cloth, and horses. The Korean court, however, still pro-Ming, broke off its tributary relations and allied itself again with the Ming in 1636. Nurhaci's successor Abahai, who now styled himself emperor of the Qing dynasty, invaded Korea to secure his southern flank as he struggled to conquer China. Crossing the frozen Yalu River in the winter of 1636–1637, Manchu cavalry forces advanced quickly and captured Seoul. Injo (r. 1623–1649) retreated to a fortress south of the capital while members of the royal family and their entourage fled to the safety of Kanghwa. Injo and his forces, after holding out against a Manchu siege for weeks, surrendered when news arrived that the Manchus, succeeding where the Mongols had failed, had captured Kanghwa and with it the royal family. Injo then pledged his loyalty to the Manchu rulers. Seven years later the Manchus captured Beijing and the Qing dynasty (1644–1911) replaced the Ming.

For the next three and a half centuries Korea served as a tributary of the Qing dynasty. The Koreans, however, entered the relationship unwillingly, and hostility toward the Manchus remained strong. Some, such as the military commander Im Kyŏng-ŏp (1594–1646), sought to renew hostilities. A number of Koreans were held hostage, including two princes, Sohyŏn and Pongnim; the latter became King Hyojong (r. 1649–1659). Hyojong upon becoming king prepared to support Ming loyalists who were fighting the Qing in China and planned for an attack. The Qing, however, eventually put down the loyalists and Koreans came to accept the reality of Manchu rule. The Koreans thereafter maintained correct if not enthusiastic relations with the new dynasty (see chapter 8).

COMPETITION FOR POWER AMONG THE ELITE

Yi Sŏng-gye (also known as King T'aejo) established the longest of Korea's dynasties, which lasted until 1910. In fact, the Yi, which ruled for over five centuries, was among the longest royal dynasties in world history. The succession to the throne, however, did not always go smoothly. Suffering from illness, King T'aejo abdicated in 1398, which led to a struggle among his sons, each backed by different powerful officials. One son reigned briefly as King Chŏngjong (r. 1398–1400) before being deposed and sent to exile in Kaesŏng by a younger brother, Pangwŏn. The latter became King T'aejong (r. 1400–1418). T'aejong was an active and able monarch, trained in and committed to Neo-Confucianist principles. His reign saw the confiscation of Buddhist monasteries and the strengthening of the military. One of his moves to consolidate royal power was the establishment of the *hop'ae* identification system in 1413. Under this system high-ranking officials wore ivory identity tags, lower-ranking officials wore tags of deer horn, and *yangban* wore yellow poplar wood tags, while commoners wore small square wooden tags. Large square wooden tags were worn by outcastes and slaves. Tags of *yangban* and officials gave their titles, those of commoners their name, place, and date of birth. Tags of slaves also provided information on the complexion and height of the tag holder. Each male from the age of fifteen was to make his own identity tag, which would then be stamped with a government seal by an official. Although only intermittently enforced, the *hop'ae* system provides an illustration of the attempt by the Yi rulers to establish an orderly, controlled society where everyone had a set place. It facilitated census taking, tax collection, and keeping track of migration and runaway slaves.

T'aejong, following the precedent of his father, abdicated in favor of his son, who became King Sejong (r. 1418–1450). Today Sejong is regarded by Koreans as their greatest monarch and his reign is seen as a high point of Korean culture. Sejong successfully strengthened the northern frontier, establishing the present boundaries of Korea. He founded the *Chiphyŏnjŏn*

(Hall of Worthies), a learned body that created the Korean alphabet, *han'gŭl* (see chapter 7). Sejong was a patron of scholarship, the arts, and sciences, which all flourished during his reign. The monarch carefully attended the Classics Mat lectures, studied the classics diligently, and generally adhered to the role of the virtuous ruler who acts as a moral exemplar. Furthermore, he was an able administrator. Dutifully seeking to ensure an heir, he fathered eighteen sons. Under his reign the throne reached a heightened prestige.

Nonetheless, Sejong was unable to ensure a smooth succession. Korean kings suffered from their involvement in court intrigue, and rather than an orderly father-to-eldest-son succession, a confused struggle for power often followed. Sejong was succeeded by a son and a grandson; the latter was deposed by his uncle who became King Sejo (r. 1455–1468). Sejo's usurpation of the throne was accompanied by bloody purges of officials from rival factions in which hundreds were executed or banished into exile. These included six distinguished scholar-officials who became known as the *Sa yuksin* (Six Martyrs) and six high-ranking officials who resigned in protest. Since the latter were not executed they became known as the *Saeng yuksin* (Six Ministers Who Lived). Later, these ministers who supported the deposed king would be held as models of loyalty and virtue. Sejo tried to concentrate power in his own hands and limit that of the high-ranking officials. To that end he abolished the State Council and had the Six Ministries report directly to him. Despite his ruthlessness Sejo was an able as well as a strong-willed ruler. His attempt to bend the monarchical-aristocratic division of power in his favor, however, did not survive him. Shortly after his death Sŏngjong (r. 1469–1494) resumed rule through the high officials and presided over a prosperous state where the arts and scholarship flourished.

While most of the early Yi dynasty monarchs were strong and capable rulers, they were not always able to secure their throne from rival factions. Two conspicuous failures were Yŏnsan'gun (r. 1492–1506) and Kwanghaegun (r. 1608–1623), both of whom were deposed. Yŏnsan'gun earned a reputation for ruthlessness. The king attempted to strengthen royal authority by abolishing the Censor-General, the Office of Special Counselors, and the Office of Royal Lectures (Classics Mat). As tension arose between the king and much of officialdom a report appeared that his mother, Lady Yun, who had died when he was only four, had been put to death as a result of court intrigue. The king responded with bloody purges of officials and other members of court. Many were killed; in some cases corpses were dug up and mutilated. His officials deposed Yŏnsan'gun and demoted him from king to prince (hence his title "gun," meaning prince, instead of the usual honorific royal ending, *cho* [progenitor] or *chong* [ancestor]). Historians have depicted him as a depraved tyrant who wasted state revenues, ravished young women, defiled temples that he turned into pleasure palaces, confiscated land and slaves of officials, and seized the homes of thousands of commoners near the capital.

Yŏnsan'gun's alleged depravity and cruelty provided a negative example for later monarchs, and his removal from office an example of the limits of royal authority. The other Yi monarch demoted to "prince," Kwanghegun, was by contrast an able monarch. He sponsored scholarship, rebuilt the historical archives that were destroyed by the Japanese, and conducted foreign policy with skill. But he fell victim to the struggles among two factions of officials—the Northerners who supported him and their rivals the Westerners (see below). The Westerners deposed him and placed their own royal candidate on the throne as King Injo. The fates of Yŏnsan'gun and Kwanghaegun were in contrast to Ming or Qing China, where officials never deposed an emperor.

The political history of Chosŏn was in good measure the saga of intrigue among aristocratic factions in maneuvering for political advantage, as well as the story of the struggle of monarchs competing for authority with powerful aristocratic families. Factionalism often made political affairs tense and dangerous during this period. The fierce competition among aristocratic factions led to four "literati purges" that are famous in Korean history: the Purge of 1498, the Purge of 1504, the Purge of 1519, and the Purge of 1545.[14] These sometimes violent power struggles led to the death and exile of many high-ranking officials. Koreans have often considered factionalism as one of the curses of their politics. The term *faction* can be misleading, however, implying that these were merely struggles for power. Factions often represented lines of policy differences, which in turn often had an ideological basis, with factional leaders claiming to represent the correct path to virtue. Some of these differences dealt with foreign policy issues such as whether to support the Ming in its conflicts with the Manchus. Korean officials often faced difficult choices in dealing with dangerous neighbors, with dire consequences if their policies failed. Passionate disputes over these issues were understandable. Factional struggles were intensified by the nature of Neo-Confucian ideology and its interpretation. Since court ritual and behavior, and the personal morality of officials, were considered necessary for a harmonious society, every activity by the members of the court and by high officials was scrutinized. The censors had the right to review and rebuke improper conduct whenever they saw it. All this led to an often oppressive atmosphere in the capital in which the performance of seemingly minor rituals and/or minor breaches of conduct could lead to demotion, exile, or occasionally execution. Exile could mean being sent for many years to live in remote places, such as on one of the many tiny islands that dot the west and south coasts.

In the late sixteenth century, these factions solidified into clearly identifiable groups. During the reign of King Sŏnjo (1567–1608) a dispute arose between factions of powerful officials, led by Kim Hyo-wŏn and Sim Ŭi-gyŏm, over appointments to influential posts in government. Since Kim lived in the eastern section of Seoul, his followers in the dispute became known as "Easterners" (*Tongin*) and Sim's followers became known as "Westerners" (*Sŏin*), names derived from places of residence in Seoul. The rivalry between these two groups soon centered over a successor to King Sŏnjo. The king had no sons by his legal wives but had thirteen sons by his concubines. A dispute arose when the Westerners backed one of his sons by a concubine as crown prince and the Easterners opposed this. Then the Easterners divided into "Southerners," (*Namin*) those who were willing to accept this decision, and "Northerners" (*Pugin*), who took a hard-line opposition to having an illegitimate son as crown prince. Thus four major factions were formed. These factions later split further into subgroups such as "Great Northerners" and "Lesser Northerners." These factional struggles become entangled in foreign policy disputes, with the Northerners in the 1620s seeking to avoid involvement in the Manchu-Ming conflict and the Westerners pursuing a more pro-Ming policy. By the mid-seventeenth century the major factions were *Noron* (Old Doctrine), *Soron* (Young Doctrine), Northerners, and Southerners. The first two were the result of a split among the Westerners. These groups, sometimes called the *sasaek* (four colors), remained the four major factions into the nineteenth century. Loyal disciples followed their masters so that the factions remained tied by family and political loyalty over generations.

Since the *yangban* had to a great extent become a service nobility and the number of high-ranking posts was limited, the factions centered on the competition for office, and the power and prestige that came with it. Ideology played a role as well, since faction members often took different sides on questions of interpretation of Confucian doctrine and its application to various situations. An example of factional rivalry over ideological disputes was the Mourning Rites controversy in the seventeenth century. This dispute arose over a disagreement on the proper mourning period for one of the wives of King Hyojong (see chapter 8). This led to a difference of opinion by the leaders of two rival factions. The dispute led to a purge of one faction and the coming of power in 1674 of another and to an eventual counterpurge in 1689.[15] Each dispute left a legacy of bitterness and resentment that was passed down over generations, making factionalism deeply rooted.

CHOSŎN POLITICS IN PERSPECTIVE

Although the voluminous historical records kept during the Yi dynasty read as a perpetual and vicious struggle for power, these conflicts and intrigues usually involved only a small number of elite officials and high-ranking aristocrats in the capital. That is, the factional conflicts were largely confined to a small upper stratum of society; they did not mean the country at large was in turmoil. Yi politics and the moral language it was couched in were convoluted, contentious, and occasionally violent. Yet, for the most part the institutions of the state worked well and functioned for nearly five centuries without breaking down. In fact, no ruling dynasty in China, Japan, Southeast Asia, or Europe (except, perhaps, the Ottomans) lasted so long without a major upheaval. The bureaucracy was staffed by well-educated people, who more often than not owed their positions as much to successful performance in the state-administered civil, and to a lesser degree military, examinations as they did to their family connections. Many took their duties and responsibilities seriously, trying to adhere to the ethical standards they had studied since childhood. In short, Korea under the Yi dynasty enjoyed centuries of stability. It was also a resilient state that survived the destructive Japanese and Manchu invasions without radical institutional or political change.

KOREA IN GLOBAL PERSPECTIVE: CHOSŎN AS AN IDEOLOGICALLY DRIVEN STATE

Chosŏn Korea underwent a long-term effort to bring government, social institutions, and personal conduct into conformity with Neo-Confucian norms. The zeal with which many Koreans adhered to Neo-Confucianism does not have a parallel elsewhere in East Asia. Chinese Neo-Confucian reformers in the Song greatly influenced their society, but they never had the command of the state. Periodic persecutions against Buddhism occurred as early as the mid-ninth century by xenophobic Chinese Confucianists. But China never experienced such a long, sustained, and systematic effort to remodel the institutions of government and society. No Chinese government enforced adherence to orthodoxy as rigidly as in Korea. Some Chinese rulers, such as the first Ming emperor Hongwu (r. 1368–1398) and the Qing emperor Qianlong (r. 1736–1796), ruthlessly suppressed any sign of subversive thought, but this was aimed at threats to their authority, not to ideological orthodoxy. In Japan, despite efforts by early Tokugawa rulers in the seventeenth century to promote Neo-Confucianism, no belief system was ever established as rigid orthodoxy. Buddhism retained an intellectual vigor lacking in Korea, Shinto was still associated with the emperor, and various nativist and heterodox Confucian schools of thought flourished. Korean visitors commented unfavorably on this. Vietnam's ruling class promoted Confucian doctrine from the fifteenth century, but there too, it blended with native religions and beliefs, and Buddhism remained stronger than in Korea.

In some ways Korean Neo-Confucianism resembled orthodox Islam in that it encompassed a code of behavior governing nearly every aspect of life. Both were intolerant of rival beliefs and of ideological pluralism, and both were intensely moral as well as political. As in the case of Sunni Islam, there was no Neo-Confucianist priesthood, but a more informal structure of learned and pious men of faith that exercised enormous influence over society. A better analogy with the Neo-Confucian revolution might be the Islamic revivals that characterized much of the Muslim world, such as the Shi'a movement of the Safavids of Persia in the late fifteenth and sixteenth century, the Wahhabi movement of eighteenth-century Arabia and the Fulani Jihad of West Africa in the early nineteenth century. All were movements to reshape every institution and custom to match religious orthodoxy. Korea's ideological zeal might also be compared with medieval Christianity or with Reformation religious reformers. Unlike the more varied religious world of India or Southeast Asia, Europeans adhered strictly to a doctrinal faith, punishing deviation with even greater vigor and ruthlessness than did Koreans; there was no Neo-Confucian Inquisition. In Europe the conflict between the secular authority of kings and the sacred authority of popes, and the creation of autonomous corporations such as universities allowed for some intellectual pluralism, limited as it was. Europe was also a larger and more ethnically diverse region with variations on local customs and practices. But the Neo-Confucianists were not as militant as these Muslim and Christian zealots in imposing total orthodoxy of belief and practice upon their lands. Buddhism continued to survive with several thousand temples dotting the countryside; even members of the elite called upon its monks at times for spiritual needs. In addition, Shamanism remained widely practiced and occasionally received official if discreet patronage. Perhaps because it was more a code of social, political, and personal conduct than religion in the conventional sense, Confucianism, even in its more mystical Neo-Confucian forms, could not satisfy all the spiritual needs of the people.

Neo-Confucianism was not the last foreign ideology that Koreans embraced with zeal. Later some Koreans would display the same fervor for Christianity and Marxism. But only under North Korea would there be such an extraordinary effort to remake society in conformity to a dogmatically held vision.

Yun Hoe: On the Harmfulness of Buddhism

Yun Hoe [1380–1436], deputy Director of the Hall of Worthies, and others submitted the following memorial [in 1424]:

We consider the harm of Buddhists to be prevalent still. Since the Han period the reverence for Buddha has been increasingly fervent, yet neither happiness nor profit has been gained. This is recorded in the historical books, which Your Majesty has certainly perused thoroughly. Must you therefore wait for your ministers to tell you?

We think of all the heterodox teachings, Buddhism is the worst. The Buddhists live alone with their barbaric customs, apart from the common productive population; yet they cause the people to be destitute and to steal. What is worse than their crimes? Beasts and birds that damage grain are certainly chased away because they harm the people. Yet even though beasts and birds eat the people's food, they are nevertheless useful to the people. Buddhists, however, sit around and eat, and there has not yet been a visible profit.

—from the *Sejong sillok* 23:27a–b[16]

Sin Ch'ŏjung: On the Deceitfulness of Buddhism

Sin Ch'ŏjung, a licentiate at the Royal Confucian Academy, and one hundred and one others went to the palace and tendered the following memorial [in 1424].

Those Buddhists, what kind of people are they? As eldest sons they turn against their fathers; as husbands they oppose the Son of Heaven. They break off the relationship between father and son and destroy the obligation between ruler and subject. They regard the living together of man and woman as immoral and a man's plowing and a woman's weaving as useless.

If monks were forced to return to their home villages; if they were treated as men fit to join the military; if they were made to settle down in order to increase their households; if we burnt their books in order to destroy their roots and branches; if their fields were requisitioned in order to distribute them among the offices; if their bronze statues and bells were entrusted to the Office of Supply in order to mint copper cash; if the utensils they use were handed over to a ceremonial office in order to prepare them for official use; if within the capital the temples of each sect were divided up among the offices without buildings; if the temples outside the capital were all torn down in order to build postal stations and school buildings; if for funerals the *Family Rites* of Zhu Xi were exclusively relied upon, then, in a few years, the human mind would be corrected and the heavenly principles clear, the households would increase, and the number of soldiers would be complete.

—from *Sejong sillok* 23:30a–32b[17]

7

✦

Chosŏn Society

Korea during the Chosŏn (Yi dynasty) period became in many ways a model Confucian society. Confucian ideas shaped family and society in profound ways. Although China was the home of Neo-Confucian ideals and they were embraced by many in Japan and Vietnam, nowhere else was there such a conscientious and consistent attempt to remold society in conformity to them. The zeal and persistence by which Koreans strove to reshape their society in accordance with Neo-Confucian ideals helped to set them apart from their East Asian neighbors. These efforts initially began at the upper levels of society, but by the eighteenth and nineteenth centuries Neo-Confucian norms had prevailed, if to a lesser degree, among all social classes. As Neo-Confucian values penetrated throughout all levels of society, they helped bind the Korean people together as members of a single culture even while sharp class divisions remained. While it moved Korea closer to many Chinese cultural norms, Confucianization was also a creative process of adapting the ideals that originated in China to indigenous social practices. Indeed, it was during this period that many distinctive features of Korean culture, such as its unique writing system, emerged.

The basic ideals of Confucianism centered on proper social relationships. Three cardinal principles (*samgang*) guided these social relationships: loyalty (*ch'ung*) of subjects to their ruler, filial piety (*hyo*) toward one's parents, and maintaining distinction (*yŏl*) between men and women. Distinction meant that women had to display chastity, obedience, and faithfulness. Another Confucian formulation that defined the relationships that held society together was the five ethical norms (*oryun*): *ŭi* (righteousness and justice), which governed the conduct between ruler and ministers (subjects); *ch'in* (cordiality or closeness) between parents and children; *pyŏl* (distinction) between husbands and wives; *sŏ* (order) between elders and juniors; and *sin* (trust) between friends.[1] The ethical norms of Confucianism emphasized the importance of family relations, the hierarchical nature of society, the necessity for order and harmony, respect for elders and for authority, the importance of a clear distinction between men and women, and the subordinate status of women. Neo-Confucianists taught that each individual was to strive to cultivate his or her virtue. This was regarded as a lifelong task that involved sincere and persistent effort. Neo-Confucianists placed great importance on rituals and ceremonies, on honoring one's ancestors, on formality and correctness in relationships, on constant study of the classics as a guide to a virtuous life, and on the importance of public service. They valued frugality, thrift, hard work, and courteousness, along with refraining from indulgence in immoderate behavior. Neo-Confucianists could be prudes, disdainful of spontaneous or sensuous behavior.

It was a philosophy that emphasized rank and status; it was important for everyone to know his or her place and role in society. Concern about rank and hierarchy had always been a feature of Korean society, Neo-Confucian thought gave that concern ethical purpose. The Korean language reinforced rank consciousness. Lower-class people addressed upper-class persons with honorific forms that Koreans call *chondaeŏ* or *chondaemal*. As they addressed their superiors, their sentences concluded with verbal endings that indicated levels of deference. The language contained many synonyms reserved for respectful usage. Superiors in age or social status spoke in turn to their inferiors in a speech style devoid of the elaborate honorific endings and special honorific terms, which came to be called *panmal*. This use of elaborate speech styles indicating levels of deference, intimacy, and formality is still part of the Korean language.

THE FAMILY

Family and lineage were fundamental to the Korean Confucian order. Lineage refers to those people who directly trace their origins to a common ancestor. In Korea these lineages were called *munjung*. Only those who were in the direct line traced through the eldest son or nearest male relative belonged to a lineage. To keep track of lineage, Koreans began to keep *chokpo*, books where births, marriages, and deaths were recorded over the generations. This started to become a common practice in the fifteenth century and eventually became a universal custom, so that most

Koreans, even today, can usually trace their ancestry back many generations. Families eventually began to keep *pulch'ŏnjiwi* (never removed tablets) with the names of their immediate ancestors at the home of the lineage heir, normally the eldest son. Many of the ceremonies and practices
associated with lineage found their way into the law code, the *Kyŏngguk
taejŏn*, compiled in 1469. Laws required all Koreans to perform the rites
to their ancestors known as *chesa*. In the *chesa* ancestral rites family members pay homage to *chosang* (ancestors). This emphasized that the ties
of kinship extended to include the dead as well as the living. Ancestral
rites became extremely important in establishing family ties. There were
three basic types of *chesa*: *kije*, or death anniversary commemorations,
which were performed at midnight on the eve of the ancestor's death day;
ch'arye, or holiday commemorations, which were performed on certain
holidays; and *myoje*, or graveside commemorations performed on visits
to a family member or to an ancestor's grave (*myo*).

At the *kije* and *ch'arye* rites, the family members offered food and drink
to the ancestral spirits. The rites came to symbolize the importance of
maintaining order and properly adhering to rituals. Every aspect of the
rituals followed a formal procedure. Food had to be arranged on an altar in a special order: fruit in the front row; then vegetables, soups, and
meats; rice and thick soups; and spoons and chopsticks in the back. Red
fruit was placed on the east and white on the west. Incense was placed in
front of the food table, and a tray for wine was placed in front of the incense. Rites were performed by the eldest direct male relative, who began
the ceremonies by kneeling and burning incense and then pouring three
cups of wine. Others, generally according to rank, followed, prostrating
themselves with their heads touching the floor three times. The eldest
male then took the cup of wine after rotating it three times in the incense
smoke. When the wine offering was completed the family members left
and allowed the ancestor to eat. The men returned and bowed and the
food was then served to the family. These rituals came to be performed
exclusively by men. *Chesa* rituals emphasized the importance of family,
lineage, and maintaining a sense of order and propriety.

Marriage in Chosŏn Korea was characterized by extreme exogamy and
a strong sense of status. Koreans generally married outside their communities and were prohibited from marrying anyone within the same
lineage, even if that lineage contained up to hundreds of thousands of
members, as the largest ones did. Yet the concern for status meant that
marriages remained confined within a social class. In early Koryŏ times,
marriages between close kin and within a village were probably common,
but they became less so in subsequent centuries. The adoption of the civil
examination system in the tenth century led to careful records of family relations and to the strengthening of Chinese influences forbidding

marriage of patrilineal kin. However, in Koryŏ such marriages still took place. During the Chosŏn period the strict rules prohibiting kin marriages were enforced. Men and women married at younger ages than Western Europeans but not as early as in many Asian societies. In 1471, minimum ages of fifteen and fourteen were legislated for men and women respectively. Men generally married between sixteen and thirty years of age and women fourteen to twenty; the age gap between husband and wife was often considerable. Commoners often married at younger ages than *yangban.*

Weddings underwent changes in Korea during the Chosŏn period as the result of the impact of Neo-Confucianism. Zhu Xi's *Family Rituals* (Chinese: *Jiali*, Korean: *Karye*) became the basis for rules governing marriage ceremonies and practices. Koreans did not always blindly adhere to them, and wedding practices were modified somewhat to conform to Korean customs. For example, Koreans had traditionally married at the bride's home. But Zhu Xi and other authors stated that it should be done at the groom's home. Scholars and officials debated whether to follow Chinese custom or *kuksok* (national practice). A compromise was worked out in which part of the ceremony was performed at the bride's home, after which the couple proceeded to the groom's family home to complete the wedding. To this day when marrying, Korean women say they are going to their groom's father's house (*sijip kanda*) and men say they are going to their wife's father's house (*changga kanda*). In Koryŏ times, many if not most newlyweds resided at the wife's family residence. This custom, contrary to notions of patrilineal family structure, gradually died out, and brides moved into their husband's home. In many cases, however, young couples lived with whomever's family was nearest or with whichever parents needed care or had land available to farm.

A variation of marriage custom was the *minmyŏnuri*, a girl bride who entered the house as a child, often at the age of six and seven. Koreans never felt entirely comfortable with this custom, boasting that, unlike the Chinese at least, they did not take girls at infancy.[2] The girl bride would be ritually sent back to her home to reenter upon marriage, although this was not always practiced. The Yi government disapproved of the custom and set minimum marriage ages, but these were not enforced. Child marriages were practiced mainly by the poorer members of society who needed the child labor and who could not afford costly weddings. Often the family of the bride could not afford a dowry. One advantage of child marriages was that the girl would be trained to be an obedient daughter-in-law, but in general it was a source of shame and a sign of poverty. Many grooms who were too poor to obtain a bride found this to be their only option. It was not unusual for the groom to be a fully grown adult so that an age gap of as much as thirty years between husband and wife was possible. Korean tales talk of the abuse these child brides received from their mothers-in-law. No doubt for some life was miserable. For much the same economic reasons, some families had *teril-sawi* or boy child grooms, although this was less common.

Great emphasis was placed on direct male descent, usually through the *changja* (first son). While this was always important in Korea, it was reinforced by Neo-Confucian thought, especially the influence of Zhu Xi. So important was direct male descent that even the posthumous adoption of a male heir (usually a close male relative) was necessary if a man died before leaving a male offspring. Men also took secondary wives, not just to satisfy their lust but to insure they had male offspring. Inheritance patterns in Korea differed from those of its neighbors. While in China land was divided equally among sons, and in Japan all rights went to a sole heir, in Korea the trend during the Yi was to exclude daughters from inheritance and to give the largest portion to the first son, although all sons had the right to some property. This meant that most of a family's property was kept intact and not divided, or at least kept in the lineage.

In short, Korean families during the Yi dynasty became increasingly patriarchal in that the authority of the males was enhanced. They became patrilineal in organization in that property was inherited through males, and that descent and the status that came with it was traced primarily through direct father-to-son or nearest male relative lines. The habit of residence in the groom's family home after marriage reinforced male dominance. Families and lineages were exclusive; nonmembers could not be adopted into families. Nor could they join lineages, although disgraced members such as traitors and criminals could be expelled from them. Family and lineage truly mattered in Korea, as evidenced by the huge number of printed genealogies produced, perhaps unmatched in volume per capita anywhere else in the world.

WOMEN DURING THE YI DYNASTY

The status of women declined during the Chosŏn period. This can be attributed at least in part, if not primarily, to the fact that Neo-Confucianists stressed direct male descent and the subordination of women to men. Women were urged to obey their fathers in youth, their husbands in marriage, and their sons in old age. Books written for women emphasized virtue, chastity, submission to one's husband, devotion to in-laws, frugality, and diligence. Moral literature, a great deal of which was published under the Yi, emphasized that women should be chaste, faithful, obedient to husbands, obedient to in-laws, frugal, and filial. Some of this literature was published by the state. To promote these values, the state in

1434 awarded honors to women for virtue. Literacy was very low among
women, since the village and county schools admitted only men. The
small proportion who could write, perhaps amounting in the eighteenth
and nineteenth centuries to only 3 or 4 percent at the most, generally did
so in *han'gŭl*, rather than in the more prestigious Chinese characters.

The decline in status was gradual. Households headed by women
disappeared early in the Yi dynasty, but women still inherited property until the seventeenth century. Widows were no longer allowed to
remarry, since they were supposed to be loyal to their husbands even
after their partner's death. As the marriage customs shifted from earlier
practices, brides usually left their families after marriage. A daughter was
a *todungnyŏ* ("robber woman"), since she carried away the family wealth
when she married. A married daughter became a *ch'ulga oein* ("one who
left the household and became a stranger").[3] This contributed to the practice of reducing or eliminating a daughter's share of her inheritance. Since
the daughter was thought to leave her family, there was less reason to
bequeath a portion of the family estate to her. Women could not divorce
men, but men could divorce women under the principle called *ch'ilgŏjiak*
(seven grounds for divorce), which legitimized the grounds for divorce.
The seven grounds for divorce were disobedience to parents-in-law,
failure to bear a son, adultery, jealousy, hereditary disease, talkativeness,
and larceny. So associated were women with their families that they were
generally referred to by their relationship to their male family members
rather than by their name. It has been suggested that by late Chosŏn,
women became "nameless entities," being referred to as "the wife of" or
as the "mother of (son's name)." They had, in other words, not only lost
their rights to divorce, to property, to participating in public life, they had
also lost any identity of their own.

Women could no longer freely mix with men socially, and their lives
were restricted in many ways. The official legal code, the *Kyŏngguk Taejŏn*,
forbade upper-class women from playing games and from partying out-
doors with penalties of up to 100 lashes. Horse riding, a common activity
among upper-class Koryŏ women, was forbidden by law in 1402. Women
had to seek the permission of husbands or family heads before participating in social activities. In later Chosŏn, women in Seoul were allowed in
the street only during men's curfew hours from 9 p.m. to 2 a.m. At other
times it became customary for women to wear veils when entering the
street. The segregation and restriction of women became reflected in the
architecture of the Korean home, which was divided between the *sarang
ch'ae*, the outer section for men, and the *anch'ae*, the inner section of the
house for women, also called the *anbang* (inner room). Even poor families
often had three rooms: one for men, one for women, and the kitchen.
Husbands and wives often lived virtually apart in their own home. Sepa-

ration of religious functions occurred as well, with the women in charge of *kosa*, offerings to household gods, and the men *chesa*, Confucian rites to the ancestors. Unlike in China, women were excluded from the rites to the ancestors. In Korea there was a clear gender division in ritual responsibilities.

Particularly tragic was the position of widows. Since a woman was not allowed to remarry, or head a household, once her husband died she became an inconvenience for her family. There were stories of widows being pressured to commit suicide, but this was probably rare. A widow was sometimes called a *mimangin* (a person who has not died yet). Among commoners and outcastes widows were sometimes married off to a poor man, sometimes to a widower who needed a wife but could not afford a marriage. The man would enter the house and carry out the woman, supposedly in a big sack, resulting in what was sometimes referred to as a "sack marriage." This might be arranged by the widow's family against her will.[4] Also difficult was the life of women in a household where a man took a concubine. This practice was an opportunity for a poor slave or commoner woman to enter an upper-class household. But her life could be made difficult by the jealous first wife and her children, and by the stain of illegitimacy given to her children (see below). First wives could also feel miserable by the entry of a new younger wife with whom they had to compete for their husband's attention.

The same Confucian demand on loyalty and chastity that made remarriage unacceptable resulted in the custom of presenting a woman with a *p'aedo*, a suicide knife. This custom, which began among the elite, became common to all social classes in the southern regions. There were reported cases of women using the knife to protect themselves from attackers. In one such case, a government slave girl, Tŏkchi, used her *p'aedo* to kill a number of Japanese who attempted to rape her during the sixteenth-century invasions. But the purpose of the knife was for a woman to protect her virtue by committing suicide. A particularly sharp knife was called a *chamal p'aedo* after another slave girl who after being embraced by her drunken master always kept her knife sharpened.[5] A woman had to not only protect her honor but, most importantly, protect her family from even the slightest hint of scandal. Sometimes even rumors of an indiscretion were enough for a woman to be pressured to commit suicide for the sake of her family's reputation.

The sign of a married woman was the *tchok*, long braided hair coiled at the nape and held together with a *pinyŏ*, a long pin. Single women wore their long hair unpinned. Ideally women were kept from public view, secluded in their women's quarters and venturing out only in screened sedan chairs or at night. In reality, only the upper class could afford this. Rural women worked in the fields, participating in all the tasks except plowing and threshing, which were men's work. Women could not engage in business, but women's loan associations, called *kye*, were an important source of income for rural women. Commoner and low-caste women mixed with men at festivals. The separate existence of men and women was an ideal most honored at the upper reaches of society.

There were also some exceptions to the restricted roles of women. *Mudang* (women shamans) were an important part of life since at least Silla. During Chosŏn times the great majority of shamans were women, although their social status declined as a result of the official Confucian disdain of traditional religions. Some women became entertainers. These were generally from outcaste and slave families from whom attractive young girls were often purchased to be trained as entertainers known in Chosŏn times as *kisaeng*. Women prevailed in some performing arts, such as singers in the nineteenth-century dramatic form *p'ansori*.

Perhaps the most interesting exception to the restricted lives of women were the *kisaeng*. The *kisaeng* were carefully trained female entertainers similar to the Chinese singsong girls and the Japanese *geisha*. *Kisaeng* often came from the slaves. Attractive ones would be taught to read and write, appreciate poetry, and perform musical instruments so that they could entertain men, especially *yangban*. Since the lives of men and women were increasingly segregated, the *kisaeng* offered men a chance to enjoy the company of women who were not only attractive but able to engage in learned conversation and witty banter. There were also common prostitutes; however, the *kisaeng* were considered more virtuous as well as highly educated, fitting companions for upper-class men. *Kisaeng* were able to engage in conversation with men and be intellectual as well as romantic companions to men in a way that good, virtuous Confucian wives could not. Some *kisaeng* were official *kisaeng*, recruited and employed by the state. These were carefully trained in government-regulated houses. During the early dynasty about 100 *kisaeng* were recruited every three years for the court while others were trained and sent to provincial capitals.

Most *kisaeng* were privately employed by the hundreds of *kisaeng* houses throughout the country. There were, however, also medical *kisaeng* who besides their duty entertaining men also served to treat upper-class women, since women of good families were unable to see male doctors who were not related to them. Others were also trained to sew royal garments. *Kisaeng*, although never entirely respectable, were often admired and loved by men. Some were celebrated for their wit and intellect as well as their beauty and charm. A few talented *kisaeng* won fame for their artistic and literary accomplishments, such as the sixteenth-century poet Hwang Chin-i (see below). Another, Non'gae, according to legend, became a heroine when she jumped in the Nam River with a Japanese general during the Hideyoshi invasions. But these were exceptions; most *kisaeng* led humble lives in which the best they could hope for was to be some wealthy man's concubine.

SOCIAL STRUCTURE

Legally Korean society was divided into *yangmin* (good people) and *ch'ŏnmin* (base people). In practice, however, Chosŏn society was divided into three basic classes: the *yangban* elite, commoners, and the "mean people," consisting of slaves and outcaste groups. Under Yi law, this threefold distinction was often obscured. For example, all *yangin* (that is, not slaves or outcastes) had the right to enter schools, take exams, and serve in office. In reality, however, the *yangban* could be distinguished from commoners. The key was family history; only those with prominent ancestors were *yangban*. The *yangban* were generally wealthier than commoners, and their wealth was derived from owning land and slaves. While there were relatively few large estates, *yangban* families tended to hold more land than commoners, although these holdings might be in scattered parcels. *Yangban* differed from earlier Korean aristocracy and from the *bushi*, or samurai, Japan's warrior-aristocracy, in that they were not a military group; they derived and maintained their status and power through office holding.

Yangban were also called *sadaebu*, derived from the Chinese term *shidafu*, meaning "scholar-official," but they differed from the scholar-bureaucrats of China in that there was a greater importance attached to heredity. Another way they differed from their Chinese counterparts was that ownership of slaves as well as landowning and office holding was a basis of status, wealth, and power. While commoners did own slaves, most census figures from the seventeenth and eighteenth centuries indicate that *yangban* families almost always had more slaves than commoners.

Wealth was important as a distinction between *yangban* and commoner, but *yangban* status was determined primarily by ancestry, and demonstrated by a display of learning and virtue. In general, *yangban* families needed to produce officials in order to maintain their prestige, if not legal status. This generally meant producing degree holders through the examinations. They also needed to display a knowledge of and regularly perform the Confucian rituals, as well as display skill in poetry and calligraphy and a mastery of the classics. While exams were usually a crucial factor in establishing or reaffirming power and status, some families of *hyangban* (rural *yangban*) were able to maintain high status even without producing higher-exam passers for generations. Yet generally the exams were a key to defining as well as securing *yangban* status. Legally commoners could take the civil exams, and a few did before 1600. As Chosŏn society became more rigid, family history and pedigree was the only basis for determining who could take the exam. The examinee's ancestors were reviewed for three generations on his father's side and one on his mother's to make sure he came from a good family. *Yangban* status was also tied to tax privileges; they were free from the household tax. They were also free from corvée and from military service.

Yangban totally dominated Chosŏn. They manned the bureaucracy and served as the moral and cultural leaders of society. From their ranks were drawn most of the nation's scholars and writers and many of its leading artists. In the countryside the *yangban* served as the local elite. They advised local officials, gave public talks that served as sermons for the local people, and provided informal leadership in the community. The *yangban* were segregated from commoners, living in different neighborhoods, and *yangban* met and socialized at private academies and at *kisaeng* houses. *Yangban* were identified with their hometowns, with which they maintained ceremonial and political ties. During the Chosŏn period single-name villages where all were at least distant kin became common. Identification with a hometown or region may have become stronger during the later centuries. During the early Chosŏn, *yangban* often relocated in far-off parts of the country, seeking economic opportunities, but later they tended to stay near their home base, moving, if at all, only to neighboring counties.

The greatest goal of a *yangban* was to serve as a high official, and the most ambitious were drawn to the capital; but even officials in the capital tended to return to their home villages. They held exclusive membership in the *Hyangch'ŏng* (Local Agency) and later in Yi the local *yangban* associations. Income from official posts was important for many; some tutored the youth of other *yangban*, but wealth mostly came from landowning. Not all *yangban* were big landowners, and not all big landowners were *yangban*. Nonetheless, most major landowners were *yangban*, and generally *yangban* were the biggest landowners in their communities. Unlike the Silla or early Koryŏ aristocrats, most *yangban* of the Chosŏn did not have military backgrounds and were contemptuous of the skills of warriors. Some scholars see the military weakness of late Yi dynasty Korea, a nation that once fiercely resisted the Chinese and the Mongols, as due to the domination of society by people who failed to value military skills. *Yangban* were also forbidden to engage in the demeaning profession of commerce.

The term *yangban* meant the two orders of officials, the *munban* (civil officials) and the *muban* (military officials). But by the sixteenth century the term had come to mean the entire elite aristocratic class of Korea. Aristocratic status, determined by birth, provided the privilege of potentially serving as a government official, with the civil examinations being the most important means of acquiring office. Society was dominated by civil officials; however, the military examinations continued to be a secondary path, despite the general disdain for warriors. The military exams included a test on the exposition of the classics and a test of martial skills such as archery, lance-wielding, polo, and field hockey. The exams were open to *yangban* and commoners. As historian Eugene Park has pointed out, many took the exam; between 150,000 and 170,000 passed it during the five centuries of the Yi dynasty, considerably more than passed the civil exams. By comparison, during the Chosŏn dynasty some 14,607 passed the highest *munkwa* exam; 47,997 passed the lower *sama* (or licentiate) exam; and over 12,000 passed the *chapkwa* (technical exams).[6] To prepare students for the military exams the state set up a number of *muhak* (military schools) throughout the country. Although the military exams were open to commoners, it was the provincial *yangban* who often turned to these exams as a secondary path to certify their status as a degree holder. By the eighteenth century, if not earlier, *yangban* who were military degree holders belonged to different lineages or sublineages from the civil officials. While proud of their status, for the most part they held few offices of significance and had little power.

Commoners were the majority of the population. There may have been some social mobility at times, but in general a wall of privilege separated them from the *yangban*. Unlike the *yangban* they had no tax exemptions, were required to perform corvée duties and to serve in the military, and in practice were barred from the examinations. Most commoners were poor farmers, working small plots of their own land or working as tenant farmers. Sometimes they both owned some plots of land and farmed plots of *yangban*-owned land for a share of the crops. Many engaged in crafts such as cloth making to supplement their incomes. A few became wealthy farmers. Others engaged in commerce, an activity *yangban* were prohibited from engaging in (see chapter 8). In theory, the government ruled in a benevolent manner, with concern about the welfare of the common people, but the tax on commoners could be very burdensome. Corvée labor could be burdensome as well; at times vast numbers of peasants were mobilized for labor on public works. They were also sometimes victimized by local officials or exploitative landlords. When conditions became intolerable they rebelled. Most of these rebellions were localized and easily contained, but they were a source of concern for the state.

SLAVES AND OUTCASTES

Although most commoners were poor, they at least enjoyed the legal protections of being *yangmin*. Below commoners were *ch'ŏnmin* ("mean

people"). The largest group of these "mean people" were slaves. Slavery
was a major social institution in Korea from the Three Kingdoms period
to its abolition in 1894. Various attempts have been made to analyze the
scope and nature of Korean slavery; however, these have been hindered
by the lack of records, difficulties in interpreting them, and the problem
of defining different levels of servitude as slavery. In general, slaves appear to have constituted a larger percentage of the population of Korea
than was the case in its East Asian neighbors. Perhaps the emphasis on
inheritance of status contributed to this. Slaves were classified into *sanobi*
(private slaves) and *kongnobi* (government slaves). The former were
owned by members of the royal household, the officials, private citizens,
and by Buddhist temples, while the latter were owned by central and
local government agencies and by the royal family. Both private and government slaves were classified into *solgŏ nobi* (household slaves) and *oegŏ
nobi* (out-resident slaves). Household slaves served on duty at palaces and
government offices, as personal retainers of military and civil officials,
and as domestic servants. Out-resident slaves often possessed their own
property and paid rents to their owners, and they were little different
than tenant farmers or commoners.

In fact, the legal status of slaves was complex. For example, there was
a system known as *chakkae* in which a slave was assigned two types of
agricultural fields: one in which all produce he cultivated was turned
over to his master and the other in which he kept all the produce for his
own consumption or sale.[7] Some out-resident slaves paid their owners a
personal tribute, sometimes as bolts of cloth, while others shared a portion of the crop much as did free tenant farmers. Slaves could purchase
their freedom or win free status through military service or government
favor. The number of slaves in Korea is difficult to determine but appears
to have fluctuated. Some estimates place the number of slaves as high as
30 percent of the population both during Koryŏ and the early Yi period.[8]

Slavery was generally accepted in Korea, although some rulers and
individuals were praised for their compassion in freeing some. For the
government, too many private slaves were a problem since it meant there
were fewer taxpaying free peasants and fewer commoners to serve in the
armed forces. Slaves were exempted from compulsory military service.
But government slaves were an important source of income and labor
for the state. Yi Sŏng-gye, following his coup in 1388, converted 80,000
slaves of Buddhist temples to government slaves. State slaves reached
about 350,000 in number by the late fifteenth century. While the origins of
slavery are not clear, many slaves were descendants of prisoners in wars
and rebellions and of criminals. Often commoners in debt wound up enslaved. Chosŏn regulations strongly reinforced the permanent hereditary
nature of slavery, going as far as declaring that if the direct family line

died out, the nearest relative in the same lineage would inherit them. If there were no near relatives to the fourth cousin, they would then become the property of the state. Marriage between slaves and commoners was prohibited under Koryŏ, and this prohibition was carried on during the Yi dynasty. Yet despite the frequent reissuing of this rule, it was widely ignored.

Slavery created concerns for the state. While no one is recorded as calling for the abolition of slavery, the moral problem of slavery was occasionally mentioned. An official in the Office of Remonstrance in 1392 said, "Even though slaves are base, they are still Heaven's people, [and yet] we usually talk of them as chattel goods and actively buy and sell them, exchanging them for oxen and horses."[9] Monarchs and officials expressed worry that too many slaves meant a loss of taxpaying, military-serving commoners. King T'aejong tried to limit the ownership of slaves to 150 for officials and 40 for commoners but abandoned this attempt after too many objections were raised.[10] Disputes over ownership of slaves created an enormous backlog, reaching 13,000 cases in the early fifteenth century. Yet slavery was important to the economy of Korea. It was one of the major bases for elite status along with land owning and office holding. Scholars such as Yu Hyŏng-wŏn (1622–1673) in the seventeenth century argued that slavery brutalized both the slaves and their masters, claiming that it did not exist in the distant past and that the ancient Chinese did not measure wealth in slaves as Koreans do. Still, even he did not call for its total abolition.[11]

Slavery did decline somewhat in late Yi dynastic times. From the eighteenth century the number of out-resident slaves appears to have shrunk despite an overall increase in population. Exactly why is not clear. Perhaps the growth of tenant farming blurred the distinctions between commoners and slaves and made slave ownership less important to the prosperity of the elite since they could make do just as well from rent collecting. It may also have been the result of the population increases in the seventeenth and eighteenth century and the resulting abundance of labor. Resident slavery did not disappear; even in the late nineteenth century most prosperous *yangban* families had at least one or two household slaves. The number of official slaves declined to less than 100,000 in the late eighteenth century. Official slavery, with a few exceptions, was abolished in 1801, and the records of 66,000 slaves were destroyed. Hereditary slavery was not abolished until 1886. All forms of slavery were legally abolished in 1894, and it disappeared in practice too.

Besides slaves, various categories of outcastes existed. These included innkeepers, ferrymen, prostitutes, entertainers, and people involved in unclean professions such as leather working and butchering. *Paekchŏng*, or butchers, are the best known of these outcaste groups, and the term *paekchŏng* has come to be applied to outcastes in general. Little is known of the origins of these outcaste groups except that they existed since at least Silla times. Some professions such as entertainers were assigned to these outcaste groups because the Confucian elite held them in low regard. The outcaste designation of others such as butchers and leather workers may have originally been influenced by the Buddhist aversion to the harming of animals. Outcastes lived apart from society and occupied a place similar to the untouchables in India. In fact, Korea can be said to have had a caste system that was not unlike that of India in practice, but without the religious sanctions and with less elaborate distinctions. It is still unclear if the social structure was as rigid in practice as it appears in the historical record. There was, no doubt, some social mobility. But in general, the life for those at the bottom of the social scale was hard, with little hope of major improvement.

Another small hereditary group in Korea, the *chungin*, did not fit into the threefold distinction of *yangban*, commoners, and "mean people." The *chungin* (middle people) was the term given to technical officials and hereditary clerks. This originally pejorative term came into use during the middle Chosŏn period. The technical specialists were those who sat for the *chapkwa* (specialized exams) for scribes, accountants, legal professionals, astronomers, interpreters, and geomancers. The line between *chungin* and the officials became more sharply drawn as the dynasty progressed, reinforced by Confucian preference for generalists with lofty moral principles and the *yangban* disdain for technical knowledge and technicians.[12] The origins of the *chungin* are not clear; some arose from lower social status groups, and some were descended from illegitimate sons of *yangban*. In a society where bloodlines largely determined status, these "middle men" were excluded from high government posts. They became a hereditary class that depended on the specialized exams to reconfirm their status and to gain access to government posts. Especially coveted were positions as interpreters and medical officers, since these brought with them the opportunity to join tribute missions where they could engage in profitable trade.

Another group that was like the *chungin* below the *yangban* but above commoners in status were hereditary local clerks known as *hyangni*, literally local officials, also known as *sŏri* or *ajŏn*. In Koryŏ times, *hyangni* were powerful local aristocrats who controlled much of the countryside, but their status declined by early Chosŏn. Despite their lower status, they were indispensable to the operation of government. It was the *hyangni* who collected taxes, kept the local and provincial government records, supervised local granaries, served as census takers, did police work, and in some localities also managed the local militia.[13] Each of the approximately 300 counties had some *hyangni* lineages. Since due to the law of avoidance magistrates could not serve in their home districts and their term of service was usually short, they were heavily dependent on the *hyangni* for information and advice. Yet they were strictly separated by status from the magistrates they served. The hereditary local clerks were prohibited by law from marrying yangban.

In later Chosŏn, the *chungin* groups—the technical specialists and the hereditary officials—formed a small sub-elite modeled somewhat on their *yangban* superiors. Some, such as those that served as technical specialists in Seoul, were wealthy. They formed their own kin organizations and lineages and compiled genealogies. In the eighteenth and nineteenth centuries many contributed to literary works and anthologies. At the same time, the *chungin* gained greater control over the local government and became indispensable to the functioning of the government. Since their salaries were often meager at best and they were not independently wealthy, they supported themselves by exacting fees on the commoners. As a result of this practice they were often the object of peasant discontent. Because some of the technical specialists were trained in foreign languages and were generally less restrained by custom than the *yangban*, some were able to play an important role in introducing Western culture into Korea in the late nineteenth century.

The social structure of Chosŏn Korea is illustrated by the problem of illegitimate sons. It was common for upper-class men to take commoner or slave concubines. This wife was known as his *ch'ŏp*. It created the problem of the *sŏja*, or children by these *ch'ŏp*. Early in the Yi dynasty if there were no sons by his legal wife, a *sŏja* could be named heir. But this was not approved of and it became customary to name a nephew or other male relation as heir instead. *Sŏja* were generally prohibited from taking the civil exams and holding office. As a result, they formed another hereditary group that became known as *sŏŏl*. The problem of *sŏja* and their discrimination in society was of great concern throughout the period. It seemed unjust to many scholars and to some Yi kings, who were also sometimes sons of concubines. But such was the growing strength of the patrilineal organization that the plight of the *sŏja* only became worse as it became harder, although not impossible, for a father to have a son by a secondary wife inherit all or some of his property. The problem illustrates the strength of the Confucian concept of family, and perhaps just as importantly, the aristocratic nature of Chosŏn society with its sharp division between the *yangban* elite and the rest of society. Allowing for a *sŏja* to take the civil examinations or inherit estates would blur this division. It also indicates that maternal lineage and inherited status in general were more important in Korea than in China, where such sons faced no comparable discrimination.

CRIME AND PUNISHMENT

Chosŏn law was based on Ming law. The major legal code was the *Kyŏngguk Taejŏn* promulgated in the fifteenth century, which followed the Ming Code *Da Ming lü*. During the Koryŏ period Koreans borrowed extensively from Chinese law. The Yi dynasty not only borrowed from Chinese legal practice, but it thoroughly followed the Ming Code. Chosŏn law, however, tended to vary from Chinese because case decisions, as well as various government pronouncements, supplemented this basic law code so that over time it became adapted to Korean circumstances and customs. The Ministry of Punishments was in charge of justice, but in Korea, as in China, there was not a separate judiciary. Instead administrative officials acted as investigators, prosecutors, and judges. Most criminal cases were handled by the county magistrates. Their assistants would make arrests and gather witnesses. The magistrate would then interrogate the defendants, plaintiffs, and witnesses, and pronounce sentence in accordance with the law code. More serious cases such as murder went before the provincial governor, who worked with a legal advisor from the Ministry of Punishments. The Ministry of Punishments also ran prisons, although the Board of War, the Office of the Censor-General, and the State Tribunal ran prisons as well. Difficult cases could be referred to the Ministry of Punishments in the capital. At the top of the judicial system was the *Ŭigŭmbu* (State Tribunal). This too was a Chinese-modeled institution; however, unlike in China it met irregularly only whenever the court was convened. It reviewed serious or difficult cases.

The legal process was based on the principle that the punishment should fit the crime. This meant that the intention of the criminal was taken into consideration. For example, courts had to determine whether the crime was one of passion, or whether it was planned, intentional, or accidental. The law served to enforce class distinction, not establish legal equality. "Mean people" were often punished for passing as commoners, commoners for insulting *yangban* or violating sumptuary laws. *Yangban* often carried out their own informal investigations and punishments for crimes, especially theft. Domestic violence was not generally a matter of judicial concern. If a husband beat his wife, it was not considered a criminal matter unless he broke her bones. Even then it was up to the wife to report the crime, navigating herself through the legal process. She was likely to receive severe punishments if she could not prove her charges. Discriminatory attitudes toward women are suggested by the fact that most wives charged with murdering their husbands were given the death penalty, while husbands charged with murdering their wives most often received a reduced sentence.[14]

Legally prescribed beatings were common. Light beatings were pre-scribed for minor punishments and were carried out by the local magis-trate, while heavy beatings for more serious crimes would be carried out by the governor or the Board of Punishments. Murder and treason were often, but not always, punished by execution. Mitigating circumstances for a murder might result in imprisonment, enslavement, or severe beatings. Torture was routinely used during interrogation, not only of suspects but also of witnesses. A uniquely Korean custom was the use of *churi*, which involved tying a suspect's legs tightly together, placing levers between the shins, and twisting. Not only was this very painful, it sometimes resulted in the breaking of the legs and even the permanent crippling of the suspect.[15] Not only suspects and witnesses but those who brought complaints to the state as well as petitioners were also tortured in order to assess their sincerity. Not surprisingly, most commoners and lower-class people avoided being entangled in the legal system. Instead, many crimes were settled informally between families or by prominent members of the community. Officials often complained about the prob-lem of finding people with information on criminal cases to step forth. Fear of the legal system was exacerbated by corrupt underlings of officials who used the threat of legal actions to extort money out of villagers.

One exception to the general avoidance of the law was the practice of petitioning high officials and the court to redress miscarriages of justice. Petitioners ran a considerable risk, for they could be held and questioned under torture and punished if the grievances were found unjustified. Many petitioners lined up along the roads whenever the king and his entourage traveled. During the reign of King Chŏngjo (1776–1800) more than 4,000 such petitions were recorded.[16] Others traveled to the capital to beat the petition drum outside the palace that was kept for this purpose. Most were illiterate peasants who no doubt desperately grabbed at any chance to save a loved one from execution or other punishment. For most quarrels, villagers simply went to village elders or the local *yangban* to informally settle their disputes with in-laws or neighbors.

Many crimes and acts of violence were caused by drunkenness, a prob-lem that was a matter of concern to many. King Sejong complained that wine undermined moral behavior: "How then can the little people of the villages be expected to avoid the suits and criminal cases which arise in such number from this?"[17] A large percentage of all the criminal cases at the village level were caused by alcohol-influenced brawls, beatings, and sometimes sexual assaults. Another problem was the huge amount of grain, especially rice that was used to make wine. To conserve food grains, the state issued prohibitions against making wine during periods of drought and famines, but these laws were widely ignored.

RELIGIOUS BELIEFS AND PRACTICES

Buddhism greatly declined during the Yi dynasty. Buddhist temples were banned from the capital and cut off from official patronage. Monasteries lost their tax exemptions and it was no longer proper for *yangban* to support temples. Yet despite the predominantly anti-Buddhist sentiment of the Neo-Confucian scholar-bureaucrats, the religion continued to play a role in the lives of many if not most Koreans. Several thousand temples and hermitages existed, mostly in the mountains and the countryside, where they offered a retreat from the pressures and concerns of everyday life. Two basic sects of Buddhism, Kyo and Sŏn, continued their line of teachings, and a few significant Buddhist thinkers emerged. Foremost among them were Sŏsan (1520–1604), who achieved fame during the Hideyoshi invasions by organizing armed resistance by Korean monks. Many later Korean Buddhist teachers traced their line of transmission to Sŏsan, who was also an impressive intellectual figure, and to Puhyu. Individual members of the upper classes, including even some members of the royal family, privately supported Buddhism. Commoners continued to visit temples, and Buddhist rituals remained part of popular culture. For example, in the eighteenth century the practice of *yŏmbul* (recitation of the name of Buddha) became popular among women. Still the religion declined, becoming more peripheral to Korean society. With much of its royal and upper-class patronage gone, Korean Buddhism declined in intellectual vigor until its revival in the first half of the twentieth century.

In addition to Buddhism a variety of folk religions flourished. Neo-Confucian thought left little room for the supernatural. Everything it taught was part of the natural interplay between *li* (principle) and *ki* (material force). There were no gods, afterlife, or an eternal soul. In practice, however, most Koreans were concerned about the world of spirits. Most believed in a complex spiritual realm and in spiritual forces. Restless spirits of the dead were a source of deep worry since they could cause diseases and other woes. Spirits of the ancestors were central to popular religion and ritual. To some Confucian intellectuals, this was symbolic, but probably to most Koreans, *kwisin* (spirits) were real.

Many elements of the popular religion were of indigenous and ancient origin. These included worship of spirits that inhabited natural phenomena such as trees, rocks, and especially mountains. Shrines to *Sansin*, the Mountain Spirit, were so prevalent that they were incorporated into Buddhism, where almost every temple had one. Other spirits, such as *Ch'ilsŏng* (Big Dipper), were and are still often found in temples. Women conducted pilgrimages to mountains to pray to the spirits for the health of children, a custom still practiced at the end of the twentieth century. Belief in the hidden spiritual power of prominent features of nature was blended with geomantic ideas imported from China. These centered on the importance of rivers and mountains. Mountains were especially venerated. Since at least the thirteenth century Paektu Mountain on the Korean-Manchurian border area was considered the most sacred mountain. A number of other mountains such as Chiri and Myohyang were also of great spiritual importance.

There was a host of household gods. *Sŏngju* (House Lord) inhabited the beams above the porch, *Samsin Halmŏni* (Birth Grandmother) the inner room, *Chowang* (Kitchen God) the kitchen, and *Pyŏnso Kakssi* (Toilet Maiden) the toilet; *Chisin* (Earth God) dwelt in the foundation; *Sumun* (Door Guard) protected the main gate; and *Ponhyang Sansin* (Mountain God) and *Ch'ilsŏng* (Big Dipper) inhabited the storage jars. Behind the house lived the *T'ŏju Taegam* (Site Official).[18] *T'ŏju Taegam*, the Site Official, was particularly important and had to be appeased with ritual offerings of food. Even in modern Korea offerings to the Site Official are common when the construction of a building takes place. Each village also had a *Sŏnghwang*, a local guardian god, and shrines were constructed for them. There were additional deities that some families worshiped. Most of these household and location spirits were derived from China, although the rituals differed in Korea.

One of the distinctive features of Korean popular religions was the extent to which ritual functions were segregated by gender. This was done to a degree not found among the Chinese and Japanese. While after the fifteenth century Confucian rites were carried out by men, women presided over the complex of household gods. Each of the household gods was given offerings at their place in the home. *Kosa*, the ritual offering to these gods, was exclusively performed by women, with the senior women generally in charge, especially of the rituals for the Kitchen God. In addition to the household gods, numerous beliefs were associated with fertility, especially having sons. Women venerated rocks shaped like genitals, rocks with vaginal-shaped holes, and two intertwined trees. Candlelight prayers by women at rocks and the hollows of trees was and is still practiced. Another object of veneration was the Marrying Tree, with a phallic-shaped rock in y-shaped branches.

Shamanism was also an important part of Korean spiritual life. Since ancient times shamans (*mudang* or *mansin*) acted as mediums between the world of the spirits and the human realm. The gods often descended into the *mudang* during the *kut*, the shamanist ceremony. These spirits included *chosang*, or ancestral spirits, who were sometimes restless and caused problems for the living. Shamanism lacks a cosmology or cosmogony, and is therefore not a systematic religious tradition, but it was important in Korean spiritual life. Shamans served as healers and as diviners, and both the Koryŏ and Chosŏn states patronized them as such. The state was ambivalent about shamanism, and most good Neo-Confucianists had disdain for them. Chosŏn officials, while tolerant of *p'ansu* (blind exorcists) and fortune-tellers, were intolerant of *mudang*. In part this was due to the fact that shamans, with their power to possess spirits, were a potential threat to the authority of the state and its officials. Yet shamans were useful as a channel of communication with the common people. The state registered all *mudang* and created an office to supervise them. Shamans were taxed, although some criticized this tax as it made the government dependent on them for income. In early Chosŏn, shamans participated in state-sponsored rituals, and monarchs and their families often consulted them. There was even a royal *mudang*, but this position was abolished in the seventeenth century as official disapproval of shamanism increased. Yet local officials to the end of Yi dynasty often hired shamans to perform ceremonies at local tutelary (*todang*) shrines and to drive malevolent spirits from the local government office. Shamans also, often at the request of officials, performed *kut* to end droughts and to ward off storms. During the Yi dynasty shamanism increasingly became the domain of women. As men turned away from shamans, women continued to seek them to help in problems such as child illness. Some shamans were men; most, at least in later times, were women. In late Chosŏn, women shamans formed *mubu*, regional associations run by their husbands, who were able to handle the business and public aspects of their professions. They frequently performed music during their wives' ceremonies.[19]

Elite and non-elite Koreans practiced geomancy. Koreans took the proper location of graves and homes seriously to make sure they were in accord with geomantic principles. *Chisa*, wandering geomancers, assisted rural folk in selecting grave sites and gave other geomantic advice. So important was this that there are stories of people illegally digging up bodies from graves so that they could bury their own family members in an auspicious site. Even the layout of Seoul was based on geomancy. It was protected from malevolent northern forces by Puksan (North Mountain) and safeguarded in the south by the Han River.

PHILOSOPHY

Chosŏn Korea saw a great flowering of philosophical scholarship. Philosophy was not simply an intellectual pursuit by a few scholars but was central to the society. The entire Yi dynasty can be said to be based on a great philosophical enterprise, an endeavor to discern the Way and bring the political and social institutions in conformity to it. Determining the Way thus was a vital activity. *Yangban* men generally saw themselves as scholar-bureaucrats. From childhood they were trained for government

service. Since government service meant mastering the Confucian classics in order to pass the civil exams, Confucian learning came early in life
beginning with such primers as *Xiao Xue* (*Lesser Learning*), a collection
of passages on ethics drawn from the classics by Zhu Xi's student Liu
Zucheng.

Chosŏn scholarship focused more exclusively on the Cheng-Zhu school
of Confucianism than was true in Ming and Qing China or Tokugawa
Japan. A constant vigilance was maintained against heterodoxy. Pak Se-
dang (1629–1703), a seventeenth-century scholar and official, for example,
was attacked for criticism of Zhu Xi. Pak came from a distinguished
line of bureaucrats and was himself an official in the Ministry of Rites.
His *Sabyŏnmok* (*Thoughtful Elucidations*) contained critiques of Zhu Xi's
interpretations and commentaries on the Daoist classics *Dao De Jing* and
Zhuangzi in which he included sympathetic remarks. He also argued that
Zhu Xi's amendments to the texts of the *Great Learning* and the *Doctrine of
the Mean* had failed to restore the original form that had been lost during
the Qin. He then provided his own corrections.[20] Also condemned for de-
viating from orthodoxy was Yun Hyu (1617–1680), a scholar and official
who took a more critical look at Zhu Xi. While seeing himself as being
in the Cheng-Zhu tradition, he suggested that civilization was continuing to develop so that it was not necessary to rigidly adhere to all Zhu's
teachings. Since most of his contemporaries saw Zhu Xi's commentaries
as representing the purest transmission of the Way, such remarks were
dangerous. Consequently, he was denounced and purged.

Philosophic debates became so intense because defending orthodox
philosophy was defending civilization against barbarism. Koreans saw
philosophy as a tradition that came down from the ancient sages of China.
It was their duty to carry on this line of transmission and see to it that it
was applied to everyday life. That Korea carried on this line in its purest
form was a source of enormous pride. It was also a matter of practical
politics. It was the duty of the scholar-official to advise the rulers and see
to it that they acted as a moral example for others. Even slight deviations
from these standards could have disastrous effects for society. Governing
meant maintaining a constant vigilance against the threats to civilization.
Naturally officials often disagreed on how rulers should act and behave.
These disagreements became the basis of political factions and power
struggles. Thus, moral ideals, philosophical interpretations, and power
politics became intertwined. An example of this was the Rites Controversy of 1659. In that year when King Hyojong died it became unclear
from the manuals on rituals how long the queen dowager should mourn.
Some officials in the State Council, such as Song Si-yŏl (1607–1689) a
leader of the *Sŏin* (Westerners) faction, argued that she should observe
a full one year of mourning, which was appropriate since she was the

mother of one of the sons of her husband. Other scholars, including those such as Yun Hyu associated with the *Namin* (Southerners) faction, insisted that since Hyojong was a king she should observe three years of mourning, the maximum period according to the rituals. The debate was joined by nonofficials from the private academies who accused the officials of not fully respecting the royal family. Fifteen years later, the Ritual Controversy took place when Queen Insŏn, Hyojong's widow, died. Since a wife was mourned according to her husband's status, Queen Dowager Chaŭi's mourning was based on her daughter-in-law's husband's status. But Korean law stipulated a one-year period of mourning for the wife of an eldest son, nine months for others. The Ministry of Rites chose a nine-month period of mourning. King Hyŏnjong (r. 1659–1674), outraged by this decision of the *Sŏin*-dominated bureaucracy, demanded one year of mourning and began punishing *Sŏin* bureaucrats, but his death shortly after brought the purge to an end.[21]

Yet within this narrow confine of orthodoxy an impressive outpouring of scholarship emerged. The sixteenth century in particular was a creative period. The century saw two of the most important Neo-Confucian thinkers of East Asia during this time: Yi Hwang (1501–1570), also known by his pen name T'oegye, and Yi I (1536–1584), also known by his pen name Yulgok. The main thrust of their thinking dealt with the relationship between matter and principle. The universe was viewed as a complex interaction between the two, but which came first? Which was more fundamental? Was the world made of primarily material stuff or were principles, vaguely analogous to the Western concept of ideals, more fundamental? What were the implications of these and how could such knowledge instruct people in their daily lives? These were some of the problems Korean philosophers dealt with. T'oegye placed more emphasis on the idea that *yi* (Chinese: *li*), the patterning principle of the universe, was fundamental, and Yulgok stressed the *ki* (Chinese: *qi*), the primal matter-energy. As abstract as these debates may seem, they occupied the attention of intellectuals for several centuries. T'oegye in particular was admired by scholars as far away as Japan and Vietnam, and he has been rediscovered by Western students of Eastern thought today, who have recognized him as a seminal thinker.

T'oegye also was involved in a debate with a young scholar-official, Ki Taesŭng (pen name Kobong, 1527–1572), on human nature, a debate known as the Four-Seven Debate. This also dealt with the problem of dualism. Human nature consisted of feelings, conventionally called the Seven Feelings: desire, hate, love, fear, grief, anger, and joy, a concept taken from a passage in the *Book of Rites*. Committed to the perfection of humanity, Neo-Confucian scholars worried that these feelings were not always good. But human nature was basically good, a natural goodness argued for by Mencius (372–289 BCE) in his "Four Beginnings." This natural goodness, Mencius had argued, was seen in the disposition for compassion, shame and dislike, yielding and deference, and approving and disapproving. The cultivation of these natural elements of goodness transformed them into the fundamental virtues of humanity, righteousness, propriety, and wisdom. T'oegye in his debates with Ki associated the Four Beginnings with *yi*, and the Seven Feelings, that may or may not be good, with *ki*. Later Yulgok argued that the Four Beginnings and the Seven Feelings are generated by *ki* but that *yi* directs them. The issue was whether one side of human nature is governed by goodness and another by feelings or passions that may not necessarily be good, or if human nature is one and good. This friendly debate was a search to establish a unity in humanity and in the universe.[22]

Although works outside of the Zhu-Cheng tradition were largely banned, many scholars discreetly read them. One heterodox school of Confucianism was the Wang Yangming (1472–1529) school of thought. Chŏng Che-du (pen name Hagok, 1649–1736) was an outstanding proponent of Wang Yangming. After Chŏng, a line of scholars continued to study the fifteenth-century Chinese writer. Buddhism still held intellectual interest for some scholars. Later in the Yi dynasty a truly heterodox teaching, Christianity, would also find a small number of adherents. Overall, there were few deep ideological divisions among Koreans, who increasingly came to share a common set of values.

ARTS, LITERATURE, AND SCIENCE

One of the greatest cultural achievements of the early Chosŏn period was the creation of *han'gŭl*, the indigenous alphabet. A number of systems had been devised to write Korean phonetically with Chinese characters, but they were cumbersome and did not gain lasting use, in part because the complex sound system of Korean made using a phonetic script difficult. Under King Sejong a group of scholars were commissioned to create a simpler script to make the written language more accessible to the common people. Analyzing the sounds of the Korean language, the scholars established a system based on sophisticated linguistic principles. The twenty-eight-character alphabet was so scientific that even the shapes of some letters were partly based on the position of the mouth and tongue making them. The script took these phonetic symbols and then combined them into syllables, no doubt influenced by the Chinese writing system in which each character represented a syllable. The result was a unique, practical system of writing. The new script was proclaimed in 1446 and was called *hunmin chŏngŭm* (correct sounds to instruct the people) or *ŏnmun* (vernacular script). The term *han'gŭl* (Korean writing) came into use only during the twentieth century.

It took a while for the new system to gain acceptance. This was because the prestige of Chinese characters was so great that scholars were reluctant to abandon them. Rather, *han'gŭl* was used mostly by women and to write popular literature. Official publications, scholarship, and most of the literature written by *yangban* were in Chinese or in Korean using Chinese characters. Gradually *han'gŭl* became the vehicle for popular literature and informal writing. Only in the twentieth century did it become the principal system of writing, although Chinese characters are still sometimes used in a mixed script form. *Han'gŭl* is the only major system of writing in use today that does not have its origins in the ancient Middle East, India, or China. It has become an important component of Korea's identity as a culture, and a great source of national pride for contemporary Koreans.

The *yangban* of Chosŏn saw themselves as scholars, not as artists, and did not pursue the arts as a profession. But an aesthetic sensibility was part of the pride of cultivated gentlemen. Many dabbled in amateur painting, producing some outstanding literati painters such as Kang Hŭi-an (1419–1464). The ideal in Korea, as in China, was that of the talented amateur who combined scholarship and literary knowledge with mastery of the brush stroke. Landscapes remained the most popular form of *yangban* painting. Chinese styles were admired and emulated, although fashions differed. Early in the dynasty the Northern Song school with its monumental landscapes was imitated; later the softer landscapes of the Southern Song and various Ming schools were popular. The court-sponsored art and a *Tohwasŏ* (Bureau of Painting) was established in Seoul. It was attached to the Ministry of Rites because painting was important for recording ceremonies and rituals. Artists in this office, sometimes with the help of *yangban* amateurs, produced elaborate books of ceremonies and rituals, some recording actual events. These not only are beautiful works of art but they provide an important visual record for modern historians. Court artists had to take a qualifying exam based on copying old masters. Artists were judged in four categories of descending importance: first, bamboo; second, landscape; third, people, animals, and birds; and fourth, flowers. These reflected the traditional Chinese order of importance. Professional artists, who were mostly from the *chungin* class, held less prestige than the *yangban* literati amateurs. These professional artists, however, appear to have been held in higher regard than their Chinese counterparts; some achieved fame as painters, such as An Kyŏn in the fifteenth century and Yi Sang-jwa (1465–?) in the sixteenth. An Kyŏn (flourished mid-fifteenth century) was especially admired for his Korean landscapes. The most famous is *Dream of Strolling in a Peach*

Garden (Mong yu towŏn to). This, the only surviving painting that can positively be attributed to him, is regarded by Koreans as one of their great masterpieces. Buddhist paintings, reflecting the decline in aristocratic and royal patronage, were of lesser importance. Still, many beautiful works were produced by anonymous artists. An interesting tradition was the *taenghwa*, or banners, that became popular from the sixteenth century. Influenced perhaps by Tibetan art, this tradition gained popularity in Korea as it was dying out in China and Japan. Calligraphy continued to be a highly esteemed art; many *yangban* dabbled in it.

Ceramic art, as in the Koryŏ period, was also highly esteemed. In the fifteenth century an official government-controlled factory near Kwangju in Kyŏnggi Province (not to be confused with the city of Kwangju in the southwestern Chŏlla Province) was established on the model of the great Chinese official production center at Jingdezhen. Kwangju is still a center for traditional pottery production. The demand for the products of these official kilns was so great that they had to be relocated every ten years when the nearby forests were cut down. *Punch'ŏng* was the predominant ceramic ware from the 1390s to the 1590s. It was made of the same gray clay used in celadon but was coarser in texture, with white slip decoration. Koreans did not follow Qing in its use of bright colors in porcelains and enamels. Instead, Yi dynasty pottery contains a simplicity and purity of design lacking the elaborate decorative embellishments of Ming and Qing ceramics. A number of deliberately rough-hewn ceramics were produced. The simplicity of Chosŏn pottery appealed to the Japanese and it was used in their tea ceremony.[23] During his invasions of Korea the Japanese ruler Hideyoshi brought back hundreds of Korean potters who established a number of kilns in Japan. Korean potters in Japan with the rough simplicity of their stoneware and porcelain established the basis for *raku* and other natural, deliberately unpolished styles that later would greatly influence the pottery of the West.

Chosŏn architecture survives today in many temples, palaces, schools, and private dwellings. It made no radical departures from established traditions. Building styles continued to follow Chinese patterns. Almost all larger structures were made of wood with characteristic curved overhanging roofs with ceramic tiles. Koreans, however, preferred their own distinctive and often less bright shades of red, blue, yellow, white, and green. Producing these colors developed into an art form known as *tanch'ŏng*. The city of Seoul was laid out on the model of Chinese imperial cities. The royal palaces, as with their Chinese counterparts, were symmetrical structures laid out behind each other facing south. The Kyŏngbok Palace best exemplifies this Chinese imperial style. Other palaces and public buildings tended to modify the rigid symmetry of Chinese official architecture. Palaces and wealthy homes often had gardens. The most famous of Chosŏn gardens is the Piwŏn (Secret Garden) in Seoul. It best illustrates the rough, natural, almost uncared-for style of Korean gardens that is quite different from the manicured gardens of China and Japan. Restricted in number in the cities, Buddhist temples took advantage of remote mountain locations so as to blend into their natural settings. Temples in Korea tended to adhere to pre-Song styles.

Poetry flourished in Chosŏn Korea. Every *yangban* was supposed to appreciate poetry, and many composed verses in Chinese and Korean. A major genre was *sijo* poetry. This was a short suggestive poem, similar to Chinese *jueju* and the Japanese *tanka* and *haiku*. The *sijo* emerged in the late fourteenth century and became the most beloved poetic form in Korea. It is still popular. The name *sijo* is a modern one; in the Chosŏn period it was usually referred to simply as *tan'ga* (short song), a name that suggests its link with lyrical songs. *Sijo* has three lines, each with fifteen syllables, although the last line varies somewhat in length. They total about forty-five syllables. Each line is divided into two parts by a pause in the middle. The first line presents the theme, and the second line either reinforces or elaborates on it. The final line, as Kichung Kim points out, often introduces a "jolting twist or counter theme."[24] Unlike Chinese poetry, Korean poems rely on alliteration or on cadence, not rhyme. This beloved form was written by Koreans of all professions. Thousands of *sijo* from the Yi dynasty survive today. Some were simply moral precepts in poetry; others extolled the beauties of nature. A famous one is the "Song to Five Companions" by Yun Sŏn-do (1587–1671), who is regarded as among the greatest masters of *sijo*:

> How many friends have I, you ask?
> The streams and rocks, the pines and bamboo;
> Moon rising over eastern mountain
> You I welcome too.
> Enough. Beyond these five companions
> What need is there for more?[25]

Kisaeng also composed a number of *sijo*. Most famous is the Hwang Chin-i (1506–1544), who was one of its great masters. Unlike most women, *kisaeng* were relatively free to express their emotions, and they were often highly literate. One of the subjects of their poetry was the sadness associated with love. Their often intense passions for clients always had an impermanent quality about them, forcing them to explore the nature of love. This is illustrated in the following poems by an anonymous seventeenth-century *kisaeng*:

An anchor lifts, a ship is leaving.
He goes this time, when to return.

Far over the sea's vast waverings
one can see a going as return.
But at the sound of that anchor lifting the night could feel her insides turn.[26]

Another poetic form was the *kasa*, a longer, open-ended type of poem. The *kasa*, which was most probably derived from lyric songs, began in the fifteenth century and was perfected by masters such as Chŏng Ch'ŏl (1537–1594) and Hŏ Nansŏrhŏn (1563–1585). A popular theme of this form of poetry was the beauty of nature. *Kasa* were written in *han'gŭl* and partly for this reason were popular among women as well as men.

Stories of the mysterious and bizarre, derived from the Chinese tradition of *quanqi* (tales of wonder), were popular in Chosŏn times. Among the best known was *Kŭmo sinhwa* (*New Stories from Golden Turtle Mountain*) by Kim Si-sŭp (1435–1493), an eccentric writer who lived part of his life as a wandering monk. Another popular work was the *P'aegwan chapki* (*The Storyteller's Miscellany*) by Ŏ Suk-kwŏn (fl. 1522–1544), a Chinese interpreter. The Yi period also saw the emergence of the Korean novel. Hundreds of Chosŏn novels survive, the majority by anonymous authors. Widely read, most were romantic tales of adventure and love. One of the first was *Hong Kil-tong chŏn* (*Tale of Hong Kil-tong*) by Hŏ Kyun (1569–1618). This is the story of an illegitimate son of a high official who suffers the discrimination of being an illegitimate son. Hong studies martial arts and then leads a bandit gang with other illegitimate sons and social outcasts called the "Save the Poor" Gang. In Robin Hood style they rob the unjust rich, including corrupt officials and greedy monks, but not the poor. The hero has magical powers that assist him. In general the novel is filled with fantastic elements and lacks the character development expected in modern Western novels. It has been called the first Korean novel, but it is rather short and it is perhaps better to call it a romantic prose tale. Very popular, it also has been viewed as a story of social protest, criticizing the Chosŏn society for valuing bloodlines over talent and virtue. The author, himself a legitimate son of a high-ranking *yangban*, appeared to identify with the society's outcasts, especially its illegitimate sons. Hŏ was executed in 1618 for allegedly plotting an uprising against the state.

Another great classic novel was *A Dream of Nine Clouds* (*Ku un mong*) by Kim Man-jung (1637–1692). It has been called the oldest major novel in *han'gŭl* but may have been originally written in *hanmun* (Chinese characters). As with so many Korean stories it was set in China, in this case during the Tang. In the novel a Buddhist monk dreams he is reborn as another person. In his new life he meets eight beautiful women in different settings; two become his wives and the others his concubines. Skilled in both martial and literary arts, he has many adventures and becomes an official in the imperial court. One day in retirement he wakes up to find it all a dream. While superficially a Buddhist tale of the transitory nature of existence, in reality it is a sexual and romantic fantasy.

TECHNOLOGY AND INVENTIONS

Koreans showed a lively inventive spirit. A number of water clocks were made. A water clock of 1398 had a bell that struck at sunrise and sunset. In the fifteenth century the inventor Chang Yŏng-sil earned fame for many mechanical devices, including a self-striking water clock. Under Sejong, a royal observatory with an elaborate armillary sphere and a forty-foot bronze gnomon to measure the exact altitude of the sun was constructed. Skilled artisans manufactured numerous other astronomical clocks, water clocks, and sundials, including imitations of Western mechanical clocks in the seventeenth century. This concern with timekeeping was stimulated in part by the widespread use of wet field agriculture, which made keeping an accurate calendar ever more crucial. Consequently, Koreans made careful studies of astronomy and the weather. In 1442, a system of rain gauges (*ch'ŭgugi*) was set up throughout the kingdom to keep accurate records of rainfall. This system was discontinued in the late sixteenth century and resumed in 1770. Korea thus maintains the longest records of measured rainfall in the world. Worried by foreign invaders, Koreans experimented with weapons such as a multibarreled cannon. The most famous invention was the "turtle ship," the world's first ironclad ship, built in the late sixteenth century.

The inventions, the outpouring of philosophical writings, and the literary and artistic achievements of Chosŏn Korea from the fifteenth through the seventeenth centuries all reflect a flourishing society. As Neo-Confucian values pervaded society and shaped its family and political life, they lent a unity and stability to Korean society. This along with improvements in agriculture made this period a prosperous and productive one in Korea's long history.

KOREA IN GLOBAL PERSPECTIVE:
WOMEN IN KOREA

During the Chosŏn period Korean women saw greater restrictions placed on their activities; they lost the rights to divorce, remarry, and inherit property; and they found themselves increasingly segregated from males. All this was in sharp contrast with earlier times. This development was not unique to Korea; it was part of a general pattern in East Asia that is often attributed to the Confucian revival that took place during the Song dynasty (960–1279) and that spread to Korea and later to Japan. Chinese women from the Song saw greater restrictions on their activities, and the cult of chastity was such that families added to their prestige by erecting monuments to particularly virtuous women. These became so popular that the Qing (1644–1911) government limited their construction. Women could not remarry or appear in public without the company of male members. As in Korea, women could not inherit property.

Koreans appeared to go a bit further than the Chinese in practicing strict segregation between the sexes; Chinese homes were never so sharply divided into male and female quarters, nor were there separate curfew hours for men and women in the cities. However, there was no Korean equivalent to the Chinese practice of foot binding that began in the Song and became a pervasive custom in Ming and Qing times. Japanese women were, as Korean visitors commented on, much freer, and the two sexes could mingle in public. But Japanese women saw a similar decline in social status—becoming less prominent in public affairs. By the seventeenth century they lost their ability to participate in village government, to divorce, and to own property. As in Korea, the lower social status of women in the seventeenth, eighteenth, and nineteenth centuries was a strong contrast to earlier times.

Some historians have seen a global decline in the status of women in the millennium before the twentieth century. Evidence from art and literature suggests that Indian women enjoyed greater social freedom before the twelfth century. Then tighter restrictions were placed on them, perhaps influenced by Islam which entered the region as a major force in the late twelfth century. The explicit sexuality and immodest dress depicted in ancient and early medieval art became offensive to the prudish tastes of Indians in more recent times. The practice of *sati*, the immolation of women at their husband's funeral, while never widely practiced, became a symbol of the total devotion a good Indian wife was supposed to display. In the Middle East, Islam gave women greater legal protection from spousal mistreatment and the right to receive alimony payments; but it also sanctified restrictions on public movement, gave the husbands the right to divorce, to have up to four wives, and in many ways made women subordinate to the authority of men. Many of these restrictions, including public veiling, were already widely practiced in the Middle East but were newly introduced with the arrival of Islam in many areas from North Africa to Indonesia. Some historians see a similar decline in the freedom and independence of women in much of Africa after 1000 CE with the spread of female circumcision and the influence of Islam. Only in Europe and in non-Muslim Southeast Asia is this pattern less clear.

Thus the decline in the status of women in Korea from the fourteenth century can be seen as part of broader trend in many parts of the Afro-Eurasian world. Some features of life for women in Chosŏn times, however, had fewer equivalents elsewhere: the arrangements of the house into separate women's and men's sections, and the quite separate world of religious rituals centered around *chesa* for men and *kosa* for women. Korea developed a women's literature different from men's. The closest equivalent of this was in Japan during the Heian period (794–1160) where women produced some of that society's greatest literary works. But this unique world of women's literature was largely absent later. China, Europe, and the Middle East produced women poets, mystics, and essayists but there were no distinctive genres of women's literature. So while the decline in the social status of Korean women and the restrictions they lived under were not so different from other societies, the degrees to which separate and segregated spheres were established for men and women from household architecture to religious ritual and literature had no exact equivalent.

KOREA IN GLOBAL PERSPECTIVE: CHOSŎN'S SOCIAL HIERARCHY

Social inequality, hierarchy, and inherited status were characteristic of almost all complex societies in premodern times. Korea very much typified the pattern. There were variations of this general structure of societies. China from the Tang times evolved into a society that allowed greater social mobility than Korea, mainly through the civil examination system. In marked contrast to Chinese practice, Koreans restricted the examinations to only those of privileged status. Thus in Korea, the civil exams reinforced inherited status. The social mobility of late imperial China is reflected in the popular tales of families rising and falling from humble backgrounds to membership in the elite and back to humble status in three generations. However, the contrast with Korea can be overdrawn, as studies have shown that while there was not an official inherited elite in China after Tang times, certain families through wealth and connections were able to produce examination holders and maintain local leadership for generations. Still, compared with China, Korea under both Koryŏ and Chosŏn was a more rigidly stratified and a more aristocratic society. Japan, perhaps, was most similar with its domination by the *bushi* class of warrior aristocrats. There too, heredity was the dominant principle. Although there were cases of people from humble background, such as Hideyoshi, emerging to the highest ranks of society, especially during times of social and political unrest, occupation, whether merchant, farmer or ruler, was determined by family background.

In can be argued that Korea's social structure resembled India's caste system with its corresponding elite, commoner, and outcaste groups. However, it differed from India in that inherited privilege was not religiously sanctified in Korea. In fact, Confucian principles regarded merit, not heredity, as the ideal basis for leadership and governance. Nor was the hierarchical social structure of Korea articulated in such a detailed and complex way. European society before the nineteenth century was probably nearly as rigidly hierarchical as Korea, dominated by aristocratic elites. Only gradually after 1500 did rising urban interests erode aristocratic domination. Indeed, most Middle Eastern, African, and Southeast Asian societies as well as pre-Columbian societies such as the Aztec and Inca were dominated by inherited elites.

Perhaps what marked Korea as distinctive was the continuity of the aristocratic elite. Recent studies have shown how many of the same aristocratic families that dominated Koryŏ maintained economic and social dominance during the Chosŏn. The thousand-year dominance of much of the aristocracy had no counterpart in China, the Middle East, or Europe. Historical events partly explain this. Middle Eastern and South Asian societies saw continued social upheaval as Turkish and other groups invaded and established dominance during the tenth through fifteenth centuries. No state in that region enjoyed the stability and institutional continuity of Korea. Southeast Asian societies saw major changes throughout the middle ages and in early modern times as Thais, Burmans, and other new ethnic groups displaced earlier dominant ones such as the Mon. Migrations of peoples roiled most of Europe until the tenth century, and violent civil wars among the warrior aristocrats help account for the smaller numbers of European aristocratic families that survived for many centuries. Only in isolated Japan was there a similar continuity of elite families. Thus while emphasis on hierarchy and inherited status in Korea was not atypical of the premodern world, few societies had such a stable social order.

The Creation of the Han'gŭl Script
King Sejong, Preface to Correct Sounds to Instruct the People

The sounds of our language differ from those of Chinese and are not easily communicated by using Chinese graphs. Many among the ignorant, therefore, though they wish to express sentiments in writing, have been unable to communicate. Considering this situation with compassion, I have newly devised twenty-eight letters. I wish only that people will learn them easily and use them conveniently in their daily life.

—from *Hunmin chŏngŭm* 1a[27]

Chŏng Inji, Postscript to Correct Sounds to Instruct the People

In general, the languages of different countries have their own enunciations but lack their own letters, so they borrowed the Chinese graphs to communicate their needs. That is, however, like trying to fit a square handle into a round hole. How could it possibly achieve its objective satisfactorily? It is, therefore, important that each region should follow the practices that are convenient to its people and that no one should be compelled to follow one writing system alone.

In the winter of the year *kyehae* [1443], His Majesty, the king, created twenty-eight letters of the Correct Sounds and provided examples in outline demonstrating their meanings. His Majesty then named these letters *Hunmin chŏngŭm*. Resembling pictographs, these letters imitate the shapes of the old seal characters. Based on enunciation, their sounds correspond to the Seven Modes in music. These letters embrace the principles of heaven, earth, and men as well as the mysteries of yin and yang, and there is nothing they cannot express. With these twenty-eight letters, infinite turns and changes can be explained; they are simple and yet contain all the essence; they are refined and yet easily communicable. Therefore, a clever man can learn them in one morning, though a dull man may take ten days to study them. If we use these letters to explain books, it will be easier to comprehend their meanings. If we use the letters in administering litigations, it will be easier to ascertain the facts of the case. As for rhymes, one can easily distinguish voiced and voiceless consonants; as for music and songs, twelve semitones can be easily blended. They can be used whatever and wherever the occasion may be.

—from *Hunmin chŏngŭm haerye* 26b–29b[28]

8

❖

Late Chosŏn, Early 18th Century to 1876

The period stretching from the late seventeenth to the early nineteenth century was one of peace, stability, and prosperity in Korea. In general this was true of East Asia as a whole. The Qing had consolidated their rule in China and presided over an era of demographic and commercial expansion. Japan under the Tokugawa entered a period of limited contact with the outside world, but it was also a time of economic growth and domestic order. The Qing had gained firm control over Manchuria, securing that region. Korea thus faced no major threats from its neighbors. Internally, several centuries of efforts to promote Neo-Confucian values and institutions had resulted in a major transformation of society. Educated Koreans were proud of this transformation that made their society a center of civilized values. Yet there was still a wide discrepancy between the ideals of society held by Confucianists and the reality around them. Consequently, many Koreans called for various reforms that would solve the problems of poverty and social injustice and strengthen the state. A large body of literature critical of society emerged and a number of reforms were carried out, although seldom as vigorously as their adherents hoped.

The eighteenth century also saw a cultural efflorescence as Koreans produced many works of art and literature, including some new genres. Koreans wrote a number of histories and studies of their own culture during this period. Some historians today see in the eighteenth century a heightening of national consciousness and a growing awareness and appreciation by Koreans of the distinctiveness and uniqueness of their culture. Koreans also began to see their land as the truest bastion of the great

Confucian tradition. More than China, it was Korea, they believed, that kept the line of transmission of civilization in its purest, most unbroken form. Yet for all the increasing pride and confidence literate Koreans felt in their society, many remained concerned about its problems.

THE POLITICS OF LATE CHOSŎN

The late seventeenth century saw Korea ridden with factional struggles centered in the capital. The *Namin* (Southerners) came to power in 1674. They were ousted by the *Sŏin* (Westerners) in 1689, who soon split into rival *Noron* and *Soron* (Old and Young Doctrine) factions. The Old Doctrine emerged as dominant. Then two very able monarchs came to power. The first, King Yŏngjo (r. 1724–1776), made a practice of appointing officials from all the major factions, a policy that brought a half century of political stability as he carefully balanced factions and exerted a strong personal influence on the court. During his exceptionally long reign he gained the experience and skill to dominate his officials. He was succeeded by his grandson Chŏngjo (r. 1776–1800), who also strove hard to provide orderly government. Factional disputes and court intrigue continued, but during their long rule the two exemplary monarchs were able to moderate the intrigue and attract many talented scholars and administrators to the central government.

In many ways Korea during the reigns of Chŏngjo and Yŏngjo came as close to being a model Neo-Confucian society as ever appeared in East Asia. As good Confucians, the Yi monarchs employed the concept and rhetoric of the sage-king. However, kings not only used the rhetoric, but also had to submit to the rigors the ideal demanded. The king was the father-ruler. Koreans believed that humans through the power of reason could make society moral, orderly, and rational on the model of and in harmony with the larger universe. In order to establish such an order the Mandate of Heaven (Chinese: *tianming*; Korean: *ch'ŏnmyŏng*) was conferred upon a certain individual to become a ruler. This idea vested every action by the king and his court with enormous importance. It was also a heavy burden since every action had major moral and cosmic significance. The ruler was at once chief priest to his people, dynastic instrument to his forebears, promoter of civilization, upholder of the classics, and exemplar and father to his people.

A Korean monarch's role as a model of Confucian conduct restricted him. His every utterance was carefully scrutinized, and he had to constantly display his virtue. His authority was also limited by the fact that the Chinese emperor, not he, was the center of the universe. The investiture ceremony of the Korean ruler by the Son of Heaven symbolized this peripheral and subservient position of Korean king. The monarch's power was further restricted by the fact that a relatively small number of powerful aristocratic families monopolized the greater portion of top posts and were power centers in themselves. In addition, Koreans took the moral authority of scholars seriously. Learned men serving as censors and private scholars issued memorials that criticized the actions of the king and his officials. Yŏngjo, in particular, availed himself of the rhetoric and ritual to fashion an image as a moral ruler. It was not an easy task, because the bureaucrats had their own claims to be wise and upright upholders of the moral order. The king had to continually and scrupulously adhere to the letter and spirit of Neo-Confucianism. Much of a king's time was spent in performing rituals, and Yŏngjo exerted his power in part by dutifully and carefully performing them. Adding to his prestige and influence, Yŏngjo created a new ritual of expressing sympathy with the people during times of famine or epidemics when he would meet with afflicted families and do what he could to ease their sufferings.[1] His grandson and successor Chŏngjo followed in his path.

But even these able monarchs could not free themselves from court intrigue. Yŏngjo's principal queen had no sons; two, however, were born from lesser wives, and one died young. The surviving son, Prince Changhŏn (also known as Prince Sado), was made crown prince and assigned duties at court. The prince's behavior became increasingly erratic and bizarre as he manifested symptoms of mental illness. In 1762, the king ordered his son placed in a rice chest and smothered to death. This became a famous episode in Korean history. Two major new factions emerged over these events: the *si* that opposed them and the *pyŏk* that accepted them. Thus for all his skill as a king, Yŏngjo created still new factions. The next king, Chŏngjo, was Changhŏn's son. He had to contend with the struggle for power between a lineage of the P'ungsan Hong and a lineage of the Ch'ŏngp'ung Kim. Accounts of his reign, while fairly uneventful, nonetheless are full of tension, for life at the royal court was often a perilous one. Every action by every member was subject to criticism. A mistake, even among members of the royal family, could lead to exile or death.

LATE CHOSŎN AND THE CONFUCIAN WORLD ORDER

Meanwhile, Korea maintained correct if not warm relations with China under the Qing (Manchu) dynasty. The Manchus had defeated Korea in 1636, forced the Koreans to pay indemnities, and held members of the royal family as hostages. Initially harsh, the tribute extracted by the Manchus, who after 1644 ruled China as the Qing dynasty, was considerably reduced in the seventeenth century. Still, each year the Koreans supplied rolls of their prized paper, furs, and bolts of cotton and other cloth. This tribute continued until the mid-nineteenth century. In addition to the inconveniences of tribute, Koreans continued to view the Qing rulers as barbarian usurpers. King Hyojong (r. 1659–1674), who had spent eight years as a hostage, harbored a hatred of the new Chinese rulers. He plotted to organize a "northern expedition" to attack the Qing that never materialized. Anti-Qing forces were encouraged by the resistance of Ming loyalist groups within China, but with the defeat of the last Ming loyalist base in Taiwan in 1683 those hopes faded. The Yi court then became reconciled with the reality of the Manchu rule of China.

Despite the contempt many Koreans felt for the new dynasty and for the way Chinese officials had compromised their integrity by serving it, relations gradually improved. Under the able emperors Kangxi (r. 1662–1722) and Qianlong (r. 1736–1796) China prospered, and Koreans came to admire the flourishing culture and economy of Qing. Trade along the border and during diplomatic exchanges prospered. Korean embassies continued to visit Beijing during New Year's, at the ascension of new emperors, and at various other occasions. Chosŏn monarchs still found the investiture ceremony by the Son of Heaven useful for legitimizing their authority. Furthermore, the diplomatic missions continued to be an important source of information and cultural exchange. Many of Korea's leading scholars and officials participated in these missions, where they had an opportunity to meet with Chinese officials and scholars and collect books. Korean officials visiting Beijing, especially in the eighteenth century, were impressed by the prosperity and by the high cultural attainment of Qing China. As in the past, they were eager to follow the latest trends from what they regarded as the world center of culture.

Most Koreans, however, felt more loyalty to the old Ming dynasty and regarded the Manchu rulers as both usurpers and part barbarian. While outwardly submitting to the Qing, they continued to discreetly honor the memory of the Ming. In 1704, King Sukchong built an altar, the Taebodan, to the Ming emperors. Court officials built another altar in 1717 to the Ming emperor Wanli, who had sent troops to assist Korea during the Hideyoshi invasions. In a number of quiet but subtle ways the Chosŏn government hinted at its disdain for its powerful neighbor. Tribute missions to China that had been called *choch'ŏn* (Chinese *chaotian,* "visiting the court of the Son of Heaven") were given the less exalted title of *yŏnhaeng* (mission to Beijing). Koreans continued to use a calendar that was dated from the last Ming emperor rather than adopt the calendar of the Qing. The Qing in turn remained somewhat suspicious of Chosŏn, and restricted trade and contact with them.

One line of thought was that Korea could do nothing but wait until Heaven sought to restore legitimacy to the celestial throne. Until that time Korea had to maintain correct relations with its neighbor, and carry the burden of being the sole inheritor of the Way of the Sages. As a result, the idea came about among Koreans that since China was ruled by a dynasty of questionable legitimacy, and since its rulers were not fully civilized, Korea remained the last true bastion of civilization (that is, of course, Confucian civilization). Yŏngjo reflected on this idea that China under the Qing was itself part barbarian when he stated that "the Central Plains [China] exude the stenches of barbarians and our Green Hills [Korea] are alone."[2] Such an idea was reinforced by the reports that in China the teachings of Wang Yangming and other "heterodox" thinkers were widely accepted. Only Korea remained firm in its adherence to "orthodox" Confucian teachings as transmitted by Zhu Xi. All this gave the Korean elite a feeling of distinctiveness or separateness from China as well as a sense of cultural superiority, even if their country was militarily weak.

Korea also maintained neighborly relations with Japan. Despite the destruction and loss of life caused by Hideyoshi's invasions, Chosŏn sought to establish peaceful relations with the new government of the Tokugawa shogunate that was established after 1600. In 1606, Seoul sent an embassy to the new ruler, Tokugawa Ieyasu, in Edo (Tokyo). In 1609 a treaty was established with the Sŏ clan of Tsushima across the Korea Straits. This allowed Japanese ships to trade at Pusan. A special walled compound was built outside that city, the *Waegwan* (Japan House), where Japanese merchants could reside and trade. From the early seventeenth century to the 1870s on average about 500 Japanese lived in Japan House.[3] The two societies carried out a modest but not insignificant trade with each other. Korean merchants sold a variety of Korean goods and some Chinese products in exchange for Japanese porcelain, crafts, and especially silver. Japan's biggest import from Korea was ginseng. In the seventeenth century, when the shogunate debased the coins, it minted a special silver money primarily to buy ginseng. Trade between the two lands declined somewhat in the later eighteenth and nineteenth centuries but was never insignificant. In addition to trade, Koreans occasionally sent embassies to Edo. Eleven were sent between 1606 and 1793. These were huge affairs including hundreds of members who traveled by ship and over land visiting cities and towns. A number of Korean scholars accompanied these embassies, where they met Japanese scholars and artists. As a result of these embassies Korean scholars had some influence on Japanese art and philosophy, and they sometimes came back impressed by Japan's prosperity and commercial development.

Despite the trade at Pusan and the occasional embassies with their friendly meetings between Korean and Japanese scholars, the Koreans remained distrustful of their island neighbors. The Chosŏn government refused requests by the Bakufu government to send embassies to Seoul, and the Japanese merchants at Pusan were confined to their walled compound. A sensitive diplomatic point was the refusal of Koreans to acknowledge the Japanese ruler's title of emperor. This would place the Japanese on equal terms with the Chinese emperor, totally unacceptable in the Korean view of the world. It would also place Korea in the diplomatically inferior position. The Tokugawa shoguns dealt with this problem by simply avoiding any reference to the Japanese emperor in their diplomatic exchanges. In their dealings with Chosŏn the shoguns assumed the title for themselves of *Taikun* (Great Prince). This term was picked up by Westerners when they came to Japan and is the origin of the English term "tycoon."

On their northern border, the Qing had incorporated Manchuria into the Chinese Empire, which meant that Koreans no longer had to worry about Central Asian invaders. In fact, as the result of the use of firearms and artillery by the Chinese and by the Russians in the west, the power of the nomads had been broken. But a new threat slowly emerged from the northwest: the Russians in the seventeenth century conquered Siberia and began to approach the frontiers of Korea. The full force of this new threat, however, would not be felt until the nineteenth century. During their embassy visits to Beijing in the seventeenth and eighteenth century Koreans had their first encounters with Westerners. Initially these contacts were no more than curiosities for Koreans, but toward the end of the eighteenth century Western ideas began to influence a small circle of intellectuals (see chapter 9).

KOREAN TRAVELERS TO CHINA AND JAPAN

Koreans continued under the Qing to send three tribute missions a year. All totaled up, about 700 missions went to Beijing during the two and a half centuries from the inauguration of the Qing dynasty in 1644 to the end of the tributary system in the late nineteenth century. The typical mission consisted of about 30 officials who along with their scribes, translators, servants, and porters added up to about 200–300 persons. They followed a prescribed land route that took up to eight weeks each way and stayed in Beijing for about two months in the Hall of Jade River in the south part of the city. Although technically these were diplomatic missions, the members privately engaged in trade with merchants along the way and in the Chinese capital. Upon arrival there were official functions to attend and the audience with the emperor to prepare for, but much of the time was spent seeing the sights, meeting with Chinese and the occasional foreigner in Beijing, and of course shopping. Other than translators, who held the humble status of *chungin*, few Koreans could speak Chinese, but they could read and write it. They therefore communicated with their Chinese counterparts in what they called "brush talk," that is, through writing.

For most Koreans the trip was a once-in-a-lifetime opportunity and they tried to make the most of it. Many educated members wrote travel accounts when they got back. About 40 of these travel diaries from the Ming, usually called *Choch'ŏnnok* (*Audience with the Emperor*), and 500 from the Qing, called *Yŏnhaengnok* (*Travel Records to Beijing*), have survived. They provide a glimpse into how Koreans saw themselves as well as what they saw in China. By the eighteenth century these travel diaries became a vehicle to critically compare Korea with China, generally with the aim of pointing to the need for reform in their society. This school of critical writing became known as *Pukhak* (Northern Learning), the north being a reference to Beijing. Thus a uniquely Korean literary form combining travelogue with criticism emerged that had no counterpart elsewhere in East Asia. The diarists were impressed by the level of commercial activity in China. Markets were open all day and night, every day, unlike in Korea where markets generally opened only on market days. And their size and variety were impressive. One observer writing in 1828 wrote, "The lengths these people will take to make a living are really ingenious. There are some who will even cut other people's hair, others will administer baths, still others will cut people's fingernails. And there is a gadget for everything, even for picking paper out of privies or for carrying horse manure."[4]

Korean travel diarists used their works to criticize their own society. Among the important travel diaries was Hong Tae-yong's (1731–1783) *Yŏn'gi* (*Beijing Record*). Accompanying an uncle to Beijing as a military aide in 1766, Hong wrote of the order and prosperity of China under the Qing Qianlong emperor.[5] Pak Chi-wŏn's (1737–1805) *Yŏrha ilgi* (*Jehol Diary*) saw China's wealth as a model for Korea. China possessed good roads, canals, and canal locks, and made use of carriages, baggage wagons, and wheelbarrows. Korea had a mountainous terrain, Pak noted, but even China's mountainous regions had good roads. Why not Korea? he asked. He was also aware of the less rigid class distinctions in China and the greater ability of men of talent to rise to high office without belonging to elite families. Another famous critique is Pak Che-ga's (b. 1750) *Pukhak ŭi* (*A Proposal for Northern Studies*), a memorial to King Chŏngjo in which he argued that Korea must emulate China's technology and commerce.

Korean travelers to China, however, also found much to be critical of. They commented on the subservience of the Chinese to their "barbarian" Manchu rulers. While Koreans proudly wore Ming-style fashions, such clothes were prohibited to their hosts. Especially notable was the custom by which Chinese men shaved the front part of their scalps and tied their hair in the back of their heads into queues. This practice, ordered by the Manchus to distinguish the Chinese from themselves, was to many Koreans a shameful sign of subservience. They could not help contrasting this to their own proud adherence to the practices of the venerable Ming dynasty and their own freedom from domination by a foreign ethnic group. Hong Tae-yong, while engaging in a "brush talk" with a Chinese scholar, for example, was explaining the Korean custom of showing respect for the former dynasty by leaving a blank line before writing the name Ming. The Chinese scholar upon seeing the character for Ming quickly tore up the paper before authorities could see it.[6] Thus, while Koreans increasingly admired the Qing, especially under the Kangxi and Qianlong emperors, they also became acutely aware of their differences, including their greater ideological purity.

Koreans also journeyed to Tokugawa Japan on twelve missions to that country between 1607 to 1811. Travelers to Japan also wrote diaries and noted the differences between their society and Japan. Since such missions were fewer and held less prestige than those to China, these diaries never developed into a Japanese equivalent of the Northern Studies literature. They do, however, provide insights into how Koreans contrasted themselves with the Japanese. Korean envoys were impressed by the prosperity of Tokugawa Japan, by the size of their cities and their cleanliness. Osaka was larger than Seoul, but almost entirely devoted to commerce, with a vast number of shops. There was no equivalent commercial center in Korea. Travelers also commented on the high quality of Japanese craftsmanship and the sophistication of agricultural technology. The cities and towns were clean and bustling, the countryside was prosperous, and the people were well dressed. Japanese steelmaking, in particular, was of a high standard. They also commented on Japan's military strength.[7]

Yet there was much they did not admire about Japan. Japanese moral standards were woefully inadequate. Men and women socialized too openly, and the women were flirtatious. Prostitution and brothels were everywhere, and people of the same surname married. Most shocking was .the sight of men and women bathing naked together. Although Koreans themselves had once practiced this custom, in Yi times this was scandalously in violation of propriety. The principle of segregating men and women was not practiced; boys and girls played together, and were not separated at the age of seven as in Korea. Also disturbing was the practice of homosexuality, which confused the distinction between men and women, a cardinal Confucian virtue. Koreans found the level of civilization in Japan to be lower than in their own country. Japanese scholarship was inferior to their own, since the Japanese showed less mastery of the Confucian classics. They had internalized less of what they did know. There were no altars to Confucius and no ritual robes at funerals, nor did the Japanese properly carry out the rites to their parents or ancestors. Koreans were unimpressed by Japanese literature. Their lack of propriety between men and women, their inferior knowledge of Confucian literature and ritual, and their practice of blackening their teeth were all signs of their semibarbarian nature. Patronizingly, some Koreans noted the Tokugawa state sponsorship of Neo-Confucianism, commenting that they were making some progress. Koreans could point out with pride that the Zhu Xi school of Neo-Confucianism had been introduced to Japan by Kang Hang (1567–1618), a Korean scholar who had been taken to Japan as a prisoner of war. Kang worked with Fujiwara Seika (1561–1619), the Japanese scholar who helped establish Neo-Confucianism as an officially sponsored school of thought during the Tokugawa period. Visitors also noted that Yi T'oegye was studied and admired in Japan. Yet visitors from Seoul also noted that Confucian scholars were lower in social status than warriors.[8] Overall the level of learning in Japan, Koreans felt, was much inferior to their own. A few scholars, notably Chŏng Yak-yong (also known as Tasan) (1762–1836), took Japanese scholarship seriously enough to study it. But for many the Japanese were "barbarians like the beasts and the birds."[9]

TAXATION AND REFORM

The Chosŏn court, the central bureaucracy, the local government officials, the military, and the many scholars and officials supported by the state derived their income from a complex system of taxes. The Chosŏn state was more successful than its predecessor in raising revenue; still, it struggled to get adequate support. Revenue came from the collection of land taxes, tribute payments in which individuals and localities were required to supply specialized products, the use of corvée labor from commoners, and the forced labor of government slaves. The state also imposed a vast array of supplementary taxes. Since Korea was an overwhelmingly agricultural society, taxes from commerce and industry made up only a small portion of the revenue. Most of the tax burden fell on the peasants.

A major source of revenue came from tribute taxes that consisted of tribute of *chinsang* (local specialties to the royal family), *kongmul* (local specialties to the central government departments), and *sep'ae* (local specialties to the Chinese emperor). Provincial governors and magistrates were required to supply tribute articles to the king, and these of course were exacted from the commoners and slaves under their jurisdiction. The state kept *kongan* (tribute ledgers) to keep track of payments. The ledgers were based on populations of different districts; however, they were not periodically revised to account for changes in population or in the local economy that may have once but no longer produced a certain product. This resulted in unreasonable levies in some areas. Special levies of tribute could be issued, and sometimes tribute was collected years in advance. *Chinsang* was especially burdensome because it could be levied frequently and unexpectedly. Tribute contracting (*taenap* or *pangnap*) became increasingly more common. Tribute contracting involved middlemen who collected rice or cloth as a substitute for tribute payments from district magistrates or from commoners and used them to purchase tribute goods. Many royal family members and high officials engaged in contracting, and sent their personal aides or slaves to forcibly collect tribute if necessary. By the seventeenth century the tribute system was, in practice, replaced by the direct purchasing of goods through contractors. As a result, most peasants and officials simply paid their tribute in the form of rice, cloth, or cash.

Peasants were also burdened by uncompensated labor service. This involved grain taxes and tribute items from villages and the transportation of them to collecting points. It also included manufacturing boats; mining; gathering husks, straw, coal, and firewood; and hunting game. It could also involve digging for coal; fishing; tending horses; building dikes, dams, city walls, and bridges; and supplying goods on demand. Peasants also had to bear the expense of putting up foreign envoys, officials who were on government business, and the king and his entourage when they were on the expeditions. These expenses could be unannounced and burdensome. Besides this formal tax system, peasants and other commoners were regularly forced to pay bribes and unauthorized fees to officials who often depended on these unofficial charges to support themselves.[10]

The inequity of the tax system and its unsystematic nature troubled many officials, who suggested a variety of reforms. Since as good Confucianists Koreans looked back to the time of the ancient sages of China for models, officials from time to time suggested various reforms based on their understanding of ancient Chinese practice. One popular idea was the well-field system of ancient Zhou China in which the state owned all the land and distributed it to the peasantry, dividing allotments into eight family plots with a ninth plot to be harvested for the state. The interesting fact is that scholars often viewed private ownership of land with suspicion. If only the state owned and could redistribute the land, some argued, the extremes of wealth and poverty would be eliminated and a prosperous peasantry could adequately support the state by paying uniform and fair land taxes. A more practical reform was the *taedongpŏp* (Uniform Land Tax Law), the new tribute replacement tax. The new tax, introduced in the seventeenth century, was designed to replace the old tribute tax. A percentage of the harvest was collected in rice, but this could also be paid in cotton cloth or in copper cash. This was carried out, first in Kyŏnggi Province and then gradually throughout the country, over the next century. The land tax fostered the accumulation of commercial capital by *kongin* (tribute men). It also contributed to the emergence of independent artisans producing the products needed by the state. The *taedongpŏp* reduced the cost of arbitrary exactions of officials and clerks, reduced the costs of government expenses in collecting tribute, enormously simplified the tax system, made it more uniform, and prohibited all sorts of irregular levies not authorized by law. Compulsory labor was replaced by paid wages. While an improvement, the new land tax did not eliminate the burdens and inequities of the tax system. Officials could still levy tribute for some items, and governors could demand rare or specialized items from their areas for use by prestigious visitors. The main problem with the reform was that regular periodical land surveys were not carried out, leading to inequities in the land tax system.

Another burden for commoners was military service. Later in the Chosŏn period local levies of peasant-soldiers were replaced by paid recruits and an annual military tax of two bolts (*p'il*, each one equaling two by forty feet) of cotton cloth. In 1750 a *kyunyŏkpŏp* (Equalized Service Law) was enacted in an attempt to levy the tax peasants paid in lieu of military service more equitably. The law reduced the tax to one bolt of cotton and added a grain surtax of about one-sixth of 1 percent of the harvest. It also imposed a number of miscellaneous taxes on fish traps, salt production, and fishing and trading vessels. This unfortunately caused a great burden on coastal communities dependent on income from fishing and salt flats. Many reformers saw a uniform household cloth tax as equitable and as a way of ensuring a secure source of revenue for the military. But there was a controversy centered on whether to tax the *yangban*. While taxing the *yangban* would enhance state revenues, it would give them the stigma attached to military service. When Yŏngjo levied a tax on the small number of *yangban* who did not register for school, about 24,000, this resulted in great protests.[11] Young *yangban* avoided the tax by registering as students. Sometimes *yangban* participated in collective village cloth payments, but this was done only occasionally and voluntarily. The burden of this tax remained on commoners. Villagers formed *kye* to share the tax burden. The *kye* is an association in which members pool their money so an individual can then withdraw from this pool when he or she is in need. It is still common today as a way of raising or borrowing money. The unfairness was increased by the fact that the quotas were not adjusted after 1750 to account for changes in the number of adult males in the districts. Neither did the military tax prove an adequate substitute for military service. It became merely another tax, while the military was allowed to deteriorate.

The grain loan system also provided the state with revenue. The state sought to stabilize prices and prevent famine by adopting the Chinese practice of buying and storing grain and then using these stocks to provide grain loans for famine relief and to tide farmers over during the spring hunger season. In the fifteenth century a move was made toward adopting Zhu Xi's *sach'ang* (village granary system), which would be in the hands of local leaders, not officials. But in Korea this was supervised by the magistrates. Although there was an aversion to charging interest, in practice a *mogok* (wastage charge) was levied that was, in fact, interest. The state had in effect become a moneylender. By the seventeenth century, grain loans became an important source of revenue for the state and subject to abuse. The state also had *Sangp'yŏngch'ang* (Ever-Normal Granaries) in major market towns for price stabilization. These too lent grain at interest, profiting the officials who managed them. The total value of loans increased in the late eighteenth century. Poor peasants were seldom able to repay the loans on time, keeping them in constant debt, and the accumulated interest payments became in fact another tax. The greatest hardship was on the poorest, who were most likely to need to borrow grain. Overall the tax system, despite reform efforts, was complex and inefficient, reinforced *yangban* privilege, and placed the heaviest burden on the poor.

AGRICULTURE

Chosŏn society was based on agriculture. At the start of the dynasty this base was strengthened by bringing in land for cultivating and by introducing new agricultural methods. Despite some setbacks such as those caused by the Japanese and Manchu invasions, agriculture continued to expand. The most important development in agriculture was the expansion of wet rice cultivation. The advantage of wet rice was its high yields per acre; it yielded twice as much grain per acre as wheat or barley on dry land. A number of irrigation projects such as building dikes and polders enabled new areas to be brought under paddy. Waterwheels were built to bring water from nearby streams, and the building of reservoirs allowed lowlands far from streams to be converted to paddies. Another important change that accompanied wet rice cultivation was the practice of growing rice in seedbeds and then transplanting them into the paddy. This was more efficient than broadcast seeding. Wet rice and transplanting led to an increase in food production. This more productive method of farming spread in some southern areas during the first two centuries of Chosŏn, and then expanded quickly again in the late eighteenth and nineteenth centuries. Although most heavily concentrated in the south, it was practiced in all provinces except for P'yŏngan in the north.

Intercropping became more important in the eighteenth century, especially in the southern provinces where a winter crop of barley was common. Other intercrops included soybeans, red beans, millet, buckwheat, and root vegetables.[12] Lighter ploughs and hoes also increased productivity. Other agricultural advances included the greater use of fertilizer and a move away from the use of fallow fields. It is not clear if these improvements actually made life more prosperous and comfortable for most peasants. Wet rice cultivation required intensive use of labor and careful attention to irrigation works. Transplantation was also risky, since a drought during the crucial transplantation time could spell disaster for the whole crop.

Evidence clearly indicates that the population of Korea expanded during the Yi dynasty, an expansion that was made possible by agricultural advances; but it is less clear if there was an increase in agricultural productivity. Korean agriculture became more sophisticated and yields per acre were higher than in Western Europe or most other parts of the world. They were not, however, as high as in late Tokugawa Japan or in the more productive regions of late Qing China. Historians debate over whether these agricultural changes led to an increase in agricultural surplus or simply meant more labor was needed. The lack of large urban centers and the rural nature of the population suggest that gains in productivity were modest. Some farmers did benefit by the greater use of cotton and tobacco as cash crops, and the introduction in the eighteenth and nineteenth centuries of New World food crops such as potatoes and sweet potatoes acted as an extra insurance against famine.

COMMERCE AND TRADE

Korea never developed a flourishing commercial economy such as Western Europe, China, and Japan had. Korea remained an overwhelmingly rural, agricultural society. There were no major cities besides Seoul, which was a government center reaching perhaps 200,000 in population in the eighteenth and nineteenth centuries. Nor was there a large vigorous commercial class. Korea was also slow to develop a money economy. Coins were minted by Koryŏ and during the Chosŏn period, but only sporadically. One reason for this was that in the fifteenth century the Ming demanded gold and silver as tribute. Koreans then avoided mining the precious metals for fear it would only encourage the Chinese to ask for bullion as tribute. But mining in general was also discouraged since it was thought that it drew peasants away from farming. Some copper was mined and the chief type of money was copper cash, produced regularly from the seventeenth century on. This came in the form of Chinese-style round coins with square holes in the center that were placed on strings. Prices of large items were calculated in standard "strings of cash" commonly numbering 1,000 coins. Without gold or silver coins or paper money, large-scale transactions could be cumbersome. Partly for this reason, these coins never replaced bolts of cloth such as silk or cotton that continued to be used as mediums of exchange. The state further discouraged a money economy before the mid-eighteenth-century by collecting tribute in kind rather than monetary payments. The Chosŏn state also contributed to the lack of commerce by discouraging navigation and shipbuilding as part of its isolation policy (see chapter 9).

One reason often given for the lack of commercial development was that in the Chinese-Confucian worldview merchants had a low social status. Wealth was thought to be derived from the land, while trade and business only diverted people from productive work. Although some commerce was needed, it was considered by the officials to be a necessary evil. Since it was held in contempt, the *yangban* were forbidden to engage in trade. Such attitudes were hardly conducive to trade, yet they do not appear to have prevented a flourishing commercial sector in China. Korea was not on any major international trade routes, but neither was Tokugawa Japan with its vigorous commercial economy, nor did international trade account for more than a small proportion of China's commerce.

The most fundamental factor contributing to the lack of a vigorous commercial sector was geography. China was a vast continental empire with regions that could specialize in producing particular products. Japan was a long if narrow archipelago with varied climatic regions that could specialize in crops best produced there. Korea by contrast was a smaller land with less regional specialization. More importantly, China had an impressive inland waterway network centered around two great rivers and a canal system that linked them, and Japan had the Inland Sea, a convenient highway linking the major population centers. In Korea there were no great waterways that linked regions. The most obvious avenue for trade was along the coasts. But there were problems, since the western coast had some of the world's highest tides and treacherous sandbars, making navigation tricky. The eastern coast had few harbors and was away from the population centers. Korea's mountainous terrain, while not formidable enough to seriously hinder communication, made the transport of goods expensive. Consequently, roads were merely footpaths and goods were carried overland on the backs of peddlers and porters.

The merchant class was small and their activities were carefully regulated. In Seoul commerce was restricted to *sijŏn* (licensed shops). There were two agencies to control them: the *Kyŏngsigam* (Directorate of Capital Markets), which regulated prices, attempted to prevent cheating and thievery, and collected merchant taxes; and the *Ch'ŏngjegam* (Directorate of Sanitation), which maintained sanitation. Outside of Seoul there were fewer shops. Instead trade was conducted primarily at periodic markets whose location and frequency were fixed by law. Most trade was conducted by *pobusang* (itinerant peddlers) who traveled from periodic market to market. The state also employed artisans to make weapons, clothing, furniture, and a variety of items for the court and officialdom. This eliminated the need for merchants to buy and sell things to the state. Most foreign trade was limited by law to diplomatic missions. After 1442 private trade was allowed among the envoys in their embassies to China, but this amounted to a very modest level. Imports from the official trade included silver, copper, tin, sulfur, swords, sandalwood, alum, sugar, pepper, water buffalo horns, sappan wood, licorice root, and elephant tusks. Some of these were of Southeast Asian origin. Exports were Korean cotton cloth, rice, hemp, ramie, ginseng, floral design pillows, sealskins, and books. Trade along the Yalu River border with China was prohibited, although smuggling existed. Imports consisted mostly of luxury goods for the elite. Trade with Japan flourished for a while in the seventeenth century. Koreans imported Japanese copper and silver in exchange for ginseng, medicine, and a variety of goods. There was also a small-scale trade with Okinawa through which Southeast Asian spices were imported. But trade with Okinawa and Japan declined in the eighteenth century.

Late Chosŏn reformers sometimes criticized their land's lack of commercial development and unfavorably compared Korea with the vigorous commercial cities of China and Japan. Some saw commerce as promoting prosperity, not distracting peasants from their farming or *yangban* from their studies. Commerce began to grow somewhat in the eighteenth century partly as a result of tax reforms. The *taedongpŏp* reform legalized state-direct purchases from merchants, and this stimulated trade. Cash was minted more regularly, and the state began to buy goods rather than have them manufactured by government artisans. Artisans, as a result, began moving toward independent production for the market. The growth of cotton production and the introduction of tobacco, which came to Korea indirectly from the Americas through its Asian neighbors, provided new sources of cash crops for farmers.

Signs of greater independent merchant activity appeared. The peddlers formed a guild in the seventeenth century to protect their interests, and some were able to accumulate capital and achieve some prosperity. In the eighteenth century the government gradually gave up opposition to unlicensed merchants. In 1791, the government restricted the monopoly privileges of the authorized Seoul shops and allowed unlicensed merchants to sell any other product not covered, which represented a modest move toward freer trade. As the state shifted from collecting tribute to buying goods, wholesale merchants called *kaekchu* or *yŏgak* emerged. They were intermediaries between peasants and the craftsmen and merchants in town. Wholesale merchants became involved in warehousing, consignment selling, and transport. They also ran inns for traveling merchants and provided banking services. Unlike the *kongin* (tribute men), some *kaekchu* served as middlemen in the international trade after 1876 and prospered. A few like Pak Sŭng-jik and Pak Ki-sun became successful entrepreneurs and pioneers of industry in colonial Korea.[13] So in some ways Korea was developing into a more commercialized economy in the eighteenth and early nineteenth century. Nonetheless, except for some scholars such as Pak Che-ga, the Confucian disdain for merchants and trade continued; and Korea remained less commercially developed than its neighbors.

CULTURAL FLOWERING OF LATE CHOSŎN

Korean culture flourished at both the elite and popular levels during the late eighteenth and early nineteenth century. Although the influence of Chinese models in literature and the arts remained strong, there was an elaboration on indigenous forms of aesthetic expression and a focus on Korean subject matter in literature, history, and painting. For example, while the *yangban* continued to write poetry and essays in classical Chinese, the seventeenth and eighteenth centuries saw the emergence of a literature written in the *han'gŭl* script. This included novels, a literary form that was very popular in the eighteenth century. The subject matter of novels varied. Some were military adventures, and some of these reflected the interest in Korea's history by heroizing those who resisted foreign aggressors. An example was the novel *The War with Japan*; another, *General Im Kyŏng-ŏp*, was based on the exploits of a general who fought the Manchus. More popular were love stories. An example of the latter, and the most famous of all Korean tales, was *The Story of Ch'unhyang*. This was an eighteenth-century tale of a young lady who falls into the clutches of an evil local official but is eventually rescued by her lover.

While novels were popular in the late Chosŏn, poetry retained its hold as the prime form of literary expression. *Sijo* remained popular. In the eighteenth century a modified form of the *sijo*, the *sasŏl sijo*, became common. This maintained the basic format of the *sijo* with its fifteen-syllable first line and third and final line, but with a middle section that could be expanded by having additional lines added. This ended the tight restriction of the form that had been so prized, and allowed for elaboration and digressions. In the nineteenth century, *Sasŏl sijo* were written by *chungin* and commoners as well as *yangban*. They tended to be more down-to-earth and often coarse and comic. Most were anonymous. Many historians see in the growth of popular novels and in the newer, freer, and less aristocratic poetry signs of social change as non-*yangban* began to give voice to their feelings and taste in written literature. However, late Chosŏn literature was still dominated by the *yangban*. Indeed most authors of novels and expanded verse poetry were *yangban* who, out of propriety, remained anonymous.

An interesting genre of literature in the eighteenth century and early nineteenth century was satirical stories written by scholars. These used humor to criticize the inequities and stupidities of Korean society. The outstanding examples came from Pak Chi-wŏn. An innovative writer, his best-known tales are still popular. Many are found in his *Yŏrha ilgi* (*Jehol Diary*, 1780), the record of his trip to China. In the *Hŏ saeng chŏn* (*The Story of Master Hŏ*), a *yangban* who takes up useful work goes into business, prospers, and offers practical solutions to social and economic problems, but finds the *yangban* elite unwilling to take up reforms. The *Yangban chŏn* (*Yangban's Tale*) is about a lazy *yangban* who is a parasite on society. He studies but does not do any useful work and is scolded by his own wife. In *Hojil* (*A Tiger's Reprimand*) a hungry man-eating tiger decides to eat Puk Kwak, a *yangban* scholar with a reputation as a moral exemplar. But encountering the tiger, the *yangban* falls in excrement after fleeing the house of a widow with whom he is having an affair. Consequently, he stinks so much that the tiger does not eat him.[14] Another story in this genre is Chŏng Yag-yong's (or Tasan) *Ch'ultong mun* (*On Dismissing a Servant*). In an anonymous story titled *Changkki chŏn* (*The Story of a Pheasant Cock*) a pheasant hen rejects her submissive role as wife. The story thus satirizes fundamental Confucian notions about the relations between husband and wife.

An interesting legacy of Chosŏn was women's literature. In recent years scholars have rediscovered much of this large body of feminine writing. The percentage of women who were literate was small, since even *yangban* girls were discouraged from learning. Nonetheless, a small number of women became quite accomplished in letters. Lady Yun, mother of Kim Man-jung (1637–1692), is said to have tutored her two sons to pass the civil exams. Lady Sin Saimdang (1504–1551), mother of Yi I (Yulgok), was reported to have been very learned. Hŏ Nansŏrhŏn (1563–1589), a beautiful and highly intelligent daughter of a high-ranking official, was so talented as a youth that she attracted the attention of well-known poets who tutored her. Tragically she died at the age of twenty-six and destroyed many of her poems before her death. Her famous brother, Hŏ Kyun, collected what remained. These proved to be enough to earn her a reputation as an accomplished poet. *Kisaeng* such as Hwang Chin-i were often accomplished poets as well.

As in Japan, Korean women wrote primarily in indigenous script while men stuck to the more prestigious Chinese characters to express themselves. Women, if they learned to write, generally wrote in *han'gŭl*, which was regarded as fitting for them. *Han'gŭl*, in fact, was sometimes referred to as *amgŭl* (female letters). Women, following cultural expectations, generally wrote about family matters. But within these restrictions Korean women produced *kyuban* or *naebang kasa* (inner-room *kasa*). These originated in the eighteenth century and were largely anonymous. They included admonitions addressed to daughters and granddaughters by mothers and grandmothers on the occasion of a young woman's marriage and departure from home. Young brides would arrive with these *kasa* copied on rolls of paper. They would pass them to their daughters with their own *kasa* added. Other inner-room *kasa* dealt with the success of their sons in taking exams, complaints about their lives, and seasonal gatherings of women relatives.[15]

Another genre of women's literature was palace literature written by court ladies about the people and intrigues of court. A large body of this literature, much of it still not well studied, survives. Among the best known are the anonymously authored *Kyech'uk ilgi* (*Diary of the Year of the Black Ox*, 1613), the story of Sŏnjo's second queen, Inmok. Queen Inmok is portrayed as a virtuous lady who falls victim to palace politics and jealousies. She struggles to protect her son and is imprisoned by Kwanghaegun. It ends when the doors of the palace where she is imprisoned are suddenly opened following Kwanghaegun's overthrow.[16] Another work, *Inhyŏn Wanghu chŏn* (*Life of Queen Inhyŏn*), tells the virtuous life of Queen Inhyŏn, who married King Sukchong in 1681. She too is victimized at the hands of the evil rival, Lady Chang. Today the most read of these palace works is the *Hanjungnok* (*Records Written in Silence*) by Lady Hyegyŏng (1735–1815). This is the autobiography of the wife of the ill-fated crown prince Changhŏn. Written in the form of four memoirs, it is a realistic and in most respects accurate story of her mistreatment at court, the tragedy of her husband's mental illness and death, and the sufferings of her natal family at the hands of political enemies. Her memoirs are a literary masterpiece, and because of their honesty and her astute insights, they are a valuable window into court life in the eighteenth century. Biographical writings by women in East Asia are very rare, and one by a woman of such high intelligence so close to the center of political life is especially important.[17]

In painting, Korean artists in later Chosŏn tended to focus on Korean landscapes rather than on scenes from Chinese literature, and departed from earlier conventions with bolder strokes, spontaneity, and liveliness. In the seventeenth century Kim Myŏng-guk (1623–1649) developed a distinctive style with strong Sŏn (Zen) influences. The eighteenth and early nineteenth centuries was an especially creative period in Korean painting. Chŏng Sŏn (1676–1759), for example, considered one of the greatest masters, painted the mountains of Korea. He is especially famous for his paintings of the Diamond Mountains located near the east coast of what is now North Korea. Sim Sa-jŏng (1707–1769) created a number of paintings from landscapes to animals characterized by spontaneity, simplicity, and liveliness. A new genre of painting appeared in the eighteenth century that was distinctively Korean. These were playful scenes of everyday life depicting *yangban* socializing, peasants' merrymaking, or just everyday activities. Among the genre painters was Sin Yun-bok (b. 1758), an artist from the *chungin* class who depicted beautiful women and *yangban* enjoying the company of *kisaeng*. The subjects of his *An Album of Genre Scenes* are girls on seesaws, housewives washing clothes in streams, women selling wine, and women and men flirting. Sin's paintings deviated too much from Confucian propriety, and he was expelled from the Tohwasŏ. Another genre painter, Kim Tŭk-sin (1754–1822), painted ordinary people at work and play.

The most famous of the genre painters was Kim Hong-do (1745–ca. 1818). He painted peasants working in their fields, harvesting, working in their shops, performing music, and engaging in *ssirŭm* (Korean wrestling) matches. A versatile artist, he also created landscapes, portraits, and bird and flower paintings. But it is his genre paintings that are most treasured today. Although he died destitute, Kim Hong-do is recognized today as one of Korea's greatest artists. These genre paintings with their playfulness and often humor have no counterpart elsewhere in East Asia. They are not only instantly charming and appealing, but are also a vivid record of everyday life in late eighteenth- and early nineteenth-century Chosŏn. Genre painting was an example of the trend among Korean artists, writers, and musicians of drawing upon their own folk traditions to develop new forms of artistic expressions. A tradition of erotic art existed as well. Well-known painters sometimes discreetly created albums of these explicit works for their patrons.

In addition to the formal art of official artists and *yangban* amateurs, a rich tradition of art flourished that dealt with folk customs and beliefs. This folk art was "popular among all classes."[18] Unlike the more formal *yangban* art paintings, *minhwa* (folk paintings) were characterized by bright colors and a sense of spontaneity and vitality. They contained symbols from Buddhism, shamanism, and folk religion traditions. Many such paintings showed scenes from ordinary life, especially festive occasions such as birthdays and New Year's celebrations. Other folk paintings depicted landscapes, tigers, and other wild animals. Another folk art tradition was the mask dance-drama. Mask dance-dramas were performed in Silla times if not earlier. In Koryŏ times, they were sometimes performed in court. During the Chosŏn period they were characteristic of village culture. The masks, generally of wood, were highly stylized. Black masks represented old men, red ones young men, and white ones young women. Some stories hint of ancient fertility festivals in which youth/summer triumphs over age/winter. Many satirized the *yangban* and monks, and provided an irreverence that bordered on social protest. Mask dances were generally performed during festivals such as at the first full moon of the year, Buddha's birthday, Tano (a summer festival), and Chusŏk, the autumn moon festival. Puppet plays were popular and also served as social satire by poking fun at the *yangban*.

A uniquely Korean art form that emerged in late Chosŏn was *p'ansori*. In a *p'ansori* performance a singer delivers a folk tale while a drummer accompanies him or her, setting the rhythm to the singer's tale and encouraging the singer by shouting out from time to time. The singer conveys the story not only by singing but also through a series of body expressions and dancelike movements. *P'ansori* combines music, drama, and dance in a unique style. It has its origins in eighteenth-century Chŏlla Province, and it emerged by the nineteenth century as a popular entertainment performed in villages and towns by traveling performers.[19] In the marketplace a singer would start with an unrelated song, a *hŏduga*, to draw a crowd. Then the performance itself could take up to eight hours, although usually only parts of a *p'ansori* work were performed. Originally there were twelve *p'ansori* works or *madang*; today only six remain. The stories were derived from folktales with many embellishments added. Among the most popular were the *Tale of Ch'unhyang* and the *Tale of Hŭngbu*. The latter is the story of selfish, greedy, cruel Nolbu and his kind, unselfish, but also unpractical younger brother Hŭngbu. Unable to provide for his huge family Hŭngbu asks Nolbu for help, but his elder brother is too selfish to assist. The contrast between the two provides great delight. The story ends happily when a magical swallow that Hŭngbu has helped provides him with money. His greedy brother mistreats the swallow to gain wealth only to be ruined. *P'ansori* has become a great art form and singers spend years of training, traditionally strengthening their voice by practicing over the roar of a waterfall. It has enjoyed a revival in contemporary Korea and has gained a small but growing international following.

The eighteenth century was a great period of historical writing in Korea. Accompanying the trend toward drawing upon local sources for artistic and literary inspiration, historians focused on the study of their own country. An Chŏng-bok (1712–1791), a disciple of Yi Ik, wrote the *Tongsa kangmok* (*Abridged View of Korean History*), the first comprehensive history of Korea from Tan'gun to the fall of Koryŏ by a private scholar. An was concerned with the importance of legitimacy and loyalty. Touching a theme that was to inspire later nationalist historians, An was also concerned with Korea's struggle against foreign invaders. He praised the achievements of those who resisted them such as Ŭlchi Mundŏk, Kang Kam-ch'an, and Sŏ Hŭi and less well-known heroes. Illustrating his professionalism, his addenda discussed historical problems and assessed the reliability of sources. Another scholar, Hong Yang-ho, in 1794 wrote the *Haedong myŏngjang chŏn* (*Biographies of Famed Generals*). It mainly focused on those who fought foreign invaders. Another private history, *Haedong yŏksa* (History of Korea) by Han Ch'i-yun (1765–1814), covered the history of Korea from Tan'gun to the fall of Koryŏ. Both An and Kang used Chinese histories as models, but their subject matter dealt with Korea's own historical development. Han used hundreds of sources, including Japanese as well as Chinese and Korean ones. He compared and evaluated them, showing the sophistication of Korean historical scholarship. His work, not quite finished upon his death, was completed by his nephew Han Chin-sŏ (b. 1777).

Another important history was Yi Kŭng-ik's (1736–1806) *Yŏllyŏsil kisul* (*Narration from the Yŏllyŏ Study*), a history of the Yi dynasty from its founding to the reign of Sukchong (1674–1720). The first part deals with the various reigns and the second part with a number of special topics such as institutions, diplomatic relations, taxes, marriage customs, penal systems, and astronomy and natural phenomena. Yi, unlike most Korean historians, refrained from presenting his personal views. Instead he often presented verbatim quotations from his sources, 400 in all, in an effort to be objective and letting "fact speak for itself."[20] Another work of significance was the *Parhae ko* (*Study of the Parhae Kingdom*), published in 1784. The author, Yu Tŭk-kong (1748–1807), challenged the idea of a unified peninsula under Silla but rather saw Parhae as part of Korean history. Yu referred to the United Silla period as the period of the "Northern and Southern Kingdoms." A number of geographies were compiled by authors such as Sin Kyŏng-jun (1712–1781), who wrote the *Toro ko* (*Routes and Roads*) and the *Sansu ko* (*Mountains and Rivers*), and Chŏng Sang-gi (1678–1752), who produced the *Tongguk chido* (*Map of Korea*).

Some scholars today see the beginnings of Korean nationalism in the renewed interest Koreans showed in their own historical tradition. An Chŏng-bok and Yu Tŭk-kong, for example, traced Korea's history to early times, essentially making it as old as that of China. Since Koreans had often dated the start of civilization with the coming of the legendary sage

Kija from China to Korea, dating their history back to Tan'gun before Kija implied that Korea was as old as its neighbor and not derivative of China, that it had its own distinctive development. While most contemporary historians regard nationalism as a modern concept not introduced to Korea until the late nineteenth century, some scholars see the antecedents of modern Korean nationalism in the writings of these late Chosŏn historians and other writers. Certainly, Koreans in late Chosŏn displayed a strong sense of possessing a distinctive culture even as they continued to identify with the greater world of Chinese-based civilization.

SIRHAK

A large body of critical scholarship emerged in the seventeenth and especially in the eighteenth century. Today this scholarship is often referred to as *Sirhak*, "Practical Learning." This, as the late historian James Palais has pointed out, is a modern term used to categorize a number of thinkers who had different concerns. They had a lively intellectual curiosity in a wide variety of areas, yet they shared a desire to correct social and political injustices. Many of these scholars came from the *sŏwŏn*, private academies that were important centers of learning. By the eighteenth century there were hundreds of these private academies. They were autonomous institutions where private scholars taught, studied, wrote, and commented on public issues. Different academies became associated with different political factions, so that they were as much centers of factional politics as scholarship. Nonetheless, they provided an institutional basis for nonofficials to scrutinize society.

One of the earliest of these practical learning scholars was Yu Hyŏng-wŏn (pen name Pan'gye). His major work, *Pan'gye surok*, completed in 1670, systematically examined the landowning system, education, the institutions of government, and the military. As he did, he carefully pointed out weaknesses and suggested reforms. Among his proposals was a sweeping land reform based on the "Tang equal-field system" in which the government would take possession of all land and then assign equal plots for cultivation to all the peasants. Yu was not a total egalitarian. As with almost all Korean thinkers, he accepted the idea of aristocratic privilege and social hierarchy. Under his proposals the state would provide modestly larger shares of land for *yangban* and bureaucrats according to their rank. But his goal was to create a society that avoided great disparities in wealth and poverty and that would strengthen both the state and society. He also advocated the replacement of the civil examinations with a new recruiting system in order to reinvigorate the government. Yu was hardly a progressive in the modern sense. He was a conservative reformer, who wanted to bring Korea closer to what he regarded as the golden age of the past.

In the eighteenth century the number of social and political critics grew. One of the most important was Yi Ik (pen name Sŏngho, 1681–1763), who in the same tradition as Yu presented detailed analysis of economics and politics, suggesting various reforms that sought to return to a simpler, more egalitarian past. A man of broad learning and many interests, Yi was concerned with establishing social justice. He also advocated land reform that would guarantee land to all peasants and create a more equitable and just society. He realistically suggested that land reforms be carried out on a gradual basis.

Two reformers, Pak Chi-wŏn, and Yi Tŏng-mu (1741–1793), of the Northern Learning School drew from their travels to China to critique their own society. They differed from thinkers such as Yu Hyŏng-wŏn and Yi Ik in that they did not seek to restore an agrarian past but were influenced by recent trends in Qing thought, commerce, technology, and literary styles. They found fault in the *yangban* for their idleness, and for their lack of appreciation of the practical benefits of commerce and technology. Pak Chi-wŏn, for example, a member of the *Noron* faction, criticized the scholar-bureaucratic class with his previously mentioned satirical narratives *Yangban chŏn, Hŏsaeng chŏn,* and *Hojil* (Tiger's Rebuke). Hong Tae-yong, who belonged to this school, also wrote on science. He suggested that the earth rotated on its axis, and in general was critical of many of the commonly accepted East Asian views on the natural world.

Perhaps the most original of these thinkers was Chŏng Yak-yong (pen name Tasan, 1762–1836), who suggested that the ancients were not always as wise as scholars thought and that changing conditions meant that new generations had to come up with new ways of dealing with problems. Tasan, also concerned with the disparities between rich and poor, called for communally owned land and an egalitarian redistribution of wealth. He was fascinated by science, and took a deep interest in medicine. Tasan was familiar with some Western science and medicine, as well as with Christianity, and drew inspiration from this new source of learning. As with many of his contemporaries, he was influenced by Qing scholarship. He also greatly admired Tokugawa Japanese scholars such as Itŏ Jinsai (1627–1705), Dazai Shundai, and Ogyŏ Sorai (1666–1728) (all of the Ancient Learning School) and their examination of ancient texts with a concern for practical information. In a short essay, *Ilbonron* (*Essay on Japan*), he praised the effort of Japanese scholars to critically examine ancient texts. He suggested that the Japanese were becoming less militaristic and more civilized, boding well for the future relations between Korea and its island neighbor.[21] Today, some see Tasan as a modernizer breaking with tradition and calling for radical change in thinking. Yet for all his wide-ranging interests and his openness to new sources of ideas, Tasan was working within the Confucian tradition. He too saw the works of Confucius, Mencius, and the other Chinese classics as sources of great wisdom and guidance. Like Yu Hyŏng-wŏn and Yi Ik, Tasan was more focused on establishing a more equitable agricultural order than promoting commerce.

Some historians today see in all this intellectual ferment the beginnings of modern thought. According to one interpretation, the "seeds of modernization" were being planted in Korea during this time. Many contemporary Korean historians such as Kang Man-gil have found the beginnings of a commercial revolution and the possibility of political and social change leading to a more dynamic modernizing society. They cite the loosening of state restrictions on trade, the growth of a money economy, the new cash crops such as tobacco and cotton, the new ideas on science and medicine, and the criticism of the *yangban* ruling class. However, despite the growth in commerce and a growing acceptance of the importance of commerce and industry among some members of the educated elite, Korea remained a very rural society. The basic contempt for merchants and business among most of the elite changed little before the end of the nineteenth century. Furthermore, most of the "practical learning" scholars were still operating within the Confucian tradition. Most cited the ancient sages and looked to the Korean or Chinese past to find precedents for their reform ideas. There were some exceptions, but Koreans at the start of the nineteenth century were still confident and proud of the fact that they were the upholders of the ancient line of transmission of civilized values. Koreans saw civilization as always being threatened by barbarism and their land as a bastion of the Way of the Sages. The origins of civilization were in China and its principles were laid down by the ancient sage-rulers. But now that China was ruled by semibarbarian Manchus, Korea was the foremost center of civilized values. Peoples outside of East Asia might have some useful things to offer, but they were outside of civilization, ignorant of the sages and of the Way of Confucius, illiterate in Chinese characters, and unable to appreciate true art and poetry or the principles of Heaven.

EVERYDAY LIFE

Everyday life in Korea did not undergo radical change either. Rather, changes occurred within tradition. Rice was the main staple for those who could afford it, although the poor and even more prosperous peasants in times of bad harvests ate "coarse grains" such as millet and barley. Living in a cold country, Koreans pickled vegetables so that they would be available in the winter and early spring. In the eighteenth century, chili peppers, of New World origin, were introduced, beginning the Korean love of spicy food that set them apart from their northern Chinese and Japanese neighbors. The national dish of *kimch'i*, pickled cabbages or other vegetables in garlic and fermented fish or shrimp seasoned with chili peppers, acquired its modern form at this time. *Kimch'i* was stored in big crockery jars and became an indispensable part of each meal. Fish and seafood was an important part of the diet, although Koreans were also fond of meat if they could afford it. Rice wine was also consumed in liberal quantities.

Chosŏn Korea was only modestly urbanized. The largest city was Seoul, whose population probably peaked in the late eighteenth century at 200,000. If the two river ports of Map'o and Yongsan and a few other adjoining communities are added, the metropolitan area was about 300,000, about the size of contemporary Berlin in Prussia but far smaller than London and Paris. Seoul in 1800 was less than a quarter as big as Edo (Tokyo) in Japan, smaller than Osaka or Kyoto or the great Chinese cities such as Beijing. Yet serving as the political, commercial, and cultural center of the kingdom it was by far the largest city in Korea. Seoul was a walled city with three main gates: the East Gate (Tongdaemun), West Gate (Sŏdaemun), and South Gate (Namdaemun). Running east to west was Chongno (Bell Street), the main avenue. It was a city of royal palaces, numerous royal shrines, government offices, and various types of housing—large houses with tiled roofs for the rich and small, thatched-roof ones for the poor. It also had two major market areas filled with private shops: Ihyŏn area near Tongdaemun and Ch'ilp'ae area outside Namdaemun.[22]

Seoul in the late eighteenth century was followed in size by P'yŏngyang and Kasesŏng, each with 30,000, and by the southern cities of Chŏnju and Sangju with 20,000 each. Ten or eleven other towns had about 10,000 people.[23] Kaesŏng near Seoul, Ŭiji on the Chinese frontier, and Pusan, the port for trade with Japan, served as commercial centers. All other cities and towns were administrative centers. Unlike those in Western Europe, Japan, or China, Korean cities, even Seoul, lacked a vibrant urban culture. Partly this was due to the humble status of merchants, the modest scale of commercial enterprise, and the Neo-Confucian emphasis on decorum that inhibited a lively cultural life. In addition, most *yangban*, even when living in Seoul or another city, identified with their country homes, where they most often returned after retiring from public office. Furthermore, much of learning and scholarship in late Chosŏn centered around the hundreds of scattered, mostly rural *sŏwŏn*.

Most Koreans lived in rural villages and supported themselves through farming. Rural life was difficult. The widespread use of rice transplanting added to the labor-intensive, strenuous nature of farm work. All family members were involved in the tasks that were made more onerous by the fact that farms often consisted of scattered parcels, many on steep hillsides. Festivals, periodic markets, and itinerant peddlers and entertainers, as well as weddings and other special occasions, added variety and diversion to rural life. The craftsmen and laborers in cities and towns may have had more amusements available, but life for them was hard as well. Estimates of the actual living standards vary (see next chapter). Evidence suggests that most late Chosŏn Koreans lived modestly, yet for the most part not in extreme poverty.

Life in small villages was often harsh. People lived in close quarters and disputes over field boundaries or any variety of personal resentments were frequent. Village gossip could create or aggravate these disputes that, when accompanied by heavy drinking, often led to violence. For example, the mere rumor that someone was sleeping with someone else's wife could and, judging by legal records, often did result in lethal assaults.[24] In county seats the most important figure was the county magistrate who served a 1,800-day term. In smaller communities the local *yangban* generally provided leadership. The magistrate gave moral lectures at special occasions and informally adjudicated local disputes. *Yurang chisigin* (wandering scholars), who were poor unemployed *yangban*, often provided instruction to village children and acted as a means of spreading the dominant Neo-Confucian values to rural areas.

Village life, however, was also enlivened by seasonal festivals. The lunar New Year's and the Autumn Moon Festival were the biggest holidays as they still are today. While the *yangban* looked down on most sports, archery was popular. Koreans are still great archers, and in the late twentieth century they often dominated Olympic archery events. Korean traditional wrestling, *ssirŭm*, similar to Japanese *sumo*, was also popular. In *ssirŭm*, at least as it is played today, each player binds his loins and the upper thigh of his right leg with a two-foot-long cloth, or *satpa*. Each player grasps the other's *satpa* in the right hand at the loins and the left hand at the thigh; the first to touch the ground with any part of body other than the feet loses. Kings sometimes sponsored wrestling events awarding honors to winners. Several styles existed, but only one style remains today. Another popular game was *yut*, played with wooden sticks thrown up in the air. Various martial arts, including those ancestral to *t'aekwŏndo*, were widely practiced in the Yi dynasty, even among common people. In the late eighteenth century the prominent scholars Yi Tŏng-mu and Pak Che-ga wrote the *Muyedobo t'ongi* (*Illustrated Treatise on the Fighting Arts*), a military and martial arts manual. Although the martial arts tradition was derived from China, the manual shows Korean innovations in techniques as

well as in the use of schematic illustrations to indicate movement.[25]
Paduk, better known in the West by its Japanese name, *go*, and also as
Korean chess, or *changgi*, was popular, especially among the *yangban*.
Most physical activities were confined to men; however, seesaws were
popular among women.

Korean medicine was derived from Chinese practice and theory.
Among the popular forms of treatment were *ttŭm* (moxibustion), *ch'im*
(acupuncture), and *hanyak* (Chinese medicine). Koreans practiced four
methods of physical observation: observing the face and overall appearance (*sijin*), listening to the sound of the person's voice (*munjin*), question-
ing the person about his medical history and symptoms (*munjin* written
with a different Chinese character), and feeling the pulse and stomach
(*chŏlchin*). There were seventeen pulses, each requiring separate treatment. The standard medical reference was the *Tongŭi pogam* (*Exemplar of
Korean Medicine*), first compiled in 1610. It ran to twenty-five volumes and
was based on Korean and Chinese treatises on medicine. Eating healthy
food was and is still an important part of Korean medicine. Healthful
foods included *posin t'ang* (dog meat stew*)*, *paem t'ang* (snake soup), *paem
sul* (snake wine), and above all ginseng, valued for its ability to preserve
health and virility. These medical foods and medicines, as is true of many
other aspects of popular and elite culture in late Chosŏn, are still part of
a clearly defined Korean tradition.

KOREA IN THE NINETEENTH CENTURY:
THE "HERMIT KINGDOM"

All the states of East Asia maintained a policy of limiting contact with
outsiders in the seventeenth, eighteenth, and early nineteenth centuries.
China limited trade with Europeans to the southern port of Canton,
where it was strictly controlled. A few Jesuits were allowed in Beijing,
and a very restricted trade existed between China and Russia. China
and Japan did not maintain direct contact with each other, but indirect
contact was sporadically maintained between the two through Korea and
Okinawa. Chinese merchants from the south traded with Southeast Asia.
Japan maintained limited diplomatic contacts and trade with Korea, and
allowed the Dutch to trade at Nagasaki, but forbade its own people from
leaving the country. Korea was the most isolated society in East Asia.
Wary from their troubled experience with the Khitans, the Mongols, the
Manchus, the Japanese, and other invaders, Koreans went even further
to keep foreigners out and minimize contact with them. As a result,
Westerners in the nineteenth century sometimes called Korea "the hermit
kingdom."

In some ways the "hermit kingdom" appellation given to Korea was unfair because Korea remained surrounded by China, the Northeast Asian forests, and the Japanese archipelago, in the center of the interconnected East Asian region. Koreans were proud of being part of the greater cosmopolitan civilization associated with institutions and values that for the most part originated in China. Yet no land pursued a policy of isolation so zealously as late Chosŏn Korea. Koreans were forbidden to travel or even to build large boats lest they sail accidentally abroad. The main exceptions were the diplomatic missions to China. But these involved a small number of trusted officials and followed a strictly prescribed route. Chinese embassies visited Korea periodically, but they also followed a special route. No unauthorized Koreans were allowed to meet and talk with them, they entered Seoul through a special gate, and once in the capital they were confined to a special walled compound. Few ordinary Koreans saw them. Koreans sent occasional embassies to Japan, but after the mid-eighteenth century these became fewer and confined to the island of Tsushima. Japanese traders came to the southern port of Pusan, but they were restricted to a walled compound, the Japan House, where only authorized Koreans were allowed to meet and trade with them. Because of its distance from international trade routes, few Westerners or other visitors from outside East Asia came to Korea, but those who did were prohibited from entering. Thus, Koreans, confident and proud of being a bastion of orthodox teachings, the most ardent adherents to the true Way, lived in a sort of splendid isolation.

INTERNAL PROBLEMS IN THE NINETEENTH CENTURY

Historians differ on whether or not Korea was entering a period of decline and of social and institutional crisis in the nineteenth century. One possible symptom of dynastic decline was the politics of the nineteenth century. After the reigns of Yŏngjo and Chŏngjo, Korea entered a period in which weak kings were dominated by powerful royal in-law families. It is sometimes called the era of *sedo chŏngch'i* ("in-law government"). When Chŏngjo died he was succeeded by his eleven-year-old second son, Sunjo (r. 1800–1834). The real power was in the hands of the dowager queen, who appointed Kim Cho-sun of the Andong Kim royal in-law family to assist her in governing. From 1801 to 1834 the Andong Kims dominated the court. When Sunjo died in 1834, her eight-year-old grandson Hŏnjong (r. 1834–1849) became king. Power now shifted to the P'ungyang Cho royal in-law families of the boy king's mother. Upon his death, the Andong Kim family engineered the ascension to the throne of a nineteen-year-old royal relation living on a farm on Kanghwa Island, who became King Ch'ŏlchong (r. 1849–1864). Ch'ŏlchong, a heavy drinker, died an early death, leaving only a daughter. The P'ungyang Cho family then made an alliance with a relative of the royal family, Yi Ha-ŭng (1821–1898), to put his twelve-year-old son on the throne, who reigned as King Kojong (r. 1864–1907). Kojong was married as a boy to a member of the Yŏhŭng Min family that through Kojong's wife, Queen Min (1851–1895), came to prominence at the court. Yi Ha-ŭng acted as regent for his son under the title of Taewŏn'gun. This struggle for power among the clans mostly involved the high officials at court, but two bloody purges in 1801 and 1839 also accompanied the changes in power (see below).

More dramatic evidence of a dynasty in decline is found in several rebellions that took place during this period. In 1812, Hong Kyŏng-nae, supposedly a *yangban* who had failed to pass the civil service exams or secure a government appointment, but perhaps a commoner, led an uprising in the northwestern P'yŏngan Province. Hong's followers attacked government offices and seized control of a number of towns. Joined by peasants and some local officials, the rebels soon had control of much of the province. After five months, government troops put down the uprising, ending with a 100-day siege of Chŏngju, a walled county seat. Government forces dug a tunnel under the city walls, set off explosives, and stormed the citadel. Hong and many rebels fought to the death. Nearly 3,000 civilians and rebel troops were caught alive; all were executed except women and boys under ten. Remnants of Hong forces continued to rebel before they were finally defeated by government forces. The remoteness of P'yŏngan Province from the central government may have been a factor in explaining the swiftness with which the uprising spread. The rebellion had a distinct regional character; a manifesto issued by the rebels complained of discrimination against people from the northwestern part of the country.[26] But other popular disturbances broke out from time to time. A major riot took place in Seoul in 1833, triggered by a sharp increase in the price of rice. Most of the disturbances were in the countryside. These usually involved attacking the local magistrate's office and burning tax records, and sometimes attacking wealthy local *yangban*. Most were small scale, but a major uprising took place in 1862 in the southern city of Chinju. Thousands of peasants wearing white headbands murdered local officials and merchants in the city. Shortly afterward another uprising took place in the town of Iksan in southwestern Chŏlla Province. Soon violence and destruction were widespread in all three southern provinces until the uprisings were finally suppressed by government forces in 1863.

A more systematic threat to the social order came with a new religious movement, Tonghak (Eastern Learning), founded in 1860 by Ch'oe Che-u (1824–1864). Ch'oe combined Confucianism, Buddhism, and Daoism in what he claimed was an attempt to counter Catholicism (Western Learning) that was entering the country. It is clear, though, that his new faith had incorporated some Christian concepts too. For this reason, and because of his call for sweeping social reform, the court saw the new religion as a threat. Fearing rebellion among his followers, the state arrested and executed Ch'oe in 1864. But the new religion did not die out. It made many converts and thirty years later, in 1894, the Tonghaks led a major revolt.

Was Korea toward the end of the Yi dynasty a society in decline? All of these developments are cited by some historians as evidence that Korea was entering into a time of troubles in the nineteenth century. According to this view, peasant unrest was brought about by rural poverty, while discontent grew among frustrated local officials and "fallen *yangban*" who had lost their opportunity for access to government office. The domination of court politics by powerful in-law families was another symptom of this decline. Some have argued that Korea was suffering from demographic pressure, as the population grew and agricultural production remained stagnant. In the arts and scholarship as well, the brilliant efflorescence of the eighteenth and the beginning of the nineteenth century was not followed by comparable cultural accomplishments in the mid-nineteenth century. In addition, new, subversive ideas from the West, in particular, Christianity, were trickling into Korea, slowly undermining the cultural unity of the kingdom (see next chapter).

Some scholars see a parallel with what was happening in China. In the eighteenth century China had a population explosion that continued into the first half of the nineteenth century. This led to overpopulation and, consequently, an enormous pressure on the land. Population pressure probably contributed to the decline of the Qing and to the massive rebellions of the second half of the nineteenth century that cost millions of lives. Some scholars have argued that Korea too was facing declining living standards in the late eighteenth century and nineteenth century due to population pressures. In support of this view, historians can point to a serious famine that took place in 1812–1813, to sporadic reports of hunger, and to the 1833 rice riot in Seoul. If this was the case, then perhaps Korea, as well as China, had a weakened and restless society at the very moment of the Western challenge.

It is not clear, however, that Korea was undergoing a rapid increase in population or a declining standard of living. Regular censuses were taken during the Chosŏn period, but the records are incomplete and their accuracy is not certain. Nonetheless, trying to work with these figures and guessing at the rate of underreporting, one scholar has come up with estimates that bring the population of Korea to 4.4 million around 1400, a number that then more than doubled to 9.8 million in 1592. This dropped to under 8 million as a result of the Japanese and Manchu invasions, re-covering by 1650. It rose to 12 million by 1693; then a famine from 1693 to 1695 caused it to drop toward the level of 10 million. The population in-creased again, reaching 13 million by 1732. According to this calculation, throughout the eighteenth and early nineteenth centuries the population probably never grew above 13–14 million, and was still around 13 mil-lion at the end of the nineteenth century.[27] Other scholars have placed the growth in population higher, with estimates of 18 million by 1750, after which it leveled out, and perhaps declined modestly in the first half of the nineteenth century to 16 million in 1850.[28]

The growth of population was accompanied by improvements in agri-culture. Korea was having a modest "green revolution." The production of rice, barley, millet, and beans increased due to the expansion of paddy land. A great number of reservoirs were built in late Chosŏn, making ir-rigation easier. Double-cropping of rice and barley fields also increased yields. Agriculture benefited from the introduction of new crops: red peppers and tobacco in the seventeenth century, and the potato and sweet potato in the eighteenth century. Tobacco provided a cash crop for farmers, and the potato and sweet potato could grow in hilly areas less suitable for other crops.

Evidence suggests that Korea's demographic pattern was similar to that of Japan rather than Qing China. After a steady rise in the seventeenth and early eighteenth centuries Korea's population probably leveled off in the mid-eighteenth century. Agricultural production kept up with popu-lation growth, and the number of famines appears to have actually de-clined after 1750. Korea in the late nineteenth century was one of the more densely populated lands in the world, but it does not seem to have been overcrowded. However, Ki-Soo Park and Donghyu Yang have recently suggested that economic conditions deteriorated in the nineteenth cen-tury. They argue that double-cropping does not appear to have become as widespread in Korea as it was in China or Japan. Nor did Koreans make nearly as much use of the new bean-cake fertilizers as did the Chinese and Japanese in the seventeenth to nineteenth centuries. By some measure agricultural productivity was stagnant or declining.[29] On the other hand, early Western visitors to Korea sometimes commented on the lack of beg-gars or signs of extreme poverty. In short, while the evidence presents a mixed picture, there does not seem to have been any great ecological or economic crisis in Korea in the nineteenth century.

Culturally as well, the traditional arts and letters still flourished, if not with the brilliance that marked the time of Yŏngjo and Chŏngjo. Tasan, one of the dynasty's most original thinkers, wrote much of his work dur-ing the reign of Sunjo. Other scholars continued the tradition of eclectic writings. Sŏ Yu-gu (1764–1845) compiled *Sixteen Treatises Written in*

Retirement (*Imwŏn simnyuk chi*), dealing with a wide variety of social, economic, and intellectual topics. Yi Kyu-gyŏng (1788–1856) wrote *Random Expatiations* (*Oju yŏnmun changjŏn san'go*), another vast compilation of scholarly treatises on government administration, economics, history, and science. Yi Kyu-gyŏng's work is marked by careful methods of empirical scholarship, reflecting the influence of the Qing school of Evidential Scholarship. Kim Chŏng-ho (d. 1864) traveled all over Korea for years and produced what has become his famous *Detailed Map of Korea* (*Taedong yŏjido*) in 1861. In literature *sijo* were composed in large numbers and *p'ansori* emerged as a new literary and dramatic form. Chang Sŭng-ŏp (1843–1897), a poor orphan who gained employment as a government painter, became regarded as one of the three great masters of the Chosŏn period.

An example of the continued vitality of traditional culture is the life and works of Kim Chŏng-hŭi (1786–1856), better known by his pen name Ch'usa. Kim came from a family of *yangban* landowners in Ch'ungch'ŏng Province.[30] Many had served as officials. His father passed the civil service examination and held the post of minister of personnel. The youthful writings of this child prodigy are said to have attracted the attention of Pak Che-ga and other scholars. In 1809 at the age of twenty-four he passed the civil service exam with a *saengwŏn* degree and in the same year traveled with his father on a diplomatic mission to Beijing. There he studied the art of epigraphy from Chinese masters Weng Fanggang and Ruan Yuan (1764–1849). Returning to Korea he examined inscriptions from the Three Kingdoms period and became the leading member of the Evidential Scholarship school in Korea. His interests extended to Buddhism as well. He made an extensive study of Buddhist texts, and unlike many earlier Chosŏn Confucian scholars he made free use of Buddhist terms in his writings. A noted painter, he specialized in orchids. He became better known as a master calligrapher, developing the "Ch'usa" style, which is still much admired. His reputation as an artist and scholar did not protect him from court intrigue. In his fifties he was exiled to the island of Cheju, where he spent nine years confined to living in a small room in a remote village. While in exile he painted and exchanged letters with friends and relatives on epigraphy, geology, history, art, and Confucian and Buddhist doctrine and texts. Eventually family fortunes in the capital changed and he was allowed to return to Seoul. He retired from political life soon after to spend time tutoring a number of young disciples in a provincial town south of the capital. Kim's life illustrates the continual near monopoly of higher culture by the elite and the vicious political intrigues that made public life precarious. His life, however, also represents the best of the Korean scholarly tradition. It was a tradition that was still capable of producing innovations in art and scholarship.

Late Chosŏn Korea, while possessing a rigid class structure, was increasingly a society with common cultural values. The vast numbers of petitions to the monarch by ordinary people suggests a wide identification if not attachment to the dynasty and the state. Village schools, *yangban* public lectures, wandering scholars, and possibly rising literacy among males assisted in the penetration of Confucian norms among the peasant majority. Folk traditions, sports, medical beliefs, popular literature, the style of homes with their heated *ŏndol* floors, and the ubiquitous kimchi jars were all part of a rich, distinctive, and shared Korean cultural tradition.

Korea in the nineteenth century, however, was coming to the end of a long tradition. The states of Western Europe and their North American transplants in the seventeenth, eighteenth, and nineteenth centuries had undergone scientific, technological, political, and social revolutions that had transformed them from peripheral players on the world stage to global dominance. Korea, under the Chinese tributary system, away from the major international trade routes, had largely gone unnoticed by the West. Koreans had become aware of Europe in the seventeenth century, but until the end of the eighteenth century it was a remote region of no real interest or relevance to them. Gradually in the nineteenth century this changed.

KOREA IN GLOBAL PERSPECTIVE: THE HERMIT KINGDOM?

Korea has been labeled the "hermit kingdom," a term popularized by the first American book about Korea by William Eliot Griffis published in 1882 under the title *Corea: The Hermit Kingdom*. The label "hermit kingdom" seemed appropriate to Westerners when Griffis wrote the work, since no major state was more closed or so little known to them. Since the Japanese invasions of the late sixteenth and the Manchu invasion of the seventeenth century, the Chosŏn state had placed severe restrictions on foreign contacts. Except on authorized diplomatic missions Koreans were prohibited from traveling abroad, and with a few exceptions foreigners were not allowed entry into the country.

Yet, the policy pursued by the late Chosŏn state differed little from that of its neighbors China and Japan, which both sought to restrict and control contact with outsiders. The Ming and Qing placed restrictions on Chinese travel abroad, although due to the scale of the country's vast empire these were more difficult to enforce. European trade was limited to an authorized port on the southern periphery; Russians could trade only on the northern border. Trade with its Asian neighbors was similarly restricted. When the British sent a mission to China in 1793 to open trade, it was politely told that the "Celestial Empire" had no need of foreign "trifles." Tokugawa Japan from the 1640s pursued a policy labeled by historians as *sakoku* (closed country). In a manner similar to Chosŏn, the shogunate prohibited Japanese from going abroad and severely restricted trade. Only the Dutch and some Chinese merchants could trade, and only at Nagasaki on its extreme southern periphery. Japan and Korea carried on trade with each other at Pusan. Only in the face of military defeats and the threat of armed force did China and Japan loosen their restrictions on foreign contact in the mid-nineteenth century. Other countries, such as Vietnam, Siam (Thailand), Burma, and Persia, at various times after 1600 expelled Westerners or placed strict limitations on their activities.

Historians of Tokugawa Japan in particular have reexamined this view of their country as "isolated" and found that even under these restrictions the country remained significantly engaged in international commerce and that ideas and various foreign influences entered during its "closed" period. Similarly some historians have reexamined Korea's contact with the rest of the world. Trade with Japan provided an important source of metal, and border trade with China was significant. Koreans continued their close relations with China and were influenced by developments that went on there. Trade goods from distant lands entered mainly via China but also through Japan and Okinawa. Seventeenth- and eighteenth-century Koreans saw the introduction of potatoes, sweet potatoes, and chili peppers, all of which significantly "internationalized" its diet, as well as the introduction of tobacco. Geographical knowledge about the larger world improved somewhat. Western ideas about science and medicine and some technologies such as clocks trickled into the country and were known by at least a few scholars. Knowledge of European mathematics led to improvements in calendar making. And from the late eighteenth century Christianity began making a few converts.

Korea was never a major international crossroads. Located on the eastern periphery of Eurasia, and off the major international trade routes, it was never exposed to the variety of foreign contacts that Southeast Asia, India, and the Middle East were. This, however, was also true of Western Europe, especially northwestern Europe. Britain, for example, before the sixteenth century, had few direct links with peoples other than those of its immediate neighbors, who shared a similar culture. Until the voyages of discovery toward the end of the fifteenth century, Europe's understanding of the larger world was little better than Korea's. So Korea's isolation was in good measure a product of geography, and its precautions against contacts with outsiders were, in light of its history of foreign intrusions, understandable. But its policy was not so radically different from other Asian countries, and it did not cut off the country from all international trade and influences.

Regulating Marriage

Author Note: The attempts to bring marriage and the family in line with the ideals of Neo-Confucianism included efforts to regulate concubinage and prohibit the remarriage of widows. Marriage to secondary wives was a common practice among the elite, but the tendency was to make a legal distinction between the offspring of first or main wives and the offspring of secondary wives. Children of secondary wives, called *sŏŏl*, were prohibited from taking the civil exams and serving as officials and had many other legal restrictions. These reforms had become general practice by the eighteenth century. They also attracted the attention of some late Yi scholars, who saw the discrimination against secondary sons to be a tragic and unfair situation. The prohibition against remarriage for widows (not for widowers), however, was generally accepted, since a woman must be a virgin when she marries, and she must be loyal to her husband even after death, and obedient to her son.

On Differentiating between Main Wife and Concubine

The Office of the Inspector-General memorializes [in 1413] as follows:

Husband and wife are the mainstay of human morality, and the differentiation between main wife and concubine may be blurred. Embodying the great principles of the one hundred kings of the Spring and Autumn period, King T'aejo accentuated the boundary between main wife and concubine devised by the scholar-officials and instituted as the law of conferring ranks and land on main wives. The distinction between main wife and concubine has thus become clear and the root of human morality straight.

At the end of the former dynasty, the influence of ritual decorum and morality was not pervasive, and the relationship between husband and wife deteriorated. The members of the officialdom followed their own desires and inclination: some who had a wife married a second wife; others made their concubine their main wife. This has consequently become the source of today's disputes between main wives and concubines.

We have carefully examined the Ming code, which reads: "The one who makes a concubine his main wife while the latter is alive is to be punished with ninety strokes of the heavy bamboo, and the situation must be rectified. Someone who already has a main wife and still gets another one is also to be punished with ninety strokes, and they must separate."

—from *T'aejong sillok* 25:13a–b[31]

Prohibition against Remarriage of Women

Marriage was largely an affair between "two surnames," and, as far as the wife was concerned, it lasted beyond her husband's death. Confucian ideology stressed the woman's devotion to one husband, and this emphasis on the exclusive nature of the marital relationship provided Confucian legislators with the arguments they needed to prohibit the remarriage of women, a custom prevalent during Koryŏ. The first version of the State Code of 1469 apparently barred the sons and grandsons of thrice-married women from advancing into the higher officialdom. The debate of 1477 makes it clear that the majority of the discussants, here represented by Kim Yŏngyu (1418–1494), were in favor of keeping the restriction to third and not extending to second marriages. How sensitive this issue was is documented by the fact that the State Code of 1485 did not directly outlaw remarriage but provided that the sons and grandsons of remarried women would not be eligible for civil or military office and would be barred from taking the lower and higher civil service examinations. The ideological and legal implications thus, in fact, made remarriage for a woman impossible.

—from *Sŏnjong sillok* 82:9b–20a[32]

9

⊏◇⊐

Korea in the Age of Imperialism, 1876 to 1910

It could hardly have been obvious to any Korean in the early nineteenth century that their society was to undergo a relentless series of upheavals and radical transformations. Theirs was a land that had twelve centuries of political unity and a social and political system that had evolved but not drastically changed in more than a millennium. Korean leaders and elites were confident in the virtuousness of their kingdom, considering it a bastion of truly civilized values, the most faithful adherent of correct ethical norms derived from the Chinese Confucian tradition. Except for a tiny number of Christians, the world outside East Asia was of little concern for them. All this changed radically as the world of Western imperialism began to intrude upon Korea. At first there were occasional, if disturbing, incidents.

EARLY CONTACTS WITH THE WEST

The world Koreans inhabited was dominated by China, the vast continental empire that contained one of the world's wealthiest, oldest, and most sophisticated societies. Then there was Japan to the east, a participant in the broader East Asian cultural world but also a warlike and dangerous society. To the northwest were the seminomadic peoples that had so often invaded. Koreans maintained sporadic contact with Vietnamese, Siamese, and other southeast Asian people. Beyond this was the world of distant barbarians that Koreans had little contact with, knowledge of, or interest in. Among these remote peoples were the Europeans. Early in

225

the sixteenth century reports of the presence of "Pullanggi" (Franks) in Southeast Asia reached Korea, and in 1597 a Jesuit, Gregorio de Cespedes, arrived in Korea accompanying the Japanese troops, but there is no Korean record of his presence. Some Korean captives in Hideyoshi's invasions were brought back to Japan and converted to Christianity. One, baptized as Antonio Corea, arrived in Italy in 1606 and married a European woman. Antonio Corea never made it back to Korea to report on what he saw. Not until the late nineteenth century did a Korean visit a Western country and come back to relate his experiences to his compatriots.

Direct contact with the West came in the seventeenth and eighteenth centuries. The Jesuits under the talented polymath Matteo Ricci (1552–1610) established a small mission in Beijing at the end of the sixteenth century. While they made few converts, they did attract admiration for their skills in perspective painting and mapmaking, their knowledge of mathematics and astronomy, and their curious mechanical devices, especially clocks. The Chinese emperors employed Jesuits to help them maintain an accurate calendar. Koreans traveling on diplomatic missions encountered these Jesuits and shared the Chinese admiration for their technical and mathematical skills. An early reference comes from Yi Su-gwang (1563–1628), who wrote the *Chibong yusŏl* (*Topical Discourses of Chibong*) in 1614, an encyclopedic work with 3,500 entries. Included in his entries were brief descriptions of Western maps, self-striking clocks, ships, prisms, grape wine, Western religion, and Matteo Ricci. Among his descriptions of the countries of the world he mentioned Portugal, which he placed southwest of Siam, and England, which he confused with the Kirghiz tribe in central Asia.[1]

A number of other scholars and officials on diplomatic missions met Jesuits and picked up some knowledge of Western science and religion. One of these, Chŏng Tu-wŏn, in 1631 brought back with him a telescope, a clock, a Western gun, maps of the world and the heavens, and books in Chinese by Western missionaries on astronomy and world geography. For the most part Koreans were dismissive of Christianity, which they viewed as nonsensical and indicative of the low cultural level of Westerners despite their technical skill. Westerners' skills at calculating an accurate calendar were another matter, since one of the most important functions of a ruler was to be able to determine when his people could plant and harvest crops. Prince Sohyŏn, while being held hostage in Beijing by the Manchus, met Adam Schall (1591–1666), one of the most learned of the Jesuits in China, and invited him to send a Jesuit to Korea. Although nothing came of this, the Koreans did adopt Western calendrical methods to determine the position of heavenly bodies over Seoul and thus make a more reliable calendar. Previously they had relied on a calendar based on the positions of heavenly bodies over Beijing.

In the eighteenth century Korean visitors to China continued to stop by the Jesuit mission, which, as historian Donald Baker has noted, became part of the standard tour of exotic sights in the imperial capital. Jesuits even complained about the Korean visitors who handled their musical instruments and wandered around the cathedral in Beijing, spitting on the floor and ignoring its sanctity. Some Koreans were impressed by Western painting, especially its mastery of linear perspective. Pak Chi-wŏn in his *Yŏlha ilgi* wrote how he and his companions when entering a Jesuit church stretched out their arms to receive babies falling from clouds on the church ceiling. The clouds looked real, and humans appeared to be alive and moving.[2] Western realism even had some influence on eighteenth-century Korean artists, but as in Qing China, the interest in Western painting techniques was a fad that waned in the nineteenth century.

Few Koreans seemed to take the Europeans very seriously as bearers of a great tradition, rather seeing them as just clever barbarians. One of the early reported exchanges between a Korean and a Westerner is preserved in the correspondence of Yi Yong-ho, a young Korean diplomat who met Joao Rodriques (1561–1633), in which Yi challenged the Jesuit scholar on his explanation of the universe.[3] China is the center of the universe, Yi informed the Jesuit. Rodrigues replied that there is no center of the world. Western cosmology, he further argued, is far superior to the Chinese view, for the Chinese astronomers did not know why celestial bodies moved but the West had an explanation. The Jesuit then went on to explain Catholic cosmology, linking the knowledge of celestial spheres with the broader cosmology of heaven, hell, and God. Yi was impressed with the Westerner's science, but found his cosmology unconvincing.[4] A few took Western knowledge seriously. Yi Ik, for example, although he never met any Europeans, read Chinese translations and extracts of Western mathematics, geography, and medicine, for all of which he had great respect. However, nothing the Koreans learned of the West shook their belief in the superiority of East Asian civilization or their Sinocentric views of the world. In fact, Yi Ik noted that Western world maps show China in the center of the world dominating its largest continent, which he regarded as evidence of China's centrality. Mostly Westerners were strange creatures with round eyes, big noses, and sometimes red hair, who as it was frequently repeatedly urinated like dogs by lifting one leg.[5]

In 1627, three shipwrecked Dutch sailors washed up on the shores of Korea. They were employed building guns for the Korean military. Two died in the Manchu invasion of 1636; a third, Jan Janse Weltevree, who married a Korean woman and adopted a Korean name, survived to greet the arrival of thirty-six of his countrymen in 1653 when their ship wrecked on Cheju. These Dutch sailors too were forcibly detained in Korea and employed for their technical skills. Eight later escaped, and one,

Hendrick Hamel (1630–1692), wrote the first account of Korea in a Western language. An accurate observer, Hamel provided a useful outsider's view of seventeenth-century Korea. Hamel reported that Koreans treated Westerners as objects of curiosity but that even educated Koreans showed little knowledge or curiosity about Western countries. "When we nam'd some Countries to them, they laugh'd at us, affirming we only talk'd of some town or village; their Geographical Knowledge of the coasts reaching no farther than Siam by reason of the little Traffick they have with Strangers farther from them."[6] After Hamel, no more Westerners are known to have arrived in Korea for nearly two centuries.

This changed dramatically in the nineteenth century as the expansive West of the nineteenth century began to intrude upon Korea. In 1832, the *Lord Amherst* of the British East India Company appeared along the coast, offering to trade, but the Koreans explained it was against their law to trade with outsiders. In 1845, the British warship *Samarang*, surveying Korean waters, visited Cheju and other Korean ports and again inquired about trade. Korean authorities again explained that they had no desire to open their country to trade. The Koreans then requested the Qing government to make it clear to the British that it did not seek trade. But the Koreans were not to be left alone. In 1846, three French warships arrived on the coast and sent a letter to be forwarded to the king and left. In 1854, two armed Russian vessels sailed off the northeast coast and clashed with Koreans.

Koreans, through their diplomatic missions in China, were aware of more disturbing events. The British went to war with China from 1839 to 1842 in what is known as the Opium War, in which they defeated the Chinese and forced them to open ports to trade on British terms. Britain and France went to war with China again from 1858 to 1860 inflicting another defeat and extracting more concessions. The Opium War could be dismissed as merely a successful pirate attack by barbarians, but the capture and pillage of Beijing in 1860 by an Anglo-French force was a truly alarming development. Koreans through their diplomatic missions in Beijing kept informed of these disturbing events. At the same time, Korea acquired a new neighbor, as the Russians expanded south, annexing territory on China's northern frontier and advancing to Korea's Tumen River border in 1860. During 1864–1865, a number of Russians came to the border town of Kyŏnghŭng insisting on trade, while in 1863, Koreans living in the northeast began to migrate across the border into Russian territory.[7] To the east, the United States forced Japan to open itself to trade with the West in 1854.

Even before these alarming events took place a small number of Koreans became attracted to Christianity, which became known as *Sŏhak* (Western Learning). It was introduced to Korea rather indirectly through written texts. A handful of Koreans on diplomatic missions to China met with Western missionaries in the seventeenth and eighteenth centuries. Most Koreans were highly dismissive of Christianity for many of the same reasons they objected to Buddhism: it promoted selfishness, honored celibacy, and gave credence to miracles. Even an admirer of Western learning such as Yi Ik dismissed these religious beliefs, which he called the "grains of sand and piece of grit" amidst their scholarship.[8] Only in the late eighteenth century did a few Koreans become genuinely drawn to the religion. In 1784, Yi Sǔng-hun (1756–1801) accompanied his father on a diplomatic mission to Beijing and was baptized by a Western Catholic priest. A small number of yangban converted, mostly from the Namin faction that was out of power and tended to produce dissidents. Some *chungin*, however, converted as well. The converts included the scholar Tasan and his two brothers, Chǒng Yak-chǒn and Chǒng Yak-chong. In many ways Christianity's progress in Korea was unique for it was not spread directly by missionaries but by intellectuals who were attracted to Catholicism through their readings of Christian tracts in translations and through sporadic contacts with Christians in China. The beginning of Christianity in Korea was thus unusual in world history in that early converts largely converted themselves. Lacking any ordained priest, they even baptized themselves with only a vague idea of how baptism should be performed.

In China the Rites Controversy had weakened the Catholic mission the Jesuits established there in the seventeenth century. The pope had ruled in 1742 that ancestor worship and belief in Christianity were incompatible. This angered the Chinese authorities since the rites honoring a family's ancestors were central to Confucian practice. As Korean officials became aware of Catholicism they too condemned it. Chǒngjo declared it a heresy in 1785; the following year all importation of books of any kind from Beijing was banned lest they contain Christian writings. In 1791, Yun Chi-ch'ung from a yangban family in the southwestern province of Chǒlla was sentenced to death for failing to prepare an ancestral tablet for his mother. Four years later, however, the first priest from China, Zhou Wenmo, entered Korea in response to appeals from the small Christian community and began making a great number of new converts. By 1801, there were an estimated four thousand Christians in the peninsula. That Catholicism could grow was in part due to the protection given by Ch'ae Che-gong, a Namin who held great influence during King Chǒngjo's last years. But with Chǒngjo's death and the ascension of Queen Dowager Kim (Yǒngjo's queen) as regent for the youthful King Sunjo, suppression of Catholicism resumed. This was intensified when a convert, Hwang Sa-yǒng, sent his "silk letter" to the French Catholic bishop in Beijing. In it he asked the Pope to request that the Chinese emperor require the

Korean king to grant religious freedom and to have Western nations send naval forces of 50,000–60,000 men to compel the Korean government to do so. It was to be delivered by another convert who was scheduled to go on a tribute mission. This only confirmed what many feared, that Catholicism was a dangerous heresy. Furthermore, that many converts like Hwang were from prominent, well-educated families was alarming. In the Catholic Persecution of 1801 300 converts were put to death, including the scholars Yi Sŭng-hun and Chŏng Yak-chong, along with Zhou Wenmo. Chŏng Yak-chong's brothers Chŏng Yak-chŏn and Tasan were exiled to remote places. This persecution became entangled in factional disputes, since the Pyŏk branch of the Noron faction that was coming to power charged its Si branch of the Namin opponents with heresy. Religion became enmeshed with factional politics.

A few years later, however, with the royal in-law Andong Kim lineage securely in power, the persecution of Catholics eased. Meanwhile, the Vatican had appointed a vicar apostolic for Korea, and in 1836, the French priest Maubant, and in 1837, two others, Chastan and Imbert, surreptitiously entered the country. The number of converts reached 9,000 by the late 1830s. But when the P'ungyang Cho came to power they began the Catholic Persecution of 1839 in which the three foreign priests and seventy-five converts were executed. A few years later the first Korean priest, Kim Tae-gŏn (1821–1846), was ordained in Macao and then smuggled into the country. His arrival was shortly followed by the arrival of three French naval ships to investigate the massacres of 1839. Assuming a connection between Kim and the arrival of foreign ships, the court executed him along with eight converts in 1846. With King Ch'ŏlchong on the throne in 1849 and the Andong Kim in power again, the persecutions let up. Twelve French Catholic priests entered, and Catholic books and pamphlets were published. The number of converts reached 20,000 by 1864. In the nineteenth century many converts were from the urban poor; many were women. Most were from the Seoul area. Christianity was by no means sweeping the country, but the presence of a Christian minority with its foreign links was troubling to Korean conservatives.

THE OPENING OF KOREA

The growing menace Westerners posed, along with internal financial problems, contributed to a growing sense of crisis. Korea responded with a vigorous reform effort led by the Taewŏn'gun. When King Ch'ŏlchong (r. 1849–1864) died without an heir, the second son of a relative, Yi Ha-ŭng, was selected to succeed as Kojong (r. 1864–1907). As Kojong was a minor, his father became regent, taking the title of Taewŏn'gun (Grand Prince). The Taewŏn'gun's program of reform was designed to strengthen the monarchy and the power of the central government. He rebuilt the main royal palace and restored royal tombs, instituted a new currency, and carried out measures to increase the state's tax revenue. Among the latter was a new household tax that was levied on the previously tax-exempted *yangban*, the herediatary aristocracy that dominated Korean society, as well as on commoners.

Initially the Taewŏn'gun was tolerant of the Christian community in Korea. The growing foreign crisis in East Asia fed fears that Christianity was a dangerous Western doctrine that would undermine the political and social order. The connection between Catholicism and the French presence in Asia resulted in a belief that Catholic missionary activities were part of hostile French designs on Korea. The regent launched a major persecution in 1866 on the advice of many of his officials. In March 1866, nine French priests who were illegally in the country were ordered to leave; when they refused, six were executed while three others fled. Forty Korean converts were also executed. The Qing government in Beijing warned Korea against hostile actions against foreign missionaries, but the regent's belief in the need for strong measures against any Western threat was only reinforced by the U.S.S. *General Sherman* incident. In August 1866, a heavily armed U.S. merchant ship with a crew of Americans, Malays, British, and Chinese entered Korean waters and sailed up the Taedong River to P'yŏngyang (Pyongyang) seeking to open trade. Ignoring orders to leave, the crew fired upon a hostile crowd and burned nearby boats. A few days later when the ship was caught in a receding tide, the local governor, the distinguished scholar Pak Kyu-su, ordered it destroyed. The *General Sherman* was burned and its crew killed. Although little known to Americans, the *General Sherman* incident would be later celebrated in North Korea as the beginning of the Korean people's resistance to American imperialism. The Taewŏn'gun then carried out further persecutions of the small Catholic minority in Korea in which several thousands of converts died—which became known as the Catholic Persecution of 1866.

In October 1866 the French sent seven ships and 600 men on a punitive expedition to Korea in response to the execution of its missionaries. After capturing a fort on the strategic island of Kanghwa near the mouth of the Han River, the French Admiral Roze delivered a letter to the capital court in the Korean capital of Seoul demanding that those responsible for the murder of the missionaries be punished. The Taewŏn'gun's response was to mobilize thousands of available forces. When the French tried to seize a fortified Buddhist temple on the southern end of the island in November they were driven back by Korean troops. With winter coming on, the French left. Meanwhile, news of the disappearance of the *General Sherman*

eventually reached the Americans in China. The United States instructed
Admiral Shufeldt to investigate. The admiral sent a ship to Korea in 1867
and another in 1868 to make inquiries, but the Koreans refused to deal
with either one. Tensions with foreigners were further aggravated by
a bizarre incident in May 1868. In an effort to open trade, the German
merchant Ernest Oppert landed on the coast of Korea and desecrated the
grave of the Taewŏn'gun's father in a failed attempt to use his father's
bones as a bargaining chip for trade concessions.

Gradually the United States became aware of the fate of the *General
Sherman*. In 1870, the newly appointed U.S. minister to China, Frederick
Low, began preparations to take firm action against the "semi-barbaric and
hostile" Koreans.[9] In May 1871 Low led five ships and 1,200 men under
Admiral John Rodgers on a punitive expedition. When on June 1 the Koreans fired upon a survey party, the Americans destroyed the shore batteries.
The Americans waited for a reply to a letter demanding an account of the
missing ship, but the Korean government replied that it was not interested
in negotiations. The Americans then attacked the city of Kanghwa and forts
on the island. The Koreans fought to the death, inflicting some casualties
on the U.S. forces. Not authorized to proceed further, and frustrated by
the Koreans' refusal to talk and their fierce resistance, Low and Rodgers
decided to withdraw. The Taewŏn'gun proudly put up stone signs proclaiming "Western barbarians invade our land. If we do not fight we must
then appease them. To urge appeasement is to betray the nation."[10] It appeared to him that the Westerners, like all pirates, could be dealt with best
by uncompromising resistance.

To the east, Japan posed another threat to Korea. Japan underwent
a sweeping change with the collapse of the Tokugawa shogunate and
the creation of the new reform-minded Meiji government in 1868. In
January 1869, an envoy from the Japanese island of Tsushima arrived in
Pusan to announce the new government. The Korean officials refused to
receive the letters. They were offended by the idea of an imperial restoration. Koreans had never recognized the Japanese ruler as an emperor,
since that would place him on a basis of equality with the Chinese emperor. Furthermore, the new Western-style uniforms of the delegation
from Tsushima were also offensive, reinforcing the old attitude that the
Japanese were semibarbarians. This impression was confirmed when
in June 1870 the German chargé d'affaires in Japan arrived in Pusan
with Japanese aboard his ship and with another Western request that
the country open itself to foreign trade. The Korean refusal to receive
the notification of the restoration of imperial rule was highly offensive
to the new leaders of Japan, who were in any case concerned about
securing their periphery. The Japanese began a vigorous colonization
of the northern island of Hokkaido, brought Okinawa under direct rule

in 1873, and secured the Kurile Islands in an agreement with Russia in 1875. The strategic importance of Korea, as well, was not lost upon the leaders of Meiji Japan, who conducted heated debates on how to deal with Korea. In 1873, some Meiji officials seriously discussed provoking an incident that would lead to an invasion of Korea, but cooler heads prevailed, and the idea was dropped.

Although the Japanese leadership decided not to invade Korea, they were determined to open diplomatic relations with their neighbor. In May of 1875, they sent the warship *Unyō* to Pusan, joined two weeks later by a second ship. The Japanese showed off these modern Western-built ships by inviting Koreans aboard and by firing their guns in demonstration. The *Unyō* and other ships then sailed along the coast of Korea, surveying the waters. When they entered the prohibited area off Kanghwa Island, they were fired upon by shore batteries. The *Unyō* returned fire, destroying the Korean guns. Japanese troops then overran a small fort on an island off Inch'ŏn, killing and wounding a number of defenders. Other warships were dispatched to Pusan with the excuse of protecting the Japanese residents there. In February 1876, Kuroda Kiyotaka landed on Kanghwa Island with a substantial military force and demanded an apology for what he claimed was an unprovoked attack on Japan's ships. Japan wanted more than an apology; it insisted that Korea open diplomatic and trade relations with its new government.

The Korean court was now in crisis. In December 1873, the Taewŏn'gun had been forced to resign, and the young king, Kojong, took personal control. Shortly after assuming power, Kojong faced this serious challenge. Most officials opposed negotiations, but some, such as Pak Kyu-su, the same official who had ordered the destruction of the *General Sherman*, argued for negotiations, as did the Chinese government. Kojong supported the latter view, and in February 1876 his government signed the Treaty of Kanghwa. In the treaty, Korea recognized the new administration in Tokyo and agreed to open Pusan and two other ports within twenty months to the Japanese. The twelve articles of the treaty had profound implications that few Koreans at the time probably understood. Korea was recognized as an independent state possessing the same sovereign rights as Japan. This contradicted the traditional view of Korea as a Chinese tributary state. The concept of an international community of equal and sovereign nations was alien to the East Asian order as Koreans had always interpreted it. The other articles permitted the Japanese to survey Korean waters, allowed Japanese to reside in treaty ports, and gave the Japanese the right of extraterritoriality; that is, Japanese in Korea would be subject to Japanese law and courts. In accordance with Article 11 of the treaty, a further agreement on trade was signed a few months later that gave additional economic privileges to the Japanese.

The Treaty of Kanghwa proved a turning point in Korean history. It ended its isolation, undermined the tributary system that had framed Korean foreign relations for centuries, began the Japanese penetration into Korea that would eventually undermine its economic and political order, and it brought Korea into the imperialist rivalries of the late nineteenth century. Korea's vigorous efforts to insulate itself from the changing world around it came to an end. It is not likely, however, that many Koreans in 1876 were aware of just how momentous a step they had taken.

EARLY REFORMS, 1876–1884

From a modern historical perspective, the years after 1876 mark a radical departure from Korean history. They may not have appeared so to Koreans at the time. The Korean state was simply adjusting itself to deal with menacing neighbors, as it had before in its history. However, the Koreans were entering a world for which their past experience had ill prepared them. It was the world of the high imperialism of the late nineteenth century, when nearly every corner of the globe was faced with the unbridled expansionist ambitions of the Western powers. Korea's situation was especially complex, since it not only had to deal with the forces of the West—Britain, France, the United States, and especially Russia—but also with its two traditional East Asian neighbors, China, which was determined to consolidate control or influence over its periphery, and a rapidly modernizing, expansionist Japan.

After the Treaty of Kanghwa was signed, the court dispatched Kim Ki-su, a respected scholar and official to head a mission to Japan. Korean kings had sent emissaries to Japan in the past to keep an eye on their troublesome neighbor, although this was the first such mission since 1810. Kim met a number of officials who showed him some of Japan's reforms carried out to "enrich the nation" and "strengthen the military."[11] After reluctantly meeting with the Japanese emperor, Kim left without Japan's modernization having made much of an impression on him. Rather than using the trip as an opportunity to introduce Korea to the rapidly changing world heralded by Japan's reform efforts, it was treated as one of the occasional missions sent to Japan in the interests of "neighborly relations" (*kyorin*). It was another four years before Seoul sent another mission. When the king sent a mission in 1880, it was headed by Kim Hong-jip, who was a keener observer of the reforms taking place in Japan. While in Japan, the Chinese diplomat Huang Cunxian presented him with a study called *A Strategy for Korea* (*Chaoxian Celue*). The work warned of the threat to Korea posed by Russia and recommended that Korea maintain friendly relations with Japan, which was at present too economically weak to be an immediate threat, work closely with China, and seek an alliance with America as a counterweight to Russia. Upon returning to Korea, Kim presented the work to Kojong, who was so impressed with it that he had copies made and distributed to his officials. Many conservatives were outraged by the proposal to seek alliance with Western barbarians or even to maintain friendly relations with Japan. Some even plotted a coup. Kojong responded to this opposition by executing one prominent official and banishing others. The document became the basis of his foreign policy.

After 1879, China's relations with Korea came under the authority of Li Hongzhang, who had emerged as one of the most influential figures in China after playing an important role in putting down the Taiping Rebellion, 1850–1864. Li was an advocate of "self-strengthening," by which China would selectively borrow elements of Western technology, especially military technology, and maintain correct relations with Western countries while adhering to traditional core values. He was appointed by the Qing in 1879 as governor-general of Zhili Province (in the Beijing area) and imperial commissioner for the northern ports. Li urged Korean officials to adopt China's own self-strengthening program to strengthen the country in the face of foreign threats. Kojong was receptive to this advice.

In 1880, following Chinese advice, Kojong decided to establish diplomatic ties with the United States, a true break with tradition. Admiral Shufeldt came to Tianjin, and in 1881–1882 negotiated with Korea through Chinese officials a Corean-American Treaty of Amity and Commerce, which was signed on May 22, 1882. In the treaty, the United States offered its "good offices" in the case of a threat from a third power. It fixed tariffs on imported goods and gave extraterritorial rights to Americans. Several elements made the treaty more acceptable to conservatives: it kept tariffs high, made extraterritoriality provisional upon the reform of Korean laws and judicial procedures to conform to America's, and it did not mention permitting missionary activity. Kojong seems to have thought it offered American protection in time of external threat. In the spring of 1883, an American minister arrived in Seoul, and an eight-man diplomatic mission was sent to the United States under Min Yŏng-ik and his deputy Hong Yŏng-sik, where they performed the traditional kowtow before a rather surprised President Arthur.

Kojong took several other steps toward reform. In early 1881, he set up an Office for the Management of State Affairs (T'ongni Kimu Amun) modeled on a similar institution created in China as part of the self-strengthening program, the Zongli Yamen. The new institution was in charge of the various areas needed to deal with the new international environment: foreign affairs, international trade, foreign language instruction, military affairs, and weapons manufacturing. Kojong also created a special Skills Force of eighty cadets under a Japanese army lieutenant to learn modern warfare. In the same year, Kojong sent twelve officials, averaging a comparatively young age of thirty-nine, to Japan on a so-called "Gentlemen's Observation Mission" to spend ten weeks studying the new modern institutions and technologies in use there. Two members of the mission stayed on in Tokyo as students, the others reported back on what they had seen and learned to an interested monarch and his court. Later that same year, an official, Kim Yun-sik, led a group of about forty students and artisans to China where they studied the modern weapons facilities in Tianjin.

None of the efforts proved highly effective. The T'ongni Kimu Amun underwent constant reorganization without actually accomplishing much. The Special Skills Force was small, incurred the jealousy of regular soldiers, and was abolished in 1882; and the study mission to Tianjin ran out of funds, the students became homesick, and it was abandoned before there was enough time to absorb the new technologies. For all their limitations, these activities, especially the trips to Japan, exposed a small number of Koreans to new ideas and institutions. These Koreans gradually formed a reform party sometimes known as the Progressive Party (Chinbo-dang) or more often as the Enlightenment Party (Kaehwa-dang), a small group committed to major reform efforts. In the meantime, the Japanese pressed Korea to open up two more ports, as required in the treaty. Wŏnsan on the east coast was opened in 1880, and only after considerable pressure was Chemulp'o (now Inch'ŏn) opened in 1883.

Although modest in scale, the reforms instituted by Kojong were too much for conservatives, who rallied around the Taewŏn'gun. An opportunity for his return to power came soon. In 1882, regular soldiers who had not been paid in months revolted when they found their grain rations had been adulterated with chaff. The soldiers, resentful of the privileged position of the special guards, murdered the Japanese officer and attacked and burned the Japanese legation. Japan's minister to Korea, Hanabusa Yoshimoto, and his staff barely escaped. After the soldiers called upon the Taewŏn'gun for support, Kojong brought his father back to help restore order. The former regent was given full authority, which he used to abolish the Special Skills Forces and the T'ongni Kimu Amun. Ominously, the military incident brought about the open rivalry between China and Japan for influence in Korea that would cause so much trouble. Hanabusa returned with Japanese military troops, but the Chinese, in their first intervention in Korea since the sixteenth century, sent a much larger body of troops, about 4,500, under General Wu Changqing. Chinese troops were now stationed at various points in Seoul. The Chinese took the Taewŏn'gun captive and brought him to exile in Tianjin. Japan then worked out the Treaty of Chemulp'o, which allowed them to station some troops at their embassy in Seoul.

The military uprising was a setback for the early reform efforts. It also brought the Chinese into Korea, where they now began to directly interfere in the country's internal affairs. The Chinese took several measures to gain a certain amount of control over Korea. They negotiated the Regulations for Maritime and Overland Trade Between Chinese and Korean Subjects in October 1882. This permitted Chinese merchants to trade in Seoul and along the border, and allowed Koreans to trade in Beijing. Thus Korea was opened to Chinese merchants. Significantly, this agreement was not a treaty but was issued as a regulation for a vassal.[12] Under Chinese advice, the monarch created the Office for the Management of Diplomatic and Commercial Affairs, better known as the Foreign Office, to handle foreign affairs and an Office for the Management of Military and National Affairs, usually referred to as the Home Office, to deal with internal matters. Also at the recommendation of the Chinese, the king appointed two advisors to the Foreign Office: the Prussian Paul Moellendorff, who had served in the Chinese Maritime Customs Service, and the Chinese diplomat Ma Jianchang. The Chinese also supervised the creation of a Korean Maritime Customs Service in 1883 with Moellendorff as its head. Again on the advice of China, Korea established a Capital Guards Command, which was to be trained by a young Chinese officer, Yuan Shikai.

In addition to the Chinese-instigated reforms, the Korean government continued on its own initiative with some modest attempts to reach out to other nations and institute further reforms. It sent Pak Yŏng-hyo to Japan in October 1882 on an apology mission. He was accompanied by Kim Ok-kyun (1851–1894), who had come under the influence of Japanese modernizers such as Fukuzawa Yukichi, and by Sŏ Kwang-bŏm, another young scholar interested in Japan's reforms. In 1883, the king sent a mission to the United States, while American diplomats arrived in Seoul. At the recommendation of Pak Yŏng-hyo and others, the state created an Office of Culture and Information, which published a thrice-monthly gazette, *Hansŏng Sunbo*, Korea's first newspaper. Forty students were sent to Japan to study military and technical subjects, and a postal administration was established.

The small group of reformers who constituted the Enlightenment Party became frustrated at the small scale and erratic pace of progress. These youthful, well-educated Koreans, most from the *yangban* class, were impressed by the developments in Meiji Japan and impatient to emulate them. In late 1884, they plotted to carry out a coup that would bring them to power so they could carry out sweeping reforms much as a group of young samurai had done in Japan in 1867–1868. Its members included Kim Ok-kyun, Pak Yŏng-hyo, Hong Yŏng-sik, Sŏ Kwang-bŏm, and Sŏ Chae-p'il (1864–1951). It was a very young group. Pak Yŏng-hyo, who came from a prestigious lineage related to the royal family, was twenty-three. Hong was twenty-nine, Sŏ Kwang-bŏm was twenty-five, and Sŏ Chae-p'il only twenty. All had spent some time in Japan. Kim Ok-kyun, at thirty-three, was the oldest. While studying in Japan he had cultivated friendships with influential Japanese figures and was the de facto leader of the group.

Their reform efforts were intertwined with factional politics in Korea. The Min clan of the royal consort, Queen Min, had been able to use the newly created institutions as bases for power. Their growing monopoly of key positions frustrated the ambitions of the Enlightenment Party. Furthermore, the Min were pursuing a pro-Chinese policy. This was partly a matter of opportunism, but it also reflected an ideological bent toward the more comfortable and traditional relationship as a tributary of China. The Min had become advocates of the "Eastern Ways, Western Machines" idea of Chinese moderate reformers. This emphasized the need to maintain the superior cultural values of the Sino-centric world while recognizing the importance of acquiring Western technology, especially military technology, in order to preserve autonomy. Thus, rather than the major institutional reforms and the adaption of new values such as legal equality or introducing modern education, the advocates of this stream of thought sought a piecemeal adoption of institutions that would strengthen the state while preserving the basic social, political, and cultural order. Most Korean adherents of this "Eastern Ways, Western Machines" school saw their aim as containing the threat of the Western barbarians. But some saw some clear practical benefits in a selective adaptation of Western technology. This was exemplified by Pak Ki-jong, a lecturer at the State Confucian Academy, who proclaimed that Western Learning (*Sŏhak*) should be rejected but that Western technology was useful for improving living standards. This could be done in accordance with the Confucian tradition of "enriching the well-being of the people by taking advantage of the useful" (*iyong husaeng*).[13]

In late 1884, the more radical reformers of the Enlightenment Party under the leadership of Kim Ok-kyun began plotting the removal of the Min clan and other obstacles to sweeping reform. The Japanese minister to Korea, Takezoe Shin'ichiro, promised to provide Japanese legation guards to support the coup plotters, although these numbered only about 200 men. The coup attempt is known as the Kapsin Chongbyŏn (the Political Disturbance of the Year Kapsin [1884]). On the night of December 4, 1884, during a banquet for the opening of the new postal administration hosted by Hong Yŏng-sik, its director, the plotters set fire to a house near the royal palace and set off some explosions in and around the palace. Taking advantage of the confusion, the leaders then entered the Ch'angdŏk Palace and removed the royal family to the Kyŏngu Palace, where they were protected by the forces of the Japanese legation. They then murdered six top officials and the leaders of the military units stationed in Seoul.

The next day, Kim Ok-kyun and Pak Yŏng-hyo proclaimed a new government and issued a fourteen-point reform program. The program called for the abolition of class distinctions, including the official ending of *yangban* status. To alleviate the plight of the poor, it called for tax reform, the punishment of avaricious and evil officials, and the permanent cancellation of debts. The program also called for the creation of a modern police system, a unified modern military through merger of the existing four military units, placing all financial affairs under the Ministry of Finance, and giving full responsibility to the State Council to formulate all laws and regulations. Reforms such as the institution of a land tax, the abolition of class distinctions, and the modernization of the police and military paralleled the early reforms of the Meiji government. The new government lasted only two days, collapsing on December 6, when 1,500 Chinese troops accompanied by Chinese-trained Korean troops intervened under the command of Yuan Shikai. They quickly overwhelmed the Japanese soldiers protecting the royal family in a brief fight. Hong Yŏng-sik and a number of the progressives were killed. Kim Ok-kyun, Pak Yŏng-hyo, Sŏ Kwang-bŏm, and Sŏ Chae-p'il fled with the retreating Japanese to Japan. All told, 180 died, including 38 Japanese and 10 Chinese. The clash between Chinese and Japanese troops was an ominous development. Eager to ease tensions between the two powers, Japanese leader Itŏ Hirobumi went to China and negotiated the Convention of Tianjin on April 18, 1885. Under this agreement, both nations agreed to withdraw their troops from Korea, neither would send military instructors, and if one party found it necessary to send troops to Korea it would notify the other.

As historian Choe Yong-ho has pointed out, the Kapsin coup was a setback to the reform movement. It left many of the leaders in exile. Yu Tae-ch'i, who was important in introducing enlightenment ideas to others, disappeared. Pak Che-hyŏng, author of a reform tract, *Mirror of Modern Korean Politics* (*Kŭnse Chosŏn chŏnggam*), was murdered by a mob. Kim Ok-kyun's and Pak Yŏng-hyo's fathers were executed. Hong Yŏng-sik's wife and elder brother committed suicide.[14] It alienated many Koreans from Japan, which as a result could less effectively serve as a model for Korea. The coup leaders sought to limit the growing involvement of China, but ironically the coup only strengthened China's role in Korea.

THE CHINESE DECADE, 1885–1894

In the decade following the failed coup, the Chinese exercised considerable influence in Korea. China's policy was one of cautious reform. Its main concern was to keep Korea from falling into the hands of another power. Beset in every direction by aggressive imperial powers, China, like Japan, was concerned with protecting its periphery. Korea's tributary relationship had long been as much symbolic as real; in all practical matters Korea was an autonomous state. However, the Chinese now exercised a direct interference in Korean affairs. Although China withdrew its troops from Korea following the Convention of Tianjin, it appointed the ambitious military commander, Yuan Shikai, to act as a sort of proconsul in Korea. He was given the vague title of commissioner of trade, which became translated by Westerners as "Resident," implying a sort of proconsul role.[15] His main concern was to limit the influence of Japan in Korea, advance the interest of Chinese merchants, make sure that in foreign affairs Korea remained subordinate to China and did not act in a way that was threatening to China, and ensure that pro-Japanese individuals were kept out of positions of authority in Korea.[16]

From 1885 to 1894 China took control over the customs service and the telegraph system. An American, Henry Merrill, a protégé of Robert Hart, the British director of the Chinese Customs Service, took over the management of the Korean Customs Service in October 1885. Since the tariff on the growing volume of foreign imports was becoming a major source of revenue for the Korean government, this gave China considerable leverage over its finances. Li Hongzhang arranged for Korea's first telegraph line, linking Inch'ŏn and Seoul; this was extended to Ŭiju, and from there it was linked with Chinese telegraph lines. When the Seoul-to-Pusan telegraph was completed in 1888, it too was placed under Chinese control. Meanwhile, Yuan, only twenty-six years of age when appointed "Resident," showed a skill at making Korean friends. However, he repeatedly interfered in Korean politics. The young official strove to keep a watch on Kojong, whom he did not trust, and to prevent officials thought to be pro-Japanese from obtaining key positions. Seeking to counter the growing Chinese influence, Kojong sought to strengthen ties with Western countries, opening diplomatic relations with Russia in 1884, Italy in 1885, and France in 1886. The king more than once requested the United States to dispatch military advisors and teachers. A small number of Americans sympathetic to Korea and concerned about maintaining its independence from China became close to the monarch. These included Horace Allen, a Presbyterian missionary and doctor attached to the U.S. legation since 1883; George Foulk, the military attaché to the legation; Hugh Dinsmore, the American minister to Korea from 1887 to 1889; and

Owen N. Denny, an advisor on Korean foreign affairs. Concerned by this American influence, Yuan in 1886 plotted to remove the king, but he was not supported by Li Hongzhang. He did succeed, however, in removing a number of officials who were in favor of closer ties to Russia that year. As a result of the removal of these officials, the power of the Min clan increased.

Korea's link with the outside world was obstructed by the Chinese, who guarded against any sign of an independent foreign policy that might place the country outside of its orbit. Following Denny's advice, the king appointed Min Yŏng-jun as the first Korean resident minister to Tokyo in 1887 as a prelude to opening up a permanent legation there. Shortly afterward, two envoys were sent to Washington and the capitals of the five European nations with whom Korea had established relations, with the purpose of opening up permanent legations in those countries. The Chinese did not object to the legation in Tokyo but tried to block the opening of Korean missions in Western countries. When the United States objected to this interference Korea was permitted to open a legation in Washington in 1888, but Beijing successfully prevented others in Europe. The effectiveness of Korea's first overseas diplomatic outposts in Tokyo and Washington, however, was limited by Chinese interference. The Chinese also sought to check foreign influence in the country by blocking several attempts by the Korean government to seek foreign loans to finance development projects. It is significant that during this period Korea did not send any major cultural mission abroad comparable to those that had been sent to Tianjin in 1881 and Japan in 1882. The Chinese, with the collusion of Korean conservatives, were able to keep Koreans from traveling abroad, thereby contributing to the country's intellectual and cultural isolation. A rare exception was a ten-member musical troupe sent to the Chicago World's Fair in 1893. All students sent abroad by the government prior to 1885 were ordered to return home.[17] While isolating Korea from other countries, Resident Yuan promoted Chinese trade in Korea to counter the rapid expansion of Japanese mercantile activities in the country. The Chinese merchant community was large enough to cause resentment among Koreans. Anti-Chinese riots broke out in 1888 and 1889 in Seoul, and Chinese shops were burned. However, the Japanese remained the largest foreign community and Korea's largest trading partner.

Very few reform efforts were carried out during this period. In 1886, the Yugyŏng Kongwŏn (Royal College) was established for sons of the elite who were to be instructed in a modern Western education. Instruction was in English, and three Americans, including the missionary Homer Hulbert, later an eloquent spokesman for Korean sovereignty, were hired as instructors, but this received little financial support. The state closed the *Hansŏng Sunbo*, a vehicle for disseminating Western ideas, in 1885, but the following year Kim Yun-sik, with the assistance of a Japanese, Inoue Kakugorŏ, began publishing *Hansŏng Chubo* (*Seoul Weekly*). This too was closed in 1888 under Chinese pressure. In the same year, American general William Dye and three others were hired to modernize the military, but they received little support, so not much was accomplished.

China was trying to reassert its role as Korea's suzerain, ignoring that the country's relationship as a vassal had been largely ceremonial. Direct Chinese intervention into Korean affairs had been rare; in fact, not since the Mongols ruled China as the Yuan dynasty in the fourteenth century had it so directly interfered in Korean affairs. China's role in Korea was not entirely negative; it provided loans, assisted in building telegraph lines, and in others ways promoted modernization. Overall, however, the attempt by Beijing to put Korea firmly under its guidance limited Korea's contact with the outside world, hindered reform efforts, weakened the position of reformers, and in general contributed to the country's lack of preparedness for the challenges to its sovereignty. By being protected by China, Korea had its fate attached to a declining power whose own failure to carry out necessary reforms was dramatically demonstrated in its clash with Japan in 1894.

While successfully hampering Korean access to outside knowledge, the Chinese were not able to isolate Korea from international intrigue. Moellendorff, who had been appointed by Li Hongzhang, soon decided that Korea needed another power to balance that of China. He worked toward establishing closer ties with Russia. In 1885, Moellendorff suggested to the Russian representative in Korea that the country be made a Russian protectorate. Russian diplomats also expressed a willingness to send military advisors to Korea. Russia's interest in Korea was growing. As Russia expanded into the Pacific region, Korea offered the possibility of ice-free ports; especially tempting was Wŏnsan on the east coast. In that year, Kojong dispatched a secret mission to Vladivostok seeking Russian assistance. Russia's growing interest in Korea alarmed the British. As a warning to the Russians, in April 1885 the British occupied the small island of Kŏmundo off the south coast of Chŏlla Province, which they called Port Hamilton. Their presence on an island the Russians had once considered for use as a coaling station met with a threat from the tsarist government in St. Petersburg to occupy some Korean territories, possibly some northern ports. Eventually Russia gave assurances that it would not occupy any part of Korea, and in 1887 the British withdrew from Kŏmundo.

The United States played a more modest role in Korea. A small community of American diplomats and missionaries in Seoul were concerned about threats to Korea's sovereignty. However, they received little support from Washington. The U.S. government, with no special interest in

Korea, was largely indifferent to requests by the Americans in Seoul to become actively involved in guaranteeing its independence.

Japan, in contrast, remained very much concerned with Korea, fearing both Chinese domination and Russian involvement in the peninsula. Japan was developing considerable economic ties with Korea, which it saw as a source of agricultural produce, but it was facing Chinese competition. Tokyo's concerns about protecting its economic interests in Korea are revealed by the "Bean Controversy." In 1889, the governor of northeast Hamgyŏng Province, fearing a food shortage caused by a drought, issued an embargo against soybean exports to Japan. The Japanese protested the embargo and demanded an indemnity to compensate its importers. The "Bean Controversy" was finally settled in 1893 when Korea agreed to pay the indemnity and end the embargo.[18] Japanese merchants and manufacturers focused on the Korean market. Paying close attention to the needs of Korean consumers, they out-competed local, Chinese, and Western merchants in capturing much of the textile trade with their cheap cotton cloth.[19] But Japan's greatest interest in Korea was strategic. As one leader remarked, it was "a dagger pointed at the heart of Japan." As it built up its Western-modeled army and navy, and as its economy grew, Japan became more inclined to act upon its anxieties over the Chinese position in the peninsula.

THE TONGHAK REBELLION

While political intrigue went on in the capital, the bulk of the population, the peasantry, was also feeling the changes brought on by Korea's entry into the international economy. Peasants suffered the burden from tax increases to pay for the country's reforms. The countryside was being penetrated by Chinese and especially by Japanese merchants, a disturbing development in a society neither used to outsiders nor experienced in a modern commercial economy. These developments contributed to peasant unrest that led to the Tonghak Rebellion, a conflict that became entangled with the rivalries of China and Japan in Korea.

The primary cause of this uprising, however, was the chronic resentment of the corruption of local officials. Peasant uprisings were not uncommon in Korea. A major uprising took place in northern Korea in 1811–1812 and in southern Korea in 1862. The Tonghak Rebellion differed in that it had its roots in the new religious movement known as Tonghak (Eastern Learning) founded in 1860 by Ch'oe Che-u (also known as Suun). Ch'oe's new line of teachings seems to have been as a response to the unsettling new ideas and developments taking place, including the spread of Christianity. Ch'oe's teaching appeared to show a Christian influence, including a belief in a Lord of Heaven, an omnipotent God. It also drew heavily from shamanism and Korean folk religions, including the practice of healing rites in which the spirit that intruded into the body and caused illness was stabbed with a sword. Paper talismans were burned and their ashes drunk, another folk religion custom. But its main roots were in Confucianism.[20] Drawing from the teachings of Mencius, who considered government an instrument for the welfare of the people, Ch'oe called for an end to corruption, the punishment of evil officials, and a more egalitarian social order. It is clear, though, that his new faith had incorporated some Christian concepts too. For this reason and because of his call for sweeping social reform, the court saw the new religion as a threat. Fearing rebellion among his followers, the state arrested and executed Ch'oe in 1864. But the new religion did not die out. He left behind a few hundred followers, and out of these a second leader emerged, Ch'oe Si-hyŏng (Hyewŏl), a man from a poor commoner family. Based on a few poems and essays the founder Suun had left, he compiled a holy book of Tonghak thought and a hymnbook. His followers gradually grew in numbers during the 1880s. Following a time-honored Korean custom of honoring one's ancestors and teachers by seeking to posthumously exonerate them if they had been disgraced or purged, Tonghak leaders urged Ch'oe Si-hyŏng to petition the court to restore the founder's good name as well as that of other victims.

In 1892, several thousand followers gathered in Samnye in Chŏlla demanding Suun's exoneration and calling for the end of persecution of Tonghak. They negotiated with the governors of Chŏlla and Ch'ungchŏng provinces, who agreed to stop the persecutions but explained they had no authority to exonerate the spiritual founder. Ch'oe Si-hyŏng then agreed to assemble with his believers outside the royal court at the Kwanghwa Gate in Seoul. Three days later, on March 31, a messenger vaguely promised their petition would be accepted if they dispersed and went home. But the persecution of members continued, and on the thirtieth anniversary of the execution, Ch'oe Si-hyŏng called a mass meeting in Poun in Ch'ungchŏng. This assembly in April 1893 was attended by 20,000 followers from all over the country. Despite Ch'oe Si-hyŏng's attempt to take a more moderate position, the Tonghak members were becoming more radicalized. Displeasure with continual persecution of the church and defamation of its founder was linked to the peasant unrest over the new taxes, local grievances with corrupt officials, resentment at the Japanese merchants, and anxiety over the growing foreign presence in the country. Members called for the punishment of corrupt officials and the expulsion of Japanese and Westerners from Korea.

The next spring, protests over taxes in the southeastern region of the country erupted into violence. The leader of the movement was Chŏn

Pong-jun, the son of a local clerk, who had supported himself by private teaching and had become a recent convert to Tonghak. Peasants were angry with Cho Pyŏng-gap, the magistrate of Kobu County, who was accused of extorting excessive taxes and forcing peasants to build a reservoir without compensation and then levying a water tax on them. With Chŏn leading, the peasants, wearing headbands and armed with clubs and bamboo poles, attacked the magistrate's office and destroyed the reservoir. Under Chŏn's leadership the rebellion grew. The Tonghaks were careful to express loyalty to the king but called for the elimination of the *yangban* class, punishment of all corrupt officials, and the end of grain exports to Japan. While the government commander in the region negotiated with the rebels, a panicky government in Seoul requested Chinese assistance on June 4. The Chinese government quickly ordered naval and land forces to go to Korea. By the time Chinese forces began to arrive, the government had negotiated a truce with the Tonghak. An office was set up in Chŏlla Province to investigate complaints, and Tonghak members were allowed to participate. The Tonghak forces were allowed to have an overseer in every county of the province. The leaders decided to wait until after the autumn harvest before deciding on further action.

With the situation apparently under control, the Chinese forces were not needed. Meanwhile, in accordance with the agreement worked out in 1885, China informed Tokyo of its intention to dispatch troops, done, it was added, "in conformity with China's ancient custom of sending troops to protect vassal states."[21] The Japanese then decided to send troops to Korea under a new minister, Ōtori Keisuke, who arrived at Inch'ŏn with eight Japanese warships on June 9 and proceeded to Seoul with 400 marines. Another 3,000 Japanese troops landed at Inch'ŏn four days later. The Chinese requested that the Japanese withdraw, but instead the Japanese government decided that it was time to bring about change in the Korean government. They proposed that the two powers take joint actions to bring about reforms in Korea, which China rejected. The Japanese ignored the Korean government's request that it withdraw its troops. On July 13, Ōtori presented Korea with a plan to reform its government. The Korean government evaded the Japanese proposal and asked their forces to leave.

Japan then took direct action to bring about political change in Korea. Its troops, now with reinforcements outnumbering the Chinese, occupied the Kyŏngbok palace, where the king resided, and disarmed the Korean forces. The king agreed to form a new government headed by Kim Hong-jip. The next day, on July 25, the Japanese attacked the Chinese warships at Asan Bay. The Sino-Japanese War, as this conflict became known, was a complete victory for Japan. Chinese forces were routed at the battle of P'yŏngyang in mid-September, and in October were driven back to the Yalu River. Japanese forces overran the Liaodong Peninsula at the southern tip of Manchuria, capturing the strategic ports of Lushun (Port Arthur) and Dalian. China's northern fleet was destroyed, and the major port of Weihaiwai in Shandong fell. On April 17, 1895, Li Hongzhang negotiated the Treaty of Shimonoseki, in which China recognized Korea as an independent state, surrendering all claims as its suzerain; ceded Taiwan and the Liaodong Peninsula to Japan; and agreed to pay a war indemnity. China was no longer able to play a role in Korean affairs; a dramatic shift in power had occurred in East Asia.

Meanwhile, after the autumn harvest, Tonghak leaders called for resistance to the corrupt officials and the Japanese Army. An estimated 100,000–200,000 peasants participated. Japanese Army officers led Korean forces in an attack on the rebels, inflicting crushing defeats on the huge but poorly equipped peasant troops, who were armed mostly with bamboo spears. Chŏn was betrayed and captured. When questioned by prosecutor Sŏ Kwang-bŏm and the Japanese consul, he insisted his only aim was to remove corrupt officials. He was executed at age forty-one along with other leaders of the rebellion. Ch'oe Si-hyŏng and his appointed successor, Son Pyŏng-hŭi, escaped to Kangwŏndo, where they hid in homes of followers.[22] Ch'oe was arrested in 1898 and died in prison, but Son lived to reorganize the Tonghak movement, which was renamed Ch'ŏndogyo. It still exists today as an organized religion. The Kabo Peasant War, as the rebellion is sometimes called, failed in its immediate aims of redressing peasant grievances. Instead, it strengthened the Japanese presence in Korea.

KABO REFORMS

From July 1894 to February 1896, Korean reformers under the sponsorship of the Japanese enacted a sweeping series of laws and regulations that marked a sharp break in the country's historical traditions. Although these efforts by some of the most talented and progressive of Korea's leaders were of great importance in bringing about necessary steps toward modernization, the fact that they were carried out under Japanese military pressure and the heavy-handedness of the Japanese interference left an ambiguous legacy.

When the Japanese troops occupied the palace, the king became a virtual prisoner under the direction of the Japanese minister, and a new government was placed in charge. In late July 1894, the Japanese-directed reformers created a Deliberative Council (Kun'guk Kimuch'ŏ) with seventeen and later twenty-three members. Until it was abolished in December, it was the principal organ for carrying out the sweeping restructuring of government and society. The new government was staffed by the leading reformers in the country. To appease conservatives and the Tonghak, the Japanese installed the aging Taewŏn'gun as the nominal head of the new government. He was also a foe of the pro-Chinese Min clan. Important conservative officials were appointed to a largely powerless Privy Council. The State Council was replaced by a cabinet-style organization with a prime minister. New ministries were created to deal with foreign affairs, home affairs, finance, justice, education, defense, agriculture and commerce, and industry. Much of the authority of the king was removed to the new cabinet and to a prime minister. The affairs of the court were separated from the rest of the government and administered by a Department of Royal Household Affairs. The government was rationalized with clear separations of judicial and military functions from civil ones. It enacted laws that established a separate hierarchy of courts, and issued decrees outlawing the torture of suspects, guilt by association, and the punishments of family members of criminals. The government created a new capital and provincial police system, and made plans to rationalize the tax system as well. It abolished arbitrary taxes and merchant monopolies.

A series of measures brought about significant social reforms. An official 1886 ban on the sale of slaves was confirmed; now, thirty-one years after the United States had done so, the government legally abolished slavery in all forms. The new administration officially eliminated social distinctions of all sorts; the *yangban* no longer had a legal status. Outcaste distinctions were also legally abolished. The council enacted the radically new principle of equality of law, opening all positions to men of talent regardless of social background. It increased the marriage age for men and women to twenty and sixteen respectively, outlawing child marriage. A long legal prohibition against widows remarrying ended. It relaxed sumptuary laws that had emphasized social distinctions. One of the most momentous actions by the council was its abolition of the civil service exams that had been central to recruiting officials and confirming elite status. To signal a break with the old Chinese tributary system, it proclaimed June 6 as Korean Independence Day; it used the Korean alphabet, *han'gŭl*, in government documents; and decreed that Korean history was to be taught in school. The old Ming Chinese calendar was replaced with the Western one. A new Ministry of Education promulgated a series of ordinances creating a Western-style education system. The Hansŏng (Seoul) Normal School was established, along with five primary schools in the capital, with plans to establish others throughout the country. The ministry created a new modern curriculum and compiled textbooks for it.

The whole program is known as the Kabo Reform (Kabo Kyŏngjang) after the year Kabo (1894). The Deliberate Council issued over 200 reform bills in total. In December, Japan sent a leading political figure, Inoue Kaoru, to supervise the reform effort. To eliminate threats to the new

government, he removed the Taewŏn'gun, who had been secretly plotting with the Chinese, seeking to dethrone his son, Kojong, who was now
cooperating compliantly with the Japanese. Inoue had also ordered Japanese troops to destroy the Tonghak. Pak Yŏng-hyo and Sŏ Kwang-bŏm
returned from exile in Japan and joined the "Coalition Cabinet," which
replaced the Deliberate Council and continued with the reforms. Another
exiled participant in the Kapsin Coup, Sŏ Chae-p'il, and the American-
educated reformer Yun Ch'i-ho (1864–1945) later joined the cabinet. It is
interesting to note that the latter two were Protestant converts, the first to
serve in Korean government.

Japan's victories over China only strengthened its prestige, aiding
those Koreans who wanted to use the Meiji reforms as a model. It now
seemed inevitable that Japan would be Korea's new big brother. But all
this changed rather suddenly with the diplomatic setback that almost
immediately followed the Treaty of Shimonoseki. In the treaty of April
17, 1895, China agreed to lease the Liaodong Peninsula, with its potential
naval base at Port Arthur, to Japan. This alarmed Russia, which had its
own designs on Port Arthur as a possible warm-water port in the region.
Russia quickly gained the support of France and Germany to issue a joint
demand by the three powers that Japan cancel the lease. Facing what was
called the Triple Intervention, Japan complied. This humiliation coming
shortly after its victory was interpreted by Koreans as evidence of Japan's
weakness. Opponents of the pro-Japanese government gained courage.
Min clan members forced Pak Yŏng-hyo back into exile in July, and the
Kabo reform effort seemed threatened. A new Japanese minister, Miura
Gorŏ, arriving in September, sought to reverse this shift in power by
eliminating Queen Min, around whom many of the pro-Russian, anti-
Japanese Korean officials rallied. Following his plan, on October 8,
Japanese thugs and some Korean collaborators broke into the palace and
murdered Queen Min, two ladies-in-waiting, and a court official. Queen
Min's body was then covered with kerosene and burned. This brutal and
shocking affair, once it became known, led to a wave of anti-Japanese
feeling. It also brought international condemnation. The Japanese government recalled Miura, promising to punish those involved, and sent Inoue
Kaoru back to Korea along with a new minister, Komura Jutarō, to sal-
vage the situation. But they were unable to reverse the anti-Japanese sentiment, and with the collapse of Japanese influence, the Kabo reformers
were unable to maintain themselves in power. The first comprehensive
effort at restructuring Korean government and society ended.

Even if the Japanese influence had not waned, it is not clear how the
Korean reformers would have been able to implement so many radical
changes. One last event symbolized both the depth of the reform effort
and the degree to which the reformers had moved ahead of most ordinary

Koreans. In late December, Kojong, following the instruction of the reform government, dutifully issued a decree (*tanballyŏng*) requiring Koreans to cut off their topknots and adopt Western-style haircuts. He himself, did so. Korean men had long worn the hair long, tying it up at the top. This was a proud custom; in fact, Korean travelers to China and Japan sometime made disparaging reports about the haircuts of their neighbors. It was an issue that both conservative *yangban*, smarting over their loss of legal privileges, and ordinary peasants could rally behind. Riots took place throughout the country; in some provincial towns government officials announcing the decree were attacked by mobs and killed. Nonetheless, the Kabo reforms were a step in the transformation of Korean society, brought on by the new international environment.

THE RUSSIAN ASCENDENCY AND THE INDEPENDENCE CLUB

The decade from 1895 to 1905 was marked by the rivalry between Russia and Japan for influence in Korea, the last Korean-initiated attempts at major reform, and the establishment of a Japanese protectorate over Korea, effectively ending Korea's independence.

In late November 1895, a group of pro-Russian officials, including Yi Pŏm-jin, attempted to remove the king from the palace and spirit him off to the Russian legation for protection. A second attempt on February 11 was successful, beginning a rather bizarre episode in which the king and crown prince reigned from the Russian diplomatic compound in Seoul for one year. Now under Russian protection, Kojong, surrounded by conservative advisors, ignored the cabinet government established by the Kabo reforms and directly appointed and dismissed ministers. Tensions between the Japanese and the Russians were eased when on May 14, 1896, Komura Jutarō and Karl Waeber, the Russian envoy, worked out an agreement in which the countries would advise the Korean king on appointment of ministers. Japan would be allowed to use military police to guard the Seoul-Pusan telegraph; both countries agreed on the number of troops stationed in Seoul, Pusan, and Wŏnsan, and to limit the number of troops in the country. Shortly afterward, the Japanese senior official, Yamagata Aritomo, went to Russia and signed the Moscow Protocol (Lobanov-Yamagata Agreement) with Russian foreign minister Lobanov, confirming this agreement. Both powers recognized the independence of Korea; any loans and assistance for internal reform would be done by mutual agreement.

The Korean court sent an envoy, Min Yŏng-hwan, to Russia in the spring of 1896 to attend the coronation of Nicholas II with the intention of obtaining an alliance with Russia. Having safely contained Japanese

influence in Korea, the Russians eventually agreed only to send a few
military advisors to Korea. Meanwhile, during the post-Kabo period,
the king and his officials approved a number of concessions to Russians
and other Westerners. The right to build a Seoul-Inch'n railway that had
been given to Japan in 1894, for instance, was revoked and given to an
American, James Morse, who also received a concession to operate a gold
mine at Unsan in North P'yŏngan Province. A Russian, Jules Bryner (the
grandfather of actor Yul Brynner), received a concession to cut timber
along the Tumen River and on the island of Ullŭngdo. In a reaction to
these concessions, the Japanese sought to discredit the Russians by making the Komura-Waeber Memorandum public. When the king returned to
his palace in February 1897, the Russian influence in the government was
strong, Russians were even employed as palace guards.

Russian and Japanese interference in Korea, and the country's continued
weakness, led to the creation of the Independence Club (Tongnip Hyŏphoe)
in 1896 by a group of Koreans eager to disseminate and implement new
social and political ideas. Its leader was Sŏ Chae-p'il. The youngest of the
Kapsin coup leaders, Sŏ fled to the United States, where he earned a medical degree from Johns Hopkins and became a U.S. citizen under the name
of Philip Jaisohn. He returned to Korea early in 1896, accepted a position
on the Privy Council, and founded a newspaper *Tongnip Sinmun* (*The Independent*). This was the first newspaper to be published solely in *han'gŭl*, the
Korean alphabet, rather than in the more prestigious Chinese characters,
itself a statement of Korean cultural independence. The paper became a
vehicle for the promotion of the concepts of representative government,
national sovereignty, and modern reforms. The paper was launched in
April, and in July Sŏ assisted in the organization of the Independence Club
whose active members included Yun Ch'i-ho, Yi Sang-jae, and a young
American missionary school graduate, Yi Sŭng-man (1875–1965; better
known to Americans as Syngman Rhee). The club carried out educational
and cultural campaigns and sponsored lectures and debates, using every
format to promote the ideals of individual freedom and national independence. The club campaigned to have the Yŏngŭn Gate in Seoul, where
the Chinese envoys traditionally arrived, torn down and replaced with
an Independence Gate. The China Adoration Hall in Seoul was renamed
Independence Hall. These symbols of subservience to a foreign power
were thus converted into symbols of national independence. The Independence Hall became a forum where public debates sponsored by the club
were held every Sunday on issues of national concern. A major campaign
was the return of the king from the Russian legation. When he did so in
February 1897, he declared himself emperor and renamed the country
Taehan Cheguk (the Great Han Empire). This, too, was of symbolic importance, since it was making him and his country equal to China, and of

course, Japan. In a new campaign, the Independence Club demanded the government stop granting leases to foreigners. A mass meeting was held at Chongno in central Seoul on February 20, 1898, to pressure the government and to arouse the interest of the public on this issue.

Conservatives in the government were concerned about the growing influence of the club and of Sŏ Chae-p'il. When in the spring of 1898, under pressure from these conservatives, Sŏ returned to the United States, the club lost its most important leader. Yun Ch'i-ho took over the leadership of the club and seemed to get some support from the king. In October, the club brought about a new organization, the Ten Thousand People's Cooperative Association, also called the People's Assembly. It held a mass rally in central Seoul. With this new tactic, the Independence Club attempted to pressure the government to stop granting concessions to foreigners, to reform the tax system, and to convert the royal Privy Council into a parliamentary assembly, among other reforms. In response, conservatives in the government created an Imperial Association consisting of members of the peddlers' guild to break up meetings and beat and intimidate club members. Cho Pyŏng-sik, a conservative official, arrested seventeen members of the club. The club held daily rallies demanding the release of its jailed members. The king, vacillating, released them and permitted the Independence Club to elect twenty-five members to the Privy Council. Then, changing his mind again, he ordered the club dissolved. Its leaders fled the country, and this spasm of the reform movement came to an end.

The Independence Club failed to bring about significant institutional change, but this organization, led mostly by young intellectuals and political activists, was important in the emergence of a new conception of the Korean state. While most historians have argued that nationalism is a modern concept born in the West in the late eighteenth and nineteenth centuries, Koreans have long had an awareness of living in a society with clear physical and cultural boundaries, of being a distinctive community. What was new in the late nineteenth century was the concept of national sovereignty and of a state existing within an international community of sovereign states. The name "Independence" taken by the club and its newspaper was an assertion of this concept and a rejection of the Sino-centric tribute system or any other orientation that would subordinate Korean sovereignty to another power.

For the next few years the Korean government drifted, making only modest efforts at self-strengthening. In the last two decades of the nineteenth century most of the country's most energetic and talented reformers had left the country or withdrawn from public affairs, some had been killed. The government at its center had an indecisive king who erratically shifted positions. Conservatives held the top positions, and incompetent and often corrupt officials made up the staff. The reform movement was also weakened by its failure to find a suitable foreign protector and model to follow. China had failed in both these purposes. Japan was the obvious model, but its usefulness had been undermined by the fact that it had emerged as the most serious threat to the nation's sovereignty. Pro-Japanese reformers could not extricate themselves from Japan's often heavy-handed and ruthless designs on the country. The United States, through its missionaries, had won a great deal of goodwill among some Koreans, but it was too distant and different to serve as a useful model and too indifferent to act as a protector. The same was largely true of Western European countries such as Britain or France. Then there was Russia. It was useful as a counter to Japan, but it too had imperialist designs on northeast Asia, including Korea. In the end, the greatest threat to Korea proved to be the swift rise of a dynamic, modernizing Japan, determined to secure its peripheries by gaining control of the Korean peninsula.

THE RUSSO-JAPANESE WAR AND THE PROTECTORATE

The end to Korea's effective independence came as a result of the Russo-Japanese War. A major imperialist power in the age of imperialism, Russia took advantage of the retreat of Japan in 1895 to advance in northeast Asia. It concluded a secret treaty with China to build part of the Trans-Siberian Railway it was constructing across Manchuria. The Russians also acquired twenty-five-year leases on Port Arthur and Dalian, and began a program to build a rail line linking these warm-water ports to the Trans-Siberian. In 1900, Russian forces entered Manchuria during the Boxer Rebellion. These forces were supposed to be withdrawn after the rebellion ended, but in fact they remained there, alarming Britain as well as Japan. In 1902, to counter Russian expansion in the East, Britain abandoned its long-held policy of avoiding formal alliances by concluding the Anglo-Japanese Alliance. Britain agreed to acknowledge Japan's interest in Korea in exchange for Japan's recognition of British rights and interests in China. With its position strengthened, Tokyo demanded the withdrawal of Russian troops from Manchuria. Russia, however, reneged on promises to do so. Instead, in July 1903, a small group of Russian soldiers entered Korea at Yongnamp'o, a trading port at the mouth of the Yalu, and started constructing a fort. At Japanese insistence, they withdrew. Many Japanese had hoped to work out an agreement with Russia—a free hand in Manchuria for Russia in exchange for a Japanese free hand in Korea—but nothing came of this. Instead Russia's provocations were such that Japan decided to take military action to prevent Korea from falling into Russian hands. In February 1904, the Japanese carried out a surprise attack on the Russian naval facilities at Port Arthur.

Korea declared its neutrality in January 1904 in the wake of rising tensions between the two imperialist powers. When hostilities broke out, Japanese troops entered Seoul, as they had done at the start of the Sino-Japanese War, and compelled the Korean government to bow to its wishes. The Korean foreign minister signed a protocol in February that in effect made Korea a protectorate of Japan. It gave the Japanese government the right to take any necessary action to protect the Korean imperial house or the territorial integrity of Korea if threatened by a foreign power and gave the Japanese the right to occupy certain parts of the country. In another agreement signed in August 1904, Korea agreed to appoint a Japanese advisor to the Ministry of Finance and a non-Japanese foreigner recommended by the Japanese government to advise the Ministry of Foreign Affairs. It also required Korea to consult with Japan before signing any treaties or agreements with other countries, or any contracts or concessions to foreigners. A Japanese, Megata Tanetarō, became financial advisor, and an American, Durham White Stevens, became the foreign affairs advisor. In effect, the Korean government had conceded control of its financial and foreign affairs to Japan. Meanwhile, a pro-Japanese association called the Ilchinhoe (Society for Advancement), under the leadership of Song Pyŏng-jun, was actively advocating the union of Korea and Japan. This group received support from nationalist, pro-expansionist groups in Japan. The purpose was to give an impression that the Japanese takeover of Korea had popular support among Koreans. Many Japanese nationalists became involved in the project to bring Korea under Japanese rule, sometimes working in tandem with their government, sometimes running ahead of it.

To the surprise of many observers and largely to the delight of the British and Americans, Japan emerged victorious in the war. Facing overly extended supply lines and revolt at home, Russia concluded the Treaty of Portsmouth with Japan in September 1905, with President Theodore Roosevelt acting as mediator. Russia withdrew from Manchuria, and Japan acquired Port Arthur and was now unchallenged in its efforts to achieve domination over Korea. The United States tacitly accepted the transfer of Korea to Japan in the Taft-Katsura Memorandum of July 1905. In this exchange of views between American secretary of war William Howard Taft and the Japanese prime minister Katsura Tarō, the United States recognized Japan's right to take appropriate measures for the "guidance, control, and protection" of Korea; in exchange, Japan recognized America's position in the Philippines. Britain, renewing its alliance with Japan in 1905, also tacitly accepted Korea as being in Japan's sphere. The way was diplomatically prepared for Japan to take a free hand in Korea.

In November 1905, Itō Hirobumi, one of the principal architects of Meiji Japan came to Seoul to conclude a treaty establishing a protectorate. On

November 17, 1905, with Japanese troops displaying a show of strength on the streets of the capital, the Korean foreign minister, Pak Che-sun, signed what has been called the Protectorate Treaty of 1905. The acting prime minister, Han Kyu-sŏl, refused to sign it. This agreement transferred all foreign relations to Japan. A Japanese resident-general (*tōkan*) was to be stationed in Seoul with direct access to the Korean emperor. According to the treaty, his role was to manage diplomatic affairs, but his authority soon expanded to include most aspects of the country's administration. Beginning with the Americans, the international community closed its legations in Seoul, and the country was now only nominally independent. Most Korean officials such as Pak Che-sun, who became prime minister, simply accommodated themselves to the new reality. A few were despondent. Diplomat and official Min Yŏng-hwan committed suicide in protest; others went into exile. In reality, Korea was under Japanese control since the start of the Russo-Japanese War in early 1904, so the formal protectorate was not a sudden change or traumatic event but simply one in a series of steps by which Japan consolidated its rule over Korea. The process, however, did not end with the protectorate; rather, it was another step in Japan's absorption of Korea.

THE PROTECTORATE, 1905–1910

In the spring of 1906 Itō returned to Korea to take up the position as resident-general. He was able to find enough Korean officials to work with him—men such as Yi Wan-yong, the minister of education—but he had some problems with Kojong, who had never signed the protectorate treaty. In 1907, Kojong sent the American missionary Homer Hulbert to Washington to gain U.S. support for Korea. Hulbert made two trips but was ignored by the Roosevelt administration, which had accepted Japan's position in Korea. In 1907, the king secretly sent three representatives to the Second Hague Peace Conference with a petition requesting international assistance in recovering Korea's sovereignty. The Western powers refused to recognize and seat them. Their petition was ignored, but it did generate publicity in the Western press. Embarrassed and annoyed, the Japanese, using a combination of pressure and trickery, got Kojong to abdicate and made his mentally challenged son Sunjong emperor. Angry Korean mobs stormed and burned the residence of Yi Wan-yong, who had become prime minister. Pak Yŏng-hyo, who held the position of minister of the imperial household and who plotted a coup to replace the pro-Japanese cabinet with those who would resist further efforts to erode Korea's sovereignty, was exiled to the southern island of Cheju. Following the abdication, Yi Wan-yong signed a new agreement requiring the resident-general's approval for virtually all laws, regulations, and appointments and removals of high officials. The protectorate issued a press law that banned books that were considered anti-Japanese and tightened control over the press. Several newspapers were closed. On July 31, 1907, the resident-general ordered the small 9,000-man Korean Army disbanded.

When the protectorate was established in 1905 a few members of the *yangban* class organized what were called "Righteous Armies" (*ŭibyŏng*). When the Korean Army was ordered disbanded in 1907, the commander of the First Infantry Guard committed suicide. Many of his troops along with the troops of the Second Infantry Guards responded by revolting. Retreating to the countryside, they were joined by some provincial units to become the core of a widespread resistance movement. Some civilians, both *yangban* and non-*yangban*, also took up revolt, forming more Righteous Armies. An example was Hŏ Wi, who had taken up a small resistance group in 1896 that was disbanded. He now organized another. In 1907 Hŏ and another resistance fighter, Yi In-yŏng, each leading over 1,000 fighters, reached within eight miles of Seoul but were then driven back with heavy losses.[23] Guerilla bands were organized in many parts of the country from Chŏlla in the southwest to Hamgyŏng in the northeast. The scale of this resistance movement and the number of casualties is not known for certain. They were large enough to require a major military operation by the Japanese. By some estimates 50,000 Korean insurgents participated, and more than 10,000 of these were killed. The resistance was divided into many small bands, mostly from 100 to 500 in number. There was little overall coordination, and for the most part the insurgents were poorly trained and equipped. Activity peaked in 1908; by 1910 the guerillas had been defeated or driven across the border to Manchuria or Siberia.

At some point the Japanese government decided to annex Korea. There was little opposition to this from Britain and the United States, since both had largely given their approval to Japan to act as it saw fit in Korea. In 1907, Tokyo also reached a secret agreement with Russia in which the latter accepted the annexation in return for Japanese recognition of Russia's special interests in Outer Mongolia. Itō Hirobumi, who had doubts about whether the time was right for annexation, resigned as resident-general in 1909 and was succeeded by the vice-resident-general, Sone Arasuke. But Itō continued to assist in the preparation for annexation by negotiating a treaty abolishing the Korean ministries of justice and defense. Shortly after, he went to Harbin, China, to confirm Russian acceptance of annexation. There on October 26, 1909, he was assassinated by An Chung-gŭn (1879–1910), a member of the resistance forces. He was not the only victim of angry Koreans. When Durham White Stevens, the Japanese-nominated advisor to the Korean government went to the United States in 1908 to promote the benefits of Japanese rule in Korea, he was shot and killed in San Francisco by two Korean students, Chang In-hwan and Chŏn Myŏng-un.

In July 1910, Terauchi Masatake, a former war minister, arrived in Seoul as the new resident-general. He banned all political discussion and assembly, imposed tight press censorship, and arrested Koreans deemed a threat to the authorities. On August 16, Terauchi presented a draft of the treaty of annexation to Korean ministers. Prime Minister Yi Wan-yong, to the condemnation of later Korean nationalists, signed it. On August 29, the Japanese government issued edicts in the name of Emperors Meiji of Japan and Sunjong of Korea announcing the merger of the two countries. The Korean kingdom established in the seventh century and the Chosŏn dynasty that had ruled it since 1392 came to an end.

The Japanese takeover has been viewed by most Koreans as one of the two great tragedies of their modern history; the other being the division of the country. Could the colonization of Korea have been avoided? Historians often assign blame to the king, to recalcitrant conservatives, to a *yangban* elite that could not rise above self-interest, and to mistakes by reformers. All are blamed for their failure to maintain Korean sovereignty by carrying out the institutional changes that would have strengthened the state and enabled it to operate more effectively in the new international environment. But Koreans had little time to absorb and adjust to the new world into which they had been thrust. For centuries Korea maintained its autonomy within the East Asian world order dominated by China. The experience of Koreans with the tributary system, their proud adherence to Confucian values and institutions, and their limited experience with the West did not prepare them well for the challenges of late nineteenth-century imperialism. The intrusion of the West came rather suddenly and left them with little time to develop adequate responses. Nonetheless, some educated Koreans were quick to grasp the realities of a changing international environment and pushed for institutional changes that would strengthen their state. Korea's geopolitical position, however, did not favor this effort. Chinese interference, Japanese expansionism, and Russian intrigue, along with the indecisive leadership of the king and the petty self-interest of many members of the elite all hampered attempts to carry out reform and maintain sovereignty. Furthermore, as has been pointed out, it was difficult to find an appropriate model for Korea. Japan was the most obvious, but its aggressive policies undermined its advocates.

More significantly, Korea's geopolitical situation was a most precarious one. Surrounded by three major expansionist powers, all of which had identified Korea as strategically important, it is difficult to see how it could have easily navigated its way safely toward modernization without inviting the intervention of its neighbors. Nor is it easy to conceive how a poor, overwhelmingly agricultural nation of perhaps 15 million could have resisted its much larger and more powerful neighbors. Few nations escaped colonization in this era, including other long-standing states such as Vietnam and Burma. Among the small number of exceptions were states such as Thailand, Afghanistan, and Persia, which did so partly as buffer states between empires, but Japan's victories over China and Russia ruled out this possibility.

KOREA IN TRANSITION

Despite the country's loss of independence, this period brought about important changes that marked the birth of a modern Korea. Korea's entry into the world of imperialism profoundly altered society. By the early twentieth century, the forces of modernization were being felt throughout the country. Railway construction, financed by Japanese and American companies, began in 1896; Seoul was being electrified, and Western-style buildings were changing the face of the city. Port cities such as Pusan and Inch'ŏn were taking on a cosmopolitan atmosphere. In the countryside, where the great majority of the population lived, farming was increasingly oriented toward the export of rice, soybeans, and other agriculture products for the Japanese market. The old rigid social structure of Korea, based on inherited status, was starting to break down. The legal privileges of the dominant *yangban* class had ended. The examination system that had been a principal vehicle for reaffirming status and gaining access to powerful government positions was abolished, as was slavery.

It would be wrong to see Koreans as the passive victims of external forces. Many ordinary farmers, as well as large landowners took advantage of the opportunities presented by the new markets for their produce. Some poor farmers found opportunities in the new mines that were opening, such as the American-owned gold mine at Unsan in the northwestern part of the country. Many sought positions in the new post offices, customs posts, telegraph offices, and the new government departments. They sent their children to the new schools, and a few took the opportunity to travel abroad. Mission schools provided a new means for social advancement for people of humble status. Members of sub-elite groups such as *chungin*, the heredity class of technical specialists, and rural clerks were able to enter higher bureaucratic positions that would have been previously closed to them. And a new small entrepreneurial class was emerging. Some of these entrepreneurs came from the small group of wholesale merchants that emerged in the eighteenth and nineteenth centuries, others came from varied backgrounds. Although most

of these changes were only just starting before 1910, the old social order
was coming to an end.

As educated Koreans sought to make sense of the changing world
around them, they were assisted by American missionaries, who played
an important role as agents of change and reform. Especially active were
the Presbyterians under the leadership of Horace N. Allen and Horace G.
Underwood, both arriving in the 1880s. The latter was able to draw on
the wealth from his typewriter business to build schools and hospitals.
A number of Korean intellectuals became Christian, including: Sŏ Chae-
p'il, Yun Ch'i-ho, Yu Kil-chun, the first Korean to travel around the world
and write an account of his travels, and a young Yi Sŭng-man (Syngman
Rhee). Korean Christians admired the United States for its strength and
for what they considered its enlightened political and social concepts.
However, America's usefulness as a model was limited by the racism they
also found there.[24]

A small class of intellectuals started publishing newspapers, forming
discussion groups, establishing educational associations, and opening
up new private schools with modern curricula. Koreans had always associated education with moral perfection, and under the civil exam system it served as a means for advancement. With the end of civil examinations, the elite were increasingly attracted to Western-style education.
Young men and some women were attending these new private schools
or those established by Western missionaries, and going to Japan and
the West for advanced schooling. Japan, because of its proximity, lower
costs, and cultural similarities was becoming a popular destination for
education among the small number of Koreans who could afford it. A
flood of new ideas about government, society, and science flowed into
the country as Koreans read Western works, often in Chinese or Japanese translations. Members of the educated elite formed educational
and patriotic organizations inspired by Western ideas. Women who
were attending some of the Western-style schools became involved in
these organizations. The very fact that many women were attending
the new schools was a sign of the radical changes in Korean society
that were starting to take place. Women's education was pioneered by
American missionaries such as Mary Scranton, who founded the first
Ewha Girls School in 1886; by 1910 many Koreans had accepted the importance of schooling for girls.

Changing too was the sense of identity that was emerging among
Koreans. As Andre Schmid has pointed out, in the years after 1895 the
new journals, newspapers, and various educational associations were
starting to create a community of educated Koreans who argued over
how to protect the nation, and after 1905 how to revive it.[25] It was a
community drawn from both the old *yangban* class and from common-

ers exposed to modern education and ideas, a community that began to think of themselves as belonging to what should be a sovereign state. The Independence Club had been an early manifestation of this new conceptualization. This feeling of being a nation, of being a people with a shared culture, history, and common destiny, when combined with the concept of national sovereignty, marked the beginning of modern Korean nationalism. Historians and political thinkers such as Pak Ŭn-sik (1859–1923) and Sin Ch'ae-ho (1880–1936) were reexamining Korea's place in the world and what it meant to be Korean. In 1908, the young Sin published an especially important essay "A New Reading of History" (*"Toksa Sillon"*), in which he borrowed the concept of "folk" (Korean: *minjok*) from Japanese and Chinese writers and placed it at the center of history. The history of Korea became a history of a Korean people with their unique cultural tradition. Other scholars were standardizing and promoting the Korean alphabet, *han'gŭl*, which was becoming a symbol of a modern, national identity.

Koreans, with their long history of borrowing abroad, began a new process of adopting and adapting foreign culture. By the time of the annexation of the country by Japan in 1910, Koreans had already begun laying the foundation for a new society with a new sense of national identity.

KOREA IN GLOBAL PERSPECTIVE: KOREA IN THE AGE OF IMPERIALISM

Many historians have challenged the older interpretations of history that see this period as one in which events are driven by the challenge of imperialism, and in which the actions of Koreans are judged in terms of how well they responded to that challenge. Instead they point to the importance of appreciating the internal changes that were taking place before 1876. Government slavery was abolished in 1801, and private slavery was declining. There were signs that the society was becoming more commercial as a result of changes in the tax system in which tribute was replaced with cash payments, and with the emergence of a new class of wholesale merchants. They point to the peasant rebellions in the nineteenth century and to the restlessness among people from more marginalized northern provinces, as well as to the emergence of the Tonghak religious movement and the growth of the small Christian community from the late eighteenth century as signs of social unrest and cultural change. Korea, as these historians have maintained, was not intellectually, economically, or socially stagnant in the nineteenth century, nor is there any clear evidence that it was in a state of decline. Nonetheless, it is not obvious that Korea was set for a major transformation or upheaval in the mid-nineteenth century; and it is clear that forces of imperialism altered the course of its history, as they did in most of the world.

How does Korea's experience with imperialism compare to other nations? In many ways it was a typical victim of the imperialist powers of the late nineteenth and the early twentieth centuries. Yet certain aspects were distinctive. As was the case with other states, such as Morocco, Korea was an object of competing imperial rivalries. Unlike most societies in the non-Western world, it was colonized by a neighboring nation, not a distant foreign power. Korea, itself, differed from most colonies. It possessed a greater coherence as a cultural and historical unit and a longer history of territorial stability than almost all other nineteenth-century states. It had clearly defined borders, and a distinctive ethnic culture and language not shared by any other peoples. It was a state that was an ethnic group, or an ethnic group that was a state. And it had many centuries of autonomy. China was theoretically its suzerain, but for all practical purposes Korea had been an independent state with little outside interference since the Manchu incursions of the first half of the seventeenth century. Few other states had such stability, such a long period of self-government, or such a homogeneous ethnicity and culture.

Furthermore, Korea had many attributes that gave it a foundation for making the transition to a modern state: a long tradition of rational bureaucratic government; a fairly high literacy rate, at least among men; a common shared set of values and customs that gave the country a sense of unity and purpose; and not least, a tradition of borrowing from abroad. In fact, considering the isolation of the country and the suddenness of its forced opening to outside intercourse, educated Koreans were quick to learn new customs. Western missionary schools after an initial slow decade became very popular from the 1890s; by the end of the nineteenth century, Koreans were establishing many private schools offering new Western-style curricula. Despite the many barriers, hundreds made it overseas to acquire learning. The enthusiasm with which Korean intellectuals became absorbed in new ideas, despite the enormous linguistic hurdles, is impressive, especially when contrasted with the much slower response of Chinese or Muslim intellectuals. Indeed, the speed with which Koreans began appreciating the strength of Western nations and the value of Western learning is more comparable with Japan.

Yet the country's modest level of commercial development, the social gap between the elite and commoners, the traditional disdain for the military, and the stubborn sense of Confucian righteousness among many of the governing class also hindered its ability to respond effectively to the imperialist threat. And the institutions of government proved woefully inadequate to the challenges that it faced. Nor was Korea a nation in the modern sense. As made clear in the work of contemporary scholars such as Gi-Wook Shin, one of the major challenges educated Koreans faced was deciding who they were, and where their society fit into the world.[26] Some, such as Kim Ok-kyun, identified Korea as being, along with China and Japan, one of the three Asian *hwa* (cultures or societies) that had to unite against Europe and America. He and others looked to Japan as the country that could lift up its neighbors to a level of civilization that could compete with the West. Some Koreans began to see race as a category and themselves as part of an Asian race. Many of these, too, looked to Japan for leadership. But by 1910, intellectuals such as Sin Ch'ae-ho and Pak ŭn-sik, influenced by Western writings on race and nation, began to see Korea as a unique land with its own history and tradition, as a member of an international community of nations with its own "folk," its own traditions, and its own history. They were establishing the basis for a new Korean nationalism that no longer saw itself as firmly rooted in a Chinese-centered Confucian civilization but as a distinctive nation.

Thus, if Korea was unusual in its cultural homogeneity, its long history as a self-governing state, and the stability of its political institutions, it was typical in the process by which it struggled to create a sense of how it fitted in the new Western-dominated world of nation-states.

Inaugural Message of the *Independent*, April 7, 1896

As we publish the first issue of *The Independent* today, we shall declare to everyone in Korea, foreigners and natives alike, what we believe.

We are impartial and nonpartisan and recognize no distinction between upper and lower classes; everyone shall be treated equally as a Korean. We shall speak only to benefit Korea, and we shall be fair. We shall speak not only for the people in Seoul but for everyone throughout the country on every subject.

We shall communicate to the people what the government does and convey the conditions of the people to the government, thereby benefitting both sides who need not feel uncomfortable or suspicious.

Since we are not publishing the paper for the sake of profit, the price of a copy is low. We write in the vernacular (*han'gŭl*) to enable men and women of all social classes to read; we also insert space between the words to make reading easier.

We shall be truthful, we shall report on those government officials who may misconduct themselves; we shall let the whole nation know about any corrupt and self-enriching officials; we shall investigate and publicize any private persons who may violate the law.

We are for His Majesty, the government of Korea, and the Korean people; there shall not be any partisan discourse nor words to benefit only one side printed in our paper.

We have a page written in English because foreigners are not well informed on the Korean situation and, therefore, are liable to be misguided in their thoughts by relying solely on biased words. In order to give them correct information we shall prepare a section in English.

It will become evident, then, that this newspaper exists only for the interests of Korea. Foreigners and Koreans, men and women, people of diverse social classes and stations, all will become informed about Korea. We will also report from time to time on the situations in foreign lands so that those Koreans who cannot travel to foreign countries may learn about them.

As today is our first day of publication, we have outlined where we stand. We believe that by reading our paper the opinions and wisdom of the Korean people will be improved.[27]

Chang Chiyŏn, "We Wail Today"

Author Note: The Korean-Japanese Protectorate Treaty was signed on the night of 17 November 1905 and was announced on 18 November. This well-known editorial was printed in the 20 November issue of *Hwangsŏng sinmun.* (Imperial Capital News), a newspaper that first appeared in September 1898.

When Marquis Itō came to Korea the other day, the innocent people of Korea said to one another that, since he had hitherto devoted himself to bringing about stability and peace among the three nations of the East, his visit this time would surely be for the purpose of recommending measures for strengthening our nation's independence. Therefore, officials and civilians alike gave him a big welcome all the way from the port to Seoul. There are, however, many unpredictable things in this world. How could these five totally unexpected articles of the treaty be proposed? Since the proposed provisions will not only affect Korea but also cause division among the three nations, one wonders about Marquis Ito's ultimate intention.

Due to the strong objection of His Majesty the emperor, we may surmise that Marquis Ito could have known of the eventual defeat of the treaty and have withdrawn it. Nevertheless, the so-called ministers of our government, who are not even worthy of being compared to dogs and swine, sought their own rewards and gains, got frightened by momentary threats, and, to our consternation, became traitorous criminals. They handed over to foreigners a nation with a four-thousand-year history and a dynasty that has lasted five hundred years, thereby reducing twenty million souls to being the slaves of foreigners. Foreign Minister Pak Chesun and other ministers are beneath the level of dogs and swine and do not even deserve the honor of serious censure.

The man whose official title is supposed to be prime minister is the head of the government, yet he only cast a negative vote as if that alone were enough to discharge his official responsibility and save his honor. Unlike Kim Sanghŏn who tore up the document and wailed or Chŏng On who disemboweled himself in protest, the prime minister is still alive and moves about. How dare he face His Majesty and his twenty million fellow countrymen?

Alas! How deplorable! Fellow countrymen, now slaves to foreigners, are you dead or alive? Should we let the national spirit that has been preserved for four thousand years since the days of Tangun and Kija (Chi Tzu) disintegrate overnight? How deplorable! How deplorable! Fellow countrymen! Fellow countrymen!

—from the newspaper *Hwangsŏng sinmun* (*Imperial Capital News*), November 20, 1905[28]

10

❖

Colonial Korea, 1910 to 1945

Korea's modern history was profoundly influenced by its thirty-five years (1910 to 1945) as a colony of Japan. The Japanese colonial regime established the basis of many of the economic, educational, and governmental institutions of Korea, while its authoritarian rule, its mass mobilization campaigns, and its attempt at forced assimilation touched the lives of almost every Korean, often in disturbing and even traumatizing ways. As Koreans responded to the demands, opportunities, and challenges presented by the colonial regime, they developed the ideological divisions that would be so important in determining the course of their history after 1945.

Japanese colonial rule was top-down centralized, direct, and intensive. The centralized nature of colonial government, Government-General of Korea (Chōsen Sōtokufu), as it was called, can be seen in the power concentrated in the hands of the governor-general (Sōtoku). Appointed by the Japanese emperor and directly responsible to the prime minister, he possessed an enormously broad authority, including the right to issue laws, ordinances, and regulations and to appoint various officials. All governors-general were military men, generals or admirals, and possessed the power to mobilize and command the troops stationed in the country. Assisted by a centralized police apparatus, they ruled with powers Adrian Buzo has likened to "a general in a theater of war."[1] A symbol of his authority was the Government-General building in front of the throne-hall of the Kyŏngbok Palace, the major royal residence. Under the governor-general there was a director-general of administration (Seimu Sōkan), the second-most important position, who was appointed by the Japanese prime minister. The colonial regime maintained Korea's administrative division of thirteen provinces, which were subdivided into over 200 counties and municipalities. Counties, in turn, were subdivided into districts, villages, and hamlets. The governor-general appointed all the provincial governors and county superintendents. These officials appointed the district and village heads. Thus, although Korea under the Chosŏn dynasty had been a centralized state with a government that appointed officials down to the county level, the colonial regime penetrated even further to the township and village level. Commanding the military forces in the peninsula, controlling a highly centralized police system, appointing all important local officials, and possessing broad legislative power as well as executive power, the governor-general was a new authoritarian figure in Korean political history. Not even the kings had had so much power concentrated in their hands.

Not only was it highly centralized, but colonial rule also became increasingly intrusive as it grew to become a vast apparatus. To administer the country, the Government-General in 1910 had about 10,000 officials. This number was to grow until it reached 87,552 in 1937, comprising 52,270 Japanese and 35,282 Koreans. If all members of the military, state, and semigovernment banks and companies are included, the figure is closer to 246,000 Japanese and 63,000 Koreans. By 1940, there were 708,418 Japanese residents of Korea, amounting to 3.2 percent of the population. About 40 percent directly and indirectly worked for the government. To impose its authority, the Japanese employed 6,222 military and civilian police in 1910, half Korean. This grew to 20,771 in 1922 and 60,000 by 1941.[2] The police had the power to judge and sentence those arrested for minor offenses. But their role went beyond that to include: tax collecting, supervising irrigation and water controlling, overseeing road construction and maintenance, enforcing health regulations, and acting as public information officers. It was a comprehensive system that grew to over 2,500 substations and one officer for every 800 households.[3]

The first decade of colonial rule was particularly harsh, what Koreans have called the "dark period" (*amhŭkki*). It was characterized by harsh political repression that stifled cultural as well as political life. The press was under tight control, police permits were required for any public gathering, and all organizations and meetings deemed political in nature were prohibited. To emphasize their authority, Japanese officials, even schoolteachers, wore swords, although Koreans were not allowed to own any type of weapon.

This harsh administration took place in an atmosphere of troubled and tense relations between Koreans and their Japanese rulers. The most publicized incident took place in December 1910 when the Japanese announced the discovery of a plot to assassinate the new governor-general, Terauchi Masatake, led by An Myŏng-gŭn, brother of An Chung-gŭn, who assassinated Itō Hirobumi. Some 700 Koreans were detained, 123 arraigned, and in 1911, 105 were convicted. Three others died during interrogations. Most of the arrested were Christians, including the prominent Protestant leaders Yun Ch'i-ho (1864-1945) and Yi Sŭng-hun. The trial, which became referred to as the "Case of 105 Persons," generated considerable international publicity, not least because it seemed to focus on Christians. Furthermore, many of the defendants gave highly improbable confessions that implicated the members of the foreign mission community.[4] Few of these confessions seemed plausible, and the heavy-handedness of the Japanese proved an embarrassment. Many were retried, given lighter sentences, and eventually released. The trial was a clear warning to Koreans that the colonial government would not tolerate any anti-Japanese activity. There were many other similar sweeps and waves of arrest by the colonial administration. Tens of thousands of Koreans were arrested from 1910 to 1919 for political reasons.

Under these repressive conditions, resistance to Japanese rule took place mainly among the exile community. During most of the long Yi dynasty period (1392–1910) very few ethnic Koreans lived outside Korea. This began to change in the late nineteenth century. From the 1860s, small numbers of Koreans began to cross the Yalu and Tumen Rivers into Manchuria and Siberia. Originally this migration was motivated by economic distress near the border regions, beginning with a drought in the 1860s. Most of the Koreans in Manchuria settled in Kando (Jiandao in Chinese), a sparsely populated area adjacent to the border. Kando had a population of 65,000 in 1894 and 109,000 in 1910. Koreans left mainly fleeing poverty, but after 1905 the desire to flee Japanese rule added to the migration. A wave of 60,000 poured into the area during the first two years of colonial rule. Their descendants formed the Yanbian Korean Autonomous Region in China today. Tens of thousands of Koreans also migrated to the Russian Maritime Province for both economic and political reasons. Another 7,000 Koreans migrated to Hawaii from 1902 to 1910 to work on the sugar and pineapple plantations until U.S. authorities restricted the migration. Small Korean communities emerged in Shanghai after 1910, mostly political exiles. In Japan there was a growing student population numbering several thousand in the 1910s. A small handful of Koreans lived in the United States and Europe, mainly as students. These Korean communities became the homes of a number of small nationalist groups, some of which later played an important role in Korean politics.

THE MARCH FIRST MOVEMENT

Although there were small nationalist exile groups and dissidents within Korea from the time of the protectorate, a truly nationwide Korean resistance movement to Japanese occupation first took place in March 1919. The end of World War I and the Versailles Peace Conference inspired hopes for colonial peoples throughout the world. In part, this was sparked by the peace settlement, and in particular by President Wilson of the United States, who in his Fourteen Points called for the principle of "national self-determination." While this was meant only to apply to European people, the Korean diaspora, like so many non-Western colonial subjects, was greatly excited by these events. An exile group led by Kim Kyu-sik (1881–1950) went to Paris to argue for Korean independence. An attempt by the small Korean community in Hawaii, through its Korean National Association (Taehan Kungminhoe), tried to dispatch a delegation led by Syngman Rhee for the same purpose, but it failed when they were denied passports. The most significant of the developments outside Korea was among Korean students in Japan. They organized a Korean Youth Independence Corps (Chosŏn Ch'ŏngnyŏn Tongniptan). In Tokyo over 600 Korean students attended a meeting on February 8, 1919, where they passed a declaration written by intellectual and writer Yi Kwang-su (1892–1950) calling for immediate independence. The group then sent members to Korea in order to agitate for independence there. In Korea, several different groups were discussing independence in early 1919: a group of Ch'ŏndogyo members including Son Pyŏng-hŭi, a group of Presbyterians based in P'yŏngyang led by Yi Sŭng-hun, Methodists in Seoul, and a group affiliated with Chungang High School that included Kim Sŏng-su (1891–1955) and Song Chin-u (1890–1945), both to later play a prominent role in Korean political life. The arrival of Korean students from Tokyo with news of their calls for independence and about activities of exile groups stimulated them into action. But the catalyst for major action came with Kojong's death on January 21, 1919. Rumors that the Japanese had poisoned him or that they had forced him to commit suicide added to unrest. Taking advantage of the large crowds that were expected to arrive in Seoul for the scheduled funeral on March 3, representatives of the various groups decided to issue a declaration of independence in Pagoda Park in Seoul on March 1. Thirty-three signed it: sixteen Christians, fifteen Ch'ŏndogyo members, and two Buddhists. A petition was to be sent to the Japanese and U.S. governments and to the Paris peace conference. The signers were careful to emphasize the nonviolent nature of their protest. They do not appear to have intended to create a mass uprising. The reading of the declaration was moved to a restaurant on February 28 for security reasons. Nonetheless, crowds met to hear the declaration on the afternoon of March 1. There, a person who happened to have a copy read it to an enthusiastic crowd that began marching down the main street in downtown Seoul. In the following days, demonstrations took place throughout the country.[5]

What is most interesting about the demonstrations that took place beginning March 1, 1919, was the large number of participants and how widespread they were. It has been estimated that 500,000 to 1 million people participated in the demonstrations that continued throughout the spring. There were 667 reported peaceful demonstrations along with hundreds of violent incidents that took place in every province and city.[6] A small radical group known as the National Congress (Kungmin Taehoe) called for more violent action, but for the most part leaders attempted to keep what became known as the March First Movement peaceful. The Japanese authorities reacted by attempting to suppress the demonstrations, often quite violently. All assemblies and street demonstrations were banned, and reprisals were taken against groups that participated. One sixteen-year-old girl, Yu Kwan-sun, who was arrested and tortured and who died in prison, became an icon of the independence movement. Much of the suppression was directed at the Christians, who, along with members of the Ch'ŏndogyo, were heavily represented in the movement; over 400 churches were destroyed. In one notorious incident a church was burned with its congregation perishing inside. Officially 553 were killed, 1,409 injured, and over 14,000 arrested during the months that followed. Korean nationalists claimed the figures were much higher, up to 7,000 deaths and tens of thousands arrested.[7]

The March First Movement was a major turning point in Korean history. It has been regarded by some historians as the birth of modern Korean nationalism. Others have seen it as not the beginning of Korean nationalism but its transformation from a small movement of isolated and scattered intellectuals and of tiny exile groups abroad to a mass movement that cut across class lines. An impressive number of women, peasants, and non-elite urban and small-town residents participated in it. A vision of Korea as a nation appeared to have emerged among many Koreans at this time. Koreans were seeing their land as one of an international community of nations, a nation that had lost its independence. The movement encouraged exiles abroad to combine efforts to achieve national independence, an effort that was centered in Shanghai. Domestically, the demonstrations were suppressed without achieving independence, but they embarrassed the Japanese government and led it to change its policy toward Korea.

THE POST–MARCH FIRST PERIOD

The March First Movement was an embarrassment to the Japanese government and resulted in a call by some political leaders for a reform of its harsh military rule in Korea. It also coincided with a more liberal atmosphere in Japan. The Japanese government had been partly modeled on the Prussian/German one. With the victory of the more democratic Allied powers in World War I—the United States, Britain, and France— there was a call for liberal democratic government at home. Thus Japan entered what is called "Taisho Democracy," a period ending after 1930. Japanese policy reflected this liberal trend. Japan's liberalism in the 1920s, however, was modest. Even more modest was its liberalism in Korea. Nonetheless, the government of Prime Minister Hara Takashi issued the Revised Organic Regulations of the Government-General of Korea in August 1919, which marked a change in policy under the new slogan "Harmony between Japan and Korea" (*Nissen yūwa*). He appointed as governor-general Admiral Saitō Makoto from the more liberal navy, with a mandate to make major administrative changes.

Saitō quickly received a reminder of the discontent in Korea—a bomb went off in Seoul Station the day of his arrival. To carry out his reform, he appointed Mizuno Rentarō, former home minister (1916–1918) to assume the duties of director-general of political affairs, the number two position, and a talented young Maruyama Tsurukichi as the head of his police. A number of changes were made. The gendarmerie was abolished, replaced by a regular police force. Many of these reforms were symbolic. Japanese teachers and civil officials no longer wore military uniforms and carried swords. Minor offenses were no longer punished by whippings. Laws regulating burials, slaughtering of animals, and peasant markets that interfered with traditional customs and were greatly resented were abolished or modified. Korean government workers were to receive the same wages as Japanese, although they still did not receive the bonuses that their Japanese counterparts did. Saitō created an advisory council with provincial Korean representation. Koreans were appointed to serve on city, county, and provincial councils. Business and trade was also liberalized. The Japanese government eliminated the tariff barriers between Japan and Korea, the Korean market was now open to Japanese trade and investment. In 1921, the Japanese invited key Korean businessmen to participate in the Chōsen (Korea) Industrial Commission.

In the spring of 1920, the Korean crown prince married Japan's Princess Nashimoto. This symbolic merger of the two royal houses was accompanied by an amnesty of several thousand political prisoners and the inauguration of what the government called its "culture policy" (Japanese: *bunka seiji*). There was a new, more tolerant attitude toward Korean cultural activities. The ban on Korean newspapers was lifted, and in that year prominent Koreans established the *Chosŏn Ilbo* and *Tonga Ilbo*, still South Korea's two leading papers. With restrictions on publishing reduced, hundreds of popular magazines and specialized publications appeared. Beginning in 1920, the lifting of harsh restrictions on organized activity resulted in an explosive growth in the youth, religious, social, educational, intellectual, labor, and farmer organizations. Many were small and local; some were large and countrywide.

This freer atmosphere was accompanied by efforts of the colonial regime to maintain tight control. The colonial administration expanded the police force and opened hundreds of new police stations throughout the country. To provide better intelligence and surveillance capabilities Maruyama created the High Police (Kōtō Keisatsu). The police presence was conspicuous in Korea with policemen stationed throughout the country, half being Japanese. These policemen assumed many roles, from enforcing detailed regulations to collecting taxes and supervising the collection and transport of rice, becoming a ubiquitous presence in the lives of ordinary Koreans. The new administration may have reflected some more liberal thinking in the Japanese government, but it also represented a more sophisticated attitude toward control. The Government-General in the 1920s co-opted Korean nationalists by providing intellectuals and others an avenue to legally express themselves, showing a greater sensitivity to Korean culture, and removing the most hated symbols of Japanese authority, while increasing the size and efficiency of the colonial administrative and police organs. Allowing Korean activists to move about more openly also made it easier to observe them.

There were limits to the freedom allowed. Koreans were not allowed to openly advocate independence; their criticisms of the administration had to be very circumspect. Failure to adhere to this resulted in the banning of organizations, the closing of publications, and arrests. A rigorous censorship was still carried out, and publications were frequently shut down. Freedom of expression began to tighten with the passage of the Peace Preservation Law in Japan in 1925, which gave police much greater latitude in imposing restrictions on any speech or activity deemed subversive. Still, compared to the years before and after, the early 1920s was a fairly liberal period.

CULTURAL FERMENT OF THE 1920S

The 1920s was an especially important time in Korean cultural history. Not only did the years immediately after World War I and the March First Movement see a burst of creative energy among artists and intellectuals who laid the foundations for modern literary and artistic expressions, but the main split among nationalists on how they envisioned a modern Korean nation took shape. Indeed, it could be argued that the intellectual foundations of the two Koreas were established at this time. External events stimulated the movement: the excitement over the Versailles Peace Treaty, the Bolshevik Revolution, and the growth of anticolonial movements around the world. The more liberal policies of the Japanese colonial administration facilitated the intellectual ferment. Furthermore, the young people who grew up after the traditional political and social order had fallen, and who were educated in modern-style schools, were coming of age.

There was an explosive burst of creative energy, as artists and intellectuals explored new ideas and new literary and artistic forms. New literature flowered in the journals *Creation* (*Ch'angjo*, 1919), *Ruins* (*P'yehŏ*, 1920) and *White Tide* (*Paekcho*, 1922). The novelists Kim Tong-in (1900–1951) and Yŏm Sang-sŏp (1897–1963), and the Buddhist poet Han Yong-un (1879–1944) pioneered modern Korean literature. Leftists wrote proletarian literature. Modern theater, which had begun with the Wŏn'gaksa Theater in Seoul in 1908, flourished. A new avenue of artistic expression, the cinema, began in the 1920s. One of the early works was the film *Arirang*, directed and acted by Na Un-gyu in 1926. The colonial authorities banned it for its nationalist theme. A number of silent films were produced from 1926 to 1935, sometimes called the golden age of Korean cinema; unfortunately few of these films have survived.

MODERATE AND RADICAL NATIONALISM

This period of cultural ferment in the early 1920s saw a division among Korean nationalists that would profoundly shape Korean history: between the moderate, Western-looking cultural nationalists, and the more radical nationalists who tended to look toward the Soviet Union and Communist movements abroad for inspiration. Modern Korean nationalism, which can be traced to the 1890s, came to maturity at this time. Nationalists held a strong sense of loyalty to a Korean nation that was defined by its distinctive culture, its language, history, and heritage. They regarded the loss of sovereignty to Japan as a great tragedy and sought eventual independence. By the 1920s, many Korean intellectuals looked to the West as a model for civilized behavior, much as the Korean intellectuals in the past had looked to China. Ironically, many of these were educated in Japan, where they read Western works in Japanese translation, although in some cases they studied Western languages, usually English or German. They were highly critical of Korea's cultural backwardness, which they saw as responsible for the fall of their country to the Japanese. Other nationalists turned to anarchism, socialism, and after 1917 to Communism.

Many advocated a moderate agenda, working within the limitations of the colonial framework. The focus of these moderate nationalists, whom historian Michael Robinson calls "cultural nationalists," was on culture, not politics. This was partly based on pragmatism, since any call for independence would result in arrest and harsh repression, and therefore be ineffective. But it was also based on a sincere conviction that Korea must develop spiritually and culturally before it could be ready for independence. It was their duty to work on uplifting society first. Cultural nationalists advocated a gradual approach to development, seeing education as a key. They propagated their ideas through the newspapers, a host of new magazines, and through various youth, women's, educational, and cultural associations. Especially important vehicles for expressing their ideas were the two major newspapers and the new intellectual magazines that emerged in the early 1920s.

Among the leaders of these moderate nationalists was Kim Sŏng-su. Kim came from a wealthy *yangban* family in North Chŏlla. Educated in Japan, Kim combined a bright intellect with a keen business sense. He took advantage of the Japanese demand for Korean rice to consolidate and expand his holdings over some of Korea's richest rice paddies. Then he invested much of this into new industrial enterprises, eventually becoming one of Korea's richest businessmen. A strong promoter of Korean education, he founded the Posŏng foundation, which supported Korean-owned schools, one of which was to become Koryŏ (Korea) University. He also established the *Tonga Ilbo* newspaper. Closely associated with Kim Sŏng-su was Song Chin-u, a prominent moderate leader and the president of *Tonga Ilbo*.

Another key figure in the moderate nationalist movement was Yi Kwang-su. Born in P'yŏngan in 1892, Yi was educated at a village school. After his parents died he lived with relatives associated with the Tonghaks. Through various connections, he received a scholarship from the Ilchinhoe to study at Japanese secondary school in 1905. Later he traveled to Shanghai and the Russian Far East. Then with financial support from Kim Sŏng-su he went back to Japan to study at Waseda University, where he earned a degree in philosophy. Yi was the principal author of the Tokyo Korean Student Declaration in February 1919. He then joined other political exiles in Shanghai but returned to Korea under the more liberal conditions in 1921. Already well established as a novelist as well as political activist, Yi, not yet thirty years old, was probably Korea's leading writer and thinker. In May 1922, he wrote a long essay in *Kyebyŏk* "Minjok Kaejoron" ("Treatise on the Reconstruction of the Nation") that articulated the agenda for moderate nationalists. It advocated working within the colonial system, not violently opposing it; and it argued for the need for national development prior to political independence.[8]

Many of these moderate nationalists were Christians. Some were from the *yangban* class, but many were of more humble background. Whatever their background, and however critical they were of Korea's cultural heritage, they tended to assume much the same role as the old premodern intellectual elite had in being the guardians of knowledge, whose role was to lead the masses. As with the old Confucian elite they often despised, they placed the highest value on moral and spiritual development through education. They criticized what was called *sadaejuŭi*, or the blind cultural subservience to China, as a source, if not the main source, of Korea's backwardness, and they looked for a distinctive Korean cultural tradition. Yet they advocated for the adoption of many aspects of Western culture, with a similar admiration for foreign models.

Many Korean intellectuals, however, began to look at their own cultural heritage with pride. Some were angered by the work of state-sponsored Japanese scholars that found Korean history characterized by stagnation in contrast to the progressive societies of Japan and the West. To counter this idea, scholars such as Ch'oe Nam-sŏn (1890–1957) sought to create national histories that pointed to the unique and dynamic nature of their nation's past. In 1934, a group of scholars established the Chindan Hakhoe (Chindan Society) to publish historical scholarship from this nationalist point of view. Another significant project by nationalists was the effort to promote and standardize the Korean written language. Since the 1890s the Korean alphabet, *han'gŭl*, had become a symbol of Korean cultural distinctiveness and was promoted by many. The pioneer in the work of standardizing the rules of grammar and spelling was Chu Si-gyŏng (1876–1914), who believed language was a fundamental form of the expression of national identity. Chu died young, but his disciples, taking advantage of the more liberal atmosphere after 1920, created the Korean Language Research Society (Chosŏnŏ Yŏn'guhoe) in 1921. Their work was made easier by the fact that Korea was a homogeneous country where everyone spoke the same language and by the fact that the regional dialects were not so marked that they posed a problem in creating uniform rules of orthography. This was in contrast to the problems encountered by the similar *baihua* movement that was going on in China. The society led mass literacy campaigns in the late 1920s and produced a *Unified Orthography* (*Matchumbŏp t'ongil an*) in 1933. In the 1930s, the society's main task was the compilation of *The Big Dictionary* (*K'ŭn sajŏn*). The principal editor of this work was arrested by the Japanese during World War II for the crime of compiling a dictionary, and he died in prison, but the society continued on and completed the dictionary after 1945. There emerged, then, among many moderate nationalists, an ambiguity toward their cultural traditions, which they viewed with both shame and pride.

One of the major attempts by moderate nationalists to rally the people in a national cause, while still working within the framework of legality, was the Korean Production Movement. It was begun in the summer of 1920 in P'yŏngyang by Cho Man-sik (1882–1950). Cho was a Presbyterian elder who studied at Waseda University in Japan, where he read about and became an admirer of Gandhi's nonviolent, noncooperation nationalist movement in British India. His own deep religious and ethical convictions, belief in nonviolence, simple lifestyle, and modest personal demeanor earned him the sobriquet "the Gandhi of Korea." Influenced by Gandhi's effort to raise national consciousness and self-sufficiency by encouraging the use of homespun cloth, Cho established the Society for the Promotion of Korean Production to encourage Koreans to buy locally made products and boycott imported Japanese goods. The idea was not entirely new; during the protectorate period some Koreans launched a National Debt Movement, a similar campaign of economic self-sufficiency. Cho's movement became national when the Society for the Promotion of Korean Production was created in January 1923. An impressive array of leaders joined the campaign, from the writer and intellectual Yi Kwang-su to the businessman Kim Sŏng-su. Christian, Buddhist, and Ch'ŏndogyo leaders; youth; and women's groups all actively participated. It had a permanent headquarters with branches in every province and published a monthly journal *Industrial World* (*Sanŏpkye*). There was an auxiliary women's association, T'osan Aeyong Puinhoe, to assist. The main aim was to encourage people to shop at Korean-owned stores and buy Korean-made products, even if more expensive and of lesser quality. Consumer cooperatives were established as alternatives to the Japanese-dominated commercial markets. The Government-General banned major rallies, especially in Seoul, and censored announcements and pamphlets for nationalist references but otherwise tolerated the movement. The Korean Production Movement rallied people throughout the country and was greeted by great enthusiasm that had not been seen since the March First Movement. From 1923 to 1924 it appeared to be somewhat effective, but then the movement ran into problems. Korean manufacturers could not meet demands for many products, while Japanese merchants were able to weather the campaign and offer lower prices. Furthermore, the colonial authorities began offering subsidies to Korean businessmen, something they had been requesting since 1920, thus weakening their support. Korean merchants also worried about competition from the consumer cooperatives the movement organized. After the initial wave of excitement, public enthusiasm waned and the movement declined. It did not disappear, but was periodically revived. With the more repressive political atmosphere after 1931, its political activities were limited. Still, it survived until 1937, when the organization and its journal were ordered closed.[9] More radical nationalists dismissed the whole movement as led by capitalist collaborators; in any case, its effectiveness was limited.

Moderate nationalists established the Society for the Establishment of a National University (Minnip Taehak Kisŏng Chunbihoe). Koreans had

always valued education, but the lack of higher educational opportunities in their own country was very frustrating, especially to members of
the elite who were forced to seek it in Japan or elsewhere. A movement
in the early 1900s to create a university had not proceeded far. This time
the movement was very popular, resulting in a nationwide fund-raising
campaign. It was led by Yi Sang-jae and Song Chin-u, editor-in-chief of
Tonga Ilbo. The Society established offices for the fund-raising campaign
in provincial cities and sent representatives to Manchuria and the United
States. Despite the widespread enthusiasm, the movement was plagued
with mismanagement, infighting among chapters, and the withdrawal
of radical nationalists, including the All Korean Youth League, from the
movement, part of the growing split between moderates and leftists. The
troubled campaign suffered perhaps a fatal blow when the Japanese government announced it would establish a Keijō (Seoul) Imperial University
by 1926.

In contrast to the moderate nationalists and their program of gradualist reform, a number of Koreans took a more radical view of nationalism.
They saw their role less as cultural reformers bringing the masses up
to modern standards of civilization than as part of the vanguard of the
"people." Under the influence of socialism, especially in its Marxist form,
they looked to the common people as embodying the essence of the nation and their own role as leaders of the people. They rejected cooperation
with the colonial regime, were suspicious of both the old landowning and
the newly emerging Korean entrepreneurial classes, and saw the overthrow of both the colonial regime and the elite as their aim. Most of these
radicals in the 1920s became associated with the fledgling Communist
movement.

The Korean Communist movement reflected the fractured, geographically dispersed, complex nature of Korean nationalism during the colonial period. The first Communist groups appeared among the exile
communities in Siberia that had a large Korean community that became
caught up by the Bolshevik Revolution of 1917. The Bolsheviks, seeking support in the region, offered aid to Korean exiles in regaining their
independence. In 1918 the first Communist organization was formed in
Khabarovsk, the Hanin Sahoe-dang (Korean Peoples Socialist Party), by
Yi Tong-hwi (1873–1945). Yi did not have a likely background for a Communist. A major in the royal army of Korea, he resigned in protest in 1905
at the Japanese takeover of Korea and was arrested in 1910 for an alleged
involvement in an assassination plot against the Japanese governor-
general; after being released he joined the exile community in the Kando
region of Manchuria.[10] Shortly afterward, he went to Shanghai to participate in the Korean Provisional Government, becoming its prime minister.
About the same time, other more assimilated Koreans in Russia, led by

Nam Man-ch'un, formed a Korean section of the Bolshevik Party in the Siberian city of Irkutsk, where they established a military academy. The two Communist groups became rivals. The Irkutsk Communists were critical of Yi Tong-hwi with his *Ŭibyŏng* (Righteous Army) and Christian past, regarding him as not a true Communist but simply a nationalist who was taking advantage of Soviet assistance. Their attempt to assert control over Yi's group led to an armed clash at Alekseyevsk in Siberia in June 1921 in what was called the "Free City Incident," killing and capturing hundreds of them. The Irkutsk faction became part of the Bolsheviks, with their own Korean regiments in the Red Army. In the 1930s, Stalin, becoming distrustful of the loyalty of the Koreans, disbanded these regiments, and purged Korean army cadres. The Korean community in the Soviet Union no longer played an active role in the nationalist movement, but they would be important in the creation of the North Korean state after 1945.

The domestic Marxist movement was born among students in Japan. In contrast to the moderate nationalist movements, the Communist movement in Korea never attracted prominent cultural figures but mainly consisted of young, educated, but not well-known activists. In 1922, one group of young people, the Friends Society of Tokyo, issued the first known public call for class struggle in Korea. About a month later, the Proletariat League (Musanja Tongmaeng-hoe) was created in Seoul to champion the rights of the working class. A public lecture in Seoul in December of that year drew 1,500 to hear speeches denouncing capitalism.[11] In 1923 some members of the Proletariat League formed the New Thought Study Society (Sin Sasang Yŏng'gu-hoe), with ostensibly all new ideas. On the birthday of Karl Marx, November 19, 1924, it was renamed the Tuesday Society; and on April 17, 1925, the Tuesday Society merged with another group, the North Wind Society, to form the Korean Communist Party (Chosŏn Kongsandang). Most of the group were arrested by the Japanese later that year. A second KCP was organized in 1926, but soon its leaders were arrested as well. A third party was organized in December 1926, but most of these were arrested in January 1928. A fourth attempt that February led to another wave of arrests in August 1928.[12] In December 1928, the Comintern leaders issued the December Theses analyzing the causes of the failures of the Korean Communists. They complained that they consisted of only intellectuals and students, that they were weakened by their factionalism, that they failed to attract industrial workers and poor peasants, and that they needed to develop a clearer understanding of Marxist-Leninist principles.

Meanwhile, secondary students became involved in nationalist protests. A number of student incidents, such as school strikes, occurred in the 1920s. From 1920 to 1926 some 386 recorded school strikes occurred. Many of these, in fact a majority, had anti-Japanese overtones, often

directed at teachers thought to be pro-Japanese. An example took place in
May 1927, when some 400 pupils at Sukmyŏng Girls School, a secondary
school, went on strike, demanding the dismissal of Japanese administrators. They were joined by the students at Chinmyŏng Girls School. Leftist organizations sometimes infiltrated the student bodies at secondary
schools. This happened at the three secondary schools in the provincial
city of Kwangju. These schools had histories of student protests. In the fall
of 1929, the students at all three went on strike over the alleged mistreatment of female Korean students by Japanese male students. This spread
throughout Korea as secondary students in protest boycotted classes
and sometimes attacked Japanese students. By the spring of 1930, 54,000
Korean students in 194 schools had joined what had become an anti-
Japanese movement. Students demanded the end of police interference in
school activities, the release of arrested students, the reinstatement of expelled students, and the reform of the educational system. Student pamphlets with slogans such as "Down with Imperialism" and "Long Live the
Proletarian Revolution" indicate the leftist influence in the movement.[13]
The movement was crushed by authorities, with many students arrested
or expelled. Sporadic student strikes and protests occurred after that date,
but these became increasingly difficult with the imposition of a harsher
colonial policy after 1931. However, the colonial period left a tradition of
student activism that would be taken up again in South Korea after 1945.

Despite the split between the moderates and radicals in the nationalist
movement, the two groups united in 1927 to form the Sin'ganhoe (New
Shoots Korea Society). The leadership consisted of moderate nationalists,
but it was supported by Communists and other leftist groups who gained
control over many of its branches. The Sin'ganhoe was a broad-based
organization consisting of youth, labor, farmer, intellectual, and women's
groups. By 1928, according to nationalist sources, Sin'ganhoe had 143
branches and more than 20,000 members. Korean Communists, having
difficulty operating due to constant Japanese repression, found the organization a way to become involved in nationalist activities. Ironically the
Japanese found it useful as well, as a means of bringing leftist activities
into the open, and therefore they tolerated it. The organization struggled
with disputes over whether to support the Kwangju Student Movement
in 1929 but survived to 1931. In that year, following Comintern directives,
it was dissolved after moderates unsuccessfully fought to save it.[14]

A shift to a more repressive policy by the colonial regime in 1931 meant
that open nationalist activities became largely confined to the exile communities. The scattered Korean diaspora was involved in the nationalist
movements. Their numbers were small and their activities were largely
ineffective, but they influenced the developments in Korea after 1945.
Some in Japan joined nationalist groups. There was also an anarchist orga-

nization, the Black Comrades Society, whose leader, Pak Yŏl, attempted to assassinate Crown Prince Hirohito on his wedding day. Police uncovered the plot, and Pak and many members of his group were arrested. Tight police surveillance made such activities increasingly difficult. A special "student section" of the Ministry of Education kept watch on Korean students in Japan. More important were fragmented nationalist groups and individuals located in China, Manchuria, Russia, and the United States. Many of these were Communists, some anarchists, and others, such as Syngman Rhee in Hawaii, were staunchly anticommunist and pro-Western. Communists were the more numerous of the active nationalists outside Korea. As was the case with other exile groups, they were never united under a single leader or organization. Some Korean Communists fought with the Chinese Communist Party. Among them were Kim Chŏng, better known by his revolutionary name, Mu Chŏng, who made the 1934–1935 Long March with Mao Zedong and the other Chinese Communist to their new base at Yanan. When war broke out between China and Japan in 1937 some Koreans joined the anti-Japanese struggle. Some fought with the Guomindang and others with the Chinese Communists. Mu Chŏng formed a Korean military unit with several hundred Koreans that was engaged in battle with the Japanese from 1939. As they found out about this military unit, many Koreans in China joined it. In 1942 it became known as the Korean Voluntary Army. Other Koreans fought with the Chinese Communist–led anti-Japanese guerilla units that sprang up in Manchuria after its annexation by the Japanese in 1931. Most of these Koreans were drawn from the Korean communities of southern Manchuria just north of the Korean border. One of these guerilla fighters, who achieved some fame, was the young Kim Il Sung (Kim Il-sŏng, born Kim Sŏng-ju) (1912–1994). Kim Il Sung and the other guerilla leaders fought in small units of 50 to 100, rarely more than 300. Kim's claim to fame was a successful raid into northern Korea and brief occupation of the Korean town of Poch'ŏnbo in June 1937. Japan began a determined effort to clear the Manchurian border areas of guerillas in the late 1930s, and succeeded in driving Kim and the other guerillas out of Manchuria into the Soviet Union by 1940. There the ex-Chinese and Korean Manchurian guerillas were organized into a brigade of the Soviet Army but saw no action during the war.

The largest non-Communist nationalist resistance movement was the Korean Provisional Government. Originally based in Shanghai, during World War II it was headquartered in Chungking (Chongqing). It had a small force of troops, the Korean Restoration Army (Han'guk Kwangbokkun). Under the leadership of Kim Ku (1876–1949), it had about 3,000 or so resistance fighters. But this was still a modest-sized group. Like the Communists, the non-Communist nationalist resistance movements were fragmented and ineffective.

Both internally and among the exile groups, a strong ideological divide split Korean nationalism. This division between the moderate "cultural" nationalists and the more radical mostly but not exclusively Marxist nationalists contributed to the radically different directions the two Koreas would take after 1945.

ECONOMIC DEVELOPMENT

Korea's economy grew considerably under colonial rule, although the extent to which the colonial period laid the foundations for its economic transformation after 1945 is controversial. The record is complex and ambiguous. Japan did build an elaborate infrastructure and industrial base in Korea and modernized agriculture, but it did so in ways that often minimized the benefits for Korea and created structural problems. And at the end of colonial rule, Korea still remained mostly rural, with the majority of Koreans very poor, arguably, in some ways more impoverished than at the start of colonial rule.

The period around 1919–1920 marked an important turning point in South Korea's economic development. Japan emerged at the end of World War I from a debtor to a creditor nation. Capital-rich Japanese companies now sought to invest in Korea and pressured the Japanese government to abolish the tariffs in 1920 that had largely closed Korea to investment. The rice riots that broke out in Japan during 1918 protesting the soaring prices of this staple also acted as an incentive to promote rice production in Korea. The period was also a turning point because merchants and landlords in Korea who had accumulated capital began to actively participate in modern industry. The Kabo Reforms ended the legal prohibition of retired government officials who were members of the landowning *yangban* elite from participating in commerce. More significantly, attitudes were changing. By the early twentieth century, the traditional disdain of the elite for business was dissipating. Instead, many formed societies for the promotion of industry and commercial activity. Most Korean intellectuals and reformers saw commerce and industry as a source of national strength, and regarded Korea's traditional disapproval of these occupations as a source of its weakness and backwardness.

Among the pioneer Korean-owned industries was the Kyŏngsŏng Cord Company, founded in 1910 by the aristocratic Yun family and becoming a joint-stock company in 1911.[15] Also prominent were the Koch'ang Kims from Kobu (now Koch'ang) County in the rich rice-growing lands of North Chŏlla Province in southeast Korea. An old *yangban* family, the Kims took advantage of their location near the port of Kunsan to expand their holdings and produce rice for export. To this they added rice mill-ing and other subsidiary businesses. Already by 1920 they emerged as a wealthy and prominent family. The leading members were Kim Sŏng-su and his brother Yŏn-su, both Japanese educated, who combined the traditional role of the scholar-gentry, being active in intellectual, cultural, and political affairs, with the new role as entrepreneurs. Their Kyŏngbang Textile Company became one of the largest and most successful Korean-owned industries. Other prominent entrepreneurs were Min Kyu-sik, of the Korean-owned Hanil Bank, and Pak Hŭng-sik (1903–1994), who owned a chain of retail stores including the Hwasin department store in Seoul. Pak, of humble background, became the richest man in Korea by the 1940s. This small Korean entrepreneur class worked closely with their Japanese counterparts. They needed access to Japanese capital, permits for establishing shops and factories, and access to Japanese suppliers. A significant point of contact was the Keijō (Seoul) Chamber of Commerce and Industry (Keishō) established in 1888 to serve the Japanese business community. Korean participation became mandatory when, in 1915, the Government-General prohibited separate chambers of commerce for Koreans. This small class of modern entrepreneurs, fluent in Japanese and accustomed to working closely with their Japanese counterparts formed the basis of South Korea's business community after liberation.[16]

Despite the emergence of a Korean entrepreneur class, the economy was dominated by Japanese firms. These worked closely with the Government-General, which provided it subsidies and loans through state-owned banks. All of Japan's major *zaibatsu* (industrial-financial conglomerates) became involved in Korea. The Noguchi *zaibatsu*, founded by Noguchi Jun, was based entirely in Korea. The Nippon Chisso plant in Hŭngnam was owned by Noguchi's Chōsen Nitrogenous Fertilizer Company, one of the largest chemical complexes in the world.

To accompany this industrialization, an impressive infrastructure was built. Before 1910, the Japanese completed the Pusan-ŭiju railway. After 1910, railway construction continued and was coordinated with the development of the Japanese-owned South Manchurian Railway Company in northeast China, which took over the management of Korea's railroads in 1933. By 1945, Korea had one of the most extensive rail networks in Asia. Most of the cities and ports in Korea were linked by rail. The total kilometers of track was a quarter of that of Japan's well-developed rail system, but considering that Korea had only half the area and a third the population of Japan, this is quite impressive. Yet it carried only a tenth as much freight and less than 3 percent as many passengers as the Japanese rail system. This is because the rail network was built as much for military purposes as for economic ones. To a large measure, it was designed to facilitate the movement of troops in Korea and, especially after 1930, to link Korea to the empire on the Asian mainland. It was, however, a stimulus to economic development.[17] There was considerable mining, mostly in the northern part of the country: gold, silver, iron, tungsten, and coal were all mined. American interests were involved in the gold mines until the Japanese bought them out in 1939, otherwise mining was largely done by Japanese companies. Originally the mines primarily served to supply Japan with raw materials, but by the late 1930s much of the output of the mines supported Korea's own growing iron and steel, chemical, and other industries.

During the 1930s, with the Japanese conquest of Manchuria and then the invasion of China, the industrialization of Korea accelerated. New industrial cities sprang up in the north. Najin, a village of 500 people in 1927, had a population of 26,000 a decade later; while Ch'ŏngjin grew from a village of 100 in 1900 to a city of 72,353 in 1938, when it was the leading port on the Sea of Japan.[18] The economic activity during the colonial period had some unfortunate ecological consequences. A particular tragic development was the deforestation of the country. A combination of aggressive logging by Japanese companies and the pressure of a growing population for firewood and land for subsistence farming resulted in a denuded mountainous landscape. Efforts by the authorities to reforest lands were not successful. A similar tragedy afflicted the nation's fisheries. Fishing, as always in Korea, was a major economic activity. Koreans had continued to rely on fishing as an important source of food, but most of the seafood caught was by larger Japanese commercial operators who through overfishing depleted the country's fisheries.

MODERNITY AND SOCIAL CHANGE

While Koreans have often been portrayed in modern histories as either passive victims of imperialism or engaged in a nationalist struggle against their Japanese oppressors, it is perhaps more accurate to see them as embracing elements of change and taking advantage of the opportunities available to them. Colonial-era Koreans were presented two versions of what it means to be modern: Japan's own version and the one from the West. If the Soviet Union is considered, it could be argued that Koreans were presented with at least three ways a society and individuals could be modern and successful. Koreans eagerly embraced them all. Intellectuals were quick to adopt liberal democratic ideals from Western Europe and America, socialist ideas from the Soviet Union, and concepts of state and society from Japan, while people of all backgrounds moved into new occupations and adapted to new institutions.

Educational development under colonial rule provides a good example of such adaptation. Koreans were hardly reluctant to accept new styles of schooling, seeing it as a way of advancing in a changing society. Education was flourishing by the last two decades of the Chosŏn period, from 1890 to 1910. Hundreds of new schools were established by Koreans and by foreign missionaries, while the state was beginning to create a national system of public education. The colonial regime sought to gain control over schooling and to channel it toward serving Japanese aims—primarily to provide basic schooling for unskilled and semiskilled laborers. In 1911 the Japanese administration created a new educational system that provided up to fourteen years of schooling for Japanese residents but limited public education for most Koreans to four years of "common school" with a few four-year "higher common schools" mostly focused on vocation education. According to the Educational Ordinance, the purpose of the educational system for Koreans was "to give the younger generations of Koreans such moral character and general knowledge as will make them loyal subjects of Japan, at the same time enabling them to cope with the present condition existing in the Peninsula."[19] Tight restrictions were placed over the hundreds of private modern-style schools that mushroomed in the early twentieth century. Many Korean-run schools were forced to close because they were unable to provide the education in the Japanese language the colonial authorities required.

With the new more liberal "culture policy," a major reform of educational policy took place in 1922 that extended elementary education from four to six (sometimes five) years and secondary education to five years, while adding a three-year college preparatory or advanced technical school. Expansion of the school system, however, proceeded very gradually. As late as the mid-1930s less than one in six Korean children of elementary school age were enrolled in officially recognized schools. The pace of educational expansion failed to meet the public needs. In response, Koreans established hundreds of unlicensed schools; many of these were night schools taught by young graduates of public or mission-run educational institutions. Traditional village schools known as *sŏdang* flourished; generally they consisted of little more than children meeting in the house of a literate but untrained teacher. Although maintaining a more traditional curriculum, they remained the principal form of schooling for most Korean children; in fact, these village schools increased in number, with enrollment peaking in the 1930s. The increase in these traditional schools and hundreds of other unlicensed institutions reported to be supplying basic education indicated a rising demand for schooling that the deliberate pace of educational expansion pursued by the Japanese was not satisfying. But unlicensed private schools could not issue certificates, and *sŏdang* were, as far as a means of social advancement was concerned, dead ends, since only a modern-style education could provide opportunities for success in the new society.

Frustration at the gradualist approach to educational development was felt most keenly by members of the elite and the small but growing urban middle class. A central issue for upper-class and upwardly mobile Korean families was higher education. Keijō Imperial University, established in 1925, remained the sole university in Korea until after 1945. The faculty was overwhelmingly Japanese, and the student body contained a disproportionate number of Japanese students. The Japanese colonial authorities did not monopolize schooling in Korea. Private schools, many operated by American missionaries or by American-trained Koreans survived. Since the Japanese state invested little in higher education for Koreans, private institutions were important at that level. In 1935, 73.6 percent of postsecondary education was carried out by private schools and nonuniversity institutions. These private colleges were regarded with suspicion by Japanese authorities, and most were eventually closed down. Overall, the Japanese record on providing opportunities for higher education for Koreans compares unfavorably with the British in India or the Americans in the Philippines. Because the expansion of higher education was too slow to meet demand, an increasing number of Korean students sought schooling in Japan. In 1925, 13.8 percent of Korean students in higher education were in Japan. By 1935, the figure was 47.3 percent, and in 1940, 61.5 percent. In 1942, there were 6,771 Koreans attending institutions of higher education in Japan, but only 4,234 in Korea. Also impressive was the number of Koreans attending secondary schools in Japan; in 1940, 71.6 percent of the 20,824 Korean students in Japan were enrolled at secondary schools. The Japanese government gave little assistance or encouragement to this educational exodus, and the higher living costs were a heavy burden for most. Yet rapidly increasing numbers of Koreans were overcoming linguistic handicaps and making financial sacrifices to achieve education because in their own country the rising demand for education was outstripping opportunities at all levels.

Limited access to the higher reaches of education was paralleled by the limited opportunities for Koreans to serve in administration and teaching. The bureaucracy remained dominated by Japanese. In 1922, 29 percent of the instructors in public schools were Japanese; ten years later, 30 percent of all teachers in public schools were Japanese, a figure that rose to 44 percent in 1938. This created serious problems after liberation in 1945, when these teachers returned to Japan. But the most serious problem for many individual Koreans and their families was being blocked from taking the traditional route to honor and privilege, advanced education, and appointment to government office. This frustration was aggravated by wartime policies after 1938 that further limited the number of schools of higher education, even as it expanded primary education, and that redirected the curriculum away from literary to less prestigious technical education and vocational training. The result was an unsatisfied desire for schooling at all levels, but especially at the higher levels, that became evident immediately after liberation in both North and South Korea.

The rising demand for modern-style schooling reflected the social changes in Korea. The country's old order began to crumble with the Kabo Reforms of 1894–1895 that legally abolished the rigid and hereditary social structure of Chosŏn-dynasty Korea. It accelerated during the colonial period with the rise of an industrial working class and a new middle class, the emergence of social movements among women and outcastes, and acceleration of social mobility. The new industrial working class grew slowly at first. Although there was an increase in industrial production in the 1920s, as late as 1928, 80.6 percent of the labor force was employed in agriculture, while only 2.1 percent was in mining and factory work.[20] In the 1930s, the numbers grew dramatically. There were 99,000 factory workers in 1933 and 390,000 in 1943. The number of mine workers during the same period grew from 70,000 to 280,000. Along with transportation and construction workers, the Korean working class numbered about 1,750,000 in 1943. The industrial workforce included large numbers of women, generally confined to menial and repetitive sectors of industry such as silk reeling and cotton fabric production. Female laborers were mostly young, unmarried girls working to help their families and to save for marriage.

This growth in industry is reflected in the urban population. Between 1935 and 1944 the urban population (living in cities over 20,000) went from 7 percent to 13.2 percent of the population. This, it should be pointed out, was far less than in Japan, which in the early 1940s was about 42 percent urban; it was, in fact, about the same as Japan in 1908. The population of Seoul increased nearly three times from 1925 to 1942, from 342,000 to 1,114,000. The greatest increase in the labor class was in Kyŏnggi Province, the area around Seoul, and in the northeastern Hamgyŏng Province. In general, industry and mining were concentrated in the northern areas while the southern provinces remained overwhelmingly agricultural. Japanese workers in Korea made up about 10 to 11 percent of the workforce until 1937. With the huge increase in Korean workers, they declined to only around 7 percent of the workforce in 1943.[21] Japanese were mostly skilled workers and were paid much better than Koreans. However, by the early 1940s an increasingly larger number of Koreans entered more skilled positions. Korean workers enjoyed few protections, since there was little regulation of working conditions and business practices. They also suffered from sharp disparities in wages with Japanese workers in the same plants and firms. Korean workers in the employ of Japanese firms not only made much less than Japanese workers but also had wages well below those of Japan's other major colony, Taiwan. In 1937, Japanese workers earned 2 yen a day, Taiwanese 1 yen, and Koreans .66 yen.

Yet Korean workers, rather than being passive victims, often showed a surprising militancy participating in labor agitation. After 1920 labor strikes increased. Most of the strikes involved day laborers on the docks, on construction projects, and in other nonfactory jobs. The most famous was the Wŏnsan General Strike that took place in 1929. Communists following Comintern directives made serious efforts to organize "red" labor unions during 1930 to 1931 with some success. Among these was the Hamhŭng Committee of the Chosŏn Red Labor Unions created in February 1931. But the police arrested more than 1,800 members of this and other red unions in the early 1930s. By the mid-1930s labor union activity continued only tenuously as an underground movement. In 1938, the government launched the Campaign for National Protection Corps of Industrial Workers (*Sanpō*); this included a labor-management council to make sure all worked together for the war effort. These wartime industrial relations programs, Soon-won Park has argued, profoundly shaped later South Korean labor practices. The politicization of labor movements in South Korea, the intervention into labor-management relations by the government, and the prevalence of company unions were all influenced by wartime colonial practice.[22]

A small modern middle class emerged in colonial Korea. This class included professionals such as teachers, doctors, accountants, businessmen, bankers, and civil servants in the colonial bureaucracy. More than any other group, they were a group open to new ideas and often eagerly embraced the modern world. They wore Western-style clothes; sent their children to modern schools; and read newspapers, magazines, and the modern literature by foreign writers in translation or by Korean writers such as Yi Kwang-su. Many came from *yangban* backgrounds, some were from the old *chungin* class, but many were of humble family origins. The latter represented the new social mobility in Korea. A key to their new status was education, and access to education would be a central concern to all those who aspired to or sought to maintain this status. Members of the middle class were urban, cosmopolitan, and open to new ideas. The members of the newly emerging middle class may have made up no more than 5 to 10 percent of the population, but they were to form the political, economic, and cultural leadership of colonial Korea.

Few social changes marked a greater break with tradition than those that concerned women. Many Korean women embraced new ideas and opportunities presented by a modernizing society. Korean progressives in the late nineteenth century saw the humble status of Korean women as symptomatic of the country's low level of civilization. The Kabo Reforms had abolished some of the legal restrictions on women. It also abolished child marriages and ended the prohibition on widows to remarry. The issue of establishing greater equality for women, begun by the tiny number of Koreans exposed to the outside world in the 1890s, was embraced by much of the intellectual community in colonial times. Many Koreans blamed the Confucian concept of *namjon yŏbi* (revere men, despise women) as emblematic of both the country's backwardness and its past uncritical adoption of Chinese customs. Of particular concern was the exclusion of women from formal education. They noted that girls attended schools in Western countries and that Japan had drawn up plans in the 1870s to make basic education universal and compulsory for girls as well as boys. An early proponent of women's education was Sŏ Chae-p'il, whose editorial in the *Tongnip sinmun* on April 21, 1896, called for equal education for men and women to promote social equality and strengthen the nation. In another editorial in September that year, he argued that gender relations were a mark of a nation's civilization. Conservatives in the late Chosŏn government were less sympathetic to the need for women's education. A petition to the king by a group of women from *yangban* families to establish a girls' school was ignored.[23] Women's education was established by American missionaries, not Koreans. After an initial slow start, many families began sending their daughters to these new schools, and the enthusiasm for education among Korean women was commented on by foreign missionaries. Women graduates of these schools became active in patriotic organizations, and thousands of women participated in the March First Movement. It was only, however, during the 1920s that the women's movement became a major force in Korea. One of its important figures was Kim Maria. Educated in Tokyo, she formed in April 1919 the Taehan Aeguk Puinhoe (Korean Patriotic Women's Society), an organization to promote national self-determination. The organization worked with the Korean Provisional Government in Shanghai and in 1920 claimed some 2,000 members. The activities of this and other, mostly Christian, women's groups helped win respect for women among Korean intellectuals.

In the 1920s men and women participated in discussions about the role of women and gender relations. Feminists included Kim Wŏn-ju, who published *Sin yŏja* (*New Woman*); artist Na Hye-sŏk (1896–1948), who wrote for *Yŏja kye* (*Women's World*); and the poet Kim Myŏng-sun. Some members of this small class of women led lives daringly defiant of tradition. They wore Western-style clothes with short skirts and bobbed hair, socialized in public, advocated free love and the right to divorce, and rejected the confinement of women to the roles of housewife and mother. These ideas, however, were too radical for Koreans, including male intellectuals. Moderate nationalists called for an educated, healthy woman whose role in society was very much like the "good wife, wise

mother" ideal promoted by the Japanese government; meanwhile, leftist male nationalists argued for the need to subordinate gender issues to
those of class.

Two individuals exemplify this new small class of "modern" women.
One is Kim Hwal-lan, known to Westerners as Helen Kim. Born in 1899 to
Christian parents in Inch'ŏn, she attended mission schools, became active
in the YWCA, went on to Boston University, and received a PhD from
Teachers College of Columbia University in 1930. After returning, she
became president of Ewha College, the most prestigious school of higher
education for women in Korea, a position she held from 1939 to 1961, except for a brief period (1944 to 1945) when the school was shut down by
the Japanese. Pak Kyŏng-wŏn (1901–1933), daughter of a rich farmer, attended an industrial arts school in Japan and took a job as a technician in
the silk reeling industry, an industry dominated by women workers. She
then returned to Japan to learn to become a driver, a rarity for a woman,
and then became one of the few women to attend an aviation school.
Korea's first woman aviator, she won a number of flying competitions in
Japan before perishing in a flight back to her home in Korea.[24]

The women's movement was quite political, since most writers linked
the liberation of women with national liberation. While this may have
made the belief in women's rights and equality more acceptable to
educated Koreans, it meant that feminists subordinated their own social
agenda to the national political agenda. It also meant that the women's
movement followed the general split between moderate, gradualist
reformers and radical leftists that characterized most political and intellectual activity from the early 1920s. Moderate women reformers were
associated with the YWCA and various church and moderate patriotic
associations, while some thirty women with socialist and Communist
leanings established a more radical group, Chosŏn Yŏsŏng Tonguhoe
(Korean Women's Friendship Society) in 1924. As part of the united front,
in 1927, moderate and radical women worked together to organize the
Kŭnuhoe (Friends of the Rose of Sharon). By 1929, the Kŭnuhoe had 2,970
women, including 260 in Tokyo.[25] For the vast majority of Korean women,
their traditional subordinate social status remained unchanged, but the
emergence of a small number of politically active and assertive women
among the educated was an important precursor of more radical changes
that would take place after 1945.

Another marginalized group that took advantage of new opportunities
were the paekchŏng, a low-status hereditary group in Korea who lived
in their own villages. While most were farmers, they also worked in
the "unclean" professions such as butchers, leather workers, sometimes
executioners, as well as other less obviously undesirable jobs such as ferrymen and wicker craftsman. Very much like the untouchables (or dalits)

of India or the *eta* (or *burakumin*) of Japan, they were socially shunned by ordinary citizens, possessing a legal status as "mean people" (*ch'ŏnmin*) below the ordinary peasants or even slaves. They were not allowed to wear the clothes and hats of nonoutcastes, and marriage between *paekchŏng* and commoners was legally prohibited, although it did occur. Even their names distinguished them, since they were not allowed to include Chinese characters with noble meanings. The status was legally abolished in the Kabo Reforms, but this did not result in any effective change in their position, since their legal rights were ignored. During the colonial period many *paekchŏng* became workers in state slaughterhouses, where, although shunned, they became exposed to new ideas and life-styles. A few managed to achieve a modern education and some prosperity. In April 1923, *paekchŏng* social activists formed the Hyŏngp'yŏngsa (Equalization Society) in Chinju. This became a national organization that at its peak in the 1930s claimed over 400,000 members, most probably an inflated figure. It campaigned for the end of discrimination in the schools, workplaces, and society at large; the end of segregated grave sites; and their inclusion in local meetings. As was so often the case, education was a major concern. Ordinary Koreans sought to exclude them from public schools; an example was the Ikchang incident in 1924, in which non-*paekchŏng* protested about their children sharing classrooms with outcaste members.[26] Despite deep-seated prejudices, their social status improved, and during the social upheavals of the 1930s through the 1950s they became assimilated into the general population. The ferment among the outcastes, like the growing movement among women, reflected a change in the old hierarchical social order of Korea and the growth of egalitarian ideals that would emerge so strong after 1945 and shape the history of North and South Korea.

RURAL SOCIETY

Korea remained an agricultural land. During most of the colonial period, three out of four Koreans were farmers. One of the first major tasks of the new colonial administration was to carry out an accurate survey of land. Korea was an agricultural society; the great majority of the population consisted of farmers, and wealth derived from agricultural rents was the principal economic basis of the *yangban* class. Agriculture was the basis of the colonial order as well. Tokyo regarded Korea as an important supplier of food, a rice producer for an industrializing Japan. The Korean state had derived much of its revenue from taxing farmers. This was true of the colonial regime as well but with a difference. Traditionally the Korean state taxed agricultural production, the colonial government taxed land.

The importance of Korea as an agricultural producer and the reliance on a land tax made the need for a careful survey and codification of land ownership a high priority of the colonial government. The Korean state undertook what became known as the Kwangmu Land Survey from 1898 to 1902, but it was highly unreliable. So the Government-General carried out a comprehensive survey of land from 1910 to 1918. With a thoroughness that Korea had not seen, at least in recent times, every plot of land was carefully recorded and classified according to type, such as dry field and wet paddy land. Each plot was also graded by productivity.

The land survey has become a subject of controversy. Many ordinary Korean farmers were unable to produce the formal documentation necessary to show ownership of their land. Many peasants held partial ownership or certain customary squatters or tenant rights that could not be documented. No doubt many were simply confused by the new unfamiliar legal procedures and did not register their lands. It is widely believed that as a result of these problems many Korean farmers lost their lands to the Japanese. However, recent research indicates that while many poor Koreans lost land or the customary use of lands, the chief beneficiaries were members of the old *yangban* class, who were able to take advantage of the survey to increase their land holdings. Indeed, Carter Eckert has described this period as part of the "halcyon era for the Korean landlord class" that began in the late nineteenth century.

But the Government-General became the largest landowner. It took possession of the lands owned by the Korean state and the Yi royal household—in short, all public lands including forests and riverbeds. In 1930, the colonial government owned 40 percent of all land. Japanese individuals and corporations also acquired a great deal of land. Some of this was purchased from the Government-General at bargain prices as part of an effort to encourage Japanese settlement in Korea. As early as 1907, Tokyo created a semigovernmental Oriental Development Company for the purpose of acquiring land and then offering it to Japanese farmers at bargain prices if they would settle in Korea, but few came.

With the industrialization of Korea in the 1930s agriculture's share of the economy declined. Yet the great majority of Koreans were still peasants. While some land did fall into Japanese hands, most landlords were Koreans, generally from the former *yangban*, who benefited by the rationing of land because it provided opportunities to consolidating their holdings. The majority of landlords owned less than 50 *chŏngbo* (123 acres) and these were mostly Koreans. In 1942, of landlords with more than 50 *chŏngbo*, 2,173 were Korean, 1,219 Japanese. Only among the very largest landowners, possessing more than 500 acres, did Japanese outnumber Koreans: 184 Japanese and 116 Koreans.[27]

Most peasants worked for landlords as tenant farmers. But the picture is complicated, since tenants sometimes owned some land that was insufficient to support their families, so they also served as tenants on additional fields. One report found that 538,000 farmers owned some land and rented some; 1,073,000 were tenants; and 971,000 were sharecroppers. About 2.5 percent of families owned 64 percent of the farmland. Overall, the majority of Korean farmers owned no land or not enough to support their families. Tenancy rates in the agriculturally rich southwest approached 80 percent. Their life was hard. On average, half the harvest went to the landowner. Tenant conditions were made more difficult by the tendency of landowners to make the cultivators pay for the costs of irrigation projects, fertilizers, tools, and seeds. Farmers were forced to borrow and often were victims of usury. Population growth also increased pressure on the land and drove up rents. Land taxes, which before the 1930s were the main source of revenue for the colonial administration, were also burdensome. Consequently, many Koreans moved into the mountains, where they cleared public forestlands to create fire fields. Land would be burned, a crop then sown, and then the farmer would move on to another field. It was a precarious, hard, uncertain way to survive and contributed to deforestation.

A major change was the commercialization of agriculture, a change that began with the opening of Korean ports after 1876 and accelerated during colonial rule. Farmers grew for the market, which often meant that rice farmers could not eat their own rice. The per capita consumption of rice actually declined even though rice production increased 140 percent from 1910 to 1939.[28] Many Koreans ate millet, mixed rice and millet, or other less desirable grains. In the 1930s, Korea imported millet to feed itself even while it was exporting rice to Japan. For a people for whom the words *meal* and *rice* are synonymous, this was a bitter hardship. Farmers had always suffered from the unpredictability of the weather. As farming became commercial, the fluctuating market prices and the often unexpected changes in government agricultural policies added to their worries. Changing market prices contributed to the growing indebtedness that burdened both landlords and peasants. Indebtedness increased with the Great Depression, forcing many owners to mortgage their cultivated lands.

Landlord-tenant disputes were frequent. In the late 1910s and 1920s there were many well-organized, reform-minded peasant groups aimed at rent reduction and securing tenancy tenure. Many of these were successful. But an agriculture depression in the late 1920s followed by the Great Depression made the position of peasants less secure. Rural Korea was hit hard by the Depression; the price of rice, the most important cash crop, fell in 1931 to 39 percent of its 1925 level.[29] Landlords, many also facing debt, began evicting tenants. Tenant disputes became more defensive, with many arguing for their right to subsist, and in a traditional Confucian manner calling upon the benevolence of the landlord. These were less successful, and many landless farmers immigrated to Manchuria, to Japan, or to the new industrial centers in the north looking for work.[30] A number of Red Peasant Unions were organized, especially in the northern part of the country. Although linked with the Communists and often brutally suppressed by the Japanese, recent studies show these to have been more concerned with local tenancy disputes than with fomenting revolution. Nonetheless, a tradition of peasant radicalism began, especially strong in the north, as well as a legacy of bitterness and frustration among tenant farmers that reemerged after the end of colonial rule in 1945.

Alarmed by peasant unrest, the Government-General in the 1930s attempted to ameliorate conditions. It enacted the Arbitration Ordinance of 1932 and the Agricultural Lands Ordinance of 1934, which attempted to reduce landlord-tenant disputes through government intervention, sometimes at the expense of the landlords. In 1932, the colonial government inaugurated the Rural Revitalization Campaign aimed at improving the economic conditions of the peasantry, made worse by the Depression, by reducing debt and promoting self-sufficiency. Modeled on a similar program to aid the plight of Japanese peasants, the campaign focused on gathering information and finding ways to better utilize labor and get villages to work together for mutual assistance. Local youths, both men and women, with some schooling, and those between the ages of eighteen and twenty-five were recruited as village leaders to promote rural improvements; 9,000 were trained between 1936 and 1940. This program achieved only modest success, but it proved useful after 1937 as part of the general mobilization of the Korean population for the war effort.[31]

All the commercialization of Korean agriculture and the various programs for rural development might be misleading. Despite the commercialization of agriculture, in many ways life for the majority of Koreans living in villages did not change radically, at least not until the 1930s. Customary dress, diet, and habits of everyday life remained the same. Much of the countryside was still economically and socially dominated by *yangban*, although they now often lived in the more exciting world of the cities, leaving stewards behind to manage their properties. When the colonial period ended, the common farmers revealed themselves to be restless, seeking to get out of indebtedness and tenancy.

WARTIME COLONIALISM, 1931–1945

Korea's colonial experience changed profoundly after 1931. Two aspects of this change deeply impacted Korea's historical development. One was a great uprooting of people. Massive dislocations took place by the wartime mobilization. Koreans were uprooted from their homes, either voluntarily or by compulsion, and they migrated to the industrial cities of the north, to Manchuria, to Japan, or to other parts of the empire to supply labor needs. Few Korean families were not affected by this mobilization and dislocation. The other feature of wartime colonial rule was Japan's effort to forcibly assimilate the Korean people, to remake them into Japanese.

The relatively liberal policies inaugurated by the colonial authorities after 1919 were replaced by a reassertion of a harsher, more repressive rule. The crackdown on Korean cultural, social, and political activities came in three steps: in 1926, in 1931, and in 1937. The Government-General began a tightening of freedom in 1926. Partly this reflected worries about Communism in the home country that resulted in the 1925 Peace Preservation Law, which gave domestic police in Japan greater authority to root out radicals. Authorities also feared a repeat of the March First demonstrations. In June 1926, the funeral of Sunjong, the last Chosŏn monarch, resulted in widespread demonstrations known as the June 10 Incident. Soon there was a crackdown on political activities; many suspected leftists were arrested and many publications shut down. The Korean press would never be as free again. A concern of the police was the effort by leftists to organize tenant farmers and labor unions. The police became increasingly effective in undermining efforts to establish these unions.

While 1926 saw a tightening of Japanese control over Korea, a much more significant change occurred in 1931. The Great Depression hit Japan hard in 1930 and tilted Japanese politics away from the more liberal and pro-Western-minded to those who advocated a more ultranationalist, militarist direction, and who viewed the Western powers, especially Britain and the United States, more suspiciously. As military and ultranationalist circles gained influence in Japan, the country resumed its imperialist expansion in Asia with a new vigor. In September 1931, the Japanese Kwantung Army created an incident as an excuse to seize control over the vast northeast Chinese region of Manchuria. In 1932, Tokyo formed a nominally independent state of Manchukuo, but the new territory was controlled by the Japanese Army and became an agricultural and industrial base for the further expansion into China. The new orientation of Japan away from cooperation with the West and toward imperial expansion in Asia greatly impacted Korea. Korea was now a link between Japan and Manchuria and a strategic base for the further expansion of the Japanese Empire. To implement changes in colonial administration in view of Korea's new position in the empire, Tokyo appointed a new governor-general, the army general Ugaki Kazushige, in 1931. His policy was to mobilize Korea for the benefit of the empire by increasing the production of food and other needed products. As Japan moved toward greater economic self-sufficiency within its empire and less reliance on world trade, which had greatly contracted with the Great Depression, its colonies became a more significant source of raw materials, investments, and trade. The colonial authorities made efforts to mediate landlord-tenant disputes, to stabilize the countryside, and to increase rice production for exports. Korean rice exports, however, were depressing prices of the rice production of the Japanese, and from 1933, the Government-General began an agricultural diversification program. Agricultural production shifted away from food to fabrics under the slogan "cotton in the south, sheep in the north."

With the outbreak of war between Japan and China in 1937, colonial rule took a radical turn toward mass mobilization of the Korean people for the war effort. The Government-General began to shut down Korean organizations of all types. In their place were a large number of state-sponsored organizations designed to control the activities of the population and direct them toward the war effort. In 1938, for example, it formed the Korean Federation of Youth Organizations as an umbrella organization to control and utilize all the country's youth groups. The authorities ran Local Youth Leadership Seminars and Training Institutes for Children's Organizations. Writers were organized into the All Korean Writers Federation, and there were similar nationwide associations for laborers, tenant farmers, and fishermen. Among the other organizations that the colonial authorities established were the Korean Defense Association, the Association for the Study of Policy Dealing with the Critical Situation, and the Korean Association for Imperial Rule Assistance. The colonial government established a Korean League for General Mobilization of the National Spirit in 1937 with branches in every county and township. In 1938, it created another all-embracing organization, the Korean Anticommunist Association, which also had branches in every province. There were local offices in police stations and associated groups in villages, factories, and other workplaces. Almost every Korean became associated with some mass organization. Beginning in September 1939, the first day of each month was Rising Asia Service Day, on which people were required to perform tasks for the sake of developing the new Asia.[32] In 1940, the entire colony was organized into 350,000 Neighborhood Patriotic Associations, each with ten households. These became the basic units for collections of contributions, imposition of labor service, maintenance of local security, and rationing.

Education became highly militarized and regimented. Compulsory military drills were introduced to all middle and higher-level schools. Political rallies became a part of schooling, as did mass mobilization of Korean youth for the war effort. In incremental stages, the colonial government brought the students into the war. In April 1938, the Japanese government organized a Special Student Volunteers unit for selected Korean students who wanted to participate in military duty. Then in May

1943, the state permitted all Korean students to volunteer for service in the army, and in October of that year for the navy. Because the numbers volunteering proved to be modest, the state made registration for military service compulsory in November 1943.[33] In October 1940, all student organizations automatically became branches of the Citizen's Total Mobilization League. Students found their time increasingly occupied by extracurricular activities, such as collecting metal for the war effort and attending patriotic rallies. College students were sent to the countryside to explain the war effort to farmers and rural folk. In the early 1940s, the school term was shortened and students of secondary schools were required to work on military construction projects. After 1942, many students were conscripted to work in Japan, while at home the *kinrōtai*, student labor groups, were formed to do "voluntary" work such as building airstrips and defense works. By the spring of 1945, virtually all classroom instruction above the elementary level was suspended and students were fully involved in labor and military service.

A few Koreans were admitted into the Japanese Military Academy in Tokyo during the 1930s and early 1940s, and a larger number into the Manchurian Military Academy. Although the total number of Korean officers in the Japanese Army was small, they were to provide the nucleus for the officer corps of the postwar South Korean Army. Most Koreans who joined or were conscripted into the Japanese Army did labor duty on airstrips or served as prison guards.

An extreme form of coercion was the comfort women, or comfort girls. These were young Korean girls who were either recruited or forcibly enrolled as sex slaves to serve the Japanese troops. The so-called comfort girls included Filipinas and Chinese, but most were Koreans. Many of these girls were recruited under false pretenses. They or their parents were told that they were to be given well-paying jobs. In practice, they were treated miserably. After the war, these girls returned home disgraced and were forced to hide their past or live lives as unmarried and unwanted women. Between 100,000 to 200,000 Koreans became comfort women. One example was Mun Ok-ju, an eighteen-year-old woman from a poor family of casual laborers in Taegu, in southwestern Korea, who was offered "a good job in a restaurant," by two civilian recruiters. Lured by the promise of a good salary to support her family, she went along with a group of seventeen other young women between the ages of fifteen and twenty-one who were shipped off to Burma, where she "serviced" thirty men a day under conditions of virtual imprisonment. Five of the girls in her group died or committed suicide.[34]

The abuse of the comfort women has become one of the most contentious issues in colonial history. It many ways it symbolizes the brutality and exploitation of Japanese colonialism at its worst. It was only one way

Koreans were victimized. Koreans also suffered from Allied bombing while working in Japan, for example. Among the more than 2 million Koreans working in wartime Japan, at least 10,000 died from the atomic bombs on Hiroshima and Nagasaki.[35]

FORCED ASSIMILATION

During World War II a vast, unprecedented experiment in mass assimilation began. The new governor-general, Minami Jirō (1936–1942), pledged to end discrimination and promote reconciliation between Japan and Korea under the slogans "Japan and Korea as one body" (*Nai-Sen ittai*) and "harmony between Japan and Korea" (*Nissen yūwa*). All Koreans were required to register at Shinto shrines, even though this was an alien religion to all Koreans and especially offensive to Christians. The authorities required students and government employees to attend Shinto ceremonies. Then in late 1939, the government issued the Name Order, which set in motion the process by which Koreans were to change their names to Japanese ones. Generally, this was done by having people select Chinese characters that could either be the same or similar to their names, but pronounced in a Japanese way, or they could select entirely new names. From 1940, all government employees, families with children in school, and others affiliated with the state were more or less pressured to adopt new Japanese names. Eventually, about 84 percent of Koreans complied and adopted new names. In a society where ancient family lineage was prized, this loss of names was a particular humiliation. Korean-language newspapers were ordered closed in 1940; except for the Korean edition of the official government daily, all remaining twelve newspapers were in Japanese. By the early 1940s, the publication of all Korean books ceased. Korean language use in the schools was extremely restricted after 1938, and by 1943 students could be punished for speaking Korean at school.

Yet the colonial regime was ambiguous about this policy, insisting that Koreans were now Japanese but also maintaining their distinct identity and status as subordinate and inferior subjects. All public documents, school records, and job applications listed the original family name as well as the place of birth and the clan. Official reports made a clear distinction between "peninsular" people and "homeland" Japanese. Japanese leaders themselves had no clear, consistent idea of exactly what the relationship between Koreans and Japanese was. There was some debate among Japanese political leaders as to whether Koreans could be allowed to participate directly in the Japanese government. From 1921 the House of Representatives, or Diet, introduced resolutions calling for extending the franchise for Koreans and allowing Korean representation in parliament. Some Koreans actively campaigned for the franchise. In the 1920s the writer Ch'oe Rin led a home-rule movement demanding that the political rights guaranteed to Japanese in their 1889 constitution be extended to Korea. A number of pro-Japanese associations flourished in the 1930s; in 1937 Minami created the National Association of Koreans to unite them. A resolution in 1939 and another in 1940 to grant the franchise to Koreans passed, but both were vetoed by the cabinet.[36] Only in December 1944 did Tokyo approve of Korean (and Taiwanese) representation in the Diet, which was to begin in 1946.

Koreans, however, were far from assimilated into Japanese culture. Most Koreans could not speak Japanese, did not have any social interaction with Japanese, or identify with Japan. One Japanese source in 1943 stated that 23 percent of Koreans comprehended Japanese, 12 percent without difficulties.[37] Some Koreans may have genuinely been attracted to Japanese culture. Among the small professional class, there were many who enjoyed Japanese literature, films, and music and enjoyed the opportunity to visit Tokyo. Yet assimilation failed. Japanese and Koreans remained two separate peoples who did not mix socially. By the early 1940s out of some 750,000 Japanese living in Korea, most of them men, fewer than 1,000 were married to Koreans. Rather than leading to assimilation, the presence of a privileged alien minority in this historically homogeneous society, and the clumsy and inconsistent efforts at erasing their culture, created a strong collective sense of ethnic and national identity among Koreans of all social classes.

A SOCIETY IN TURMOIL: THE LEGACY OF COLONIAL RULE

Historians debate over how to evaluate Japanese colonial rule. To what extent did Japan establish the foundation for modern Korea? How much credit or blame Japan can take for developments in the history of North and South Korea is still debated, but there is no doubt that Japan's colonial rule left a complex legacy. In so many ways, the bases for a modern society were established during colonial rule. Japan provided high standards of government efficiency, established much of the infrastructure for a modern industrial society, and laid the foundations for a modern school system. Its administration saw the erosion of the old social order, the emergence of a modern middle class, and the beginnings of an industrial working class. The Japanese provided a model of a closely related people who had appropriated Western science, technology, and some institutions and values, and had established a nation that could successfully compete in the world. The Japanese introduced a government both more efficient and more authoritarian than Koreans had previously known.

Korean society was most profoundly impacted by the last years of Japanese rule. The state became more coercive, and every aspect of life more
politicized and militarized when Japan's imperialist adventure in China
put the colony on a wartime basis.

The lives of almost all Koreans were deeply affected by the colonial
experience. Many of the leaders of postwar Korea—industrialists such as
Chung Ju-young (Chŏng Chu-yŏng) (1915–2001), the founder of Hyundai, and Yi Pyŏng-ch'ŏl (1910–1987), founder of Samsung, and leaders
such as Park Chung Hee (Pak Chŏng-hŭi) (1917–1979), who as South
Korean president oversaw the big push for industrialization in Korea, and
the North Korean dictator Kim Il Sung—were profoundly shaped by their
experiences growing up in colonial Korea. The impact of Japanese rule
upon Korea was especially traumatic after the occupation of Manchuria
in 1931 and the creation of the puppet Manchukuo state the following
year. Korea's position in the Japanese Empire changed from peripheral to
central, as the peninsula became a bridge from the Japanese archipelago
to the Chinese mainland. Industrial development in Korea increased,
particularly in the north, and jobs in the newly industrializing centers
in northern Korea and in Manchuria became available to many Koreans,
setting into motion a great social migration as hundreds of thousands left
their villages to take advantage of these new opportunities. This process
accelerated in 1937, when war broke out between Japan and the Republic
of China. At first the movement of farmers and laborers was mainly voluntary on the part of many poor Koreans, who left their villages in search
of employment in the mines and factories that were mushrooming in the
northern part of the country and in Manchuria, but this soon involved a
forced mobilization of millions of Koreans to work where needed in Korea, Japan, China, and elsewhere in the expanding empire.

The scale of this great social upheaval, which continued to accelerate
in the early 1940s, is extraordinary. The Korean population of Manchuria
swelled after 1931 to perhaps 1.5 million. The fastest growing immigrant
community during the colonial period was in Japan. Korean population
in Japan increased from 26,000 in 1919 to 276,000 in 1929 and 543,000
in 1934.[38] These included students, some of whom settled in Japan, and
laborers working in factories and mines. Life for them in Japan's homogeneous and often xenophobic society could be harsh. Koreans in Japan
were not assimilated but remained outsiders. Thousands of Koreans were
murdered by hysterical Japanese mobs in the aftermath of the Kantō (Tokyo region) earthquake of September 1923. Then, after 1937, a huge number of Koreans came to work in the mines and factories, most voluntarily;
some were simply conscripted as laborers. In 1945 there were 2.4 million
Koreans in Japan, making up a quarter of the industrial labor force. By
1944, as Bruce Cumings has pointed out, 11.6 percent of all Koreans were

residing outside of Korea; and 20 percent were living abroad or in Korea but outside their home provinces.[39] According to Cumings, "forty percent of the adult population was part of this uprooting."[40] This mass movement of people served to break down routines of ordinary life and open up new experiences and possibilities to millions of Koreans. The last years of colonial rule, especially, had shaken up traditional Korean society. This society would be further shaken by the political turmoil and civil war that followed liberation.

Japanese rule, especially its last years, would provide both North and South Korea with a model of state-directed economic development, with the examples of mass mobilization of the population for national purposes, and massive propaganda campaigns. The cult of the Japanese emperor and the many Shinto shrines was to have an echo in the cult of the ruling Kim family of North Korea. Thirty-five years of Japanese rule also helped to foster and shape a powerful sense of Korean nationalism. Significantly it also resulted in an ideologically divided nationalist movement.

KOREA IN GLOBAL PERSPECTIVE:
THE KOREAN NATIONALIST MOVEMENT

The colonial period saw the emergence of an intense Korean nationalism. Chronologically, the growth of nationalist movements within and outside the country coincided with nationalist movements elsewhere in the colonial world, but was perhaps embraced more widely and more passionately than was the case in many other countries. The strong sense of Korean cultural identity, the homogeneity of Korean society, and the intrusive and intense nature of Japanese colonial rule help account for this. The exclusive nature of Japanese culture and their presence in a land that was unaccustomed to foreigners contributed to the sense of Koreans as a distinct and different group. Some Koreans did accept an identity as members of a greater Japanese Empire, but discriminatory practices only reinforced the fact that they were not Japanese. Even the efforts at assimilation were contradicted by all sorts of legal distinctions that were still imposed on Koreans.

In many ways, the nationalist movement in Korea was a typical one among colonial peoples in the first half of the twentieth century. Japan's rule, while allowing some scope for activities expressing ethnic and cultural sentiments, placed severe limits on overt political activity. Furthermore, the colonial authorities often were able to involve prominent Koreans in the public life of the colony, undermining the nationalist credentials of many leading figures in Korea. In its suppression of any calls for independence, and with its insistence on the active participation of everyone in the war effort during the 1930s and 1940s, the Japanese weakened the ability of most of the members of the professional class to serve as effective and credible national leaders. As a result, it was mostly the exiled members of the independence movement that emerged in 1945 with the most unblemished reputations. These included both conservatives such as Syngman Rhee and radicals such as the Communist guerilla Kim Il Sung. In this way, the Japanese colonial administration resembled the Dutch in the East Indies and the French in Indochina more than the British in India. As with Vietnam, the Communists proved to be highly effective organizers. Korea, however, lacked vast remote regions that could provide guerilla strongholds, and the Japanese police and military establishment was more formidable and effective than those of most other colonies. The exile community was also at a disadvantage, since it was so geographically fragmented. Unlike many independence movements, there was no logical base or center for opposition. However, in contrast to many independence movements—Burma, Indonesia, India, or much of Africa—Korean nationalists did not have to deal with separatist movements; the boundaries and unity of Korea were taken for granted.

KOREA IN GLOBAL PERSPECTIVE: KOREA'S COLONIAL EXPERIENCE

How unique was Korea's colonial experience? In many ways it was a typical colony. The Japanese had modeled much of their colonial administration on that of the major European powers. In fact, Japanese colonialism can be seen as a late, imitative form, part of that nation's efforts to achieve parity with the great Western powers. The Japanese promoted industrial development in Korea far more than was the usual case for a colonizer. As a result, Korea in 1945 was industrialized to a greater extent than most colonies, more than any in Asia or Africa. But the nature of the industrialization and economic development in general fit a typical colonial mold. It was designed to produce raw materials and products needed by the mother country, which directed and controlled its development. And in spite of this industrialization, Japan, until World War II at least, saw Korea primarily as a producer of commodities for the home country. The push to grow rice and soybeans and later cotton and wool for the Japanese market, for example, conformed to the conventional pattern of colonial development.

Yet Korea's colonial experience differed from most others in that Korea was neither a contiguous appendage to a land empire nor ruled by a distant overseas power. Only 115 miles from Japan's shores, Korea had a long history of interaction with its colonizer, including the sixteenth-century invasions and attempted conquest. It was a familiar, often menacing neighbor. But Japan shared a common East Asian cultural heritage with Korea. Like Korea, much of its legal, literary, political, and artistic traditions were derived from China. Although Confucianism was not the all-embracing ideology that it was in Korea, Japan remained throughout the colonial period a society profoundly influenced by Confucian values and concepts. Its rule reinforced some of these values, including emphasis on rank, hierarchy, authority, and respect for education, and it married them to Western concepts of science, industry, technology, and bureaucratic efficiency. Japanese propaganda often touted the nation as the vanguard of modern progress for the rest of East Asia, and to some extent it was. Korea could and did often follow Japan's lead in adapting to Western institutions and values—a task made easier by the fact that their languages were similar, not just in grammatical structure but in the commonly shared vocabulary borrowed from Chinese.

Yet few people have shown more bitterness toward their former occupier than have the Koreans. Contemporary Koreans, both in the North and South, almost universally condemn the Japanese rule of Korea as a cruel, brutal occupation. There is little of the open sentimentalism that is sometimes found in other countries toward former colonial rulers. In few former colonies has there been such lingering hatred. Both North and South Korea, to a degree uncommon among postcolonial states, consciously attempted to rid their societies of Japanese influences. The Shinto shrines that dotted the countryside and cities were completely destroyed almost immediately after liberation. In both Koreas, Japanese films, videos, and books were banned after 1945. Japanese words were purged in "language-purification campaigns," despite the fact that Korean, especially as used in South Korea, has absorbed a vast number of foreign loan words, mostly from English.

There are many reasons for this lingering animosity: not the least is that governments in North and South Korea have made anti-Japanese sentiment a rallying point for patriotism. The Koreans have historically been not a little xenophobic and especially wary of the Japanese. The bitterness toward the Japanese was also a result of the intense nature of Japanese rule. In the late 1930s nearly a quarter of a million Japanese served in Korea as bureaucrats; police; garrison soldiers; and employees of state banks, companies, and schools. By way of comparison, the French colony of Vietnam, with a slightly smaller population of 17 million versus 20 million for Korea, in 1937, had 2,920 French administrative personnel; 10,776 French troops; and about 38,000 indigenous personnel.[41] The Japanese personnel in Korea were equal in number to that of the British in India, which had twenty times the population. The vast bureaucracy and police system penetrated down to the village level. While most European colonies were administered by a fairly small number of officials who governed through native underlings and pliant local elites, Japanese colonial rule was direct all the way down to the local neighborhood policeman. Especially important in generating a legacy of hatred were the last years of the colonial regime, which witnessed coercive mass mobilization of the Korean people and the strange attempt at forced assimilation. And it was this wartime aspect of Korea's colonial experience that was historically unique.

Son Pyŏnghŭi et al., Declaration of Independence

We hereby declare that Korea is an independent state and that Koreans are a self-governing people. We proclaim it to the nations of the world in affirmation of the principle of the equality of all nations, and we proclaim it to our posterity preserving in perpetuity the right of national survival. We make this declaration on the strength of five thousand years of history as an expression of the devotion and loyalty of twenty million people. We claim independence in the interests of the eternal and free development of our people in accordance with the great movement for world reform based upon the awakening conscience of mankind. This is the clear command of heaven, the course of our times, and a legitimate manifestation of the right of all nations to coexist and live in harmony. Nothing in the world can suppress or block it.

For the first time in several thousand years, we have suffered the agony of alien suppression for a decade, becoming a victim of the policies of aggression and coercion, which are relics from a bygone era. How long have we been deprived of our right to exist? How long has our spiritual development been hampered? How long have the opportunities to contribute our creative vitality to development of world culture been denied us?

Alas! In order to rectify past grievances, free ourselves from present hardships, eliminate future threats, stimulate and enhance the weakened conscience of our people, eradicate the shame that befell our nation, ensure proper development of human dignity, avoid leaving humiliating legacies to our children, and usher in lasting and complete happiness for our prosperity, the most urgent task is to firmly establish national independence. Today when human nature and conscience are placing the forces of justice and humanity on our side, if every one of our twenty million people arms himself for battle, whom could we not defeat and what could we not accomplish? We do not intend to accuse Japan of infidelity for its violation of various solemn treaty obligations since the Treaty of Amity of 1876. Japan's scholars and officials, indulging in a conqueror's exuberance, have denigrated the accomplishments of our ancestors and treated our civilized people like barbarians. Despite their disregard for the ancient origins of our society and the brilliant spirit of our people, we shall not blame Japan; we must first blame ourselves before finding fault with others. Because of the urgent need for remedies for the problems of today, we cannot afford the time for recriminations over past wrongs.

Our task today is to build up our own strength, not to destroy others. We must chart a new course for ourselves in accord with the solemn dictates of conscience, not malign and reject others for reasons of past enmity or momentary passion. In order to restore natural and just conditions, we must remedy the unnatural and unjust conditions brought about by the leaders of Japan, who are chained to old ideas and old forces and victimized by their obsession with glory.

From the outset the union of the two countries did not emanate from the wishes of the people, and its outcome has been oppressive coercion, discriminatory injustice, and fabrication of statistical data, thereby deepening the eternally irreconcilable chasm of ill will between the two nations. To correct past mistakes and open a new phase of friendship based upon genuine understanding and sympathy—is this not the easiest way to avoid disaster and invite blessing? The enslavement of twenty million resentful people by force does not contribute to lasting peace in the East. It deepens the fear and suspicion of Japan by the four hundred million Chinese who constitute the main axis for stability in the East, and it will lead to the tragic downfall of all nations in our region. Independence for Korea today shall not only enable Koreans to lead a normal, prosperous life, as is their due; it will also guide Japan to leave its evil path and perform its great task of supporting the cause of the East, liberating China from a gnawing uneasiness and fear and helping the cause of world peace and happiness for mankind, which depend greatly on peace in the East. How can this be considered a trivial issue of mere sentiment?

Behold! A new world is before our eyes. The days of force are gone, and the days of morality are here. The spirit of humanity, nurtured through the past century, has begun casting its rays of new civilization upon human history. A new spring has arrived prompting the myriad forms of life to come to life again. The past was a time of freezing ice and snow, stifling the breath of life; the present is a time of mild breezes and warm sunshine, reinvigorating the spirit. Facing the return of the universal cycle, we set forth on the changing tide of the world. Nothing can make us hesitate or fear.

We shall safeguard our inherent right to freedom and enjoy a life of prosperity; we shall also make use of our creativity, enabling our national essence to blossom in the vernal warmth. We have arisen now. Conscience is on our side, and truth guides our way. All of us, men and women, young and old, have firmly left behind the old nest of darkness and gloom and head for joyful resurrection together with the myriad living things. The spirits of thousands of generations of our ancestors protect us; the rising tide of world consciousness shall assist us. Once started, we shall surely succeed. With this hope we march forward.[42]

11

✠

Division and War,
1945 to 1953

The liberation of Korea from Japanese rule was accompanied by its great national tragedy—the division of the country. Several developments during the closing days of World War II proved crucial in creating this division. Most important of these were: the contingencies of the allies as the war was coming to an end, the emerging rivalry between the Soviet Union and the United States, and the scattered and divided nature of the Korean nationalist movement.

The Korean Provisional Government (KPG), which had become virtually moribund by the mid-1920s, revived during Japan's invasion of China and had become closely associated with its sponsor, the Nationalist regime. The Nationalist regime of Chiang Kai-shek in Chungking (Chongqing) promoted the KPG. Chiang wanted a friendly, reliably anticommunist, independent Korea. In April 1942, Chungking proposed that all the allies recognize the KPG as the government of Korea. But this was ignored by the United States. Instead, in early 1943 President Roosevelt and the British foreign secretary, Anthony Eden, agreed that Manchuria and Taiwan (or Formosa, as it was commonly called in the West at that time) would be returned to China and that Korea would be placed under a trusteeship with China, the United States, and one or two other countries.[1] Later that year when Chiang Kai-shek, Franklin Delano Roosevelt, and Winston Churchill met in Cairo to discuss the future of Asia, they issued a communiqué on December 1, in which they stated that China, the United States, and Britain, "mindful of the enslavement of the people of Korea, are determined that in due course Korea shall become free and independent."[2] Roosevelt's plan was for a long trusteeship. Stalin appeared to have gone along with the plan for a trusteeship at the Teheran Conference, which followed the meeting at Cairo.[3] Roosevelt's idea was for a forty-year tutelage, but this was reduced to twenty or thirty years at Yalta.

The Cairo Declaration was important because it was the first public statement on what the allies were planning for Korea. Korea was not of great interest or concern for the United States or Britain, but Roosevelt did have the idea that it should be placed under a trusteeship. The idea may have been influenced by the model of the U.S. role in the Philippines, where Americans saw themselves as tutors preparing that colony for its full independence, which was scheduled for 1946. It was not based on any real knowledge of Korea, its history, culture, or the strong nationalist aspirations of its people. Most Koreans who became aware of the declaration interpreted the phrase "in due course" to mean immediate independence, totally unaware of Roosevelt's well-meaning but, as history would prove, unrealistic plans.

While the idea of some sort of U.S. and other allied-power occupation of Korea had been for a long time part of the plan for the postwar settlement, the division of Korea was the product of expediency. On August 6, 1945, the United States dropped an atomic bomb on Hiroshima; on August 8 the Soviet Union declared war on Japan and immediately began an offensive along Japan's northern frontier in Sakhalin, Manchuria, and along the extreme northeast corner of Korea that borders Siberia. On August 9 the second atomic bomb was dropped on Nagasaki. The Japanese government began signaling its desire to surrender, and on August 15 it did so unconditionally. This rush of events leading to the final surrender of Japan came with an unexpected suddenness. Urgently, the State-War-Navy Coordinating Committee assigned Colonel Dean Rusk and Charles Bonesteel on the night of August 10–11 to draw up a line for the occupation of Korea by Soviet and American forces. While Soviet forces were already entering the northeast of Korea, the closest American forces were 600 miles away in Okinawa and would not be able to reach Korea for several weeks. It was therefore urgent that the United States work out an agreement to prevent the entire peninsula from falling into Soviet hands. As they later explained, Rusk and Bonesteel looked at their map and saw that the thirty-eighth parallel split the country into roughly equal halves but kept Seoul in the southern half. They decided that was where to draw the line. George M. McCune, chief of the Korean section in the Office of Far Eastern Affairs in the U.S. State Department wrote that it was "an arbitrary line, chosen by staff officers for military purposes without political or other considerations."[4] Truman approved the proposal on August 13, and it was sent to Moscow. To the surprise of many, the Soviets almost immediately accepted the line, even though they were in a position to occupy all of the country. Perhaps Stalin hoped by agreeing to a joint military occupation that the door would be left open for a Soviet role in the occupation of Japan and perhaps Europe as well. Recent research suggests he was also concerned about avoiding a potential conflict with the United States in Korea.[5]

It is important to note that the thirty-eighth parallel was an arbitrary line on the map and did not correspond to any geographical, cultural, or historical division of the country. It cut across the two provinces Kyŏnggi and Kangwŏn, across counties, and across natural geographic features. Korea had been a unified country since the seventh century; no Korean had ever proposed a division of their land. Interestingly, outside powers had made similar proposals before. In the 1590s the Japanese military hegemon Hideyoshi had proposed a division of Korea following his unsuccessful attempt to invade and conquer the peninsula in 1592 (see chapter 6). His offer to the Chinese, who had come to Korea's rescue during the invasion, was that the four southern provinces would be ceded to Japan and the northern provinces would be made a sort of buffer kingdom under the Korean monarch. Japan again in 1896 proposed a division, at the thirty-eighth parallel, into a Russian and Japanese sphere, but Russia rejected this. As Japan's position in Korea grew stronger, Russia proposed a division at the thirty-ninth parallel in 1903. It is unlikely that the Americans were aware of these earlier precedents.

The Korean nationalist movement, as discussed earlier, was divided ideologically, fractured organizationally, and geographically dispersed. The Communist movement in Korea had fallen victim to relentless and effective repression by the colonial government. Most of the Communists had been killed, jailed, or driven underground. Yet, while no organized party structure existed, there was a loose network of underground Communists, largely isolated from the internationalist movement and often from each other. The head of the Korean Communist Party was Pak Hŏnyŏng (1900–1955), who had been arrested in 1933 but released in 1939 because he was thought to be insane and harmless. All moderate nationalist movements in Korea had also been repressed during the war. Virtually every prominent Korean had been forced to support the war effort and the Japanese imperialist cause, so there were few non-Communists in Korea with an untarnished nationalist record.

Outside of Korea, the Korean Provisional Government in Chungking had a small force of troops—the Korean Restoration Army (Han'guk Kwangbokkun) under the leadership of Kim Ku. It had about 3,000 or so resistance fighters, who were geographically far removed from Korea. After 1942, these Koreans had been cooperating with U.S. military intelligence officials and advisors in China. In the north of China, a few thousand Koreans were fighting with the Chinese Communist Party, most notably those led by Mu (Kim) Chŏng (1905–1952). He had joined the

Chinese Communists in 1928, participated on the legendary Long March, and operated out of the CCP headquarters in Yanan. Besides these two groups of Koreans in China, there were the former Manchuria-based guerillas that had retreated into Siberia by 1939–1940 and were serving with the Soviet Army. There were also some Korean exiles in the United States; most prominent was Syngman Rhee, who spent the war in Washington promoting Korean independence among any American officials who would listen. But none of these exile groups were regarded very seriously by the great powers or consulted by them, nor did they play much of a role in the events at the immediate end of the war.

THE END OF COLONIAL RULE IN KOREA

As these events were taking place abroad, in Korea the Japanese governor-general, Abe Nobuyuki, aware of the gravity of the situation, began to look for prominent Koreans to work out some sort of postwar transition. On August 9 he started contacts with Song Chin-u, discussing the postwar situation and the possibility of heading a transitional body of prominent Koreans to insure domestic order and prevent anti-Japanese violence until the occupation forces arrived. Song seemed an ideal candidate to lead a transition, since he was well respected, and was less tainted with collaboration activities than most of his contemporaries. He was also conservative and therefore less threatening to the Japanese. Song, however, refused to work with the colonial authorities, so on August 15 they turned to Yŏ Un-hyŏng (1886–1947). Yŏ agreed, but only after insisting that the Japanese release all political prisoners, allow Koreans to carry out peacekeeping and independence-preparation activities without interference, and ensure food supplies.[6] Yŏ had unblemished nationalist credentials that few Koreans not in exile could match. Well educated, a charismatic speaker, he was a leftist but not a Communist, a man of socialist leanings, a proponent of democracy and equality, but an opponent of violent revolution. His choice to head some sort of interim Korean authority might have seemed appropriate, especially as at the time no one in Korea or Japan was aware of the decision by the United States to divide the peninsula into two occupation zones. Soviet forces had begun amphibious landings in Korea by August 14 and quickly overran the industrial northeast of the country; on August 16 they landed at Wŏnsan farther down the coast. It was probably assumed that all of Korea would be under Soviet occupation. From that point of view, the Government-General saw in Yŏ someone who could work with the Communists but who could be trusted to oppose violence against the Japanese. Yŏ then set up the Committee for the Preparation of Korean Independence.

The emperor's August 15 radio announcement of Japan's surrender came to most Koreans as a shock, followed almost immediately by joyous celebration. Koreans fondly recall these first days; people danced, partied, and wept with joy. Symbols of Japanese authority such as the Shinto shrines were destroyed, and everywhere the long-banned Korean flag was displayed. It appears that almost all Koreans felt that independence was imminent; none suspected Allied plans for a trusteeship. Local people of all political persuasions met to plan for independence. People's committees (*inmin wiwŏnhoe*) were organized throughout the country. In a little over two weeks Koreans set up people's committees in every one of the country's thirteen provinces, as well as local people's committees in cities and counties. A controversy over these people's committees has arisen among historians. The speed by which they emerged has suggested to some that there was a secret network throughout the country, perhaps led by the Communists. However, it appears that they were in most cases spontaneous responses to the liberation. Many Communists released from prison or emerging from hiding actively participated in the committees, but they do not seem to have dominated or directed them.

On September 6 several hundred delegates from the people's committees met in Seoul and declared the Korean People's Republic (KPR). Syngman Rhee was named the chair, and Yŏ Un-hyŏng and the conservative businessman Kim Sŏng-su were given prominent positions. The Korean People's Republic appears to have been a broad coalition with Communists and non-Communist leftists being the most active participants. Six days later, the delegates of the KPR drew up a program calling for confiscation of land owned by Japanese and national traitors. They also called for the limiting of rents to 30 percent, an eight-hour workday, a minimum wage, and other reforms. It is interesting to note just how pressing the issue of land reform was. While the KPR may be a good indication of the hopes for quick independence and the demands of tenant farmers, agricultural and industrial laborers, and others, it was a powerless organization, since the authority resided with the U.S. military occupation forces, which never recognized it.

NORTH KOREA UNDER SOVIET OCCUPATION

In P'yŏngyang, local Koreans set up a twenty-member local council of the Committee for the Preparation of Korean Independence (CPKI) that was based in Seoul and headed by the well-known Presbyterian leader Cho Man-sik. The committee was dominated by Christians, although it did contain two Communist members. This is not surprising. While only 2 or 3 percent of Koreans in 1945 were Christians, P'yŏngyang was a center of

Christian activity. Cho, probably one of the most respected leaders in the north, was a natural choice to lead the government there. On August 26, the headquarters of the Soviet Twenty-fifth Army arrived at P'yŏngyang. The Soviets worked with the CPKI, appointing a number of Communists, while maintaining the conservative Cho as its head. On October 19, the Soviets organized a Five Provinces People's Committee with a Five Province Administrative Bureau to administer the country with Cho Man-sik as head. As the Communists took effective control of the organization and the local people's committees, Cho and other Christian leaders organized a Korean Democratic Party in November. In February 1946, Ch'ŏndogyo members organized a Friends Party. The existence of these two parties gave the illusion of a multiparty government in the north, but in reality all power fell into the hands of the Communists.

The Soviets, by working with the people's committees, were able to carry out a relatively smooth and peaceful transfer of power. Moscow brought in several hundred Soviet-Koreans, (Koreans of Soviet citizenship who were the descendants of earlier migrants to Siberia), to assist them in their administration. Initially they had a problem finding appropriate Communist leaders. The local Communist leader, Hyŏn Chun-hyŏk, was too independent, and most of the Communist exiles were in China, far removed from Soviet control. Therefore, they turned to the ex-guerilla soldiers of the Eighty-eighth Red Army Brigade, which included Kim Il Sung and sixty-some others, which had entered North Korea at Wŏnsan on September 19.

Kim was born in 1912 in a family of modest means near P'yŏngyang. His mother was Christian and he seemed to have grown up in a Protestant Christian household. Sometime when he was a boy his family moved to Manchuria, perhaps to escape poverty, as was the case of many others. His education stopped after completing middle school in Manchuria. As a young man, he became involved in anti-Japanese nationalist groups and joined the Northeast Anti-Japanese Army in 1935. After leading a small guerilla band, Kim, like most of the guerillas fighting along the Manchurian border, was forced by the Japanese to flee to Siberia. There, from 1940 to 1945 he sat out the remainder of the war. In September 1945 he was one of several prominent guerilla leaders, such as Kim Ch'aek (1903–1951), Ch'oe Hyŏn, and Kim Il (1910–1984), who became his close associates. Exactly why the Soviet occupation forces decided to support him is not clear. He had achieved some notoriety for his successful raid at Poch'ŏnbo and was familiar to some Soviet officers, while the local domestic Communists were weak and largely unknown to the Russians. For whatever reason, in October the Soviets eventually decided to promote him as the Communist leader in the North. He was publically introduced on October 14, and he began to gain control of the local Communist movement with the support and assistance of the Soviet Union. As the Soviets promoted Kim Il Sung, they removed local Communists who opposed him. In October 1945, the Soviets created the North Korea Branch Bureau of the Korean Communist Party, still headquartered in Seoul. In December of that year Kim Il Sung was appointed to its chairmanship.

SOUTH KOREA UNDER U.S. OCCUPATION

In contrast to the orderly, well-organized Soviet occupation in the North, the American occupation was marked by confusion of purpose, lack of preparation and planning, mixed signals from Washington, and the more open and chaotic politics of the South.

General John R. Hodge, commander of the XXIV Corps in Okinawa, was selected to head the occupation force. Hodge was assigned the task simply because his forces were closest to Korea and Washington felt it was important not to wait too long before establishing a presence there. Still it was not until September 6 that the Americans arrived. Hodge was a competent and honest military man with little background or knowledge of Korea. In fact, the United States in general was not well prepared for the occupation; it had made plans for the occupation of Japan but not Korea. As historian Bruce Cumings has pointed out, South Korea got the occupation meant for Japan. This was demonstrated almost from the beginning, when a number of serious errors were made, and by the lack of translators and interpreters, making the Americans heavily dependent on the few Koreans who were competent in English.

U.S. forces arrived, landing at Inch'ŏn, on September 8. Acting under instructions from Washington, Hodge ignored a delegation from the KPR that sought to meet him at Inch'ŏn. The Americans received an enthusiastic greeting from the jubilant Koreans, who regarded them as liberators. While the role of the United States in defeating Japan left a residual goodwill, the enthusiasm quickly dissipated when the U.S. authorities ordered Koreans to obey Governor-General Abe and his 70,000 Japanese officials. Realizing this was an error, the Americans removed Abe on September 12 and gradually over the next three months the Japanese officials were repatriated back to Japan. Power was transferred to the United States Military Government in Korea (USAMGIK). This awkward start reflected the woeful unpreparedness of the U.S. military for the occupation of Korea. American military and civilian officials lacked clear orders from Washington, especially in the early days, and they found the situation in Korea confusing and chaotic. U.S. military officials were highly suspicious of the local people's committees that were springing up throughout the fall of 1945 and were effectively taking control of much of the countryside. The

Americans feared or suspected Communist infiltration and subversion, and most simply did not fully appreciate the depth of the Korean desire for independence. The Japanese occupation, especially during its last years was a bitter, hateful experience; it was now the time, Koreans felt, to govern themselves without foreigners.

Meanwhile, conservative landowners and businessmen, many linked to Kim Sŏng-su and Song Chin-u, formed the Korean Democratic Party (KDP) on September 16. Looking for Koreans he could work with, Hodge found this group reasonable and, of course, anticommunist. On October 5, he created a Korean Advisory Council with Kim Sŏng-su as head. As Hodge began working with conservatives, he criticized the KPR, declaring on October 10 that it had no authority. This helped to undermine the organization. As conservatives and moderates then left, it became an increasingly radical, Communist-dominated organ. On December 18, Hodge outlawed KPR and it collapsed, although some local peoples committees survived for a while. Adding to the political turmoil was the return of two prominent anticommunist exiled leaders. On October 16, Syngman Rhee arrived in Seoul, managing to finagle a ride on MacArthur's private plane. Four days later, General Hodge introduced Rhee to the Korean public, giving an air of official American endorsement to the longtime U.S.-based exile. At Hodge's request, Kim Ku, the president of the Korean Provisional Government in China, and its vice president, Kim Kyu-sik, returned to Korea in November.

By the late fall, the South Korean political scene included: the Communists under Pak Hŏn-yŏng, still hoping to work with non-Communists to bring about an eventual socialist revolution; the conservatives of the KDP, representing the landowners, businessmen, and wealthy elite; moderate leftists such as Yŏ Un-hyŏng; moderate conservatives such as Kim Kyu-sik; the radical rightist Kim Ku; and Syngman Rhee, who while conservative preferred not to ally with anyone but had his own organization, the Committee for the Rapid Realization of Korean Independence. Then there was the U.S. occupation authority, both fearing the spread of Communism and looking for moderate democrats with a political agenda comprehensible to and comfortable for the Americans.

TRUSTEESHIP

Meanwhile, the allied powers met at the Moscow Conference that began on December 27, 1945, to discuss the postwar settlement. There it was agreed that a four-power trusteeship of the United States, the USSR, China, and Britain would be set up for four to five years. This was a considerable and more realistic reduction for the earlier twenty to thirty years agreed to at Yalta, but it was still four to five years too long for most Koreans. Koreans of all political persuasions, who were still expecting immediate independence, were outraged at the news of a planned trusteeship. Massive demonstrations took place, with all major groups participating. Koreans were united in their opposition to the trusteeship idea. In the midst of the agitation, a potential leader of high standing, Song Chin-u, was assassinated on December 30. The unity of all Koreans in their opposition to the trusteeship was short lived. The Soviet Union ordered the Communists to support the trusteeship, which they dutifully did by switching their position on January 3, a move that cost them much popular support in the South. In North Korea, Cho Man-sik, who criticized the trusteeship, was removed from office on January 4, 1946.

At the conference, an American-Soviet Joint Commission was created to work out details of the trusteeship. Before it met in March 1946, preliminary talks were held in Seoul in January. A number of basic issues were brought up, such as the problem of electricity. Most of the South's electricity came from the North, and the USAMGIK wanted to guarantee its supply; it also wanted to allow free movement across the thirty-eighth parallel where the Soviets had set up roadblocks, but no progress was made on this or on other issues. When the Joint Committee met in March, the Soviets refused to allow representatives of any organization that did not support the proposed trusteeship to participate. This, in practice, meant that almost all political groups in the South other than the Communists were excluded from any consultative role in the trusteeship. Deadlocked, the talks were postponed indefinitely on May 8.

By early 1946, the outlines of separate occupational zones, with their own administrations had already appeared. This was an unintended outcome of the military occupation. No Korean wanted or foresaw such a development. Nor does it appear to have been the initial intention of either the USSR or the United States to create two separate states.

ESTABLISHING A SEPARATE REGIME IN THE NORTH

In retrospect, it is clear that a Communist regime was rapidly being put in place in the Soviet zone by early 1946. There is evidence that the Soviets were genuinely interested in the trusteeship and preferred to work through a National Front government with the Communists in ultimate control. It is even possible that Moscow would have settled for a neutral and united Korea.[7] But with the opposition of Cho Man-sik and other non-Communists to the trusteeship during the Moscow Conference, the Soviets began rapidly pushing for a communization of the North. On February 8, 1946, the Soviets created a North Korea Provisional People's Committee to carry out a number of reforms. It was supposedly a broad coalition of all political groups, but in reality it was dominated by the

Communists, who were rapidly consolidating their control over the country. The Provisional People's Committee carried out the nationalization of Japanese industry. The most important reform, the Law on Land Reform, was enacted in March. It confiscated all lands owned by Japanese and national traitors and limited all other holding to 5 *chŏngbo* (12.25 acres). This was, in effect, a redistribution of land from large landlords to individual farm families. Taxes on farmers were fixed to 25 percent of the crop. The land reform addressed an important concern of millions of rural poor who made up a majority of the population. Although there were not as many large landlords in the North it was still a sweeping change. Its implementation was also made easier by the fact that thousands of rich landlords, fearing repression, had already fled south of the thirty-eighth parallel. The regime carried out a number of important measures in the spring and summer of 1946, creating large-scale social organizations that aimed at mobilizing women, peasants, workers, and other groups that had previously had little power in Korea, and granting equality to women.[8] The provisional government also announced plans for universal primary education. At the same time, movement across the border was further restricted and the rudiments of a defense force established.

In June the North Korean Branch Bureau of the Korean Communist Party headed by Kim Il Sung became the North Korea Workers' Party. It merged with another Communist party, the Sinmindang (New People's Party) made up of Korean Communists returning from China and led by Kim Tu-bong. The North Korea Workers' Party held its first party congress in August of 1946. Then in December 1946, a Korean National Democratic Front (KNDF) consisting of all northern parties, plus representatives of all southern workers parties was formed. Shortly afterward, elections were held for local people's committees and the KNDF received 97 percent of the vote. Delegates from these people's committees met in February 1947 as a Congress of People's Committees, which elected a People's Assembly. Thus, step-by-step, a centralized government with branches at every local level took shape. This new government organized women, youth, labor, and intellectuals in support of a new social and economic order under the guidance of the North Korean Workers' Party. Meanwhile, the Soviets continued to promote Kim Il Sung as the leader, placing his picture in public places alongside that of Stalin. In October 1946 they named the main university Kim Il Sung University.

THE BEGINNINGS OF A NEW REGIME IN THE SOUTH

In the South, the USAMGIK had a less sure sense of the direction than the Soviets, but it too moved toward setting up a separate, centralized regime acting under U.S. guidance. On February 14, 1946, a Representative Democratic Council was formed with the intention of representing various points of view; but it was dominated by conservatives and had little power. In August, the USAMGIK announced plans to establish an Interim Legislative Assembly. This had ninety members; forty-five elected and forty-five appointed by the USAMGIK. Elections were held, but these were boycotted by leftists. Kim Kyu-sik, a moderate conservative, was made the head. This assembly was riddled with factionalism and accomplished little. Political problems were complicated by economic ones. Economic conditions in the South were a major challenge. One and a half million refugees from China, Manchuria, Japan, and North Korea arrived from August 1945 to August 1946.[9] Inflation was a serious problem, undermining savings and adding to economic uncertainty. Industries were idle and much of the population unemployed.

To maintain law and order the USAMGIK created the Korean National Police (KNP) headed by KDP member Chang T'aek-sang (1893–1969). Its members were mostly Korean police who had served under the Japanese. Unfortunately, they employed the same brutal methods that they had learned from their former colonial masters. In January 1946, the USAMGIK created a 25,000-member constabulary force, a paramilitary force that became the nucleus for the South Korean Army. To train officers, the USAMGIK established a Korean Military Academy. Initially it selected twenty veterans of the Japanese Army, twenty from the Kwantung Army, and twenty from the Restoration Army to serve as the first class. However, most the members of the Restoration Army refused to serve with those who had participated in the Imperial Japanese cause, so that the new officer corps was largely composed of those who had served in the Japanese forces during World War II. Thus, in the view of some Korean nationalists, both the police and the emerging military forces were staffed with collaborators, not true Korean patriots.

A major problem for the USAMGIK was the shift in tactics by the Communists from an attempt to work with other groups in the South to one of attempting to disrupt the military government. Those angry over the proposed trusteeship joined the Communists and other leftist groups. Discontent from workers suffering from inflation and economic hardships and peasants impatiently waiting for land reform contributed to the tensions and disorder that characterized the American occupation zone. In June 1946, the military banned trade unions but strikes continued. On September 24, a Pusan railway strike spread and led to large uprisings in Taegu, the South's third-largest city. The uprising was put down with much loss of life, and afterward, most of the Communist leaders were jailed or fled to the North.

The most effective political leader was Syngman Rhee, who used the antitrusteeship movement to advance his political stature. Rhee started out with his impeccable nationalist credentials, his personal prestige, and the impression that he was somehow the favorite of the Americans. As the Koreans were losing patience with the U.S. occupation, he was able to become a champion of immediate Korean independence over American trusteeship. The United States found him too nationalistic, too antileftist, too authoritarian, and too difficult to work with. They looked for more moderate leaders with strong anticommunist credentials. In October, Yŏ Un-hyŏng and Kim Kyu-sik formed a Coalition Committee of Rightists and Leftists to create a moderate center away from the increasingly repressive conservatives manning the police and constabulary and the leftist agitators. Hopes by some Americans that this organization would emerge as a new force were dashed when the charismatic Yŏ was assassinated by an unknown assailant on July 19, 1947. The rightists, who controlled the police, made no real effort to find the assassin. Desperate to find a moderate leader, Hodge welcomed the return to Korea of Sŏ Chae-p'il, the participant in the 1884 Kapsin Coup and the leader of the Independence Club in the 1890s. Hodge wanted Sŏ to take a leadership role and challenge Rhee. But Sŏ, a very old man, arrived in Seoul in July 1947 dying of cancer and soon returned to the United States.

TOWARD DIVISION

The American-Soviet Joint Committee met again from April to July 1947 in another attempt to work out ways to cooperate on establishing a unified independent Korea. The Soviets continued to insist that those organizations or parties that opposed the trusteeship must not be allowed representation. The U.S. government did not want to stay in Korea for long, and the talks with the Soviet Union were not making any progress, so in September it turned to the UN. The United Nations created a UN Temporary Committee on Korea (UNTCOK) to move the country toward independence. The UN plan was to hold elections throughout Korea for a unified National Assembly no later than March. Power would be transferred to this new political authority, the Soviet and American forces would then withdraw, and Korea would achieve its full sovereignty. In retrospect this plan seems to have been doomed, since it was clear that two separate political systems were already taking shape on the peninsula. It was unrealistic to think that the U.S.-supported regime in the South that had been repressing the Communists would accept a Communist victory or that the Soviets would accept a non-Communist government on their side of the border. The Communists who dominated the government in the

North and the conservative, anticommunists who dominated the South were moving along very different paths.

Since the Soviet Union did not recognize the authority of UNTCOK, there was no way it could sponsor elections in the North. It therefore decided on February 26 to hold elections in "accessible" areas, in other words in the South. Many southern Koreans worried that such elections would in fact create a separate government in the South. They still did not give up hope of unity. Nonetheless, elections were held May 10 for a 200-member National Assembly. Many people boycotted it, as they realized the elections meant the end of achieving a unified government. Although there were more than 300 registered political parties, nearly half the members were independents. The largest party, the conservative Korean Democratic Party, received only twenty-nine seats. Syngman Rhee was made chair of the Assembly. On July 17, the National Assembly adopted a constitution, which required elections for the National Assembly every two years. Every four years the Assembly elected a president, who had strong executive powers. Three days later it elected Rhee by an overwhelming margin as the Republic of Korea's first president. The only other person to receive any votes was Kim Ku; sixteen Assemblymen voted for him. On August 15, 1948, the Republic of Korea (ROK, Korean: Taehan Min'guk) was proclaimed.

The U.N. General Assembly on December 12 accepted the UNTCOK report that the elections were "a valid expression of the free will of the electorate" of that part of the country where they could be monitored; and it declared that the ROK was not only a "lawful" government but also "the only such government in Korea."[10] Authorities in the North then went ahead with their own elections to a new Supreme People's Assembly, which included delegates representing the South as well as the North, the former supposedly chosen through secret "illegal elections." The new assembly declared the Democratic People's Republic of Korea (DPRK, Korean: Chosŏn Inmin Minjujuŭi Konghwaguk) on September 9, 1948. Thus what came to be called in the West North Korea and South Korea came into being as sovereign states.

THE REPUBLIC OF KOREA

The new Republic of Korea began in a precarious state. The North Koreans had cut off the electric power supply, contributing to an already shattered economy. It was an economy that had been geared toward supplying Japan with its needs. Japan, however, was no longer importing Korean products. The South had been the rice basket, but there were no external markets for its production. Most of the industry was in the

North. What was located in the ROK was in a sorry state. With its Japanese suppliers and markets gone, the Japanese technicians repatriated, erratic power supplies, and the confusion that followed the government takeover of Japanese enterprises, the meager industrial base was in shambles. Half the country's industries had ceased to operate; the remainder were working at only 20 percent of capacity. South Korea, instead, was heavily reliant on U.S. aid, which amounted to $116 million in 1948–1949, but the Americans were wary of a heavy economic commitment and cut the aid in half during the 1949–1950 period.

President Syngman Rhee governed the state in an authoritarian style. Despite his American education and his decades spent in Hawaii and the U.S. mainland, his manner was autocratic rather than democratic. He carried an antagonistic attitude toward the National Assembly, where his supporters numbered hardly more than a quarter of the 200 seats. To maintain his authority, he relied on the bureaucracy, the police, and the military, all dominated by members who had loyally served in their posts under the Japanese. All six divisions of the ROK Army formed to replace the constabulary had commanders who had served in the Japanese forces. One, Kim Sŏk-wŏn (1893–1978), headed a special unit to hunt down Kim Il Sung in the late 1930s.[11] Thus the government was open to charges that it was staffed by collaborators, which the many independents in the National Assembly were quick to point out. Since Rhee's own nationalist, anti-Japanese credentials were impeccable, he was able to shield his officials, and they in turn served him. This he had to do when in September 1948 the Assembly passed a National Traitors Act and began investigations of those guilty of serving the colonial authority. Rhee resorted to intimidation and the arrests of assemblymen to protect his base.

To maintain his government's grip on power Rhee made use of the various youth organizations that flourished after the war. Among these was Yi Pŏm-sŏk's (1899–1972) Korean National Youth Corps. Yi himself had an interesting career. Born in Kyŏnggi Province in 1899, he fought as a guerilla on the Sino-Korean border in the 1920s. In 1933, he went to Germany to study and then to China, where he became an admirer of the Nationalist leader Chiang Kai-shek and of his paramilitary Blueshirts (modeled after the Italian Fascist Blackshirts and the Nazi Brownshirts).[12] Under the slogan "*minjok chisang, kukka chisang*" (nation first, state first), Yi's Korean National Youth Corps became the largest and most impressive of the many youth groups after the war. In order to keep Yi under control and to utilize his youth corps, Rhee made him his prime minister. There were other youth groups as well, such as the Sŏbuk (Northwest) Youth, a violent anticommunist group containing many refugees from the North. Thus the politics of South Korea was dominated by fear of Communist subversion, a desire and intent to unify the country by force

if necessary, and by quarrels and tensions over the question of collaboration during Japanese rule. The presence of so many who had served and
even profited under the Japanese threatened to undermine the legitimacy
of the government. Compounding all these problems were the severe
economic slump, the difficulty of absorbing huge numbers of refugees,
and continual clashes along the border.

An example of the new state's instability was played out tragically
on Cheju, now a popular resort island off the southern coast of Korea,
"Korea's Hawaii." Cheju was the scene of perhaps the most horrendous
civil conflict in Korea. There in May 1948, protests against the holding of
separate elections in the South became a violent insurrection. The island-
ers, numbering about 100,000, were able to utilize caches of small arms
and the miles of defensive tunnels left by the Japanese, who had prepared
to make a stand there against allied invaders. A long campaign in which
the population was herded into fortified villages or concentration camps
took place before the rebellion was subdued in April 1949. Estimates of
casualties vary, but some place the figure has high as 30,000, an astounding 30 percent of the population.

A further example of the fragility of the new regime became apparent
only weeks after the Republic of Korea was proclaimed. On September 13,
1948, the American military completed the transfer of administration to
the Koreans, and on October 13, the United States began its withdrawal of
troops. A week later, units of the newly formed Army of the Republic of
Korea, which were assembled in the southern port of Yŏsu on their way
to put down the rebellion on the island of Cheju, themselves rebelled.
After a few days of heavy fighting, the revolt was quelled, although some
soldiers and supporters continued to hold out in nearby mountains. The
Yŏsu Rebellion, occurring almost immediately after responsibility for
national security was transferred from the U.S. military to the republic's
forces, was a powerful blow to the confidence of the new government,
which reacted with a heightened emphasis on internal security.

On October 27, 1948, the National Assembly passed a Law for Special
Punishments for Rioters, and on November 20, a more sweeping National Security Law was issued; both gave the National Police, which
had proven itself a reliable instrument of control at Yŏsu, broad authority to arrest those who were endangering the security of the state. This
law worded antistate activities in such a vague way that it could be used
against all kinds of real and perceived enemies. It would remain as one of
the most often used and controversial laws in South Korea. Almost every
administration for the next half century used it at times for its political advantage. Consequently, a staggeringly large number of Koreans became
victims of these measures. More than 700 persons were arrested as subversives in the first week of November alone. American sources estimated

that by mid-1949 there were more than 30,000 political prisoners in South Korean jails. Rumors of North Korean infiltrators and conspiratorial activity by subversives were a pervasive part of the South Korean scene in late 1948. On December 1, 1948, for instance, the Seoul chief of police had posters placed on the city streets proclaiming "the North Korean People's Army has already begun its invasion of South Korea. . . . Persons inciting civil disturbances will be shot on sight."[13]

Purges were carried out in the schools, where hundreds of teachers were arrested; in government offices; and in every institution. By some estimates, in the spring of 1950 the number of people in jail had swelled to 60,000, the majority for violating the National Security Act. Meanwhile, the National Assembly elections of May 1950 resulted in only 31 incumbents winning another term. A new, less educated and less politically experienced Assembly was elected. Of these only 57 were Rhee supporters, 27 came from minor parties, and 126 were independents, many anti-Rhee. Anticipating an unfavorable outcome, Rhee attempted to postpone the elections but was forced to hold them as scheduled due to U.S. pressure. Such was the troubled and unstable situation of South Korea on the eve of the Korean War.

THE DEMOCRATIC PEOPLE'S REPUBLIC OF KOREA

North Korea during the 1948–1950 period was a contrast to the instability of the Republic of Korea. The Communist regime was firmly in command. The North Korea Workers' Party, renamed in 1949 the Korea Workers' Party after its merger with the South Korea Workers' Party, consisted of Kim Il Sung and his partisans, who shared key positions with the Yanan Communists such as Kim Tu-bong, some prominent Soviet Koreans, and Pak Hŏn-yŏng and other southern Communists who had fled north. The North Korean government had begun to carry out sweeping reforms. The regime launched massive programs to promote adult literacy. It nationalized major industries and made a start at developing a viable economy under the 1949–1950 two-year economic plan, the product of Japanese-trained economists. North Korea benefitted from the array of Japanese-built industrial plants it inherited, its rich mineral resources, and its ample sources of electric power generated by the hydroelectric dams built by the colonial administration. Most importantly, perhaps, was the land reform that had been carried out during 1946, in which large holdings were confiscated and redistributed among tenant farmers and small landholders. This provided a basis for rural support and helped legitimize the new state.

Furthermore, the North Korean regime of Kim Il Sung had few of the problems of legitimacy that weakened the South Korean government, since Kim Il Sung, his guerilla partisans, and the other Communists had untarnished credentials as patriotic, anti-Japanese resistance fighters. Kim Il Sung was not yet the absolute dictator he would later become, but he had the backing of the Soviets and was clearly in overall command of the state. He was aided by a corps of several hundred Soviet-Koreans, who provided administrative and technical expertise, and by the veterans who had fought with the Chinese Communists and thus possessed considerable military experience. Unlike the South, there was no significant internal opposition. The Korean Workers' Party (KWP) was a mass organization of 700,000 members under his control. The Stalinist-model command economy that was constructed under Soviet tutelage was well suited for mobilizing the population for war. A confident North Korean government then sought to unify the country.

ON THE EVE OF THE KOREAN WAR

One of the great controversies in recent history has been the origins of the Korean War. The war has been seen as inevitable by some, a tragic and avoidable mistake by others. The division of Korea into North and South was an unanticipated and unacceptable outcome to almost all Koreans. Leaders in both North Korea and South Korea viewed the establishment of separate regimes as tragic but only temporary. In the South, Syngman Rhee called for reunification, as did Kim Il Sung. Frequent clashes took place along the thirty-eighth parallel.

The volatile situation was only made worse by Korea's entanglement in the Cold War. U.S.-Soviet rivalry already existed in 1945 and intensified over the next several years. The Soviet Union's support of international Communist movements, its view of world history as the inevitable struggle between the socialist and capitalist world, with the former eventually victorious, clashed with the American fear of Communism and desire to establish and maintain a peaceful world order with governments amenable to the U.S. and allied trade and investment. The Cold War came into clear focus with the Truman Doctrine of March 1947 and the American policy of containment. The U.S.-Soviet rivalry focused on Europe, where American and Soviet forces faced each other. The Berlin blockade of 1948–1949 sharpened these tensions; the creation of NATO in April 1949 gave the U.S.-led alliance in Europe an institutional form. While U.S. attention was mainly directed at Europe, Asia was an area of increasing concern for the United States and its allies. The Chinese civil war (1946–1949) ended with the Chinese Communist victory and the proclamation of the People's Republic of China on October 1, 1949. In February 1950, Mao Zedong signed the Sino-Soviet Treaty of Friendship, Alliance and Mutual Assistance, making China and the USSR formal allies. The United States, which had invested considerable military aid in an unsuccessful bid to support the Nationalists under Chiang Kai-shek, now largely wrote him off as he fled to Taiwan. By early 1950, the United States saw the fall of this last stronghold as inevitable. The "loss" of China to the Communists put pressure on the Truman administration to draw the line of containment in Asia, but at the same time, most U.S. policy makers wanted to avoid a land war in Asia, which was less important to them than Europe.

There was consequently a somewhat ambiguous American position on South Korea. The United States supported the state and wanted to prevent Communism from spreading closer to Japan, which all agreed was vital to U.S. interests; however, the American political leaders in the Truman administration and in Congress did not want to invest too much in a land that remained of peripheral concern. When the United States withdrew its troops from Korea it allocated funds for the establishment of a 65,000-man ROK Army and also left behind a 500-member Korean Military Advisory Group (KMAG) to help train this new South Korean force. The United States also provided generous economic aid to Seoul. But this generosity waned; economic aid after 1949 was considerably reduced; and funding for the South Korean Army was limited. Americans were particularly wary of President Rhee's strident nationalism and were concerned over reports of ROK raids along the northern border, as they wanted to avoid the risk of conflict on the peninsula. Only small arms were provided for the ROK forces, and no significant aircraft. Even in small arms, the ROK Army had only a fifteen-day supply in June 1950.[14] The United States was unclear about the extent of its commitment; the most famous example was Secretary of State Dean Acheson's January 1950 press conference in which he excluded South Korea from the U.S. defensive perimeter; it would instead have to rely on the UN.

The Soviet Union, as well, sought to limit its commitment to Korea and was reluctant to see a war start there, but this changed. From the start, the USSR provided an earlier and more extensive buildup of the North Korean armed forces. After the Soviet forces pulled out at the end of 1948, they provided more heavy military equipment including tanks and artillery. Thousands of Koreans were sent to the USSR for training in the use of this equipment. But the key factor in North Korea's military buildup was the determination of its leadership, especially Kim Il Sung, to unify the country by force.

North Korean leaders had hopes that the inevitable armed conflict could be carried out at least in part by Communist guerillas in the South.

There were some active groups in the southern part of the country, particularly in the mountainous areas in the southwest. The insurgency was geographically confined to a small area and suffered substantial losses to South Korean counterinsurgency campaigns during 1948–1949 and 1949–1950. Certainly by 1949, if not earlier, Kim was convinced that an invasion by his forces was necessary for unification. North Korea's army was large and grew larger, with 150,000 men under arms by June 1950 compared to less than 100,000 in the ROK. It had many more experienced troops than South Korea's military. In late 1946, North Korea began sending recruits to Manchuria to aid the Chinese Communists in that crucial area. In 1947, Kim Ch'aek led 30,000 Koreans across the border to assist Mao's forces. About 15–20 percent of all Communist forces in Manchuria were Korean.[15] With the Communist victory in 1949, tens of thousands of veterans began streaming back into North Korea. With his tanks, artillery, and other arms, and his troops fresh from combat, Kim was convinced any invasion of the South would be easy, a matter of a few days. Seoul was not far from the border and would fall shortly after the invasion, and the ROK would collapse before the Americans could intervene. He was further persuaded by Pak Hŏn-yŏng and his South Korean colleagues, who argued that thousands of South Koreans would rise up in support of an invasion by the North.

In June 1949 the North Koreans created the Democratic Front for the Unification of the Fatherland, a coalition of Communists and the small token non-Communist political groups whose aim was to unify the Korean peninsula and remove both the "Rhee clique" and the Americans. Meanwhile Kim and Pak made visits to Moscow to persuade Stalin to support an invasion. At first Stalin was reluctant to get involved, but he came to believe that this was a low-risk, sure victory. The Soviets may have also liked the idea of unifying Korea as a strategic buffer state on its border, and of drawing American attention away from Europe. In January Stalin signaled his support of the plan. Moscow made it clear that it would assist with military planning and training but not with troop support, and it wanted Mao Zedong to commit himself to assist if necessary. Despite some reservations, Mao agreed in April. It appears that not all the North Korean leadership was so eager for the invasion. Moscow sent a team of military experts to assist in drawing up the plans. Finally Stalin gave the final go-ahead for approval; Kim was to set the date. Some historians have argued that the Korean War had begun before the North Korean invasion on June 25, 1950. Armed clashes involving thousands of troops and hundreds of casualties took place along the border. These were often initiated by ambitious young officers of the ROK Army, and a North Korean–supported guerilla insurgency existed in the South. But these were all dwarfed by the immensity of the conflict that began with P'yŏngyang's invasion.

THE KOREAN WAR

South Koreans often call the Korean War the "June 25th Incident," for it was on June 25, 1950, that this horrendous conflict, perhaps the bloodiest of the Cold War, began. On that day, predawn artillery barrages began on the troublesome Ongjin Peninsula. Within hours, North Korea launched a full-scale offensive along the border. The KPA was initially focused on capturing Seoul. Kim Il Sung's plan was to quickly capture the capital; he apparently believed the rest of the state would then soon crumble. The attack took the United States, the ROK, and most of the world by surprise. Just two days earlier, a UN team of observers had completed an inspection tour of the border without suspecting an imminent invasion. Better equipped with heavy artillery and tanks and better trained with thousands of veterans of the Chinese civil war, the KPA had a clear military superiority over the more poorly equipped and trained South Korean Army. ROK forces defended Seoul for two days and then began to crumble. Seoul quickly fell amid horrendous scenes of thousands of panicked, fleeing civilians. Hundreds were killed as the South Koreans prematurely blew up the Han River Bridge while it was packed with civilians heading southward. The Truman administration reacted almost immediately as soon as the scale of the invasion was confirmed. On June 27, Truman authorized General MacArthur to use U.S. air and naval forces at his disposal to support the ROK Army. Uncertain of support from a Republican-dominated Congress, he went directly to the United Nations and called for a resolution giving the United States authority to intervene. This passed quickly, as the Soviet Union was boycotting the UN to protest the refusal of the organization to allow the new Communist regime in Beijing to take China's seat, still held by the Nationalist government now headquartered on Taiwan. The UN Security Council resolution called for the withdrawal of forces by the Democratic People's Republic of Korea (DPRK) and called for UN members to assist the ROK. On July 7, the UN Security Council established a unified military command under the United States. Eventually sixteen nations contributed forces. By the spring of 1951, this included 12,000 British, 8,500 Canadian, 5,000 Turkish, and 5,000 Filipino troops.[16] But the U.N. action would mainly be an American operation, with the United States supplying the bulk of the troops, paying the cost, and taking total command.

U.S. troops from occupied Japan, where about 100,000 American forces were stationed, began to arrive in Korea on June 30. America at this time was not well prepared for the conflict. The occupation forces in Japan were largely involved in administrative duties and had little combat readiness. The U.S. armed forces had been downsizing since the end of World War II from 12 million men and women in uniform in 1945 to 1.6

million in June 1950. There were less than 600,000 in the army and many of these were in Europe. When the first American troops saw action at Osan, south of Seoul, on July 5, they were forced into retreat along with their accompanying ROK forces.

By this time, the KPA was advancing steadily south. The DPRK's forces captured Taejŏn in early July, then advanced toward Pusan, where the South Korean government had fled. Although the ROK forces were totally outmatched by the KPA and Seoul fell in days, the retreating South Korean troops did not collapse as fast as the North Koreans had expected but often put up stubborn resistance. Nor did large bands of guerillas appear, although there was some Communist guerilla activity in the southeastern mountains, remnants of those that had not yet been subdued. Most active leftists in the South had been killed or imprisoned or had fled to the North by June 1950. By and large, the South Korean population fled or acquiesced to the North Koreans but with some minor exceptions did not rise up in arms against their own government. So Kim's expectation that the war would be over in a matter of days was wrong. By early August, the ROK had shrunk to a small area in the southeast corner of the country around Pusan, the so-called Pusan perimeter. But enough U.S. forces had arrived to halt the KPA offensive, and the war temporarily stalemated.

By early August, the Chinese were already becoming concerned, and Mao had decided to send Chinese volunteers to assist P'yŏngyang if the U.S. forces were to reverse the tide of war. Meanwhile, General Douglas MacArthur, who had been put in command of the UN forces, came up with a daring plan to launch a surprise landing at Inch'ŏn, totally outflanking and trapping the KPA. Over the objections of many military officials in Washington, who feared it was too risky, MacArthur brought 80,000 marines and 260 ships to Inch'ŏn, negotiating the treacherous tides and sandbars, and landed. Although Soviet and Chinese warnings had been made to Kim Il Sung that the Americans might land on the west coast, he was focusing on the Pusan perimeter and taken completely by surprise. U.S. and ROK forces fought their way back into Seoul, and by the end of September most of the KPA was in nearly total disarray, although some KPA forces managed to retreat intact up the east coast. Had the United States been willing to accept the prewar status quo, the war could have ended soon after. North Korean forces had been defeated at a heavy cost for South Korea. One estimate is that 111,000 South Koreans had been killed, and 57,000 were missing. Over 300,000 homes were destroyed. UN forces lost about 7,000 killed or missing.[17] But the North Korean forces in the South largely disintegrated and were no longer a threat.

Unfortunately, the war did not stop at the end of September. MacArthur, as well as Syngman Rhee, was determined to "roll back" the North Koreans. MacArthur wanted the complete destruction of the DPRK;

the South Korean leaders wanted reunification, which now seemed so close. The UN resolution had only authorized that the North Koreans be repelled. Some in the United States and some allies, especially Britain, feared widening the war, for there was the possibility of Chinese or even Soviet intervention. China, which maintained no diplomatic relations with the United States, sent a warning in early October through India's ambassador in Beijing that China would not tolerate a U.S. presence on its border. On September 30, ROK forces crossed the thirty-eighth parallel in pursuit of the KPA troops. Perhaps overconfident after the success of Inch'ŏn, Washington now gave MacArthur permission to destroy all KPA forces, and on October 7, the UN passed a vaguely worded resolution that approved the use of UN troops to cross the thirty-eighth parallel for the purpose of establishing a unified government. On October 9, UN forces moved north of the parallel. Throughout October, UN and ROK forces, which were under UN authority, swept across North Korea capturing P'yŏngyang and other major cities while the DPRK government fled to the mountainous strongholds near the Manchurian border. A concerned Stalin, not yet certain of China's military intention, ordered Kim Il Sung to retreat to Manchuria. On October 20, a triumphant President Rhee visited P'yŏngyang.

Just as Korea appeared to become reunified under UN forces, the Chinese forces intervened. When the UN forces crossed into North Korea, the Chinese immediately made the decision to begin sending troops. Some members of the Chinese leadership hesitated about intervening, fearing a conflict with the United States, but Mao prevailed. He argued for the need to have a buffer to protect China; he did not want U.S. troops on his border. Mao also hoped to drive the American imperialists out of the Korean peninsula altogether and promote the revolutionary cause in Asia. Moreover, a war would be useful in consolidating the new regime's hold over China and mobilizing the population.[18] The Chinese forces came in as the Chinese People's Volunteers (CPV), not as the regular People's Liberation Army, but they were in fact regular forces led by veteran general Peng Dehuai. On October 19, the Chinese forces under Peng began entering Korea; they did so discreetly, avoiding drawing attention to their large numbers. The UN forces meanwhile fought scattered units of the KPA, guerillas, and some CPV units, but they did not expect a massive intervention by the Chinese. Chinese warnings to the Americans through diplomatic channels were dismissed, and intelligence analysts disagreed as to the significance of troop buildups along the Manchurian border. In November 24, MacArthur began an offensive to complete the war before Christmas; in response, the Chinese counterattacked in force on November 27. Overextended and overconfident, the UN troops were forced into a full retreat. Chinese forces advanced as swiftly as the UN and ROK forces had done weeks earlier. On December 6, Chinese and North Koreans troops retook P'yŏngyang; within two weeks, almost all of North Korea was under Communist control. The Chinese advanced south, crossing the thirty-eighth parallel and retaking Seoul on January 4. But by late January their offensive was losing momentum. Driven back to the thirty-seventh parallel, the UN forces regrouped and stopped the Chinese. A new offensive in February was repelled with enormous Chinese losses. The Chinese sought to compensate for their inferior firepower by launching massive assaults, the so-called "human wave" tactic, but the UN forces were able to repulse these and retake Seoul on March 15. The city had changed hands for the fourth time in less than a year.

The Truman administration, having pushed the Communist forces back to roughly around the thirty-eighth parallel, was willing to negotiate a truce. Efforts in this direction, however, were undermined by MacArthur, who stated his position in a public "no substitute for victory" letter that called for widening the war. On April 11, 1951, Truman dismissed MacArthur as commander, replacing him with General Matthew Ridgeway, a competent and more obedient commander. By spring, Mao was ready to accept a stalemate with the peninsula divided approximately where it had been before the outbreak of the conflict. With Stalin's approval, he signaled his willingness to begin armistice talks. In July, formal negotiations began as representatives of the Chinese People's Volunteers, the Korean People's Army, and the United Nations command met. The war, however, would continue for two more years. The initial problems— the creation of a line of demarcation for the two Koreas, the establishment of a demilitarized zone (DMZ), and the creation of a Military Armistice Commission—were agreed on. It was clear that the boundary line would be roughly similar but not exactly the same as the thirty-eighth parallel, extending a little below it to the west and above it to the east. The main stumbling block was the issue of prisoner exchange. The UN held 95,000 KPA and 20,000 CPV prisoners; the Communists held 16,000 ROK and a small number of UN prisoners. The UN command insisted that the prisoner repatriation be voluntary, while the Chinese and North Koreans insisted on a general exchange. Many North Korean prisoners and some Chinese did not want to return. The small number of North Koreans and Chinese who opted for exchange was unacceptable to the Communists. By early 1952 the talks were at a logjam.

The first year of the war had a horrific impact on Korea. When the North Koreans retook Seoul and other parts of the South, they set up people's committees. DPRK officials confiscated the property of the ROK government, its officials, and "monopoly capitalists," and drew up plans to redistribute land in the countryside, completing the partial land reform that had begun under the U.S. occupation. They released political prisoners from the jails, many of whom sought the opportunity to get revenge on the police and others who had persecuted them. Thousands of young men were impressed into the North Korean Army. The Communists committed a number of atrocities. In general, few South Koreans showed much enthusiasm for their liberators, and many fled. Pusan and other southern cites swelled with refugees. Pusan became the wartime capital of the ROK. When the ROK forces occupied the North they in turn carried out ruthless purges of Communists, committing their own share of atrocities. Most people in North Korea showed as little enthusiasm for their liberators as southerners had. As with most civil wars, this was a vicious, unpleasant conflict. For the millions of Koreans caught up in the conflict such as Lee Young Ho, it was a true and confusing nightmare. Lee was a seventeen-year-old high school student in Seoul when the North Koreans occupied the city. His frightened family attempted to stay at home but Lee, venturing on the street, was taken into custody by the occupiers and, without his family knowing his whereabouts, was forced into the North Korean Army, only to desert during the hasty retreat in the fall of 1950. He then wound up fighting in the South Korean Army. He and his family survived, and can therefore be counted as among the fortunate.[19]

The last two years of conventional fighting was largely confined to a narrow strip of land. The allies carried out an extensive bombing of the North. Cities in the DPRK were totally destroyed, as was most of the infrastructure. U.S. planes, looking for targets, bombed the elaborate irrigation system with its many reservoirs that the country's agriculture was dependent on. More allied bombs were dropped on North Korea than on Germany or Japan in World War II. With limited air defenses, the North Koreans endured the conflict in underground shelters, somehow surviving.

One of the surprising developments in the war was the survival of the Kim Il Sung regime. In spite of Kim's disastrous failures in launching a war that not all of his comrades were eager for, he appeared to have consolidated his power. When the war went against him, he was quick to put the blame on his rivals in the leadership. At a party meeting in December 1950, in the provincial town of Kanggye, where his government had retreated, he carried out a purge of the party. Mu Chŏng, the veteran of Yan'an, was dismissed in late 1950 and died shortly after. The Soviet Korean Hŏ Ka-i (1904–1953) came under attack and committed suicide in the spring of 1953. The Communist leaders from the South were given special blame for the great guerilla uprising that had failed to appear. A show trial convicted the top southern Communists led by Pak Hŏn-yŏng, and most were eventually executed. The former Communist leader in the South was arrested, tried, and convicted of treason in August 1953. He was put to death two years later. Half the old Korean Workers' Party had

been lost through death, desertion, or expulsion. Many of these were expelled for cooperating with the ROK or UN when they reoccupied much
of the North. Kim Il Sung dealt with this by rebuilding the party during
the war, so that by 1953 it had 1 million members, truly a massive party in
a nation of less than 10 million. Nearly one in four adults became a party
member. The majority of these were uneducated farmers and workers
selected out of their loyalty to the state and party during the war. Thus
it was virtually a new party, a party of common people, not of the more
educated as the old party had been.

The South Korean government carried on as best it could during the
war from its temporary capital of Pusan. All southern cities were swollen
by hundreds of thousands of refugees. Just keeping people alive was a
major problem. The UN and other aid agencies did heroic work with the
help of Koreans. The war effort in the South brought forth considerable
examples of courage and heroism in overcoming incredible odds. Tent
schools were set up, for example, with massive classes so that the school
year could continue, and most children somehow kept up on their lessons.
Unfortunately, the war brought out some horrible incidents of violence,
corruption, and thuggish politics. President Rhee, always of authoritarian
nature, used the conflict to try to strengthen his hold on government. To
many Koreans, he was a symbol of national resistance. But the reputation of his administration was seriously damaged by scandals. One was
the massacre in February 1951 of over 700 villagers in Koch'ang in South
Kyŏngsang Province during antiguerilla operations there. Attempts by
National Assemblymen to investigate were met with repression. To mobilize all available men for the war effort, Rhee created a National Defense
Corps, but this was so riddled with incompetence and corruption it caused
a great uproar, and Rhee had its director arrested and executed.

More than fifty years later, other atrocities would emerge that were
committed by North Korean forces in the South, South Korean forces in
the North, by the ROK government against its own people, and by U.S.
forces. North Korean forces executed thousands during their brief occupation of Seoul and other parts of the ROK. They also took thousands
of South Koreans with them when they retreated north; most were never
heard of again. The ROK government, for its part, carried out the execution of thousands of political prisoners in June 1950 as North Korean
forces advanced south. By some current estimates, up to 100,000 South
Koreans were killed by their own government. Nor were the Americans
entirely innocent of atrocities. In one highly publicized event that came
to light in 1999, U.S. troops in July 1950 deliberately fired into civilians
fleeing from the KPA in the central village of No Gun Ri (Nogun-ri), killing a disputed number. And there were the huge civilian casualties from
American bombings in North Korea. The United States was accused by

the Communist powers of using bacteriological weapons in the North, but this has generally been dismissed as a false charge.

Rhee attempted to appear above political parties, so he associated himself with none. But worried about the 1952 election, he created his own Liberal Party in December 1951. He then tried to pass a constitutional amendment that would call for a direct popular election for president under the assumption that the National Assembly would not support his reelection. When the National Assembly refused to pass the amendment, he had martial law declared in Pusan and arrested the members. Intimidated, they voted for the amendment and in a direct election with no credible opponent, Rhee was easily elected to another four-year term. Thus, as was the case with Kim Il Sung, Rhee was able to use the wartime conditions to consolidate his power despite setbacks on the battlefield.

The conflict ended in the summer of 1953. The election in November 1952 of President Eisenhower, who had promised to end the conflict, was followed by his visit to Korea. The Soviet Union, however, may not have minded its continuation. The Soviets were careful not to get directly involved in the conflict. They supplied equipment to the North Koreans and Chinese and flew some reconnaissance aircraft but in general did not commit troops. This was in good part because Stalin was not eager to get into a conflict and did not want to take forces away from Europe, which was the area of confrontation with the West that mattered most to the USSR. The war from the Soviet point of view tied the U.S. forces down in the east, lifted pressure from Europe, drained American resources, and cost the Soviets little, since it was fought by the Chinese and North Koreans. However, there was a concern that an Eisenhower administration would place great military pressure to end the war. Mao may have found the cost of the conflict bearable because it was fought with troops from the civil war, there was no shortage of cannon fodder, and the war was useful for rallying support for his new regime. Furthermore, having fought the Americans to a stalemate added to his prestige. Yet as the war dragged on, indications are that Mao was willing to bring it to an end. In the spring of 1953, the United States carried out the most extensive bombing of the war, raining horrific destruction upon the civilian population of North Korea as well as on the CPV and KPA forces. Stalin's death in March removed an obstacle to peace, as his successors showed little interest in continuing the conflict. North Korea needed a respite from the constant American bombing; its hope of reunifying Korea was clearly dashed, at least for the near future. So in the spring of 1953 all parties were ready to bring the war to an end.

A major exception was Syngman Rhee. The stubborn South Korean leader was both an asset and a liability for the Americans. His personal charisma and oratorical skills were important in rallying the South

Korean people for the war effort. However, Rhee quarreled with the Americans over the aims of the conflict. He was unwilling to let go of the hope of reunifying his country and pressured the United States to push the war to complete victory. He was adamantly opposed to a negotiated truce that left the country divided as it had been before. Rhee gave speeches, organized mass rallies, and used every opportunity to call for the continuation of the war until Korea was reunified. He even threatened to continue the war alone if the UN called a truce. So difficult had he become that in 1952 the U.S. government began a secret plan, "Operation Plan Everready," to remove him and replace him with someone thought to be easier for the Americans to deal with. At one point in the spring of 1953 he tried to sabotage the negotiations for prisoner exchange by releasing 25,000 North Korean Communist prisoners being held in the South. Eventually, however, an armistice was agreed to by the UN, North Korea, and China, who signed it on July 27, 1953. It came into force without Rhee's signature.

Historians have debated both the cause and the nature of the Korean War. Could it have been prevented? Who was responsible for it? Given the unacceptability of a divided Korea to most nationalists and Kim Il Sung's determination to reunify the country, it seemed almost inevitable. In fact, had South Korea's military been stronger, the ROK may have been tempted to invade the North. Some have argued the war could not have occurred without Stalin's approval and Mao's acceptance. Stalin appears to have been initially reluctant to approve an invasion but eventually backed it, perhaps seeing it as a low-risk gamble after having been assured by Kim and Pak Hŏn-yŏng that victory would be swift and certain. The United States has been criticized for not making its willingness to defend South Korea clear. It has often been charged that Secretary of State Dean Acheson's ambiguity about the U.S. commitment to defend South Korea in his famous January 12, 1950, press conference encouraged Kim Il Sung and Stalin to invade, but recent archival evidence does not suggest this influenced their decision. However, the U.S. did not provide adequate preparations for the country's defense. Clearly Kim Il Sung is most immediately responsible, as well as Pak Hŏn-yŏng. Hotheads on both sides of the peninsula contributed to the tensions that preceded the war. The United States is to blame for its role in the division of Korea, the USSR for its part in that division and its support of the invasion. China bears some responsibility, and one can even assign responsibility to Japan for creating the situation that led to the allied occupation of Korea that created the division.

Scholars have also debated whether it should be considered a civil war or an international conflict. It was a civil war that became an international conflict, with both North and South Koreans acting as manipulators as well as victims of the great powers. Historians will, no doubt, long be debating these issues.

THE IMPACT OF THE KOREAN WAR

No one knows for certain the extent of the losses; one estimate places the toll at 750,000 military and 800,000 civilian deaths. Of the military deaths, 300,000 were from the North Korean Army, 227,000 from the ROK Army, 200,000 from the Chinese People's Volunteers (some estimates place this figure much higher, as many as 500,000). About 37,000 Americans and 4,000 UN allies were killed. Civilian casualties are hard to estimate. On the high end, one UN estimate places the number of South Koreans who died of all causes including disease, exposure, and starvation at 900,000. North Korean casualties were probably higher.

The Korean War contributed to the upheaval of Korean society that had begun in the 1930s. In South Korea it expedited the land reform (see chapter 10) and wiped out the wealth of many, acting as a great social leveling process. It also enhanced the power of the South Korean state. The massive U.S. aid that arrived in the wake of the war provided an invaluable economic prop to the Rhee government, since it gave the state access to foreign currency, which it was able to use to reward or discipline businesses and industries, and other potential supporters and opponents. More importantly, the Korean War provided the state a means of legitimizing itself through the use of the ideology of anticommunism. Anticommunism provided a rationale for state power and gave a purpose and raison d'être for the South Korean state. South Korea was on the front line of Communism, a member of the free world that had to be ever vigilant against Communist aggression and subversion. The three-year conflict created a huge military force, which grew from 100,000 troops on the eve of the conflict to 600,000 at the end. After the war, the military forces were kept at this level, well equipped by the United States and increasingly well trained. It was, in fact, one of the ten largest armed forces in the world. The war continued and greatly enhanced the economic and cultural influence of the United States on South Korea. The United States provided $200 million in aid annually for the decade after the war, a figure that accounted for a tenth of the total economy. While most of this economic support was in the form of immediate relief, not industrial investment, it did at least sustain the state until South Korean policy makers were able to work out successful strategies for economic development. The presence of hundreds of thousands of GIs and civilian officials, and the long-term stationing of troops in this historically homogeneous and sometimes xenophobic society insured that American culture would flow into the country. It also insured that South Korea would be linked with the Western world, economically as well as culturally.

The Korean War created the bunker mentality that characterized North Korea. The regime's bunker mentality was not surprising, since for two and a half years much of North Korea literally lived in underground bunkers. This bunker mentality manifested itself in several ways: an obsession with mass mobilization and continual ideological indoctrination; an ideology that increasingly centered on ultranationalism and self-reliance; a constant war footing; and a relentless hostility toward South Korea and its allies. Stalin's apparent willingness to abandon North Korea to the UN forces when he ordered Kim to retreat into Manchuria may only have reinforced his need to be militarily self-reliant. These features of North Korea contributed to its isolationist and truculent nature and kept the Korean peninsula and indeed Northeast Asia in a constant state of tension.

The war that started in order to reunify Korea ended by hardening its division. For all Koreans the division was an unacceptable and temporary condition. The regimes in both Seoul and P'yŏngyang in 1950 were committed to end this aberration at almost any cost. The tragedy of the Korean War for Koreans was that they suffered so much but failed to achieve the unity they all desired. Instead, the conflict drove the two Koreas bitterly apart and consolidated their separate systems.

KOREA IN GLOBAL PERSPECTIVE: DIVIDED COUNTRIES

Korea was not the only country to be divided in the twentieth century. India, Ireland, and Palestine were all partitioned, but these were along ethnic or sectarian lines. Germany and Vietnam provide better analogies, since they were also divided as a result of Cold War conflicts. The division of Germany into East and West is best known and in some ways most resembles that of Korea, since it was the result of the lines of occupation drawn by the Western powers and the Soviet Union at the close of World War II. After a short occupation—four years versus the three for Korea—two rival regimes were set up, with the Communist East Germany having a smaller population than the non-Communist West Germany. In Germany, too, the two regimes were also partly based on preexisting ideological divisions. But the parallels end there. East Germany was much smaller than West Germany, with only a quarter of the latter's population, versus North Korea, which had half the population of South Korea. Since the North was much more industrialized than the South, the disparities in size and economic potential were less pronounced than between the two Germanys. East Germany was far more the creation and puppet of the Soviet Union and never posed a serious military threat to

West Germany. There was no bitter civil war between the two, and in spite of the construction of the Berlin Wall in 1961, East Germany was not hermetically sealed from the West; people from the West did visit relatives in the East, and many Easterners were able to receive West German television. While the desire for reunification remained strong, Germany itself had been created out of various states only seventy-four years before it was divided. The division, while tragic, occurred in a land with stronger regional identities, and a shorter history of unification. Furthermore, the Germans themselves bore some measure of responsibility for their situation, having been a menace to their neighbors.

Vietnam might be a closer analogy. It was divided roughly equally into north and south halves in 1954 following a long war against the French. As in Korea, the division in part reflected ideological divisions inside the independence movement. And like Korea, the division was not acceptable, especially to the North, which waged a long, ultimately successful struggle for reunification. But there were some pronounced differences. Vietnam's divisions reflected a certain historical and geographical logic. Although in each half the overwhelming majority was ethnically Vietnamese, the two population centers in the Hong River Basin in the north and the lower Mekong River Basin in the south were separated by a long, narrow coastal plain and rugged highlands. Lifestyles differed in the two regions, which were in reality separate states for several centuries before reunification in 1802. As tragic and unacceptable as its division was, Vietnam simply did not have a comparable history of unity or the same degree of cultural homogeneity, nor was the division so arbitrarily drawn and imposed. And unlike Korea, North Vietnam and its South Vietnamese Viet Cong supporters prevailed after two decades of fighting.

In short, there is no case truly comparable to the division of Korea, to its suddenness, its arbitrariness, and to the tragedy it resulted in. The border between the two states became the most tense, most sealed, and perhaps most unacceptable of all political boundaries in the second half of the twentieth century.

KOREA IN GLOBAL PERSPECTIVE: THE KOREAN WAR

The Korean War had a considerable impact on not just Korea but on its neighbors and the world. China's historical course was profoundly affected by the Korean War. The Chinese paid a high price for their entry. According to Chinese statistics 152,000 were killed or missing, including Mao's son Mao Anying.[20] Most Western scholars believe the actual figures were far greater. China also paid for the war with the loss of Taiwan. On the eve of the war China was preparing to invade Taiwan, but when the war started Truman sent the seventh fleet into the Taiwan Strait blocking the invasion. Thus the emergence of an effectively independent, prosperous, and democratic Taiwan and the ongoing two-Chinas issue was a product of the Korean War. Furthermore, the war had another very significant impact on China. The United States responded to the war by building a defensive wall around the country, with military bases in South Korea, Taiwan, Japan, the Philippines, and Thailand, and with the ships of the Seventh Fleet off the coast. This led to isolation and a siege mentality that contributed to the path of China's development for more than a quarter of a century. Only after 1978 did China break out of this wall and begin to enter extensive intercourse with the West, Japan, and rest of the non-Communist world.

For Japan, the Korean conflict was the turning point in its postwar economic development. During the first five years after its surrender, the Japanese economy languished, and was heavily dependent on American support. Then, the outbreak of the Korean War turned the economic situation around. The U.S. government at the onset of conflict made the decision to take advantage of Japan's proximity, low costs, and recovery needs to use it as a supply base for the war effort. Consequently, the Americans made $2.37 billion worth of special procurements in the four years starting with June 1950, creating a huge demand for ammunition, trucks, uniforms, communications equipment, and other products from Japanese companies.[21] The president of Toyota would later remark "These orders were Toyota's salvation, I felt a mighty joy for my company and a sense of guilt that I was rejoicing over another country's war."[22] The president of the Bank of Japan, drawing a comparison to the "divine wind" (*kamikaze*) that saved Japan from the Mongols, called the war procurement "divine aid."[23] Yoshida Shigeru, the dominant political figure of the era, agreed, calling the Korean War "a gift of the gods."[24] The war consolidated the power base of the political conservatives and helped to shape Japan's postwar relationship with the United States. It unfortunately had a tragic consequence for the remaining Koreans in the country, who found it difficult to be repatriated to a North Korea hostile to Japan or to a devastated South Korea. They remained a marginalized and mistreated minority.

The Korean War shaped the political alliance system in East Asia for most of the rest of the century. When the war ended, the United States sought to shift some of the effort to contain Communism in Asia to a NATO-like regional collective security alliance including Japan, Taiwan, and South Korea. South Korea became a long-term U.S. client state; the 1954 ROK-U.S. mutual defense treaty formalized this relationship, and 30,000 U.S. troops remained in the country a half century later. The war reinforced the arguments for a continued U.S. presence in Japan that was incorporated into the peace settlement. Already the coming of the Communists in China in 1949 and the February 1950 alliance with the Soviet Union made any friendship between Beijing and Tokyo unlikely, and the U.S. alliance with Japan perhaps inevitable. The war made the arguments for the U.S.-Japan relationship more compelling. A bilateral treaty between Japan and Taiwan in April 1952 and a peace treaty between Japan and South Korea in 1965 completed the American-led alliance system in East Asia. It also led to two decades of hostility and suspicion between the United States and China, with images of China's "human wave" tactics in the conflict contributing to American fear of aggression by fanatic Chinese Communists. The Korean conflict colored U.S. perceptions of the need to contain Communism in Asia, and influenced the U.S. involvement in Vietnam.

The Korean War had another less direct or obvious impact on East Asia, with global significance as well. The war created two U.S. client states: South Korea and Taiwan, which, while under the U.S. military umbrella, were also economically linked with the U.S., Japanese, and global markets. Following a decade of massive U.S. aid, they became a favorite place for American, Japanese, and European investment. Partly by emulating Japan's post–World War II developmental state, they flourished and became third-world success stories, providing a model for China after 1978, as well as for other developing nations. Thus, in an indirect way, the Korean War created the political, military, and economic order in East Asia and contributed to the region's rise as a center of the global economy.

Summary of the Instructions of Commanding General Chistiakov at the Meeting of the Five Provinces (November 1, 1945)

To you Koreans. For thirty-six years, the Japanese Imperialists plundered Korean financial resources, limited the freedom of speech, effaced racial independence and national existence, pillaged your language, and in addition dragged you into the war. But now you have been liberated from slavery under the Japanese oppression.

The time for the Korean people to plan their own living has arrived. The Red Army has absolutely no intention to plunder, but rather to restore the independence of Korea. All private properties are under the reliable protection of the Red Army, so there is no cause for fear. We are not going to compel our principles of government on this land. Though we are establishing a democratic form of government here, you have the right to express your own point of view. Every organization must guarantee the freedom of religion. Leaders must settle rapidly all matters concerning mining enterprises. Make a detailed examination of all mining machineries, also of raw materials, and take preparation to train mining technicians as soon as possible. Immediate steps much be taken to convert production of war machineries to production of machineries used in peacetime. All factories must be kept operating. All problems concerning food supply and raw materials must be settled. The Japanese took away most of the food raised by the farmers and made them miserably poor.

In short, this meeting was held to solve the necessary problems for independence and then:

1. Agriculture production and curtailments must be discussed.
2. Problems arising in business must be solved.
3. Financial problems must be solved. Concentrate all individual capital in banks, guarantee monetary payment and capital circulation.
4. There is no central or local administrative organization. You are working temporarily. You must select directors of villages, county and city committees. For discussion, this bill must be divided into four sections.
   a. Agriculture and commerce
   b. Industry
   c. Administration

This meeting must be held again.[25]

12

⬦

North Korea: Recovery, Transformation, and Decline, 1953 to 1993

THE DIVERGENT PATHS OF THE TWO KOREAS

In the half century after the Korean War, North and South Korea continued on the divergent paths that they had embarked upon in the immediate postwar years. History has no parallel to this development. What had been one of the world's most homogenous cultures, with a long historical tradition, became two radically different societies.

South Korea struggled in the 1950s to recover from the war, relying on massive U.S. foreign aid to ward off hunger and economic collapse. It had an increasingly authoritarian government under President Syngman Rhee that within the bounds permitted by its dependency on the United States attempted to subvert the country's political institutions to maintain power. Rhee was overthrown in a popular uprising in 1960; a short-lived attempt at parliamentary democracy ended in 1961 with a military coup. The military-led regime of Park Chung Hee then embarked upon a government-directed economic development program based on export-led growth, which achieved impressive success. Tied economically to the United States and, to a lesser extent, Japan, South Korea was transformed from a rural to an urban, highly literate society. Park's rule also became increasingly more authoritarian. Assassinated in 1979 amid growing political unrest due to his dictatorial rule, he was succeeded by a new military regime under Chun Doo Hwan. By the 1980s, an expanding and increasingly sophisticated middle class sought direct participation and accountability in government. Spearheaded by student radicals, labor activists, and political dissidents, popular restlessness led to a transition to more democratic government that began in 1987 and resulted in the election of a former political dissident, Kim Young Sam, as president in 1992. Throughout these years South Korea's economy continued to grow, catching up with the more industrialized North by 1970 and surpassing it thereafter. By the 1990s, South Korea was becoming one of the third world's success stories.

North Korea followed a very different trajectory. In contrast to the volatile and dynamic South, the basic institutions in place by 1953 were solidified, and the leadership became more entrenched. Kim Il Sung consolidated power in the 1950s and 1960s, became the absolute leader of the country, and created a personality cult that went beyond that of Stalin or Mao. North Korea under Kim was single-mindedly devoted to reversing the outcome of the Korean War and invested its resources and energies in the military. In contrast to South Korea's export market economy, North Korea focused on self-sufficiency. It became one of the world's most isolated countries and increasingly an anachronism, adhering to a rigid totalitarianism based partly on the Stalinist model that became discredited in the USSR and China. After some impressive recovery, the concentration on military buildup, the concern with self-sufficiency, and the emphasis on political control over technical expertise led to a stagnating economy, then to a decline into poverty and famine.

Meanwhile, the two Koreas remained suspended in a state of war. No peace followed the Korean War, only an uneasy armed truce that lasted for decades. Tensions between the two led to occasional armed clashes, often sparked by North Korean provocation. These took place between intermittent but short-lived attempts to negotiate some sort of peaceful coexistence.

NORTH KOREA'S RECOVERY

Three years after it launched its invasion of the South, North Korea was in ruins. While the death and destruction in South Korea was enormous, the DPRK suffered disproportionately greater casualties and destruction. The level of devastation inflicted upon the country was horrendous. In early November 1950, General MacArthur ordered intensive bombing along the northern area near the Chinese border that would destroy every structure, and he declared that the northwest region would be a "wilderness of scorched earth."[1] The bombing leveled virtually every city and sizeable town in North Korea; all of the industry and most of the nation's infrastructure was destroyed. Casualties suffered by North Korea are not known for certain, but were most likely higher than in the South, although it had only half the population. According to one study, 406,000

North Korean civilians and 294,000 military were killed out of a population of 9 million.[2] This is at the low end of estimates. Others calculate the total deaths in North Korea to be much higher. Even if the lower estimates are accepted, this is an incredible figure matched by few modern conflicts. North Korea is likely to have lost a greater proportion of its population than did Germany or Japan in World War II.

Yet North Korea recovered quickly from the physical destruction. The immediate postwar years were focused on rebuilding. A Three-Year Plan, 1954–1956, aimed at economic reconstruction, appears to have been successful, with industrial production in 1957 reaching pre-Korean War levels. The major features of the plan were outlined in a speech by Kim Il Sung in 1953, a week after the cease-fire agreement. Economic development would be focused on "everything for the postwar rehabilitation and development of the national economy."[3]

Immediately after the war, the campaigns of mass mobilization succeeded in clearing the destruction, rebuilding houses, schools, factories, and other facilities. Following a pattern that would characterize the DPRK for decades, people were organized military-style in mass campaigns to accomplish state-directed goals. This system was apparently effective for the initial rebuilding efforts after the war. P'yŏngyang then launched a Five-Year Plan for 1957–1961 that sought not recovery but strong positive growth in industry, agriculture, and infrastructure. The state proclaimed that this plan was so successful that it ended one year early. North Korea had the advantage of possessing 80 percent of Korea's 1945 industry, and 90 percent of its electric power, mostly hydroelectric. Therefore, much of the initial recovery was a matter of rebuilding the existing structures using the Japanese blueprints. Possessing three-quarters of Korea's mines, it had a variety of minerals such as iron, tungsten, silver, uranium, and others it could export to its Communist allies. Still, the recovery was an impressive achievement, and with some new plants under construction it put the country on the road to rapid industrialization.

Kim Il Sung followed a path of development similar to and no doubt greatly influenced by that of the Soviet Union under Stalin. It was totally centralized and state directed in adherence to the development plan, with no scope for private industry or agriculture. By the late 1950s all private businesses and industries had been eliminated. The state collected all basic commodities and redistributed them. The few remaining private enterprises were taken over by the state. There was virtually no local or regional autonomy; all decision making down to the basic allocation of food and clothing to each household through the public distribution system was made from the center. In other ways, too, he followed the model of the Soviet Union in its push for rapid growth after 1928. Shortly after the death of Stalin in 1953, the Soviet Union embarked on what it called its "new course," which emphasized a more balanced approach between heavier and lighter consumer industries and encouraged or pressured allies to follow suit. But Kim focused on developing heavy industry that could increase the industrial base of the economy and support a strong military, rather than on consumer goods. The aim was also to achieve as much economic autonomy as possible in order to make the country ready for war, should it resume, and to make the DPRK an industrial showcase that would eventually gain the admiration and support of the South Korean public. Yet foreign aid was crucial to the recovery effort. The Soviets and their Eastern European allies supplied technical help and material on a large scale. Some of the prewar infrastructure was rebuilt, such as the chemical fertilizer complex from the colonial period at Hŭngnam.[4] Soviet contributions included the Sup'ing hydrolectrical power plant, the largest in Asia; a large steel mill at Sŏngjin (renamed Kim Ch'aek) in the northeast; and the rebuilding of the port of Namp'o. In 1954, aid supplied 33 percent of the state revenues. Soviet aid to North Korea was smaller proportionally than the U.S. aid given to South Korea, which was half of the government budget in the 1950s. It also was over a shorter period of time—South Korea remained heavily reliant on U.S. aid until the mid 1960s, but by 1960 Soviet aid accounted for only 2.6 percent of the DPRK's revenues.[5] Nonetheless, it was crucial for the recovery efforts in the years after the Korean War. Furthermore, the Soviets supplied military aid and important resources such as oil at subsidized prices. Although North Korea had a small number of Japanese-trained technicians, it was greatly assisted in the 1950s by several hundred Soviet Koreans who were able to provide valuable expertise. China also assisted, by use of its troops, who remained in the country until 1958 to provide labor for construction projects.

A key part of the DPRK economic program was the collectivization of agriculture, where farmers were reduced to laborers. Few other changes impacted so many people. While some Communist countries allowed for small-scale markets for private produce, Kim opted for total collectivization. This was part of the pattern of the highly centralized command economy that conformed to the Soviet model. The land reform of 1946 had divided the countryside into small family farms. Tenancy had been ended, but farmers did not have full control over their land—it could be inherited but not alienated. Geography and labor shortage may have contributed to this decision. Food supplies were a problem, since the best agricultural land was in South Korea. Most of North Korea was very mountainous, and the growing season was short. Nor did the DPRK's allies have the large food surpluses to be given as aid, as the United States was able to give the ROK. Food shortages appeared early. Both in the late 1940s and in 1954 the state had to temporarily ban private trade in foodstuffs and forcibly requisition crops.[6] Furthermore, the Korean War had created a shortage of manpower and of draft animals. Kim and his planners saw the solution in collectivizing and mechanizing agriculture by consolidating the small plots of land into big farms that could be worked by tractors and other machinery.

Farming was collectivized in stages. Compared to the Soviet Union or China under Mao, the process went rather smoothly without upheavals and disasters. In 1954, the state created mutual aid teams called *p'umassiban*. Then rural villages were organized as cooperatives where the majority of farm families lived and worked. These in turn became collective farms. Collectivization was completed by the end of 1957, ahead of the original plans. By this time, all private trade in grain was prohibited; all production was sold to the state. In 1958, these collective farms, based on preexisting villages, were consolidated into even bigger ones containing 300 households and about 500 hectares of land.[7] Larger farming units were established in order to create large fields that could be worked by tractors and other mechanical equipment. Collective farms administrated by party cadres were given a quota of agricultural products to be supplied to the state. The state provided them with tools, fertilizers, seeds, and fuel. Farm families were allowed to cultivate tiny plots of land that could be used to grow a few garden crops for personal use. Thus, a decade after land reforms largely ended tenancy, farmers found they had become landless agricultural laborers.

Besides making the need for the mechanization of agriculture more convincing, the loss of life in the Korean War may have contributed to the mass entry of women into the workforce.[8] The latter feature of the DPRK's development amounted to a major social revolution.

The prominent place of women in all industries was a contrast to the South, where women generally continued their role as homemakers. Few women, however, rose to positions of authority. The near total destruction of the cities allowed the state to totally rebuild them in accordance with the principles of the new order. P'yŏngyang and other cities were completely rebuilt. The conflict had virtually erased the physical evidence of the past and provided a blank slate for the regime to rewrite history.

To stimulate industrial workers and farmers to increase output, Kim Il Sung relied on inspiring them with revolutionary fervor through mass campaigns. In this he followed the Soviet Union's Stakhanovite campaigns of the 1930s, similar campaigns by Mao in China, and the mass mobilization movements of imperial Japan. He launched the Ch'ŏllima movement in December 1956, named after a flying horse from Korean mythology that could travel vast distances in short times. The Ch'ŏllima movement focused on organizing large numbers of people to work long hours in teams, mainly on construction and heavy industry. In 1958, perhaps under the influence of Mao's Great Leap Forward, the program was expanded. Groups of workers who surpassed their production targets were given medals and honored as Ch'ŏllima riders. Kim Il Sung personally visited production sites for moral support and to give instructions in what became known as "on-the-spot guidance." These efforts were probably effective in the initial phase of industrialization, which depended on carefully supervised mass labor. And some workers were probably inspired by being told they were building a social paradise.

The DPRK made eliminating illiteracy and providing universal education a priority, and it appeared to have achieved both in the 1950s and 1960s. Night schools were set up in the villages and cities to teach basic literacy. And beginning in the late 1950s, the state established a number of two-year technical schools. In 1956, a law for universal and compulsory primary education was promulgated. At first this was limited to four years, but it was soon expanded to seven years, and in 1959, a nine-year compulsory education system was announced. The latter took nearly a decade to fully implement due to a shortage of teachers and facilities. Educational development advanced further when Kim Il Sung at the Fifth Party Congress in 1970 unveiled plans for a new eleven-year education system: two years of kindergarten, four years of elementary school, and five years of middle school; the plan was to be implemented in 1976.[9] To deal with the shortage of teachers and facilities, classes ran on a two-shift basis, as they also did in many South Korean schools. Overall, North Korea made impressive strides in providing a comprehensive primary and secondary education. The state also expanded higher education, mainly creating a number of two-year technical colleges; the most prestigious of these was Kim Ch'aek University. The elite institution was Kim Il Sung University in the capital; this was the only four-year comprehensive university. By the 1980s it had about 12,000 students and graduated 3,000 a year. Thus, while North Korea was able to provide basic literacy and technical training, it had very few university graduates with a broad-based education.

Although problems were soon to arise and the early rapid growth slowed down, North Korea had by the early 1970s become an industrial state with only 30 percent of the population engaged in agriculture.

POLITICAL CONSOLIDATION

North Korean leader Kim Il Sung used the Korean War to consolidate power, eliminate rivals, and rebuild the party. At the end of the war, Kim eliminated the domestic Communists who had remained in Korea working underground during the colonial period and their leader Pak

Hŏn-yŏng. When the UN forces had entered the North, many citizens, to the dismay of the regime, had cooperated with them. Hŏ Ka-i, a leader of the Soviet-Koreans and an expert on party organization, carried out a purge of the collaborators. But so many had collaborated that Kim found he would need to rebuild the party and state. The dispute over collaboration also reflected the different views of the party. Hŏ sought a balance between workers and peasants and wanted to restrict membership to a small vanguard on the Soviet model, while Kim argued for a broad-based party whose membership reflected the fact that 80 percent of all North Koreans were peasants. In short, he opted for a mass party rather than the Soviet-style elite membership. Kim had Hŏ expelled from the party in November 1951; he was reported to have committed suicide two year later. Thousands who had been purged for collaborating with the enemy were reinstated. But it was mostly a new party membership. Hundreds of thousands of new recruits were drawn from those who had served the regime during the conflict. By the late 1950s the Korean Workers' Party had 1.1 million members, about a tenth of the population. In no other Communist country did the party membership embrace such a large proportion of the population. It was mostly a party of poor Koreans drawn from workers and peasants with little formal education. Party membership brought the opportunity for social and economic advancement for many ordinary Koreans. With little knowledge of Marxism-Leninism, little or no foreign experience or contacts, its membership was unsophisticated but loyal to the regime.

As he built up the party, Kim ruthlessly eliminated all other possible rivals. Although he was the unchallenged leader, he could only count on his fellow ex-guerillas for absolute loyalty. Kim first turned on the domestic Communists, conducting the regime's show trial of their leaders just one week after the July 1953 armistice, in which they confessed to having plotted a coup against the regime and to have collaborated with the United States. Pak Hŏn-yŏng, the most prestigious of the domestic Communists, was arrested and executed two years later as an American spy. There were 200 Soviet Koreans who still had important positions. Similarly, there were a number of officials who had served in prewar China, sometimes referred to as the Yan'an group. The influence of both groups was enhanced by their links with North Korea's two principal allies.[10] The Soviet Koreans appear to have been somewhat critical of the rapid pace of industrial development and collectivization, preferring a more cautious policy of gradually building up the country's economy through technical training. In December 1955, Kim Il Sung openly criticized Pak Ch'ang-ok (d. 1958), the State Economic Planning Commission chair. The following month he had him removed from his post. Meanwhile, the denunciation of Stalin by Khrushchev at a closed party congress in Moscow in February

1956 emboldened some of the KWP leadership to meet in August of 1956 while Kim was out of the country. Led by some Soviet Koreans under Pak Ch'ang-ok, they criticized his cult of personality, much as Khrushchev had criticized Stalin's cult, and attacked Kim's economic policies. Kim Il Sung quickly countermoved, but an intervention by the Soviet Union and China initially protected Pak and his allies, which included members of the Yan'an group.

The intervention did not protect Kim's opponents for long. Beginning in late 1956, Kim moved against the Yan'an group, removing Ch'oe Ch'ang-ik (1896–?), the most prominent member, and eventually purging nearly all the others by the end of 1957. The following year he moved against the Soviet Koreans, arresting Pak and others, although most were allowed to return to the Soviet Union. There were now no groups within the party that had their own power base. Between the time of the Third Party Congress of the Korean Workers' Party in 1956 and the Fourth Party Congress in 1961, most of the top leadership had been replaced. So thorough were the purges of party leaders that only twenty-eight of eighty-five members of the Central Committee of the KWP at its Fourth Party Congress in 1961 were returning members from the last party congress five years earlier.[11] Only those whose loyalty to Kim was unconditional remained, these being mostly ex-guerillas. Kim Il Sung, despite the disastrous invasion of the South and the military setbacks early in the war, had been able to consolidate his power and transform the party and state into his personal instruments.

Kim continued to tolerate no opposition, frequently removing officials throughout the 1960s. When some party officers questioned his economic policies, he removed them at a special Party Conference in October 1966. At the Fifth Party Congress in 1970, only 4 of 16 members of the 1961 Politburo, the top-ranking leaders, remained, as did only 39 of the 172 members of the 1961 Central Committee. By this time, the party leadership was reduced mainly to Kim's fellow ex-Manchurian guerillas, their children, and others related to them or to the Great Leader. The innermost circle consisted mostly of those who had served in the Eighty-eighth Brigade, followed by other former Manchurian guerillas who were not Eighty-eighth Brigade members. There were few purges after 1970. Thirteen of the fifteen Politburo members in 1970 were still around in 1994.[12] The small group of ex-Manchurian guerillas and their families monopolized almost all the key positions in the party and government. Unfortunately, few of these had any technical expertise or intellectual background. In a final formal assumption of power, Kim drew up a new constitution in 1972 to replace the 1948 one. It created a new powerful presidency, which he assumed. He was now the head of state as well as of the party.

As the ruling circle narrowed, Kim Il Sung began to groom his son Kim Jong Il (Kim Chŏng-il) (1942–) as his successor. Kim Jong Il was born in Siberia in 1942 to his father's first wife Kim Jong Suk (1917–1949). He graduated from Kim Il Sung University in 1964 and emerged as an important figure in the party when he led the Three-Revolutions Teams movement in 1974. Interestingly, he was referred to in the media only as "the Party Center" (*Tang chungang*). When at the Sixth Congress of the Korean Workers' Party in October 1980 he was publicly mentioned by name for the first time, it became clear he was the designated successor. His role in the state continued to increase. When Kim Jong Il published a theoretical work, *On the Juche Idea*, the North Korean media heaped endless praise on it. He now joined his father as the great authority on all ideological matters. Honored as the Dear Leader (*Ch'inaehan Chidoja*) to distinguish him from his father, the Great Leader (*Widaehan Suryŏngnim*), he assumed much of the day-to-day operation of the state. Except for Kim Jong Il, no new generation of leaders was emerging. Of the ten positions at the 1980 Party Congress, the aging Manchurian comrades of Kim Il Sung still held eight.[13]

THE CHANGING INTERNATIONAL SITUATION

The Korean War solidified North Korea's alliance with its Communist neighbors, while its hostility and bitterness toward the ROK and the United States was an obstacle to reconciliation with the West. Close ties with the Soviet Union and China were crucial to North Korea's economic recovery and development. According to one study, direct Soviet aid to North Korea from 1945 to 1970 totaled US$1.146 billion while direct Chinese aid during the same period came to US$541 million.[14] The major part of this aid came in the decade after the Korean War. Even more important was the gas and oil supplied at artificially low prices; the weapons and military technology supplied by the two Communist allies, also at artificially low prices; and the technical training the Soviet Union and, to a lesser extent, China provided. North Korea was economically dependent on the aid from its Communist neighbors, a fact made plain by the economic contraction that came with the end of Soviet aid in the early 1990s. However, by balancing its relations with the two Communist powers, the country was able to avoid becoming a political or economic satellite of either.

Despite the heavy reliance on Soviet economic support, relations with Moscow were often troubled. Kim Il Sung was critical of the de-Stalinization policy launched at the Twentieth Congress of the Soviet

Communist Party in 1956. In that same year, Politburo member Leonid Brezhnev, representing the USSR at the Third Korean Workers' Party Congress, launched a veiled criticism of Kim by suggesting the adoption of "collective leadership."[15] This is when some Soviet-linked North Koreans made the only known attempt to challenge Kim Il Sung's leadership. Subsequently, relations between the two nations were rarely smooth.

The Sino-Soviet rift challenged P'yŏngyang to avoid becoming entangled in the dispute and risking alienating one of its benefactors. But it was also an opportunity for North Korea to remain neutral while seeking the favor of both regimes. The split in the two Communist powers contributed to North Korea's ability to pursue an independent foreign policy, enabling it to avoid becoming a satellite of either while seeking economic aid from both. Soon after the split became open, P'yŏngyang carefully signed treaties of friendship, cooperation, and mutual assistance with Beijing in July 1961, only days after signing a similar treaty with Moscow. Both treaties went into effect at the same time. However, this balancing act proved difficult as the dispute between the two powers grew sharper. In addition, the revolutionary ties with China, the Chinese participation in the Korean War, historic cultural ties between Koreans and Chinese, the unease with the Soviet policies of peaceful coexistence and collective leadership, and the Soviet link with the challenge to his leadership in 1956 all made Kim lean more toward China. In 1962, the North Korean media ceased to cite Soviet examples, and the official newspaper, *Rodong Sinmun*, began to take the Chinese side, even criticizing the Soviet Union. The Soviet Union responded by sharply reducing economic and military aid to P'yŏngyang in 1962 and 1963. In October 1963 the *Rodong Sinmun*, in an editorial "Let's Defend the Socialist Camp," openly criticized the Soviet Union, accusing it of putting economic and military pressure on China.[16]

A major reason for North Korea's tilt toward China was that Kim Il Sung felt comfortable with the virulent anti-Western, anticapitalist rhetoric from Maoist China. In almost all cases, P'yŏngyang took a more truculent stance toward non-Communists than Moscow. It vigorously endorsed China's actions in the Sino-Indian border conflict of 1962 and criticized Soviet "capitulation" in the Cuban missile crisis. The DPRK praised the Cuban response to U.S. imperialism when Havana mobilized its population, which inspired North Korea to launch a new military mobilization campaign at home. However, the reality of the dependency on Soviet aid and the inability or unwillingness of China to make up the difference, as well as the advantages of political neutrality, led to patching up relations with the Soviet Union. In 1965 Premier Aleksey Kosygin visited the DPRK, a sign of improving relations. Three years later the DPRK supported the Soviet invasion of Czechoslovakia. At this time, tension grew with China during the Cultural Revolution. There were clashes over the disputed boundary at Paektu Mountain (Changbaishan in Chinese), considered the most sacred of Korean mountains. The border had remained unclear despite the attempt to settle it in 1712 and again in 1909. In addition, the instability of the Cultural Revolution made Kim Il Sung uneasy. During 1967 and 1968, the Red Guards, young revolutionary zealots Mao had unloosed to promote his Great Proletarian Cultural Revolution, attacked Kim Il Sung by name, calling him "Korea's Khrushchev." This was ironic for a man who had so much contempt for Khrushchev and his reforms. However, after 1969 the Cultural Revolution began to moderate, and relations between the two countries became more comfortable. The boundary issue was settled in Kim Il Sung's favor.

From 1970, P'yŏngyang was strictly neutral in the dispute between the two Communist giants. In that year, both Soviet Premier Kosygin and Chinese Premier Zhou Enlai visited P'yŏngyang, and relations were improved with both. Both Beijing and Moscow came to accept the independence of North Korea. This policy of neutrality served the regime well, since it was able to receive substantial aid from both and be a truly independent state. This ensured the supply of oil and other commodities at extremely low "friendship" prices. The North Koreans, however, remained more comfortable with China. During the 1970s and 1980s China provided an estimated 15 to 25 percent of North Korea's foreign trade, most of it on very favorable terms to Kim Il Sung's regime.[17] China's involvement in the war, which extended to the final withdrawal of Chinese forces in October 1958, and the fact that so many senior officers and officials had served there, gave China a special interest in that country and an emotional tie between the leaders of both countries.[18] October 25, the day that the Chinese People's Volunteers officially entered the war, and July 27, the anniversary of the armistice, were commemorated with ceremonies including ritual visits to the Resist America and Aid Korea Martyr's Cemetery in Shenyang.[19] A large number of senior PLA officers who served in the Korean War held high posts in the Chinese government. Seven served in the Politburo between the mid-1950s and the late 1980s, and during 1969–1983 between 15 and 17 percent of the Central Committee members were Korean War veterans.[20] P'yŏngyang often followed Chinese models. The Ch'ŏllima movement in the late 1950s paralleled the Great Leap Forward. And the Three-Revolutions Teams in the early 1970s were at least partially inspired by the Cultural Revolution. Beijing's own talk of self-reliance encouraged the regime, which adopted the Chinese slogan of "relying on one's own strength" (*Charyŏk kaengsaeng*) in the late 1950s. Relations were not without problems, but North Korea was China's principal ally in Asia, and after 1991 P'yŏngyang's only reliable supporter in the world community. Even the Chinese, however, tended to show impatience with the regime's isolation and intransigent hostility to the West.

In the 1970s, the North Korean regime made an attempt to court the nations of the third world, even going so far as joining the Nonaligned Movement. Leaders from various Asian and African nations were invited to P'yŏngyang, and a large number of embassies were opened. In good part this was another front in the ongoing Korean War. The DPRK sought to isolate South Korea diplomatically and win recognition as the legitimate government of Korea. This was also an assertion that it was far from being a satellite of either of the major Communist powers. Little came of this effort, however, and most developing nations became more interested in trade and assistance from Seoul, while the missions abroad were costly to maintain. By the 1990s, the regime largely abandoned its efforts to gain support and credibility in the developing world, a failure that only emphasized the isolation of the regime.

CONFRONTATIONAL STANCE TOWARD
THE SOUTH AND THE UNITED STATES

The Korean War never ended for North Korea, a fact that explains much of its truculent and confrontational foreign policy. For all the horror of the war, its indecisive conclusion did not alter the aims of the North Korean regime. Kim Il Sung and his comrades appeared to have concluded that the battle was lost but the overall strategy was sound. Their policy was one of waiting for the United States to withdraw and for internal crises in South Korea to provide an opportunity for intervention and unification. This explains the constant state of military preparedness and the hostility to regimes in Seoul. The ceasefire in July 1953 was merely that—a ceasefire, not a peace. The border between the two Koreas, separated from coast to coast by a four-kilometer-wide no-man's land, the Demilitarized Zone (DMZ), became the most fortified and armed border in the world. In the first two decades after the ending of hostilities, North Korea maintained a policy of unrelenting hostility toward the Republic of Korea, and its allies the United States and Japan. It periodically carried out acts of provocation that kept the border tense and made the possibility of a new outbreak of fighting appear real. Accompanying these tensions was the constant stream of vitriolic anti-American propaganda that emanated for half a century from P'yŏngyang.

The tensions with South Korea and the United States increased in 1967 when North Korea created a number of incidents along the DMZ. Following a purge of technocrats who were critical of Kim Il Sung's economic buildup, a number of military men were appointed to high positions. This seemed to have resulted in a shift to more active confrontation with the ROK and its American ally. In January 1968, the DPRK sent thirty-one commandos to assault the "Blue House," the presidential residence in Seoul. Twenty-seven of the commandos were killed, one was captured, and three escaped. But the incident was the most provocative since the end of the Korean War. Two days later, North Korea seized the U.S.S. *Pueblo*, an American intelligence-gathering ship in international waters. The crew was released after one year of negotiations. On April 15, 1968, the birthday of the Great Leader, North Korean fighters shot down an American reconnaissance plane, killing its crew. In October of that year, another group of North Korean soldiers landed on the east coast of South Korea with the intention of establishing a guerilla base. They were eventually killed or captured by ROK forces. The DPRK also organized the Revolution Party for Reunification, an underground group, in 1964. South Korean authorities destroyed the party and executed its leader, Kim Chong-t'ae, in 1969. From these provocations, North Korea learned it had little support among the South Koreans, who showed no enthusiasm for the DPRK troops that entered remote villages. They also found that rather than respond militarily to its provocations the Americans were willing to negotiate with them.

Kim Il Sung then changed tactics again. Most of the military men who had risen to high party positions were absent from the 1970 KWP Congress, and tensions between North and South lessened. Besides the failure to gain anything from the confrontational tactics, Kim may have been influenced by the U.S.-China rapprochement. In July 1971, President Nixon announced that he would be visiting Beijing, which he did in February 1972. This may have been the event that helped Kim to decide on a change in policy toward the ROK. In August 1971, talks began between the Red Cross committees of the two Koreas. Among the humanitarian issues discussed was the location and reunion of families separated by the conflict and the establishment of postal exchanges. This was followed by secret missions by high-ranking officials from both sides. On July 4, 1972, the two Koreas issued a joint communiqué announcing that both sides agreed that reunification should be negotiated peacefully and without foreign interference and calling for locating and carrying out reunions of families separated by the Korean War. South Korea sought to concentrate on humanitarian issues such as reuniting divided families and to eventually work toward bigger issues. North Korea, however, insisted on the withdrawal of all U.S. forces as a first step for further agreements. The uncompromising stance of the DPRK resulted in the collapse of the talks in 1973. This began a pattern in DPRK-ROK relations in which promising starts at reducing tensions and developing some measure of cooperation were followed by reverse shifts in policy by P'yŏngyang.

North Korea kept tensions along the Demilitarized Zone high. In August 1976 North Korean soldiers attacked and killed two American officers who were trimming a tree in the area. The DPRK constructed tunnels under the border capable of providing passage for as many as a division of men in an hour. The first was discovered in 1974; three more were found in 1975, 1978, and in 1990. The North Korean regime provoked a major crisis on October 9, 1983, when it attempted to kill the South Korean President Chun Du Hwan during his visit to Burma. A platform where ROK and Burmese leaders were to speak was blown up, killing seventeen senior ROK officials including four cabinet ministers as well as members of the Burmese government, although failing to harm Chun. China, apparently alarmed at this incident, encouraged Kim Il Sung to open up a dialogue with the United States and the South. The United States also indicated that it would talk directly with P'yŏngyang if the talks included the ROK. North Korea agreed to the three-way talks between the DPRK, ROK, and the United States. Little, however, came of this, since North Korea insisted that the talks lead to a bilateral agreement with the Americans, excluding the ROK, a demand that was acceptable to neither Seoul nor Washington. A dialogue did resume between the two Koreas, leading to an exchange of art performances and family union visits in the summer and fall of 1985. But this minor thaw in relations soon ended when the DPRK demanded a nonaggression pact between the two countries and the ending of joint military exercises between the ROK and U.S. forces. Terrorist acts against the South continued, most notably the bombing of a Korean Air flight in 1987. A new round of talks between the two sides took place again between 1990 and 1991, but this too ended with little progress.

Kim Il Sung's militant stance toward the South was not irrational. He never accepted the outcome of the Korean War as anything other than a temporary setback, and he never gave up the goal of reunification. There were a number of encouraging signs for North Korea that it might achieve its goal of reversing the result of the Korean War, such as in 1960 when a student-led uprising overthrew the Syngman Rhee government and the political and social unrest that followed suggested a possible collapse of order and perhaps a revolutionary upheaval in the ROK. Signs were encouraging again in the mid- and late 1970s with the American withdrawal from Vietnam, the decision of the Carter administration to remove troops from South Korea in 1977, and the political unrest that followed South Korean President Park Chung Hee's assassination in 1979. These all may have suggested that history was working on P'yŏngyang's side. The reality was that from the late 1980s "the correlation of forces" was working against North Korea.[21] South Korea's economic growth from the 1960s on and its transition to democracy from the late 1980s only made the country stronger. North Korea's economy, by contrast, slowed down, stagnated, and then declined (see below). And the collapse of the Soviet Union and China's move toward a market system only isolated the regime.

If the Korean War never ended for Kim Il Sung, neither did the anti-Japanese struggle. The DPRK also carried out anti-Japanese propaganda and raised fears of Japanese remilitarization. All North Koreans learned of the Japanese "atrocities and crimes" committed and the heroic achievements of the resistance led by the young Kim Il Sung. It maintained hostile rhetoric toward Japan so that the liberation struggle against colonial Japan merged with the post–Korean War struggle against U.S. imperialists, their South Korean puppets, and their Japanese allies. The two countries had no diplomatic relations. Japan, however, was an important source of income, which came in the form of remittances sent by Koreans in Japan to family members in North Korea. To keep an eye on the Japanese, the regime kidnapped Japanese citizens and used them to train spies in language and customs.

RELENTLESS MILITARIZATION

As he prepared for the eventual renewal of hostilities, Kim Il Sung kept his country in a perpetual state of war. The mobilization of the nation for war never ceased and in fact tended to intensify over the years. The armed forces were enlarged after the withdrawal of the Chinese People's Volunteer Army in 1958. In the following year the regime created the Worker and Peasant Red Guard, a militia that embraced much of the adult population. All men from eighteen to forty-five and single women from eighteen to thirty-five were required to serve. In late 1962, Kim Il Sung, in response to the Cuban missile crisis, announced a four-point program at a meeting of the Central Committee of the Workers' Party that called for arming the entire population and fortifying the whole country. At this time, Kim adopted a "people's defense" military strategy that required turning the entire country into an armed camp. All able-bodied adults and children received military training. Later, in 1970, the Young Red Guard was established, which enrolled young people from fifteen to seventeen. By the early 1970s the Young Red Guard (Pulgŭn Ch'ŏngnyŏn Kŭnwidae) numbered 1.25 million members. The Young Red Guards in each province formed a corps, those in each county formed a regiment, and at the village or hamlet level they formed squads.[22] Almost every worker and peasant received military training, and children from the age of seven were taught how to use handguns. Eventually, about a quarter of the population was in the reserves. Military checkpoints were established throughout the country. To prevent the destruction of the nation's infrastructure, as happened in the Korean War, hundreds of military factories were constructed underground. South Korean intelligence believed that 8,000 underground factories and military installations were eventually constructed with 500 kilometers of tunnels.[23] If North Korea were again bombed, it could still operate under the ground as it did during the Korean War, but this time on a massive scale.

A number of factors explain why militarization tended to intensify over the years. As Kim Il Sung purged potential rivals, he increasingly surrounded himself with fellow former guerilla fighters whose experience was in waging war. In addition, the withdrawal of Chinese troops in 1958 and a decline in Soviet trade in the 1960s led to sharp increases in military spending. The troubles he had in balancing relations between China and the Soviet Union also encouraged military self-reliance. The Soviet retreat in the Cuban missile crisis led to a belief that the nation could not rely on its help if war broke out. Mass mobilization and military preparedness were also effective in maintaining tight control over the country. Another reason may have been Kim's concern to prevent a repeat of the North Korean population's failure to resist when UN and ROK forces invaded the North in 1950. In addition, the regime generally felt threatened by the presence of U.S. forces along its southern border.

To make sure the population was at military readiness and possessed the will to resist an invasion with the ferocity that was absent in 1950, the population was subjected to constant training and propaganda. Military drills and preparedness exercises were carried out on a far greater scale than in South Korea. Government rhetoric suggested that an invasion was imminent. Music, dramas, school lessons, every medium was used to promote a militarily ready society. The vocabulary of public announcements, no matter what subject, was laced with fierce, militant rhetoric. International events were interpreted as either a sign that the United States and its allies were planning an invasion or were used as warnings for the need for preparedness. In the wake of the Cuban missile crisis, Kim argued that the nation must be prepared to expel the "Yankee Imperialist" invaders and their South Korean allies as well as aid revolutionaries in the South. The increased U.S. involvement in Vietnam, the breakdown of talks with the South in 1972–1973, and the Gulf War of 1990–1991 also were occasions to increase combat readiness.

Despite having only half the population of the South, P'yŏngyang was able to match the South in the size of its military and even overtake it in the 1970s. By 1972, its army numbering 485,000 troops was one of the largest in the world in proportion to its population, which was only about 12 million at the time. In the mid-1970s it was expanded again, reaching 680,000 in 1978. The latter figure included 41,000 commando forces. In the 1970s P'yŏngyang established the Second Economic Commission to be in charge of military industry. The economy was now divided into the military and the nonmilitary sector. The military industry was turning out a considerable number of weapons, including tanks, artillery pieces, antitank missiles, amphibious vehicles, patrol boats, multiple rocket launchers, and submarines.[24] There was an early effort to develop more unconventional weapons. In 1976, P'yŏngyang bought Soviet Scud missiles from Egypt and around the same time began to modernize a small nuclear reactor supplied by the Soviets. The DPRK began constructing a 200-megawatt and a 500-megawatt reactor and large processing plants at Taechon and Yongbyon (Yŏngbyŏn), an obvious effort to develop nuclear weapons. In the 1980s, working from Soviet Scud missiles, the North Koreans began to develop longer-range missiles. They developed the Rodong-1 missile with a range of 1,000 kilometers in 1993. Starting in the 1960s, the state started a biological weapons program, developing a number of strains of bacteria.[25] Thus, despite the slower economic growth after 1970, North Korea remained militarily formidable.

THE IDEOLOGY OF SELF-RELIANCE

North Korea's leadership was driven by an intense nationalism. Kim Il Sung sought to make his country militarily and economically strong while preparing to reunite his nation. He relentlessly pursued a policy of economic nationalism and self-reliance, much as Japan did after 1931. In pursuing his policies, he made intensive use of indoctrination. Perhaps no Communist regime ever emphasized ideology as much as North Korea. Originally the state was founded on the principles of orthodox Marxism-Leninism. Marxism-Leninism provided Kim Il Sung and the other North Korean leaders with a vocabulary, and the Soviet Union a model, for achieving the goal of establishing a strong and independent Korea. It linked its national aspirations with a universal philosophy. Just as Korea in the past sought to borrow and adopt the most civilized patterns for society from China, North Korean leaders sought to appropriate the most progressive set of ideas for their society. Thus Marxism-Leninism was adopted to achieve the nationalist goals of economic and military strength and national sovereignty and to place the Korean people in the vanguard of history. In the process, North Korea gradually evolved an ideology of its own: *juche* thought (*chuch'e sasang*). *Juche* can be translated as "self-reliance." At its core was an emphasis on political independence, economic and military self-reliance, and Korean nationalism. North Korean publications explained it as an adaptation of Marxism-Leninism to conditions of the country. Eventually *juche* came to have little to do with Marxist ideology. One authority on North Korea, Dae-sook Suh, has called it "nothing more than xenophobic nationalism that has little relevance to Communism."[26]

Juche first appeared in a speech by the great leader on December 28, 1955. Kim expressed his criticism of those in his party who blindly followed Soviet and Chinese ways, urging them to be more self-reliant. This speech was a prelude to his successful effort to eliminate Soviet- and Chinese-connected members from the leadership. Gradually Kim Il Sung developed *juche* until by the 1970s it became the reigning system of thought. *Juche* at first meant a creative adaptation of Marxism-Leninism without slavishly imitating Moscow or Beijing. It was an ideology that argued the country could shape its own destiny. Kim Il Sung in 1972 explained *juche as* meaning "one is responsible for one's own destiny and one has also the capacity for hewing out one's own destiny."[27] Its origins were fictitiously traced backed to his guerilla days and even to his youth in the 1920s. In the 1960s the term was used in public pronouncements of all sorts. By then, official publications began to suggest that *juche* was a complete system of thought. It was the ideological basis of a way of socialism more appropriate to North Korean conditions. *Juche* emerged as a comprehensive ideology in North Korea in the early 1960s when the Soviet Union reduced its aid to the regime, making it less secure. Thus the rise of the ideology to a central place in state propaganda coincided with the shift of economic allocation to military expenditures at that time. P'yŏngyang emphasized self-reliance when it felt it could depend less on its allies.

The elaboration of *juche* continued throughout the 1970s. By then, theorists sometimes argued that it was a universal philosophy. It was interpreted in increasingly broad if vague ways, and volumes were written on it. Its study became the core curriculum in the schools and the subject of weekly study sessions at workplaces throughout the country. According to the 1972 constitution, *juche* was the "guiding principle of politics."[28] In 1979, an Academy of Juche Sciences was established in P'yŏngyang under the direction of party ideologist Hwang Jang Yop (Hwang Chang-yŏp) (1923–). The universal principle of *juche* was applied to every field: music, sports, science. It was deliberately vague and meant to be somewhat incomprehensible to foreigners. North Korea developed an ambiguity about its role in the world at large. At times its universality was highlighted. *Juche* study societies were organized around the world under the supervision of the Juche Research Center created in Tokyo in 1978.[29] The DPRK made grandiose claims that it was a "mighty beacon of hope for all humanity." Yet at other times it appeared to be very much an indigenous Korean ideology by and for Koreans. From the early 1980s its uniquely Korean character was emphasized more. Its universal elements were less often mentioned. At that time, references to Marxism-Leninism and to the international socialist movements also began to disappear from public pronouncements.[30] By then the ideology of the DPRK under the label of *juche* began to be narrowly restricted to a blend of extreme nationalism and the cult of the Kim family.

North Korean official histories presented an increasingly xenophobic racial-nationalist history depicting the constant struggle of a racially pure, virtuous people against outside invaders. This narrative could be found in South Korean textbooks and in popular culture in the South as well. But North Korea's version of history was more extreme. The acknowledgment of foreign borrowing or assistance was rarely given. For instance, texts dropped all references to even the Soviet Union's role in liberating the country from the Japanese. Full credit was given to the heroic Korean people under the great leader, Kim Il Sung. Those in Korea's past who had sought foreign support were criticized for failing to rely on the Korean people instead. Kim Il Sung used this accusation of being subservient to foreign powers to attack his opponents. In this, the regime was influenced by the rejection by the colonial-era nationalist writers of *sadaejuŭi* (flunkyism), the Korean tradition of serving the great that had made Korea a loyal tributary state of China until the nineteenth century. Koreans in both North and South viewed these former tributary relations as a sign of their past weakness and a national failing. In the South as well, dissidents frequently accused the South Korean regime of being subservient to the United States. The DPRK's emphasis on self-reliance was thus motivated by a fiercely independent strain in twentieth-century nationalism that was strengthened by being thwarted by the Americans from reunifying the country, and by humiliation over its reliance on the Chinese support and Soviet aid for its survival.

The realities of the small nation meant that it was never able to achieve economic autonomy. For instance, North Korea remained reliant on Soviet technology and on Soviet oil. The regime was only able to avoid being totally reliant on a single patron. However, the regime did eventually achieve an ideological autonomy by having its own system of thought. Drawn from Kim Il Sung's guerilla experience and by the Korean War, *juche* was in fact the ideology of the bunker and an instrument Kim used to achieve unquestioned and unchallenged authority for himself and later his son. As an ideology of the bunker, it was closely linked with the drive for militarization. To be independent and secure meant to be militarily prepared. Self-sufficiency was not unique to North Korea. In fact, the idea of import substitution was common in developing countries. India in the 1950s and 1960s is another example. Concerns about avoiding economic dependence are reflected in the intellectual discourse and political rhetoric of Latin America and other developing states in the decades after World War II as well.[31] But in North Korea it was carried out with a particular urgency that, coupled with the country's isolation, its authoritarian ruthlessness, and its ultranationalism, gave it a unique quality.

In the past, Korea had borrowed beliefs from abroad—Buddhism, originally from India and Confucianism from China—and then made some adaptations to suit Korean needs or cultural dispositions. But Korean Buddhism and Confucianism, especially the latter, still very much adhered to orthodox forms. In fact, scholars and officials in Chosŏn Korea were very proud to have firmly adhered to the letter of the Confucian classics. Thus, the radical ideological evolution of North Korean Communism was historically unprecedented.

THE CULT OF THE KIM FAMILY

The ideology of *juche* was linked with the cult of Kim Il Sung and his family. The cult of Kim Il Sung went beyond that of Stalin in Russia or even Mao. Adoration of the Great Leader and his family, especially his son, came to pervade every aspect of North Korean society to an extent that has struck most foreign observers as incomprehensibly bizarre. Kim Il Sung initially followed the example of Stalin as the leader of the party and revolution, and he was critical of Khrushchev's de-Stalinization campaign that began in 1956. His own cult of personality emerged gradually. It increased with the publication of his *The Selected Works of Kim Il Sung* in 1956 and intensified in the 1960s. Kim's propaganda organs began calling him *widaehan suryŏng* (Great Leader) in 1967. Soon his name was preceded by such honorifics as "Ever-victorious iron-willed brilliant commander," "the sun of the nation," "the red sun of the oppressed people of the world," "the greatest leader of our time."[32] Kim Il Sung became the infallible leader, and his *juche* thought the infallible truth. The intensity of this cult of personality can be illustrated by the announcement of his election to party secretary in 1971:

> When it was announced that Comrade Kim Il Sung, the founder of our Party, peerless patriot, national hero, ever-victorious iron-willed brilliant commander, one of the outstanding leaders of the international communist movement and working-class movement and the great Leader of our Party and the forty million Korean people, had been elected General Secretary of the Central Committee of the Party, the entire delegat[ion] to the Congress and the observers all rose and loudly shouted "Long live Comrade Kim Il Sung, the Great Leader."[33]

In April 1972, Kim Il Sung reached sixty, an important landmark in Korean tradition. Sixtieth birthdays, known in Korean as *hwan'gap*, are often elaborately celebrated. The fanfare that accompanied the Great Leader's sixtieth birthday, however, was unprecedented in Korean history. Amid enormous, well-choreographed demonstrations, a massive statue painted in gold was unveiled on Mansudae, a high hill overlooking the Taedong River in P'yŏngyang. A spot that was, ironically, once the site of a shrine for the Japanese emperor.[34] A vast marble museum opened dedicated to recording the heroic deeds of the great leader. Its ninety-two exhibition rooms dealt with the milestones in recent Korean history: Kim's heroic and successful anti-Japanese resistance, his liberation of Korea, his direction of national defense during the Korean War, and his construction of the socialist state after the Korean War. Most interesting were the rooms filled with gifts sent from all over the world to honor the great leader, a tribute to his global stature and his many admirers abroad. At this time officials began to wear badges with his picture. Eventually all North Koreans wore these badges. In fact, a way of punishing people became removing the badges, marking the individual as less than a reliable revolutionary, a person best avoided. There were three types of badges—for students, adults, and party members. They bound the Korean people to their leaders. By the time of his seventieth birthday in 1982 the entire country became dotted with shrines to Kim Il Sung. The places he visited, and he traveled frequently throughout the small country, became sacred sites marked with commemorative plates. His quotes were carved into prominent rock outcroppings and mountainsides throughout the country. Songs in praise of him dominated the airwaves. To celebrate this new milestone in his life, an Arch of Triumph, larger than the original arch in France it was modeled on, was constructed. In addition, a Tower of *Juche* was constructed to honor his contribution to human thought. It was the highest stone structure in the world, and it is topped with a red torch. The Kim Il Sung Stadium, a massive sports arena holding 100,000, was opened with an international competition that attracted all of six countries.[35]

So many statues, mosaics, portraits, and shrines to the Great Leader existed that it was almost impossible to be out of sight of one. In every classroom, office, and home his portrait was hung in a prominent place. At the base of these portraits was often a small cloth to clean the glass plate over his picture.[36] Workers and students began their days bowing before his portrait and placed wreaths at his statues on holidays. The holidays themselves centered on his life. The big holidays were April 15, his birthday, and later February 16, his son Kim Jong Il's birthday. His hometown of Mangyŏngdae was a place of pilgrimage. His life and his various heroic activities were the subjects of most of the nation's output of movies, plays, and operas. Kim Il Sung was portrayed as an international figure admired by the oppressed throughout the world. North Koreans were told of tributes to the Great Leader that constantly came in from abroad.

Although clearly modeled on the cult of Stalin, Kim Il Sung's cult took on elements that some have identified with Confucianism and some with Christianity. Perhaps it was influenced by both traditions, since not only was Kim Il Sung a product of a Confucian society, he also came from a Christian family. Kim was not just the "iron-willed commander," and "incomparable genius of the revolution," but a benevolent, loving figure. North Korean propaganda showed him surrounded by crowds of adoring subjects basking in his benevolence, or as it was often stated, "bonded in his bosom." He was the "parental leader" (ŏbŏi suryŏng) of the Korean people who loved and cared for his people, who ruled them with benevolence and protected them from the hostile Yankee imperialists. On his sixtieth birthday it was stated in the paper *Kŭlloja* (*the Worker*), "Comrade Kim Il Sung, a genius of revolution and great Marxist-Leninist, has lived his entire sixty years only for our people's freedom and happiness and the victory of the Korean and world revolutions."[37] Koreans were taught that under his guidance they were marching "on the road to paradise." Already they had achieved the essential material basics for happiness. "Throughout the nation's history, our ancestors thought a paradise to be a society where people enjoy three things: being able to eat white rice, live under a clay-roof, and educate their children. These three 'privileges' were the life-long aspiration for our ancestors. Now we have achieved all three under the wise leadership of the Great leader."[38] Children were taught to sing "we have nothing to envy in the world."

North Korean propaganda often used familiar terms, describing him as the parental or fatherly leader of the people. The use of family and kinship terms to describe the relationship between Kim Il Sung and the people provided an ideological context for the transfer of power to his son. The cult of Kim Il Sung became a family cult with the rise of his son Kim Jong Il. The elder Kim, worried by his succession, decided to make his son his successor, perhaps sometime in the early 1970s. The rise was a slow and cautious one. In 1975, at the time of the Three-Revolutions Teams, reports began of the "party center." Then in the late 1970s, Kim Il Sung carried out more purges, perhaps eliminating opposition or potential opposition to his son. In 1980, at the Sixth Congress of the Workers' Party, Kim Jong Il was named to the Presidium of the Politburo, the Secretariat of the Central Committee, and the Military Commission. He ranked fourth in the party hierarchy. It was clear that he was the designated heir. In 1983, he then moved up to rank second in the official leadership hierarchy after his father; and in 1988 he was receiving a level of honorifics in public pronouncements similar to his father. The timing of this rise is not clear, but most probably the problems that followed the death of Mao Zedong in 1976 only highlighted the importance of insuring a smooth succession of power. With the rise of the son, the entire Kim family was glorified in all media. Texts were rewritten to make the modern history of Korea the history of the Kim family.[39] His great grandfather was reported to have led the attack on the U.S.S. *General Sherman* in 1866. This now became a major incident in Korean history, the beginning of the struggle against American and Western imperialism with the Kim family in the forefront. Kim Jong Il's birth was now located on the sacred Paektusan mountain along the Korean-Manchurian border, although most outside observers agree that at the time in 1942 the family was in Siberia. His mother, Kim Jong Suk, was elevated to the status of a national hero who had fought the Japanese alongside her husband. Monuments to the Kim family appeared throughout the country.

Not the least of the influences on the cult of Kim Il Sung and his family was the imperial cult of prewar Japan. North Korean school children paid their daily obeisance to the Great Leader at the school's shrine to him much as colonial Korean school children attended shrines to the semi-divine Japanese emperor. The practice of bowing ceremoniously in the direction of the imperial palace in Tokyo, the ubiquitous Shinto shrines, and tone of reverence expressed when referring to the emperor all had strikingly similar manifestations in North Korea. Even the glorification of the Kim family resembled that of the Japanese imperial family and its ancestors. Like the Japanese imperial cult, the cult of Kim Il Sung sought to inculcate an almost mystical sense of unity among the people and demanded their total loyalty to the leader.

Indoctrination reached a level of intensity perhaps found nowhere else. Virtually all art, literature, film, and music was directed at glorifying Kim Il Sung, the revolution, and the great leader's philosophy of *juche*. North Koreans learned very little of the prerevolutionary culture, or of art, music, and literature from outside Korea. The cult was accompanied by a severe isolation that prevented the populace having even a minimum of knowledge of the outside world. International news consisted mainly of reports of foreign praises of the Great Leader and meetings of *juche* study clubs in various countries. Foreign visitors to North Korea after 1980 were often amazed by the near total ignorance of the outside world by a generation that had grown up after the conflict. While many of these developments grew out of the pre-1950 ideology and dynamics of the North Korean state, the Korean War contributed to this ideological hothouse by isolating the state from the West and from their compatriots in the South. Ultimately *juche* combined with the cult of Kim Il Sung effectively isolated North Korea ideologically from its neighbors and helped insulate it from the upheavals and collapses that swept the Communist world in the late 1980s and early 1990s. It contributed to the ease by which P'yŏngyang was able to ignore the winds of reform in China and elsewhere in the remaining socialist countries. North Korea had become a cultist state, where the people were intensely bonded to the leadership and isolated from the rest of the world.

SOCIETY

Despite the egalitarian ideology of Communism, the DPRK developed in ways that mirrored the rigidly hierarchical, hereditary society of premodern Korea. The consolidation of the regime was not accompanied by violent class warfare. Partly this was due to the fact that most of the landlord and business class fled to the South after 1945. However, the educated that remained were used by the regime. There was no war against intellectuals and people with technical skills, such as that characterized by Maoist China. Interestingly the Korean Worker's Party had for its logo the hammer and sickle plus a writing brush. The latter represented a class the North Koreans called the *samuwŏn*, essentially white-collar professional people such as teachers, government officials, and clerks. But there was a great social upheaval. Those who had served at the bottom of the social scale—peasants and workers—now emerged at the top of society. The social mobility of the early years of the regime was striking. Most of the leadership, like Kim Il Sung, came from rather modest backgrounds. The KWP's membership in the late 1940s was drawn largely from the peasantry, and this was even more so when the party was rebuilt after the Korean War.

However, it was far from a classless society. An elaborate system of classification based on family background developed from 1957 to 1960. Everyone was placed in three basic groups: core, wavering, and hostile. The core class, about 30 percent of the population, comprised those who came from families of urban workers, Communist Party members, or those who had contributed to the Communist movement. The hostile class, also about 30 percent, came from families of landlords, businessmen, Japanese collaborators, members of Christian religious groups or others who had opposed the regime. The rest, about 40 percent, belong to the in-between category, the wavering class. This system was further refined during 1964–1969 when the regime undertook another series of careful background checks on their citizens. The population was further classified into fifty-one *sŏngbun*, or ranks; twelve belonged to the core class group, nine to the wavering, and the remainder to the hostile class.[40] All were based primarily on family background. Members of the hostile class led miserable lives excluded from higher education and positions of responsibility and were discriminated against in many other ways. Many were resettled in remote areas, primarily the northeastern part of the country, far removed from the capital. These categories were hereditary and they profoundly mattered. Food rations, access to desired goods, housing, jobs, career advancement, and admittance to higher education were determined by the classification, which was very difficult to change.

Although family background was the main determinant of social class, people could be downgraded as a result of improper political behavior. The primary test of behavior was the loyalty to the Great Leader. A sign of privilege was to live in P'yŏngyang. In contrast to the noise, dirt, and chaos of Seoul, it was a clean, quiet city with some attractive buildings, efficient public transportation, and trees and parks. It was also a city devoid of cars, busy markets, or nightlife, striking many foreigners as grimly sterile. And everywhere were the monuments to the Great Leader, dominating parks, squares, and the skyline. People lived in apartments assigned by rank. A considerable gap existed between the relatively comfortable life in the capital and the rougher, harder living conditions in provincial cities and in the countryside. An even greater gap existed between the lives of the official elite of higher-ranking KWP members, top bureaucrats, and military officers. This became more pronounced over time. By the 1980s, if not earlier, the very top lived in great luxury, driving expensive German cars, drinking French cognac, and having access to other imported luxuries. The hereditary nature of the ruling elite became more pronounced over time. By the time of Kim Il Sung's death in 1994, most of the younger high-ranking officials were the sons, nephews, or in-laws of the old guard. Despite the early and progressive move toward women's equality, few women held high positions.

Just as in traditional Korea, the education system reflected the hierarchical nature of society. There was the elite school, Kim Il Sung University in P'yŏngyang, followed by the technical Kim Ch'aek University. Other schools were of lower rank. Admission was by family background and ideological purity as much as merit. Thus, just as in premodern Korea, when the civil examinations were used to select high officials but were only opened to members of the *yangban* elite, the DPRK school system functioned in a similar way. Prestige degrees were a means of reaffirming status rather than acquiring it. Youths from twelve to eighteen could try to join the Socialist Youth Organization, an important gateway to better opportunities later in life. But membership in this too appeared to be linked to family status. Thus the egalitarianism and social mobility of the first years was replaced by a rough replication of the rigid, hierarchical structure of society based largely on inheritance that was characteristic of traditional Korea.

No country better deserved to be called totalitarian. Children were given toy guns to play with and were taught military marches. Young people practiced carefully choreographed dances and marches for which the country became famous. These were much like massive military drills. Military service was a major part of life. Young men served from the age of sixteen to twenty-eight—twelve to thirteen years, later shortened to only eight years; after this was completed they served in the reserves. Daily life for most citizens was tightly organized. The public distribution system set up at the onset of the regime allocated food, cooking oil, clothes, and other essentials. In the capital most people went to work early in the morning. They attended sessions where they read and discussed the newspapers before actually working. There were breaks for calisthenics and frequent after-work political study sessions that could last into the evening. Women were allowed to leave early to pick up children from schools or day care centers and then prepare dinner. Others stayed at their worksite to attend meetings or sessions where they reviewed the day's work and discussed future plans and how they would meet the goals assigned in the economic plans. The meetings included self-criticisms and ways to adhere to *juche* principles in their work. Less is known about rural life, where conditions were harder. Farmers, too, attended discussion centers. It is reported that there were thirty-minute daily sessions in which the newspaper was read and discussed. Radios and later televisions were adjusted so they could only receive the official Central Korean Broadcasting Service. The chief newspaper, the *Rodong Sinmun*, was devoid of any real news but was a vehicle for disseminating the official line on various aspects of life. Provincial newspapers were virtually identical in content to the main newspaper in the capital. It was difficult to change jobs or move without special permission. Movement was strictly monitored; special passes were required to travel. Few societies in the world were as regimented and controlled as the DPRK under Kim Il Sung.

Art and literature served the state. Writers and artists were under the direction of the Federation of Literature and Art. From 1948 to 1962 this was headed by the novelist and short story writer Han Sŏrya (1900–1970?), one of a number of prominent cultural leaders who had voluntarily come to the North after 1945. Literature, originally in the socialist realist mode, came under increasing restrictions until by the 1960s it consisted mainly of panegyrics and crude, often violent tales glorifying the deeds of the Great Leader or the heroic struggles of peasants fighting the Japanese or other agents of oppression. Han, who had been a successful writer associated with the proletarian literature movement in colonial times was purged in 1962 as too bourgeois.[41] Artistic expression was so constricted that it was difficult for any creative individual to flourish. Ch'oe Sŭng-hŭi (1911–?), an internationally acclaimed dancer who introduced modern Japanese influences into Korean traditional dance during the colonial period went to the North in 1946. She adopted Korean and modern dances to revolutionary themes, but she also fell out of favor in the 1960s and disappeared from the public. From the 1970s the stage was dominated by collectively composed revolution operas such as *P'i Bada* (*Sea of Blood*) first performed in 1971, the story of mass killings under the Japanese with lyrics said to have been composed by Kim Il Sung. Another work, *Kkot p'anŭn ch'ŏnyŏ* (*The Flower Girl*), the story of oppressed villagers under the Japanese and a peasant woman turned revolutionary, first appeared in 1973 and remained a staple for the next three decades. Movies followed the same themes, the same mix of brutality and sentimentality. Kim Jong Il famously took great interest in filmmaking and is reported to have visited the main film studio outside of P'yŏngyang hundreds of times to offer on-the-spot guidance to the actors and film crews and to have authored *The Theory of Cinematic Art* in 1973. Most music output consisted of songs extolling the leadership, such as "Song of General Kim Il Sung," "Long Life and Good Health to the Leader," and "We Sing of His Benevolent Love."

While almost all art and entertainment was focused on glorifying the regime and its Great Leader, some traditional cultural forms survived. Korean curved roofs topped some buildings, and women wore traditional *hanbok* dresses on special occasions and learned to play traditional instruments such as the *kayagŭm*, a Korean zither, along with Western ones. Perhaps, the most important survival of tradition in this society molded to the will and vision of its leader was the Korean love of family. North Koreans with official approval displayed their fondness for children, the state boasted of its preschools and kindergartens, and family ties were still important for most ordinary people.

ECONOMIC PROBLEMS

After an impressive decade of recovery and growth, the North Korean economy began to slow down. In 1961, the regime launched a Seven-Year Economic Plan (1961–1967) to accelerate industrialization. Initially there were signs that there was to be a bit more emphasis on consumer goods to improve the living standards. But this changed in 1962 when relations with the Soviet Union temporarily soured, and with the Cuban missile crisis in October 1962. When the Soviet Union backed down and removed its missiles in the face of U.S. threats, its reliability as an ally came into question. Lacking confidence in the Soviet Union as an ally, Kim Il Sung focused more of the economy on military-related production. He was also concerned about the hard-line anti-Communist stance of the military government of Park Chung Hee that ruled in the South from 1961. As a result, up to 30 percent of economic resources were allocated to military production, perhaps the highest of any country. When some of his technocrats expressed concern over the effects of this on economic development, Kim removed them from their positions. Subsequently, the Seven-Year Plan began to run into trouble and was extended three years. It was followed by a Six-Year Plan (1971–1976). Although declared a success, it too was extended one year, suggesting that the state was having trouble meeting its economic targets.

To promote economic production Kim attempted to kindle revolutionary zeal and launched military-style campaigns. The economy was treated as a series of military campaigns with such slogans as "capturing the six hills" of production. Industries were organized on a military basis with companies and battalions, and workers were given military ranks.[42] An early attempt at this was the Taean system, inaugurated in 1961. This transferred the decision making at factories and shops from managers to committees of party zealots. Kim himself traveled frequently around the country giving on-the-spot guidance to encourage productivity. Also in the early 1960s in a bid for agricultural self-sufficiency the regime adopted the Ch'ongsan-ri method. This was named after an agricultural village near P'yŏngyang where Kim Il Sung spent fifteen days in February 1960 providing "on-the-spot guidance" to the local farm cooperative. The movement emphasized self-sufficiency and the revolutionary spirit of self-reliance, using guerilla units as a model. Private garden plots were denounced; instead farmers were told, much as industrial workers had been, that they were in a battle in which each person must sacrifice selflessly. In 1974, the regime launched the Three-Revolutions Teams movement. Inspired, at least in part, by the Red Guards in China's Cultural Revolution, teams of young revolutionaries went into mines, factories, and other production centers to increase output by stimulating the revolutionary enthusiasm of the workers. They attacked "bureaucratism" and called on workers to develop innovative solutions to problems. Speed battles were launched in which workers and farmers were urged to labor tirelessly for days on end to spur production. After 1978, China abandoned this approach for a more market-oriented economic development. North Korea, however, persisted in it.

During the 1960s the government ceased issuing meaningful statistics on economics. Because of this near total statistic blackout it is difficult to know what the economic growth rate or the real condition of the economy was. Official pronouncements gave obviously exaggerated figures such as the 16 percent growth rate of the 1971–1976 Six-Year Plan, despite the fact it had been extended an extra year. One indication of trouble was the food shortages that took place in the early 1970s despite a heavy investment in agriculture. In the 1960s Kim had launched his "four modernizations" in agriculture, which consisted of mechanization, electrification, irrigation, and chemicalization (chemical fertilizer and pesticides).[43] Still, even with this heavy and costly investment, agriculture production lagged behind basic needs.

By the early 1970s, the North Korean leadership had come to realize how dated its technology was. Most of the country's power plants and steel mills were from the colonial period. Kim Il Sung may have also become concerned over South Korea's rapid industrialization under Park. In 1972, he began a buying spree of Western plants and machinery. Petrochemical, textile, concrete, steel, pulp, and paper manufacturing plants were purchased, but the equipment was too sophisticated, the country lacked parts or money to buy them, and the electricity supply was often unreliable, rendering many of these purchases of limited use. Furthermore, North Korea was unable to earn the foreign exchange to repay the loans. Unfortunately for the regime, this tepid venture into buying technology from the capitalist world coincided with the oil shock of 1973, which depressed the price of its mineral exports. The state, unable to pay its debts, defaulted on them in late 1974.[44] Foreign debt payments were stretched out, but eventually P'yŏngyang was unable to pay even these and defaulted again in the mid-1980s. Remittances from Koreans living in Japan provided some hard currency, but in the 1970s the DPRK began to engage in counterfeiting and in drug smuggling through their foreign embassies, under the cover of diplomatic immunity, to acquire badly needed foreign exchange.

Up to the 1970s, North Korea had still maintained an impressive level of economic development. By that time, no more than a third of the population was rural; only Japan was as urbanized. Foreign observers were often impressed with the country's degree of industrialization. Harrison Salisbury, the first prominent American journalist to enter North Korea since the Korean War, reported of his 1972 visit that the country had made a "tremendous technical and industrial achievement." Visiting the Hamhŭng-Hŭngnam area on the east coast, he saw "endless vistas of industrial smokestacks."[45] Several years later another Western journalist contrasted the orderly industrial society of North Korea with South Korea, noting the lack of slums, prostitution, or children selling gum that could be seen in Seoul.[46] But much of its industry was labor intensive. Rather than developing improvements in productivity, Kim Il Sung was still relying on mass mobilization such as *ch'ŏllima* campaigns in which workers competed for metals and fought speed battles to increase output. North Korea made full use of all its potential labor, including employing women in light industry, sending soldiers to help with industrial production or construction projects, and making use of the large prison population as industrial labor. Despite these efforts, production stagnated by the 1980s. The government claimed the Second Seven-Year Plan, 1978–1984, was a success, with a 12.1 percent yearly growth rate, but it was obvious to outsiders that this was false, which was suggested by its extension to 1986. North Korea appeared to be reaching a limit as to what it could achieve under its command economy.

The bunker state that was first constructed in the Korean War created what one writer has called a "strange socialist fortress."[47] Kim Il Sung used techniques of mass mobilization to rebuild the war-ravaged country and as a means of control. But there was no further evolution in economic and social development. Rather, the state continued to rigidly adhere to relentless political indoctrination, mass campaigns, and emphasis on military over civilian needs.

KOREA IN GLOBAL PERSPECTIVE:
NORTH KOREA AS A COMMUNIST COUNTRY

How can we characterize North Korea? Some observers, such as Adrian Buzo and Paul French, have labeled North Korea a Stalinist state. In fact, this is a most common characterization of the DPRK. It is argued that Kim Il Sung took Stalinist Russia as his model, with its highly centralized command economy, its emphasis on autarkic development rather than international trade, the priority given to heavy industry to support a large military, the complete collectivization and mechanization of agriculture, and the use of both propaganda and state terror to promote production. Even Kim Il Sung's cult of personality resembled Stalin's. This is not surprising since almost every Communist regime established in the years after 1945 was influenced by the Soviet example. Besides, Kim Il Sung lived in the Soviet Union during World War II, was put in power by the Soviets, and depended on them for aid.

However, Kim Il Sung's regime also resembled Maoist China. Like Mao, he was enamored of the potential of mass mobilization to achieve development targets, used self-criticism campaigns to instill correct thinking, and made use of the "mass-line" methods in which cadres both taught and learned from the people. His cult of personality, in which his "thought" was viewed as among the highest ideological achievements of humanity, can also be seen as Maoist. It is clear that the DPRK borrowed and was influenced by some aspects of Maoism—the Three-Revolutions campaign of the mid-1970s is an example. However, much of the Maoist-type features of North Korea appear to have been independent developments, perhaps not so unusual considering the similar cultural backgrounds of the two societies. North Korea deviated in many ways from Maoism. There were no campaigns against intellectualists; although, of course, independent thinkers were not tolerated. There was less suspicion of technocrats, no backyard steel mills, and no Cultural Revolution. Nor were they any attacks on the family. In contrast to the radical swings in policy that characterized the PRC after

1949, the DPRK adhered rigidly to the same methods and policies from the 1950s to the 1990s. In this way, North Korea resembled Albania under the four decades of Enver Hoxha's Communist dictatorship more than it did China.

Some aspects of North Korean Communism appear to be sui generis. There was the Korean belief in the transformative power of education, a tradition derived from Confucianism as practiced in that country, which is evident in the constant "learning sessions" and other propaganda lessons. Familial language was used to an extent not found in other Communist regimes and was a contrast to Mao's own war on the family. In fact, the Confucian way in which the leadership was portrayed as benevolent rulers and society was described as an extended family bound together by reciprocal love was distinctive. So was the degree in which the regime was openly nationalist. Only North Vietnam was similar in being so nationalistic, but Hanoi's nationalism never displaced Marxism-Leninism to the degree it did in the DPRK. Other Communist regimes sought to isolate themselves from the world economy; none ideologically isolated themselves to such a degree by evolving such a self-referential, all-encompassing system of thought as *juche*.

North Korea differed from most other Communist states in others ways as well. The rivalry between Moscow and Beijing enabled North Korea to achieve a degree of political autonomy to pursue its own path, which was absent in Mongolia or the Eastern European states. It could be argued that none went through such a bitter colonial experience. Certainly none suffered from anything on the scale of the self-inflicted humiliation and destruction that resulted from the Korean War. North Korea was much more industrialized and urbanized than China or Vietnam. As late as the 1970s nearly four out of five Chinese lived in the countryside compared to only one in three in North Korea. It was also a small state, with a sense of its vulnerability, that was locked in competition with a larger claimant to the mantle of heir to national unity. And although the leaders of the DPRK had more impressive anti-imperialist, independence-fighter credentials, the ROK had two-thirds of the population and the traditional capital. The DPRK without Seoul was like a claimant to being the real France without having Paris.

North Korea continued to call itself socialist and maintained many features reminiscent of Stalinist Russia. However, with its elaborate hierarchical structure based on family background, its Kim-family cult, its extreme ultranationalism, and its *juche* ideology that eventually ceased to be Marxist in any meaningful way, it had evolved along its own path.

Kim Il Sung, from "Report on the Work of the Central Committee to the Fourth Congress of the Workers Party of Korea," September 11, 1961

Author Note: With the successful carrying out of the anti-imperialist, anti-feudal democratic revolution in the northern part of the country after the Liberation, North Korea gradually embarked on the path of transition to socialism; socialist transformation began at that time.

Before the war, however, because the necessary social, economic and material conditions were not yet fully mature, socialist transformation was only partial, the main work being to prepare for it. In the post war years socialist transformations of agriculture, handicrafts, capitalist trade and industry was undertaken on a full scale and in 1958 it was completed in all these fields almost simultaneously.

The Chollima Movement

The splendid achievements in socialist reconstruction of our country have been scored in the midst of the great upsurge of socialist construction and in the course of the Chollima movement.

The Chollima movement is a manifestation of the tremendous creative power of our people who have firmly rallied around the Party. It is a nationwide popular movement for the utmost acceleration of our social construction.

Our country had inherited a backward economy and culture from the old society and, in addition, went through a fierce war of three long years. We are building socialism in the conditions of north-south division of the country, standing face to face with the U.S. imperialists, and at the same time we are struggling for peaceful unification. In such a situation our struggle was bound to be exceedingly intense. Quickly to get rid of the backwardness left us by history, to accelerate the unification of the country, which is our supreme national task, we had to march ahead much faster than other people.

In view of this requirement of the development of our revolution, our Party mapped out a plan for definitely speeding up socialist construction in the North, and, on this basis, organized and mobilized the entire working people in the heroic struggle for socialist construction.

The working people of our country, educated and trained by the Party, were fully aware of the urgent requirement of the development of our revolution and of the historic mission they were entrusted with, and gave unanimous support to the Party's line of speeding up socialist construction.

In active response to the appeal of the Party, "Dash forward at the speed of Chollima!" our working people dashed ahead through thick and thin to carry out the task put forward by the Party. They rushed on and on, emulating each other, overcoming all obstacles and difficulties.

Thus, innovations were made and world-shaking miracles wrought almost every day on all fronts of socialist construction.

Our heroic working class built 300,000- to 400,000-ton-capacity blast furnaces, each in less than a year, laid a standard-gauge railway more than 80 kilometers in length in 75 days, and set up a huge, up-to-date vynalon factory on a spot which had been only a waste land in a little over one year. Our working people turned out more than 13,000 extra machine tools over and above the state plan within a year by initiating the machine tool multiplying movement. Within a period of three to four months they erected over a thousand factories for local industry by utilizing idle material and manpower in local areas. [48]

Kim Il Sung, from "Socialist Construction in the Democratic People's Republic of Korea and the South Korean Revolution." Lecture at the Ali Archam Academy of Social Sciences of Indonesia, April 14, 1965
The South Korean Revolution

Being a revolution for liberating one half of our country's territory and two-thirds of its population still held in bondage by foreign imperialists, the revolution in South Korea is an important component part of the Korean revolution as a whole. For the unification of our fatherland and the victory of the Korean revolution, it is necessary to strengthen the revolutionary forces in South Korea while promoting socialist construction in the North.

Since the first days of their occupation of South Korea, the U.S. imperialists have pursued the policies of military aggression and colonial enslavement. As a result, South Korea has been turned entirely into a colony, a military base of U.S. imperialism.

The South Korean "government" is a puppet regime set up with the armed support of the U.S. imperialists; it is nothing but a tool faithfully executing the instructions of its U.S. overlords.

Through this puppet regime and the use of so-called "aid" as a bait, the U.S. imperialists have placed all the political, economic, cultural and military affairs of South Korea under their control.

U.S. imperialism has thus set up a system of colonial rule following its occupation of South Korea, and, on this basis, has been enforcing an unprecedented military dictatorship over the South Korean people.

Today the national economy of South Korea is totally bankrupt and its industrial output stands at no more than 85 per cent at the time of Liberation.

Today there are roughly seven million unemployed and semi-employed in South Korea. And each year more than one million peasant households suffer from lack of food during the lean spring months.

The people are entirely denied political rights and are exposed to terrorism and tyranny.

Therefore, to attain freedom and liberation, the South Korean people must drive out the U.S. imperialist forces of aggression and overthrow the landlords, comprador capitalists and reactionary bureaucrats who are in league with them. U.S. imperialism is target No.1 of the struggle for the South Korean people.

There can be neither freedom and liberation for the people in South Korea, nor progress in South Korea society, nor the unification of our fatherland, unless the U.S. imperialist aggressive troops are driven out and colonial rule is abolished.

Thus the revolution in the South is a national liberation revolution against the foreign imperialist forces of aggression, and a democratic revolution against feudal forces.

The motive force of this revolution in South Korea is the working class and its most reliable ally—the peasantry—together with the students, intellectuals and petty bourgeois who are opposed to the imperialist and feudal forces. The national capitalists, too, may have a share in the anti-imperialist, anti-feudal struggle.[49]

13

ㅁ◇ㅁ

South Korea: From Poverty to Prosperity, 1953 to 1997

In March 1961, the *New York Times* reporter A. M. Rosenthal did a series on South Korea. It concluded with an article entitled "Outlook Dreary for South Korea." "South Korea," the report starts, "the poorer half of one of the poorest countries in the world, is trying to exist as a nation with too many people and too few resources." No one knows the answers to the country's economic woes, the author reported, except for "a Korea dependent for the foreseeable future, perhaps for decades, upon the self-interest and charity of . . . the United States."[1] This was not an unusually pessimistic assessment; for most outside observers, South Korea's prospects for the future looked grim. Overcrowded, possessing modest resources, artificially severed in half and cut off from the more industrial and developed North, riddled with official corruption and political instability, few countries must have seemed a less promising candidate for an economic takeoff. So how was it possible that South Korea could have become an economic powerhouse in just several decades? How could it have become one of the few postcolonial states to enter the ranks of developed countries? How could it have become not only one of the most prosperous, but also most democratic societies in Asia?

THE SYNGMAN RHEE YEARS, 1953–1960

Certainly there was little in the first years after the Korean War to hint at South Korea's dramatic economic transformation. In 1953, it was a nation shattered by three years of war. Seoul was in ruins, and a great deal of

373

infrastructure had been destroyed. Thousands of families were returning from refugee camps to ruined homes; many were separated from relatives in the North with whom they had no contact. Almost every family had a member or close relative killed or missing. Economically the southern provinces of Korea that made up the Republic of Korea were poorer than they had been before World War II. The country was dependent on massive economic assistance from the United States and also the spending of the large number of American forces in the country.

It was also a changed society. South Korea was still a mostly rural, agricultural country where traditional values were strong and loyalties were still primarily focused on family, clan, and locality. But the land reform that took place during the Korean War (see below) created a countryside of small family farms no longer dominated by the *yangban* class. And the Korean War had accelerated the growth of the urban population, as many refugees fled to the city during the conflict and stayed there. Although less than one in four people lived in urban centers, this was still a significant increase. The urban population, mostly poor, was more open to new ideas, influenced by democratic concepts, and concerned with opportunities for economic and social advancement. In short, the countryside was still conservative, but it was no longer dominated by the old aristocratic landholding families; and the cities were filled with a restless, volatile population.

Politically South Korea was dominated by the seventy-eight-year-old President Syngman Rhee. Still intellectually bright, energetic, and politically shrewd for his advanced age, he was unfortunately too rigid, authoritarian, stubborn, and concerned with maintaining his power to be the effective leader that South Korea needed to create a stable political system and pull itself out of poverty. His Liberal Party had no real ideology other than perpetuating Rhee's rule and using his administration to personally advance the political and economic fortunes of its members. Rhee and his Liberal Party supporters did not refrain from using bribery, intimidation, manipulation, and thuggery to maintain themselves in power. In the May 1954 elections, the Liberal Party received 114 seats, a modest majority. The conservative opposition Democratic Party won only 15 seats, with independents filling most of the other seats. The Liberal Party then pushed for a constitutional amendment that would enable Rhee to run for a third term. In November 1954, the proposed amendment received 135 votes, one short of the two-thirds needed. Then, under pressure, the presiding officer at the Assembly ruled that since technically 135.3 were needed for a two-thirds majority, this could be rounded off, and the amendment passed.

Rhee then went on to win a third term in 1956. However, his corrupt regime was gradually losing its hold. A long-time nationalist hero, his support among the urban population was declining. The aging president was also facing a more effective opposition. In September 1955, the Korean Democratic Party merged with various anti-Rhee groups to form the Democratic Party. This began the dominant pattern of South Korean politics for the next half century: a basic two-party system, with the two parties marked less by clear ideological difference than by different coalitions of factions, most of the factions centered on an individual leader. In the 1956 elections, huge political rallies were held in support of the Democratic candidate, another aging political veteran, Sin Ik-hǔi (1894–1956). Sin died weeks before the election; still, Rhee received only 56 percent of the votes, compared to 72 percent in 1952. In rural areas the Liberal Party was able to maintain its support, often by playing on the naivety of voters, in many cases pressuring schoolteachers, respected figures in villages, to instruct their students' parents to vote for Rhee. Many urban voters cast their ballots for a third-party candidate, Cho Pong-am (1898–1959), a socialist and principal architect of the land reform. Cho received 30 percent of the votes and carried a number of southern cities including Taegu, the third largest and the scene of leftist violence in 1946. Rhee later had Cho arrested on charges of treason and executed him in 1959. The Liberal Party candidate for vice president, Yi Ki-bung (1896–1960), lost to the Democratic candidate, Chang Myǒn (1899–1966), by 41.7 to 39.6 percent. Significantly, Chang won overwhelmingly in urban areas.

A growing urban population, the increasing disgust with corruption, and the disappointments over the slow pace of economic recovery and growth made Rhee's hold on power increasingly tenuous. Social changes were taking place that were working against the regime. The urban population doubled from 15 percent in 1945 to 30 percent in 1960. The growth of an increasingly literate class is indicated by newspaper circulation that had grown five times in the fifteen years after liberation to more than 2 million by 1960.[2] In May 1958 the Liberals received only 38.7 percent of the vote against 29.5 percent for the Democrats, despite use of voter manipulation and vote fraud. To counter these trends, the Liberal Party pushed through a new National Security Law in December 1958 that made it easier for the government to crack down on critics under the name of endangering national security. In 1960 Rhee ran for a fourth term and the Democrats nominated Cho Pyǒng-ok (1894–1960) as their candidate. But he too died just before the election. Attention then shifted to the vice presidential race, where Chang Myǒn faced the Liberal party challenger, Yi Ki-bung. Yi had become Rhee's designated successor; Rhee had even adopted his son to seal a family connection. Since Rhee was eighty-five and thought not likely to live much longer, the general feeling was that the vice president would most likely end up being the next president. With no opposition, Rhee received 88.7 percent in the official count, while Yi Ki-bung, who was widely unpopular and who had lost in 1956, was officially announced the winner by an absurdly large landslide. The

blatant vote rigging led to riots in the southern city of Masan. The demonstrations protesting the elections spread to Seoul, where thugs from the
Anticommunist Youth Corps attacked students from Korea University. It
was a common tactic of Rhee to use thugs to break up demonstrations,
much as King Kojong had done before him. The next day, April 19, some
30,000 university and high school students marched toward the presidential mansion, where police fired on them, killing 139 and wounding
hundreds of others. This event later became an annual day of commemo-
ration, "Student Revolution Day." When demonstrations continued in the
following days and the students were joined by their professors, the military commander in Seoul, General Song Yo-ch'an (1918–1980), refused to
obey orders to fire on them. Under intense U.S. pressure and with public
support clearly lost, Rhee resigned on April 26 and left for exile to Hawaii, dying there five years later. Yi Ki-bung, his elder son who had been
adopted by Rhee, his younger son, and his wife killed themselves. Chang
Myŏn had earlier resigned, so as the highest-ranking official, Foreign
Minister Hŏ Chŏng (1896–1988) formed an interim government that drew
up a new constitution.

The legacy of the Rhee regime is mixed. It is easy to dismiss it as corrupt, authoritarian, and inept. Decades later, however, some South Koreans have a more charitable view of Rhee as an effective and patriotic
leader. Many of the problems his administration faced were enormously
daunting. His government did secure vast amounts of U.S. aid, valuable
in recovering from the devastation of the Korean War. His refusal to
reestablish ties with Japan was counterproductive economically, but this
stemmed from a real fear of reestablishing the country's dependency on
and its domination by the former colonial ruler. His virulent anticommunism made any kind of reconciliation with North Korea impossible. Yet it
is unlikely that any reconciliation was possible in any case, in light of the
deep differences between the two states and North Korea's determination
to reunify the country on its own terms. His regime saw the rapid expansion of education that was so crucial to the country's transformation, although it is debated how much credit his administration deserved for this
development. Whatever his achievements, his use of thugs, intimidation,
and vote rigging to maintain himself in office, and his abuse of power to
eliminate opponents left an unfortunate political legacy.

THE DEMOCRATIC EXPERIMENT, 1960–1961

South Korea then had a brief experiment with a more democratic government. On June 15, 1960, a new constitution was drawn up that created a
parliamentary, cabinet form of government, which the Democratic Party

had been calling for. There was a bicameral National Assembly. The president was chosen by the National Assembly, not by popular election, and his powers were greatly reduced, with much of it going to the new post of prime minister. National Assembly elections were then held on July 29, with the Democratic Party receiving 175 of the 233 seats in the lower house. The Democratic Party consisted of two major factions: the New and the Old Faction. Chang Myŏn of the New Faction was selected as prime minister, Yun Po-sŏn (1897–1990) of the Old Faction as president. This power sharing did not prevent a party split, with Yun's Old Faction forming the New Democratic Party in September. Thus Chang Myŏn headed the cabinet without a majority of the seats in the Assembly. His weakened government was constantly seeking allies, reshuffling the cabinet, and changing ministers.

The Chang Myŏn administration labored under many disadvantages. Besides lacking a solid working majority, it worked within a constitution that had created a weak executive and a strong legislature, a reaction to Rhee's abuse of executive powers. But there was little party discipline among the legislators, making it difficult to carry out programs for reform. Nor was there a desire to carry out sweeping changes, since conservatives dominated the government. The new government of the Second Republic, as it was called, was largely made up of members of the elite. It was out of touch with the more radical calls for social justice that were advocated by labor, student, and other dissident groups. It did respond to the public calls for the investigation and removal of members of the bureaucracy and the police who had abused their power under Rhee. The government was initially reluctant to carry out a major purge, but bowing to public pressure, it dismissed 17,000 police officers. Unfortunately, this had the effect of weakening the effectiveness of the police, needed to control the disorder in Seoul. The crime rate soared.

A series of strikes plagued the country as labor leaders, teachers, and other called for the removal of all members of the old regime and the enactment of laws addressing their grievances for better pay, improved working conditions, more freedom to organize, for immediate national unification, and direct negotiations with P'yŏngyang. The demands for higher wages became more strident as workers faced galloping inflation. The decision by the Chang government to devalue the *hwan* (South Korea's currency, later renamed the *won* [*wŏn*]), from 650 to 1,300 to the U.S. dollar, resulted in inflationary pressures, adding to the distress of wage earners as well as making the business community uneasy. Support from the business community further eroded when the Assembly moved to pass legislation punishing corrupt businessmen with ties to the Rhee regime, although the final bill was fairly innocuous.[3]

An illegal teachers union sprang up that carried out in-school hunger strikes calling for better pay, recognition of their union, dismissal of unpopular principals, and other reforms. Students who had spearheaded the overthrow of the Rhee administration were emboldened to pressure the government for more reforms. In South Korea's Confucian society there was a long tradition of remonstrance—public expressions of moral outrage by students and young scholars over official conduct. This tradition was reinforced by the successful student-led uprising against Rhee. Yet student demonstrations, many calling for radical and unrealistic measures, added to the sense of turmoil and ineffectiveness of the democratic government. With demonstrations in Seoul an almost daily event, there was an impression that the government was unable to establish order. This was particularly true after militant students broke into the Assembly to pressure the members to act on their demands. Already plagued by instability, inflation, and a sense that the country was edging toward chaos, the government faced a new challenge when student leaders and other radicals decided to meet with North Korean representatives. Early in 1961, several small radical parties were formed calling for the withdrawal of all foreign troops from Korea, a demand supported by student radicals. In May of 1961, students called for a meeting with their fellow students from the North at P'anmunjŏm. The call for dialogue with the North made conservatives nervous. They distrusted P'yŏngyang and saw any attempt to open a dialogue with them as playing into the DPRK's hands. The instability was also seen as a possible invitation to the North to invade again. Not only was the democratic government struggling to cope with the volatile situation, it is not clear how committed most South Koreans were to democracy. The Democratic Party leaders themselves often acted in an undemocratic manner, reissuing the National Security Law that Rhee had used to silence political opponents.

THE MILITARY COUP

At the same time, the military was becoming restless. South Korea had vast armed forces numbering 600,000. Trained and equipped by the United States, its military was in many ways the most modern, effective institution in the country. Under Rhee the military had little political influence. Rhee skillfully played the factions in the army off against each other, especially the northeast and northwest factions consisting of Japanese-trained officers from these two regions of the country. Underneath the higher-ranking generals were more youthful officers trained in the Korean Military Academy during the late 1940s; some also had military training under the Japanese. Mostly they were young, under forty years of age. Their promotion and advancement in the ranks was blocked, since their superiors monopolized the higher ranks. The most important group of dissident officers came from the eighth class of the Korean Military Academy, who graduated in 1949 just before the Korean War. This class of officers had seen much action in the war and had formed a strong bond. Their leader was Kim Jong Pil (Kim Chong-p'il) (1926–), a former member of the ROK Army Counterintelligence Corps. One of the few college-educated military officers with important rank, the thirty-five-year-old had begun recruiting and planning for the coup before the April 1960 student revolution.[4] Kim was married to a niece of General Park Chung Hee (Pak Chŏng-hŭi), a major general respected and trusted by the junior officers. He and his junior officers were concerned about more than the reform of the military and the removal of senior corrupt or incompetent officers. They also were concerned about the growing strength of the leftist movement among labor, students, and teachers; about the corruption of businessmen; about the venality and ineffectiveness of the civilian politicians; and about the country's weakness in the face of the North Korean threat. In the spring of 1961, Kim and his coconspirators plotted to overthrow the state under the leadership of General Park Chung Hee.

In the predawn hours of May 16, 1961, some 1,600 troops occupied key positions in Seoul. The military conspirators then took over the major government buildings. Chang Myŏn fled to a Catholic convent, while the plotters announced over Radio Seoul that the country was under military rule. Martial law was declared and a strict curfew was imposed. A Military Revolutionary Committee was then organized. Chang came out of hiding to serve on the committee, hoping to avoid bloodshed and not wishing to create an incident that would encourage a North Korean attack. President Yun also agreed to support the committee. Chang soon resigned, and the Military Revolutionary Committee, which was firmly in military hands, took over. The Second Republic had ended and a period of military rule had begun that was to last three decades.

The new military rulers created the Supreme Council for National Reconstruction (SCNR). In June they issued a Law for National Reconstruction that gave the SCNR control over the government, and the National Assembly was dissolved. The military detained Chang Myŏn and most of his colleagues and carried out a purge and dismissal of over 40,000 members of the bureaucracy.[5] Political activity was banned and 4,000 politicians were prohibited from political activity for six years. The military rulers established a Revolutionary Tribunal that tried thousands of offenders for corruption or for activities favorable to the enemy (North Korea).

The key figure in the new government was Park Chung Hee. Park was from a humble background and rose through intelligence and a remarkable self-discipline. Born in 1917, the youngest of seven children in a poor peasant family, he excelled as a young pupil and gained entry to the elite Taegu Normal School in 1932. After graduating, he taught school for three years, and there remained in Park's personal style something of the stern schoolmaster lecturing to his students. He later enrolled in the Manchukuo Military Academy, and in 1944 was commissioned as a second lieutenant in the Imperial Japanese Army, returning to Korea in 1946 as a captain. Park was never involved in nationalist politics but appeared to be a loyal Japanese subject. However, he had a brother involved in leftist politics after the war and was himself implicated in the Yŏsu military rebellion in 1948, where he was sentenced to life imprisonment. He was pardoned but dismissed from the army and then reinstated at the start of the Korean War. Park finished the war as a brigadier-general.

In the army he did not join any fraternal organizations and was not associated with any faction, remaining aloof with an unblemished reputation for honesty. Small in stature, Park was not charismatic but was respected for his intelligence and discipline. The new military leader did not plot to seize power but was selected by the coup plotters as their leader. Once in power, he assumed the role of leadership with efficiency and skill. Park proved a pragmatist; he wanted to create an orderly and strong ROK but was open to advice from experts. Under this leadership the military government ran the country with an efficiency and purpose not previously seen.

The SCNR imposed law and order, arresting members of criminal gangs and parading them down the streets. Even "corrupt businessmen," including many of the leading business figures, were arrested, publicly humiliated, and released after they paid fines. With puritanical zeal they cleaned up red light districts and closed dance halls, bars, and coffee shops. Many newspapers and other publications were shut down. Anyone suspected of being a Communist was arrested.

To consolidate power, coup leaders purged the military, forcing many senior officers to retire and placing members of the eighth military academy class in key positions. One of the most important actions at the time was the creation of the Korean Central Intelligence Agency (KCIA) by Kim Jong Pil, whose own background was in the Army Counterintelligence Corps. This was developed into a sophisticated organization for domestic and international intelligence. It eventually grew into a vast apparatus with tens of thousands of agents. The KCIA was financed by a variety of funds, ranging from government kickbacks to money from rightists in Japan to its own business operations, including Walker Hill, a gambling resort for foreigners used to gain access to foreign exchange. Its tentacles reached into almost every school, business, and political or social organization. It even extended overseas, where the KCIA kidnapped dissident Koreans to bring them back home for punishment and bribed foreign officials to shape policies favorable to the ROK.

ECONOMIC TRANSFORMATION

South Korea's economic takeoff, its spurt of rapid industrialization and economic growth, began in the early 1960s under the direction of the military government. It was under the nearly three decades of military-led governments that the economic transformation that pulled the country out of poverty occurred. This economic transformation is sometimes referred to as the South Korean "economic miracle" or the "miracle on the Han," the latter referring to the Han River that flows through Seoul. The years before 1961, by contrast, are dismissed as a time of stagnation, inflation, corruption, and dependence on foreign aid. However, there was some real economic growth under the Rhee regime, much of it due to U.S. aid. In the 1950s, South Korea was one of the largest recipients of American assistance; Washington financed most of the ROK operating budget, paying the entire cost of its large military. With such aid, South Korea's basic infrastructure was largely rebuilt by the late 1950s, bringing the country back up to its prewar level. Still, real economic growth was only 4 percent a year, less than 2 percent per capita when the high birthrate is factored in. This real but modest rate of growth meant that in 1960 the country was still extremely poor.

Rhee followed an import substitution industrialization policy typical of many postcolonial states after World War II. The United States encouraged Seoul to establish trade relations with Japan, whose own economy was undergoing a strong recovery in the 1950s. But Rhee would not sign a peace treaty or establish diplomatic relations with the former enemy. His anti-Japanese sentiments, while shared by most Koreans, went to extremes. ROK patrol boats frequently clashed with Japanese fishing vessels that were violating the country's territorial waters. These minor disputes were played up in the media and dramatized with government-sponsored anti-Japanese rallies, giving the impression at the time that the ROK was in a two-front conflict with North Korea to the north and Japan to the south. Rhee's policies, nonetheless, reflected genuine fears that their country would become an economic colony of Japan. For this reason, his administration resisted the advice of American advisors who encouraged the production of agricultural products such as rice and seaweed for the Japanese market. If he had followed this advice it would have largely re-created the economic structure of the colonial period.

Reasonable as his refusal to be a supplier of raw materials to Japan was, Rhee did not have a truly constructive alternative. Instead, he largely

relied on U.S. aid and an overvalued currency to keep the country economically afloat and himself in power. American aid was essential. The
massive amounts accounted for nearly 80 percent of all government revenues and a substantial portion of South Korea's entire GNP. Much of this
went to the economic recovery efforts, including rebuilding infrastructure destroyed in the war. Foreign aid, along with the inflated exchange
rate, was also used to support crony capitalism. The government gave
out import licenses to favored businessmen to buy commodities. Since
the official exchange rate of the *hwan* did not reflect any market reality,
this meant that import licenses were highly profitable. Part of the profits
would go to Rhee's Liberal Party. Among the goods imported were items
such as sugar and flour supplied at bargain prices through a U.S. food aid
program known as P.L. 480. Yi Pyŏng-ch'ŏl, who later founded Samsung,
exemplifies how this system worked. He purchased imported sugar at low
prices for his Cheil Sugar, using his government-issued foreign exchange
license to become the country's largest refiner while also becoming an
important financial contributor to the pro-government Liberal Party. In
this manner, the small capitalist class became dependent on the regime.
Meanwhile, the country exported little. In 1956, exports amounted to $25
million and imports $389 million, the huge deficit made up for by the
infusion of U.S. aid funds. The slow pace of economic recovery in South
Korea despite massive aid was worrisome to the Americans, who by 1956
had become aware of the much faster recovery in North Korea.[6] In 1957,
they began cutting aid and insisting on a program that involved limiting
the budget deficit to curb inflation, and they pressured Rhee to devalue
the currency. These measures weakened the regime in the later 1950s but
did not result in any economic improvements.

Nonetheless, some of the basic foundations were being established for
the country's later economic growth. As riddled with self-serving, corrupt
officials as it was, the Rhee administration also had many able and talented people in the areas of economics, education, and finance. To these
were added a steady stream of South Koreans who were going to the
United States to study science, engineering, economics, education, and a
variety of other fields. They often were employed as young technocrats by
the government. In 1958, the administration created the Economic Development Council, a body of these technocrats that began to draw up plans
for long-term economic development. Although the Rhee administration
collapsed in 1960, before they could be implemented, these plans formed
a basis for those of the Park Chung Hee regime after 1961.

In addition, two fundamental changes took place in South Korean society before 1961 that contributed enormously to the country's economic
takeoff. One was the rapid expansion of education (see below). The other
was land reform. As John Lie and others have pointed out, land reform

was a crucial element in South Korea's economic as well as social modernization. The powerful popular demand for land reform was only partially satisfied by the U.S. occupation authorities when they redistributed Japanese holdings. Rhee's conservative supporters were largely from the landlord class and were less than enthusiastic about a more comprehensive redistribution of land. Worried by the effect of North Korean propaganda on restless peasants and pressured by the United States, the National Assembly passed a land reform act in 1949, but it was only during the Korean War that this was carried out. Under the land reform, property holdings were limited to 7.5 acres; farmers receiving redistributed acreage had to pay 150 percent of the annual value of the land received over a ten-year period. The result was dramatic. In 1944, 3 percent of landowners owned 64 percent, but in 1956 the top 6 percent owned only 18 percent; tenancy had virtually disappeared.[7] The land reform not only ended peasant unrest, it changed rural society. Land reform in South Korea delivered a major blow to the old order, perhaps not as completely and as suddenly as in North Korea, but it was still revolutionary. The domination of the countryside by the landowning elite had finally come to an end.

But whereas land reform in the North was followed by collectivization, in which the state replaced the *yangban* as landlords and much of the old landed class fled south or disappeared, the results were different in South Korea. Traditional peasants became small entrepreneurial farmers. The conservative landlords, rather than disappearing completely, now directed their capital and energy toward business or education.[8] Since the 1910s some members of the landed aristocracy had been entering business; the land reform accelerated this trend. Many others established private schools, universities, and private educational foundations. In this way, land reform contributed to the foundations of a prosperous society. It brought stability to the countryside and redirected much of the capital and entrepreneurial energy of the old landlord class toward commerce, industry, and education.

ECONOMIC GROWTH UNDER PARK CHUNG HEE

The military government that came to power in 1961 inherited a poor nation with only a modest rate of economic growth that was embarrassingly dependent on the United States for aid. It faced a rapidly industrializing North Korea and an economically expanding Japan that threatened to absorb the country as part of an East Asian economic sphere. The slow pace of growth was not just frustrating to the Americans but to many Koreans. It was clear that the country was falling behind North Korea. It was also frustrating to see the nation mired in poverty while Japan boomed, and to see the contrast between its impoverished citizens and the well-fed American troops.[9] South Korea possessed a military that was strong in manpower but like the economy in general was totally dependent on U.S. equipment and aid. Freeing the nation from its "mendicant" status and lifting it out of poverty became the military government's highest priority. Park himself seemed to understand the importance of making South Korea economically strong. In a sense, his vision was not too different from the military leaders that ruled Japan during the Meiji period with the slogan "rich country, strong military." Indeed he modeled himself in part on the Meiji leaders and on other strong leaders who modernized and developed their countries, such as Pasha Kemal (Ataturk).[10] South Korea's small and fragile industrial base compared unfavorably with the more industrial North and its strong recovery. The ROK's economic dependence on U.S. aid was not only a sign of its weakness and a national humiliation, but also a limitation on its sovereignty. The desire to free the nation from its economic dependence on the United States was reflected in the motto of the First Five-Year Plan, *charip kyŏngje* ("self-reliant economy"), proclaimed from public billboards and on numerous placards.[11] In this respect he resembled Kim Il Sung as well. Both were at heart economic nationalists who sought a Korea economically strong enough to be capable of supporting a large military and to be free from dependence on outside powers. Park later questioned whether South Korea could preserve its "self-respect as a sovereign nation, independent, free and democratic," being so dependent on the Americans. Park was troubled that the United States had "a 52 percent majority vote with regard to Korea."[12] This referred to the fact that the American aid accounted for over half the government's budget. The similarity in the way leaders of both Koreas saw economic development linked with military strength and self-reliance is seen in a slogan Park used in his industrialization effort: "construction on the one hand, national defense on the other" (*ilmyŏn kŏnsŏl, ilmyŏn kukpang*), which echoed Kim Il Sung's contemporary call for "arms in the one hand, hammer and sickle in the other."[13]

Park admired the Japanese state-directed economic development he witnessed as a young man. Thus the influence of the North, with its ambitious economic plans for rapid industrialization, the influence of prewar Japan, and his own experience in a disciplined modern army led him to support a state-directed, planned program of economic development. Yet, initially, the coup leaders appeared not to have had clear ideas about what to do about the economy. At first they issued decrees regarding rural debt relief and price support for rice to alleviate the plight of farmers. Disgusted with the corrupt relationship between businessmen and the government, they detained and fined fifty-one of the leading business figures, including the country's richest, Yi Pyŏng-ch'ŏl. But this quickly changed as the military leaders soon realized that they needed the skills of the entrepreneurs to promote economic growth. They released the businessmen after each signed an agreement stating "I will donate all my property to the government if it requires it for national reconstruction."[14] Park then appointed thirteen of them to the Promotional Committee for Economic Reconstruction, with Yi Pyŏng-ch'ŏl as chair.[15] Thus began the military government's partnership with the country's entrepreneurial elite that continued for a generation. It was a partnership in which the state in the early years was firmly dominant.

Then the SCNR issued a Five-Year Economic Development Plan. The need for long-range economic planning had become apparent to many government bureaucrats. The SCNR's Five-Year Plan was largely based on the one that the Chang Myŏn administration had outlined the previous year, which in turn was based on the one being drawn up in the waning days of the Rhee administration. So in this sense, it was not a radical break but part of a general move by the technocrats for comprehensive government-directed planning. Several steps were taken to direct the state toward economic growth, perhaps the most crucial being the nationalization of all commercial banks and the reorganization of the banking system to give the state control over credit.[16] Money could now be lent out to businesses according to the needs of the economic plan. To direct the overall economic development the government established an Economic Planning Board (EPB) staffed by young talented technocrats to work out the details of the plan. To insure that the economic plan would be under technocrat supervision, Park made the EPB head a deputy prime minister, outranking all other cabinet members. The plan called for a 7.1 percent economic growth rate for 1962–1966 by encouraging the development of light industries for export. This target would have been a large improvement over the 4 percent growth of the previous few years. Although many foreign advisors were skeptical about reaching this goal, the state exceeded it. After expanding only a modest 4.1 percent in 1962 the economy grew 9.3 percent in 1963, and boomed each of the next three years. The final result was that under the First Five-Year Plan economic growth averaged 8.9 percent, launching South Korea on its path to rapid industrialization. Exports grew 29 percent a year, manufacturing 15 percent a year.[17] It was followed by a Second Five-Year Plan, 1967–1971, which placed greater emphasis on improving the basic infrastructure, including transportation and electric power.[18]

In addition to directing low-interest loans to businesses fulfilling the plan, the government also created a number of centers to promote research and the dissemination of technical knowledge to business enterprises. One of the first established in 1966 was the Korean Institute of

Science and Technology. It also promoted technical education, building a number of new vocational middle and high schools and two-year technical colleges. Students were encouraged to study abroad, although many of these did not return.

Since Park's economic development policies were driven by economic nationalism and the desire to achieve autonomy for his country, he was concerned about avoiding foreign economic control. Consequently, he initially limited direct foreign investment into the country. But then, on the advice of his economists, he began easing up on these restrictions. And he was still heavily reliant on the United States, which held considerable economic and political leverage. This was highlighted when the United States forced Park to restore civilian rule in 1963. He then ran and was elected president, and reelected in 1967. From 1963 to 1971 he ruled in a semi-authoritarian fashion, with his official party, the Democratic Republican Party, maintaining a majority in the National Assembly. Park managed to keep just enough semblance of democratic government to please the Americans, while remaining effectively in control of the country. Gradually, as the economy grew, the United States began to scale back aid, but in the 1960s and 1970s, U.S. aid and technical assistance was still absolutely indispensable to South Korea's economic development. Moreover, throughout the 1960s, 1970s, and 1980s, the United States absorbed the majority of the country's exports.

Park, may have resented Washington's interference in the country's internal affairs, but he also was able to use political and military relations with the Americans for economic development purposes. A significant example was the ROK participation in the Vietnam War. Park made an agreement with the Johnson administration in 1965 to provide troops for Vietnam in return for considerable concessions. These were formally worked out in the 1966 Brown Memorandum, named after the U.S. ambassador to the ROK. A bill authorizing the sending of troops was passed in 1965 when the opposition was boycotting the National Assembly because of Park's efforts to normalize relations with Japan. Park committed the country to supplying 20,000 troops to support the U.S. military effort, a number that increased over the next several years. Eventually 300,000 ROK troops did tours of duty there between 1965 and 1973. In the 1966 Brown Memorandum, the U.S. formally agreed that South Korean firms were to be given lucrative contracts to supply goods and services to the South Vietnamese, American, and allied military forces. South Korean firms constructed many military installations, helping to establish a new overseas industry for South Korea that proved useful for earning foreign exchange. South Korean firms such as Hyundai gained valuable experience in completing construction and transportation projects for the United States in Vietnam. Later Hyundai and other Korean construction companies applied their experience in building to meet short timetables to win contracts in the Middle East and elsewhere. In addition to these contracts, the United States further agreed to modernize the ROK armed forces and provide military and other aid.

Economic development was greatly facilitated by normalizing relations with Japan. By 1964, Japan was emerging as a great economic power, showcased by the Olympics it hosted that year. Japan had a booming economy, rising labor costs, and capital for foreign investment. Korea, next door, in the same time zone, with historical ties, with many in its business community fluent in Japanese, was a natural place for investment. Korean cheap labor and Japanese capital and technology were a good match. Yet there was bitterness in Korea toward Japan, a fear that close economic partnerships with its former colonial ruler would replicate the preliberation dependent status and would lead to an economic recolonization. For this reason, Syngman Rhee was not the only South Korean to reject the resumption of trade and economic ties with Japan. Normalization, therefore, was a sensitive issue. Koreans demanded reparations from Japan, and safeguards, as well as Japanese admissions of injustices done in the past. The Park administration saw how clearly advantageous, even necessary, normalization would be to economic development. Opponents of the regime, and there were many who resented the rule by military or ex-military men, found this a useful issue, since Park's and many of his supporters' past links with Japan made his administration vulnerable to charges of pro-Japanese sentiment. Attempts to begin normalization in 1964 led to massive student demonstrations. In June, Park had to declare martial law and sent two combat divisions into the streets to restore order. The National Assembly approved normalization on August 14, 1965, only after the opposition walked out in protest and troops had cleared the streets of protesters. The treaty went into effect in December 1965. Japan agreed to pay $800 million in aid. The fishing dispute was settled by both sides agreeing to twelve-mile (twenty-kilometer) economic zones; Koreans living in Japan were guaranteed residency rights and equal rights to public education or welfare, although some social welfare benefits were not granted in practice for another two decades.[19]

With this agreement the reparations issue was closed. Far more important than Japanese reparations money, which was modest, was the flow of investments that contributed to the already strong growth of the ROK economy. In the years after the treaty, Japan was a major foreign investor in South Korea, second only to the United States. In a decade after the treaty, trade between the two countries expanded more than ten times; Japan supplied nearly 60 percent of the foreign technology between 1962 and 1979.[20] Without the U.S. market and Japan's investments and technology transfers, it's difficult to imagine how South Korea's economic transformation could have been accomplished.

There was a shift in economic policies in the early 1970s associated with the more authoritarian turn in the Park regime. After declaring martial law and writing a new constitution in 1972 that gave him nearly dictatorial powers, Park pushed the country more ruthlessly in the direction of heavy industrial development. His new Third Five-Year Economic Plan for 1972–1976, unlike the two earlier plans, called for investment to be channeled into heavy and chemical industries. This is often referred to as the HCI (heavy and chemical industry) phase of South Korea's economic development. In place of textiles and footwear, the ROK would focus on developing steel, shipbuilding, petrochemical, and automotive industries. In 1973, six industries were targeted: steel, chemical, metal, machine building, shipbuilding, and electronics. This stage of industrial development was concentrated in five small provincial cities, four of them in Park's home Kyŏngsang area in the southeast part of the country: Yŏsu-Yŏchŏn for petrochemicals, Ch'angwŏn for machine-building, P'ohang for steel, Okp'o for shipbuilding, and the Kumi complex for electronics.[21] To oversee this new stage of economic development he created a Corps for Planning and Management of Heavy and Chemical Industries, headed, significantly, not by a technocrat but by a political appointee. The shift to these heavy and chemical industries required the government to play an even greater role in aiding and guiding industrial development. Favored companies expanded, some into industrial giants.

Park ignored many of his technocrats as well as foreign experts, who felt that Korea was not ready or large enough for these types of industries. He did not want to stay with an expanded textile industry. While light industries such as manufacturing of textiles and wigs were important for economic growth, they could not provide the basis to support a militarily and economically strong state that would be less dependent on the Americans. A desire to be able to eventually supply most of its own military equipment and to be economically autonomous was a major incentive for this push. In some ways, in its emphasis on heavy industry, South Korea resembled its northern rival. This is not surprising, since the desire for heavy industry was also part of the South's desire to match developments in North Korea. How could South Korea continue to pursue the manufacture of apparel, shoes, and wigs when the North was producing steel? There was also a sense of competing with Japan. The HCI program was another manifestation of economic nationalism and South Korea's need to compete with its neighbors, which drove so much of its economic development.[22]

South Korea again did better than most foreign observers expected. The economy grew by double digits despite a less favorable international situation in the 1970s. In the decade from 1972 to 1982 steel production increased fourteen times. Some industrial sectors such as the petrochemical did not become that competitive; however, others did. Pohang Iron and Steel Company (POSCO), a state-owned corporation, opened the world's largest steel-making complex. Under its capable manager, Pak T'ae-jun, it proved to be an efficient operation that successfully competed in the world steel markets. Similarly, South Korea emerged in the 1980s as the world's second-largest shipbuilder, with a reputation for being able to complete orders for new ships quickly and on time. Still there were many problems. The timing was unfortunate, since these energy-intensive industries were launched at the time of sharp increases in petroleum prices. The 1973–1974 oil shock, when the price of crude oil quadrupled, hit the South Korean economy hard, since it had to import all its energy. Inflation soared to 40 percent in 1974. However, the flow of foreign exchange to pay for more costly imported oil was soon compensated in part by the flow of the earnings from Korean construction companies and their workers in the Middle East. Thus South Korea weathered the economic crisis quite well. A more serious problem was the mounting foreign debt, as the country was a major borrower to finance not just new investments but huge infrastructure projects such as expanded power generation, telecommunications, port facilities, and roads. An example of the last was the new express highway linking Seoul with Pusan. Foreign debt rose from $2.2 billion in 1970 to $27.1 billion in 1980.[23]

CHAEBŎLS

The policies of the 1970s contributed to one of the distinctive features of South Korea's development, the concentration of so much of the economy into huge family-owned conglomerates known as *chaebŏls*. The term itself is the Korean pronunciation of the Chinese characters used to write *zaibatsu*, the prewar 1945 Japanese conglomerates that in many ways they resembled. The growth of *chaebŏls* was due to more than just the entrepreneurial skill of a handful of talented businessmen, it was also the product of government policy. Banks, all state owned after 1961, poured credit into a few companies to develop industries targeted for development. The state gave the *chaebŏls* exemptions from import duties on capital goods and offered special rates for utilities and the state-owned rail system. Smaller firms and those engaged in enterprises not favored by the development plans found it difficult to gain access to credit, nor could they receive all these special discounts and exemptions. Each *chaebŏl* leader found it necessary to work closely with the government and contribute generously to government political campaign coffers and to pet projects favored by the Park and later Chun regimes. However, a key to understanding the South Korean system is that the *chaebŏl* had to be efficient. It was not by political connections but by their ability to produce results, that is, to efficiently meet economic targets and compete in the domestic and foreign marketplaces, that brought about government support. The government did not allow any *chaebŏl* to achieve a monopoly but rather encouraged competition among several in each industrial sector to keep them efficient.

In the 1970s, when the state pushed for heavy industry, the *chaebŏls* grew at the fastest rate. The top ten conglomerates grew at 27 percent a year, three and a half times the GDP growth rate.[24] As they grew, they tended to expand horizontally, branching out into a highly diversified range of activities often far removed from their original core businesses. Samsung branched out from food processing to enter electronics, heavy equipment, and automobiles; Hyundai from construction to shipbuilding and automobiles. The *chaebŏl* founders were an extraordinary group of talented entrepreneurs driven by nearly limitless ambition and often possessing considerable personal charisma. Although it is possible to see them as the product of government economic policies, it is hard to imagine South Korea's economic takeoff without them. This was in sharp contrast with Taiwan, or later with China, where small and medium-size industries dominated the export economy.

One of the most dynamic of these entrepreneurs was Chung Ju-yung (Chŏng Chu-yŏng). Born of humble rural background in Kangwŏn Province in what later became North Korea, Chung attended a traditional village Confucian school. He came to Seoul in his teens, worked on the docks, and then started an auto repair business in 1940 that grew during the war to about seventy employees. After 1945, he established a construction company that worked for the U.S. Army and the Korean government. A hardworking efficient entrepreneur, he prospered with state support in the 1960s. Chung became one of the favored entrepreneurs of the Park regime for his ability to complete tasks ahead of schedule, such as a bridge over the Han River. After 1965, Hyundai Construction received many contracts to build in Southeast Asia during the Vietnam War, and in the 1970s in the Middle East. Chung established Hyundai Motors in 1967 to build the first South Korean car, which became known as the Pony. He established Hyundai Shipbuilding and Heavy Industries in 1973 in response to the HCI initiative. Later in the early 1980s Hyundai entered the electronics industry. By then, the Hyundai Group was the largest *chaebŏl* in Korea.

Lee Byung-chull (Yi Pyŏng-ch'ŏl), unlike Chung, came from a wealthy landowner family. In 1938, after a brief unsuccessful attempt to run a rice mill, he founded a small trading company in Seoul. He used his entrepreneurial experience to establish the Cheil Sugar Refinery in 1953. He also established the Cheil Textile Company. Closely associated with the Rhee regime, he received profitable import licenses in return for contributions to Rhee's Liberal Party, becoming the country's wealthiest entrepreneur and controlling several commercial banks and insurance companies. As Korea's richest businessman and closely associated with Rhee, Lee became a prime target of Park's anticorruption campaign. After paying a fine in 1961 and having his bank holdings expropriated, he was enlisted by Park Chung Hee to help encourage other businessmen to cooperate with the military government's plans for industrial development. In fact, Lee is often given credit for helping to convince Park and the other members of the junta of the need for a cooperative relationship between the business community and the military government. Lee's Samsung (Three Stars) group acquired a reputation for being efficient and well managed. Involved in many areas, in the later 1960s Lee made electronics his prime focus. By the early 1980s Samsung was one the world's largest manufacturers of TV sets. In the mid-1980s it moved into the semiconductor business being promoted by the government.

Kim Woo Jung (Kim U-jung) (1936–) was born near Taegu in 1936, thus was a generation younger than most of the *chaebŏl* founders. He established the Daewoo trading company in 1967 when he was barely in his thirties. Exporting fabric and other materials, he attracted the attention of Park, who was looking for aggressive entrepreneurs for his HCI push. In 1975, with government financial assistance, Kim established the Daewoo group. He acquired Shinjin, an unsuccessful automotive company, and began building cars for General Motors, then acquired the failing Okp'o shipyard and become a major shipbuilder. Kim's relative youth and his education made him an attractive symbol of the go-getting Korean entrepreneur. He was famous for working 100-hour weeks and never taking off a day except for one morning of truancy for his daughter's wedding. His autobiography was a best seller.

Koo In-hwoi (Ku In-hoe) (1907–1969) was one of the oldest of the *chaebŏl* founders. He founded Lucky Chemical Company in 1947, said to be named after the popular American cigarette Lucky Strike.[25] It became the country's major toothpaste manufacturer. In the 1960s he went into the electronics business under the Goldstar label. In 1995, the Lucky-Goldstar company changed its name to LG, eventually becoming one of the world's largest consumer electronics firms.

Ssangyong (Twin Dragons) was founded by Kim Sung Kon (Kim Sŏng-gŏn). It began as a textile company in 1939. In the 1950s Kim prospered in the cement business, obtaining like his fellow entrepreneur, Lee Byung-chull, import licenses from the Rhee government. The Park regime found him an efficient, resourceful entrepreneur, and Ssangyong branched out into many industries, including trading, construction, and automobiles, becoming one of the six largest *chaebŏls* in the 1970s and 1980s. The *chaebŏls* at their core were essentially family-run businesses. The top managerial positions were held, in roughly hierarchical order, by family members, followed by high school and college classmates, and people from the same hometowns. The immediate family members were most important. Chung Chu Yung had eight sons, the so-called "eight princes" that constituted the upper management of the various Hyundai companies.[26] Modest inheritance taxes and strategic marriages kept much of the ownership in family control. Most were products of the post-liberation period. Of the fifty largest *chaebŏls* in 1983, ten predated 1945, nineteen were established in the 1950s.[27] A few new conglomerates appeared in later years; most, however, were well established by 1980.

TRANSFORMATION OF THE COUNTRYSIDE

The industrialization of South Korea was accompanied by a transformation of the countryside. At first, rural areas lagged behind in development, then, in part to shore up his rural base of support, Park launched the New Village (Saemaul) Movement in the winter of 1971–1972. The rural population had not enjoyed the economic boom of 1961–1971; most still lived in poverty. The Saemaul Movement was an attempt to mobilize the rural communities for the purpose of carrying out modernization efforts. Local governments were enlisted in programs to educate farmers to modernize their farms and their homes. To symbolize this change, all rural households had to replace their thatched roofs with tiles, which were more fireproof and considered more modern, although the poor often had to settle for corrugated metal roofs painted blue or orange to look like tiles. The movement encouraged self-help and the adoption of new progressive values in ways similar to the government-sponsored rural movements of the 1930s. In its rush to promote modernization, many traditional customs that the Park administration regarded as wasteful or backward were discouraged. This has led critics to accuse the Saemaul Movement of undermining traditional rural culture. Certainly some of the policies were heavy-handed, such as forcing farmers to grow new high-yield varieties of rice even though consumers preferred more traditional rice. But the program brought many benefits to farmers. Village committees were established to formulate and carry out their own improvement schemes. This proved a path for social mobility for the elected men and women that served as Saemaul leaders. And many of the leaders were women, some drawn from the 1960s rural birth control movement (see below).[28] Most important was the price support given to farm crops, especially rice. It meant higher food prices for urban workers, who often struggled on low wages, but it produced higher income for farmers and eventually reduced rural poverty. By the mid-1970s the Saemaul Movement was a model for other similar movements—factory saemauls, school saemauls, saemauls in offices—but these were not very effective. And even the original Saemaul began to lose its momentum.

General economic growth might have been as important or more important in transforming the countryside as specific programs targeting farmers. The construction of roads, the completion of rural electrification, the introduction of telephones and of televisions all ended rural isolation and also contributed to the greater information about and access to markets. Chemical fertilizers, mechanized equipment, and the demand for agriculture products in the urban centers made farming more lucrative. Meanwhile, industry produced a far greater percentage of the economy. Expanding industry and services provided many opportunities. As a result, millions of Koreans left their rural homes to find work in the cities. Parents sent their kids to the cities to get a better education, and their children seldom returned. In 1960, farmers made up 61 percent of the population. This fell dramatically to 51 percent in 1970 and to 38 percent in 1980. By the end of the Park era, South Korea caught up to the North in the percentage of nonfarming population. In both Koreas little more than a third of the people worked the fields by 1980. For the first time in its history, Korea was primarily an urban, nonagricultural land.

Families became smaller. The International Planned Parenthood Federation introduced family planning to Korea, forming the Planned Parenthood Federation of Korea in 1961. The Park administration made family planning part of its Five-Year Plans. South Korea's technocrats accepted the argument by Western advisors that cutting the birthrate was essential for fast economic growth and modernization. Working with the Planned Parenthood Federation of Korea, the state sent family planning staff to local clinics. Especially effective was a program to recruit women in rural communities to receive training and spread knowledge of birth control to their neighbors. These efforts were accelerated in 1966, which the government, promoting IUDs and vasectomies, declared the Great Year of Family Planning. In 1968, the Ministry of Health and Social Welfare created Mother's Clubs for Family Planning and introduced oral contraceptives.[29] The family planning movement was incorporated into the Saemaul Movement in the 1970s. Again, in 1974, the state launched a renewed campaign for birth control, declaring it another Family Planning Year, and began a female sterilization campaign in the 1980s. But by the late 1980s the birthrate had fallen so sharply that family planning was no longer a worry. It is not clear how much these efforts to promote birth control contributed to economic development. With increased women's literacy and urbanization, the birthrate would have fallen in any case. Furthermore, some economists in recent years have questioned the importance of birth control in assisting economic growth. What is clear is that South Korea made the demographic transition with the same speed that it made its economic transition into a modern industrial state.

ECONOMIC DEVELOPMENT IN THE 1980s

In 1980, South Korea faced a serious economic crisis. The second oil shock of 1979 contributed to an already double-digit inflation rate. Inflation reached an alarming 44 percent in 1980, threatening the competitiveness of the country's exports. Then there was the turmoil and uncertainty that followed Park's assassination in October 1979. A poor rice harvest due to unfavorable weather compounded problems. The nation's GNP, which had been growing in excess of 8 to 10 percent annually contracted to 6 percent in 1980. The country's economic woes appeared to be more than just a temporary problem. Foreign debt was mounting. The HCI policy resulted in huge loans, since Park relied heavily on foreign borrowing to finance the necessary expenditures on infrastructure that accompanied it. Corporate debt was also rising as the *chaebŏls* borrowed to finance expansion. It also appeared that the highly centralized command structure of the economy in which businessmen were directed by a few high-placed officials in the EPB, the Ministry of Finance, and the Ministry of Industry and Commerce was showing its limitations. South Korea's economy was becoming more complex, the business groups larger and stronger, and its exports more diverse. To some foreign observers, South Korea seemed to have reached a plateau, as far as it could go with its export economy based on cheap labor and foreign investment.

As they had been earlier, these foreign observers proved unduly pessimistic. The South Korean economy recovered in 1981 and resumed its impressive growth rates. Some reforms were carried out to make the economy slightly less centralized and more flexible. The government forced a number of mergers and closures in some deeply indebted sectors such as heavy industry and shipping to make them more efficient. The country began moving into more high-tech industrial areas such as consumer electronics, computers, and semiconductors. A surge in the U.S. economy beginning in 1982 helped exports, oil prices dropped, and foreign investments continued. In 1983, the first Hyundai cars were exported. By 1986–1988 the growth rate reached its peak, when with an average of 12 percent, it was the highest in the world.

Problems remained. Throughout the 1980s the country suffered from huge trade deficits with Japan. Korean firms bought capital equipment and industrial parts from their former colonial occupier. These were essential to the manufacturing of the export goods they sold to the United States. The results were trade surpluses with America that were negated by deficits with Japan, and the country seemed stuck at the intermediate technology phase. Lingering anti-Japanese sentiment made this reliance on Japanese technology humiliating. South Korea, however, maintained its ability to work out technology transfer arrangements so that this dependency on imported technology lessened. Government-funded research centers, meanwhile, made impressive strides in promoting technological and scientific expertise.

EXPLAINING SOUTH KOREA'S ECONOMIC MIRACLE

South Koreans often attribute their nation's economic growth to traditional values loosely associated with Confucianism. By this they mean hard work, discipline, respect for learning, frugality, and the importance of family. In the past, Western scholars associated traditional Confucian values with conservatism, hierarchy versus equality, and conformity to group versus individualism, and they held it responsible for the economic backwardness of Korea and China. Then in the 1980s, some writers started to refer to a "Confucian ethos" that contributed to the economic success of South Korea, Singapore, Hong Kong, and Taiwan. South Koreans also came to attribute much of their success to these traditional values. It is possible to make an argument linking traditional values to hard work, the emphasis on education, the high esteem in which civil servants were held that attracted talented technocrats to serve the state, and even to the willingness to delay gratification that resulted in the high savings rate that characterized the period of rapid economic growth. Yet South Koreans possessed this "Confucian" heritage before 1961, as did North Koreans. It is therefore necessary to look at specific development policies and historical contingencies for explanations of the economic transformation.

U.S. aid is often cited as a source for South Korea's economic miracle. Vast amounts of aid were poured into the country. From 1946 to 1976 the United States provided $12.6 billion in economic assistance, only Israel and South Vietnam received more on a per-capita basis. To put this into comparative perspective: $6.85 billion was given in this period to all of Africa, and $14.89 billion for all Latin America.[30] Much of the assistance to Korea was relief, not development aid. The greatest amounts of aid came in the decade that followed the Korean War, for reconstruction, food aid, and supplies of building materials. Aid also provided much of the fiscal support for the ROK government, especially under Rhee. Besides the aid money, South Koreans received technical training from the United States.

This ranged from a program to train statisticians to the many economists and engineers that received a U.S. education. While this was only a small proportion of the aid programs, it provided the country with a large core of well-educated and trained bureaucrats, educators, and other skilled, professional people.

Perhaps more important than aid was the stability offered by the U.S. troops stationed in that country, which made it less risky for foreign investors, and the openness of the American market to South Korean exports. These two factors were important after 1961, when the country began promoting foreign investment and export-oriented industries. In other words, it was not only direct American aid but also the favorable conditions created by the United States that South Korea was able to take advantage of during the crucial years of economic growth from the early 1960s through the 1980s. South Korea's position on the frontline of the Cold War also helped, such as the participation in the Vietnam War that provided aid and construction contracts. The ROK vigorously sought every useful support it could get from the United States by having an effective embassy and active lobbying interests in Washington. Korean immigrants sometimes were helpful; they provided a link to the American wig business, to name one industry.[31] U.S. advice was not always helpful. Americans were often skeptical of South Korean plans for economic development. For example, the Korean government was forced to reject advice that the First Five-Year Plan focus on the export of rice, pork, laver (edible seaweed), tungsten, iron, and graphite.[32] This type of commodity-exporting economy was exactly what Korean economic planners sought to avoid. One can only imagine what would have happened if South Koreans had decided to emphasize rice exports to Japan in the 1950s. In the 1970s, the United States through the World Bank pressured the country to temporarily drop its plans for a steel industry. South Koreans learned a lot from their U.S. counterparts, but it was often when they ignored U.S. advice and forged their own path that they were most successful.

Japan has often been given a great deal of credit for South Korea's economic development. Some observers of the country's economic development have attributed much of it to the colonial legacy, which, they argue, left some fine infrastructure such as the rail network, a number of skilled workers, experienced bankers and entrepreneurs, and high standards of education and bureaucratic efficiency. Certainly many features of South Korea's industrialization bore a major imprint of the Japanese colonial model: the close government-business relations, the role of the state in directing the economy to achieve national goals, and the concentration of capital into big *chaebŏls*, which closely resembled the pre-1945 Japanese *zaibatsu*. However, one has to be cautious in attributing too much of the country's economic development to Japanese rule, which was harsh, exploitative, and left the country still primarily agricultural and impoverished, with an economy directed toward and dependent on Japan. Furthermore, most of the top skilled jobs were done by Japanese who left, and the education system they established fell far short of the nation's needs or the public's demand. Nonetheless, South Korea did benefit from its proximity to a booming Japan that was looking for overseas investments. South Korea was nearby and shared many cultural similarities; furthermore, there were Japanese entrepreneurs with experience doing business in Korea in prewar times. Japanese investment, joint ventures, and crucial technology transfers were important, but total Japanese investment in Korea was smaller than U.S. investment. Perhaps as important as investment, was the example of Japan as a successful model. The desire to emulate Japan's success was both an incentive as well as a practical example to follow. Japan, like North Korea, was also a competitor that spurred South Korean leaders to push for economic development by linking it to national security.

A popular explanation for South Korea's economic success was the fact that it had a strong state capable of overriding vested interests.[33] The general interpretation is that South Korea inherited a powerful centralized bureaucracy and national police from the Japanese colonial administration, and that the security-minded American military occupation and the Syngman Rhee regime that followed made use of these instruments to suppress leftist dissent and maintain internal security. After 1961, the military rulers further centralized authority and directed the state toward economic development. The state then was able to achieve autonomy and impose its will on society. This argument appears most valid for the 1960s and 1970s when the military government was able to exercise discipline over the business class and suppress labor movements. It was less true after 1980 when the *chaebŏls* became powerful interests, when labor became more restless, and when the middle class became more insistent in its demand for greater say in policy making. Even under Park, the state never had complete autonomy; it had to make concessions to public opinion to maintain support, and it was never free from corruption.[34] Bribery, kickbacks, secret political funds, and bank accounts by officials and businessmen under false names were very much a part of the South Korean system. The state still had the ability to favor or undermine *chaebŏls*. This was demonstrated in 1985 when the Pusan-based Kukje group, the seventh largest, ran afoul of Chun Du Hwan, who succeeded Park Chung Hee. When the group's head refused to provide the requested financial contributions to the regime, Chun decided to punish him by pressuring banks to demand repayment of loans, forcing the firm to liquidate. The collapse of Kukje was a disturbing reminder of the close political links between corporations and state. But this incident was an exception. By the

1980s the *chaebŏls* were becoming too big to fail, since a collapse of a major group could bring down the entire economy with it.

South Korea's economic transformation was also made possible by the social transformation that was occurring in the country. Old social classes and social barriers were breaking down; the society was opening up to talent, becoming both highly competitive and more literate. While economic development contributed and accelerated this process of social transformation, many fundamental changes preceded it. The upheavals that resulted from the colonial period, the Second World War, the partition, and the Korean War had created a more fluid and unsettled society, a society open to change. It was a society in which millions had left home to work in the northern regions before 1945 or in Manchuria, China, and Japan. These millions of people had been exposed to a world beyond the village and were restless and open to new opportunities. There was also a sense of optimism, a belief in the possibility of a better life, noted by foreign observers and often regarded by them as unrealistic.

EDUCATION

Another important factor in explaining the economic miracle was the creation of a highly literate population. The optimism and belief in the possibility for individuals and families to improve their status and condition in life was reflected in the desire for education. Immediately after liberation in 1945, new schools mushroomed and enrollments exploded. There was clearly a pent-up demand for education, since the expansion of schooling under the Japanese had proceeded so slowly. In response, the framers of the 1948 constitution made primary education a right. The Rhee administration in 1949 adopted an educational system patterned after the U.S. system and on the one the American occupation had established in Japan. Six years of elementary school was followed by three years of middle school, three years of high school, and four years of college. Secondary schools were divided into academic and vocational, but graduates from both were eligible to enter university. Unlike the more restrictive elitist education of colonial times, South Koreans opted for an open-ended system to maximize access to higher levels of schooling.

The country faced enormous problems. Half the teachers were Japanese who returned home, there were few textbooks in Korean, and many school buildings were destroyed in the Korean War. Also, there were only limited funds to support a comprehensive educational system. Nonetheless, enrollments expanded spectacularly. Between 1945 and 1960 primary school enrollment grew by three times, secondary schooling eight times, and higher education ten times. Class sizes were enormous, with as many as 100 students in a class, and with two and even three shifts a day. During and after the Korean War, classes often were conducted in tents. By 1960, primary schooling was nearly universal for boys and girls, and the dropout rate was minimal. To finance the schools the government simply transferred the burden to children and their families by charging various fees. Since the state concentrated on primary education, half the high schools and three-quarters of the colleges and universities were established by private foundations. Many foundations were supported by former landowners seeking new opportunities now that they had lost their agricultural estates. After 1961, the state shifted its attention to secondary education. In 1960, 29 percent of those of secondary school age were enrolled in middle and high schools; by the late 1980s that figure was over 90 percent. Extensive in-service training programs kept the level of professionalism high. So successful was the ROK's educational development that by the 1990s other nations began to see the system as a model of excellence.

As with the case of the "economic miracle," South Korea's education "miracle" needs some explaining. The state provided some help with its teacher-training programs. It contributed to educational expansion with its open-ended educational system and its emphasis on trying to maintain fairly uniform standards throughout the country, even in remote rural areas. The main engine of educational expansion, however, was a nearly universal popular demand for schooling. The state could never build schools fast enough to meet this demand. Parents were willing to make enormous sacrifices to obtain schooling for their children. A farmer who sold his only ox to pay school fees became a stereotype based on the reality of the sacrifice the majority of Koreans unhesitatingly made. Families often sent sons and daughters to live with relatives where schools were better.

This social demand for schooling created considerable problems. Great pressure was placed on students to pass the middle school entrance exam and then the university exam. The former was eliminated in the late 1960s, but this only increased the focus on the all-important college entrance exam. Middle-class families spent considerable sums on after-school lessons at cram schools, and on private tuition. These private lessons, combined with the numerous fees and parent-teacher association contributions, made the education system quite costly. While the South Korean government spent a smaller percentage of its annual budget on education than many developing countries, the average family spent a higher percentage of its income on schooling than almost anywhere else. The education itself was focused on rote memorization and examination preparation, much to the disapproval of American educational advisors. Efforts by the state to limit the number of university students and to promote vocational education met with public resistance and were consequently only modestly successful.

Despite these problems, the transformation of South Korea into a highly literate, well-schooled nation was a key component of its economic and social development. Educational development did not just keep pace with economic development, it preceded and outpaced it. While it is difficult to establish a direct correlation between education and economic development, South Korea in the 1960s, 1970s, and 1980s was able to offer a labor force that was literate, numerate, and used to learning while still low wage. As the country developed, the high levels of schooling made it better prepared to enter the information age. Furthermore, the sequential nature of educational development—the emphasis on first pushing for universal primary education, then middle, then high school, and then finally making higher education broadly available—differed from most developing countries, which often establish fine universities while leaving many children with inadequate or no available basic schooling. This did much to insure a balanced, broad-based social and economic modernization without leaving pockets of underdevelopment. It also meant a well-informed population. By the 1990s newspaper readership was among the highest in the world. South Korea's educational transformation by providing a well-educated citizenry not only contributed to its economic growth but also probably facilitated the transition to democracy.

KOREA IN GLOBAL PERSPECTIVE: EDUCATIONAL DEVELOPMENT

After World War II there was a worldwide expansion of education; historically it was a revolution of sorts. Between 1950 and 1990, for the first time, most of the world's people became literate and education was almost universally accepted as a norm for all children. South Korea's educational development can be seen as part of this revolution in literacy. Few nations, if any, however, saw such a dramatic rise in education. In 1945 the majority of the adult population was illiterate, a little over half were enrolled in primary school, and only 5 percent had a secondary education. By 1960, the ROK had an extremely high rate of school enrollment of children in elementary school for a poor developing country. The nation continued to improve educational standards at a rate outpacing its economic performance. At every stage from 1950 to 2000, South Korea had the highest rate of educational attainment of any country within comparable GDP per-capita range. As a result, South Korea began its industrial takeoff with a better-educated population than most other nations, including China, Vietnam, Thailand, or India. Educational development, in general, correlates well with economic development, but in few other places does this correlation seem so dramatic.

Other aspects of South Korean education were distinctive as well. The dropout rate in schools after 1945 was extremely low, in fact, the lowest of any developing country with reliable statistics. Compared to most developing nations, the school system was fairly open, with relatively little tracking. Teacher-training standards were unusually high. Perhaps the most distinctive features of South Korean education were the sequential nature of educational development, the uniformity of educational standards, and the extent that the cost was shifted from the state to the families of students. Only a relatively small number of countries such as Japan in the late nineteenth and early twentieth centuries and later Taiwan so focused on developing schooling in stages—providing universal primary education, then secondary school, and finally higher education. There was less regional disparity in schooling than in most other developing countries. Statistics in the 1960s through 1980s showed a much narrower gap between urban and rural levels of schooling than in most developing countries or than in many developed nations. The vigorous pursuit of uniformity of standards may not have served the more gifted students well, but at least it brought the population up to comparatively high overall standards of literacy and numeracy. In this respect, the ROK's educational development was similar to Japan's but differed from most other nations such as all those of Latin America or from India or China. Overall state expenditures on education were about average for a developing country. Much of the expense was borne privately, especially at the higher levels. Charging school fees is a common practice in poor countries; what was unusual was how universally families somehow managed to pay them. There was little resistance to sending children, including girls, to school; even poor farmer parents seemed willing to make whatever sacrifices were necessary.

KOREA IN GLOBAL PERSPECTIVE:
ECONOMIC DEVELOPMENT

South Korea's economic takeoff was one of the most dramatic in modern history. Foreigners after 1945 pointed to the country's lack of resources and its dense population as great obstacles. But history has shown there is little correlation between natural resources and development. In fact, reliance on commodities such as mineral and agricultural products has often proved to be an ineffective path to development, since commodity prices are subject to sharp swings, resulting in a boom-bust cycle, and they do not necessarily lead to the development of important technical skills. The path to development the ROK followed: export-led growth focusing on manufacturing, has been the most successful in achieving long-term sustained economic growth. South Korea's growth rates were not unique. Japan's growth rates before World War I and after the Korean War were also impressive. Indeed, Japanese growth rates from 1950 to 1970 were similar to South Korea's from 1965 to 1995. Taiwan and Singapore grew at comparable rates. None of these societies, however, was as poverty-stricken or had such dismal prospects as did the ROK in 1960. China might be more comparable, but its growth, due to its vast size, has been more regional, with large segments of the country and its people left behind.

It is difficult to compare South Korea's economic development with other nations. The country has been labeled one of the "Little Tigers" along with Taiwan, Hong Kong, and Singapore. Yet, each was quite different. Hong Kong and Singapore were cities without large numbers of rural peasants, and were already international trading centers before their industrial booms. Taiwan, with half of South Korea's population, is more comparable, but it too differed. It had a large professional class that fled from the mainland of China in 1949, often with some capital, an advantage South Korea did not have. It followed a somewhat different development trajectory, focusing on small family firms, not large business concentrations, and there were more state enterprises. Thailand and Malaysia have also been considered later members of the Pacific Rim boom-economies. The economic growth of these countries, however, was based on commodities—rice for Thailand; oil, tin, and rubber for Malaysia—as well as on manufacturing; and their economic rise was less dramatic. In short, there were a number of factors that were distinctive to South Korea's success: the intense rivalry with North Korea; its strategic value to the United States, which poured in so much aid, opened its markets, and provided enough security to attract investors; its proximity to Japan at a time when the Japanese were looking for places to invest; the existence of Japan as a model; the openness of Korean society to change; and the universally held zeal for education as a means of advancing social status.

Park Chung Hee

Why were we obliged to carry out the revolution? [the military coup of May 16, 1961] why did the people support the revolution? . . .

The April 19 Student Uprising and the May 16 Military Revolution signify the most decisive political disruption during the 16 years following the Liberation. These two revolutions, by students and by the Army, were successful because the courage, passion and strength necessary to save the nation and people could not be found anywhere but in these two special communities. Communities which ordinarily must remain detached from politics. For what reason did students put their studies aside? For what reason did soldiers leave their primary duty to defend the country to take part in this march of revolution?

At this point, two years after the event, there is no need to emphasize afresh that without the revolution the country would have fallen! National morality would, at this moment, have completely disappeared! It was too late, by far.

It was too late, by far, to expect the miracle of national salvation from boastful politicians. Too, it would have been foolish to expect this from civilians. What was the situation which, at that moment was so pressing, so desperate?

I will recall fragments of the past—a past which I felt to the depth of my bones at the time of the revolution, and await your candid and honest judgment.

In human life, economics precedes politics or culture.

In this light, the economic situation of Korea is most urgent.

The national economy was completely devastated by internal poverty throughout the Yi Dynasty and the cruel colonial extortion under Japanese rule. More recently it was the result of the unbalance of natural resources, due to the division of the nation, after the Liberation and the Korean War in the 1950s. The treasures of the country were on the point of exhaustion.

Just as an individual, without ability to help himself financially, has to depend on others, so the hope for the wholeness of a nation without its economic independence is literally to look for fish in a forest. What was our economic situation? Statistics show the following.

Every year countless numbers of people had to fight hunger. The ideas that a man has the right to eat and live is no luxury, no excessive ambition. It is a minimum right that should be guaranteed absolutely. Even that this idea has to be brought into question, signifies that we have other aims than merely to extend our barest existence. . . .

The key industries of the nation were in a pitiful state. Farming villages were impoverished and miserable beyond description. The crowd of unemployed intellectuals in the cities was a heart-breaking sight. . . .

We say the country was poor. How poor? Here is a living proof! It is none other than the Supplementary Budget of the Democratic Party government in 1961; the year of the revolution!

The total size of the budget was 608,800 million hwan, of which the United States counterpart funds supplied 316,900 million hwan, including 13,000 million hwan in the proceeds of $10 million worth of surplus farm products, to finance national construction development projects. This represents 52% of the total budget when compared with the 291,900 million hwan in domestic resources.

Thus, more than half of the national budget, the basic housekeeping of national management, depended upon the United States.

Though nominally independent, the real worth of the Republic of Korea, from the national statistical point of view, was only 48%. In other words, the U.S. had a 52% majority vote in regard to Korea, and we were dependent to that extent. . . .

We have to accomplish, as quickly as possible, the goal of an independent economy. We must manage our own affairs as our own responsibility. Before May 1961 this was the primary objective which made me undertake the revolution. Independence! There is no other net to catch this elusive goal except economic independence.

—from *The Country, the Revolution and I* [35]

14

-⊏◇⊐-

South Korea: Creating a Democratic Society, 1953 to 1997

There was no more radical way in which South Korea evolved differently from the North than its transformation from an authoritarian state to a democracy. And this transformation was just as unpredicted as its economic "miracle." The early years of the Republic of Korea did not offer much promise for the emergence of flourishing democratic institutions. Although it had the outer appearance of a multiparty democracy, the Rhee administration was authoritarian, and its Liberal Party used bribery and intimidation to remain in power. South Korean prisons held thousands of political opponents, and the elections of 1960 were blatantly rigged. Following a student-led uprising in 1960, the one-year experiment in a parliamentary democracy produced a somewhat chaotic, weak, and ineffective government followed by a military coup and nearly three decades of military-dominated government. Yet despite this saga of political instability, authoritarianism, and military coups that was so characteristic of developing nations, South Korea developed a stable, democratic political order.

MILITARY AUTHORITARIANISM

The military coup in 1961 had been welcomed by much of the public. After the corruption of the Rhee administration and the perceived incompetence of the short-lived government of Chang Myŏn, 1960–1961, most South Koreans were hopeful that the military could bring some improvement. Many South Koreans were skeptical of democracy. In a poll conducted in 1963 among students who had participated in the revolt against Syngman Rhee, 86 percent thought that Western-style democracy was not suitable for Korea.[1]

Yet from the beginning the United States exerted pressure on the military rulers to return the government to civilians. In August 1961, Park announced plans to restore civilian rule by May 1963. In December 1962, the military leaders drew up a new constitution that restored the strong executive presidency that existed under Rhee and the unicameral legislature. That month, Park announced he was retiring from the military in order to run for president. In January he lifted the ban on political activity. In February 1963, he created the Democratic Republican Party (DRP). Park, reluctant to give up power, decided in March to extend military rule for four more years. This brought a sharp reaction from the United States, on whom his government was heavily dependent, making Park's room for action very limited. At that time, U.S. aid still accounted for 50 percent of the national budget and 72 percent of the defense budget.[2] Bowing to American pressure, Park agreed to go ahead as planned with the elections, which inaugurated what was known as the Third Republic.

The elections in 1963 were reasonably fair, although funding from the Korean Central Intelligence Agency (KCIA) and government support gave the pro-government DRP an advantage. The opposition was also disadvantaged because the October 15 date for the presidential election was not announced until a few weeks earlier, giving the opposition less time to organize. Park ran as the DRP candidate and Yun Po-sŏn, the former president, ran as the opposition candidate. Park received about 47 percent of the vote to Yun's 45 percent. In November, elections were held for the National Assembly. It is interesting that for all its advantages, the DRP won only a third of the vote, but because the opposition was divided it was the largest share of the vote. Under the complicated election rules, the party that won the largest share of votes received two-thirds of the at-large seats. This ended up giving the DRP 110 of the 175 seats. While there was considerable freedom of the press and free scope for political activities, Park maintained control of the army, the bureaucracy, and the powerful KCIA to effectively carry out policy.

With real evidence of economic development Park was able to win a second four-year term as president in 1967, again defeating Yun Po-sŏn, this time 51 percent to 41 percent. In 1969, Park decided to seek a third term. As in 1954, the ruling party sought a constitutional amendment, and as in 1954, this was strongly resisted by the political opposition. Students and others demonstrated, and finally the amendment was passed by the dubious method of the DRP meeting secretly in an annex to the National Assembly and passing it without the presence of the opposition members. A referendum was then held approving the third term. Nonetheless,

Park's position was not entirely secure. As under Rhee, a clear difference was seen between the urban and rural populations. Most farmers were poor, but due to the land reform most owned their farms; therefore, they were more accepting of the status quo. They also maintained the traditional respect for authority and held firm anticommunist attitudes. With the movement of young people to the cities, rural communities were older and more conservative. This was the political base of the Park regime, much as it had been for Rhee. And like Rhee and his Liberal Party, Park and the DRP did not do well in the cities. In 1971, the opposition united under a young, charismatic politician from South Chŏlla Province, Kim Dae Jung (Kim Tae-jung) (1925–2009). Kim represented part of a new leadership among politicians. The older generation was drawn from the conservative elite, who were wealthy and often foreign educated. Kim, like Park, was from a humble background and was a self-made man. In 1971, he ran an effective campaign. Park won 51 percent to 44 percent but again did poorly in the cities, a bad sign in a country that was rapidly urbanizing. Shortly after the election in December 1971 Park issued a state of emergency.

THE YUSHIN ERA, 1971–1979

A number of developments in 1971 appeared to make the world a bit more precarious for the ROK. President Nixon announced in the previous year his intention to withdraw two combat divisions, about 20,000 troops from Korea. In 1971, the U.S. rapprochement with China began, and it was clear that the United States intended to eventually withdraw from Vietnam. All this suggested that the U.S. commitment to South Korea might not be as secure as the ROK had thought. American decline was also suggested by Nixon's decision to take the United States off the gold standard, creating economic uncertainty. And then there was America's protectionist pressure on South Korea to limit textile exports. Textiles were Korea's biggest export, and the United States was its biggest market, so this was a serious blow. These factors, plus the new energy shown by the opposition, may have contributed to Park's decision to suspend the constitution and declare a state of emergency. On October 17, 1972, he proclaimed martial law, suspended the constitution, dissolved the National Assembly and the political parties, and prohibited all political activities. All this came as a shock to much of the public. Park placed restrictions on free speech and other civil liberties. The Third Republic was at an end. The eight years in which a semi-authoritarian military regime operated under the veneer of a democratic multiparty system was replaced by a more thoroughly authoritarian state. Park's government was now a dictatorship with only the thinnest veneer of an open society. Even before this, Park had made use of the KCIA and the National Security Law to threaten and arrest dissidents. In one notorious case, more than 200 Koreans living in Europe in 1967 were kidnapped and sent to Korea for trial in what became known as the East Berlin Spy Incident. From 1972 on, he became less restrained in the pursuit of perceived threats to his power or to national security.

The new government he created was called Yushin, the name of a series of "revitalizing" (*yusin* in Korean) reforms that created a new Yushin Constitution. The term itself, interestingly, was the same given by Japan (pronounced *Isshin* in Japanese) for the reforms carried out in the late nineteenth century. The new constitution gave the president almost total powers. He was not elected directly by the voters but by a National Council for Unification. Since this was a body created by the president, who headed it, this meant the president, in practice, elected himself. The National Assembly had little power to check the president, who appointed one-third of its members. Important matters could be carried out through national plebiscites. A public referendum in November 1972 approved the constitution and the so-called Fourth Republic was launched. Park also strengthened his authority by issuing a number of emergency decrees. Most notorious of these was Emergency Measure No. 9 in May 1975, which prohibited criticism of the president. With the aid of the KCIA, Park ruthlessly went after enemies, arresting and torturing them, and forcing confessions. Even Koreans overseas were sometimes kidnapped or murdered by his agents. The most notorious case was the kidnapping of Kim Dae Jung, who had gone into exile in the United States and then in Japan. He was abducted from his hotel room in Tokyo, placed on a boat, and tied with weights as if to be thrown overboard. At the last minute, an American official who had gotten word of his abduction issued a warning to Park, and Kim's life was spared.

Park was able to justify his political repression as part of the need for national security. In this he was aided by North Korea. There were the DPRK's aggressive incidents along the DMZ in 1967; the 1968 commando attack on the Blue House, the presidential mansion; and later that year the landing of commandos along the northeast coast. Some promising exchanges took place between the two powers in 1972, but when these broke down in 1973 the government could point to the insincerity of the enemy. The discovery of the tunnel built by the North Koreans under the DMZ that had been constructed during the talks reinforced this argument. Indeed, the tension with the DPRK made for a dangerous situation and may have helped people tolerate a higher level of political restrictions in the name of national security. The Park regime also sought legitimacy through economic performance. And this too was creditable, since economic growth was improving the standards of living for most citizens and creating a large middle class able to enjoy a degree of material comfort previously confined to the privileged elite. Much of the business community was supportive of the regime. Park himself was personally honest, hardworking, much respected, and dedicated to lifting the country out of poverty. The assassination of his wife at a public event in 1974 added a measure of personal sympathy for him. The assassin, a Communist agent, had been aiming at Park.

Park also navigated international relations competently, which was important, as South Korea was highly dependent on the United States militarily and economically. Park sought to achieve as much political autonomy from Washington as possible while at the same time maintaining America's commitment to defend the ROK, to keep its markets open to Korean goods, and to provide technical assistance and loans. He skillfully aligned South Korea with the United States when President Johnson needed support in the Vietnam War, gaining, as we have seen, considerable benefit in return. Conditions soured a bit under the Nixon administration, with its measures to protect textiles, its plans to reduce its troop commitments in Korea, and its opening with China. They were especially tense under the Carter administration, which announced plans for troop reductions and made a point of promoting human rights. On balance, Park managed to weather rough spots in relations with the Americans reasonably well. Relations with Japan following the normalization of relations in 1965 mainly focused on economic issues, with Tokyo being an important source of foreign investments and loans. The Korean public remained, however, resentful of Japan, a resentment encouraged by South Korean history textbooks that highlighted the victimization of Korea by its neighbor. The Japanese government's reluctance to accept responsibility for its colonial rule, as well as Tokyo's approval of history textbooks that whitewashed Japan's imperialist past, provided fuel for lingering anti-Japanese sentiments. Meanwhile, South Korea gradually expanded its diplomatic relations with nations around the world, but until the 1980s the country was very much in the shadow of the United States and focused on its rivalry with the North.

Even though the threat of North Korea, economic growth, the support of the business community, and its general competency in managing both economic and foreign affairs worked to the Park regime's advantage, and despite the often ruthless persecution of its opponents, a vigorous dissident movement emerged. This movement consisted of students, intellectuals, labor activists, Christian groups, and people from the southwestern part of the country who felt left behind in development projects that favored Seoul and Park's home region in the southeast. The students were carrying on a long Confucian tradition of being upholders of moral righteousness. Taking advantage of the years of relative freedom from family and work responsibilities, they often devoted time to political and social issues. Participating in a political movement eventually became almost a rite of passage for young Koreans before graduating and entering business, government, and the professions. There was also the legacy of the April Student Revolution that had toppled Syngman Rhee in 1960. Major student protests erupted during the 1964–1965 normalization treaty controversy and in 1969 over the attempt to amend the constitution to allow Park a third term. The more oppressive rule of the Yushin government drove the student movement underground but did not smash it. Violent student protests erupted from time to time, followed by harsh suppression. By 1979, the student movement was becoming more violent and more openly opposed to Park's continual rule. Students were not the only ones to protest. In December 1973 opponents of the regime launched a One Million Signatures Campaign for Constitutional Change that called for the end of the Yushin system, freeing of political prisoners, press freedom, and an independent judiciary.[3] Nothing came of it, but this showed that there was still a significant opposition.

The increasingly better-educated South Korean society produced not only more students but also more intellectuals and artists. Kim Chi-ha (1941–), a poet, became the most famous of these dissident artist-intellectuals. His poems "Groundless Rumors" and "Cry of the People" became generally known and were a highly effective way of pointing out the social inequities of society for a poetry-loving people. He attacked the Park regime's political abuses and the economic growth at the expense of the poor laborers and others left behind. His most famous long poem "Five Thieves" (1970), summarized the frustrations and anger of many South Koreans over the political-industrial system Park had created. His five thieves were: military generals, the bureaucrats, rich industrialists, cabinet ministers, and national assemblymen.

South Korea had a small but politically active labor movement after 1945 but this had largely died out in the 1960s. After 1970, labor became more politically active again. A key incident was the self-immolation on November 13, 1970, of Chŏn T'ae-il, a poor garment worker in Seoul. His shocking act of protest over labor conditions drew attention to the plight of the country's growing labor force. Union members grew in numbers and assertiveness in the 1970s. Two Christian groups, the Young Catholic Organization and the Protestant-sponsored Urban Industrial Mission, were important in supporting labor. A number of dissidents were drawn from the North and South Chŏlla provinces. The general development of Korea under Park was focused on the Seoul area and on the southeastern North and South Kyŏngsang provinces. This was part of the natural Seoul-Pusan axis, which linked the capital with its most important port and the traditional gateway to Japan, South Korea's second-largest trading partner. But the focus of development on this area was also due to the fact that Park and much of the key leadership came from the southeast and favored their home area. The agriculturally rich Chŏlla region, once the most important rice basket in Korea, was relatively neglected. Regional resentments became strong. Contributing to this resentment was the fact that Kim Dae Jung, the country's best-known dissident was from the area. Together these groups formed a growing dissident movement.

Park himself seemed to have become more isolated by the late 1970s, even from his supporters. In 1975, he removed Kim Jong Pil as his premier and replaced him with a professional bureaucrat of no political ambition, Choi Kyu Hah (Ch'oe Kyu-ha) (1919–2006). Personal access to him was controlled by his head of the Presidential Security Force, Ch'a Ch'i-ch'ŏl. Meanwhile, relations with the United States had soured, in part because of the "Koreagate" scandal in spring of 1975. A Korean businessman, Tongsun Park, had been involved in bribing U.S. congressmen. This led to an investigation by Congress of the activities of the KCIA in the United States, including the kidnapping and harassment of Korean-Americans and ROK nationals in America. Korea was also hit by the second oil shock of 1979. This blow to the economy coincided with an increase in political unrest including a more vigorous political opposition by a faction of the New Democratic Party led by Kim Young Sam (Kim Yŏng-sam) (1927–). In August 1979, the brutal treatment of 200 female textile workers of Y. H. Trading Company who were holding a demonstration in the opposition party's headquarters triggered a new round of militant activity of students, labor, and opposition politicians. In early October, Kim Young Sam gained control of the NDP. When he called Park a dictator in a *New York Times* interview, the DRP reacted by expelling him from the Assembly. This led to a walkout by the opposition and a new round of demonstrations by students, workers, and others calling for his reinstatement. The demonstrations spread to the Masan-Pusan area, the home of Kim Young Sam and a major industrial area with many restless workers. Martial law was declared there. Kim Chae-kyu, head of the KCIA, is said to have urged Park to work out a compromise with the opposition, while Park appears to have leaned toward using the military to put demonstrations down. On October 26, Kim Chae-kyu shot and killed Park and his bodyguard Ch'a Ch'i-ch'ŏl as they were dining in a KCIA compound near the Blue House. Choi Kyu Hah then became acting president.

SEOUL SPRING, 1979–1980

The assassination of Park led to a brief period of political openness sometimes called "Seoul Spring." Initially shocked by the sudden death of the man who had governed the country for eighteen years, most of the politically active population was eager to bring the repressive Yushin era to an end and move to a more representative government and freer atmosphere. Choi Kyu Hah was elected under the Yushin constitution by the National Council for Unification on December 6. He was considered by most a caretaker until the transition to a new government could take place. Choi moved quickly to free hundreds of political prisoners, including Kim Dae Jung, who had been under house arrest; abolished Emergency Measure No. 9; and promised that a referendum would be held on a new constitution within a year. In February, full civil rights were restored to Kim Dae Jung and hundreds of other political figures.

The new atmosphere led to political jockeying for power among the factions of the Democratic Justice Party and the New Democratic Party. In the DRP, Kim Jong Pil, who had long been thought a successor to Park Chung Hee, fought for leadership with Lee Hu Rak, who had also served as head of the KCIA. And Kim Young Sam and Lee Cheul Seung contested for leadership in the New Democratic Party, a contest joined by Kim Dae Jung when he was released from house arrest. Meanwhile, a small clique of generals began consolidating power within the army. The leader was Chun Doo Hwan (Chŏn Tu-hwan) (1931–), a two-star general who headed the Defense Security Command. His principle allies were General Roh Tae Woo (No T'ae-u) (1932–) and Chŏng Ho-yong, all major generals of the eleventh class of the Korean Military Academy who had graduated in 1955. They were from the Taegu-Kyŏngsang Province region, the same region as Park Chung Hee, hence they became known as the "T-K faction." In South Korea, school and regional ties were extremely important, and this group shared both. The generals seized control of the army in a coup on the night of December 12–13 that became known as the 12-12 Incident. Chun, in charge of Army Security Command, ordered the arrest of Chŏng Sŭng-hwa, army chief of staff and head of the Martial Law Command, for alleged complicity in the assassination. The Capital Garrison Commander and Commander of the Special Forces were also arrested as a regiment from Roh's Ninth Division moved into Seoul. In contrast to the bloodless coup of Park Chung Hee in May 1961, this was a violent incident involving exchanges of fire at the ROK Army Headquarters and Ministry of Defense in central Seoul. Some high-ranking commanders fled for their lives to the nearby U.S. military base in Seoul. Having taken command of the army, Chun and his group took control of the KCIA in the spring, while gradually assuming control of the government that was still nominally under the civilian leadership of Choi Kyu Hah.

In March, the universities reopened. Students began demanding greater campus autonomy and the purging of administrators and professors associated with the Park regime. They also protested the continuation of martial law and the Yushin constitution, and demanded the immediate implementation of democratic government. Students also wanted to address issues of economic and social inequality. When in April 1980 Chun illegally assumed control of the KCIA, student demonstrations began to spill into the streets; by May massive demonstrations in Seoul were presenting an atmosphere of instability, just as they had in 1960 and the spring of 1961. In mid-May, Chun moved troops and armored vehicles into the streets to protect government buildings as up to 100,000 students carried out boisterous demonstrations calling for his resignation and that of Prime Minister Sin Hyŏn-hwak, the lifting of martial law, and more rapid abolition of the Yushin system. With the encouragement of Kim Young Sam and Kim Dae Jung, the students called off further demonstrations on May 16. The next day, May 17, Chun proclaimed Martial Law Decree No. 10, extending martial law throughout the country, closing universities, and banning labor strikes. All political activity was prohibited, and twenty-six opposition leaders including Kim Dae Jung were arrested.

Anti-Chun feeling was especially strong in Kwangju. Kwangju was the largest city in South Chŏlla, the center of government opposition and resentment at the domination of government by the military from the southeast and the consequent economic neglect of their region. On May 18, Chŏnnam National University students in Kwangju demanded the release of Kim Dae Jung, who was a local hero from the nearby port of Mokp'o. Offices of the government-controlled broadcaster were burned. Special Forces commander Chŏng Ho-yong sent paratroopers who brutally attacked protesters. The alienated citizenry supported the students in a full-scale insurrection, seizing weapons, forcing the paratroopers to withdraw, and taking over the city. A Council of Citizens then attempted to negotiate with the armed forces; appeals to the United States for mediation were ignored. On May 27, Chun sent in regular troops of the Twentieth Division to retake the city in a bloody campaign with heavy civilian casualties. The official number killed was 200. The actual number killed is not known for sure, but is most likely much higher, with the figure of 2,000 often cited. The Kwangju Incident remained as an important legacy and left a stain on the Chun regime that it never quite recovered from. The official pronouncement that it was a Communist rebellion that had been crushed was believed by very few and only damaged the credibility of the regime. Kwangju became a symbol of civilian resistance to military rule and helped to radicalize the student and dissident movement and alienate much of the middle-class population from the government. It also led to anti-U.S. sentiment. A 1978 agreement creating the U.S.-ROK Combined Forces Command gave control of selected units of the ROK regular army to the commander of American forces in Korea. Many South Koreans came to believe that the American military commander and therefore the

U.S. government must have given at least tacit approval to the movement of troops to quell the rebellion. However, this was not the case, since the dispatched paratroopers were outside the control of the commander.

Chun then took the final steps in consolidating his power. In late May he organized a Special Committee for National Security Measures with Choi as nominal head. It contained both civilian and military officials, but Chun and his clique were clearly in charge. In August, Choi resigned and the National Council for Unification elected Chun. Chun then revised the constitution, creating what became known as the Fifth Republic. The revised constitution gave a bit more authority to the National Assembly but was not radically different from the Yushin constitution. This constitution was then approved by plebiscite in October, and in February 1981 a new National Assembly was elected. The Democratic Justice Party, as Chun's party was called, received 35 percent of the vote, but due to the proportional voting system it won a solid majority of seats.

THE FIFTH REPUBLIC

Chun, like Park, was born in rural poverty, the sixth of nine children in a peasant family. Also like Park, he was from Kyŏngsang Province and had chosen a military career as a way to advance out of his poor, rural background. He graduated from the Korean Military Academy, where he married the commandant's daughter. Rising up through the ranks, he proved to be an able military man, distinguishing himself in Vietnam. In many ways he was similar to Park. He was pragmatic, more interested in practical results than ideology, with the same vision of an economically strong ROK. His administration continued Park's developmental policies, which gave priority to economic development. However, Chun never commanded the respect that Park Chung Hee did. Partly this was a product of his personality; he had little charm and did not display the intellectual acuteness of his predecessor. Moreover, unlike Park, he was surrounded by scandal. His wife and family members were constantly rumored to be involved in shady financial deals (which later proved true), and in general he seemed less able to control corruption in his administration. Unlike Park's wife and daughter, who were widely admired, Chun's wife and family were treated with derision and contempt for their influence peddling. Perhaps his greatest liability was the messy way he seized power, from the heavy-handed coup of December 12, 1979, to the bloody Kwangju Incident.

The discontent with the new administration was due to more than Chun's unpopularity and lack of charisma. South Korean society had changed in the two decades between Park's military coup and Chun's consolidation of power. It was now more educated and affluent; there was a large middle class and a general feeling that while Korea was making great economic progress it was still politically backward. Most middle-class Koreans wanted a say in how their country was run. The quick resumption of military rule in 1980 came to many as a disappointment, much more so than in 1961, when the military seizure of power was actually welcomed as a relief from chaos and corruption. Many South Koreans were tired of military rule. While many Koreans accepted the argument that the dangerous security problem with North Korea called for order, stability, and a strong military, they did not interpret this to mean military rule. There was also a feeling that if South Korea wanted to join the ranks of advanced countries such as Japan, the United States, and Western Europe, it had to move beyond the politics of military coups and strongmen to more representational government, more political freedom, and orderly process.

Chun, despite his unpopularity, received some credit for the economic recovery that began in 1981. While much of this recovery was due to the drop in oil prices and strong economic growth in the key export markets of the United States and Japan, his administration did manage the economy competently. The decision in 1981 by the Olympic Committee to award the 1988 games to Seoul gave another boost to the regime. Chun also attempted to give a veneer of liberalism to his rule. The midnight-to-four curfew that had been in place for decades as a security measure in all but the inland province of North Ch'ungch'ŏng was lifted in January 1982. Other measures included easing travel restrictions and ending the requirement that school children wear militaristic-style uniforms and keep their hair short. People on the street no longer had to stand at attention when the national anthem was played at 5 p.m. But in reality South Korea remained an authoritarian state. Arrests and closed trials of dissidents were common; the press was censored; editors, reporters, and broadcasters were given official "guidance"; and the judiciary was subservient to the administration. The ruling Democratic Justice Party held a solid majority in the National Assembly due to the use of proportional seating. The party benefitted from a steady flow of financial donations from business interests. Deprived of its leadership, the opposition was rather tame.

1987: A POLITICAL TURNING POINT

The major turning point in South Korea's political evolution took place in 1987 when power began to shift away from the military-dominated regime and a genuine transition to democracy began. The events of that year caught some observers by surprise; however, they were preceded by developments that gradually weakened the Chun government, which in the early 1980s had seemed securely in power. In May of 1982 a financial scandal broke out that implicated some of Chun's in-laws, the first of a series that would undermine his credibility. The opposition became more active, assertive, and willing to work together to resist the government. Kim Young Sam, under house arrest, held a hunger strike, and Kim Dae Jung, who was allowed to go to the United States "for medical treatment" as a result of U.S. pressure, began to issue statements from exile critical of the government. In 1984 Kim Dae Jung, while still in exile, and Kim Young Sam formed an umbrella group of opponents of the regime, the Consultative Committee for the Promotion of Democracy, to bring about democratization. In January 1985, members of this group formed a new united opposition party, the New Korea Democratic Party (NKDP). This party was able to capture 102 of the 299 seats in the National Assembly elections of February 1985. Early in 1985 Kim Dae Jung returned to Korea and was immediately placed under house arrest, but his return intensified the opposition to the regime.

The Chun administration was also increasingly plagued by labor and student unrest. The anti-Americanism of student protesters, who blamed the United States for what they believed was its complicity in the Kwangju massacre, was also troubling. In 1984, Chun ended the heavy-handed police surveillance on college campuses and released many students who had been arrested. About 1,000 expelled students were reinstated. As with his loosening of restrictions on political activity, the ending of the late-night curfew, and other modest moves toward liberalization, these measures were not effective in reducing the hostility of the opponents of the regime. Despite more conciliatory measures, student demonstrations only grew in frequency.

Meanwhile, Chun stuck to his pledge to limit himself to a single seven-year term. With a growing opposition and concern about a smooth transition to his heir, Roh Tae Woo, his government began negotiations with the New Korea Democratic Party in 1986 on a new constitution. The main issue was whether to adopt a cabinet-style government with a titular head of state. The NKDP wanted a direct election of an executive presidency. The government wanted a strong National Assembly, which it felt it could control through its well-funded and well-disciplined party, the Democratic Justice Party (DJP). The opposition fragmented into competing factions; despite the current coalition, it had less chance of controlling the Assembly. Therefore the opposition favored a strong presidency, which it felt it could win if united behind a single candidate. The deadlock, which seemed to jeopardize the smooth transition to the end of military rule, resulted in a split when NKDP leader Lee Min-woo decided to seek a compromise with the administration. Kim Dae Jung and Kim Young Sam then left the party and formed their own, the Reunification Democratic Party, with Kim Young Sam as the party leader and Kim Dae Jung still officially banned from political activity as the unofficial coleader. With the opposition taking a hard line against the government, Chun decided to end the negotiations over the new constitution. Meanwhile, the death in January 1987 of Pak Chong-chŏl, a Seoul National University student, while being questioned by police, led to a new round of student demonstrations and public disgust with the administration's handling of them. In addition, international events had already added to internal tensions in 1986 when the People Power uprising overthrew the Marcos dictatorship in the Philippines, an event the Korean public followed with great interest.

On April 13, 1987, Chun announced that a new president would be decided by the National Council for Unification. In other words, he would, in effect, keep the presidential system with the strong executive presidency and handpick his successor, which everyone knew would be Roh Tae Woo. The April 13 announcement set in motion a period of political turbulence as students and political activists held increasingly larger and more massive protests. Much of the middle class, dismayed at not being able to select the next president, sympathized with the demonstrations. Every sign was that most citizens wanted some meaningful participation in the political process. The student demonstrations continued to grow in number and size, further inflamed by incidents of police brutality. On June 10, the DJP nominated Roh as their candidate, a fact that made his ascension to power a matter of course. Thousands of office workers and sympathetic citizens from various walks of life now joined the street demonstrations. They grew so disruptive that only military intervention could restore order. It was clear to many in the government that much of the public supported the demonstrators and that a crackdown could have dangerous consequences. To add to the government's concerns, the International Olympic Committee threatened to relocate the games if there was further unrest. Not only Chun but especially Roh, who chaired the ROK Olympic committee and had staked much of his prestige on successfully hosting the games as a way of displaying South Korea's economic development and maturity as a nation, could not afford to risk losing the games. American and other international opinion was sympathetic to the democratic movement, and a crackdown would be an enormous loss of face. Nor was there full assurance that the government could count on the conscript army to take extreme measures if necessary to end the protests. Yet further demonstrations could threaten stability and embolden North Korea into a rash action. Chun offered to compromise with the opposition on June 22, but this had little effect. On June 26, over 100,000 ordinary

Koreans joined a peace protest march in Seoul. Three days later, on June 29, Roh with Chun's approval issued a declaration that the DJP would accept a new constitution with provisions for direct presidential elections. The government also announced it was ending censorship, releasing political prisoners, and removing all obstacles to political activities.

TRANSITION TO DEMOCRACY

The events of 1987 launched a transition toward democracy. The presidential elections were freely contested, but the rivalry between Kim Young Sam and Kim Dae Jung split the opposition. In addition, Kim Jong Pil, one of the former leaders of the 1961 military coup also ran, so Roh Tae Woo faced the "three Kims" in the December presidential election. Roh, carrying the rural areas and receiving the support of many conservative working- and middle-class voters concerned about stability, won with 37 percent of the ballots cast. Kim Young Sam, carrying his home Pusan area and receiving much of the white-collar vote, received 28 percent. Kim Dae Jung carried his home Chŏlla region, where he obtained 90 percent of the vote in Kwangju, and captured support from labor and the left for a total of 27 percent. Kim Jong Pil received 8 percent of the votes, much of it in his home area in Ch'ungch'ŏng in the central part of the country. Under the new constitutional amendments the president was elected for a single five-year term.

Roh's five-year administration, which began in 1988, was a transitional period. A member of Chun's military clique and probably the second most important person in the Fifth Republic after Chun, Roh accepted the restrictions on his authority imposed by a more democratic political order. He avoided the aloof style of his predecessors, carrying his own briefcase to work, posing as the *"pot'ong saram"* (ordinary person). His power was further restricted when the opposition parties gained control of the National Assembly in the April 1988 legislative elections. The DJP pulled just 25 percent of the vote, obtaining only 125 of the 299 seats; the remainder were held by major opposition parties. With opposition parties holding a majority for the first time in history, the National Assembly began to play a more assertive role in governance, carrying out investigative and oversight functions. The judiciary, too, began to assert itself. In June 1988, 300 judges demanded that the judicial independence lost under Park Chung Hee be restored.[4] A new chief justice was appointed who was not tied to government officials. All this suggested that South Korea was becoming a representative democracy with independent branches of government. However, much of the governing structure, including the close ties between the ruling party, the bureaucracy, and the major *chaebŏls* remained. One product of this link was a hostile attitude to organized labor; the government showed little reluctance to use force to put down strikes. The Roh government also continued to make use of the National Security Law, intended to deal with North Korean subversion and to clamp down on leftist dissidents. Nor was the military completely free from interference in domestic matters. In 1990, for example, it was revealed that the Army Counterintelligence Corps was engaged in illegal surveillance of civilians.

The first year of the Roh administration saw one of the major turning points for South Korea: the successful hosting of the 1988 Summer Olympics in September. After the Western boycott of the Moscow games in 1980 and the Soviet boycott of the Los Angeles games in 1984, these were the first in twelve years in which almost all nations attended. For Koreans it was a way of showcasing the country's rise from the rubble of the Korean War to a modern, industrial state. As a public relations event, it was highly effective. Most visitors were surprised at how modern and prosperous Seoul was, including its newly completed, clean subway system. The games provided an opportunity to broaden its relations with other nations, most importantly the Soviet Union and China. After the Olympics, the government further lifted travel restrictions, and South Koreans began to travel overseas in great numbers. The country was emerging as a presence in the world, and its people were becoming more cosmopolitan. The economy was also booming at double-digit rates at this time, benefiting from what Koreans called the "three lows,"—the low price of oil, reducing the country's energy bill; the low interest rates abroad, which reduced the costs of borrowing; and the low Japanese yen, that is, the strong yen that made Korean products more competitive.

But from 1989, things became more difficult for the Roh administration. It faced an upsurge in radical student activity. The most dramatic incident was a student disturbance at Dongeui University in Pusan that left seven riot policemen dead. Violent student activities brought on a government crackdown that threatened to derail the democratization process. Labor activity also challenged the administration. The sharp rise in labor strikes that accompanied the events of 1987 continued into 1988 and 1989. Labor union membership grew quickly. In June 1987, only 22 percent of the workforce was unionized and of these 82 percent belonged to the government-approved and politically tame Federation of Korean Trade Unions. Only 3 percent belonged to the illegal and radical labor federation known as the Chŏnnohyŏp, which often led violent strikes. After 1987 union membership and strike activity grew at an explosive rate. Labor strikes were often violent and threatened to hamper the country's economic growth. Overall wages rose sharply in the late 1980s and early 1990s, in part due to the greater power of labor unions, increasing about

15 percent a year. This contributed to inflation, leading to the appreciation of the *won* and to the subsequent loss of competitiveness for South Korea's products overseas. Massive trade imbalances with the United States, the biggest overseas market, led to American pressure on the ROK to force it to adopt a code of voluntary restraints on exports. A boom in real estate and a soaring stock market proved unsustainable. Land prices had begun to reach absurd levels. In 1990, the total value of land was equal to 70 percent of that of the United States, which had ninety times the area of the ROK.[5] Land prices were more than twice as high as those in famously expensive Japan. Stock prices surged. This not only brought up fears of an economic bubble but also threatened to undermine the trend toward greater economic equality. The public grew concerned over conspicuous consumption. The government launched a campaign of avoiding "excessive consumption" to allay these concerns and to prevent a flood of consumer imports that would weaken the balance of payments. Stock prices began to fall in 1990, and as the real estate market cooled, so did the economy.

South Korea's foreign policy under Roh was aimed at developing closer ties with the Communist nations. Roh called his policy *Nordpolitik*, and it was modeled in part after the West German policy of *Ostpolitik*, which had similar aims. The policy was well timed, since under Gorbachev the Soviet Union was eager to develop economic ties with booming South Korea. The two countries exchanged trade offices in 1989 and full diplomatic relations in September 1990. China moved more cautiously, but it too was attracted to the prospects of trade and investment with South Korea. Despite the ideological differences, the two countries shared cultural ties and geographical proximity. For the ROK, China presented great opportunity for investment and trade. In the autumn of 1990 the two countries opened trade offices; in August 1992 they established full diplomatic relations.

The principle aim of *Nordpolitik* was to isolate the DPRK, removing any objections for North Korea's allies to establish closer ties. In a much stronger position, and with North Korea's economy entering a crisis, Seoul hoped to work toward closer ties with its nemesis. From July 1990 to December 1991 the two Koreas engaged in talks at a fairly high administrative level. This led to the Agreement Concerning the Reconciliation, Nonaggression, Exchanges and Cooperation in December 1991. But little came of this, and the talks stalemated as North Korea resumed its customary confrontational public statements. However, the new relations with the Soviet Union, China, and Eastern Europe were psychologically important to South Korea. For decades the country had been perceived as a client state of the United States. South Korea was now developing its own foreign policy and being respected as an important economic power and political player in the international arena.

The political calm of 1988 ended after the Olympics, when the opposition-controlled National Assembly began investigating corruption under the Chun regime. Many of Chun's aides and in-laws were indicted, and Chun himself was forced to apologize on television for the corruption and the abuse of power under his administration. Then he retreated to a remote Buddhist monastery. In January 1990, Kim Young Sam worked out a deal merging his party with the DJP and the smaller party led by Kim Jong Pil to form the Democratic Liberal Party (DLP). The new party now had a solid majority in the Assembly. The DLP, however, was weakened by internal rivalries, so it was not an effective vehicle for Roh to push through his agenda. In the March 1992 Assembly elections the DLP lost a number of seats to the political party of Kim Dae Jung. As part of the deal, Kim Young Sam was to be the DLP candidate in the 1992 presidential election. Roh became a lame duck.

In December 1992, the DLP ran Kim Young Sam as its candidate against his old-time rival Kim Dae Jung. A third candidate entered the race, the seventy-six-year-old Hyundai founder, Chung Ju Yong. Chung, angry with the government over disputes with his company, used his vast personal wealth to finance his campaign, but he never had a serious chance of winning. He received 16 percent of the vote. Kim Dae Jung, with a loyal following in his home of Chŏlla and among many in the moderate left, received 37 percent. Kim Young Sam won with 42 percent of the vote, gaining the support of conservatives and liberals, benefitting from the considerable resources of the government machine that endorsed him, and winning overwhelmingly in his home province, South Kyŏngsang. Regional affiliation was the greatest factor in voting, not ideology. Kim Dae Jung, for example, received 88 percent of the vote in Chŏlla and an extraordinary 95 percent of the vote in Kwangju. Kim Young Sam was inaugurated president in February 1993. It is interesting to note that there was no military man or ex-military man running for the office. The integrity of the voting process was largely accepted by all parties; the idea of military intervention in the political process was becoming unthinkable. The transfer of power to a former political dissident was smooth, orderly, and already seemed normal. Without the drama of 1987, voters were more complacent or less excited, with only 77 percent casting ballots compared to 87 percent five years earlier.

Democratization was a process that was far from complete by the 1990s. Government institutions were still not as transparent as in most Western democracies. The National Security Law was still in effect and the internal security organs were still powerful, though reined in a bit. Surveys done from the late 1980s through the mid-1990s by Doh C. Shin and Geir Helgesen suggest that traditional values were still strong. While most Koreans had become committed to the ideals of democracy and political equality, Koreans still placed greater importance on the judgments of morally upright leaders than on democratic process and attached greater importance to social harmony than to political and social pluralism.[6] Nonetheless, South Korea had moved a long way toward developing an orderly democratic system.

UNDERSTANDING THE DEMOCRATIC TURN

The events of June 1987 were a turning point in the history of South Korea. The country now began a clear, if sometimes rocky, transition to democracy. Thus South Korea had a democratic transformation to match its economic one. This political shift away from an authoritarian regime to a more open political system had many causes. The experience of 1960–1961 when democracy was associated with social disorder had faded, and there was a widespread desire to end nearly three decades of military-dominated government. A culture that had traditionally disdained the military with the old Chinese adage "the best iron is not used to make nails and the best men are not used to make soldiers" underwent major changes. The Korean War created a huge army and the need for all men to serve in it. A military conscription was enacted in 1949, but it was in full effect only after the Korean War. All men were required to serve three years, then another eight years in the Homeland Reserve Force with annual military training. Later the period of active service was reduced to between twenty-six and thirty months, according to type of service. Universal conscription promoted a sense of national solidarity and eroded class barriers to some extent. It did not, however, fully overcome Korean traditional attitudes toward the military. Park, Chun, and their generals-turned-cabinet ministers donned civilian clothes to gain respect and acceptability, but the public was never completely comfortable with rule by military or ex-military men. By the 1980s, most were eager to see a return to civilian rule.

Another factor that helped foster the end of military rule was the strengthening of big business. The *chaebŏls* had a close relationship with the ruling parties. But as the economy grew, the leaders of big business felt confident enough to compete in the international markets without the close supervision of the state. They came to view a civilian government as being more conducive to their pursuit of profit without excessive bureaucratic restraint. Furthermore, many in the business community shared the public perception that democratic government was a necessary development for the country's continued progress.

The democratization was also brought about by major cultural and social changes in South Korean society. This included two dramatic breaks with the Korean past important for understanding the evolution of democracy in the ROK: the spread of egalitarian ideals and the increase in social mobility. The upheavals of Japanese colonialism, especially during World War II when millions were mobilized for the war effort; the dislocations following the collapse of the Japanese empire and the partition of the country; the land reform; and the destruction caused by the Korean War all had a social and economic leveling effect. The old rigid hereditary-based hierarchical society dominated by the *yangban* class and its descendents had come to a final end. At the same time, the democratic ideals promoted by both leftists and by conservatives who proclaimed their adherence to American-style liberal democratic ideals took deep root. This can be seen in education where the public clamored for an open access to all levels of education, where even the humblest families sacrificed for the chance that their son or daughter might achieve a higher level of schooling and move up the social ladder. A popular belief that by industriousness and talent people could rise to wealth and power was an important factor in the country's development. People worked hard and made personal sacrifices in the belief in a better future for themselves or their children. As Laura Nelson has observed, "the carrot of a better, more equitable, wealthier, democratic (and unified) Korea was dangled before the population."[7] Egalitarian ideals were reflected in the education system, where government policies promoted equal opportunity in education and uniformity of school standards.

There were also countertrends to the establishment of an egalitarian society. Industrialization led to the rise of an extremely wealthy entrepreneurial class. It was a class enriched in part by access to low-interest credit denied to small businesses or private individuals, and reinforced by low inheritance taxes. Many married within that class, with CEO sons marrying the daughters of CEOs, threatening to create a new hereditary elite. Real estate prices also posed a threat to equality. While wages rose sharply in the 1970s and 1980s, real estate prices rose even faster. Added to the similar rise in the cost of education, the entry into a middle-class lifestyle was often frustratingly difficult.[8] Nonetheless, the overall trend, especially in the 1980s and early 1990s was toward greater income equality. In fact, during this period South Korea had one of the most equitable distributions of wealth of any developing country.

This more egalitarian society was becoming increasingly middle class in its identification and values. The economic boom and the expansion of education had expanded the ranks of well-informed, urban middle-class voters who were often embarrassed about the status of their country as a military-style authoritarian state. Most Koreans by the 1980s identified themselves as middle class even if in many cases this was as much an aspiration as a reality. They were literate and widely read;

newspaper circulation had risen to among the highest in the world, and Korean newspapers gave excellent international news coverage. By the mid-1980s almost every household had a TV and most watched the well-produced nine o'clock news on the major networks. South Koreans were curious about the world. They were also a rank-conscious culture, concerned about how they stood in the world. They knew which countries were at the top: the United States, Japan, and the nations of Western Europe. South Koreans wanted their nation to measure up to that group. The Park administration had boasted in its last days that South Korea would be a fully industrialized first-world nation before the end of the century. Although regarded by outsiders and some Koreans as unrealistic, there was no doubt for most Koreans that it would be possible. But being a "first world" nation to most Koreans meant not just economic development but reaching political maturity.

Most of South Korea's middle class accepted an open, democratic society as part of what it meant to be a "successful" first-world nation. Thus, the goal of being a rich and strong nation that Park Chung Hee and almost every Korean nationalist aspired to had become linked in the minds of the public with being a democratic society. South Korean textbooks discussed democracy and identified the country with the Western democracies, and democratic ideals of representational government, popular sovereignty, and human rights had won wide acceptance as important, desired values. They were all perceived as the traits of a modern society. When it came time to vote, many were quite conservative, but they did want to vote, and in a meaningful way.

U.S. influence also contributed to the democratization in South Korea. As Gregg Brazinsky has pointed out, to a considerable extent the political evolution of the country was shaped by the way American nation-building efforts interacted with Korean internal developments.[9] American culture deeply penetrated South Korea. Much of this was in the form of pop culture—movies, music, and fashions—but it also included education and ideas about society and politics. Korean textbooks taught U.S.-inspired principles of human rights and democracy, often with American examples as models. The thousands of Koreans who studied in America generally came back with favorable impressions of American values and culture, even if they were sometimes critical of specific U.S. policies. The ROK's client status with the United States in some ways resembled Korea's pre-1876 relations with China. While determinedly independent, South Koreans looked to the United States as a big brother—the major buyer of its exports; its military guarantor; and the source of the most advanced learning, technology, and culture.

American political influence came in many ways. Koreans went to the United States for higher education, not only in science and engineering but also for degrees in social sciences, humanities, and education. The United States sponsored in-service training programs for bureaucrats. Washington funded publications such as *Sasanggye*, an influential journal of political and social thought. A U.S. Leader Program inaugurated after the Korean War brought government officials and political figures to the United States for three months to observe America's economic and political system. Among the important figures that came out of that program were political opposition leaders and later presidents Kim Young Sam and Kim Dae Jung.[10] The United States had a major role in educational development, too; U.S.-trained officials dominated the Ministry of Education and often inserted American political values and ideas into the curriculum and teacher-training programs. American influence and the American model contributed to the acceptance of ideas of human rights, individual freedom, and democratic accountability of political leaders.

The rise of Christianity in South Korea also added to the pluralism of society and provided an institutional basis for political opposition. Christian missions were an important vehicle for the spread of new ideas, and Christians were disproportionately active in the pre-1945 nationalist movement. Yet in 1945, Christians made up only a small percent of the population, with the greatest concentration in the north, especially in the P'yŏngyang area. After 1945, millions of South Koreans converted. According to a 1983 survey, there were 1.6 million Catholics and 5.3 million Protestants.[11] Other estimates are higher, and the numbers grew until leveling off in the early 1990s, by which time a quarter to one-third of the population described themselves as Christians (the estimates vary). Crosses lit up the skylines of major cities at night. Many were small storefront churches, but there were some mega-churches, most notably the Yŏŭido Full Gospel Church in Seoul. With 800,000 members, it was the world's largest. Converts to Christianity cut across social classes, with many of the middle class as well as the working-class poor joining churches.

Most churches were not centers of social and political activism; more often they preached the gospel of material success. But some Christian ministers contributed to the rise of the labor movement and led human rights campaigns, and Myongdong Cathedral in downtown Seoul became a center used by political protesters. Both Catholic and Protestant groups had been active in organized labor. Cardinal Stephen Kim (Kim Su-hwan) (1922–2009), the Catholic archbishop of Seoul, was an important moderate voice in the opposition to government oppression and to the social injustices caused by the country's rapid industrialization. Another sanctuary was provided by the Presbyterian minister and ecumenical movement pioneer Kang Wŏn-yong (1917–2006). His Christian Academy, a seminar house, was a safe meeting ground for intellectuals and political activists.

The fact that churches had international links provided considerable protection to political dissidents and social activists, as they had to a lesser extent during colonial rule. A roughly equal number of Koreans called themselves Buddhist and there was a rise in smaller religious groups as well. Most non-Christians were less involved in politics, but a few Buddhist groups also became active in human rights movements.

STUDENT ACTIVISM

While the democratization of South Korea was primarily the product of an emerging pluralistic, middle-class society culturally linked with the West, the events of 1987 were spearheaded by the student movement. South Koreans were often tolerant of student activism, accepting that students had a right to point out injustices and the moral shortcomings of those in public life. Student remonstrance against government misconduct was a Korean tradition with premodern roots, reinforced by the contributions of student demonstrators in colonial times. The repressive nature of the Yushin government in the 1970s, by not allowing students to air their grievances, had the effect of radicalizing them, creating an underground movement that felt increasingly alienated from the political and economic system. This radicalization and the formation of strong underground organizations intensified under the Fifth Republic. There were several strands to the ideology among the students as well as other dissidents. One was nationalism. The early nationalist intellectuals of the late Chosŏn had criticized the Yi dynastic government for what was called *sadaejuŭi*, or flunkyism, in the face of China; and in the colonial period radical nationalists saw the moderates and conservatives guilty of being Japanese flunkies and collaborators. Many saw Park's normalization treaty with Japan in 1965 in this light, as toadying to Tokyo. Some radical Koreans after 1980 accused the Chun administration and its supporters in the current military-political-economic establishment of being U.S. flunkies. A deep anti-Americanism developed among student radicals in part due to the belief in U.S. support for or involvement in the Kwangju Incident. This impression was reinforced when in early 1981 the newly inaugurated President Reagan honored Chun as the first foreign head of state to be invited to the White House. Remarks by the man Reagan appointed as his ambassador, Richard Walker, who criticized the opponents of the regime and called the students "spoiled brats," also contributed to the growing hostility toward the United States by young people. The anticommunist rhetoric of the Reagan administration, although directed at the Soviet Union, seemed to echo that of the military rulers who had used the threat of Communism to strengthen their rule. In part, this anti-Americanism was the product of a young generation born after the Korean War, less concerned with the threat of North Korea, with none of the images of the Americans as liberators from the Japanese or the North Korean invaders. Instead they saw the United States as an imperialist bully that had divided their country and propped up oppressive military regimes that were economically and militarily dependent on Washington. Student radicals launched attacks on American targets, most notably on the U.S. information office and library in Pusan, which they burned in March 1982. Every American facility, even libraries, took on the appearance of armed fortresses.

Another element in student radicalism was neo-Marxism. Western critics of international capitalism were being translated and read. These included thinkers such as the South American dependency theorists, who saw the world economy as structured in such a way as to keep the poor nations of Asia, Africa, and Latin America dependent on the rich nations; American Immanuel Wallerstein, whose world-systems theories argued along similar lines; and the Italian Marxist Antonio Gramsci, with his ideas of hegemony. The fact that this radical literature was sometimes banned only added to its appeal. In sum, many radicals saw South Korea's capitalist system as benefitting only the rich, based on exploitation of the poor, and linking the ROK to the international capitalist system that was led by the United States and Japan. Thus, criticism of capitalism and the economic inequalities it created was connected to the nationalist criticism of a government subservient to foreign interests. This sometimes led to a more sympathetic view of North Korea and its *juche* philosophy. It also led to student involvement in the labor movement.

A key concept in radical ideology that was emerging in the 1970s and 1980s was *minjung*. The word can be translated as "the masses," or simply as "the people." The term was used in several ways. It was seen as defining the non-elite of society, the ordinary people within whom the national spirit was embodied in its purist form. *Minjung* thinkers saw Korean history as the struggle of the common people, ordinary men and women, against political repression, economic exploitation, and social injustice. It was thus linked to the concept of the nation as understood by the old radical nationalists. For some Christians, *minjung* became associated with the social justice movement within some churches, especially Catholic liberation theology. For others it was a way to capture the essence of what it was to be Korean. It led to a renewed interest in Korean folk culture and traditions. Student protestors would often dance to traditional folk instruments as if calling upon the spirit of nationalism before charging out into the street to make battle with the riot police. *Minjung* thought, neo-Marxism, nationalism, antiforeignism, and even Christian social activism often became fused into the struggle against not just the military regime but the entire political, social, and economic system. Although few outside student, intellectual, and radical political circles shared this basic critique of society, the highly motivated students were able to act as the vanguard of political dissent. In 1985, student radicals organized the Sammint'u (Struggle Committee for Minjung Democratization), which demanded the withdrawal of the U.S. military presence from South Korea, the destruction of the military-capitalist regime, and the unification of Korea. In 1986, this organization split into the Minmint'u, which focused on anti-imperialism and antifascism, and the more radical Chamint'u, which focused on organizing a domestic revolution. The latter organization was less interested in organizing students than in organizing the "masses."[12] These organizations effectively operated to organize protests despite police crackdowns. Although student radicals were a small minority, a much greater number of university students participated in their protests. In 1984, it was estimated that 10 percent of all college students were involved in political protests, and this percentage grew over the next three years. It was, however, only in 1987, when middle-class Koreans joined or actively encouraged them, that student demonstrations posed a major threat to the government.

ORGANIZED LABOR

The rise of labor also contributed to the ending of the authoritarian political system. Democratization took place in a society that was undergoing rapid social change. In the decades after the Korean War, millions left the countryside to move into the city, and industrialization and universal education created a large literate industrial working class. Out of the working class came the labor activists, who formed another element in the dissident movement that helped bring an end to the military regime. While organized labor appeared to have suddenly emerged in the late 1980s as a major force in the country's economic and political life, South Korea's labor movement had roots back in the colonial period. Labor unions were active in the 1920s, including a major labor strike in the port of Wonsan in 1929. Because of government repression in the 1930s, the labor groups survived only covertly and were affiliated with the Communist movement. Organized labor reemerged immediately after liberation as a major force. The chief organization was the leftist-dominated National Council of Korean Trade Unions (Chŏnp'yŏng). Established soon after the Japanese surrender, from August 1945 to March 1947 it carried out 2,500 labor demonstrations involving 600,000 participants.[13] Labor unrest reached a peak in the fall of 1946 when a quarter of a million workers were on strike at one time. The American occupation authorities and their conservative Korean allies organized the Korean Federation of Trade Unions (Noch'ong or KFTU) in 1946 to counter its influence. The Chŏnp'yŏng was eventually outlawed, and the KFTU served for the next four decades as the only legally recognized labor organization. The latter was largely controlled by centralized government with little grass-roots support. The pent-up demand for a truly effective and representative labor organization became clear when the National Council of Trade Unions (No Hyŏp) was organized in 1960, following the fall of President Rhee. It quickly developed a large and militant membership that carried out a number of strikes and demonstrations until banned by the military government in 1961.

The labor force grew rapidly in the 1960s under Park's drive for industrial development, but the workers were kept under tight restrictions. South Korea had a system of company unions that were easy for large employers to control. All these company unions also belonged to the KFTU. Efforts to organize strikes were brutally repressed by the police. Conditions for labor reached their nadir when Park in December 1971 decreed the Law Concerning Special Measures Safeguarding National Security, which suspended the right of collective bargaining and collective action.[14] While the government used manipulation of the official labor union and police intervention to control labor, Korean industrialists used Confucian terminology of paternalism, loyalty, and harmony to try to create a sense that the company was a big family where the management was concerned for its workers who in turn should be loyal. In theory, the two: labor and management, worked in harmony. In practice, corporate heads were quick to call upon riot police to break up demonstrations. They also employed thugs called *kusadae* (save our company group) to beat labor organizers, a practice that became common in the 1980s.[15]

Working conditions were often appalling, with scant regard to safety and long hours. Korean workers had what was probably the longest workweek in the world. In the 1970s the average South Korean worker put in 53.1 hours, compared with 51 hours for those in Taiwan and 39.7 hours and 38.8 hours per week for American and Japanese workers, respectively. The workweek peaked at 54.5 hours in 1986.[16] Twelve-hour shifts six days a week were common at many companies. Some workers received only every other Sunday off. Long hours and minimal concern for safety resulted in an appalling accident rate that was fifteen times that of Japan in 1976.[17] The willingness of South Koreans to work long hours and the relative lack of labor unrest as a result of government control was one of the attractions to foreign investors. The American Chamber of Commerce and *Forbes* magazine, among others, advertised South Korea as a good place for investment, where Korean workers "cheerfully" worked sixty hours a week for low pay.[18]

Industrial workers not only had to deal with government oppression and the ruthless business practices of a country hell-bent to increase industrial output at all costs, but also traditional Korean prejudices against manual labor. Industrial workers were referred to by the pejorative terms *kongsuni* (factory girl) and *kongdori* (factory boy).[19] Such sentiments meant that, whenever possible, Korean workers sought to pass themselves off as members of the middle class and pushed their children to achieve white-collar status through schooling.

Despite the tame company unions and government measures to repress worker activism, labor unrest periodically resurfaced. The most dramatic incident took place in 1970, when Chŏn Tae-il, a worker in the P'yŏnghwa Market—a block-long four-story complex of small garment factories and clothing shops employing some 20,000 workers—burned himself alive out of protest of the treatment of laborers. But there were many other less-publicized acts of violent protest. Christian groups became important in organizing labor starting in the 1960s, especially the Urban Industrial Mission (UIM). Originally this group, drawn from Presbyterian and Methodist churches, formed to proselytize among factory workers, but the pastors became increasingly concerned about the working conditions of their converts.[20] As small groups gathered for Bible readings, they discussed their hardships. This proved an effective vehicle for labor organization, since the UIM had international links, including foreign pastors, making open suppression by the South Korean government difficult. There was also a Catholic group, the Young Christian Workers, established in 1958, that also became involved in labor activities. With its international links, it enjoyed a similar advantage.[21]

An interesting feature of the South Korean labor movement was the important role women played. About one-third of industrial workers in the 1970s and 1980s were women, most young and single. They often lived in company dormitories, nicknamed "beehives" for their tiny, cramped rooms. Women workers were disproportionately represented in the huge, labor-intensive garment industry. They played an important role in fanning the flames of labor unrest, carrying out high-profile strikes at the Dongil Textile Company in 1972 and at the Y.H. Trading Company in Pusan in 1979.

The pent-up frustration of laborers was seen in the outburst of some 400 strikes and demonstrations during the "Seoul Spring" of 1980. This was followed by another wave of repression with the consolidation of the Chun Du Hwan regime that year. But labor unrest grew in the 1980s. It was abetted by a modest lessening of political control in the mid-1980s, because the regime sought to achieve legitimacy and deflect international criticism as it prepared to host the Asian Games in 1986 and the Olympics in 1988. Two hundred independent labor unions were organizing in

1984, and the number of strikes increased. A turning point was the strike in Kuro, the industrial section of Seoul, in which workers from many industries participated. It started among apparel workers but was joined by many others in that busy manufacturing zone.[22] Many of these strikes were spontaneous outbursts of protests, but they were also organized by college students and other political dissidents, and by increasingly effective labor organizers. During this time, student radicals began joining labor unions after graduating or by leaving school, and they helped to spread the antigovernment ideology. In 1986, the number of strikes more than doubled from the previous years. An especially violent protest over labor conditions occurred in Inch'ŏn that year when student radicals joined with labor activists. The biggest outburst in labor unrest came in 1987. In that year there were 3,749 labor strikes compared to 276 the previous year.[23] The sharp upswing in labor unrest in 1987 became part of the political upheavals of that year.

SOCIAL AND CULTURAL TRANSITION

The democratization of South Korea was part of a broad social and cultural change that included the rise of the middle class, of an industrial working class, and of Christianity, and the spread of egalitarian ideals. Another important component of the social and cultural change was the movement for greater legal and social equality for women. At first, attitudes about the role of women in society and the nature of the family changed slowly. After liberation, many South Korean officials and intellectuals were more concerned about preserving or restoring what they sometimes called "laudable customs and conduct" (*mip'ung yangsok*).[24] This concern was reflected in what was known as the Family Law, the parts of the civil law code that governed family relations. The Family Law, compiled in the 1950s and finished in 1958, was in many ways very conservative: it preserved the patriarchal family structure with the husband as head of the household; favored the eldest son in inheritance; and in divorce, which was uncommon, men generally received custody of children. The maintaining of these practices was important, it was argued, to preserve the essential nature of Korea's cultural traditions.

In the 1950s and 1960s women organized to challenge these traditions and the laws that protected them in the name of women's equality. A Federation of Korean Women's Groups (Taehan yŏsŏng tanch'e hyŏphŭihoe) led by Lee Tai-young (Yi T'ae-yŏng) (1914–1995) fought during the 1950s and 1960s for legal reforms establishing the equality of men and women in marriage, divorce, child custody, and inheritance. Lee, the daughter of a miner, worked as a seamstress before becoming South Korea's first woman lawyer in 1952. She founded the Korea Legal Aid Center for Family Relations, a nonprofit that provided assistance to poor, uneducated women and was a champion of equal justice and rights for women. Early women's rights advocates were up against entrenched patriarchal attitudes. With the expansion of women's education, however, and the gradual acceptance of the ideas of equality, attitudes toward these matters began to change. Even under the very conservative Yushin period in the 1970s, a Pan-Women's Group for Revision of the Family Law succeeded in revising the law in 1977 to give greater rights to women in these four areas: marriage, divorce, inheritance, and child custody.[25]

More significant changes took place when women's rights became part of the great upsurge in political and social activism of 1987. In that year, female activists created the Korean Women's Association (Han'guk Yŏsŏng Tanch'e Yŏnhap).[26] In 1989, the Family Law, in part due to the pressure from this and other groups was again revised, with most of the old patriarchal provisions eliminated or modified. Up to that time the eldest son was still expected to succeed as the head of the house, receive extra property in inheritance, and take care of his parents in old age. Under new legal revisions, complicated by court rulings, this was no longer automatically the case. Other changes were slowly taking place. The emphasis on universal education meant literacy rates among women were as high as for men, and there was no significant difference in the percentage of women completing secondary education. But in higher education women tended to be confined to nonprofessional programs, studying home economics, English, and fine arts. South Korea lagged far behind most industrial nations in the early 1990s in the percentage of women represented in law, medicine, and the other professions. Few served in government, and they were still expected to resign from work when they married.

Intellectual and cultural life in South Korea reflected the turbulent social and political transformation of society. Among the best-known political dissidents was the poet Kim Chi-ha. The South Korean government promoted officially favored artists in much the way that the North did, building large theaters such as the huge Sejong Cultural Center in downtown Seoul in the 1970s. Most artists and writers operated outside this official sphere and were often alienated from the state until the transition to democracy. Few could escape the political and social upheavals of their time, which often informed their work. An example was Yi Chung-sŏp (1916–1956), a Japanese-trained artist who died in poverty. Some of his paintings were officially disapproved of as too erotic, but he came to be recognized as an important modern artist, especially for his paintings of the ox representing Korean fortitude and hardship.[27] Pak Su-gŭn (1914–1965), a self-taught oil painter also struggled with poverty most of his life but won public acclaim in his last years for his works that depicted ordinary people in everyday Korean life. Painter Whanki Kim (Kim Hwan-gi) (1913–1974), architects Kim Chung-ŏp (1922–1988) and Kim Su-gŭn (1931–1986), and video artist Nam June Paik (Paek Nam-jun) (1932–2006) received international recognition.

Writers struggled with the country's rapidly changing society and turbulent history. Ch'oe In-hun (1936–), novelist and playwright, wrote *The Plaza (Kwangjang)* (1964), the story of a captured soldier disillusioned by both North and South Korean political and social systems. He was the first prominent writer to criticize both Koreas. Another writer was Yi Mun-yŏl (1948–) whose father defected to the North in 1950. Consequently, his family was socially stigmatized, watched by the police, and forced into poverty. He gained acceptance to the prestigious Seoul National University but dropped out and began his career in the 1970s as a writer of short stories and novels that attempted to come to an understanding of Korea's recent history. In his novel *Son of Man (Saram ŭi Adŭl)* (1979) he questioned the uncritical acceptance of Christian dogma by many Koreans. Yi Mun-gu (1941–2003), through his series of novels *Our Town (Uri Tongnae)* (1977–1981), dealt with the modernization penetrating rural life in his home Ch'ungch'ŏng region, while generating an appreciation for its dialect. Pak Wan-sŏ (1931–) known for her novel *Naked Tree (Namok)* (1970) set during the Korean War, later wrote *Lean Years of the City (Tosi-e Hyungnyŏn)* (1979) about the urban middle class dealing with modernization. Cho Se-hŭi (1942–) wrote a series of novels, *A Dwarf Launches a Little Ball (Nanjangi ka Ssoa Ollin Chagŭn Kong)* (1976–1978), about slum dwellers who were victimized rather than uplifted by the rush for industrialization. Pak Ki-p'yŏng (1957–) a labor activist, better known by his pen name Pak No-hae, was called the "faceless labor poet" for his underground poems dealing with the hardships and injustices experienced by workers. He was arrested under the National Security Law and spent eight years in prison.

Government censorship of literature and the arts was lessened starting in 1988. On the eve of the summer Olympics the Roh Tae Woo administration lifted the ban on thousands of works of art, music, and literature. Previously underground works by dissident South Koreans were now openly published, displayed, and performed. North Korean writers such as Han Sŏr-ya were published, and works of artists like Yi K'wae-dae (1913–?) who had gone to the North were exhibited in Seoul in the early 1990s. Chŏng Chi-yong (1902–1950), an apolitical poet whose works had been banned simply because he had been taken captive by the North Koreans during the Korean War were now published. Chŏng's poem "Nostalgia" (1939) became included in school textbooks. Shortly afterward the bans were also lifted on the works of the European-based artist Yi Ung-no (1905–1989) and the composer Yun Yi-sang (1917–1995), who were involved in the East Berlin Spy Incident. South Korea still had a ways to go to honestly deal with its past, but by the 1990s it enjoyed more political and cultural freedom than Koreans had known since the late Chosŏn.

KOREA IN GLOBAL PERSPECTIVE:
DEMOCRATIZATION

South Korea's political development in many ways followed a pattern typical of postcolonial states after World War II. Constitutions were written and ignored, authoritarian regimes followed each other, leaders established cults of personality, and the military intervened. As with most developing nations, governments faced the problem of political legitimacy. But in South Korea the problem of political legitimacy was especially difficult since it faced a rivalry for the mantle of Korean nationalism with the North, whose leaders possessed more impressive anticolonial credentials. Just as North Korea sought to win legitimacy by presenting itself as part of a universal, progressive system that offered great promise for the future, South Korean leaders linked their state to the West, to the "free world," and its promise of progress and prosperity. Yet, the governments of the ROK could never feel entirely comfortable with the liberal democratic system of government promoted by the United States. Furthermore, unlike North Korea's *juche*, South Korean leaders had no uniquely Korean ideology. Rhee relied principally on anticommunism as a means to rally support for the state. Park continued the anticommunist tradition but also made use of economic nationalism and economic performance. After 1961, governments sought support through achieving economic growth and prosperity in much the same way as the contemporary government of Taiwan also did and Beijing has done since the 1980s.

South Korean administrations also used the external threats to justify political repression, much as many developing countries or as North Korea's government did. The fact that the threat of renewed conflict was real and necessitated an elaborate security apparatus made it especially easy to justify political repression. The monthly air-raid drills and late-night curfews were constant reminders of a state under siege. In the name of national security, ROK governments jailed opponents, kidnapped some abroad, and carried out judicial murders. The KCIA, which Chun renamed the National Security Bureau, provided a vast system of internal espionage. Indeed, South Korea had many of the elements of a thorough police state. But unlike North Korea it could not isolate its people, since it was committed to the international marketplace and its alliance with the United States compromised the ability to tighten control over all dissent.

Each regime had to make some concessions to representative government and to an open society.

South Korea's democratic transition has been linked with the so-called "third wave" of democracy. According to this interpretation of world history put forward by Samuel Huntington, the spread of democratic governments has occurred in waves when certain international conditions seem favorable. A wave of democracy took place after World War I; another started in the mid-1970s with Portugal and Spain and continued in the 1980s as democracy was restored in some Latin American countries such as Brazil and Argentina. Then in Eastern Europe with the fall of Communist regimes in 1989. South Korea and Taiwan were part of this "wave." However, it is not clear how influenced the ROK's democratic transition was by these external events. While the People Power movement in the Philippines may have provided some encouragement to protesters in South Korea, its transition to democracy was due to its own internal developments. In this it most resembled Taiwan. Both states had identified with the Western democracies but were in reality ruled by authoritarian regimes suffering from a problem of legitimacy in the face of a Communist rival. Governments of both sought to gain support through economic development. Both countries were highly influenced by the United States, had increasingly well-educated populations, avoided the enormous disparities in income and education characteristic of most developing nations, and had by the 1980s become predominantly middle-class societies. As was the case in Taiwan, Korea's authoritarian traditions seemed unpromising soil for the flourishing of a truly pluralistic, democratic society; yet in retrospect, it appears that by the late twentieth century the social and cultural changes that had taken place in the country had prepared it well for a successful transition to democracy.

Kim Chi-ha

Five Thieves

And there lived five thieves
In downtown Seoul.
Their den at Tongbingo-dong is located high upon the bank of the Han River.
It is built at the foot of a naked mountain,
Bare as a plucked chicken-butt.
To the south it commands
A good view of the river,

Where dung floats on the putrid water,
And to the north it boasts its magnificence
Towards Sungbook-dong and Suyou-dong.
And, in between, a row of crowded shacks,
Small as hermit-crab shells and dirty as boogers.
The five thieves built splendid flowery palaces
With high gates on Changchung-dong and Yaksoo-dong.
There, where the kisaeng music never stops
And the sounds of cooking never cease,
Is the very den of the notorious "Five Thieves,"
That sonuvabitch Plutocrat, sonuvabitch Aristocrat, sonuvabich Tech-
nocrat, sonuvabich Autocrat,
And sonuvabith Bureaucrat,
Their conceited heads as big as Nam Mountain
And their necks as tough as Dongzhuo's navel.
. . .

[*Author Note:* The poem goes on to describe each of the five thieves; the
last is the Bureaucrat.]
The last contestant appears,
That sonuvabitch thief named Bureaucrat.
Having waxy eyes suffering from cataracts,
His dirty face is beyond comparison,
But he looks around with glaring eyes,
While he controls the army
With his golf club in his left hand.

When he caresses his mistress' breasts
And writes slowly on them
"More produce, more exports, and more construction," she responds
by saying
"Ah! Oh! It tickles."
"Are you saying national affairs are
Ticklesome, you ignorant bitch?"
Export more goods, even if we die of hunger.
Produce more goods, even if they don't sell.
Let's build a bridge over the Straits of Korea
With the bones of the people who starved to death
And have an audience with the Japanese gods.
                              —from *Heart's Agony: Selected Poems*[28]

15

❈

Contemporary North Korea, 1993 to 2010

In the 1990s, the two Koreas experienced major changes that both re-flected and highlighted the contrasts in their separate, divergent paths. In North Korea, Kim Il Sung died in 1994 and was succeeded by his son Kim Jong Il. The country maintained its militant, isolationist, totalitarian system, while the economy went into a decline. The economic decline became a crisis when the population was devastated by a massive famine in 1995–1997, and the country had to seek foreign aid to prevent collapse. This was in contrast to South Korea, where the transition to democracy proceeded with the orderly elections of Kim Young Sam in 1992 and another opposition leader, Kim Dae Jung, in 1997, and where economic growth continued if at a slower rate.

IN DECLINE

Up to the 1970s, North Korea maintained an impressive level of economic development. However, by the 1980s its economic stagnation became a sharp contrast with the booming South Korean economy. There were some hints that the DPRK would follow the reforms being carried out in China under Deng Xiaoping. Under the encouragement of China the DPRK issued a Joint Venture Law of September 1984 that appeared to welcome foreign trade and investment and give more emphasis on light industries. The government launched a People's Consumer Goods Pro-duction Movement with the aim of improving living standards. But like a similar movement in the early 1960s little came of this. What may have

437

been a hesitant move toward following China's path in carrying out economic reform was quickly aborted when relations with the Soviet Union improved. The Soviet Union appeared to court North Korea as a way of countering its strategically weakening position in East Asia where the United States and Japan were strengthening ties with China. Following Kim Il Sung's six-week visit to the Soviet Union in the spring of 1984 Moscow began offering an increase in trade on favorable terms. This enabled Kim to resume the pattern of economic development he was comfortable with. Buoyed by Soviet aid, he launched the Third Seven-Year Plan, 1987–1993, which adhered to the highly centralized economic development model with its focus on military-related production. The increased Soviet support was short-lived, however, as the Soviet Union under Gorbachev became interested in improving relations with the West, reforming its own economy, and reducing military commitments. As a result of this change in policies, the Soviet Union established economic ties with South Korea. The USSR's trade with the ROK increased after 1988, while its trade with the DPRK sharply declined. By 1989, the Soviet Union had stopped major weapons shipments and ended its joint military exercises.

Facing the decline in Soviet aid and pressure from China to open itself up to Western trade and investment, North Korea in 1991 created the Free Trade and Economic Zone in the Rajin-Sŏnbong area. The very remoteness of this site in the extreme northeast perhaps reflected the regime's ambivalence about the project. At any rate, this, like the 1984 initiative, was not followed up, and there was no significant economic reform. For two decades the North Korean economy had stagnated. Instead of opening up to foreign trade and investment or experimenting with private markets, it continued to adhere to its highly centralized command economy. In the 1980s and early 1990s, for example, the focus was on "Ten Major Targets for Socialist Construction in the 1980s," aimed at increasing electricity generation; coal, steel, cement, and mineral production; fertilizer and grain production; fabric production; and tidal-land reclamation. All were to be accomplished without significant importations of technology and expertise, and all involved large-scale, state-directed efforts, not private initiative. A number of overly ambitious projects were embarked on at great cost. Some of the most costly were the vast construction works that were carried out in preparation for the Thirteenth World Festival of Youth held in P'yŏngyang in 1989. These included a virtually unused P'yŏngyang-Kaesŏng Express Highway, huge shopping arcades, and the world's tallest hotel, a 106-story monster that was never completed due to structural flaws. Meanwhile, consumer shortages were dealt with by encouraging the people to get by with less. This effort to reduce consumption had already begun with the Second Seven-Year Plan of 1978–1984, which stressed frugality.

Much of the country's resources went toward supporting its vast military forces. By the 1990s the number of troops in the armed forces was enormous. P'yŏngyang claimed to have only 400,000, but most outside observers calculated their forces at 1.2 million troops including a 50,000-person navy. The estimates were largely based on the fact that since 1975 military personnel had been excluded from the censuses. Analysts have then extrapolated the numbers from the missing ones in population figures. While it is not clear how accurate these numbers really are, all agree that the trend toward ever-greater military buildup that had characterized North Korea since the early 1960s had probably continued through the 1990s, making North Korea's armed forces by then one of the largest in the world. Perhaps 5 percent of the total population or 8 percent of the adult population was on active duty in the 1990s, a percentage unmatched elsewhere in the world. In addition, 7.5 million were in the reserves. Kim Il Sung continued to view the economy from narrow military lenses, surrounding himself with ex-guerilla fighters and becoming, as Japanese scholar Wada Haruki has called the DPRK, a "guerilla state."

A PERIOD OF CRISIS

The early 1990s was a period of steep economic decline. The most severe blow to North Korea's economy was the fall of the Soviet Union in 1991 and the loss of its principal economic patron. With the new Russian government more interested in trade and investment with South Korea than in propping up the North, the DPRK economy began to contract. Severe energy shortages, along with aging equipment, led to a decline in industrial output. P'yŏngyang did not have the foreign exchange to pay for imported oil, and it was no longer receiving cheap, below-market-value oil from Russia. China provided some, but not enough. These problems only added to an agriculture threatened by flooding from deforestation; the unproductive, ill-conceived projects; and the burden of a vast defense system. In 1993, the regime was no longer hiding the fact that its Seven-Year Plan had not been successful in meeting its targets. In January 1994, Kim Il Sung admitted to his own people that there were economic problems. Previously such an admission would be unthinkable.

As the DPRK's position grew more unfavorable, it became more reliant on the development of weapons of mass destruction as compensation—primarily on nuclear warheads and a missile delivery system to compensate for its economic weakness. The missiles also provided a source for foreign revenue, being one of the country's few marketable products. North Korean technicians increased the capacity of the nuclear research reactor at Yŏngbyŏn and constructed a new one. In 1977, P'yŏngyang allowed the International Atomic Energy Agency (IAEA) to inspect its first reactor, but in the 1980s it began a secret project to build a facility for reprocessing fuel into weapons-grade material; it also began testing chemical high explosives. After the United States became aware of this, North Korea agreed to join the Nuclear Non-Proliferation Treaty. In 1990, satellite photos revealed a new structure that appeared to be capable of separating plutonium from nuclear fuel rods. The United States was becoming increasingly worried that the DPRK was developing nuclear weapons. This along with a DPRK program to develop missiles was making Washington, as well as Tokyo and Seoul, nervous. Under international pressure, North Korea signed safeguards with the IAEA in 1992. But in January 1993, inspectors were prevented from going to two previously unreported facilities. The Clinton administration announced that if North Korea reprocessed plutonium, it would be crossing a "red line" that could result in military action. And indeed, the administration was so concerned that it seriously considered a military strike on the main reprocessing facility. The arrival of former president Jimmy Carter in P'yŏngyang in the summer of 1994 led to a defusing of the crisis, as the two sides began working out an agreement satisfactory to both nations.

North Korea was not the only state on the peninsula to have a nuclear and missile program. Park Chung Hee in the mid-1970s began secretive programs to acquire advance weaponry, including nuclear weapons. In 1975 he worked out an agreement to have France build South Korea a nuclear processing facility, but Washington pressured France to cancel the deal. A second nuclear deal between South Korea and France in 1978 was also blocked by the United States. The South Korean government then continued a clandestine project to develop its own nuclear weapons, but this too was eventually terminated, as the Americans found out about it. The Park government managed, however, to develop a guided missile, which it tested in 1978 to the surprise and anger of the United States. South Korea in the 1980s began the construction of nuclear energy plants, which by the end of the century generated much of its electricity, but its dependency on the United States for military protection, as well as public opinion after 1987, inhibited the development of weapons of mass destruction. South Korea, instead, sought to keep the peninsula free of nuclear weapons.

No sooner had the 1994 nuclear crisis passed when the DPRK faced another crisis, the death of Kim Il Sung from a heart attack on July 8. His death, which came only two weeks after Carter's visit, was a shock. Kim Il Sung, although eighty-two, seemed in vigorous health. He was, as he had so carefully planned, succeeded by his son Kim Jong Il.

UNDER KIM JONG IL

Following the death of his father on July 8, 1994, Kim Jong Il assumed power in what appeared to be a smooth transition. He had been groomed as his father's successor for more than two decades and by the early 1990s shared power with him. Those who had expressed the slightest reservations about this unusual father-to-son transfer of power had been removed years earlier. This is suggested by the fact that no purges or changes in leadership accompanied the son's ascension.

In 1997, following the end of a customary Korean three-year period of mourning, Kim Jong Il assumed the position of General Secretary of the Korean Workers' Party. His assumption of power was accompanied by a more prominent role for the military. The key positions in the state were increasingly held by military men. When the Tenth Supreme People's Assembly met in September 1998, it amended the 1972 state constitution and made the chair of the National Defense Council, a position held by Kim Jong Il, the head of state. Political power appeared to be shifting away from the Korean Workers' Party and toward the military. In 1998, Kim Jong Il began to espouse the "Military First" (*sŏn'gun*) policy, which made it clear that military needs would have priority. While this policy was not a break with North Korea's military-centered society, the structural change in government was new. By establishing his power base in the military and keeping his generals happy, Kim Jong Il was probably securing his own position. The other major change in the formal structure of government was the elimination of the presidency. This was done by declaring that the late Kim Il Sung held the position eternally.

Contrary to the predictions of many foreign observers, Kim Jong Il appeared to be firmly in power. Lacking the revolutionary credentials or physical stature of his father, he seemed an unlikely candidate for supreme leader. His heavy drinking and fondness for women and luxurious living, his artistic temperament, his elevated shoes and bouffant hairstyle compensating for his short height, and his sometimes bizarre behavior made him the subject of ridicule and contempt abroad. One example of his strange behavior was linked with his great love of cinema. He reportedly possessed a vast movie collection. In 1978 he allegedly had agents kidnap a famous South Korean movie actress, Choi Eun Hee (Ch'oe Ŭn-hŭi) (1926–), in Hong Kong and then lured her husband, the well-known director Shin Sang-ok (Sin Sang-ok) (1926–2006), to North Korea. The couple was reintroduced at a party, and Kim Jong Il asked them to make movies for him, complaining about the quality of North Korean films. After making several movies for him, they managed to defect while shooting a film in Prague and return to South Korea. There have been other reports of his heavy drinking and his lavish and decadent parties. Yet he has a shrewd intelligence and has learned well how to firmly grasp and maintain his hold on power.

Following his stroke in August 2008 and his increasing frail appearance, the problem of who would succeed Kim Jong Il became urgent. The Korean Workers' Party had deteriorated as an effective organization and his eldest son Kim Jong Nam (Kim Chŏng-nam) (1971–) had fallen from favor after his arrest in Japan in 2001 for trying to illegally enter the country to attend Tokyo Disneyland. In 2009, it was reported he had designated his third and youngest son Kim Jong Eun (Kim Chŏng-ŭn) (1984–) as his successor, but he was only twenty-five. Another prominent figure that was considered a possible transitional leader was Kim Jong Il's brother-in-law Chang Sŏng-t'aek (1946–) but as of 2010 the future seemed uncertain.

IDEOLOGY

While still vaguely calling itself socialist North Korea became a nationalist-militarist state with little connection to Communism. No Communist state, for example, had ever made the military the highest governing organ. With the collapse of Communism, the regime all but abandoned any pretense to being a Marxist-Leninist state. By the early 1990s, almost all references to Marxism-Leninism ceased. Instead, references were made to "our way of socialism (*urisik sahoejuŭi*)." *Juche* continued as the "guiding principle." A new *juche* calendar was adopted in 1997, with the year of Kim Il Sung's birth, 1912, the year one. *Juche* was defined in more explicitly nationalist terms. In 1997, Kim Jong Il declared that *juche* "clarified that the country and nation are the basic unit for shaping the destiny of the masses"[1] Citizens were not only to study and follow *juche* but also to have *juche*. And having *juche* meant they must "submerge their separate identity into the collective identity of the Korean nation."[2] The centrality of ethnic-racial nationalism as the basis for both the state and for national unity was made clear in a speech the following year when Kim Jong Il declared that "the Korean nation is a homogeneous nation that has inherited the same blood and lived in the same territory speaking the same language for thousands of years." The people of both North and South share the "same blood and soul of the Korean nation," and are "linked inseparably with the same national interests and a common historical psychology and sentiment." Therefore "the reunion of our nation that has been divided by foreign forces is an inevitable trend of our nation's history and the law of national development."[3] The family cult has continued unabated, Kim Jong Il, the former Dear Leader, becoming the Great Leader but with a different Korean term (*Widaehan Ryŏngdoja*) to distinguish him from his father (*Widaehan Suryŏngnim*), also translated in English as Great Leader. While extrava-gant praise has been heaped on Kim Jong Il, there is no diminishing of the veneration of his father, Kim Il Sung, the founder, builder, and tow-ering figure of the Democratic People's Republic of Korea. Kim Il Sung remains the "eternal president."

An extreme manifestation of nationalism and the family cult was the revival of interest in Tan'gun, the mythical founder of the first Korean state, who, according to tradition, was born in 2333 BCE. In South Korea, October 3 is a national holiday celebrating Tan'gun's birth, and his name is conjured up from time to time by politicians and editorial writers as a symbol of the uniqueness and antiquity of the Korean nation. Most textbooks and professional historians, however, treat him as a myth. In the DPRK, Tan'gun, regarded by North Korea's Marxist historians as a feudal myth, was ignored. It therefore came as a surprise when North Korea announced on the eve of National Foundation Day 1993 that its ar-chaeologists had excavated remains believed to be those of Tan'gun from a site near P'yŏngyang. According to a North Korean radio broadcast, eighty-six bones had been dug out of the ancient royal tomb together with a gilded bronze crown and some ornaments, and these were believed to belong to Tan'gun and his wife. The bones were further stated to be 5,011 years old; Tan'gun was estimated to have been about 170 centimeters tall. Few scholars outside North Korea took these claims seriously. South Ko-rean archaeologists, for example, voiced suspicions about the authenticity of the claim, agreeing among themselves that the finding probably had been fabricated. The existence of bronze ornaments found in the tomb shed doubt on the dates, since no bronze work more than 3,000 years old had previously been found on the peninsula.[4]

Furthermore, these findings by North Korea were also linked to the re-ported discoveries of early human remains, Pithecanthropus, suggesting that Tan'gun and the Korean nation had descended from a distinct line of humans. The DPRK announced, "Scientific evidence therefore supports the claim that there is a distinctive Korean race and that the foundation of the first state of the Korean nation by Tan'gun was a historic event, which laid the groundwork for the formation of the Korean nation."[5] By 1998, the DPRK became more emphatic in this claim. "Tan'gun is now a histori-cal figure who founded the first Korean state about 3000 BCE, which cen-tered around P'yŏngyang." The basin of the river Taedong, they declared, was "the cradle of mankind," since the remains of Pithecanthropus were found dating back to 1 million years ago.[6]

North Korea has long claimed that Kim Jong Il was born in Paektusan on the China–North Korea border, a sacred spot and considered the birth place of Tan'gun. Thus, in a very indirect way, the Kim dynasty was linked to the ancient progenitor of the Korean people. Now this connection was made more explicit. The DPRK, in establishing this link, most probably sought to bolster its legitimacy over the peninsula by showing that Tan'gun was born near P'yŏngyang and built a state there. The regime implied it was a successor to the founder of the Korean nation and upholder of the national spirit. By the late 1990s Tan'gun's name was frequently asserted as a symbol of the Korean nation. The third of October, long celebrated in South Korea as National Foundation Day, became in the North "the nation's day," with memorial services to "King Tan'gun." Official statements from P'yŏngyang often termed Korea as the "Tan'gun nation." For example, when North Korea launched the Taepo-dong 1 missile on August 31, 1998, it announced the launch as "a great pride of the Tan'gun nation."[7] Kim Jong Il in public statements urged the Korean people to follow the "spirit of Tan'gun." Kim Il Sung was called "a great sage of Tan'gun's nation born of heaven, and [the] sun of a reunified country."[8]

Sixty years after the establishment of the Democratic People's Republic of Korea its ideology amounted at its core to little more than glorifying the leader and the nation and demanding absolute loyalty to both. The nation was defined in ethnic-racial terms. Kim Il Sung and Kim Jong Il were viewed as the great protectors of the Korean race, a race that throughout its history had been subject to invasion and violation from outsiders, such as the Japanese in colonial times and the United States in more recent years.[9] The unity of the Korean race meant the division of the country was unnatural, its reunification a necessity and inevitable once the South Koreans were free from their enslavement by the Americans.

FAMINE

Soon after becoming the sole ruler, Kim Jong Il faced a horrific food crisis. The immediate cause was the widespread flooding in August 1995 that destroyed much of the nation's rice crop. North Korea possessed limited farmland and a short growing season. To overcome this handicap the regime spent large efforts on elaborate irrigation systems, expanding the arable acreage by filling in the shallow seas along the west coast and by clearing forested mountainsides. Some progress was made in creating new farmland from the sea, but at a great expenditure of resources. Geographic limitations were made worse by years of economic mismanagement. The irrigation systems often required pumps that needed imported fuel oil, which created problems when the supply of cheap Soviet oil ended. Other unsound agricultural practices only made things worse. Seeds were closely planted, making the crops vulnerable to pests and exhausting the soil. To compensate, intensive use was made of pesticides and chemical fertilizers, the latter also falling victim to petroleum short-ages. Mechanized agriculture meant that tractors became idle for lack of oil. Shortfalls of food grew worse during Kim Il Sung's last years, when the country may have produced only 60 percent of its needs.[10] In the late 1980s rice rations were cut 10 percent, the government announcing the cut as "patriotic rice" donations to the military. The idea of getting by with less reached a grim point in 1991 with the "Let's eat two meals a day" slogan.[11] China supplied some food, but due to rising agricultural prices Beijing cut food supplies in the mid-1990s. The greatest problem was deforestation. The forested hillsides of this mountainous country were cleared to plant crops, even in areas too steep to be suitable for farming. One aid official in 1997 observed entire hillsides torn away from erosion due to these shortsighted policies.[12] The state also encouraged livestock raising, especially poultry and pigs, but these required feed. In a measure to deal with the scarcity of meat, Kim Il Sung launched a campaign to encourage goat raising, although the country has limited grazing land and goats further contributed to erosion.[13] Deforestation and erosion resulted in the disastrous floods that were the immediate cause of the severe famine of the 1990s. Particularly hard hit was the northeastern part of the country.

North Korea responded to the famine in an unprecedented man-ner—by publicly reporting the floods. It then openly sought foreign aid, perhaps a sign of desperation. A number of foreign relief agencies came in, such as the UN-related World Food Program, the Food and Agricul-tural Organization (FAO), the United Nations International Children's Emergency Fund (UNICEF), and the World Health Organization. Some European countries also offered aid. By 2000, these international agencies were providing 40 percent of North Korea's food needs. International aid workers confronted a historically unprecedented situation. There was massive starvation, but unlike the usual chaotic conditions that ac-company famine, they found a tightly controlled police state determined to limit the interactions between relief workers and the people they were helping. DPRK officials insisted on managing the distribution of food. Aid workers complained about lack of access to victims and were frus-trated over their inability to determine just where the food was going.[14] Rumors circulating among donors, often proved correct, were that food aid was being diverted to the military, whose needs were the highest priority for the regime. This led to a controversy over whether food aid was being used to feed the army and party at the expense of others in more dire need, especially children; but the extent to which this was true could not be verified.[15] There were also some disturbing reports that rice being supplied by Japan and South Korea was being resold abroad to earn foreign exchange.

Malnutrition was already becoming a problem, the sudden food short-age only made things worse. By the end of 1995, many thousands of people, mostly the elderly, the ill, and young children had died of starva-tion. In that year it was estimated that half the country's crop was lost. The situation only worsened in 1996, when perhaps a much larger num-ber died of causes related to food shortages; more perished in 1997–1998, although the food shortage was becoming less severe. Estimates of the number of people that died run as high as 2 million; although a more probable figure is that between 600,000 and 1 million of the total popula-tion of 20 million people perished in the famine.[16] This was, nonetheless, a truly appalling number. It should be pointed out that these numbers are just estimates, since no statistics have been published. All agree that the famine was horrific. A survey in 1998 by United Nations experts es-timated that 63 percent of all North Korean children exhibited signs of long-term undernourishment, including lassitude, susceptibility to minor illness and infection, increased mortality, impaired cognitive functions, and stunted growth.[17] Foreign aid workers commented that children often appeared several years younger than their real age. Just how bad condi-tions in the northeast were could not be verified, since international relief staff were not permitted into the area.

After 1998, conditions improved and starvation was rarer, but chronic undernourishment remained a problem, especially for children. Mean-while, many aid organizations, exasperated by the restrictions placed on their activities, the insistence that they use only non-Korean-speaking personnel, and the lack of information over where food was being distrib-uted, began to pull out. Other groups, by accepting these limitations and by carefully steering away from politics remained in the country.

CRISIS AND SUMMITRY

Meanwhile, tensions between North Korea and its neighbors continued over the problem of nuclear weapons. During Kim Il Sung's last days, war had narrowly been averted as the Clinton administration considered taking military action against North Korea. After Kim's death, negotia-tions continued, and in October 1994 what became known as the Agreed Framework or the Geneva Framework Agreement was signed. Under this, the first bilateral agreement signed between the United States and North Korea, P'yŏngyang agreed to suspend its nuclear program and permit its nuclear plant at Yŏngbyŏn to be opened to inspection by the International Atomic Energy Commission. Since the DPRK claimed the program was needed for nuclear energy, the United States agreed in exchange to supply North Korea with heavy fuel oil. An international consortium consisting of the United States, South Korea, and Japan would build two light-water nuclear reactors that could not be used to make weapons-grade material. Japan would chip in, paying for part of the cost of the fuel and the nuclear reactors. This left unanswered the question of how much weapons-grade plutonium North Korea had already extracted before it shut down the plant. Most experts believed it was enough to build one or two nuclear bombs.

Another issue was the DPRK's missile program. North Korea already possessed short-range missiles and was developing a medium-range one. In August 1998 it test-fired a medium-range Taepo-dong 1 ballistic missile that flew over Japan and crashed into the Pacific Ocean 1,500 kilometers away. U.S. intelligence believed it was a failed attempt to launch a satellite, but the military implication was clear. Short-range missiles threatened South Korea, and this medium-range missile was capable of targeting Japan's major cities. The provocative testing led to government and public outrage in Japan, where North Korea was perceived as its most serious security threat. Japan responded by suspending its 20 percent contribution to the nuclear reactor program. In September 1999, the United States, in what was called the Perry Report, offered food aid, economic relations, and full diplomatic recognition if the DPRK would agree to discontinue its development of weapons of mass destruction.

While tensions were again easing between the United States and North Korea, the new South Korean president, Kim Dae Jung, inaugurated what he called the "Sunshine" policy toward North Korea in 1998. It was an attempt at peaceful engagement that aimed to expand trade and economic and cultural links between the two countries and to gradually coax the DPRK toward reform, thus reducing tensions and easing the transition to the day when the two Koreas could unite. In April 1998, the two Koreas began talks in Beijing. P'yŏngyang wanted Seoul to supply it with fertilizer. The ROK insisted that any food-related aid would have to be accompanied by the exchange of home visits by divided families. The DPRK refused. Instead it criticized South Korea for not sending a condolence mission to Kim Il Sung's funeral, for politicizing rice deliveries during the famine, and for obstructing its effort to improve relations with the United States and Japan. Relations deteriorated further when on June 15, 1999, a North Korean torpedo boat was sunk and five other vessels damaged in a naval clash off South Korea's west coast.

Nonetheless, South Korean president Kim Dae Jung was determined to improve relations with North Korea. In March 2000 he gave his "Berlin Declaration," in which he offered North Korea security guarantees, economic assistance, and help in supporting the DPRK internationally. He then secretly arranged an aid package to encourage a summit conference. On April 10, the surprise announcement came that the leaders would meet for the first summit conference between the two Koreas. In June, Kim Dae Jung traveled to P'yŏngyang with an entourage of South Korean reporters and concluded a five-point agreement on peace; reunion visits for separated families; and for the expediting of economic, social, and cultural exchanges. For the first time, the two sides accepted that creating one system of government for all of Korea was a task for a future generation, agreeing only to work for a federation. It was, on the surface, an acceptance that the division of Korea into two very different states was a long-term reality. An exchange of family reunions occurred in August and September, and the North and South Korean Olympic teams marched together at the games in Sydney in the fall of 2000. Meanwhile, Kim Dae Jung's visit was followed by visits from Russian president Vladimir Putin in July, American secretary of state Madeleine Albright in October, and officials from China and the European Union. It appeared North Korea was breaking out of its long isolation.

The unprecedented visit of Kim Dae Jung to the DPRK caused great excitement in South Korea. But the high expectations that followed the summit were not met. When a groundbreaking ceremony took place in September 2000 for the construction of a rail link between the two countries, no DPRK officials showed up. Nor was there a follow-up visit by Kim Jong Il to South Korea as promised. Instead the DPRK placed more missiles near the border, apparently in an attempt to extract more economic aid from South Korea.[18] Relations became more strained in late 2001. Planned family reunions did not take place, and there was no significant progress in dialogue between the two Koreas. Partly this was due to the hard line the new George W. Bush administration took toward North Korea. The new administration was critical of the Sunshine policy, which they thought rewarded bad behavior. With the new focus on anti-terrorism after September 11, 2001, this policy only hardened.[19]

TENTATIVE REFORMS

In the wake of the economic crisis, major changes took place in North Korean society. Famine conditions in the mid- and late 1990s resulted in a partial breakdown in the carefully controlled public distribution system by which food and goods of various sorts were allocated. People were forced to look for food where they could find it. Small private plots appeared, and an informal market for agricultural products emerged. Even the movement of people, once strictly controlled, broke down as individuals wandered to wherever they could find food or work. Thousands of North Koreans illegally crossed into China, where they took whatever work they could find and smuggled money and goods back into North

Korea. Many of these refugees in China lived under appalling conditions, but they often managed to earn money to bring back with them as they returned home. This contributed to a flourishing black market in food and smuggled goods. Authorities tended to ignore these developments. Still, those who crossed into China were subjected to extortion, intimidation, and arrest.

At first it did not appear that the famine would generate any basic reforms. Rather, the government's response to economic decline was to launch a new Ch'ŏllima campaign in 1998. This changed four years later with the currency reform. Partly to regain their tight grip over the economy and to obtain revenue by taxing this private market, the DPRK announced a series of radical economic measures on July 1, 2002. The reforms sought to bring the artificially low prices in line with real market values. Citizens were billed for items such as housing, food, and fuel that had previously been provided by the state at virtually no cost. Wages increased twenty times to compensate for these changes. The reforms placed North Korea on a more money-based economy and introduced economic incentives and accountability for managers. It appeared that the types of economic reforms that were introduced in China over the span of a decade were implemented here all at once.[20] The price reforms of 2002 were designed to end the distortion in the relative prices of goods, to eliminate the gap between state and market prices so that farmers would sell their products to the state instead of only in private markets, and to encourage the production of goods that could be sold abroad for hard currency. They may have also been intended to alleviate the drain on state finances caused by heavy subsidies on certain staples such as rice.[21] It also enabled the state to gain some control over the growing black market and to be able to tax it. The price reforms resulted in severe inflation. Wages could not keep up with items such as rice that increased fifty times in cost over the next year. This reform was followed by the creation of a Sinŭiju Special Economic District near the Chinese border, but this proved to be an aborted effort.

The change in direction was suggested by the elections in August 2003 for the new Supreme People's Assembly, which saw the emergence of more reform-minded technocrats. Pak Pong-ju (1939–), a former minister from the chemical industry, for example, replaced the older, less economically experienced Hong Song Nam (1929–2009) as premier. Pak had visited Seoul in the fall of 2002 for a tour of South Korean industries and was regarded as representing a younger, more pragmatic, and technically knowledgeable generation.[22] Instead of the highly centralized system of previous years, some economic decision making was transferred from the central government to local production units. Workers were evaluated on their productivity and the profit of their factories, and factory managers were now able to directly export products.²³ Already the state had permitted the sale of farm products, but by 2003 it was allowing the sale of consumer and industrial products. A mini-consumer boom appeared, at least in P'yŏngyang, where the ownership of bicycles and electronics increased. Even a few privately owned automobiles were sold, although traffic in the capital was still extremely light. There was even an underground market for videos from South Korea, as well as a black market for used VCR players to watch them on. The food situation improved somewhat, as the economy experienced modest growth. Private markets were not limited to farmers selling their goods but state organizations and even the military engaged in market activity to raise revenue.

By 2005, the DPRK was asking the World Food Program to switch from relief assistance to development aid. Nonetheless, North Korea was still dependent on food aid. In 2006 this food aid still made up a substantial portion of its basic needs. Trade with the South increased, growing six-fold from 2000 to 2005. One thousand South Koreans crossed the border per day in 2005, and 3,000 were working in the North.²⁴ The year 2004 saw the opening of the Kaesŏng Industrial Zone, where a number of South Korean companies were opening plants that promised thousands of jobs for North Koreans. By 2009 there were 40,000 North Koreans at Kaesŏng working for South Korean companies, although in that year troubles with the North Korean government and lack of profitability caused doubt about the long-term prospects for the industrial zone. The number of South Korean tourists coming to the North was expanding also, mostly to the Kŭmgang (Diamond) Mountain area near the west coast. Direct flights from Seoul to P'yŏngyang were inaugurated by the DPRK's state airline, Air Koryo.

There were, however, also signs that the DPRK was still less than fully committed to fundamental market reforms. In 2005, there was a partial revival of the state distribution system. The government tried to limit the private markets by prohibiting women under fifty and men from participating in them. Furthermore, in 2006, more floods, always a great threat due to the deforestation of the country, resulted in hundreds of reported deaths. The South Korean–based Buddhist NGO Good Friends, however, suggested the real death toll was 50,000.²⁵ If true, it indicates both the continued reluctance of the regime to report bad news and its ecological fragility. Meanwhile, South Korea suspended tourism to Kŭmgang Mountain after a South Korean woman visitor was shot and killed by North Koreans in 2008 for straying beyond the area open to tourism, closing a lucrative source of foreign exchange for the DRPK.

North Korean society itself seemed to be changing. The division of the population into three classes: loyal or core, wavering, and hostile, and the *sŏngbun* system had begun to break down in the 1990s. By the early 2000s, it was gradually being replaced by more informal status categories based not on party membership and family background but on access to hard currency; connections with friends and family across the border; access to private markets and to private kitchen gardens; and money earned by women peddling greens, homemade food, and private livestock. Those with relatives in Japan that could send money or gifts also had an advantage. Thus many people of formerly low status were able to advance economically if not socially.[26] But not everyone benefitted. Most remained very poor and malnutrition and the threat of famine were prevalent.

Especially tragic was the plight of North Korean refugees. The border between North Korea and China was never hermetically sealed. During Mao Zedong's disastrous Great Leap Forward, which brought about mass hunger in China, some ethnically Korean residents in Manchuria crossed into North Korea in search of food. With the famine in the late 1990s, thousands of North Koreans began crossing into China, walking across the frozen Tumen and Yalu rivers, bribing border guards and risking arrest to look for food and work in China. Many returned or made multiple trips, so the population was not stable, but at any one time there were as many as 200,000 North Koreans living in China, mostly near the border. They faced arrest when returning; many were sent to prison camps. The remainder became caught in an uncertain limbo, fearing punishment if they went back but living miserable and dangerous lives as illegal aliens in China. Many of the women entering China became victims of human traffickers, working in brothels, or becoming unwilling brides of Chinese suffering from a shortage of women.[27] Beijing refused to acknowledge them as political refugees or grant them asylum. China also denied NGOs seeking to offer assistance access to the North Korean community.

CONFRONTATIONS AND THE POLICY OF SURVIVAL

While North Korea was carrying out its peculiar economic reforms, tensions with the United States increased. Conditions for improved relations with Washington seemed less likely with the Bush administration, which was critical of South Korea's Sunshine policy of seeking accommodation with P'yŏngyang. President Bush labeled North Korea as one of the "axis of evil" in a January 2002 speech, and he told a reporter, "I loathe Kim Jong Il." Trouble with Tokyo also emerged. In September 2002, the prime minister of Japan, Koizumi, made a historic visit to P'yŏngyang, where the two sides signed the DPRK-Japan P'yŏngyang Declaration, in which North Korea accepted that Japan "keenly reflected" upon its past and "apologized from the heart" for the damage and pain inflicted by colonial rule.[28] In an ill-calculated gesture of good will, Kim Jong Il admitted that the DPRK had kidnapped thirteen Japanese citizens; eight had died and the remaining five could return to Japan. Japanese public opinion reacted strongly to this admission of what had long been suspected—that North Korean agents had come to Japan and abducted its citizens. This led to a deterioration in relations as Japanese public opinion became outraged over the DPRK's reluctance to repatriate the remains or allow children of abductees to visit Japan. As a result, Tokyo found it publically difficult to provide any significant aid concessions.

The following month, a new crisis arose with the visit by the U.S. envoy James Kelly. Before the signing of the Agreed Framework, North Korea had clandestinely extracted about twenty-four kilograms of plutonium, enough for two or three twenty-kiloton bombs. Many foreign observers suspected that P'yŏngyang already possessed a couple of weapons. From 1994 to 2002 spent fuel was kept in storage ponds, and as late as July 5, 2002, the U.S. national security advisor, Condoleezza Rice, stated that her country was keeping to the 1994 agreement, although it was delaying the full implementation of the Agreed Framework until all parts of the agreement could be certified by IAEA inspectors. In November 2001, however, American analysts completed a report asserting that North Korea had begun construction of an enriched uranium plant. Kelly presented the North Korean authorities with the evidence that American intelligence had found of a program to produce highly enriched uranium. When the North Koreans appeared to admit (accounts of this are confusing) that they had been secretly working on what was a second path to developing nuclear materials, the United States reacted strongly and suspended the Agreed Framework.

One of the first casualties of this new crisis was the construction of the light-water nuclear reactors in North Korea. In 1995, the United States, South Korea, and Japan created the Korean Peninsula Energy Development Organization (KEDO) to construct light-water nuclear reactors with a planned completion date of 2003. The countries ran into problems arranging the financing of the corporations, so construction did not get underway until 2000, a delay that angered North Korea and raised doubts about the sincerity of Washington, Seoul, and Tokyo. By 2002, several hundred South Koreans workers were on the site pouring concrete, but soon after, work halted due to the crisis of 2003.

North Korea announced its decision to lift its freeze on nuclear facilities in Yŏngbyŏn and told IAEA inspectors to leave by the end of the year. On January 10, 2003, P'yŏngyang declared it was withdrawing from the Non-Proliferation Treaty of Nuclear Weapons (NPT), the second time since 1993. Perhaps nervous after the U.S. invasion of Iraq in March 2003 that removed the regime there, North Korea attempted to use the crisis as an opportunity to establish bilateral talks with the United States. In what it termed its "bold bid," it offered to eliminate its nuclear program in exchange for economic assistance, security guarantees, and diplomatic normalization. Bush's response was to state, "See they are back to blackmail"[29] Meanwhile, the United States pushed for the Proliferation Security Initiative designed to impede the illicit trade of WMDs. Although the United States refused to meet in bilateral talks, seeing this as a reward for bad behavior, it did engage in a series of six-nation talks starting in August 2003. These involved China, South Korea, Russia, and Japan. All of North Korea's neighbors sought to cool the crisis. Over the next several years there were several rounds of six-party talks, but little progress was made. North Korea sought diplomatic recognition from the United States and an agreement not to use military force against it, while the Americans insisted on nuclear dismantlement first before any agreements were made. Meanwhile, the U.S. Congress passed the North Korean Human Rights Act of 2004, committing the United States to aid and protect North Korean refugees.

On July 4, 2006, North Korea test-fired a series of missiles including, unsuccessfully, a long-range missile potentially capable of reaching parts of the United States. In the fall of that year it detonated a small nuclear bomb. These actions were probably intended to increase P'yŏngyang's leverage in talks, as well as to draw U.S. attention to the need to negotiate with the DPRK. Both China and South Korea reacted angrily to the nuclear test, which created fears of a Northeast Asian nuclear arms race, since South Korea and Japan might feel pressured to develop their own nuclear forces. Yet there were no real reprisals. China, concerned that too much pressure on North Korea might lead to its collapse, followed by chaos on its border and huge numbers of refugees, was reluctant to place too much pressure. Consequently, it continued to provide some cheap oil and some economic support. Seoul shared the same fears, hoping that its trade and investment in the North would bring about a gradual transformation in that society, ease tensions, and make a future reunification less costly. Consequently, the South Koreans maintained their Sunshine policy, although it did make some cuts in aid. When the six-party talks resumed in 2007, the United States showed more willingness to meet bilaterally with North Korean officials.

In February 2007 North Korea agreed to shut down the nuclear reactor at Yŏngbyŏn and to permit IAEA inspectors to return. P'yŏngyang also agreed to "disable" all nuclear facilities and give a full accounting of all their nuclear programs. Hailed by the United States and other countries as a great breakthrough, Washington agreed to return frozen assets held by the Banco Delta Asia in Macao; to supply heavy fuel oil; and, along with Japan, to move toward normalization. The United States also held out the carrot of taking the DPRK off the list of state sponsors of terrorism.

There was concern among many nations that the DPRK might sell its nuclear technology abroad. This concern was reinforced by a nuclear facility the North Koreans were helping Syria to construct until it was destroyed by an Israeli air strike in September 2007. In a further agreement in the fall of 2007, the DPRK promised not to transfer nuclear materials, weapons, or weapons-making knowledge, suggesting the country was moving toward greater cooperation with the United States and other nations. IAEA inspectors returned, and in 2008 the main nuclear cooling tower at Yŏngbyŏn was destroyed. Still there was some skepticism within the United States, South Korea, and Japan over whether P'yŏngyang would ever give up its nuclear weapons or even cease production of more.

Relations with South Korea appeared to move in a generally positive direction, with exchanges between the two continuing. The increased trade and contact that followed the summit conference in 2000 between ROK president Kim Dae Jung and Kim Jong Il in P'yŏngyang continued. In 2007 the two Koreas reached an agreement on a joint fishing area off the west coast of the peninsula and on developing the port of Haeju south of P'yŏngyang. The election of Lee Myung-bak (1941–) as president of the ROK in December 2007, however, changed the tone of the relationship. The new president was critical of the large but poorly monitored aid it was supplying and the DPRK's lack of significant political or substantial economic and social reform. Others also wondered if the South's generous aid was simply propping up the regime and providing it with less incentive to reform. The shooting of a South Korean tourist in the summer of 2008 by a North Korean guard angered the South Korean public, contributing to doubts about how much the North really sought better relations.

What seemed apparent was that the North Korean leadership had no clear plan except to survive. Their foreign policy had degenerated into little more than blackmail. Attempts were made to extract as much aid from South Korea and the United States and other countries as possible, creating crises and then moderating their behavior when concessions of food, fuel, and financial aid were offered. Meanwhile, North Korea's modest reform efforts begun in 2002 also seemed to be slowing down. Driven by fear of losing control of society, the government banned private trading in grain in 2005. Other attempts were made to limit the extent of the marketization of the economy, and restrictions were placed on the ability of workers to leave failing state-owned enterprises to seek work elsewhere.[30]

The DPRK still remained one of the most repressive societies in the world, possibly the most repressive. The elaborate system of state security developed under Kim Il Sung continued to keep watch over the population. A Ministry of Public Security administered the police and watched over citizens. Those found guilty of political offenses were turned over to the State Security Agency, whose task was to monitor political behavior and thoughts and to oversee the prison system for political prisoners. The prisoner system was divided into reeducation camps for ordinary criminals and others for political prisoners. Life in the former was brutal, often involving forced labor in logging, mining, and tending crops. Prisoners reeducated themselves by such means as attending political sessions and memorizing the speeches of Kim Jong Il. Hunger, malnutrition, and starvation were common in prison camps, although they were also common among the general population. A separate system of camps for political prisoners existed that was estimated to hold 200,000 people. These were even harsher, with prisoners unable to wash and wearing clothes until they were rags. Entire families were imprisoned, including children. Reports by refugees suggested these political prisons amounted to virtual death camps. According to the testimony of one survivor most of the 6,000 persons that were in her prison in 1987 had perished by the time she was released in 1992.[31] Public execution of prisoners was common, especially in the late 1990s. The practice was reportedly renewed in 2007, after becoming less common after 2000. According to unconfirmed accounts, entire stadiums were filled with spectators required to watch them.

It was also an increasingly corrupt government. Evidence suggested that members of the elite, the military, and the police, were increasingly involved in black marketing and smuggling activities or taking bribes from those who were. Informal transportation systems, using military or civilian government vehicles or the railway, distributed food and black market goods. The market had become so lucrative for the country's elite that it was difficult for the state to control it. Various regulations to restrict market hours and limit the goods that could be sold proved to be difficult to enforce. Men were forbidden to engage in market activities, but an earlier ban to limit markets to women over fifty was modified to women over forty, and even this was not regularly enforced. By some accounts, private markets accounted for nearly half of all the food families received, much of it food aid stolen by officials. Other estimates are that more than half the household income of families came from private markets. However, the regime, apparently uncomfortable with the idea of flourishing private markets, made another attempt to control them. In late 2009 the government suddenly announced currency reform. The old notes were devalued by 99 percent, and people were allowed to exchange only forty dollars worth of old notes for the new, the rest becoming worthless, an attempt to wipe out capital accumulation. This announcement was reported to have been greeted by rare displays of public anger. The government also banned the possession of foreign currencies.

At the same time, after having been told for years that they were the envy of their southern cousins, the North Korean people began acquiring knowledge of the outside world via those who had traveled to China, through pirated videos, through South Korean stations that could be heard on imported radios smuggled into the country, and through cell phones. This along with the pervasive corruption by civilian and military authorities threatened to undermine whatever public support there was for the regime. The scale of public cynicism was suggested by a series of interviews of refugees in China published in early 2008. The interviewers found that there was a widespread belief among the refugees that officials regularly stole or otherwise denied food aid to those in need.[32] In 2010, however, it was difficult to determine just how much cynicism, disillusionment, or even latent hostility to the regime existed.

Life for most North Koreans only became harder in 2008 as relations with South Korea entered a more troubled phase under the administration of Lee Myung-bak. South Korea had become a vital source of food aid. The refusal by DPRK officials to allow access to the food recipients had resulted in the UN World Food Program cutting off food aid. Some private charities provided relief, but it was insufficient to compensate for the severe shortages the country was facing from 2006. By some estimates the DPRK was producing only half as much rice and other cereal grains as it optimally needed. Much of the shortfall was made up for by South Korea, which under the previous administration had supplied food without conditions. This amounted to about a half million tons of rice and other cereal grains, feeding as many as one in every five or six North Koreans, as well as a large amount of desperately needed chemical fertilizer. In the spring of 2008 the Lee Myung-bak administration began insisting on the same monitoring procedures that the UN World Food Program had required. North Korea responded angrily, cancelling military agreements and ratcheting up tensions along the peninsula. It threatened to close down the industrial complex at Kaesŏng, even though this would hurt it more than the ROK, and began to order South Korean businessmen to leave the country. Facing another mass famine, the DPRK government turned to such desperate measures as a mass mobilization campaign to collect human feces from public and private toilets in order to mix it with ash to make fertilizer. Food was reportedly being more severely rationed even in the armed forces, where rank and file soldiers were restricted to two meals a day.[33] The United States under the Bush administration, eager to improve relations with North Korea before it left office, agreed to step in and supply food but only after it worked out an agreement to allow Korean-speaking relief workers. After appearing to reach an agreement, DPRK officials would not issue visas to Korean-speaking aid workers who were Americans. In the spring of 2009, the North Koreans were rejecting American aid when Washington insisted on allowing the Korean-speaking aid workers into the country as had been agreed on.

This rejection of food aid came at a time when the World Food Program estimated that 9 million of the nation's 23 million people were in urgent need of food aid, mostly women and children. Tensions were again raised as P'yŏngyang launched a multistage rocket on April 5, 2009, in a trajectory that sent it over Japan. Officially described as a successful effort to put a satellite into orbit, foreign intelligence services reported no evidence for a satellite, nor did the missile, potentially capable of reaching Alaska, travel as far as intended. But it sent a signal to the new Obama administration in Washington of North Korea's capacity to stir up trouble if ignored. On May 25, 2009, North Korea tested a second and larger nuclear bomb.

In 2010, the future of North Korea was increasingly uncertain. Despite growth in mineral exports to China, its economy was desperately poor. The effects of years of chronic malnutrition were becoming startlingly evident: young North Korean adults were considerably shorter than those in the South by as much as four inches in men and two and a half inches in women. The sinking of the South Korean naval vessel the ROKS Cheonan in March 2010 only added to its international isolation. The rare public protests against the currency reforms at the end of 2009, followed by an unprecedented official apology, suggested that the regime might be losing its ability to command total obedience from its people. Kim Jong Il was ailing; his frail appearance mirrored the frailty of his regime. Signs were that he was preparing for the succession of power to his untested twenty-seven-year-old youngest son, but it was not clear how smooth the transition to a third generation of the Kim family would be. Meanwhile, the 23 million people of North Korea continued to survive as best they could, taking enormous risks to smuggle goods, bribe officials, and search for food.

KOREA IN GLOBAL PERSPECTIVE: NORTH KOREA'S FAMINE

As of this writing (spring 2009), it is impossible to get a good idea of the scale of North Korea's 1995–1998 famine. Estimates of deaths vary from 200,000 to an unlikely 4 million and every point in between, although the careful estimates made by Marcus Noland place it between 600,000 and 1 million. The lack of official statistics and the limited access granted to foreigners make for much guesswork. Still, the world was horrified at the sheer scale of starvation at a time when the state continued its nuclear weapons and missile program and extravagantly celebrated the birthdays of Kim Jong Il and Kim Il Sung and other special events glorifying the regime. The callousness of the regime to the suffering of its own people shocked outsiders.

Mass famines resulting from failed policies happened in other Communist regimes. The number who died from the collectivization of agriculture during the First Five-Year Plan in Russia 1928–1932 was appalling. Estimates vary from 6 to 8 million peasants perished. At least 1 million out of a population of 6 million died in Cambodia under Pol Pot in 1970–1975, most from starvation. The Great Leap Forward in China in 1958–1962 resulted in the greatest famine of modern times—20 million may have died from starvation in rural China; some calculations are even as high as 30 million or more. Proportionately, the scale of North Korea's famine may be no greater than that of Russia or China, and less than Cambodia. And unlike China, which never publically admitted its famine, the DPRK eventually called for help from the international community. The nature of North Korea's famine also differed. While these other famines took place in the midst of upheavals caused by sudden implementation of radical new economic policies, North Korea's transition to socialist agriculture went fairly smoothly. It was only after several decades of accumulated failed economic policies that the country plunged into catastrophe. Furthermore, North Korea's famine, unlike the other cases, was partly caused by external developments, primarily the Soviet aid cutoff. It was also preceded and followed by a long period of chronic hunger. The greatest tragedy may be the long-term consequences of years of chronic undernourishment among the nation's youth.

KOREA IN GLOBAL PERSPECTIVE:
NORTH KOREA AS A FAILED STATE

North Korea has often been described as a failed state whose demise was frequently predicted. With the collapse of the Communist regimes in Eastern Europe and the Soviet Union in 1989–1991, some in the West expected the DPRK of Kim Il Sung to go the way of the Romania of Nicolae Ceauşescu, overthrown in a violent upheaval. The economic meltdown that followed the loss of Soviet aid in 1991 was also seen as a sign of a pending collapse. Yet the regime survived. Partly this was due to the ideological autonomy of North Korea, its *juche* thought increasingly stressed the uniqueness of the state, insulating it from the fall of Communism elsewhere. And North Korea was never part of the Soviet Warsaw Pact alliance. Like the People's Republic of China, and the Communist regimes in Vietnam and Cuba, it was able to survive. China's assistance greatly helped, and South Korea emerged as an economic prop, supplying generous aid. North Korea also made attempts at reforms. It appeared to experiment with a number of things: fenced-off tourist resorts for South Koreans to spend hard currency; the industrial zones for South Korean firms, also carefully fenced off; currency reforms; limited private markets; and some educational exchanges. Ideology was not an obstacle, since it had deviated so far from orthodox Marxism that almost any change of policy could be justified.

Yet if the DPRK did not collapse like the USSR, neither did it carry out sweeping economic reforms, as did China in the 1980s or Vietnam in the 1990s. There are a number of reasons for this. The country was too small to experiment with special economic zones that could be placed far from the capital and insulated from most of the country, as China was able to do. But more fundamentally, reforming the economy of North Korea would have been a much more difficult task than it had been in China or Vietnam. Both of those countries remained predominantly rural at the start of their reform process, with over 70 percent of the population still peasants; and their industrial infrastructure was relatively small. The DPRK, by contrast, was a highly urbanized, industrial society with only 30 percent living in the countryside and with a huge industrial labor force. Transitioning from state enterprises to the private market would have been more complicated. Furthermore, the country was to some extent trapped by its confrontational stance toward the major sources of foreign investment and trade: the United States, Japan, and South Korea. Nor did North Korea have a Deng Xiaoping who had been a victim of the erratic and disastrous policies of the previous leader. Kim Jong Il and his leadership were all products of the Kim Il Sung regime, had benefitted by it, and were less likely to undermine a system that had personally served them well. Nor was there any great upheaval in North Korea, only an economic decline.

Another reason there were no major changes was that unlike the other Communist regimes North Korea was locked in a rivalry with South Korea over claims to be the true Korea. The growing disparity in wealth between the two countries—by 2006, the World Bank estimated the per capita income of the South was twenty times that of the North—threatened the survival of the regime. It was unlikely that the DPRK could compete for the loyalty of its citizens with the dynamic consumer economy and popular culture of South Korea, the latter being immensely popular throughout much of Asia. Then there was the fate of East Germany, which collapsed within days of letting its people travel to West Germany. In other words, the risks of opening the country were just too great for the leadership. The result was a survival strategy, using small concessions and nuclear blackmail as a way of coaxing maximum aid from South Korea and the United States.

North Korea is a failed state in terms of its inability to provide a decent living standard for its people or to adjust to the global economy. But the ruling elite maintain a firm grip on power. In this respect it most resembles Burma, with its secretive, isolationist, and repressive rulers firmly in control of an economically failed state. Its inexperience in dealing with the outside world led to clumsy miscalculations, and it has shown a callous disregard for the welfare of its citizens. Its leadership, however, seems adept at survival. Its foreign policy is characterized by confrontation, but it shows no desire for a real conflict, in which the DPRK's antiquated armed forces would suffer disastrous defeat. The sheer scale of repression makes any kind of open opposition impossible. The general population does not have the organizational means or the access to knowledge to form a large-scale resistance and is too preoccupied with survival. Kim Jong Il is careful to attend to the concerns of the military and there are no other obvious internal threats to his authority. Eventually the regime might collapse or undergo internal reform, but in the spring of 2010 neither was obviously on the immediate horizon.

"Publishing Comrade Kim Jong Il's *Brief History*," foreword to *Biography of Kim Jong Il*: The Democratic People's Republic of Korea Official Biography

Comrade Kim Jong Il, General Secretary of the Workers' Party of Korea is the most faithful successor to the revolutionary cause of Juche, the Supreme Commander of the revolutionary armed forces of Korea and the great leader of the Workers' Party of Korea and the Korean people. In the first days of his revolutionary activities he set it as his lifetime task to complete the cause of Comrade Kim Il Sung, the great leader of the Korean people, and has scored immortal exploits [of] the Party and the revolution, for the country and the people.

The historical course of his leadership over the Workers' Party of Korea has covered the arduous and trying period in which the internal and external situation of the revolution was very complex and the Party and the revolution were faced with tasks more difficult and enormous than ever before. In the arduous days when the fierce class struggle between socialism and capitalism was waged amid the protracted confrontation with the allied forces of imperialism of the world, Comrade Kim Jong Il, as the closest comrade and most faithful assistant of Comrade Kim Il Sung, has always held fast to the banner of socialism, the banner of the revolution, and turned misfortunes into blessings and adversities into favorable conditions, thus leading the Korean revolution to continuous upsurge and brilliant victory.

Through energetic ideological and theoretical activities he systematized Comrade Kim Il Sung's revolutionary ideology into the ideology, theory and methodology of Juche, developing it to be the immortal revolutionary banner of the era of independence. He also worked out powerful ideological and theoretical weapon[s] for the Korean revolution by giving scientific and theoretical answers to the urgent problems arising in the revolution and construction.

He advanced the idea that the working-class party must become the party of the leader and put the idea into practice. In this way he brought about a fundamental change in the building, activities and work of the Party, strengthened the Workers' Party of Korea founded by Comrade Kim Il Sung to be a revolutionary party of the Juche type and improved its militant efficiency and leadership.

In command of the overall revolutionary armed forces he developed the Korean People's Army to be the genuine armed forces of the Party and the leader and to be the invincible revolutionary armed forces that staunchly safeguard the Party and the cause of socialism by force of arms and turned the country into an impregnable fortress in which the entire population are under arms.

He put forward a fresh line to imbue the whole society with the Juche idea and stepped up the three revolutions—ideological, technological and cultural—strengthening the single-hearted unity of the revolutionary ranks to be invincible. He ushered in a new economic and cultural construction.

Sharing joy and sorrow with the people at all times and through genuine popular politics, he has made the whole country a large revolutionary family in which all people are united around the Party and the leader. He has also shown deep concern [for] providing the Korean people with worthwhile and happy lives.

Through tireless revolutionary activities spanning over 30 years he ushered in a new era of prosperity for Kim Il Sung's nation of Korea.

The editorial board publishes Comrade Kim Jong Il's *Brief History* to help those who want to know the history of Comrade Kim Jong Il's activities.[34]

An Account of the Famine

By about 1996, the numbers of beggars thronging the markets had burgeoned. Tired, ragged children wandered through the city. People gave these beggar gangs the name—*chebi*—"swallows"—because this bird, which leaves in the autumn and comes back in the spring, is constantly in search of warmth and food. First of all there were the *kotchebi*: the very young street children. They were called this because *kot* means "the bud of a flower." And Kim Il Sung, as I have said before, had announced that children were the "flower-buds of the nation." Then there were the adolescents, called *chongchebi* (*chong* means "youth"). Finally, the old people who begged for their food were called *nochebi* (*no* means "old"). The ones called *kotchebi* were children abandoned by parents who could no longer feed them, or who wandered the streets because there was nothing left to eat at home. Unless they had deliberately left the family home, tired of seeing their parents tearing each other apart in constant arguments over the shortage of food. Since it is traditional in Korea for a husband to expect his wife to cook for him, he would accuse her of mismanaging the household budget, of being lazy . . . and the argument would follow on from that. Famine-related rows were very common.

The famine encouraged the most selfish kinds of behavior. My grandmother sold soya dishes and soups, a little trade that helped her to survive. She worked not at the market but in her own home, and customers came to see her there. I remember one father who regularly came to my grandmother's house in secret to eat his fill far from the eyes of his family. He paid her with sacks of coal that he went and collected in the mines that had been spared from flooding, and urged my grandmother not to mention his visits to anyone. My grandmother preferred to be paid in money, but since this rather special customer had the same surname as us, she treated him sympathetically.

The customers who dropped in at the house sometimes spoke of the prostitution that had spread as a result of the famine, and the presence of wealthy Chinese traders. In many of the towns in the north—the border town of Namyang, but also Chongjin, Wonsan, Hamyung—girls of fourteen or fifteen were selling themselves for practically nothing. Prostitutes risked being sent to a penal labor colony, and recidivists could be sent to prison. Nonetheless, many of them continued to ply their trade, especially with army officers and Party cadres. Most of the cadres also had mistresses, usually widows, whose husbands had died of hunger. Everyone knew this, but no one spoke of it; particularly not the legitimate wives of the cadres, who feared that kind of opprobrium more than anything.

Apart from the market, the station was also a hideout for *kotchebi*. In normal times there was a daily train for Chongjin, but the shortage of petrol and electricity had reduced the rail service to one departure every two weeks. The Onsong-Pyongyang line sometimes took a month to reach the capital—as opposed to five hours under normal conditions. So the station was filled with people waiting for trains that never came. It had turned into a big dormitory, where destitute crowds slept night and day on plastic sheets that they had found who knows where. Skeletal children wandered through the waiting room, all of whom suffered from skin complaints. Some of them were very young: I remember kids of one or two who couldn't even stand upright. They walked on all fours on the filthy floor, picking up whatever they could with their black fingers. They put anything they found into their mouths to see if it was edible. There were so many of them that people no longer paid them any attention. At night some of these children, left to their own devices, slept in the station, and others took refuge in houses deserted by their occupants, who had either died of hunger or left in search of food. But in winter, the station was the favored spot for these desperate souls. Even if the building was not heated, at least the walls were a shelter against the freezing north wind.

—from *This Is Paradise! My North Korean Childhood*[35]

16

ᴇ◊ᴇ

Contemporary South Korea, 1997 to 2010

By the early 1990s South Korea was entering the ranks of the developed countries and successfully negotiating the transition to a democratic society. But this did not mark an end to the society's rapid evolution. Many of the social and cultural changes that had been taking place in previous decades began to accelerate, creating a society that in many ways was a profound departure from its past.

RETURN TO CIVILIAN GOVERNMENT

The transition to democratization continued under the Kim Young Sam administration. In February 1993, Kim Young Sam was inaugurated president of the Republic of Korea, an important step in the country's democratization. Long one of the country's leading dissidents, he was now the first democratically elected civilian president in more than three decades. Kim was elected on the ticket of the Democratic Liberal Party, a coalition of the old supporters of the Fifth Republic, including those associated with Chun Doo Hwan and Roh Tae Woo, as well as a variety of other conservatives and moderate reformers. Kim Young Sam, an experienced and able politician, soon proved to be no puppet of the former military rulers. Using a corruption probe into the military, he forced many high-ranking officers to resign. In particular, he removed from key posts those associated with the secret and powerful Hanahoe society within the military, whose members included Chun Du Hwan and Roh Tae Woo. Kim reformed the Agency for National Security Planning, as the KCIA had been renamed

465

under Chun, curbing its domestic surveillance. As part of his reform image, he publicly disclosed his financial assets and had the members of the
cabinet and other high-ranking officers reveal theirs. This resulted in the
resignation of many holdovers from the Roh administration, including
the head of the National Police.[1] Kim Young Sam's main reform program
was aimed at the pervasive corruption in business and government that
not only offended the moral sensibilities of the public but was also seen as
a hindrance to the nation's transition into a modern first-world state. His
own reputation for personal honesty was his most important asset in this
campaign. In the summer of 1993, he passed the "Real Name" reform that
ended the practice of opening up financial accounts under false names.
This practice had been used to provide a channel for tax evasion, money
laundering, and bribery. All sorts of illicit financial activities by private
and public officials were carried out secretly through these accounts. The
reform was a step toward making South Korean business more transparent. These measures proved popular; his approval ratings soared to 90
percent in the first months of his administration.

After his first year in office, there was a lull in reforms; in fact, there was
relatively little fundamental reform under Kim Young Sam. This was especially true in the economic structure. Some red tape was cut, some state-
owned companies were privatized, most importantly the Korean Electric
Power Company. But the reforms were limited. No major restructuring
of industry or the banking world took place, despite the fact that many
businesses had become overextended financially. There were some half-
hearted efforts to deal with this. A Chaebŏl Specialization Reform was incorporated into the current Five-Year Plan, and in line with this, in January
1994 the top thirty *chaebŏls* had to list core industries that would be their
focus. But this effort to prevent overexpansion and needless duplication of
investments was not implemented. The number of subsidiaries owned by
the major *chaebŏls* actually increased 10 percent between 1993 and 1996.[2]
Most significantly, the same alliance of big business supported by loans
from the state-owned banks, the bureaucracy, and the ruling government
persisted. Labor continued to be restive, with some violent labor strikes by
the militant unions. Wages rose much faster than productivity, threatening
the competitiveness of Korean exports. One change was brought about by
international forces—South Korea was receiving increasing pressure from
the United States and the signatories of the Uruguay Round of the General
Agreement on Trade and Tariffs to open its markets. However, there was
strong opposition from farmers and their sympathizers against lifting the
restrictions on the importation of many agricultural products, especially
rice. Kim Young Sam's administration also faced student protests against
government corruption or against what they perceived as the administration's anti-North Korean positions.

The limited nature of the reforms was highlighted by the fact that Kim Young Sam did not repeal the National Security Law. Like his predecessors, he found the broad powers it gave him and the vague definitions of antistate activity useful. And Kim was not afraid to use the police against protestors, including organized labor. To many observers the Kim Young Sam administration was looking more like the previous one. His popularity began to wane. Contributing to his declining approval ratings was in-fighting among members of his own party, which weakened his administration, and an economy that continued to grow but not at as fast a rate as in the past.

In one democratic reform, a local autonomy law was passed in 1994 that made mayors and county and provincial administrators elective and gave local government greater powers to collect revenue independently of the central government. This was a historical reversal for the highly centralized government of Korea. In the local elections in June 1995 that followed this reform, Kim Young Sam's DLP did poorly.

Perhaps to shore up his sagging support, in the summer of 1995 Kim began bringing charges against former presidents Chun and Roh, accusing them of corruption, of military insubordination, and of treason. The bitterness over Kwangju remained, and much of the public wanted those involved to be punished. Disgust at the former presidents was fueled by revelations that they had been guilty of stashing away vast sums of money. Roh, who was not as personally disliked as Chun, was found to have squirreled away $650 million in a so-called "governing fund" (*t'ongch'i chagŭm*). Investigations also revealed the close connections between the former presidents and the major *chaebŏls*. All nine of the leading *chaebŏls* had contributed funds, illustrating the depth of crony capitalism. Kim Woo Jung, the head of Daewoo, and Lee Kun Hee (Yi Kŭn-hŭi) (1942–), the head of Samsung, were indicted.[3] Chun was sentenced to death and Roh to life imprisonment, although both were later released.

The move buoyed support for Kim Young Sam's administration, and his party did well in the April 1996 National Assembly elections. His popularity soared in the opinion polls, but then, largely hurt by scandal, declined again. The president tried to reform business by introducing tougher campaign finance laws and requirements for high-ranking bureaucrats to register assets, but he was undermined by the Hanbo scandal that broke in early 1997. A number of his close associates were involved in accepting payments from the Hanbo Iron and Steel Company, which was seeking their help in keeping the heavily indebted, troubled company from liquidation. The taint of corruption was made worse by the conviction of Kim Young Sam's second son for influence peddling. Meanwhile, labor unrest grew in 1996–1997, accompanied by a revival of student radicalism. In August 1996, 3,500 members of a radical student group that adhered to the North Korean position on unification and inter-Korean relations were arrested. Of these, 280 were charged under the National Security Law.[4]

Still, for all the problems, the economy was doing well. South Korea's GNP grew 7 percent in 1996, and that year marked its membership in the Organization of Economic Cooperation and Development (OECD), a thirty-member group of developed nations. Symbolically, South Korea had graduated from a developing country to the ranks of the wealthy developed nations. But the following year, events suggested that its graduation might have been too soon. The Hanbo affairs turned out to be indicative of deep financial trouble in many South Korean companies. Many had overexpanded, supported by low-interest loans from the state-controlled banks. The size of corporate debt by 1997 reached frightening proportions, just as the national foreign debt had in the 1970s and early 1980s. At the same time, South Korea was dealing with rising labor costs and competition from China. Several large companies, including Sammi and the distiller Jinro, were facing bankruptcy in 1997. In the summer of that year, Thailand underwent a financial meltdown, as its currency collapsed and the stock market plummeted. This set off a domino effect, as worried foreign investors in Asia's fast-growing developing economies began to take their money out. In October, the Hong Kong stock market collapsed. Stock prices fell sharply in Seoul, and then there was a run on the won, which as a result lost nearly two-thirds of its value. Suddenly running out of foreign currency, the ROK government in November was forced to call upon the International Monetary Fund (IMF) for help. An emergency package of $57 billion in loans and backup was quickly put together, the largest such measure ever created up to that time.

In the midst of the this financial crisis, Kim Dae Jung was elected president on December 18, 1997, defeating the conservative candidate Lee Hoi Chang (Yi Hoe-ch'ang) (1935–) by only one-half of a percentage point. The election marked the first true peaceful and orderly transition of power from one political party to another. It was an important step in the process of democratization. The very fact that a politician so hated by the former military regime could be elected and inaugurated in an orderly manner, and that it was all taken routinely, was a sign of how far the country had moved in the past decade. In fact, the election was largely devoid of excitement. Kim Dae Jung was now in his seventies, making his fourth try at the presidency. He had his strong supporters in the southwestern Chŏlla region but was viewed with less enthusiasm elsewhere. Enough voters, however, wanted a change that they were willing to vote for him rather than a member of Kim Young Sam's party.

ECONOMIC CRISIS AND RECOVERY

Kim Dae Jung had to deal with one of the country's worst economic crises. He began negotiating with international financial officials and working out a recovery plan before his inauguration. He then navigated the "IMF" crisis, as South Koreans called it, with considerable skill. Kim was aided by the gravity of the financial crisis, which engendered a national consensus that the economic structure of the nation needed major reform. Under the "Korea Inc." system, economic growth had centered on the government-*chaebŏl* axis. This axis had to be broken. A number of measures were recommended by both Korean and foreign experts: leaner *chaebŏls* focused on core businesses with less diversification, more transparency in banking practices, and more flexible labor. Each of the big companies, Daewoo, LG, Samsung, Hyundai, and Ssangyong (SK), had expanded their tentacles into so many different businesses that they over-invested in plants, resulting in wasteful and unnecessary competition. Previous attempts at reform had proved difficult since the big *chaebŏls* regarded themselves as too big to fail, and they could usually rely on politicians who were concerned about protecting constituents' jobs and investments to intervene on their behalf. No matter how indebted the big conglomerates became, the banks could be counted on to lend them more money, since neither the banks nor the government felt they could afford to have the huge companies go bankrupt, thus their debts kept mounting. But restructuring businesses was difficult, since firms "doctored" their financial statements so much that it was difficult for banks to distinguish between good and bad loans.

Initially, the Kim Dae Jung administration made some real progress at economic reform. A number of banks were forced to close or merge, and there was some business restructuring. In the past, administrations had boasted of South Korea's negligible unemployment rate, and they were reluctant to see employees let go or companies go under. But this changed by necessity. President Kim Dae Jung worked out an agreement with the labor unions to accept cuts and layoffs. A tripartite presidential panel for labor, capital, and government reached agreement on reducing working hours from forty-four to forty hours starting in 2001. In a major concession to foreign pressure, the country's stock market and its real estate markets were opened to foreign investment. Foreign companies were allowed to take over Korean companies, including hostile takeovers. In a society that had long feared foreign economic domination, this was a radical break with the past.

The reforms were painful. Unemployment rose from 2 to 8 percent in a country with little in the way of a social safety net, where most households had a single breadwinner. Perhaps the personal embarrassment at losing a job was most difficult. The suicide rate went up 50 percent. A phenomenon known as *nosukja* appeared. These were unemployed men who slept in subway stations rather than go home jobless. Women seeking income turned to prostitution full- or part-time, until they numbered an estimated 1 million, and layoffs were sometimes accompanied by violence.[5] The won settled at a rate that was worth only half of what it had been, making the imports and overseas travel that Koreans so loved very costly. The economy contracted 5.8 percent in 1998; only once since the Korean War, in 1980, had this happened.

Yet, assisted by the low won, which made exports more competitive, the economy recovered. South Korea soon surprised the international community by paying off the emergency loans quickly. The GDP rose 10 percent in 1999 and 9 percent in 2000. The privatization of the huge Pohang Iron and Steel Company was completed, and a start was made at privatizing the electric power company, KEPCO. Both were important, since the reduction of the public company workforce was regarded as a necessary reform. The government attempted to improve the social safety net by expanding industrial compensation insurance to all types of workplaces, increasing the number of public pension recipients, and separating the prescription and dispensing of drugs to control costs. In August 2000, the IMF declared Korea's graduation from its emergency loan program. Unfortunately, the economic reforms ended too soon. After the initial emergency reforms, the banking and industrial sector did not undergo further substantive changes. Furthermore, before 1998 was over, the labor unions began resisting any further layoffs. And there remained a deep uncertainty about the future. A second round of financial restructuring in early 2000 was not completed. It was clear that the government was losing momentum in corporate reform. Other drags on the economy were the protracted sale of Daewoo Motors, which eventually General Motors bought; a decline of semiconductor prices; and oil price hikes. Efforts at economic reform also ran into problems over issues such as regulations on ceilings on investments and on the debt-capital ratio. Both business and opposition politicians opposed these proposed measures designed to contain corporate debt.[6]

Despite the incomplete economic reforms, and the tough competition South Korea faced from Chinese manufacturers, the economy in the early twentieth century continued to grow, if at a slower rate than in previous decades. By 2006, Koreans achieved what they called the *imanbul sidae* ($20,000 per-capita income era) regarded as a benchmark, meaning it had a level of economic development close to the OECD average. The government began a campaign to become the ninth member of the group of eight major world economies (G-8). It did succeed in becoming part of a G-20 of the major world economies during the economic summit in late 2008.

Its exports in the 2000s surged, and it began accumulating a large foreign reserve. By 2008, it had become one of the world's major holders of U.S. debt, an impressive achievement for a country that had been itself in serious debt a decade earlier. South Korean products, especially consumer electronics, telecommunications equipment, and automobiles had begun to acquire a reputation for quality. Indeed, the country was becoming a technical innovator that could compete with its Japanese and Western rivals in quality, design, and innovation. Yet the country had suffered from unemployment rates, although modest by European standards, that were historically high; its rate of investment was low enough to cause worry about future competitiveness; and it was still a manufacturing-based economy that was slow in making a structural shift toward a service economy. There was also a concern that the move to a more flexible labor policy and the neoliberal economic policies that the government had pursued, even if only partly carried out, were creating greater income inequality. Future growth was also clouded by the fact that the "crony capitalism" that saw big business and government working in collusion had not yet disappeared.

DOMESTIC POLITICS

Kim Dae Jung's swift response to the economic crisis earned him respect among domestic and foreign observers. Long labeled a dangerous radical by his opponents, he proved to be cautious and moderate. He sought to reform the economic structure but not to change it. Ironically, for someone who had strong support among labor, Kim was forced to impose some sacrifices on labor by getting unions to accept layoffs and asking them to refrain from strikes. To the disappointment of some, he retained the National Security Law that had been used in the past as a means of jailing dissidents under its broad authority and vague definition of national security.

His party, the Millennium Democratic Party, or MDP, formed a coalition with the United Liberal Democratic Party of his former opponent, Kim Jong Pil. This very coalition with one of the stalwarts of the Park Chung Hee regime suggested the nonradical nature of his administration. In the April 2000 National Assembly elections, the two parties combined fell short of a majority, while the main opposition Grand National Party (GNP) also failed to get a working majority, so Kim Dae Jung's government ruled without control of the Assembly. After the elections, the heads of the two major parties, Kim's MDP and the GNP, met and agreed to the "politics of mutual survival." Nonetheless, the parties quarreled, and the result was that Kim Dae Jung's ability to govern was somewhat weakened. The need for the president to work with many different parties meant that Kim Dae Jung could not exercise the same degree of power as some of his predecessors, although the president still had enormous authority. The low voter turnout—only 57 percent voted in the 2000 Assembly elections—indicated both complacency and apathy. This was partly because the stakes seemed less momentous than in the past, but there was also a cynicism about the ability of politicians to make important changes. Another feature that was apparent was the strong hold of regionalism. The GNP won sixty-four of sixty-fve seats in Kyŏngsang, the traditional southeast stronghold of the establishment, and the MDP twenty-five of twenty-nine seats in Chŏlla, the southwest support base of Kim Dae Jung and the region that had long been a bastion of political opposition. South Korean politics thus was based less on ideological divides than on emotional appeals to ties of home region and personal loyalty to individual politicians. A more promising sign was the active role of civic groups in discrediting candidates they saw as unfit to hold office and in rewriting election laws and monitoring the election process; especially active was the Civic Alliance for the 2000 General Elections.

The summit with North Korea and the awarding of the Nobel Peace Prize in the fall of 2000 momentarily boosted his popularity, but soon Kim Dae Jung's support began to decline. A number of problems, including the usual scandals, began to mar his administration. Close confidants were involved in insider trading, embezzlement, and stock-manipulation scandals. All three of his sons were involved in financial irregularities; one was sentenced to four years imprisonment. His investigation of tax evasion by twenty-three newspapers in 2001, announced at a televised town hall meeting, drew charges of attempting to intimidate a mostly conservative and critical press.[7] A new medical prescription program was passed to assist with the country's modest and inadequate social safety net, but this ran into problems, as it quickly became apparent that there were not adequate funds for the program. Labor became restless and labor stoppages increased. And there was a general disappointment over the failure to follow up on the initial reforms of the country's business and banking structure. His administration also suffered from disappointment over the failure to see marked improvement in relations with North Korea following his summit and the opposition's continual criticism of his Sunshine policy. A particular blow was the resignation of the unification minister, who was thought of as the chief architect of the Sunshine policy, following the visit of some legislators to Mangyŏngdae, Kim Il Sung's birthplace.

In 2002, the ruling party held an American-style primary to select its presidential candidate. To the surprise of many, the winner was Roh Moo-hyun (No Mu-hyŏn) (1946–2009), a fifty-six-year-old human rights lawyer who won over Rhee In-je (Yi In-je) (1948–), the favorite of most of the party. Roh (pronounced No) was popular among what became known as the 386 generation: people in their thirties who had entered college in the 1980s and had been born in the 1960s. This generation was tired of the old-style politicians, many of whom had been active for a generation or more, and they were attracted to Roh, a political outsider, born in poverty, largely self-educated, with only modest experience in national politics but with a long and distinguished record as a fighter for social justice. His mostly young supporters formed the *No (Roh) sa mo* (gathering of those people loving Roh), an Internet fan club to generate interest in their candidate and as a vehicle to express their political views. Large numbers of young people campaigned for him bearing piggy banks, representing the small collections of money from ordinary people with which they sought to finance his campaign. Roh's nomination was challenged by Chung Mong-jun (Chŏng Mong-jun) (1951–), youngest son of Hyundai founder Chung Ju-young. Chung Mong-jun, handsome and charismatic, had served as cochair of the Organizing Committee for the 2002 World (Soccer) Cup that was held jointly in South Korea and Japan. South Korea did surprisingly well, coming in fourth place, and the games went smoothly. Chung was given much credit and was able to bask in the glory. The two agreed to a television debate in which the viewers would then decide who won, Roh agreeing to step down if he lost. The results were that viewers, by 46.8 to 42.2 percent, thought Roh won, so Chung withdrew. Chung then, at the last moment, withdrew his support for Roh.

Roh faced Lee Hoi-chang of the GNP, a sixty-seven-year-old former Supreme Court judge and veteran politician who had narrowly lost to Kim Dae Jung. Lee had strong support from older and more conservative voters but suffered from a series of embarrassing revelations. To the old problems of his two sons avoiding military conscription for dubious reasons were added new reports of his luxurious lifestyle. Also damaging was the revelation that his daughter went to Hawaii to give birth in order for his grandchild to acquire U.S. citizenship.[8] Roh had many liabilities as well. In a country that respected education Roh had never gone to college, although he had passed the bar exam. He held many unconventional views, made anti-American remarks, had a politically radical past, and had little administrative experience. He had a father-in-law who died in prison without ever renouncing Communism. Nor did he seem to have much knowledge of the world; he had never been outside of Korea. Nevertheless, the "Roh wind," as his enthusiastic support was called, was strong enough, and Lee Hoi-chang was damaged enough to give him a very narrow win: 48.91 to 46.59 percent.

Roh Moo-hyun, an establishment outsider, created an administration of outsiders. He filled his administration with people who had long records in activism, many had gone to prison, but with little or no political experience. Many of his personnel came from the Lawyers for a Democratic society (*Minbyŏn*), an organization of young progressive lawyers. Among his appointees drawn from this organization were his minister of justice, a forty-year-old woman, and the director of the National Security Agency. He also appointed professors from provincial universities and members of various political watch groups to his administration. As did every president, Roh created his own political party, the Uri (Our Open Party) out of former members of the MDP and others.

Unfortunately the inexperience of Roh and his staff quickly became apparent when he made many embarrassing remarks and political blunders. Members of his administration also got involved in scandals, including illegal political contributions from LG and Hyundai. He also faced a rise in labor unrest. Farmers protested his efforts to establish a free trade agreement with Chile as a prelude to further agreements, including with the United States. Korean farmers with small farms depended on generous state price supports for their crops and feared their livelihoods would be threatened by cheap imported foodstuffs. They carried out dramatic protests, both at home and abroad. Although the farmers and their families made up less than a tenth of the population in this now overwhelmingly urban society, as in Japan and Taiwan, they formed a powerful political lobby. Roh continued with Kim Dae Jung's Sunshine policy, but his efforts were undermined by the revelation that in his eagerness to arrange the summit in 2000 with Kim Jong Il the former president had the Hyundai Group secretly offer North Korea $500 million in economic development projects. Slumping in the opinion polls, Roh announced that he would hold a referendum on December 15, 2003, on his performance and would step down if the voters disapproved of it. Opinion polls suggested he would win, since the voters did not want to go through selecting another president so soon after the last election, and also suggested that they did not want the referendum; neither did the opposition, and it was cancelled.[9] An effort to impeach the president by the GNP backfired when public opinion strongly opposed it and contributed to a strong showing by the Uri Party in the April 2004 National Assembly election, when it received a bare majority of 152 out of 299 seats. With allied parties, Roh now had a comfortable majority. Following this election, the constitutional court reinstated Roh, who had had to temporarily step down during the impeachment proceedings. But in 2005, the opposition GNP won almost all the by-elections, and Roh's standing in public opinion fell to new lows; by 2006 he began to be viewed as a weak, ineffectual lame duck president.

Roh's party had carried out what has been described as an "ongoing cultural war in the South over policy toward the North."[10] The culture refers to the generation gap. Older voters looked at North Korea with great suspicion, memories of the June 25, 1950, invasion and the terrorist acts committed since shaped much of their perception; while younger voters had much less hostility. The latter viewed the North Koreans as their poor cousins needing assistance. But although there were some nominal attempts to rehabilitate former radical patriots and other symbolic acts, the Roh administration marked no sharp change in South Korea's domestic or foreign direction. He sent troops to Iraq, supporting the alliance with the United States despite his history of anti-American rhetoric, and did not abolish or radically modify the notorious National Security Law. He even showed symptoms of the authoritarian tendency, seeking to intimidate the predominantly conservative major newspapers by threatening to pass laws that would limit their market share and make it easier for the government to sue them.[11]

There were some positive signs of a maturing democracy. Previously buried topics from the past were examined. The government established a Truth and Reconciliation Committee to deal with mass murders during the Korean War. The commission uncovered more than 1,000 executions, including 200 committed by U.S. troops (see below).[12] An investigation into the 1973 kidnapping of Kim Dae Jung revealed that Park Chung Hee approved it. However, some of the Roh administration's attempts to right the wrongs of the past were politically motivated; in particular, the examination of Korean collaborators in colonial times was directed at the new opposition leader Park Geun Hye, (Pak Kǔn-hye) (1952–), daughter of Park Chung Hee, reminding the public that her father had served as a military officer in the Japanese Army.

In April 2007, the administration worked out a free trade agreement with the Americans, but this ran into opposition in the United States, where there was growing sentiment against open-ended free trade agreements, and in the ROK with strong opposition among farmers and various citizen groups. Meanwhile, 2007 saw a major scandal involving Samsung, now the nation's largest *chaebǒl*. Samsung was the symbol of a sophisticated, competitive, innovative, high-tech Korea. Yet, the scandal, which involved the bribing of government officials for favors on a considerable scale, showed that crony capitalism was still alive and well.

In the December 2007 presidential election, Lee Myung-bak (Yi Myǒng-bak), the Grand National Party candidate, easily defeated the ruling party candidate, Chung Dong-young (Chǒng Tong-yǒng) (1953–), who was handicapped by President Roh's unpopularity. A former Hyundai executive and popular mayor of Seoul, Lee Myung-bak had been nicknamed "the bulldozer" for his assertive, energetic, can-do attitude. Lee promised to accelerate economic growth and to close the economic gap between South Korea and the richest countries. His pledge to put the nation back into the fast track of economic development appealed to many voters, as, despite the 5 percent growth rate, the public was worried about the economy. Lee won in a landslide election and then saw his public approval plunge in the first several months in office. Promising to set a 6 percent annual growth rate, he called for streamlining the bureaucracies, selling off state enterprises, and pushing for a number of major infrastructure projects, including an inland canal system. The heavy-handed authoritarian manner in which he attempted to implement these policies infuriated many citizens. In April 2008, when he unilaterally ended the ban on imported U.S. beef, the anger spilled out into massive public protests. In addition, the high fuel, food, and commodities prices that the resource-poor nation was facing meant that rather than entering another boom, the ROK was looking to face slower growth, if not recession. The demonstrations, mostly peaceful candle-lit affairs, were still disruptive, and the efforts by some organizers to use mass mobilization to bring down a newly elected president disturbed some observers who saw them as a sign of South Korean democracy's lack of maturity. However, there was no serious likelihood that the verdict of the polls would be overturned, and Lee's unpopularity was largely the product of his style of governing, which reminded the public of its authoritarian past.

An interesting development in South Korean politics was the growth of NGOs, which had become a major force in South Korea. Exploding in number in the 1980s, NGOs were instrumental in shaping national debates and policies on key issues. Some were quite large and powerful. The Citizen's Coalition for Economic Justice, formed in the summer of 1989, campaigned for a more equitable distribution of income and against corruption in government. The Korean Women's Association, formed in 1987, became an effective champion of women's equality. The Korean Federation of Environment Movements, organized in 1993, conducted several successful antipollution campaigns and forced Taiwan to cancel a nuclear waste deal with North Korea.[13] In 1992, the Citizens Coalition for Fair Elections kept close track on this and future elections, investigating the dubious connections and qualifications of candidates. In 1999, a group organized the Citizens' Groups' Solidarity Roundtable for Judicial Reforms, and later a number of small groups coalesced to form the Citizens Solidarity for the General Election, which created lists of politicians not to be nominated or elected because they had been involved in corruption, bribery, or human rights abuse activities. After 2000 there was a marked growth of NGOs based outside of Seoul. Very few South Korean NGOs had foreign links; they were locally organized, for the most part led by moderate middle- and working-class Koreans, and played an important role in consolidating democracy within the country.[14]

Possessing a stable if contentious democracy and a prosperous if no longer booming economy, South Korea had much to be pleased about in the twenty-first century. Nonetheless, there were serious concerns about the direction in which the country was heading. The anger over U.S. beef imports was partly a product of a disinformation campaign by the local agricultural industry, which suggested American beef was unsafe because of the possible threat of mad-cow disease. But this protest and the opposition to a free trade agreement with Washington also had an undertone of anti-Americanism, reflecting ambiguity about the country's long-term relationship with the United States. And its economic woes pointed to the vulnerability of a country so reliant on the international economy, and increasingly on China. China's economy was absorbing ROK's imports, but its demand for food and materials was contributing to the upward surge in the cost of these items, which was straining South Korea's economy.

FOREIGN POLICY

South Korea's foreign policy in the early twenty-first century largely revolved around three issues—how to deal with North Korea, how to adjust itself to the realities of a rising China, and how to define its relationship with the United States. Kim Dae Jung's major initiative in foreign policy, his so-called Sunshine policy, resulted in the summit conference with Kim Jong Il in P'yŏngyang in June 2000 and earned Kim Dae Jung the Nobel Peace Prize that fall. The aftermath of the summit resulted in a lively debate in the South. Conservatives were skeptical of any real change in the North, viewing this as only one in the long series of tactical moves that had led to many false starts in improved relations, such as in 1972, 1984–1985, and 1990–1991. The government countered by arguing that there was no reasonable alternative but to try to gradually open the North to international trade and investment. The Sunshine policy was a truly radical shift in foreign policy, a break with the nearly half century of hostility South Korea had maintained toward the North. It was in part a product of growing confidence in the ROK, as well as a concern for the possibility that the DPRK could collapse and bring chaos to the peninsula. Initially, there was great excitement; among some, especially the young, there was even a short-lived enthusiasm for Kim Jong Il. From 2001, however, the Sunshine policy was bringing a disappointing return, and it became clear that the summit that had excited the South Korean public would not be a turning point. It was, however, not an entirely false start, and trade and investment between the two countries grew, haltingly but significantly.

Besides his North Korean policy, Kim Dae Jung initially maintained good relations with China, Japan, and the United States. However, with the inauguration of the Bush administration in 2001, relations with the United States became more strained. The Bush administration was scornful of the Sunshine policy, which it regarded as rewarding bad behavior, and sought to take a hard line against North Korea. After September 11, 2001, the U.S. focus on terrorism and its labeling of North Korea as a terrorist state and a member of the "axis of evil" provided a less comfortable international environment for the Kim Dae Jung administration's foreign policy. To some extent, the ROK worked at cross-purposes with the United States after 2002. South Korean presidents Kim Dae Jung and Roh Moo-hyun held to the idea that the best way to deal with North Korea was to open the country up into trade and development. They encouraged South Korean investment in the North and provided generous foreign aid, while the United States sought to isolate the regime. Under president Roh, aid and investments in the North continued to grow, despite mixed results in improving relations. He rejected conservative critics in his own country that this had to be linked to demonstrative progress on the part of the DPRK in improving its human rights record, reducing its military buildup along the border, working toward denuclearization, carrying out substantial economic reforms, and allowing more family reunifications. The last was still a sensitive issue, especially for the older generation. Many South Koreans, perhaps as many as three-quarters of a million, had relatives in the North.[15]

While there was little progress in these areas, Roh went ahead with a second summit meeting in P'yŏngyang in October 2007. Roh Moo-hyun and Kim Jong Il agreed on the construction of two shipyards in the North; on improvements in North Korea's railway system, which would make future rail links between South Korea and China easier; and to work toward more joint representations at international events. Tensions increased in 2008 with the inauguration of President Lee Myung-bak, a critic of the Sunshine policy. Lee made public comments critical of the North's human rights record, its failures at reform, and its military-first policies. This in turn resulted in angry and threatening responses from P'yŏngyang. Yet trade between the two continued to slowly expand.

Several other issues made for difficulties in foreign relations. Seoul had to deal with the issue of the tens of thousands of North Korean refugees in China. Many of them made spectacular and dangerous attempts to make it into the ROK's Beijing embassy in an effort to seek asylum in the South. The refugee problem was a touchy issue. The Chinese were strongly opposed to granting asylum, and Seoul did not want to anger China or jeopardize improved relations with the DPRK, so at first it ignored the plight of these desperate people fleeing poverty and repression. The ROK, however, was forced to accept refugees in light of international publicity about their plight. South Koreans remained ambivalent about these new arrivals to their country, fearing their settlement might encourage even more to come.

Controversies over history troubled South Korea's relations with its neighbors China and Japan. In April 2001, a new Japanese-government-approved history textbook angered Koreans, who claimed it presented distortions about the past. Japanese history textbooks' depiction of Korea and in particular their failure, in the view of Koreans, to fully acknowledge the injustices Japan had perpetrated against Korea in the past was a chronic source of contention between the two nations. The new history text rekindled this old complaint by reflecting a conservative, nationalist trend in Japan, more likely to feel pride and less likely to feel shame in its militaristic and imperialist past. This was reinforced by the Japanese prime minister's visits to the Yasukuni Shrine where a number of World War II military leaders were buried. The dispute over the island of Tokto in the Sea of Japan, which the Japanese called Takeshima and held a territorial claim to, was another irritant. In China, the work produced by the Northeast History Project, a government-funded program that supported archeological and historical research in Manchuria, led to Chinese claims that the ancient kingdom of Koguryŏ was a Chinese state. This angered many Koreans, not only extreme nationalists who used the boundaries of Koguryŏ as a basis for claiming that most of Manchuria was once Korean territory, but all Koreans, for it implied that northern Korea itself was once Chinese. The issue aroused passions in Korea. By 2004, it had become a thorn in the relations between the two countries and a cause of concern among Koreans over their increasingly powerful neighbor.[16]

The problems with China pointed out a major dilemma for South Korea. Its foreign policy had always been closely aligned with U.S. foreign policy. But disagreement with the United States over how to deal with North Korea, concern about rising Japanese nationalism, and the increasing importance of China all called this into question. There was also a belief that the geopolitics in Asia was shifting, with an emerging Chinese superpower likely to play the dominant regional role in the near future. Rather than rely on the U.S.-Japanese alliance, some South Koreans felt that they should seek to create a more independent military force and that the country's foreign policy should accommodate or at least recognize China's needs and interests more. The growing importance of China was most striking in its economic relations. Trade with China grew dramatically in the 2000s. In 2004, exports to China, led by the country's demand for steel, were up 48 percent in that year alone; China by then had displaced the United States as South Korea's largest trading partner. South Korean firms were moving much of their manufacturing to China, taking advantage of lower labor costs and geographical proximity. Yet there was no consensus over exactly what direction the country's foreign policy should be regarding its huge neighbor, with some Koreans worried about possible Chinese attempts to establish hegemony over the region.

South Korea's relations with the United States were complex. Most of the older generation remained pro-U.S., distrustful of the DPRK, and cautious about relations with China. But anti-Americanism was strong among the younger generation. Yet when the United States announced in 2003 and 2004 its plans to reduce troops in Korea by a third, opinion polls showed that most Koreans accepted the need for a U.S. alliance and were not enthusiastic about the withdrawals. Economic ties with the United States were still important, with American firms by far the top investors in the country. The South Korean government, even under the left-of-center president Roh Moo Hyun, supported the Global War on Terror, including $45 million during 2002–2004 for reconstruction in Afghanistan. In February 2004, the National Assembly voted 155 to 50 to dispatch 3,600 troops to Iraq, the third-largest contingent, despite strong public opposition to the war. The enormous unpopularity of President Bush contributed to troubled relations. There were hopes for improvement when Barack Obama was elected president in November 2008 but also concerns about the protectionist economic policies he and his Democratic Party often espoused.

RETHINKING REUNIFICATION

A significant change in South Korea was the attitude toward reunification. The public was no longer as enthusiastic about reunification as it had been in the past. In the years after 1953 nearly every South Korean dreamed of uniting the two states. They began to reconsider this after the reunification of Germany in 1990, when the problems and costs of unification became apparent. The growing disparity in income and the widening gap in culture and lifestyles between the two societies made the process and costs of absorbing the North and its 23 million people even more daunting. Whereas East Germans had a per-capita income of over one-third of West Germans at the time of reunification, it was estimated that North Korea had only one-twentieth the GDP per capita of the South in 2008. The differences in the two economies can be seen in the volume of international trade. In 2007, the total foreign trade, exports and imports, of North Korea was about US$5 billion compared to South Korea's more than US$700 billion. The total power generation of North Korea was only 1 percent of that of the ROK. This shocking disparity would be enormously costly to overcome. In 2008, some estimates were that reunification would cost at least US$1 trillion. What South Koreans now sought was reform in the DPRK and a gradual integration of the economies of the two Koreas. But indications were that cultural integration would be difficult as well. In 2008, there were already about 10,000 North Korean refugees living in the South, where they where handicapped by the lack of appropriate job skills and work habits and suffered discrimination from their South Korean neighbors.

A SOCIETY UNDERGOING RAPID CHANGE

South Korea in the first decade of the twenty-first century was a society still undergoing rapid change. As was the case with its economic development, a social transition that took decades in most other countries occurred over a relatively few years. One of the most dramatic changes was demographic. The once high birthrate fell sharply in the 1960s with a government-sponsored birth-control program. By 1983, it was only slightly above the replacement level, with women having an average of about 2.1 children. Other changes also contributed to the creation of a two-child norm by the end of the 1980s. The urbanization of the population, now crammed into small apartments and townhouses; the enormous expense of education; and the high literacy rate of women were important. Cultural norms changed as well in what was still a rather conformist society. Increasingly, a small family with a son and a daughter had become the ideal. However, by the late 1990s the birthrate continued to fall, dropping below the natural replacement rate. The sharpest drop was in the five-year period 1997–2002, blamed on the economic crisis of the late 1990s. But the return of good economic conditions did not reverse this trend. In 2004, the birthrate had fallen to 1.08, one of the lowest in the world, even lower than Japan's 1.3 rate, which was the cause of so much concern there. Although this rose a bit in 2008 to 1.26, it was still alarmingly below the replacement rate. As a result, South Korea's population, which stood at just under 48 million in 2008, was expected to increase only by 1 million in the next ten years and then to decline to 42 million by 2028. This led to a related problem of an aging society. South Koreans were living longer; life expectancy had reached about seventy-five for men and eighty-two for women in 2008 and was still rising, but the birthrate was dropping. As a result, South Korea was expected to be an "aging society" by the 2020s, when a quarter of the population would be over 65. More alarming were projections that placed the over-sixty-five population at 38 percent by 2050, which would be one of the highest, if not the highest in the world. At that time there would be only 1.4 adults of working age for every senior citizen.[17]

Even with unemployment at relatively high rates in 2006 and 2007 the planners began to worry about a looming labor shortage.

By 2008 officials and media commentators began to sense an urgency about the aging issue. One solution was a plan in early 2007 to increase both the retirement age from sixty to sixty-five and to reduce the average age Koreans entered the labor market from twenty-five to twenty-three.[18] The government began providing financial subsidies for parents with multiple children. Local governments came up with many incentives, offering bonuses for a second and third child, and offering free baby-sitting services. The government discouraged abortions, threatening to take away licenses of doctors who performed them.[19] None of these measures appeared likely to produce significant results.

A major factor contributing to the low birthrate was the cost of education. The zeal for education, what Koreans called their "education fever," was a factor in the country's remarkable economic and social transformation, and it remained in the early twenty-first century one of its greatest assets. Educational levels, in terms of percentage of students completing secondary school and going on to tertiary education, were among the highest in the world. The quality of education improved as well. In its second Program for International Student Assessment, given in 2003, the OECD ranked South Korea first out of forty-one nations in problem solving, second in reading, third in math, and fourth in science. As impressive as these achievements were, they had many problems.[20] Education remained strongest at the lower levels, but at the tertiary level research facilities had not reached the standards of the world's best universities. Importantly, this educational achievement came at enormous costs. The financial burden of education on families was heavy. In addition to private tutoring and after-class cram schools, many middle-class parents began sending students abroad to attend high school with families in the United States or other English-speaking countries so that they could master English, an important skill. As a result, Korea had the highest education deficit of any OECD country; the flow of money overseas on education was a serious drain on foreign reserves.[21] Surveys in 2003 and in 2006 found that South Korean families spent a higher proportion of their income on schooling than any other people in the world: two to three times more than Americans or Japanese, the next highest spenders among the major industrial countries.[22] And the expenses were going up faster than any other major household expense, rising 100 percent between 2000 and 2005. The costs threatened to undermine efforts at promoting equal opportunity in a society concerned not to replicate its long history of hereditary inequality.

But these were not the only costs of education. The preoccupation with education placed enormous stress on young people, who studied from early morning to late at night, causing some experts to wonder if South Korean students were being robbed of childhood. Furthermore, it was a major contributing factor in the low birthrates. Most studies suggested that the high cost of educating children resulted in Koreans putting off marriage until fairly late and deciding to have only one child. Since the mother's role in supervising education became almost a full-time job this also inhibited women from entering the job market and the professions. Much of the preoccupation with education focused on obtaining prestige degrees. The national obsession for academic credentials is common in many societies but it seemed to have reached an extreme in South Korea. The problem was highlighted in 2007 in what was called the "Shin-gate scandal." A thirty-five-year-old art professor, Shin Jeong Ah, who had risen to prominence in the Korean art world in large part due to the influence of her lover, a presidential advisor, was found to have a fake degree from Yale.[23] This led to revelations of many prominent people who had falsified their degrees. In many cases they possessed genuine credentials that seemed quite acceptable, but in a society that rewarded "brand" diplomas, these otherwise qualified people found it worth the risk of faking more prestigious degrees.

The rising costs of education contributed to a disturbing trend toward greater income inequality. One of South Korea's proud achievements after the Korean War was a burgeoning middle-class society with a more even distribution of wealth than was found in most countries. The 1997 economic crisis reversed this trend. More frequent layoffs, the greater use of temporary workers who received less pay and fewer benefits than permanent employees, and the move toward a more knowledge-based society all contributed to a shrinking middle class, greater poverty, and an ever-wealthier upper-middle class. In 1995, the bottom 10 percent of the population earned 41 percent of the national income average; by 2003 they earned only 34 percent. The top 10 percent income earners made 199 percent of the national average in 1995, and 225 percent in 2003. The percentage of people officially listed as living below the poverty line went from 8 percent in 1997 to 16 percent in 1998. Another measure of income equality was the Gini coefficient, based on disposable income. In this measurement, the lower the number, the more equitable the income distribution. The number had lowered steadily since the 1970s, and in 1997 at .283 it was low by international standards. Then in 2000 it rose to .358, the third highest in the OECD; only the United States and Mexico at .368 and .494, respectively, were higher.[24]

According to the Development Institute, the country's middle class shrank 5 percent between 1997 and 2004.[25] More ominously, the number of citizens who saw themselves as middle class shrank. As early as the 1980s, most of the public called themselves middle class in surveys. A myth emerged that all South Koreans were becoming part of a single, large middle class, with economic and social class lines disappearing. However, the number of those who regarded themselves as middle class fell from 70.7 percent in 1994 to 56.0 percent in 2005.[26] There were various signs that reality was moving away from the dream of a single middle-class society. People from well-to-do families tended to marry others from wealthy families. In a country where a prestige degree still offered so many advantages, the accelerating cost of tutoring placed children with less wealthy parents at a growing disadvantage. While disparities in South Korea were still less than in many other countries, including the United States, Koreans were fearful of replicating the inherited privileged status groups that had characterized so much of their past. It was not an unreasonable fear, since the economic elite tended to intermarry, and an enormous amount of wealth was controlled by a relatively small number of these families. By one measure, thirty leading *chaebŏl* families controlled 40 percent of the economy in the 2000s. Meanwhile, as was common with many developed nations, South Korea's move into the knowledge economy was threatening to create a huge gap between highly skilled professionals and less educated industrial and clerical workers. Industries were moving production offshore, to China, Vietnam, and elsewhere, while trying to be lean and efficient at home by reducing payrolls and hiring more temporary workers. Meanwhile, the upper-middle class, a large group but smaller than the older concept of middle class, enjoyed a new cosmopolitan lifestyle, which included sending their children overseas to learn English, buying imported brand-name products, joining health clubs, and taking frequent vacations abroad.

This problem of inequality was compounded by an undeveloped social safety net. Unemployment in 2006 was only a modest 4 percent, but most experts believed the real figure was much higher. And it did not include senior workers forced to work part-time or take "honorary" retirements. This problem was related to the practice by South Korean firms of promoting employees according to seniority. As older workers were expensive, they were forced to retire early to reduce costs. Many who were unable to support themselves on retirement savings became part-time workers. Many young people also found themselves in temporary jobs. Since after two years temporary employees by law became permanent, with mandated benefits and protections, companies often dismissed workers before two years were up. South Korea lagged behind in social welfare benefits. The ROK in the 2000s was spending only 10 percent of its annual budget on social welfare, the lowest of the thirty OECD nations and only half as much as the second-lowest, Mexico.[27] Focused on economic growth, the state gave less priority to social welfare needs. Kim Dae Jung had promised radical increases in what he called "productive welfare," but the IMF financial crisis and the prevalence of neoliberal free-market thinking in the governing circles meant that this promise was not kept. In 2000, the government implemented the National Basic Liveli-hood Security System, in which everyone below poverty would receive financial benefits. The catch was that they had to prove they were unable to receive support from family, this being unlikely in a society that was so family oriented. So in practice, social support was left to the family, a heavy burden on the poor.

CHANGING GENDER RELATIONS, CHANGING FAMILIES

Among the profound social changes in South Korea none were more dramatic than those concerning gender and family. The legal codes had been amended to allow women to head households, inherit property, and initiate divorce, and gender discrimination was legally prohibited by the early 1990s. Enrollment of women in colleges and universities soared past that of men in the 2000s. Higher education was no longer a finishing school where girls majored in home economics, English, and art. Women, however, still faced discrimination in the workplace and elsewhere. In-creasingly educated, organized, and empowered, Korean women were no longer accepting the patriarchal traditions of their society. Under pressure from women's groups the Kim Dae Jung administration created a Ministry of Gender Equality in 2001, renamed the Ministry of Gender Equality and Family in 2005, to deal with this problem. Women in the 1990s dealt more openly with previous taboo issues such as spousal abuse and sexual harassment. During the military regimes, some women had protested against Japanese sex tourism. After 1990, women's groups refocused on these issues, brought attention to the South Korean govern-ment's complicity in making prostitution available in base camps used by American troops in Korea, and in other ways confronted the whole issue of sexual exploitation of women.[28]

From the perspective of its historical legacy of male domination, the changing role of women in South Korea was almost revolutionary, yet by most measures Korean women still lagged behind their counterparts in other developed nations. In 2006, women made up only 3 percent of exec-utives in companies of over 1,000 employees; major corporations such as Samsung had only 12 women out of 1,300 officers and managers; Hyun-dai Motors and POSCO had no women in top positions. Women made 50 percent less than men, and the gap actually widened between 2000 and 2005.[29] In one international study in 2007 only 34 out of 131 countries where sufficient data was available had a wider wage gap between men and women. The gender gap in wages was not only greater than in all

Western countries but in most other Asian countries as well.³⁰ Women
did make some progress in politics, although here too they lagged behind
their sisters in most industrial states. Still, the change in politics was impressive. In 1992, only 1 percent of legislators were women; by 2006, 13
percent were.³¹ In the spring of 2006, Han Myung-suk (Han Myŏng-suk)
(1944–) became the first female prime minister, a position much less important than in most countries but still a significant post; and in that year
Park Geun Hye (Pak Kŭn-hye), the daughter of Park Chung Hee, was the
leader of the main opposition party.

Another break with ancient tradition was ending the prohibition in the
Civil Code against people who share the same surname and ancestral
home from marrying. Most Koreans share one of a small number of family names, nearly half named Kim, Lee (or Yi or Rhee), or Park (or Pak).
The surnames were broken down into clans who shared the same ancestral home and reputed ancestral descent. Members of some clans such as
the Gimhae Kim, the Miryang Park and the Chŏnju Lee had hundreds
of thousands of members—there were 1.5 million members of Gimhae
Kim, creating hardship for young people sharing a remote and theoretical
ancestry who happened to fall in love. Marriages between them were not
recognized, and their children were regarded as illegitimate. A court ruling declared this law unconstitutional in 1997, and in 2002 after lobbying
by reformers, the National Assembly formally repealed it.

A truly unprecedented change in Korea's social history was the rise in
the divorce rate. Up through the 1980s, divorce brought great shame and
was uncommon, but by 1990 this had begun to change. Between 1995 and
2005 the divorce rate tripled. By 2005, the rate was 2.6 divorces per 1,000
people, a little higher than Japan's 2.3 or the European Union average of
1.8, although less than the U.S. rate of 4.0 per 1,000. Many women were
opting out of marriage. In one survey of college women, a third said
they did not want to get married.³² For men the problem was not enough
women. This was the product of Korean preferences for sons. In the 1980s
and 1990s the use of sonograms resulted in increased abortion of female
infants. The result was that there were more boys than girls. The imbal-
ance reached a peak in the mid-1990s when there were 115 baby boys
per 100 girls. That surplus of boys began to be a serious problem in the
early twenty-first century. Public awareness of the problem and changing attitudes saw a reversal of this trend in 2002. Five years later, the
gap between male and female births narrowed to just slightly above the
natural ratio of 105 males to 100 females. The use of sonograms resulted in
similar sexual imbalances in China, India, Vietnam, and other nations. Yet
this was beginning to change after 2000. South Korea was the first Asian
nation to show this sharp reversal. And surveys in the early twenty-first

century suggested that the age-old preference for sons over daughters no longer prevailed.

Families themselves were changing. In 2007, the average household contained only 2.8 members, half the size of a generation earlier. A quarter of Korean households were headed by women. Another new phenomenon was the single, never-wed mother, called "Miss Mom." While still uncommon, they were no longer a rarity. According to one poll in 2007, one in six single women said they would be happy to have children without having husbands.[33] Even adoptions were becoming more common. Because Korean culture placed such emphasis on bloodlines, it was rare to adopt children. As a result, agencies sprang up after the Korean War to arrange for adoption to the United States and Europe. Embarrassingly for many, Korea continued to be a source of adoptees for Westerners at the start of the twenty-first century. This was beginning to change, although slowly. Still, in some ways South Koreans were socially conservative. In international surveys, they were less likely to approve of cohabitation without marriage or believe that people can be happy without marrying than people in most Western nations or in other developed Asian nations such as Japan and Taiwan.

ETHNIC HOMOGENEITY

South Korea's low birthrate contributed to one of the most radical changes in Korean society in centuries—the end of ethnic homogeneity. A factor contributing to this was the shortage of women due to the preference for males. This hit rural men hard. Few young women wanted to live on a farm, and with the supply of marriage-age men greater than that of women they were able to avoid doing so. Consequently, many rural men sought wives from abroad. By 2006, more than a third of male farmers married foreign women, mostly Chinese and Vietnamese, but also from other Asian countries such as the Philippines and Uzbekistan. According to the National Statistical Office in Seoul, marriage to foreigners accounted for 13 percent of all marriages in 2005; over 70 percent were between Korean men and women from other Asian countries. According to one study, by 2020 Kosians (bi-ethnic children) would make up one-third of children born in South Korea.[34] In a homogeneous society such as Korea this was a startling statistic. Public awareness of the idea of interethnic and interracial marriage and the implications for what it meant to be Korean was highlighted by the visit of Hines Ward, a Korean-speaking American football hero whose parents were a Korean mother and a black American father, and by a popular TV drama "The Bride from Hanoi."

Another development ending the nation's homogeneity was the influx of migrant workers from poorer Asian nations—including Bangladesh, China, Nepal, the Philippines, and Mongolia. They numbered 400,000 in 2007, half undocumented. They were often treated harshly, doing what Koreans called "3-D" jobs, dirty, difficult, and dangerous. The influx of foreign workers began in the 1990s and increased in the 2000s. Finding immigration procedures cumbersome, many employers hired workers on tourist visas, which they overstayed, hence over half the foreign labor force was in the country illegally and subject to exploitation. In 2004, the government introduced an Employment Permit System to make it easier for businesses to legally bring in foreign workers. While these were all temporary workers, the threat of severe labor shortages in the future meant that a permanent nonethnic Korean population was very likely to be another challenge to the conception of Koreans as constituting a "pure-blooded" nation.

Meanwhile as more nonethnic Koreans moved into the country, some Koreans continued to emigrate. The South Korean government estimated in 2007 that there were about 6.5 million Koreans and people of Korean descent living overseas. This included the 1.8 million Koreans living in China, mostly in the border areas of Manchuria, where they formed the Yanbian Autonomous region. About 600,000 lived in Japan, where in contrast to the economically successful Chinese minority they were hindered by discrimination. A half million lived in the states of the former Soviet Union. The largest overseas community was the nearly 2.5 million Korean-Americans. These had become very successful immigrants, with one of the highest education and income levels of any ethnic group. About 150,000 Koreans or people of Korean descent lived in Canada. Smaller numbers of Koreans were found in Australia, Europe, and South America. By 2001, there were, for example, 30,000 Koreans residing in Buenos Aires, where they ran much of the garment industry.

Almost everywhere, Korean immigrants prospered. Many of these were truly international Koreans who were bilingual or multilingual and sometimes went back and forth between Korea and their adopted home. These included business people, scientists, and technicians who were sometimes lured back to South Korea for high-paying jobs. Emigration became significant with the easing of restrictions on emigration by the ROK government after 1970 and peaked in the 1980s. Economic prosperity and political stability resulted in a decline in numbers after 1990; however, many Koreans were still attracted by economic opportunities and a chance for a better or more promising lifestyle for themselves or their children. Many were simply joining family members who had emigrated earlier; some were students who went abroad for study and then accepted job offers there or romantics seeking a new adventure in a new land. Many Koreans had family members and close friends overseas whom they visited. This only added to the increasing internationalism of Korean society.

FACING HISTORY AND PRESERVING HERITAGE

As the society underwent rapid change, the South Korean government became concerned about maintaining its cultural heritage. In 1962, it passed a Cultural Properties Protection Law patterned after a similar law in Japan. In 1972, a Cultural and Arts Promotion Law gave further financial support to preserving the nation's architecture and maintaining arts and crafts. Various structures were assigned as cultural treasures, and certain individuals skilled in traditional handicrafts, art, and music traditions were named "living cultural treasures" and supported, with the idea that they would train others to pass on their skills. The government established the Academy of Korean Studies in 1979 devoted to studying and preserving the past. The public also developed a keen interest in the past. Historical novels were popular, as were historical dramas on television. Major classics from the past were translated into modern Korean, and *p'ansori*, a traditional dramatic form, had a revival. By the 2000s the middle class, especially the upper-middle class, began to take a deeper interest in their cultural heritage. Traditional furniture, the *ondol* floor-heating system, Korean patterns and decorations, craft items, and even traditional hearty peasant foods became fashionable. The fact that these Korean products were often more expensive than foreign imports or more modern ones may have added to their desirability.[35]

Koreans also began to deal with their troubled recent past. One of the most interesting developments in coming to terms with the past was the Truth and Reconciliation Commission that President Roh Moo-hyun had established in 2005. With 15 commissioners and a staff of 239, it investigated political movements under Japanese colonial rule and all acts of political violence, terrorism, and human rights violations in Korea from 1945 to the democratization of the country in the late 1980s. Although the Roh Moo-hyun government may have had some political motives, seeking to discredit conservative opposition figures with links to past military regimes, the commission was nevertheless an experiment in coming to terms with the past that was unprecedented in East Asia.

Writers dealing with the country's recent history found a large audience for their works. Pak Kyŏng-ni (1926–2008), in her popular twenty-one-volume, 9,000-page saga *T'oji* (*The Earth*) (1969–1994), traced the history of Korea from 1860 to 1945 through four generations of what had been originally a wealthy landowning family from southern Korea. Cho

Chŏng-nae (1943–), in his popular ten-volume novel *T'aebak Mountains* (1983) examined the partisans in southern Korea from 1945 to 1953. Sin Kyŏng-suk (1963–), in her novel *Solitary Room* (*Wae Ttan Bang*) (1995), drew upon her own experience growing up during the years of military rule and rapid urbanization. The emotionally charged Kwangju Incident was explored in Im Ch'ŏl-u's (1954–) novel *Spring Days* (*Bom Nal*) (1998).

At the start of the twenty-first century, many Korean writers were moving away from ideological and political issues, dealing either with more universal themes such as sexual orientation and the limitations of consumer society or with fantasy. Kim Yŏng-ha (1968–) looked beyond Korea for subject matter. His *Dark Flower* (*Kŏmŭn Kkot*) (2007) chronicles Korean immigrants in Mexico in the early twentieth century. Pak Min-kyu (1968–) populated his novels such as *Earth Hero Legend* (2003) with characters from computer games and animation, while breaking grammatical and stylistic conventions. Kim Ae-ran (1980–), in her *Tallyŏra Abi* (*Father Keep Running*) (2005), deals with those on the margins of Korea's competitive, consumer society in a cheerful and accepting manner. Many younger readers have turned to Internet novels and *manhwa* (manga). Facing this phenomenon, some established literary figures have experimented with online novels, including internationally recognized Hwang Sŏk-yong (1943–), with his successful *Dog's Supper Star* (*Kaebap Paragi Pyŏl*) (2008). Celebrating the 100th anniversary in 2008 of the first modern play, *Silver World* (*Ŭnsegye*), Korean theater was also becoming more universal in its themes and global in its activities.

While Koreans were taking an interest in their cultural heritage, they were not only embracing contemporary culture but also becoming a dynamic exporter of it, a phenomenon called the "Korean Wave" (*Hanryu*). Korean movies and television programs in the early 2000s not only regained a domestic audience that had long preferred foreign entertainment, especially Hollywood movies, but they also became popular in China, Japan, and Southeast Asia. The TV serial melodrama *Winter Sonata* began airing in Japan in 2003, where it became a huge hit. Hundreds of thousands of Japanese fans came to visit the film site, and a photo book of lead actor Bae Yong Joon (Pae Yong-jun) sold 100,000 copies at $160 each. Korean movie directors Im Kwŏn-t'aek, Yi Ch'ang-dong, and Park Chanwook (Pak Ch'an-uk) have received critical acclaim, and Kim Ki Duk (Kim Ki-dŏk) has attracted some attention in international film festivals. Big-budget films such as the spy thriller *Shiri* by the director Kang Je-Gu (Kang Che-gyu) were box-office hits in much of Asia. Korean popular music, or "K-pop," became a major export. K-pop singers such as Bi (also known as Rain) drew mass crowds on tours of China, Japan, Vietnam, and elsewhere. Korean animation began competing with Japanese anime for audiences abroad.

The government helped to promote movies by passing the Motion Picture Promotion Law of 1995, which provided state subsidies to Korean filmmakers. In 1999, a Basic Law for Culture Industry Promotion was enacted to assist film and television producers. A more important factor contributing to this boom in pop culture was the repeal of restrictions limiting imports of foreign films, music, videos, and comic books, especially those from Japan. It was feared that the country's domestic entertainment industry could not compete with that of its former colonial ruler. In the late 1990s, when the policy was liberalized, the flood of Japanese popular culture imports acted instead as a great stimulus to South Korea's creative youth. Perhaps the most successful cultural exports were South Korean TV dramas. So popular were they in Asia that governments in some countries such as China and Vietnam moved toward imposing quotas on them to protect their own less popular television industry. *The Jewel in the Palace* (*Tae Chang Kŭm*), for example, a series loosely based on a Chosŏn-era woman physician, became the number one rated show in almost every country along the Pacific Rim of Asia and some beyond. It was estimated in 2007 that 60 percent of the entire adult population of Iran tuned in to it, and it was a big hit in other countries from Russia to Mexico. Whether the Korean Wave was a passing phenomenon or not, it was clear that South Korea had become a dynamic, sophisticated society.

NEW CRISES AND NEW PROBLEMS

In the early twenty-first century, Koreans were living in a new globalizing era and were becoming a cosmopolitan people. Once labeled the "hermit kingdom," Koreans now traveled across the world in large numbers. Spending time abroad was becoming a routine part of a college education, and an overseas vacation was now becoming something that the average South Korean could afford. More than 100,000 South Koreans were studying in foreign countries in 2008, and thousands were working in business. There were also thousands of Korean missionaries active in countries from Africa to China. Korea was emerging out of its historical obscurity. Samsung, LG, and Hyundai were internationally known brands, taekwondo (t'ae kwŏndo) was practiced everywhere and was an Olympic sport, and then there was Korean pop culture, which had an enormous audience in Asia and parts of the Middle East and Latin America. Notably, a Korean, Ban Ki Moon, (Pan Ki-mun) (1944–) was elected Secretary-General of the United Nations in 2006.

But the very degree to which South Korea was connected to the world made it vulnerable to developments beyond its control. This became clear during 2008 and 2009, when the country became caught in the worldwide financial meltdown. In 2009 the economy contracted by 0.8 percent. By the end of the year it was showing a robust recovery fueled by export growth, low interest rates, and government stimulus measures. South Korea's membership in the new G-20 group of the world's major economic powers established in 2008, and its planned hosting of the G-20 summit in November 2010 symbolized its importance in the world. Yet, the country's dependence on manufacturing for export earnings, its rigid labor market, and most of all its aging population were causes for concern. Even more troubling for the nation's long-term future was the prospect of having to deal with, and perhaps absorb, a failed North Korean state.

KOREA IN GLOBAL PERSPECTIVE: SOUTH KOREA'S PLACE IN THE WORLD

A status-conscious society, South Koreans could look at their place in the world with some contentment. In 2008, they ranked about twelfth or thirteenth in GNP. Although the country's economic growth was slowing down, it was still an economic powerhouse. Its firms included the two top makers of DRAM chips, the three biggest shipbuilders, the second-largest consumer electronics manufacturer, the third-largest steel producer, and the fifth-largest automaker. The trillion-dollar economy was the fourth largest in Asia after China, Japan, and India. With a population not likely to grow beyond its 48 million, in fact scheduled to decline after 2018, the total size of the economy was likely to be overtaken by much more populous nations—Indonesia, Mexico, Vietnam, perhaps eventually nations such as Pakistan or even Nigeria. But it was less likely that any of these other developing nations would match the per capita income of South Korea for a long time. Ranked in the top thirty richest countries in the first decade of the twenty-first century, the economy was still growing at a faster rate than most developed nations, although not as fast as previously or as fast as China or India. By 2008, South Korea had one of the world's lowest infant mortality rates, and the average life span of its people was among the longest, longer than the Americans, longer than the collective OECD, but slightly shorter than the Japanese or some Western Europeans. Education levels were among the highest in the world, being among the five highest in level of educational attainment among people in their mid-twenties. In the OECD's 2007 international tests of math, science, and analytical skills among secondary school students, South Korean youths overall scored higher than all other young people with the exception of those of Finland.

South Koreans in 2008 ranked second in the world in newspaper readership per capita, only Finns had more cell phones per capita, and South

Korea had the highest percentage of homes with broadband Internet access. South Korea was one of the most wired societies. In 2007, a new form of wireless broadband, Wibro, covered the entire country so that even passengers riding between cities on trains would have high-speed access. Broadband service rates were the second-lowest in the world. And the country was now a major exporter of popular culture, its fashion styles being imitated in other Asian nations. Still there was progress to be made in improving the quality of life. The country lagged behind most developed nations in parks and recreational facilities. South Koreans worked longer hours and lived in smaller homes than most citizens of developed nations. And there was still a small stream of South Koreans seeking a better life abroad. South Koreans had made many achievements in education, but few if any of their national universities ranked among the top 50 or 100 in most international surveys. And not a single South Korean scientist had earned a Nobel Prize. Korean artists, architects, and writers, with a few exceptions, were still not well known outside their country.

South Korea's place in modern world history was an example of how a poor nation can climb out of poverty and develop stable political institutions accountable to the people, without jettisoning too many of its cultural traditions and without losing its strong sense of national and cultural identity. It followed a path influenced by the one Japan had taken, and in turn, it influenced other developing nations such as China. Koreans may have helped in providing an answer to the question that historians have asked and many in the non-Western world worried about: Does modernization mean Westernization? Koreans have created what is in most measures a modern society (two versions of it if North Korea is included) while not losing touch with their cultural heritage or becoming Westerners.

The struggle to become a strong and rich nation, however, was not a smooth one. The South Korean people went through terrible tragedies from the Korean War to Kwangju, worked in appalling industrial complexes for incredibly long hours, went through the confusion of a rapidly changing society, and made mistakes along the way. The several million who left after the loosening of emigration restrictions in the late 1960s to seek a better life abroad were a testimony to the hardships that seemed too great for many. And in contrast to their many accomplishments, there was the failure to achieve national unity. The unresolved conflict with North Korea has left a sense of frustration and anxiety about the future. Most South Koreans no longer fear a military threat from the North, but instead worry about the possibility of chaos in the event of the DPRK's collapse. They worry about how to bridge the economic and cultural gap with their fellow Koreans, and they are pained at the hunger, human rights abuses, and suffering the people in the North are experiencing.

The hope of reformers in the late nineteenth century to see their country survive intact as a progressive member of the modern world has not yet been fulfilled.

Kim Dae Jung
"A Father's Guilt"

November 24, 1980

To my dear son Hong-up,

I feel a heavy weight as I think of you—a feeling of guilt. Though you have passed the age of thirty, because of your father your hopes for marriage have twice been destroyed and you have not been able to find a job in the business world, where you have always wanted to work. It is not just that I have been unable to help you; I have repeatedly been an obstacle to your happiness and future. How could my heart not ache? And when I see how you persevere without any sign of resentment, I feel even more distressed. I pray to God for your future happiness. I can only hope that the bitter experiences you have undergone will become an asset to you in the future.[36]

"For Life in the Twenty-first Century"

September 23, 1981

In the twenty-first century there will be political and social changes that simply cannot be imagined at this juncture. It does not seem likely, however, that there will emerge a regimented society in which humans are destroyed by the machine and held at bay in slavery such as Aldous Huxley envisioned in his *Brave New World*. I believe it to be much more likely instead that an era of popular freedom and justice will come into being, an age in which, for the first time in our history, human beings will be able to maximize use of their personal characteristics and abilities under conditions of equality of education and a secure economic life. It goes without saying that this will require our efforts and sacrifice, especially for posterity.[37]

"The Strengths and Shortcomings of Our Nation"

September 30, 1981

With love and respect to you and my beloved children:

Because my August letter did not reach you, I asked the prison authorities for permission to write another. . . .

In my letter of the 23d, I wrote about the history of mankind, but today I want to jot down some observations on the strength and shortcomings of our nation, based on my reading of our own history. Our greatest strength has been the astounding ability to maintain independence for 1,300 years—from the time of unification under Silla until the Japanese occupation in 1910. This record is unparalleled in world history. . . .

We tend to treat any signs of dependency on foreign powers as shameful. But one American scholar who has the benefit of an objective broad view of world history has commented that such a tendency in Korea reflects the prudent wisdom to survive when faced with the pressure of the Continental powers. Even though our nation formally adapted to foreign influences, our people have stoutly preserved their identity. Despite the overwhelming influence of Chinese civilization, for example we have retained unique characteristics in our culture. We have kept a distinct life-style in such things as clothing, food, language, and shelter and have completely prevented the penetration and domination by the notorious overseas Chinese. . . .

We also have to acknowledge our ancestors for their intense desire for learning. Although we belong to the hemisphere of Chinese civilization, we do not by any means lag behind China in terms of our levels of education and culture. Such a tradition of independence has given us the resourcefulness to join the ranks of middle-tier nations, such as Hong Kong, Taiwan, and Singapore, all of which are also located within the sphere of Chinese influence. . . .

We have shortcomings, however, that stand in rather shameful contrast to our strengths. First, our political culture is narrow-minded and lacking in magnanimity. . . .

Second, although our nation has distinguished itself in preserving its fundamental attributes, it is quite lacking in progressive tendencies. Our history abounds in conclusive proofs. For example, King Changsu of Koguryo moved the capital from Kungnaesoong, located across the Yalu, to Pyongyang, which is on the peninsula. When Silla unified the peninsula, it voluntarily relinquished the eastern half of the Manchurian lands to the north of Taedong River and would not budge an inch northward in the location of the traditional capital city of Kyongju. Finally, even though Yi Sung'gye participated personally in the northward policy of the Koryo dynasty in its last years, he moved the capital south of Kaesong, misled as he was by the superstition against the north.

In spite of the fact that our country faces the ocean on three sides, we have refused almost completely to recognize this reality. This is why we have been bothered so persistently by the Japanese. If we were to try to identify the great navigators or others engaged in maritime activities, Chang Po-go from the late Silla period is about the only one that comes to mind. . . .

Third, we can take note of the formalist tendencies of our nation. We are so concerned with formal appearances that we quite disregard practical benefits, while our excessive sensitivity to the issue of losing face often leads us to pretensions that we cannot sustain and ultimately to waste. This sort of formalism only aggravates bureaucratic abuses and serves as a major suppressant of creativity.[38]

—from *Prison Writings*

Conclusion

Korea's past century, its intensive colonial occupation, its arbitrary division, and most striking of all, the radically different trajectories pursued by the two halves is without a comparable example in modern history. No modern nation ever developed a more isolated and totalitarian society than North Korea, nor such an all-embracing family cult. No society moved more swiftly from extreme poverty to prosperity and from authoritarianism to democracy than South Korea. Modern history offers no other example of such an ancient, homogeneous society growing so far apart in such a short span of time. By the beginning of the twenty-first century the border separating the two Koreas marked a boundary between two lifestyles and living standards more sharply divergent than any border in the world.

Until it had entered the world of the late nineteenth century, Korea was a remarkably stable society with twelve centuries of political unity. Politically the aristocratic-monarchical system had undergone some modifications but remained fundamentally the same since the Silla period. And the Yi (Chosŏn) dynasty was the third-longest-ruling dynasty of any major state; only the imperial houses of Japan and Ottoman Turkey among major states were older. Socially most of the great families traced their ancestry back many centuries; some, such as the Kyŏngju Kim lineage, had been prominent since at least as early as the fifth century. This was an ancestry several centuries longer than that of any royal or aristocratic family in Europe.

Within this relatively stable political framework a well-defined Korean society, possessing a sense of its own identity as a people with their own culture, had emerged. Korea was an ancient land characterized by change within tradition, a strong sense of continuity, and stability. Politically independent, suspicious of outsiders, and remarkably homogeneous with no ethnic minorities, Korea was a land apart. Yet the Koreans were participants in a great cosmopolitan civilization centered in China. Koreans were aware of their distinctiveness as a people with a language very different from their neighbors and their own style of dress, housing, cuisine, and folk customs. However, before the end of the nineteenth century, Korea was not a "nation" in the modern sense; it was, rather, a clearly defined political, ethnic, and cultural unit within East Asian civilization.

The great civilization that the Koreans were so proud to be a part of underwent a severe challenge in the late nineteenth and twentieth centuries. This challenge fundamentally altered Korean culture and brought the old order to an end. Yet the rich and ancient cultural tradition of Korea did not die out so much as it was transformed by the exposure to the Western-dominated world of the late nineteenth and twentieth centuries. Just as in the past Koreans had looked to China as a cultural model, they now sought to take the best in the achievements of Western civilization and adopt and adapt them to their culture. Twentieth-century Koreans were to look to Japan, the United States, and Europe. Just as they proved to be China's most studious pupils, they would be among the twentieth century's most ardent and eager students, absorbing and bringing back ideas on society, politics, art, literature, music, science, economics, philosophy, and fashions. These they developed into a unique Korean synthesis. In North Korea the result of this synthesis was the creation of one of the most totalitarian and oppressive systems of government the world has ever seen. In South Korea this led to the emergence of a vigorous if contentious democratic society with an internationally competitive economy.

Due to this common historical inheritance, the two Koreas share many features. Both have been driven by a passionate Korean nationalism. While nationalism has been a globally dominant force in shaping societies, few developing nations have had such a long history as a clearly defined political and cultural entity. As the centuries-old political system crumbled along with the Sino-centric world with which it was associated, members of the educated elite grappled with new forms of identity. They began examining their state and its place in the modern global community; in the process, they gave birth to modern Korean nationalism. This new sense of being part of a Korean nation quickly took root among the general population. A powerful ethnic nationalism emerged in the first half of the twentieth century, unencumbered by racial or linguistic minorities, regional separatism, or strong sectarian identities. Colonialism assisted in this process, since the harsh and intrusive nature of Japanese rule in this ethnically homogenous society contributed to a collective sense of victimization. Both North and South Korea were able to draw upon this Korean nationalism to mobilize their populations for state-directed goals.

Both Koreas are the product of the highly turbulent middle third of the twentieth century. The mass uprooting of the Korean people caused by wartime Japan's mobilizations, the dislocations that followed division, and the Korean War all helped to shake up society and break up traditional, rigid class lines, making society more fluid, more open to change and mobility. In North Korea, that social mobility was initially revolutionary, but then that society began to rigidify as a new hierarchical social order emerged. The social revolution in South Korea was at first less marked, as old elites consolidated power, but the Korean War, land reform, mass education, and rapid industrialization established a semimeritocracy, provided many avenues for upward mobility, and created a new middle-class society. In both cases the social upheavals eased the task of pursuing development agendas.

The two states were shaped by the unique geopolitical situation of Korea. The modest-size Korean peninsula is almost completely encircled by three of the most formidable states in history: China, Russia, and Japan. Korea has no neighbors its own size. With the American occupation of Japan in 1945, Korea acquired a fourth powerful neighbor: the United States. Each of these much more populous and powerful states intervened and occupied at least part of Korea in the century after the country was forced to open its doors to the world. Korea could only survive and flourish as an independent entity by skillfully playing the surrounding great powers off one another or seeking one as a protector. Each of the Koreas after 1945 sought two of these powers for economic support and military protection, not without considerable ambivalence and prickliness. The fear of foreign domination and the frustrations of dependency partly account for the intensity of Korean nationalism and the determined efforts of the North and the South to acquire military and economic strength.

The ROK and the DPRK also have been shaped by Korea's long history of centralized, bureaucratic rule. During the Chosŏn period, 1392–1910, an elaborate system of government was administered from the capital down to the county level. There was little local autonomy. The colonial administration reinforced this pattern, with the state organs penetrating to the township and village level. It was also more authoritarian and militarized than the dynastic state, and it introduced the practice of mass mobilization to achieve state goals. Both Koreas, consequently, were highly centralized states. In North Korea everything was decided from the center, from the allocation of resources for industry to the food and clothing rations issued through the public distribution system. There was a complete absence of provincial autonomy or culture. South Korea also had a remarkable lack of local authority. Until the local autonomy laws of the early 1990s, the Ministry of the Interior appointed all local officials from governors to local mayors, the Ministry of Education imposed uniform and detailed regulations on every local school, and there were no local police forces or any other significant administrative organ that was not directed from Seoul. The centralized nature of both states is reflected in their capitals. P'yŏngyang totally dominates North Korea, it is where all the members of the elite live, and although the size has been kept to a modest 2–2.5 million by strict internal migration controls, it is still much larger than any other city in the country. Seoul, lacking such internal migration controls, grew into a megacity with a population that has reached 10 million, more than 18 million if the suburban "satellite cities" are included, two-fifths of the country's total. It is the largest industrial center, the financial hub, and the political capital. It is also the educational center, with all the best universities located there, and the cultural and intellectual center.

Both Koreas have pursued policies of economic nationalism in which the state directs the economy using centralized planning. This was in part a legacy of the colonial economic experience, the logical outcome of centralized bureaucratic states, and the influence of the Soviet model in North Korea—which in turn influenced South Korea. The goals of the governments in both Koreas remained similar: to make their states strong and independent through economic development. Both were able to tap into a strong sense of national pride to mobilize the population for these aims. The slogan of Meiji Japan after 1868, "rich nation, strong military," could have very well been the motto of the DPRK under Kim Il Sung or the ROK under Park Chung Hee. Both Koreas motivated their populations by appealing to the same sense of ethnic-racial nationalism. This mind-set became increasingly explicit in the North from the 1970s, eventually becoming more central to the state ideology than Marxism-Leninism.

Yet the shared inheritance of the two Koreas led them onto different paths. North Korea pursued a model of development that proved to be an economic and historical dead end. The desire to be self-sufficient, to be free from foreign domination despite its precarious geopolitical terrain and modest size, had disastrous consequences for the North. It could not flourish in a world dominated by global capitalism. Attempts by Kim Il Sung and Kim Jong Il to do so began to resemble the futile efforts at isolation pursued more than a century earlier by the Taewŏn'gun.

South Korea's more chaotic but more pluralistic society proved more successful in bringing prosperity if not self-sufficiency. This was in part because its economic and political links to the United States and Japan proved more effective in developing its economy. Here the crucial role of the United States needs to be acknowledged. The American legacy in modern Korea is an ambiguous one. Despite the important influence that American missionaries had as agents of modernization in the late nineteenth and early twentieth centuries, the U.S. government was largely indifferent to Korea, willing to let it become part of the Japanese Empire. When the United States did actively intervene in Korean affairs, the result was catastrophic, since it was the United States that was initially responsible for the division. The American military intervention in the Korean War turned what would have been a short if nasty civil war, into a three-year global conflict that devastated the country and left it divided. Washington tolerated military governments, American firms took advantage of the suppression of labor movements, and the U.S. military presence may have contributed to the tensions between the two Koreas. Yet South Korea enormously benefitted by the U.S. involvement. The United States opened its markets to Korean exports and poured in development aid. Its universities educated many tens of thousands of Koreans. It plugged Korea into the global society and provided the security needed to attract foreign investment. And for all its tolerance of military rulers, the United States acted as a check on authoritarianism, allowing space for a pluralistic society to grow. North Korea, by contrast, had no similar external check on the ambitions and visions of its authoritarian leaders; and the regime effectively eliminated any element of pluralism.

None of this detracts from the strengths of South Korean society, which made possible its transition to developed status in just several decades. South Korean leaders, while sometimes brutal, corrupt, and self-serving, also made some wise choices, sometimes against American advice. The South Korean people endured many hardships and made many sacrifices, and they were able to draw upon many resources from their cultural heritage and recent history. Their preoccupations with educational attainment, pursuit of status, sense of national purpose, and openness to change were all crucial elements. Especially important was the Korean tradition of looking outside their society for examples of excellence and then trying to emulate them. Tragically, although North Korea shared the same historical inheritance and its people exhibited the same sense of hard work and national purpose, the interplay of historical contingency and policy choices brought about very different outcomes.

The great tragedy of modern Korean history has been the nation's division. In the six decades since the two states were created, the Koreans have continued to think of themselves as one people. Almost universally, the division of the country has been regarded as "unnatural" and unification at some point inevitable. However, as the sixtieth anniversary of the establishment of the two republics passed, there was no obvious path to reunification. Nor was it clear just how far the two Koreas have pulled apart and become not only two states but also two cultures. Only if and when the two Koreas become one nation-state will we be able to truly comprehend the significance of this division and the insights into history it provides; and only then will the hopes of Koreans to create a modern nation be fulfilled.

Appendix

Romanization

The Korean language has a rather complex sound system that has posed challenges to romanization. This book follows the McCune-Reischauer system that is used by the Library of Congress and with minor variations in most scholarly English language texts. Below is a basic guide to the pronunciation of the McCune-Reischauer system used in this book. *Note:* The Korean sound system is very different than in English so the equivalents below are only rough approximations.

CONSONANTS

ch is as in English but unaspirated, sounding a bit more like a j
ch' is pronounced as in English but more aspirated
k as in English but unaspirated, sounding a bit like a hard g
k' as in English but more aspirated
kk a very tense unaspirated k sound
l as initial l in English, never as a final l such as in well
p as in English but unaspirated and sounding a bit like a b
p' as in English but more aspirated
pp a very tense unaspirated p sound
s softer than an English s, but if followed by i pronounced as sh
ss more tense than an English s
t as in English but unaspirated, sounding a bit like a d
t' more aspirated then in English

tt a tense unaspirated t
tch a tense unaspirated ch sound

Other consonants are pronounced more or less as they are in English.

VOWELS

a as the a in father
ae a bit like the a in cat
e roughly as in get
i between the i of tin and the ee of teen
o as in hope
ŏ between the sound of u in fun and the aw in fawn
oe roughly as "way"
u as the u in tune
ŭ similar to the oo in book
ŭi sometimes as in eh

In 2000 the South Korean government adopted a new official Revised Romanization that is also coming into use. The following list shows some of the differences.

McCune-Reischauer	*Revised Romanization*
ch	j
ch'	ch
k	g
k'	k
p	b
p'	p
t	d
t'	t
ŏ	eo
ŭ	eu

In Revised Romanization hyphens between syllables in names are optional. Many users of McCune-Reischauer also delete hyphens between syllables in names although they are used in this book.

The following list presents some names and terms written in (1) McCune-Reischauer, (2) Revised Romanization, and (3) the Korean alphabet.

ch'ŏnmin	cheonmin	천민
Chosŏn	Joseon	조선
Han'gŭl	Hangeul	한글
kisaeng	gisaeng	기생
Kim Pu-sik	Gim Bushik	김부식
Koryŏ	Goryeo	고려
kwagŏ	gwageo	과거
Paekche	Baekje	백제
p'ansori	pansori	판소리
Silla	Silla*	신라
Tan'gun	Dangun	단군
T'oegye	Toegye	퇴계
yangban	yangban*	양반
Yi Sŏng-gye	Yi Seonggye	이성계

* Some Korean names and terms are spelled identically in McCune-Reischauer and Revised Romanization.

Notes

CHAPTER 1 THE ORIGINS

1. Gari Ledyard, "How the Linguist's Tail Wags the Historian's Dog: Problems on the Study of Korean Origin," *Korean Studies Forum* 5 (Winter–Spring 1978–1979): 80–88; for an example of linguistic evidence used to explain the origin of the Korean peoples, see Roy Andrew Miller, "Linguistic Evidence and Japanese Prehistory," in *Windows on Prehistoric Japan*, ed. Richard J. Pearson et al. (Ann Arbor: University of Michigan Press, 1986), 101–20.

2. Sarah M. Nelson, "The Politics of Ethnicity in Prehistoric Korea," in *Nationalism, Politics, and the Practice of Archaeology*, ed. Philip L. Kohl and Clare Fawcett (Cambridge, UK: Cambridge University Press, 1998), 218–31.

3. Sarah Nelson, "Korean Interpretations of Korean Archaeology," *Asian Perspectives* 27, no. 2 (1990): 185–92.

4. Choe Chong-pil, "Origins of Agriculture in Korea," *Korea Journal* 30, no. 11 (November 1990): 4–14.

5. Choe Chong-pil, "The Diffusion Route and Chronology of Korean Plant Domestication," *Journal of Asian Studies* 41, no. 3 (May 1982): 513–18.

6. Martin Bale, "The Archaeology of Early Agriculture in the Korean Peninsula: An Update on Recent Developments," *Indo-Pacific Prehistory Association* 21 (2002): 77–84.

7. Sarah Nelson, "The Neolithic of Northern China and Korea," *Antiquity* 64, no. 2 (June 1990): 234–48.

8. Sarah Nelson, "Social Dimension of Burials in Prehistoric Korea," in *Proceedings of the Seventh International Symposium on Asian Studies 1985* (Hong Kong: Asian Research Service, 1986), 247–56.

9. This interpretation of the meaning of Chaoxian has been challenged in recent years. The "chao" can be translated as "court" rather than "morning." And in

any case the characters were probably chosen for their pronunciation rather than meaning.

10. This ancient Chosŏn state, usually called Old Chosŏn, is not to be confused for the official name of the Korean state from 1392 to 1897 (see chapter 6).

11. Gina L. Barnes, *State Formation in Korea: Historical Archaeological Perspectives* (Richmond: Curzon Press, 2000), 14–15.

12. Barnes, *State Formation in Korea*, 19–20.

13. Gina L. Barnes, "Early Korean States: A Review of Historical Interpretation," in *Bibliographical Review of Far Eastern Archaeology 1990: Hoabinhian, Jomon, Yayoi, Early Korean States* (Oxford: Oxbow Books, 1990), 125.

14. Kenneth H. J. Gardiner, *The Early History of Korea: The Historical Development of the Peninsula up to the Introduction of Buddhism in the Fourth Century C.E.* (Honolulu: University of Hawaii Press, 1969), 29.

15. Written with a different character from the Chinese Han, the latter a name derived from the Han dynasty.

16. Barnes, *State Formation in Korea*, 27–31.

17. Yi Ki-moon, "Language and Writings Systems in Traditional Korea," in *The Traditional Culture and Society of Korea: Arts and Literature*, ed. Peter H. Lee (Honolulu: Center for Korean Studies, 1975), 16.

18. Gardiner, *Early History of Korea*, 42, 52–58.

19. Peter H. Lee and William Theodore De Bary, eds., *Sources of Korean Traditions*, vol. 1, *From Early Times through the Sixteenth Century* (New York: Columbia University Press, 1997), 5–6.

CHAPTER 2 THE PERIOD
OF THE THREE KINGDOMS, 4TH CENTURY TO 676

1. This statement needs some qualification, for most of the old Koguryŏ state became part of the state of Parhae, but Parhae was more of a Manchurian power than a peninsular one.

2. Kenneth H. J. Gardiner, *The Early History of Korea: The Historical Development of the Peninsula up to the Introduction of Buddhism in the Fourth Century A.D.* (Honolulu: University of Hawaii Press, 1969), 31–34.

3. Gina L. Barnes, "Early Korean States: A Review of Historical Interpretation," in *Bibliographical Review of Far Eastern Archaeology 1990: Hoabinhian, Jomon, Yayoi, Early Korean States* (Oxford: Oxbow Books, 1990), 137–38.

4. Kenneth H. J. Gardiner, "Beyond the Archer and His Son: Koguryŏ and Han China," *Papers on Far Eastern History* 20 (September 1979): 57–82.

5. The term *kan* here may be of Central Asian origin and related to the later term *Khan* used by the Mongols and others.

6. Russell J. Kirkland, "The 'Horserider' in Korea: A Critical Evaluation of a Historical Theory," *Korean Studies* 5 (1991): 109–28; Obayashi Taryo, "The Ancient Myths of Korea and Japan," *Acta Asiatica* 61 (1991): 68–82.

7. J. H. Grayson, "Excavations of Late Kaya Personal Tumuli in Koryong, Korea: Chisan-dong Tombs 32–35 and Associated Burials," *Indo-Pacific Prehistory Association Bulletin* 5 (1984): 64–73.

8. Namio Egami, "The Formation of the People and the Origin of the State in Japan," *Memoirs of the Research Department of the Toyo Bunko* 23 (1964): 35–70; see also Wontack Hong, *Paekche of Korea and the Origin of Yamato Japan* (Seoul: Kudara International, 1994).

9. Hatada Takeshi, "An Interpretation of the King Kwanggaet'o Inscription," *Korean Studies* 3 (1979): 1–17.

10. Gina L. Barnes, *State Formation in Korea: Historical Archaeological Perspectives* (Richmond, UK: Curzon Press, 2000), 134–142.

11. Barnes, *State Formation in Korea*, 195, 209–11.

12. Ki-dong Yi, "Shilla's Kolp'um System and Japan's Kabane System," *Korean Social Science Journal* 11 (1984): 7–12.

13. Sarah Nelson, "The Queens of Silla: Power and Connections to the Spirit World," in *Ancient Queens: Archaeological Explorations*, ed. Sarah Nelson (Walnut Creek, CA: Altamira Press, 2003), 77–92.

14. Richard Rutt, "The Flower Boys of Silla," *Transactions of the Korea Branch of the Royal Asiatic Society* 37 (October 1961): 1–66.

15. Vladimir Tikhonov, "Hwarang Organization: Its Functions and Ethic," *Korea Journal* 38, no. 2 (Summer 1995): 318–38.

16. The *li* was the principal unit for measuring distances in East Asia; its length varied with time and place but a rough rule of thumb is three *li* to one mile.

17. John Charles Jamieson, "Collapse of the T'ang-Silla Alliance: Chinese and Korean Accounts Compared," in *Nothing Concealed: Essays in Honor of Liu Yu-yun*, Occasional Series No. 4, ed. Frederick Wakeman (Taipei: Chinese Materials and Research Aids Service Center, 1970), 81–94.

18. Peter H. Lee and William Theodore De Bary, eds., *Sources of Korean Traditions*. vol. 1, *From Early Times through the Sixteenth Century* (New York: Columbia University Press, 1997), 55.

19. Lee and De Bary, *Sources of Korean Traditions*, vol. 1, 27.

CHAPTER 3 LATE SILLA, 676 TO 935

1. The translations of the names of Korean institutions in this text generally follow those in Ki-baik Lee, *A New History of Korea*, trans. Edward W. Wagner with Edward J. Shultz (Cambridge, MA: Harvard University Press, 1984).

2. Chin Kim, "The Silla Village Registers and Korean Legal History: A Preliminary Inquiry," *Korean Journal of Comparative Law* 7 (November 1979): 99–127.

3. Ki-baik Lee, *A New History of Korea*, 109.

4. Kim Chong Sun, "Slavery in Silla and Its Sociological and Economic Implications," in *Traditional Korea—Theory and Practice*, ed. Andrew Nahm (Kalamazoo: Center for Korean Studies, Western Michigan University, 1974), 29–43.

5. Martina Deuchler, "Thoughts on Korean Society," in *First International Conference on Korean Studies*, Chŏngsin Munhwa Yŏn'guwŏn (Yongnam, Republic of Korea: Chŏngsin Munhwa Yŏn'guwŏn, 1980), 643–52.

6. Martina Deuchler, *The Confucian Transformation of Korea: A Study of Society and Ideology* (Cambridge, MA: Council on East Asian Studies, Harvard University, 1992), 81.

7. Werner Sasse, "Trying to Figure Out How Kings Became Kings in Silla," *Cahiers d'Etudes Coreenes* 7 (2001): 229–41.

8. Peter Lee, ed., *Sourcebook of Korean Civilization*, vol. 1 (New York: Columbia University Press, 1993), 209.

9. Robert E. Buswell, Jr. "Imagining Korean Buddhism" in *Nationalism and the Construction of Korean Identity*, ed. Hyung Il Pai and Timothy R. Tangherlini (Berkeley: Institute of East Asian Studies, University of California Press, 1998), 73–107.

10. Ik-jin Koh, "Wonhyo and the Foundation of Korean Buddhism," *Korea Journal* 21, no. 8 (August 1981): 4–13.

11. Nha Il-Seong, "Silla's Cheomseongdae," *Korea Journal* 41, no. 4 (Winter 2001): 269–81.

12. Yi Ki-moon, "Language and Writing Systems of Traditional Korea," in *The Traditional Culture and Society of Korea: Art and Literature*, ed. Peter H. Lee (Honolulu: The Center for Korean Studies, University of Hawaii, 1975), 15–32.

13. William E. Henthorn, *A History of Korea* (New York: Free Press, 1971), 65.

14. Edwin Reischauer, *Ennin's Travel in T'ang China* (New York: Ronald Press, 1955).

15. Song Ki-ho, "Current Trends in the Research of Palhae history," *Seoul Journal of Korean Studies* 3 (December 1990): 157–74.

16. William H. McCullough, "The Heian Court, 794–1070," in *Cambridge History of Japan*, vol. 2, *Heian Japan*, ed. John Whitney Hall et al. (Cambridge: Cambridge University Press, 1988), 20–96.

17. Not all historians agree on the extent to which Parhae can be considered a part of Korean history. In the eighteenth century, Korean scholar Yu Tŭk-kong in his *Parhae ko* argued that Parhae was a successor state to Koguryŏ and a part of Korean history. Since then, many historians of Korea have regarded the eighth and ninth centuries as the period of the "Two Kingdoms."

18. C. Cameron Hurst, "The Good, the Bad and the Ugly: Personalities in the Founding of the Koryo Dynasty," *Korean Studies Forum* 7 (Summer–Fall 1981): 109–25.

19. Kenneth H. J. Gardiner, "Korea in Transition: Notes on the Three Later Kingdoms (900–935)," *Papers on Far Eastern History* 36 (September 1987): 139–61.

20. Peter H. Lee and William Theodore De Bary, eds., *Sources of Korean Traditions*, vol 1, *From Early Times through the Sixteenth Century* (New York: Columbia University Press, 1997), 27.

21. Lee and De Bary, *Sources of Korean Traditions*, vol. 1, 114–16. Kyunyŏ (923–973) was a monk who revived the Flower Garland school of Buddhism. His collected works include eleven poems written in the *hyangch'al* system and are among the surviving twenty-five poems in this early form of writing in Korean.

CHAPTER 4 KORYŎ, 935 TO 1170

1. John B. Duncan, *The Origins of the Chosŏn Dynasty* (Seattle: University of Washington Press, 2000), 16–19.

2. Hugh W. Kang, "The First Succession Struggle of Koryŏ, in 945: A Reinterpretation," *Journal of Asian Studies* 36, no. 3 (May 1977): 411–28.

3. Duncan, *Origins*, 40–44.

4. H. W. Kang, "Institutional Borrowing: The Case of the Chinese Civil Service Examination in Early Koryŏ," *Journal of Asian Studies* 34, no.1 (January 1974): 109–23.

5. Duncan, *Origins*, 79.

6. Duncan, *Origins*, 46–47.

7. Yong-ho Ch'oe, *The Civil Examinations and the Social Structure in Early Yi Dynasty Korea: 1392–1600* (Seoul: Korean Research Center, 1987), 3.

8. Duncan, *Origins*, 42–43.

9. Michael C. Rogers, "National Consciousness in Medieval Korea: The Impact of Liao and Chin on Koryŏ," in *China among Equals: The Middle Kingdom and Its Neighbors, 10th–14th Centuries*, ed. Morris Rossabi (Berkeley: University of California Press, 1983), 151–72.

10. Keith L. Pratt, "Politics and Culture Within the Sinic Zone: Chinese Influences on Medieval Korea," *Korea Journal* 20, no. 6 (June 1980): 15–29.

11. William E. Henthorn, *A History of Korea* (New York: Free Press, 1971), 100.

12. Edward J. Shultz, "Twelfth Century Koryŏ Politics: The Rise of Han Anin and His Partisans," *The Journal of Korean Studies* 6 (1988–1989): 3–38.

13. Robert E. Buswell, *The Korean Approach to Zen: Collected Works on Chinul* (Honolulu: University of Hawaii Press, 1983), 1–72.

14. Buswell, *Korean Approach to Zen*, 18.

15. Pratt, "Politics and Culture within the Sinic Zone," 24.

16. Jane Portal, *Korea: Art and Archaeology* (London: British Museum, 2000), 91.

17. Portal, *Korea: Art and Archaeology*, 84.

18. Kim Kichung, *Classical Korean Literature* (Armonk, NY: M. E. Sharpe, 1996), 54–56.

19. Duncan, *Origins*, 56–57.

20. Much of this discussion of marriage and family is based on Martina Deuchler, *The Confucian Transformation of Korea: A Study of Society and Ideology* (Cambridge, MA: Harvard University Press, 1992).

21. Peter H. Lee and William Theodore De Bary, eds., *Sources of Korean Traditions*, vol. 1, *From Early Times through the Sixteenth Century* (New York: Columbia University Press, 1997), 154–56.

CHAPTER 5 MILITARY RULERS AND MONGOL INVADERS, 1170 TO 1392

1. The major study of this topic is Edward J. Shultz, *Generals and Scholars: Military Rule in Medieval Korea* (Honolulu: University of Hawaii Press, 2000).

2. Edward J. Shultz. "Ch'oe Ch'unghŏn: His Rise to Power," *Korean Studies* 8 (1984): 58–82.

3. Shultz, *Generals and Scholars*, 54–109.

4. Robert E. Buswell, *The Korean Approach to Zen: Collected Works on Chinul* (Honolulu: University of Hawaii Press, 1983), 1–2.

5. Edward J. Shultz, "Ch'oe Ch'unghŏn and Minamoto Yoritomo," *Japan Review* 11 (1999): 31–53. Much of the comparison between Koryŏ and medieval Japan is drawn from this article.

6. See Jeffrey Mass, *Warrior Government in Early Medieval Japan* (New Haven, CT: Yale University Press, 1974).

7. William Henthorn, *Korea: The Mongol Invasions* (Leiden, UK: Brill, 1963); William Henthorn, "Some Notes on Koryŏ Military Units," *Transactions of the Korea Branch of The Royal Asiatic Society* 35 (1959): 66–75; Gari Ledyard, "The Mongol Campaigns in Korea and the Dating of *The Secret History of the Mongols*," *Central Asiatic Journal* 9 (1964): 1–22.

8. Kim Kichung, *Classical Korean Literature* (Armonk, NY: M. E. Sharpe, 1996), 62.

9. Peter Yun, "Foreigners in Korea during the Period of Mongol Interference," in *Proceedings of the 1st World Congress of Korean Studies: Embracing the Other: The Interaction of Korean and Foreign Cultures*, the Korean Academy of Korean Studies (Seoul: July 2002), 1221–28.

10. Paik Nak Choon, "Tripitaka Koreana," *Transactions of the Korea Branch of the Royal Asiatic Society* 32 (Seoul: 1951): 62–78.

11. J. R. McNeill and William H. McNeill, *The Human Web* (New York: W. W. Norton & Company, 2003), 180.

12. Peter H. Lee, *Anthology of Korean Literature: From Early Times to the Nineteenth Century* (Honolulu: University of Hawaii Press, 1981), 51.

13. Choe Yong-ho, "An Outline History of Korean Historiography," *Korean Studies* 4 (1980): 1–27.

14. Kim, *Classical Korean Literature*, 66–67.

15. Kim, *Classical Korean Literature*, 69–71.

16. Peter H. Lee and William Theodore De Bary, eds., *Sources of Korean Tradition*, vol. 1, *From Early Times through the Sixteenth Century* (New York: Columbia University Press, 1997), 200.

CHAPTER 6 THE NEO-CONFUCIAN REVOLUTION AND THE CHOSŎN STATE, 1392 TO THE 18TH CENTURY

1. Ch'oe Yong-ho, *The Civil Examinations and the Social Structure in Early Yi Dynasty Korea: 1392–1600* (Seoul: Korean Research Center, 1987), 67.

2. Chai-sik Chung, "Chŏng Tojŏn: 'Architect' of Yi Dynasty Government and Ideology," in *The Rise of Neo-Confucianism in Korea*, ed. William Theodore De Bary and Jahyun Kim Haboush (New York: Columbia University Press, 1985), 59–88.

3. Michael C. Kalton, "The Writings of Kwon Kun: The Context and Shape of Early Yi Dynasty Neo-Confucianism," in *The Rise of Neo-Confucianism in Korea*, ed. William Theodore De Bary and Jahyun Kim Haboush (New York: Columbia University Press, 1985), 89–123.

4. This outline of institutions and translations follows Edward W. Wagner, *Literati Purges: Political Conflict in Early Yi Korea* (Cambridge, MA: East Asian Research Center, Harvard University, 1974).

5. Choe Yong-ho, "An Outline History of Korean Historiography," *Korean Studies* 4 (1980): 1–27.

6. Choe, *Civil Examinations*, 79–80.

7. Choe, *Civil Examinations*, 34.

8. Choe, *Civil Examinations*, 19.

9. Michael J. Seth, *Education Fever: Society, Politics and the Pursuit of Schooling in South Korea* (Honolulu: University of Hawaii Press, 2002), 8.

10. Yi Tae-jin, "The Influence of Neo-Confucianism in the 14th–16th centuries," *Korea Journal* 37, no. 4 (Summer 1997): 5–23. A *kyŏl* was actually a unit of crop yield that varied from two to nine acres depending on the fertility of the land. The figures do suggest an overall increase in acreage.

11. William E. Henthorn, *History of Korea* (New York: The Free Press, 1971), 132.

12. Kenneth R. Robinson, "From Raiders to Traders: Border Security and Border Control in Early Chosŏn, 1392–1450," *Korean Studies* 16 (1992): 94–115.

13. Henthorn, *History of Korea*, 158.

14. Wagner, *Literati Purges*, 23–120.

15. Jahyun Kim Haboush, "Constructing the Center: The Ritual Controversy and the Search for a New Identity in Seventh-Century Korea," in *Culture and the State in Late Chosŏn Korea*, ed. Jahyun Kim Haboush and Martina Deuchler, 46–90 (Cambridge, MA: Harvard University Asian Center, 1999).

16. Peter H. Lee and William Theodore De Bary, eds., *Sources of Korean Tradition*, vol. 1, *From Early Times through the Sixteenth Century* (New York: Columbia University Press, 1997), 312–13.

17. Lee and De Bary, *Sources of Korean Tradition*, vol. 1, 313.

CHAPTER 7 CHOSŎN SOCIETY

1. Andrew Nahm, *Korea: Tradition and Transformation* (Elizabeth, NJ: Hollym International, 1988), 113.

2. Youngsook Kim Harvey, "Minmyŏnuri," in *Korean Women: View from the Inner Room*, ed. Laurel Kendall and Mark Peterson (New Haven, CT: East Rock Press, 1983), 46.

3. Mark A. Peterson, *Korean Adoption and Inheritance: Case Studies in the Creation of a Classic Confucian Society* (Ithaca, NY: East Asian Book Program Cornell University, 1998), 3.

4. Research Center for Asian Women, Sookmyung Women's University, *Women of the Yi Dynasty* (Seoul: Sookmyung University, 1986), 169.

5. Hyun-key Kim Hogarth, "The Widow's Suicide in Pre-Modern Korean Society," *Korea Journal* 36, no. 2 (Summer 1996): 33–48.

6. Eugene Y. Park, "Military Examinations in Late Chosŏn: Elite Substratification and Non-elite Accommodation," *Korean Studies* 25, no. 1 (2001): 1–49.

7. James B. Palais, *Views on Korean Social History* (Seoul: Institute for Modern Korean Studies, 1998), 39.

8. James B. Palais, *Confucian Statecraft and Korean Institutions: Yu Hyŏngwŏn and the Late Chosŏn Dynasty* (Seattle: University of Washington Press, 1996), 4.

9. Palais, *Confucian Statecraft*, 218–19.

10. Palais, *Views on Korean Social History*, 33.

11. Palais, *Confucian Statecraft*, 235.

12. Palais, *Views on Korean Social History*, 33.

13. Kyung Moon Hwang, "Bureaucracy in the Transition to Korean Modernity: Secondary Status Groups and the Transformation of Government and Society, 1880–1930" (PhD diss., Harvard University, 1997), 381–417.

14. William Shaw, *Legal Norms in a Confucian State* (Berkeley, CA: Institute of East Asian Studies, University of California, Center for Korean Studies, 1981), 3.

15. Shaw, *Legal Norms*, 97.

16. Han Sang-kwon, "Social Problems and the Active Use of Petitions during the Reign of King Chŏngjo," *Korea Journal* 40, no. 4 (Winter 2000): 227–46.

17. Shaw, *Legal Norms*, 82–83.

18. Descriptions of these household spirits are given in Laurel Kendall, *Shamans, Housewives, and Other Restless Spirits: Women in Korean Ritual Life* (Honolulu: University of Hawaii Press, 1985).

19. Boudewijn Walraven, "Popular Religion in a Confucianized Society," in *Culture and the State in Late Chosŏn Korea*, ed. Jahyun Kim Haboush and Martina Deuchler (Cambridge, MA: Harvard University Asia Center, 1999), 160–98.

20. See Mark Setton, *Chŏng Yagyong: Korea's Challenge to Orthodox Neo-Confucianism* (Albany: State University of New York Press, 1997).

21. Jahyun Kim Haboush, "Constructing the Center: The Ritual Controversy and the Search for a New Identify in Seventh-Century Korea," in *Culture and the State in Late Chosŏn Korea*, ed. Jahyun Kim Haboush and Martina Deuchler, 46–90 (Cambridge, MA: Harvard-Hollym, 1999).

22. See Michael Kalton, *The Four-Seven Debate: An Annotated Translation of the Most Famous Controversy in Korean Neo-Confucian Thought* (Albany: State University of New York Press, 1994).

23. Jane Portal, *Korea: Art and Archaeology* (London: British Museum, 2000), 137–41.

24. Kichung Kim, *Classical Korean Literature* (Armonk, NY: M. E. Sharpe, 1996), 78.

25. Ki-baek Lee, *A New History of Korea*, translated by Edward W. Wagner with Edward J. Shultz (Cambridge, MA: Harvard University Press, 1984), 220.

26. Constantine Contogenis and Wolhee Choe, *Songs of the Kisaeng* (Rochester, NY: Boa Editions Limited, 1997), 14.

27. Peter H. Lee and William Theodore De Bary, eds., *Sources of Korean Tradition*, vol. 1, *From Early Times through the Sixteenth Century* (New York: Columbia University Press, 1997), 295.

28. Lee and De Bary, eds., *Sources of Korean Tradition*, vol. 1, 295.

CHAPTER 8 LATE CHOSŎN, EARLY 18TH CENTURY TO 1876

1. See Jahyun Kim Haboush, *A Heritage of Kings: One Man's Monarchy in the Confucian World* (New York: Columbia University Press, 1988), 39.

2. Jahyun Kim Haboush, "Constructing the Center: The Ritual Controversy and the Search for a New Identity in Seventeenth-Century Korea," in *Culture and the State in Late Chosŏn Korea*, ed. Jahyun Kim Haboush and Martina Deuchler (Cambridge, MA: Harvard University Asia Center, 1999), 46–90.

3. James B. Lewis, *Frontier Contact between Chosŏn Korea and Tokugawa Japan* (London: RoutledgeCurzon, 2003), 192.

4. Gari Ledyard, "Korean Travelers in China over Four Hundred Years, 1488–1887," *Occasional Papers on Korea* (March 1974), 1–42.

5. Gari Ledyard, "Hong Taeyong and His Peking Memoir," *Korean Studies* 6 (1982): 63–103.

6. Ledyard, "Korean Travelers," 26.

7. Hur Nam-lin, "Korean Officials in the Land of the Kami: Diplomacy and the Prestige Economy, 1607–1811," in *Proceedings of the 1st World Congress of Korean Studies: Embracing the Other: The Interaction of Korean and Foreign Cultures*, The Academy of Korean Studies (Seoul, July 2002), 82–93.

8. Chai-shik Chung, "Changing Korean Perceptions of Japan on the Eve of Modern Transformation: The Case of Neo-Confucian Yangban Intellectuals," *Korean Studies* 19 (1995): 39–50.

9. Hur Nam-lin, "Korean Officials," 88.

10. James B. Palais, *Confucian Statecraft and Korean Institutions: Yu Hyŏngwŏn and the Late Chosŏn Dynasty* (Seattle: University of Washington Press, 1996), 49.

11. Palais, *Confucian Statecraft*, 567.

12. Hochul Lee, "Agriculture as a Generator of Change in Late Chosŏn Korea," in *The Last Stand of Asian Autonomies: Responses to Modernity in the Diverse States of Southeast Asia and Korea, 1750–1900*, ed. Anthony Reid (New York: St. Martin's Press, 1997), 111–13.

13. Carter Eckert, *Offspring of Empire* (Seattle: University of Washington Press, 1991), 12–13.

14. Kichung Kim, *Classical Korean Literature* (Armonk, NY: M.E. Sharpe, 1996), 177–78.

15. Kim, *Classical Korean Literature*, 123–24.

16. Kim, *Classical Korean Literature*, 99.

17. JaHyun Kim Haboush, *The Memoirs of Lady Hyegyŏng: The Autobiographical Writings of a Crown Princess of Eighteenth-Century Korea* (Berkeley: University of California Press, 1996), 6–10.

18. Jane Portal, *Korea: Art and Archaeology* (London: British Museum, 2000), 143.

19. Marshall R. Pihl, "*P'ansori*: The Korean Oral Narrative," *Korean Studies* 5 (1981): 43–62.

20. Choe Yong-ho, "An Outline History of Korean Historiography," *Korean Studies* 4 (1989): 1–27.

21. Mark Setton, *Chŏng Yagyong: Korea's Challenge to Orthodox Neo-Confucianism* (Albany: State University of New York Press, 1997), 128–29.

22. Kim Dong Uk, "The City Architecture of Seoul," *Korea Journal* 34, no. 3 (Autumn 1994): 54–68.

23. Hochul Lee, "Agriculture as a Generator of Change in Late Chosŏn Korea," in *The Last Stand of Asian Autonomies: Responses to Modernity in the Diverse States*

of Southeast Asia and Korea, 1750–1900, ed. Anthony Reid (New York: St. Martin's Press, 1997), 122.

24. William Shaw, *Legal Norms in a Confucian State* (Berkeley: Institute of East Asian Studies, University of California, Center for Korean Studies, 1981), 81–85.

25. Andrew Pratt, "Change and Continuity in Chosŏn Military Techniques during the Later Chosŏn Period," *Papers of the British Association for Korean Studies* 7 (2000): 31–48.

26. Anders Karlsson, "Challenging the Dynasty: Popular Protest, *Chŏnggamnok* and the Ideology of the Hong Kyongnae Rebellion," *International Journal of Korean History* 2 (2001): 255–77.

27. Tony Michell, "Fact and Hypothesis in Yi Dynasty Economic History: The Demographic Dimension," *Korean Studies Forum*, no. 6 (Winter–Spring 1979–1980): 65–93.

28. Donald Baker, "Sirhak Medicine: Measles, Smallpox, and Chang Tasan," *Korean Studies* 14 (1990): 135–66.

29. Park, Ki-Joo and Donghyu Yang. "The Standard of Living in the Choson Dynasty Korea in the 17th to the 19th Centuries," *Seoul Journal of Economics* 20, no. 3 (Fall 2007): 297–332.

30. Ch'oe Wan-su, "A Study of Kim Chŏng-hŭi," *Korea Journal* 26, No. 11 (November 1986): 4–20.

31. Peter H. Lee and William Theodore De Bary, eds., *Sources of Korean Tradition*, vol. 1, *From Early Times through the Sixteenth Century* (New York: Columbia University Press, 1997), 312–17.

32. Lee and de Bary, *Sources of Korean Tradition*, vol. 1, 319–20.

CHAPTER 9 KOREA IN THE AGE OF IMPERIALISM, 1876 TO 1910

1. Donald Baker, "Cloudy Images: Korean Knowledge of the West from 1520–1800," *B.C. Asian Review* 3, no. 4 (1990): 51–73.

2. Yi Sŏngmi, "Western Influence on Korean Painting of the Late Chosŏn Period," in *Proceedings of the 1st World Congress of Korean Studies: Embracing the Other: The Interaction of Korean and Foreign Cultures*, The Academy of Korean Studies (Seoul: July 2002), 576–84.

3. Donald L. Baker, "Jesuit Science through Korean Eyes," *Journal of Korean Studies* 4 (1982–1983): 207–29, 213.

4. Baker, "Jesuit Science through Korean Eyes," 217.

5. Baker, "Cloudy Images," 68.

6. Gari Ledyard, *The Dutch Come to Korea* (Seoul: Royal Asiatic Society, 1971), 223.

7. Key-Hiuk Kim, *The Last Phase of the East Asian World Order* (Berkeley: University of California Press, 1980), 44–45.

8. Baker, "Cloudy Images," 63.

9. Key-Hiuk Kim, *The Last Phase of the East Asian World Order*, 56.

10. Ki-baik Lee, *A New History of Korea*, translated by Edward W. Wagner with Edward J. Shultz (Cambridge, MA: Harvard University Press, 1984), 266.

11. Martina Deuchler, *Confucian Gentlemen and Barbarian Envoys: The Opening of Korea, 1875–1885* (Seattle: University of Washington Press, 1977), 53.

12. Deuchler, *Confucian Gentlemen and Barbarian Envoys*, 141.

13. Deuchler, *Confucian Gentlemen and Barbarian Envoys*, 151.

14. Yong-ho Ch'oe, "The Kapsin Coup of 1884: A Reassessment," *Korean Studies* 6 (1982): 105–24.

15. Jerome Ch'en, *Yuan Shih-k'ai* (Stanford, CA: Stanford University Press, 1961), 33–34.

16. Young-ick Lew, "Yuan Shih-kai's Residency and the Korean Enlightenment Movement (1885–1894), *The Journal of Korean Studies* 5 (1984): 63–107.

17. Lew, "Yuan Shih-Kai's Residency," 63–107.

18. Andrew C. Nahm, *Korea: Tradition and Transformation* (Elizabeth, NJ: Hollym International, 1988), 173.

19. Kirk W. Larsen, "Trade, Dependency, and Colonialism: Foreign Trade and Korea's Regional Integration, 1876–1910," in *Korea at the Center: Dynamics of Regionalism in Northeast Asia*, ed. Charles K. Armstrong, Gilbert Rozman, Samuel S. Kim, and Stephen Kotlin (Armonk, NY: M.E. Sharpe, 2006), 51–60.

20. Susan Shin, "The Tonghak Movement: From Enlightenment to Revolution," *Korean Studies Forum* 5 (Winter–Spring 1978–1979): 1–79.

21. Nahm, *Korea: Tradition and Transformation*, 176.

22. Shin, "The Tonghak Movement," 51–52.

23. Carter J. Eckert, Ki-baik Lee, Young Ick Lew, Michael Robinson, and Edward W. Wagner, *Korea Old and New: A History* (Cambridge: Korea Institute, Harvard University, 1990), 243.

24. Hahm Chaibong, "Civilization, Race or Nation? Korean Visions of Regional Order in the Late Nineteenth Century," in Charles K. Armstrong, Samuel S. Kim, and Stephen Kotlin (eds.), *Korea at the Center: Dynamics of Regionalism in Northeast Asia* (Armonk, NY: M.E. Sharpe, 2006), 35–50.

25. Andre Schmid, *Korea between Empires, 1895–1919* (New York: Columbia University Press, 2002).

26. Gi-Wook Shin, *Ethnic Nationalism in Korea: Genealogy, Politics, and Legacy* (Stanford, CA: Stanford University Press, 2006).

27. Yŏng-ho Ch'oe, Peter H. Lee, and William Theodore de Bary, eds., *Sources of Korean Tradition*, volume 2, *From the Sixteenth to the Twentieth Centuries* (New York: Columbia University Press, 2000), 279–89.

28. Ch'oe, Lee, and de Bary, *Sources of Korean Tradition*, vol. 2, 312–13.

CHAPTER 10 COLONIAL KOREA, 1910 TO 1945

1. Adrian Buzo, *The Making of Modern Korea: A History* (London: Routledge, 2002), 20.

2. Bruce Cumings, *Origins of the Korean War*, vol. 1 (Princeton, NJ: Princeton University Press, 1981), 53–61; Carter J. Eckert, Ki-baik Lee, Young Ick Lew, Michael Robinson, and Edward W. Wagner, *Korea Old and New: A History* (Cambridge: Korea Institute, Harvard University, 1990), 259; Andrew J. Gradjanzev, *Modern Korea* (New York: Institute of Pacific Relations, 1944), 75–76.

3. Chen, Ching-chih, "Police and Community in Control System in the Empire," in *The Japanese Colonial Empire, 1895–1945*, ed. Ramon H. Myers and Mark R. Peattie (Princeton, NJ: Princeton University Press, 1984), 213–34.

4. Kenneth M. Wells, *New God, New Nation: Protestants and Self-Reconstruction Nationalism in Korea, 1896–1937* (Honolulu: University of Hawaii Press, 1990), 76.

5. Frank Baldwin, "Participatory Anti-Imperialism: The 1919 Independence Movement," *Journal of Korean Studies* 1, no. 1 (1979): 123–62.

6. Baldwin, "Participatory Anti-Imperialism," 135.

7. Gradjanzev, *Modern Korea*, 55–56.

8. Michael Robinson, *Cultural Nationalism in Colonial Korea, 1920–1925* (Seattle: University of Washington Press, 1988), 64–65.

9. Robinson, *Cultural Nationalism in Colonial Korea*, 100.

10. Lee, Chong-sik, *The Korean Workers' Party: A Short History* (Stanford, CA: Stanford University, Hoover Institution Press, 1978), 3-4.

11. Lee, Chong-sik, *The Korean Workers' Party*, 19.

12. Lee, Chong-sik, *The Korean Workers' Party*, 28–29.

13. Andrew C. Nahm, *Korea: Tradition and Transformation* (Elizabeth, NJ: Hollym International, 1988), 286–88.

14. Kim Ch'ang-su, "How the Shin'ganhoe Society Came to Be Dissolved," *Korea Journal* 27, no. 9 (September 1987): 23–33.

15. Carter J. Eckert, *Offspring of Empire: The Koch'ang Kims and the Origins of Korean Capitalism* (Seattle: University of Washington Press, 1991), 29.

16. Dennis L. McNamara, "The Keishō and the Korean Business Elite," *Journal of Asian Studies* 48, no. 2 (May 1989): 310–23.

17. Gradjanzev, *Modern Korea*, 185–86.

18. Bruce Cumings, *Korea's Place in the Sun: A Modern History* (New York: W.W. Norton, 1997), 166.

19. Government-General of Chosŏn, *Annual Report on Reforms and Progress in Chosŏn 1910–1911* (Keijö [Seoul]: Sötokufu, 1911), 201.

20. Soon-won Park, "Colonial Industrial Growth and the Emergence of the Korean Working Class," in *Colonial Modernity in Korea*, ed. Gi-wook Shin and Michael Robinson (Cambridge, MA: Harvard University Press, 1999), 128–60, 133.

21. Soon-won Park, "Colonial Industrial Growth," 135–41.

22. Soon-won Park, "Colonial Industrial Growth," 155–57.

23. Kenneth M. Wells, "The Price of Legitimacy: Women and the Kŭnuhoe Movement, 1927–1931," in *Colonial Modernity in Korea*, ed. Gi-wook Shin and Michael Robinson (Cambridge, MA: Harvard University Press, 1999), 191–220, 198–99.

24. Theodore Jun Yoo, *The Politics of Gender in Colonial Korea: Education, Labor, and Health, 1910–1945* (Berkeley: University of California Press, 2008), 192–94, 202–4.

25. Wells, "The Price of Legitimacy," 200–207.

26. Joong-Seop Kim, "In Search of Human Rights: The Paekchŏng Movement in Colonial Korea," in *Colonial Modernity in Korea*, ed. Gi-wook Shin and Michael Robinson, (Cambridge, MA: Harvard University Press, 1999): 311–35.

27. Cumings, *Origins of the Korean War*, vol. 1., 46.

28. Gradjanzev, *Modern Korea*, 295.

29. Gi-wook Shin and Do-Hyun Han, "Colonial Corporatism: The Rural Revitalization Campaign, 1932–1940," in *Colonial Modernity in Korea*, ed. Gi-wook Shin and Michael Robinson (Cambridge, MA: Harvard University Press, 1999), 70–96, 78.

30. Gi-wook Shin, *Peasant Protest and Social Change in Colonial Korea* (Seattle: University of Washington Press, 1996), 174–89.

31. Shin and Han, "Colonial Corporatism," 70–96.

32. Nahm, *Korea: Tradition and Transformation*, 233.

33. Michael J. Seth, *Education Fever* (Honolulu: University of Hawaii Press, 2002), 27.

34. George Hicks, *The Comfort Women: Japan's Brutal Regime of Enforced Prostitution in the Second World War* (New York: W.W. Norton & Company), 12–15.

35. Cumings, *Korea's Place in the Sun*, 183.

36. Nahm, *Korea: Tradition and Transformation*, 231.

37. Gradjanzev, *Modern Korea*, 269.

38. Nahm, *Korea: Tradition and Transformation*, 324.

39. Cumings, *Origins of the Korean War*, vol. 1, 53–61.

40. Cumings, *Korea's Place in the Sun*, 177.

41. Cumings, *Origins of the Korean War*, vol. 1, 53–61.

42. Peter H. Lee, ed., *Sourcebook of Korean Civilization*, vol. 2, *From the Seventeenth Century to the Modern Period* (New York: Columbia University Press, 1996), 432–34.

CHAPTER 11 DIVISION AND WAR, 1945 TO 1953

1. Soo Sung Cho, *Korea in World Politics: 1940–1950* (Berkeley: University of California Press, 1967), 16.

2. Cho, *Korea in World Politics*, 19.

3. Cho, *Korea in World Politics*, 22.

4. Jongsoo Lee, *The Partition of Korea after World War II: A Global History* (New York: Palgrave Macmillan, 2006), 38.

5. Jongsoo Lee, *The Partition of Korea after World War II*, 40–42.

6. Gregory Henderson, *Korea, the Politics of the Vortex* (Cambridge, MA: Harvard University Press, 1968), 114–15.

7. See Jongsoo Lee, *The Partition of Korea after World War II*.

8. Charles K. Armstrong, *The North Korean Revolution, 1945–1950* (Ithaca, NY: Cornell University Press, 2003), 71–74.

9. Andrew C. Nahm, *Korea: Tradition and Transformation* (Elizabeth, NJ: Hollym International, 1988), 353.

10. Cho, *Korea in World Politics*, 220.

11. Bruce Cumings, *Origins of the Korean War*, vol. 1 (Princeton, NJ: Princeton University Press, 1981), 38.

12. Cumings, *Origins of the Korean War*, vol. 1, 506.

13. George McCune and Arthur L. Grey, *Korea Today* (Cambridge, MA: Harvard University Press, 1950), 243.

14. Adrian Buzo, *The Making of Modern Korea: A History* (London: Routledge, 2002), 77.

15. Bruce Cumings, *Korea's Place in the Sun: A Modern History* (New York: W.W. Norton, 1997), 239.

16. Cumings, *Korea's Place in the Sun*, 265.

17. Cumings, *Korea's Place in the Sun*, 276.

18. Jian Chen, *China's Road to the Korean War: The Making of the Sino-American Confrontation* (New York: Columbia University Press, 1994), 212–15.

19. Richard Peters and Xiaobing Li, *Voices from the Korean War: Personal Stories of American, Korean and Chinese Soldiers* (Lexington: University Press of Kentucky, 2004), 185–98.

20. Shu Guang Zhang, *Mao's Military Romanticism: China and the Korean War, 1950–1953* (Lawrence: University Press of Kansas, 1995), 247.

21. Chalmers Johnson, *MITI and the Japanese Miracle: The Growth of Industrial Policy, 1925–1975* (Stanford, CA: Stanford University Press, 1982), 227.

22. John Dower, *Embracing Defeat: Japan in the Wake of World War II* (New York: W.W. Norton and Company, 1999), 542–43.

23. Roger Dingman, "The Dagger and the Gift: The Impact of the Korean War on Japan," *The Journal of American-East Asian Relations* 2, no. 1 (Spring 1993): 43.

24. John Dower, *Empire and Aftermath: Yoshida Shigeru and the Japanese Experience, 1878–1954* (Cambridge, MA: Harvard University Press, 1979), 316.

25. Armstrong, *The North Korean Revolution*, 252–53.

CHAPTER 12 NORTH KOREA: RECOVERY, TRANSFORMATION, AND DECLINE, 1953 TO 1993

1. Bruce Cumings, *The Origins of the Korean War*, vol. 2, *The Roaring of the Cataract, 1947–1950* (Princeton, NJ: Princeton University Press, 1990), 753.

2. B. C. Koh, "The War's Impact on the Korean Peninsula," *The Journal of American-East Asian Relations* 2, no.1 (1993): 57–76, 57–58. Estimates of casualties vary.

3. Hy-Sang Lee, *North Korea: A Strange Socialist Fortress* (Westport, CT: Praeger, 2001), 24.

4. Stephen Kotlin and Charles K. Armstrong, "A Socialist Regional Order in Northeast Asia after World War II," in *Korea at the Center: Dynamics of Regionalism in Northeast Asia*, ed. Charles K. Armstrong, K. Gilbert Rozman, Samuel S. Kim, and Stephen Kotlin (Armonk, NY: M.E. Sharpe, 2006), 110–25.

5. Kotlin and Armstrong, "A Socialist Regional Order in Northeast Asia after World War II," 121.

6. Stephan Haggard and Marcus Noland, *Famine in North Korea: Markets, Aid, and Reform* (New York: Columbia University Press, 2007).

7. Kongdan Oh and Ralph C. Hassig, *North Korea: Through the Looking Glass* (Washington, DC: Brookings Institution Press, 2000), 37–38.

8. Koh, "The War's Impact on the Korean Peninsula," 68.

9. Helen-Louise Hunter, *Kim Il-song's North Korea* (Westport, CT: Praeger, 1999).

10. James F. Person, *"We Need Help from Outside": The North Korean Opposition Movement of 1956* (Washington, DC: Woodrow Wilson Center, Cold War History Project, August, 2006).

11. Dae-sook Suh, *Kim Il Sung: A Biography* (Honolulu: University of Hawaii Press, 1989), 171.

12. Adrian Buzo, *Guerilla Dynasty: Politics and Leadership in North Korea* (Boulder, CO: Westview), 84.

13. Adrian Buzo, *The Making of Modern Korea* (New York: Routledge, 2007), 146.

14. Andrei Lankov, *From Stalin to Kim Il Sung: The Formation of North Korea, 1945–1960* (New Brunswick, NJ: Rutgers University Press, 2002), 63.

15. Suh, *Kim Il Sung*, 146–47.

16. Lankov, *From Stalin to Kim Il Sung*, 65.

17. Lankov, *From Stalin to Kim Il Sung*, 66.

18. These ties are examined in detail in Chae-jin Lee, *China and Korea: Dynamic Relations* (Stanford, CA: Hoover Institution Press, 1996), 73–87.

19. Chae-jin Lee, *China and Korea*, 73.

20. Chae-jin Lee, *China and Korea*, 74–75.

21. Nicholas Eberstadt, *The End of North Korea* (Washington, DC: American Enterprise Institute Press, 1999), 6.

22. Hy-Sang Lee, *North Korea*, 54–55.

23. Oh and Hassig, *North Korea: Through the Looking Glass*, 108.

24. Hy-Sang Lee, *North Korea*, 85.

25. Joseph S. Bermudez, *Shield of the Great Leader: The Armed Forces of North Korea* (London: I.B. Taurus, 2001), 231.

26. Suh, *Kim Il Sung*, 313.

27. Oh and Hassig, *North Korea*, 19.

28. Charles Armstrong, "A Socialism of Our Type: North Korean Communism in a Post-Communist Era," in Samuel S. Kim (ed.), *North Korean Foreign Relations in the Post–Cold War Era* (Oxford: Oxford University Press, 1998), 32–55, 33.

29. Han S. Park, *North Korea: The Politics of Unconventional Wisdom* (Boulder, CO: Lynne Rienner, 2002), 108.

30. Park, *North Korea*, 106–7.

31. Park, *North Korea*, 24.

32. Suh, *Kim Il Sung*, 322.

33. Joungwon Alexander Kim, *Divided Korea: The Politics of Development, 1945–1972* (Cambridge, MA: Harvard University Press, 1975), 320.

34. Suh, *Kim Il Sung*, 317.

35. Suh, *Kim Il Sung*, 321.

36. Hunter, *Kim Il-song's North Korea*, 16.

37. Bruce Cumings, *Korea's Place in the Sun: A Modern History* (New York: W.W. Norton, 1997), 411.

38. Park, *North Korea*, 43.

39. Oh and Hassig, *North Korea*, 25.

40. Andrei Lankov, *North of the Dmz: Essays on Daily Life in North Korea* (Jefferson, NC: McFarland & Company, 2007), 66–69.

41. See Brian Myers, *Han Sŏrya and North Korean Literature: The Failure of Socialist Realism in the DPRK* (Ithaca, NY: Cornell University Press, 1994).

42. Lankov, *From Stalin to Kim Il Sung*, 69; Oh and Hassig, *North Korea*, 108.

43. Haggard and Noland, *Famine in North Korea*, 26.

44. See Erik Cornell, *North Korea under Communism: Report of an Envoy to Paradise*, Rodney Bradbury, trans. (London: RoutledgeCurzon, 2002), 61–73, dealing with the smuggling crisis of 1976.

45. Harrison E. Salisbury, *To Peking — and Beyond: A Report on the New Asia* (New York: Quadrangle, 1973), 200.

46. Bradley Martin, *Under the Loving Care of the Fatherly Leader: North Korea and the Kim Dynasty* (New York: St Martin's Press, 2006), 164.

47. Hy-Sang Lee, *North Korea*. As stated in the book's subtitle: *A Strange Socialist Fortress*.

48. Kim Il Sung, *Revolution and Socialist Construction in Korea: Selected Writings* (New York: International Publishers, 1971), 30, 42–44.

49. Kim Il Sung, *Revolution and Socialist Construction in Korea*, 99–103.

CHAPTER 13 SOUTH KOREA:
FROM POVERTY TO PROSPERITY, 1953 TO 1997

1. A. M. Rosenthal, "Outlook Dreary for South Korea: Crowded Nation Has Few Resources—Long Reliance on U.S. Held Inevitable," *New York Times*, March 21, 1961.

2. Joungwon Alexander Kim, *Divided Korea: The Politics of Development, 1945–1972* (Cambridge, MA: Harvard University Press, 1975), 157.

3. Han Sung-joo, *The Failure of Democracy in South Korea* (Berkeley: University of California Press, 1974), 169.

4. Joungwon Kim, *Divided Korea*, 229.

5. Joungwon Kim, *Divided Korea*, 233.

6. Gregg Brazinsky, *Nation Building in South Korea: Koreans, Americans, and the Making of Democracy* (Chapel Hill: University of North Carolina Press, 2007), 103–4.

7. Cho Jae Hong, "Post-1945 Land Reforms and Their Consequences in South Korea," PhD dissertation, Indiana University, 1964.

8. John Lie, *Han Unbound: The Political Economy of South Korea* (Stanford, CA: Stanford University Press, 1998), 9–18.

9. Laura C. Nelson, *Measured Excess: Status, Gender, and Consumer Nationalism in South Korea* (New York: Columbia University Press, 2000), 11.

10. Park Chung Hee, *The Country, The Revolution and I* (Seoul: Hollym Corporation, 1970), 17–120.

11. Eun Mee Kim, *Big Business, Strong State: Collusion and Conflict in South Korean Development, 1960–1990* (Albany: State University of New York Press, 1997), 103.

12. Park, *The Country, The Revolution and I*, 28.

13. Hyung-A Kim, *Korea's Development under Park Chung Hee: Rapid Industrialization, 1961–79* (London: RoutledgeCurzon, 2004), 111.

14. Hyung-A Kim, *Korea's Development under Park Chung Hee*, 81–87.

15. Hyung-A Kim, *Korea's Development under Park Chung Hee*, 87.

16. Jung-en Woo, *Race to the Swift: State and Finance in the Industrialization of Korea* (New York: Columbia University Press, 1991), 84.

17. Eun Mee Kim, *Big Business, Strong State*, 105.

18. Lie, *Han Unbound*, 73.

19. Stewart Lone and Gavan McCormack, *Korea Since 1850* (New York: St Martin's Press, 1993), 147.

20. Lone and McCormack, *Korea Since 1850*, 148.

21. Woo, *Race to the Swift*, 132.

22. Linsu Kim, *Imitation to Innovation: The Dynamics of Korea's Technological Learning* (Boston: Harvard Business School Press, 1997), 48.

23. Linsu Kim, *Imitation to Innovation*, 32.

24. Woo, *Race to the Swift*, 128–29; Eun Mee Kim, *Big Business, Strong State*, 51.

25. Chan Sup Chang and Nahm Joo Chang, *The Korean Managerial System* (Westport, CT: Quorum Books, 1994), 40.

26. Chang and Chang, *The Korean Managerial System*, 40.

27. Eun Mee Kim, *Big Business, Strong State*, 114.

28. Lone and McCormack, *Korea Since 1850*, 150.

29. Seungsook Moon, *Militarized Modernity and Gendering Citizenship in South Korea* (Durham, NC: Duke University Press, 2005), 84–85.

30. Woo, *Race to the Swift*, 45

31. Lie, *Han Unbound*, 66–67.

32. Lie, *Han Unbound*, 56.

33. See Alice Amsden, *Asia's Next Giant: South Korea and Late Industrialization* (London: Oxford University Press, 1989); Stephan Haggard and Chung-in Moon, "Institutions and Economic Policy: Theory and a Korean Case Study," *World Politics* 17, no. 2 (January 1990): 210–37; Chalmers Johnson, "Political Institutions and Economic Performance: The Government-Business Relationship in Japan, South Korea, and Taiwan," in *The Political Economy of the New Asian Industrialism*, ed. Frederic C. Deyo (Ithaca, NY: Cornell University Press, 1987), 136–64; Edward S. Mason et al., *The Economic Social Modernization of the Republic of Korea* (Cambridge, MA: Harvard University Press, 1980).

34. Michael J. Seth, "Strong State or Strong Society?" *Korean Studies* 21 (1997).

35. Park, *The Country, the Revolution and I*, 25–29.

CHAPTER 14 SOUTH KOREA: CREATING A DEMOCRATIC SOCIETY, 1953 TO 1997

1. Hyung Gu Lynn, *Bipolar Orders: The Two Koreas Since 1989* (Halifax, NS: Fenwood, 2007), 29.

2. Joungwon Alexander Kim, *Divided Korea: The Politics of Development, 1945–1972* (Cambridge, MA: Harvard University Press, 1975), 233.

3. Sunhyuk Kim, *The Politics of Democratization in Korea: The Role of Civil Society* (Pittsburgh: University of Pittsburgh Press, 2000), 59.

4. Adrian Buzo, *The Making of Modern Korea* (New York: Routledge, 2007), 162.

5. Hong Yung Lee, "South Korea in 1991: Unprecedented Challenge, Increasing Opportunity," *Asian Survey* 32, no. 1: 64–73.

6. Doh C. Shin, *Mass Politics and Culture in Democratizing Korea* (New York: Cambridge University Press, 1999); Geir Helgesen, *Democracy and Authority in Korea: The Cultural Dimension in Korean Politics* (New York: St Martin's Press, 1998).

7. Laura C. Nelson, *Measured Excess: Status, Gender, and Consumer Nationalism in South Korea* (New York: Columbia University Press, 2000), 20.

8. Nelson, *Measured Excess*, 15.

9. Gregg Brazinsky, *Nation Building in South Korea: Koreans, Americans, and the Making of Democracy* (Chapel Hill: University of North Carolina Press, 2007).

10. Brazinsky, *Nation Building in South Korea*, 59–62.

11. Chae-Jin Lee, "South Korea in 1983: Crisis Management and Political Legitimacy," *Asian Survey* 24, no. 1: 112–21.

12. Stewart Lone and Gavan McCormack, *Korea Since 1850* (New York: St Martin's Press, 1993), 161.

13. Hagen Koo, *Korean Workers: The Culture and Pattern of Class Formation* (Ithaca, NY: Cornell University Press, 2001), 26.

14. Koo, *Korean Workers*, 29.

15. George E. Ogle, *South Korea: Dissent within the Economic Miracle* (London: Zed Books, 1990), 62.

16. Koo, *Korean Workers*, 48–49.

17. Koo, *Korean Workers*, 55.

18. Ogle, *South Korea: Dissent within the Economic Miracle*, 23.

19. Koo, *Korean Workers*, 15.

20. Koo, *Korean Workers*, 71–73.

21. Ogle, *South Korea: Dissent within the Economic Miracle*, 88.

22. Ogle, *South Korea: Dissent within the Economic Miracle*, 88.

23. Koo, *Korean Workers*, 159.

24. Ki-young Shin, "The Politics of the Family Law Reform Movement in Contemporary Korea: A Contentious Space for Gender and the Nation," *The Journal of Korean Studies* 11 (Fall 2006): 93–126.

25. Shin, "The Politics of the Family Law Reform Movement," 104.

26. John Lie, *Han Unbound: The Political Economy of South Korea* (Stanford, CA: Stanford University Press, 1998), 161.

27. Keith Pratt, *Everlasting Flower: A History of Korea* (London: Reaktion Books, 2006), 258.

28. Chiha Kim, *Heart's Agony: Selected Poems*, Won-Chung Kim and James Han, translators, (Fredonia, NY: White Pine Press, 1998), 103–4.

CHAPTER 15 CONTEMPORARY NORTH KOREA, 1993 TO 2010

1. Hyung Gu Lynn, *Bipolar Orders: The Two Koreas Since 1989* (Halifax, NS: Fenwood, 2007), 108.

2. Charles Armstrong, "A Socialism of Our Type: North Korean Communism in a Post-Communist Era," in *North Korean Foreign Relations in the Post–Cold War Era*, ed. Samuel S. Kim (Oxford: Oxford University Press, 1998), 32–55, 36.

3. Gi-Wook Shin, *Ethnic Nationalism in Korea: Genealogy, Politics, and Legacy* (Stanford, CA: Stanford University Press, 2006), 93.

4. "Tan'gun Remains Reportedly Found," *Korea Newsreview*, October 16, 1993, 30–31.

5. "Pyongyang—Capital of the Korean Nation," *Korea Today*, no. 2 (1995), 43–45.

6. Korean Central News Agency, broadcast March 13, 1998, *BBC Worldwide Monitoring*, March 14, 1998.

7. "North Korea Decries South Korea's Response to Satellite Launch," *BBC Monitoring Asia Pacific*, September 11, 1998.

8. "Progenitor Abused in Both Koreas," *Korea Herald*, October 3, 2000.

9. Brian Myers, *The Cleanest Race: How North Koreans See Themselves—and Why It Matters* (Brooklyn, NY: Melville House, 2010).

10. Adrian Buzo, *The Making of Modern Korea* (New York: Routledge, 2007), 175.

11. Kongdan Oh and Ralph C. Hassig, *North Korea: Through the Looking Glass* (Washington, DC: Brookings Institution Press, 2000), 52.

12. Andrew S. Natsios, *The Great North Korean Famine* (Washington, DC: United States Institute of Peace Press, 2001), 12.

13. Han S. Park, *North Korea: The Politics of Unconventional Wisdom* (Boulder, CO: Lynne Rienner, 2002), 93.

14. See L. Gordon Flake and Scott Snyder, eds., *Paved with Good Intentions: The NGO Experience in North Korea* (Westport, CT: Praeger, 2004).

15. John Feffer, "North Korea and the International Politics of Famine," *Japan Focus* (October 2006).

16. Marcus Noland, "Famine and Reforms in North Korea," Institute for International Economics, WP 03-5, July, 2003).

17. Buzo, *The Making of Modern Korea*, 176.

18. Samuel S. Kim, "North Korea in 2000: Surviving through High Hopes of Summit Diplomacy, *Asia Survey* 41, no. 1 (January/February, 2001): 12–29.

19. Yinchay Ahn, "North Korea in 2001: At a Crossroads," *Asia Survey* 42, no. 1 (January/February, 2002): 46–55.

20. Yinchay Ahn, "North Korea in 2002: A Survival Game," *Asia Survey* 43, no. 1 (January/February, 2003): 49–63.

21. Ruediger Frank, "Economic Reforms in North Korea (1998–2004): Systematic Restrictions, Quantitative Analysis, Ideological Background," *Journal of the Asia Pacific Economy* 10, no. 3 (August 2005): 278–311.

22. Kyung-ae Park, "North Korea in 2003: Pendulum Swing between Crisis and Diplomacy," *Asia Survey* 44, no. 1 (January/February, 2004): 139–46.

23. Meredith Jung-en Woo, "North Korea in 2005: Maximizing Profit to Save Socialism," *Asia Survey* 46, no. 1 (January/February, 2006): 49–55.

24. Jung-en Woo, "North Korea in 2005," 52.

25. Feffer, "North Korea and the International Politics of Famine."

26. Feffer, "North Korea and the International Politics of Famine."

27. Kathleen Davis, "Brides, Bruises and the Border: The Trafficking of North Korean Women into China," *SAIS Review* 26, no. 1 (Winter-Spring 2006): 13–41.

28. Yinchay Ahn, "North Korea in 2002: A Survival Game," *Asia Survey* 43, no. 1 (January/February, 2003): 49–63, 55.

29. Kyung-ae Park, "North Korea in 2003: Pendulum Swing between Crisis and Diplomacy," *Asia Survey* 44, no. 1 (January/February, 2004): 139–46.

30. Stephan Haggard and Marcus Noland, "North Korea 2007: Shuffling in from the Cold," *Asian Survey* 48, no. 1 (January/February 2008): 107–15.

31. U.S. Department of State, *Country Reports on Human Rights Practices: Democratic Republic of Korea* (Washington, DC: U.S. Department of State, February 25), 205; see also Kang Chol-Hwan, and Pierre Rigoulot, *The Aquariums of Pyongyang: Ten Years in the North Korean Gulag*, Yair Reiner, trans. (New York: Basic Books, 2001).

32. Yoonok Chang, Stephan M. Haggard, and Marcus Noland, "Exit Polls: Refugee Assessments of North Korea's Transition" (Working Paper No. 08-1, Peterson Institute for International Economics, Washington, DC, January 2008).

33. Blaine Harden, "At the Heart of North Korea's Trouble, an Intractable Hunger Crisis," *Washington Post*, March 6, 2009.

34. Democratic People's Republic of Korea, *Biography of Kim Jong Il* (Pyongyang: Foreign Languages Publishing House, 1998).

35. Kang, Hyok, with Philippe Grangereau and Shaun Whiteside (translator), *This Is Paradise! My North Korean Childhood* (London: Little, Brown, 2007), 121–25.

CHAPTER 16 CONTEMPORARY SOUTH KOREA, 1997 TO 2010

1. Chong-Sik Lee and Hyuk-sang Sohn, "South Korea in 1993: The Year of Great Reform, *Asia Survey* 34, no. 1 (January/February, 1994): 1–9.

2. Young Whan Kihl, *Transforming Korean Politics: Democracy, Reform, and Culture* (Armonk, NY: M.E. Sharpe, 2005), 120.

3. B. C. Koh, "South Korea in 1995: Tremors of Transition," *Asia Survey* 36, no. 1 (January/February, 1996): 53–60.

4. B. C. Koh, "South Korea in 1996: Internal Strains and External Challenges," *Asia Survey* 37, no. 1 (January/February, 1997): 1–9.

5. Tong Whan Park, "South Korea in 1998: Swallowing the Bitter Pills of Restructuring," *Asia Survey* 39, no. 1 (January/February, 1999): 133–39.

6. Yong-Chool Ha, "South Korea in 2001: Frustration and Continuing Uncertainty," *Asia Survey* 42, no. 1 (January/February, 2002): 56–66.

7. "Joong Ang Ilbo Chief Questioned," *Korea Herald*, March 5, 2008.

8. "Lee Hit over Grand Daughter's U.S. Birth," *Korea Times*, July 25, 2002.

9. Hong Yung Lee, "South Korea in 2003: A Question of Leadership?" *Asia Survey* 44, no. 1 (January/February, 2004): 130–38.

10. John Lie and Myoungkyu Park, "South Korea in 2005: Economic Dynamism, Generational Conflicts, and Social Transformations," *Asia Survey* 46, no. 1 (January/February, 2006): 56–62.

11. "Roh Urges Newspapers to Be More Responsible," *Korea Times*, May 31, 2005.

12. John Lie and Andrew Eungi Kim, "South Korea in 2008: Scandals and Summits," *Asian Survey* 48, no. 1 (January/February 2008): 116–23.

13. Hyung Gu Lynn, *Bipolar Orders: The Two Koreas Since 1989* (Halifax, NS: Fenwood, 2007), 47.

14. Sunhyuk Kim, "Civil Society in Democratizing Korea," in *Korea's Democratization*, ed. Samuel S. Kim (Cambridge: Cambridge University Press, 2003), 81–106.

15. James A. Foley, "'Ten Million Families': Statistic or Metaphor?" *Korean Studies* 25, no. 1 (January 2001): 108.

16. Andrei Lankov, "The Legacy of Long-Gone States: China, Korea and the Koguryo," *Japan Focus*, October 2006.

17. "South Korea's Population to Shrink," *Korea Times*, January 20, 2009.

18. "Seoul to Raise Retirement Age," *Korea Times*, February 6, 2007.

19. Andrew Eungi Kim, "Demography, Migration and Multiculturalism in South Korea, *Japan Focus* (February 9, 2009).

20. "Study Finds Korean Students Best at Solving Problems," *Korea Herald*, December 8, 2004.

21. "Korea Suffers Greatest Education Deficit Among OECD Countries," *Korea Times*, February 7, 2005.

22. "Koreans Top Spenders in Education," *Korea Times*, January 15, 2005; "Rising Education Costs Put Greater Burdens on Families," *Korea Herald*, January 14, 2008.

23. "Roh's Aide Tried to Cover Up Diploma Forgery," *Korea Times*, August 24, 2007; John Lie and Andrew Eungi Kim, "South Korea in 2008: Scandals and Summits," *Asian Survey* 48, no. 1 (January/February 2008): 116–23.

24. Hyung Gu Lynn, *Bipolar Powers*, 70.

25. "A Social 'Time Bomb,' Behind Façade Income Inequality a Growing Problem," *Newsweek International*, January 23, 2006.

26. Hagen Koo, "The Changing Faces of Inequality in South Korea in the Age of Globalization," *Korea Studies* 31 (2007): 1–18, 4.

27. Young Soo Park, "Comparative Perspectives on the South Korean Welfare System," *Japan Focus*, May 5, 2008.

28. Moon, Katharine H. S., "South Korean Movements against Militarized Sexual Labor," *The Journal of Asian Studies* 39, no. 2: 473–500.

29. "Gender Gap Widens Over 50% at Large Firms," *Korea Herald*, September 21, 2005.

30. World Economic Forum, *The Global Competitiveness Report, 2007–08*, available at: www.weforum.org/en/initiatives/gcp/Global%20Competitiveness%20Report/index.htm (accessed October 6, 2008).

31. "South Korean Parliament Approves First Female PM," *Yonhap*, April 19, 2006.

32. "One in Three Korean Women Reject Motherhood," *Korea Herald*, March 23, 2006.

33. "Social Changes Lead to Various Types of Family," *Korea Times*, October 31, 2007.

34. Andrew Eungi Kim and John Lie, "South Korea in 2006: Nuclear Standoff, Trade Talks, and Population Trends," *Asia Survey* 47, no. 1 (January/February, 2007): 52–57.

35. Hagen Koo, "The Changing Faces of Inequality in South Korea in the Age of Globalization."

36. Kim Dae Jung, *Prison Writings*, Choi Sung-il and David R. McCann, translators (Berkeley: University of California Press, 1987), 4.

37. Kim Dae Jung, *Prison Writings*, 76–77.

38. Kim Dae Jung, *Prison Writings*, 79–84.

Glossary of Korean Words

ajŏn local officials, also called *sŏri*
amgŭl "female letters," another name for *han'gŭl* (see below)
amhŭkki "dark period" (of colonial rule)
anbang "inner room" (see *anch'ae*)
anch'ae the section of the house for women also called the *anbang*
bunka seiji "culture policy" (of colonial administration)
chaebŏl corporate conglomerate in South Korea
Chaech'u Privy Council in Koryŏ later called *Todang*
changgun general called
changja first son
chapkwa specialized technical exams
ch'arye holiday commemorations to ancestors
Charyŏk kaengsaeng "relying on own strength"
chesa rites to ancestors
chesul ŏp Composition Examination in Koryŏ
chikchŏn "office-field" allocated to officials
ch'ilgŏjiak "seven evils," legitimate grounds for divorcing a wife
Ch'ilsŏng Big Dipper, widely worshiped Korean spirit
ch'im acupuncture
ch'in Confucian principle of cordiality or closeness between parents and
   children
Ch'inaehan Chidoja "Dear Leader" (Kim Jong Il)
Chinbo-dang Progressive Party, another name for Kaehwa-dang
chin'gol true bone or true-bone, hereditary elite of Silla
chinsa literary exam in Chosŏn

Chiphyŏnjŏn Hall of Worthies
Chipsabu Chancellery Office during Silla period
chisa wandering geomancers
Chisin Earth God
cho "progenitor," used as an element in Korean royal names
choch'ŏn tribute missions to China also called *yŏnhaeng*
chok a large descent group in Silla
chokpo books kept by lineages where births, marriages, and deaths were recorded
Ch'ŏllima mythical flying horse, movement to speed up product in North Korea
ch'on villages
chondaeŏ or **chondaemal** Korean speech style for addressing superiors
chong "ancestor," used as an element in Korean royal names
Chŏngbang Personnel Authority political institution during military period of Koryŏ
chŏngbo unit of land (approximately 2.5 acres or one hectare)
chŏngbyŏng conscripts
chŏnghye ssangsu twofold training in quiescence [meditation] and activity
Ch'ŏngjegam Directorate of Sanitation
chŏngjŏnje "able-bodied land system"
ch'ŏn'gŏ recommendation system
ch'ŏnmin "base people"
ch'ŏnmyŏng Mandate of Heaven
chŏnsi palace exam
chŏnsi-kwa Field and Woodland, system during the Koryŏ by which officials received fixed incomes from certain lands
ch'ŏp commoner or slave concubine (also called a "secondary wife")
chosang ancestors or ancestral spirits
Chōsen Sōtokufu Government-General of colonial Korea
ch'osi preliminary exam
Chosŏn (Chinese: Chaoxian), lit. "Land of the Morning Calm," name of an early kingdom and of the Korean state from 1392–1910
Chosŏn Minjujuŭi Inmin Konghwaguk Democratic People's Republic of Korea (official name of North Korea since 1948)
Chowang Kitchen God, one of the Korean household gods
chuch'ae See **juche**
chuch'e sasang juche thought
ch'ŭgugi system of rain gauges
ch'ulga oein "one who left the household and became a stranger": term for daughter who left her natal home after her marriage

chŭlmun prehistoric comb-patterned Korean pottery, also known as *pitsal munŭi*

ch'ung loyalty

Chungbang Supreme Military Council

Ch'ungch'uwŏn Royal Secretariat in Koryŏ, later called the *Ch'umirwŏn*

chungin "middle men," a subelite class of technical specialists in Chosŏn

chungsi chief minister in Silla

Chungsŏ-Munhasŏng combined Secretariat-Chancellory in Koryŏ

Chungsŏsŏng Secretariat in Koryŏ

Hallyu (hanryu) "Korea Wave" the fad for Korean popular culture in Asia during the late 1990s and 2000s

han'gŭl the indigenous Korean alphabet (lit. "Korean writing")

hanmun Chinese characters, also called *hanja*

hanyak Chinese medicine

hojang local headmen

hop'ae identification system using special tags in Chosŏn

hunmin chŏngŭm "correct sounds for the instruction of the people," another term for the indigenous Korean alphabet (*han'gŭl*)

Hwabaek Council of Notables

hwan unit of currency (in South Korea)

hwan'gap sixtieth birthday celebration

Hwaŏm "Flower Garland," a school of Buddhism

hwarang lit. "flower boys," military bands of aristocratic youth that served as elite units in the Silla army

hwarangdo the way of the *hwarang*

hyangan local yangban rosters

hyangban rural yangban

Hyangch'ŏng Local Agency

hyangga a form of Korean-language poetry

hyanggyo state-sponsored local schools

hyangni the local hereditary elite in Koryŏ, local non-elite functionaries in Chosŏn period

hyangyak ŭisul medical prescriptions

hyo Confucian principle of filial piety

hyŏnhakkŭm "black crane zither," a modified Chinese seven-string instrument

i (Chinese: *li*), the patterning principle of the universe

idu or **kugyŏl** transcription system used to facilitate the reading of the Chinese classics

ilmyŏn kŏnsŏl, ilmyŏn kukpang "construction on the one hand, national defense on the other"

inmin wiwŏnhoe people's committees

isagŭm "successor princes," rulers of early Silla

iyong husaeng "enriching the well-being of the people by taking advantage of the useful"

juche (chuch'e) North Korean ideology based on the thought of Kim Il Sung, sometimes translated "self-reliance"

kadong house slaves

Kaehwa-dang Enlightenment Party

kaekchu wholesale merchants in Chosŏn, also called *yŏgak*

kammugwan a central government office that oversaw rural jurisdictions

kasa a genre of Korean poetry

kayagŭm a kind of zither

ki (Chinese: *qi*), the primal matter-energy of the universe

kije death anniversary commemorations

kijŏn format used in official histories

kimch'i pickled cabbages or other vegetables in garlic and fermented fish or shrimp seasoned with chili peppers

kinrōtai student labor groups

kisaeng female entertainers

kŏbuksŏn "turtle ship," early Korean iron-clad warship

kogok "curved jewel," stylized bear claws that served as signs of royal authority in Silla

kolp'um bone-rank system of Silla

kongan tribute ledgers

kongdori factory boy

kongin tribute men

kongjŏn public land

kongnobi government slaves

kongsuni factory girl

kosa offerings to household gods

Kosian, bi-ethnic child

Kōtō Keisatsu "high police"

kun-hyŏn prefecture-county, administrative unit under the Koryŏ

Kukhak National Academy

kuksok "national practice," term used to distinguish Korean from non-Korean customs

kun administrative subdivision of province often translated as county

kun (Chinese: jun) commandery in Chinese-ruled Korea

Kun'guk Kimuch'ŏ Deliberative Council

kusadae save our company group

kut Korean shamanist ceremony

kwagŏ civil service examinations

Kwanggun Resplendent Army

kwisin spirits

kye informal loan associations
Kyo Textual Buddhism
Kyojŏng Togam Office of Decree Enactment
Kyŏngguk Taejŏn official legal code dating from the fifteenth century
Kyŏngjaeso Capital Liaison Office
Kyŏngsigam Directorate of Capital Markets
Kyŏngyŏn Classics Mat
kyorin neighborly relations (Japanese term)
kyuban kasa or **naebang kasa** inner room *kasa*, women's writings about family life
kyunyŏkpŏp Equalized Service Law
mansin another term for shaman
maripkan a title for early Silla rulers
mimangin "a person who has not died yet," said of a widow
minhwa folk paintings
minjok people or nation
minjok chisang, kukka chisang "nation first, state first"
minjung "the masses" or "the people"
minmyŏnuri a girl bride
mip'ung yangsok "laudable customs and conduct"
mogok wastage charge, fees charged by state granaries
muban military officials
mudang shaman
muhak military schools
mukwa military exam
mumun plain pottery style of early Korea
munban civil officials
mun'gaek retainers
Munha-sijung supreme chancellor
Munhasŏng Chancellery
munjung descent groups
munkwa highest level of civil service examinations
Munmyo National Shrine to Confucius
myoje graveside commemorations to ancestors
myŏnggyŏng ŏp Classics Examination in Koryŏ
Namin "Southerners," political faction in Yi Korea
namjon yŏbi revere men, despise women
Nissen yūwa. "Harmony between Japan and Korea"
nogŭp stipend villages in Silla
nongjang landed estates
No (Roh) sa mo gathering of those people loving Roh
Noron Old Doctrine political faction in Yi Korea

nosukja unemployed, homeless workers

oegŏ nobi out-resident slaves

ondol style of heated floors in Korean houses

ŏnmun vernacular script (another term for the indigenous Korean alphabet, *han'gŭl*)

oryun the five ethical norms of Confucianism

Ŏsadae censorate in Koryŏ

Owi Toch'ongbu Five Military Commands Headquarters

paduk Korean name for the game of *go*, also used to designate a style of dolmen in early Korea.

p'aedo a suicide knife

paekchŏng outcaste group

paem sul snake wine

paem t'ang snake soup

pando lit. "half island," peninsula

pangnap (or *taenap*) tribute contracting

panmal Korean speech style for addressing inferiors

p'ansori distinctive Korean form of folk tales presented by a singer/dancer accompanied by a drummer

p'ansu blind exorcists

pap cooked rice

pinyŏ a long pin used by Korean women to tie hair

pobusang itinerant peddlers

pon'gwan ancestral-seat system established under the Koryŏ

Ponhyang Sansin Mountain God, one of the Korean household gods

Popŏp Paired Provisioner system

pot'ong saram "ordinary person"

pu rhyme-prose

Pugin "Northerners," political faction in Chosŏn

Pukhak Northern Learning term for late Chosŏn reform minded writers

pulch'ŏnjiwi "never removed tablets" containing names of ancestors

Pulgŭn Ch'ŏngnyŏn Kŭnwidae Young Red Guards

Pumaguk "Son-in-law Nation," term used for Korea during Mongol period

p'umassi-ban mutual aid teams (North Korea)

punch'ŏng predominant ceramic ware from the 1390s to the 1590s

p'ungsu geomancy

pyŏl distinction between husbands and wives

Pyŏlmuban special military force developed to defend Korea against invading Jurchen

p'yŏngin "good people" or socially respectable people

p'yŏnnyŏn annalistic format

Pyŏnso Kakssi Toilet Maiden, one of the Korean household gods

sach'ang village granary system

sadaebu derived from the Chinese term *shidafu*, meaning scholar-official

sadaejuŭi "flunkyism" or the blind subservience to a great power

Saemaŭl new village

saenae-mu mask dances in Silla

saengwŏn classics exam in Chosŏn

Saeng yuksin Six Ministers Who Lived

Saganwŏn Censor-General

Sahŏnbu Office of Inspector-General

Sajŏn "private land"

sama lower-level civil service examinations

Sambyŏlch'o Three Elite Patrols

samgang "three cords" or basic principles of Confucianism

Samsa "three institutions," the censorate organs in Chosŏn

Samsin Halmŏni Birth Grandmother, one of the Korean household gods

Samsŏng Three Chancelleries term for the three highest administrative organs in Koryŏ

sang changgun grand general, top military post in Koryŏ

sangdaedŭng the chief of the *Hwabaek*

Sangp'yŏngch'ang "Ever-Normal Granaries"

Sangsŏsŏng Secretariat for State Affairs in Koryo

sangsuri Silla system of having non-Sillan tributaries send hostages to serve at court in rotation

sanobi private slaves

Sansin the Mountain Spirit

sarang ch'ae the section of the house for men

sasaek four colors, another term for the major political factions in Chosŏn

sasŏl sijo later expanded form of *sijo*

Sa yuksin Six Martyrs

sedo chŏngch'i "in-law government," term used for nineteenth domination of court politics by royal consort families

Seimu Sōkan Director-General of Administration

Sibi to Twelve Assemblies, private schools that trained young men for civil service examinations in Koryŏ

sigŭp tax villages in Silla

sijo a "short, suggestive poem" consisting of three lines, each with fifteen syllables

sijŏn licensed shops

Sillok Veritable Records, the official history of the reign of a Korean king

sin Confucian principle of trust between friends

Sinŭigun Army of Transcendent Righteousness

sip chŏng ten garrisons

Sirhak "Practical Learning," modern term for reform minded scholars in late Chosŏn

sŏ Confucian principle of order between elders and juniors
Sŏbang Household Secretariat
sŏdang oath banner Silla military units, see also *sŏjae*
sŏdang village schools (written differently in Chinese characters)
Sŏhak "Western Learning," Korean term for Christianity
Sŏin "Westerners," political faction in Yi Korea
sŏja sons born to a *ch'ŏp* (see above)
sŏjae or **sŏdang** village schools
sok subordinate prefectures in Koryŏ
solgŏ nobi household slaves
Sŏn meditative Buddhism (Japanese: Zen)
sŏngbun grades in which society is divided (North Korea)
sŏnggol hallowed bone or sacred bone, ruling elite of early Korea
Sŏnggyun'gwan National Confucian Academy
Sŏnghwang a local guardian god
sŏngju castle or walled-town lord
Sŏngju House Lord, one of the Korean household gods
sŏŏl children born to ch'ŏp
sŏri local functionaries performing clerical duties
Soron Young Doctrine, political faction in Yi Korea
sŏsa general supervisory authority possessed by Censorate
Sōtoku Governor-General (of colonial Korea)
sŏwŏn private academies in Chosŏn
ssirŭm Korean-style wrestling
Sumun Door Guard, one of the Korean household gods
Sŭngjŏngwŏn Royal Secretariat in Chosŏn
taedongpŏp tribute replacement tax
Taehan Cheguk Empire of Korea
Taehan Min'guk Republic of Korea (Official name of South Korea since 1948)
taekwa refers to both the *munkwa* or *mukwa* exams
T'aep'o Festival of Wine
t'akcha "table" style of dolmens in early Korea
tanballyŏng order to cut off topknots
Tang Chungang Party Center
tan'ga "short song," another word for *sijo*
tangsanggwan those of senior third rank and above
tan'o chŏmsu sudden enlightenment and gradual cultivation taught by Chinul
tchok long, braided hair worn by women
teril-sawi boy child grooms
todungnyŏ "robber woman," said of a daughter
Tohwasŏ Bureau of Painting

T'ŏju Taegam Site Official, one of the Korean household gods

tōkan resident-general

t'ongch'i chagŭm "governing fund'

Tonghak "Eastern Learning," nineteenth-century religious movement

Tongin "Easterners," political faction in Chosŏn

T'ongni Kimu Amun Office for the Management of State Affairs

tongnyŏnhoe classmate organizations

toryŏng military commander

ttŭm moxibustion

tup'um head-ranks, a heredity status system of Silla

ŭi righteousness and justice

ŭibyŏng "righteous armies," resistance bands during the Japanese invasions of Korea

Ŭigŭmbu State Tribunal

Ŭihŭng Samgunbu Three Armies Headquarters

Ŭijŏngbu State Council of Chosŏn

ŭm privilege by which close male relatives of high ranking officials received appointments

Waegu term for Japanese pirates

wang Korean term for king

Widaehan Chidoja "Great Leader" (used for Kim Jong Il)

Widaehan Ryŏngdoja "Great Leader" (term used for Kim Jong Il)

Widaehan Suryŏngnim "Great Leader" (Kim Il Sung)

wŏn unit of currency

wŏnhwa lit. "original flowers," female leaders of the *hwarang*

yangban lit. "two sides," the aristocratic elite of Korea

yangin "good people," not slaves or outcastes

Yemun'gwan Office of Royal Decrees

yŏl Confucian principle of distinction between men and women

yŏmbul recitation of the name of Buddha

yŏnhaeng mission to Beijing

Yugyŏng Kongwŏn Royal College

yuhak student status that included exemption from military duty and eligibility for taking the civil service exams

yuil people of merit and integrity, civil service appointees through recommendation system

Yukcho Six Ministries

Yukpu Six Ministries

yuktu-p'um head-rank six, highest of the head-ranks of Silla

Yurang chisigin wandering scholars

yusin "revitalization"

yut popular game played with wooden sticks

zaibatsu Japanese industrial-financial conglomerates

Annotated Selected Bibliography

PREMODERN KOREA

Barnes, Gina L. *State Formation in Korea: Historical Archaeological Perspectives*. Richmond, Surrey: Curzon Press, 2001.

A summary of archaeological and historical scholarship on the early states in Korea from Old Chosŏn through the Three Kingdoms period. More for the serious student of early Korea than the general reader.

Best, Johnathan W. *A History of the Early Korean Kingdom of Paekche*. Cambridge, MA: Harvard East Asia Center, 2006.

Written for the serious scholar of Korea and early East Asia, the work contains annotated translations of *The Paekche Annals* in the *Samguk sagi*.

Bishop, Isabella Bird. *Korea and Her Neighbors*. New York: Fleming H. Revell, 1897.

The intelligent observations of the wife of a late nineteenth-century British diplomat, entertaining but also useful for her insights into Korea in the last days of the old order.

Buswell, Robert E. Jr. *Tracing Back the Radiance: Chinul's Korean Way of Zen*. Honolulu: University of Hawaii Press, 1991.

Translations and analysis of the writings of the important Koryŏ Buddhist monk. Contains a lengthy introduction to Chinul's life and thought as well as background information on Buddhism in premodern Korea. Aimed at a fairly high scholarly level.

Buzo, Adrian, and Tony Prince, trans. *Kyunyo-Jon: The Life, Times and Songs of a Tenth Century Korean Monk*. Sydney: Wild Peony Press, 1994.

A translation of the eleventh-century biography of a tenth-century Koryŏ Buddhist monk of the Hwaŏm school of Buddhism. It has a short text with lengthy scholarly annotations and appendices. A rare glimpse into Korean Buddhist hagiography with a useful nineteen-page introduction. Contains translations of the eleven *hyannga* poems for which this work is chiefly famous.

Byington, Mark E. *Early Korea: Reconsidering Early Korean History through Archaeology*. Cambridge, MA: Korea Institute, Harvard, 2008.

The first of a projected series of scholarly forums, this collection of essays examines how the field of archaeology influences perceptions of Korea before the tenth century. While aimed at serious scholars, it is rich in illustrations.

Ch'oe Pu. *Ch'oe Pu's Diary: A Record of Drifting across the Sea*. Translated and with an introduction by John Meskill. Tucson: University of Arizona Press, 1965.

The account of a fifteenth-century Korean official who was shipwrecked off the coast of China, describing his stay in China and his return home. Provides an insight into the values and attitudes of an early Chosŏn Confucianist and his observations about China.

Ch'oe, Yong-ho. *The Civil Examinations and the Social Structure in Early Yi Dynasty Korea: 1392–1600*. Seoul: Korean Research Center, 1987.

A controversial study of the civil examination system that argues that the civil exams were open to commoners and even to some slaves.

De Bary, William Theodore, and Jahyun Kim Haboush, eds. *The Rise of Neo-Confucianism in Korea*. New York: Columbia University Press, 1985.

A collection of essays by scholars analyzing Neo-Confucianism and its impact on Korea. The fifteen essays are of a high standard but are often demanding for the nonspecialist. The introduction by De Bary, one of the foremost East Asian scholars, provides a helpful entry into the topic of Neo-Confucianism and its importance.

Deuchler, Martina. *The Confucian Transformation of Korea: A Study of Society and Ideology*. Cambridge, MA: Council on East Asian Studies, Harvard University, 1992.

A detailed examination of the impact of Neo-Confucian ideology on Korean society during the transition period from late Koryŏ to mid-Chosŏn. The work focuses on ancestor worship, funerary rites, succession and inheritance, the position of women, the institution of marriage, and the formation of descent groups. This major study argues that a radical social transformation occurred, driven by ideological concerns.

Duncan, John B. *The Origins of the Chosŏn Dynasty*. Seattle: University of Washington Press, 2000.

An important work that analyzes the elite families of the Koryŏ and early Chosŏn to determine the extent of social and political continuities. The author argues that the change from Koryŏ to Chosŏn did not involve a radical change in Korea's social structure. Clearly written with many insights into premodern Korean history.

Eckert, Carter J., Ki-bail Lee, Young Lew, Michael Robinson, and Edward W. Wagner. *Korea Old and New: A History*. Cambridge, MA: Korea Institute, Harvard University, 1990.

The standard English language survey text on Korean history. Especially useful as a survey of Korea since 1876.

Gardiner, Kenneth H. J. *The Early History of Korea: The Historical Development of the Peninsula up to the Introduction of Buddhism in the Fourth Century C.E.* Honolulu: University of Hawaii Press, 1969.

   A short analysis of the early history of Korea to the fourth century C.E., based almost entirely on the textual sources. Still useful on the written sources for early Korean history but now dated by the wealth of archaeological evidence that has been uncovered in recent decades.

Griffis, William Eliot. *Corea: The Hermit Nation.* 9th ed. New York: AMS Press, 1971.

   Originally published in 1883, the first work on Korea by an American scholar. Interesting as a summary of what was known about Korea in the West on the eve of its opening to Westerners.

Haboush, Jahyun Kim. *A Heritage of Kings: One Man's Monarchy in the Confucian World.* New York: Columbia University Press, 1988.

   An excellent study of Chosŏn-period politics and society, and especially of kingship, through the study of the eighteenth-century monarch Yŏngjo. Clearly written with a wealth of insights and information.

———. *The Memoirs of Lady Hyegyŏng: The Autobiographical Writings of a Crown Princess of Eighteenth-Century Korea.* Translated and with an introduction and annotations by JaHyun Kim Haboush. Berkeley: University of California Press, 1996.

   The most readable translation of this fascinating work consisting of four memoirs by an eighteenth-century court lady. Contains a lengthy and informative introduction. Extremely helpful in understanding Chosŏn politics and society.

Haboush, Jahyun Kim, and Martina Deuchler, eds. *Culture and the State in Late Chosŏn Korea.* Cambridge, MA: Harvard-Hollym, 1999.

   A collection of informative essays on the politics, religion, and society of late Chosŏn.

Han, Suzanne Crowder. *Notes on Things Korean.* Seoul/Elizabeth, NJ: Hollym International, 1995.

   An entertaining, nonacademic introduction to traditional Korean customs, art forms, and crafts.

Han, Woo-keun. *The History of Korea.* Translated by Kyung-shik Lee. Edited by Grafton W. Mintz. Honolulu: University of Hawaii Press, 1974.

   A survey history by an eminent Korean historian. Now dated by more recent scholarship.

Henthorn, William E. *A History of Korea.* New York: The Free Press, 1971.

   A narrative survey of Korean history to the nineteenth century. Somewhat outdated as a result of recent research and literature on premodern Korea.

Hong (Lady). *Memoirs of a Korean Queen.* Translated and edited by Choe-Wall Yang-hi. London: KPI, 1985.

   A serviceable translation of the memoirs of Lady Hyegyŏng.

Hoyt, James. *Songs of the Dragons Flying to Heaven.* Seoul: Royal Asiatic Society, Korea Branch, 1971.

   An English translation of the fifteenth-century didactic cycle of poems concerning the establishment of the Yi dynasty. This was the first work to be written in the new alphabet, *han'gŭl*. The Korean text is placed next to the English translation. Well annotated with an informative introduction.

Hulbert, Homer. *The Passing of Korea*. Seoul: Yonsei University Press, 1969.

Originally published in 1906, an opinionated description of Korea at the end of the Chosŏn by a Christian missionary who admired much of the culture.

Illyŏn. *Samguk yusa: Legends and History of the Three Kingdoms of Ancient Korea*. Translated by Tae-Hung Ha and Grafton K. Mintz. Seoul: Yonsei University Press, 1972.

Uneven translation but does provides a look at this rich depository of myth, legends, and history from thirteenth-century Korea.

Janelli, Roger L., and Dawnhee Yim Janelli. *Ancestor Worship in Korean Society*. Stanford, CA: Stanford University Press, 1982.

A study of an important aspect of Korean culture by two anthropologists.

Jeon, Sang-woon. *Science and Technology in Korea: Traditional Instruments and Techniques*. Cambridge, MA: MIT Press, 1974.

A comprehensive survey of science and technology in Korea mostly from the Chosŏn period. Includes astronomy, shipbuilding, pottery, metallurgy, printing, papermaking, gunpowder, and weapons technology.

Kalton, Michael. *The Four-Seven Debate: An Annotated Translation of the Most Famous Controversy in Korean Neo-Confucian Thought*. Albany: State University of New York Press, 1994.

A translation of an exchange of letters between two sixteenth-century philosophers, Yi Hwang (T'oegye) and Ki Taesŭng (Kobong). Introduction provides a clear analysis of Neo-Confucian thought in Korea.

Kendall, Laurel. *Shamans, Housewives, and Other Restless Spirits*. Honolulu: University of Hawaii Press, 1985.

A work by an American anthropologist on the religious rituals and activities of Korean women. Although her study deals with modern Korea, it provides a good introduction to shamanism and traditional "folk" religion.

Kendall, Laurel, and Mark Peterson, eds. *Korean Women: View from the Inner Room*. New Haven, CT: East Rock Press, 1983.

Ten essays by anthropologists and historians dealing with Korean women in a Confucian society. Several of the essays are concerned with the Chosŏn period, while others deal with women in the twentieth century. Most essays are readable and insightful.

Kim, Key-hiuk. *The Last Phase of the East Asian World Order: Korea, Japan, and the Chinese Empire, 1860–1882*. Berkeley: University of California Press, 1980.

Although this book deals largely with events after 1860, the first chapter provides a good survey of the East Asian world order in late Chosŏn times and Korea's place in it.

Kim, Kichung. *Classical Korean Literature*. Armonk, NY: M.E. Sharpe, 1996.

A series of essays that provide an excellent introduction to the literature of Korea before the late nineteenth century.

Kim-Renaud, Young-Key, ed. *King Sejong the Great: The Light of Fifteenth Century Korea*. Washington, DC: George Washington University, International Circle of Korean Linguistics, 1992.

Fourteen short illustrated essays on aspects of Korean culture during the time of or associated with King Sejong. Topics include rites, Confucianism, *han'gul*, innovations in printing, the arts, ceramics, science and technology, and medicine.

Lancaster, Lewis, and Chai-Shin Yu, eds. *Introduction of Buddhism to Korea: New Cultural Patterns*. Berkeley, CA: Asian Humanities Press, 1986.

A collection of articles dealing with the introduction of Buddhism in Korea and its subsequent spread from there to Japan.

Ledyard, Gari. *The Dutch Come to Korea*. Seoul: Royal Asiatic Society, 1971.

A translation and commentary of the seventeenth-century account of Korea by the shipwrecked Dutch merchant Hendrick Hamel.

Lee, Ki-baik. *A New History of Korea*. Translated by Edward W. Wagner with Edward J. Shultz. Cambridge, MA: Harvard University Press, 1984.

A translation from what has probably been the most widely used college textbook on Korean history in South Korea by one of that country's most eminent historians. Mainly focuses on pre-nineteenth-century Korea. It contains a large number of names and terms that may overwhelm a non-Korean being introduced to Korean history. Perhaps most useful as a reference work.

Lee, Peter H., ed. *Anthology of Korean Literature: From Early Times to the Nineteenth Century*. Honolulu: University of Hawaii Press, 1981.

Translated with useful introductions by a leading scholar and translator of Korean literature. This anthology provides more than one hundred and fifty short poems, songs, and excerpts from biographies and prose tales, essays, and myths. Presents a good overall introduction to premodern Korean literature.

———, ed. *A History of Korean Literature*. Cambridge, UK: Cambridge University Press, 2003.

Combining a narrative history with criticism, this work offers a learned introduction to Korean literature by leading scholars. Approximately two-thirds of the essays are devoted to premodern literature.

———, trans. *Lives of Eminent Korean Monks: The Haedong Kosŭng Chŏn*. Cambridge, MA: Harvard University Press, 1969.

An annotated translation of the extant chapters of this collection of short biographies of famous monks first compiled by the monk Kakhun in 1215. Contains brief accounts of eighteen Korean and foreign monks from the Three Kingdoms period. A fascinating glimpse into Korean Buddhism in this period with a helpful introduction by the author.

Lee, Peter H., and William Theodore De Bary, eds. *Sources of Korean Traditions*. Vol. 1, *From Early Times through the Sixteenth Century*. New York: Columbia University Press, 1997; and Choe, Yong-ho and William Theodore De Bary, eds. *Sources of Korean Traditions*. Vol. 2, *From the Sixteenth to the Twentieth Centuries*. New York: Columbia University Press, 2000.

An indispensable collection of primary sources on Korean history, edited and translated by some of the leading scholars of premodern Korea.

Lee, Sang-Oak, and Duk Soo Park. *Perspectives on Korea*. Sydney: Wild Peony Press, 1998.

A collection of scholarly essays, some providing good insights into premodern Korea.

Lee, Soyoung. *Art of the Korean Renaissance, 1400–1600.* New York: The Metropolitan Museum of Art, 2009.

Beautifully illustrated collection of Korean art from this period. Essays by Jahyun Kim Haboush, Sunpyo Hong, and Chin-Sung Chang provide the historical and cultural context of these works.

Lewis, James B. *Frontier Contact between Chosŏn Korea and Tokugawa Japan.* London: RoutledgeCurzon, 2003.

A study of the contacts and perceptions Koreans and Japanese had of each other from the seventeenth to the late nineteenth centuries. Aimed at the specialist, it provides detailed information of the Waegwan near Pusan.

Pai, Hyung Il. *Constructing "Korean" Origins: A Critical Review of Archaeology, Historiography, and Racial Myth in Korean State-Formation Theories.* Cambridge, MA: Harvard University Press, 2000.

Mainly concerned with the use of archaeology, ancient myths, and texts by twentieth-century Korean historians and writers to create various versions of national identity. It is useful for understanding the historiographical issues surrounding early Korean history as well as better understanding the sources that our historical knowledge is based on. Much useful material on the Tan'gun myth.

Palais, James B. *Politics and Policy in Traditional Korea.* Cambridge, MA: Harvard University Press, 1975.

An examination of the reforms of the Taewŏn'gun in the 1860s and early 1870s that provides considerable information on the political, social, and economic problems of the late Chosŏn. Some of this study has been superseded by the author's later work, *Confucian Statecraft and Korean Institutions: Yu Hyŏngwŏn and the Late Chosŏn Dynasty* (see below).

———. *Confucian Statecraft and Korean Institutions: Yu Hyŏngwŏn and the Late Chosŏn Dynasty.* Seattle: University of Washington Press, 1996.

This massive study of over 1,000 pages uses the writings and concerns of the seventeenth-century scholar Yu Hyŏng-wŏn to examine a variety of political, economic, and social issues debated among the educated elite during the Chosŏn period. A bit unwieldy as a narrative text, this work by one of the leading American scholars of Korea contains a wealth of information and insights on premodern Korea.

———. *Views on Korean Social History.* Seoul: Institute for Modern Korean Studies, 1998.

Two essays given by James Palais in 1997 at the Graduate School of International Studies at Yonsei University. Deals with some controversial issues in Korean history.

Peterson, Mark A. *Korean Adoption and Inheritance: Case Studies in the Creation of a Classic Confucian Society.* Ithaca, NY: East Asia Program Cornell University, 1998.

Examines adoption and inheritance documents from the fifteenth to the nineteenth centuries for evidence of social change during Chosŏn Korea.

Portal, Jane. *Korea: Art and Archaeology.* London: British Museum, 2000.

Chronological account of the art and archaeology of Korea from the Neolithic period to the twentieth century, primarily focusing on premodern art traditions. Covers a wide sampling of art forms including folk art as well as the art of the elite. Well illustrated with an informative commentary, this book provides a good introduction to Korea's rich artistic heritage.

Pratt, Keith. *Korean Painting*. Oxford, UK: Oxford University Press, 1996.
   A survey of Korean painting from the fourth-century tomb paintings to the twentieth century.

————. *Everlasting Flower: A History of Korea*. London: Reaktion Books, 2006.
   A history of Korea from earliest times with an emphasis on cultural history. Mostly deals with the premodern period but has some insights on modern cultural history.

Pratt, Keith, and Richard Rutt. *Korea: A Historical and Cultural Dictionary*. Richmond, Surrey: Curzon Press, 1999.
   A compact but comprehensive dictionary of names, terms, and topics dealing with Korean history and culture. A handy reference work.

Ro, Young-chan. *The Korean Neo-Confucianism of Yi Yulgok*. Albany: State University of New York Press, 1988.
   A somewhat technical study of the important sixteenth-century Korean philosopher.

Setton, Mark. *Chŏng Yagyong: Korea's Challenge to Orthodox Neo-Confucianism*. Albany: State University of New York Press, 1997.
   Study of one of late Chosŏn's most important and original thinkers. Contains a clear, insightful explanation of his thought and the Qing and Tokugawa influences on it.

Shaw, William. *Legal Norms in a Confucian State*. Berkeley: Institute of East Asian Studies, University of California, Center for Korean Studies, 1981.
   A well-informed study of legal theory and practice in Yi-dynasty Korea, based primarily on the *Siminrok*, a late eighteenth-century collection of judicial reviews of difficult criminal cases. Contains one hundred of these short reviews of legal hearings.

Shultz, Edward J. *Generals and Scholars: Military Rule in Medieval Korea*. Honolulu: University of Hawaii Press, 2000.
   An important study of the often neglected period of military rule in the twelfth and thirteenth centuries by a leading specialist.

Toby, Ronald P. *State and Diplomacy in Early Modern Japan*. Princeton, NJ: Princeton University Press, 1984.
   An important study of Japanese foreign relations during its "seclusion period" (*sakoku*) from the early seventeenth to the nineteenth centuries, much of it focusing on Japanese-Korean relations.

Turnbull, Stephen. *Samurai Invasion: Japan's Korean War, 1592–98*. London: Cassell & Co., 2002.
   Well-illustrated account of the sixteenth-century Japanese invasion of Korea, aimed at the general reader.

Vermeersch, Sem. *The Power of the Buddhas: The Politics of Buddhism during the Koryŏ Dynasty (918–1392)*. Cambridge, MA: Harvard University Asia Center, 2008.
   A scholarly work examining the role of Buddhism in the Koryŏ period.

Wagner, Edward W. *Literati Purges: Political Conflict in Early Yi Korea*. Cambridge, MA: East Asian Research Center, Harvard University, 1974.

A detailed study of the four literati purges in the fifteenth and sixteenth century. Contains an outline of the institutional structure of the early Chosŏn.

Yi Chung-hwan. *Yi Chung-Hwan's T'aengniji: The Korean Classic for Choosing Settlements*. Translated with an introduction by Inshil Choe Yoon. Sydney: University of Sydney East Asian Series Number 12, 1998.

A translation of the influential eighteenth-century text on geomancy. The original text was written to help the *yangban* find a desirable place to live.

Yi Sun-shin. *Nanjung Ilgi: War Diary of Admiral Yi Sun-shin*. Translated by Ha Tae-hung. Edited by Sohn Pow-key. Seoul: Yonsei University Press, 1977.

A translation of the war diary of this now venerated sixteenth-century admiral.

Yi T'oegye, and Michael C. Kalton. *To Become a Sage: The Ten Diagrams on Sage Learning*. New York: Columbia University Press, 1989.

An examination of the diagrams drawn by the sixteenth-century Korean philosopher to illustrate his Neo-Confucian concepts.

MODERN KOREA

Amsden, Alice. *Asia's Next Giant: South Korea and Late Industrialization*. New York: Oxford University Press. 1989.

A favorable examination of South Korea's economic development. Now a bit dated but still useful.

Armstrong, Charles K. *The North Korean Revolution, 1945–1950*. Ithaca, NY: Cornell University Press, 2003.

An important study of the formation of the early North Korean state based on documents captured during the Korean War. The author persuasively argues that the North Korean government developed into a nationalist regime from its early days.

Brandt, Vincent. *A Korean Village between Farm and Sea*. Cambridge, MA: Harvard University Press, 1971.

An anthropological study of a South Korean village just before the country's economic transformation. A fascinating glimpse into rural Korea.

Brazinsky, Gregg. *Nation Building in South Korea: Koreans, Americans, and the Making of Democracy*. Chapel Hill: University of North Carolina Press, 2007.

An important study of the contributions of the United States in the evolution of South Korean democracy. Indispensable for understanding the political development of South Korea.

Buzo, Adrian. *The Guerilla Dynasty: Politics and Leadership in the DPRK 1945–1994*. Sydney: Allen & Unwin, 1999.

A readable, reliable study of North Korea under Kim Il Sung.

———. *The Making of Modern Korea: A History*. London: Routledge, 2002.

An often insightful political history of North and South Korea from 1910 to 2000.

Chen Jian. *China's Road to the Korean War: The Making of the Sino-American Confrontation*. New York: Columbia University Press, 1994.

Useful work for understanding the reasons for China's intervention into the Korean War.

Cho, S. S. *Korea in World Politics, 1940–1950: An Evaluation of American Responsibility.* Berkeley: University of California Press, 1967.

A still-valuable study of diplomacy and politics during this period.

Clark, Donald N. *Living Dangerously in Korea: The Western Experience, 1900–1950.* Norwalk, CT: Eastbridge, 2003.

An interesting account of the foreign community in Korea in the first half of the twentieth century, focusing on the American missionaries.

———, ed. *The Kwangju Uprisings: Shadows Over the Regime in South Korea.* Boulder, CO: Westview Press, 1988.

An examination of this bloody and tragic South Korean political uprising.

Clifford, Mark. *Troubled Tiger: Businessmen, Bureaucrats, and Generals in South Korea.* Armonk, NY: M.E. Sharpe, 1994.

Written by a journalist who covered Korea, it gives a somewhat dark picture of South Korea's economic miracle, emphasizing government-corporate collusion and corruption.

Conroy, Hilary. *The Japanese Seizure of Korea, 1868–1910.* Philadelphia: University of Pennsylvania Press, 1960.

A controversial study of the Japanese takeover of Korea, now a bit dated.

Cumings, Bruce. *The Origins of the Korean War.* Vol. 1, *Liberation and the Emergence of Separate Regimes, 1945–1947.* Princeton, NJ: Princeton University Press, 1981.

———. *The Origins of the Korean War.* Vol. 2, *The Roaring of the Cataract, 1947–1950.* Princeton, NJ: Princeton University Press, 1990.

These two volumes are an important study of Korea in the five years before the Korean War. Some of the author's arguments have been undermined by more recent evidence, but this is still valuable as a source of information on Korean political developments prior to the war. The first volume includes an especially valuable detailed study of South Korean politics immediately after liberation.

———. *Korea's Place in the Sun: A Modern History.* Updated edition. New York: W.W. Norton and Company, 2005.

An engagingly written, if somewhat opinionated, history of modern Korea by one of the most prominent American historians of Korea.

Deuchler, Martina. *Confucian Gentlemen and Barbarian Envoys: The Opening of Korea, 1875–1885.* Seattle: University of Washington Press, 1977.

A reliable diplomatic study of the first decade after South Korea was "opened."

Duus, Peter. *The Abacus and the Sword: The Japanese Penetration of Korea, 1895–1910.* Berkeley: University of California Press, 1995.

A study of Japanese politics and diplomacy behind Japan's annexation of Korea by a prominent historian of Japan.

Eckert, Carter J. *Offspring of Empire: The Koch'ang Kims and the Origins of Korean Capitalism.* Seattle: University of Washington Press, 1991.

An important study of the colonial origins of Korea's industrialization focusing on one of Korea's influential entrepreneurial families. Argues for the importance of the colonial period in understanding South Korea's economic development.

Eckert, Carter J., Ki-baik Lee, Young Ick Lew, Michael Robinson, and Edward W. Wagner. *Korea Old and New: A History*. Cambridge: Korea Institute, Harvard University, 1990.

A standard one-volume history of Korea from earliest times to the late 1980s.

Flake, L. Gordon, and Scott Snyder, eds. *Paved with Good Intentions: The NGO Experience in North Korea*. Westport, CT: Praeger, 2004.

Several essays by aid workers active in North Korea during the famine. Contains many interesting insights.

French, Paul. *North Korea: The Paranoid Peninsula*. New York: St Martin's Press, 2005.

One volume in a growing body of literature on North Korea. Generally reliable, with an emphasis on economics.

Gradjanzev, Andrew H. *Modern Korea*. New York: Institute of Pacific Relations and John Day Company, 1944.

A survey of Korea under colonial rule with many statistics that is still a valuable source. The well-informed author's identity remains a mystery.

Gragert, Edwin H. *Landownership under Colonial Rule: Korea's Japanese Experience, 1900–1935*. Honolulu: University of Hawaii Press, 1994.

An important study of landownership during colonial times.

Haggard, Stephan, and Marcus Noland. *Famine in North Korea: Markets, Aid, and Reform*. New York: Columbia University Press, 2007.

The best study to date of this tragic episode in Korean history, with some insights into North Korea under Kim Jong Il.

Halliday, Jon, and Bruce Cumings. *Korea: The Unknown War*. New York: Pantheon Books, 1988.

A popular and critical history, the basis for a PBS documentary.

Han, Sung-joo. *The Failure of Democracy in South Korea*. Berkeley: University of California Press, 1974.

An important analytical study of the short-lived experiment in parliamentary government during the Second Republic, 1960–1961.

Harrington, Fred Harvey. *God, Mammon, and the Japanese: Dr. Horace N. Allen and Korean-American Relations, 1884–1905*. Madison: University of Wisconsin Press, 1944.

Examines the career of an influential American in late Chosŏn Korea.

Henderson, Gregory. *Korea: The Politics of the Vortex*. Cambridge, MA: Harvard University Press, 1968.

Although now somewhat dated, it is still a provocative and at times insightful history of South Korea in the first two decades after World War II.

Hicks, George. *The Comfort Women: Japan's Brutal Regime of Enforced Prostitution in the Second World War*. New York: W.W. Norton, 1995.

The first major work in English on this controversial topic.

Hulbert, Homer B. *The Passing of Korea*. Reprint [1906] Seoul: Yonsei University Press, 1969.

This is a generally sympathetic account by an American missionary in Korea. Despite the prejudices and limitations of the author, it is worth reading for his firsthand accounts of events and life in Korea at the end of the Chosŏn dynasty.

Hunter, Helen-Louise. *Kim Il-song's North Korea.* Westport, CT: Praeger, 1999.
    Based on intelligence reports from the closed society that may prove to be in need of revision, it nonetheless provides a fascinating portrait of life in North Korea.

Kang, Chol-Hwan, *The Aquariums of Pyongyang: Ten Years in the North Korean Gulag.* Yair Reiner, trans. New York: Basic Books, 2001.
    The firsthand account of a survivor of the North Korean prison system and an international bestseller. It gives a glimpse into this dark and little-known aspect of the DPRK.

Kihl, Young Whan. *Transforming Korean Politics: Democracy, Reform, and Culture.* Armonk, NY: M.E. Sharpe, 2005.
    A study of the geopolitics of the two Koreas.

Kim, Alexander Joungwon. *Divided Korea: The Politics of Development 1945–1972.* Cambridge, MA: East Asian Research Center, Harvard University Press, 1975.
    Still a good analysis of Korean politics from liberation to Yushin.

Kim Choong Soon. *The Culture of Korean Industry: An Ethnography of Poongsan Corporation.* Tucson: University of Arizona Press, 1992.
    A case study of a medium-size South Korean industry during the years of rapid industrialization.

Kim, C. I. Eugene, and Han-kyo Kim. *Korea and the Politics of Imperialism: 1876–1910.* Berkeley: University of California Press, 1967.
    Provides a detailed factual account of the international diplomacy and great-power maneuvering during this period.

Kim, Eun Mee. *Big Business, Strong State: Collusion and Conflict in South Korean Development, 1960–1990.* Albany: State University of New York Press, 1997.
    A useful account of big conglomerates and the state in South Korea's economic development, accessible to the general reader.

Kim, Key-Hiuk. *The Last Phase of the East Asian World Order.* Berkeley: University of California Press, 1980.
    One of the most detailed and best analyzed accounts of the diplomacy and politics surrounding the opening of Korea.

Kim, Richard. *Lost Names: Scenes from a Korean Boyhood.* Berkeley: University of California Press.
    A semiautobiographical novel providing a vivid picture of life during the last years of colonial rule.

Koo, Hagen. *Korean Workers: The Culture and Pattern of Class Formation.* Ithaca, NY: Cornell University Press, 2001.
    An important study of the South Korean working class.

Lancaster, Lewis R., and Richard K. Payne. *Religion and Society in Contemporary Korea.* Berkeley: University of California Press, 1997.
    Ten essays on the topic of religion in modern South Korea—includes studies of shamanism, Buddhism, and Christianity.

Lankov, Andrei. *From Stalin to Kim Il Sung: The Formation of North Korea, 1945–1960.* New Brunswick, NJ: Rutgers University Press, 2002.
    An insightful political history of early North Korea by one of the best-informed scholars writing on that country.

———. *North of the DMZ: Essays on Daily Life in North Korea.* Jefferson, NC: McFarland & Company, 2007.

A series of essays, many on North Korea, by a leading historian of that country. Provides the best summary of North Korean society available in English, with many valuable insights. Highly recommended for anyone interested in North Korea.

Larsen, Kirk W. *Tradition, Treaties, and Trade: Qing Imperialism and Chosŏn Korea, 1850–1910*. Cambridge, MA: Harvard University Press, 2008.

Well-written revisionist study of this period. Argues that Qing was an imperial power using modern diplomacy, international law, telegraphs, and steamboats to aggressively assert itself in Korea.

Lee, H. B. *Korea: Time, Change, and Administration*. Honolulu: East-West Center Press, 1968.

This is still a useful introduction to the bureaucratic culture of South Korea.

Lee, Hy-Sang. *North Korea: A Strange Socialist Fortress*. Westport, CT: Praeger, 2001.

One of a number of useful studies of North Korea. This and many similar books are likely to become outdated if and when North Korea becomes more accessible to scholars.

Lee, Jungsoo. *The Partition of Korea after World War II: A Global History*. New York: Palgrave Macmillan, 2006.

An important recent study of the diplomacy around the division of Korea that makes use of Soviet archival material. Argues that there is no evidence that the Soviet Union immediately after the war had a set plan to create a separate state in the north.

Lett, Denise P. *In Pursuit of Status: The Making of South Korea's "New" Urban Middle Class*. Cambridge, MA: East Asian Research Center, Harvard University Press, 1998.

An insightful study of the emergence of South Korea's new middle class and the persistence of traditional Confucian values and attitudes.

Li, M. *The Yalu Flows: A Korean Childhood*. East Lansing: Michigan State University Press, 1956.

A very readable autobiography providing a glimpse into Korea under Japanese colonialism.

Lie, John. *Han Unbound: The Political Economy of South Korea*. Stanford, CA: Stanford University Press, 1998.

A readable and insightful history of the economic and social transformation of South Korea after 1945.

Lowe, Peter. *The Origins of the Korean War*. New York: Longman, 1986.

A solid, standard history.

Lynn, Hyung Gu. *Bipolar Orders: The Two Koreas since 1989*. Halifax, NS: Fenwood, 2007.

An insightful sketch of contemporary Korean history.

MacDonald, D. S. *The Koreans: Contemporary Politics and Society*. Boulder, CO: Westview Press, 1990.

A basic introduction to South Korea of the 1980s.

McNamara, Dennis L. *The Colonial Origins of Korean Enterprise, 1910–1945*. Cambridge: Cambridge University Press, 1990.

Focuses on Min Tae-sik and his brother Min Kyu-sik, who controlled Hanil Bank and its successor in 1931, Tongil Bank; Pak Hŭng-sik of the Hwasin Chain

Stores Company; and the brothers Kim Sŏng-su and Kim Yŏn-su, leading manufacturers.

Moon, Seungsook. *Militarized Modernity and Gendering Citizenship in South Korea.* Durham, NC: Duke University Press, 2005.

Provides some interesting analyses of gender and the militarization of South Korean culture.

Myers, Brian. *Han Sŏrya and North Korean Literature: The Failure of Socialist Realism in the DPRK.* Ithaca, NY: Cornell University Press, 1994.

Examines the career of North Korea's most prominent writer with insights into the early years of the Kim Il Sung regime.

———. *The Cleanest Race: How North Koreans See Themselves—and Why It Matters.* Brooklyn, NY: Melville House, 2010.

A provocative examination of North Korea's worldview based primarily on examination of North Korean literature and other internal publications. A highly readable, fascinating and important, if controversial, work.

Myers, Ramon H., and Mark R. Peattie, eds. *The Japanese Colonial Empire, 1895–1945.* Princeton, NJ: Princeton University Press, 1984.

Contains some useful essays on colonial Korea.

Nahm, Andrew C. *Korea: Tradition and Transformation.* Elizabeth, NJ: Hollym International, 1988.

A good introduction to Korean history, especially modern Korean history, now becoming a bit dated.

Natsios, Andrew S. *The Great North Korean Famine.* Washington, DC: United States Institute of Peace Press, 2001.

Contains some eyewitness accounts of the famine in North Korea.

Nelson, Laura C. *Measured Excess: Status, Gender, and Consumer Nationalism in South Korea.* New York: Columbia University Press, 2000.

A mixture of personal accounts and scholarly analysis of how the increasing affluence of South Korea is impacting society, especially how it is shaping the identities of women.

Oberdorfer, Donald. *The Two Koreas: A Contemporary History.* New York: Basic Books, 1998.

A very readable work on recent politics and foreign affairs by a veteran journalist.

Ogle, George E. *South Korea: Dissent within the Economic Miracle.* Atlantic Highlands, NJ: Zed Books, 1990.

An important study of labor and political dissent by someone with firsthand knowledge of the topic.

Oh, Kongdan, and Ralph C. Hassig. *North Korea: Through the Looking Glass.* Washington, DC: Brookings Institution Press, 2000.

Readable study of North Korea.

Osgood, C. *The Koreans and Their Culture.* New York: Ronald Press, 1951.

Anthropological study done in the late 1940s with good insights into Korean culture on the eve of the Korean War.

Park, Chung Hee. *The Country, The Revolution and I.* Seoul: Hollym Corporation, 1970.

President Park Chung Hee's justification for his rule. Worth reading for the insights it brings into the thinking and aims of his regime.

Park, Han S. *North Korea: The Politics of Unconventional Wisdom.* Boulder, CO: Lynne Rienner, 2002.

One of a number of useful studies of North Korea.

Park, Soon-won. *Colonial Industrialization and Labor in Korea: The Onoda Cement Factory.* Cambridge, MA: Harvard University Press, 1999.

This book is a study of labor relations and the first generation of skilled workers in colonial Korea, a subject crucial to the understanding of modernization in twentieth-century Korea.

Robinson, Michael E. *Cultural Nationalism in Colonial Korea, 1920–1925.* Seattle: University of Washington Press, 1988.

This monograph introduced the concept of "cultural nationalism." It is indispensable for understanding the rise of modern Korean nationalism.

———. *Korea's Twentieth-Century Odyssey.* Honolulu: University of Hawaii Press, 2007.

Excellent survey of modern Korean history, especially useful on the colonial period.

Schmid, Andre. *Korea between Empires, 1895–1919.* New York: Columbia University Press, 2002.

An important if challenging work of intellectual history. Argues for the beginnings of modern Korean nationalism in the emergence of a community of educated Korean readers of journals and newspapers.

Shin, Gi-Wook. *Peasant Protest and Social Change in Colonial Korea.* Seattle: University of Washington Press, 1996.

An important study of social and economic history in colonial Korea.

———. *Ethnic Nationalism in Korea: Genealogy, Politics, and Legacy.* Stanford, CA: Stanford University Press, 2006.

A sophisticated analysis of the emergence of Korean national identity from the end of the nineteenth century to contemporary North and South Korea.

Soh, C. Sarah. *The Comfort Women: Sexual Violence and Postcolonial Memory in Korea and Japan.* Chicago: University of Chicago Press, 2008.

An important study of this controversial subject by an anthropologist. Examines how the comfort women found themselves victimized by Japanese colonialism and Korean patriarchy.

Stueck, W. *The Korean War: An International History.* Princeton, NJ: Princeton University Press, 1995.

A standard work by a noted historian.

Suh, Dae-sook. *The Korean Communist Movement, 1918–1948.* Princeton, NJ: Princeton University Press, 1967.

Although somewhat dated, still a useful source for understanding the development of Korean Communism.

———. *Kim Il Sung: A Biography.* Honolulu: University of Hawaii Press, 1989.

The standard biography of Kim Il Sung by a leading authority on North Korea and Korean Communism.

Wells, Kenneth M. *New God, New Nation: Protestants and Self-Reconstruction Nationalism in Korea, 1896–1937.* Honolulu: University of Hawaii Press, 1990.
 A study of the role of Korean Christians in the emergence of nationalism.
———, ed. *South Korea's Minjung Movement: The Culture and Politics of Dissidence.* Honolulu: University of Hawaii Press, 1995.
 Nine essays essential for understanding this important political and intellectual movement in South Korea.
Woo, Jung-en. *Race to the Swift: State and Finance in the Industrialization of Korea.* New York: Columbia University Press, 1991.
 One of the best studies of South Korea's economic takeoff.
Yoo, Theodore Jun. *The Politics of Gender in Colonial Korea: Education, Labor, and Health, 1910–1945.* Berkeley: University of California Press.
 A clearly written examination of how the roles and attitudes of many Korean women underwent radical transformation during the Japanese colonial period. Contains an excellent summary of gender relations in premodern and early modern Korea.
Zhang, Shu Guang. *Mao's Military Romanticism: China and the Korean War, 1950–1953.* Lawrence: University Press of Kansas, 1995.
 Provides some insights into China's role in the Korean War.

Index

About the Author

Michael J. Seth is associate professor of East Asian and world history at James Madison University in Harrisonburg, Virginia. He received his PhD from the University of Hawai'i and his MA and BA from the State University of New York at Binghamton. Dr. Seth has lived and worked in South Korea and is the author of *Education Fever: Society, Politics and the Pursuit of Schooling in South Korea* (2002), *A Concise History of Korea: From the Neolithic Period through the Nineteenth Century* (Rowman & Littlefield, 2006), and *A Concise History of Modern Korea: From the Late Nineteenth Century to the Present* (Rowman & Littlefield, 2010).